Fundamentals of
Criminal Practice

ASPEN COLLEGE SERIES

Fundamentals of Criminal Practice
Law and Procedure

Thomas E. McClure

Assistant Professor
Illinois State University

Thomas E. Eimermann

Emeritus Professor
Illinois State University

Wolters Kluwer
Law & Business

Published by Wolters Kluwer Law & Business in New York.

Wolters Kluwer Law & Business serves customers worldwide with CCH, Aspen Publishers, and Kluwer Law International products. (www.wolterskluwerlb.com)

To contact Customer Service, e-mail customer.service@wolterskluwer.com, call 1-800-234-1660, fax 1-800-901-9075, or mail correspondence to:

Wolters Kluwer Law & Business
Attn: Order Department
PO Box 990
Frederick, MD 21705

Printed in the United States of America.

1 2 3 4 5 6 7 8 9 0

ISBN 978-0-7355-7094-8

Library of Congress Cataloging-in-Publication Data

McClure, Thomas, 1954-
   Fundamentals of criminal practice : law and procedure / Thomas McClure,
Thomas E. Eimermann.
      p. cm.
   Includes index.
   ISBN-13: 978-0-7355-7094-8
   ISBN-10: 0-7355-7094-9
   1. Criminal law—United States. 2. Criminal procedure—United States. 3.
Legal assistants—United States—Handbooks, manuals, etc. I. Eimermann,
Thomas E. II. Title.

   KF9219.85.M38 2011
   345.73'05—dc23
                                                                2011018424

About Wolters Kluwer Law & Business

Wolters Kluwer Law & Business is a leading global provider of intelligent information and digital solutions for legal and business professionals in key specialty areas, and respected educational resources for professors and law students. Wolters Kluwer Law & Business connects legal and business professionals as well as those in the education market with timely, specialized authoritative content and information-enabled solutions to support success through productivity, accuracy and mobility.

Serving customers worldwide, Wolters Kluwer Law & Business products include those under the Aspen Publishers, CCH, Kluwer Law International, Loislaw, Best Case, ftwilliam.com and MediRegs family of products.

CCH products have been a trusted resource since 1913, and are highly regarded resources for legal, securities, antitrust and trade regulation, government contracting, banking, pension, payroll, employment and labor, and healthcare reimbursement and compliance professionals.

Aspen Publishers products provide essential information to attorneys, business professionals and law students. Written by preeminent authorities, the product line offers analytical and practical information in a range of specialty practice areas from securities law and intellectual property to mergers and acquisitions and pension/benefits. Aspen's trusted legal education resources provide professors and students with high-quality, up-to-date and effective resources for successful instruction and study in all areas of the law.

Kluwer Law International products provide the global business community with reliable international legal information in English. Legal practitioners, corporate counsel and business executives around the world rely on Kluwer Law journals, looseleafs, books, and electronic products for comprehensive information in many areas of international legal practice.

Loislaw is a comprehensive online legal research product providing legal content to law firm practitioners of various specializations. Loislaw provides attorneys with the ability to quickly and efficiently find the necessary legal information they need, when and where they need it, by facilitating access to primary law as well as state-specific law, records, forms and treatises.

Best Case Solutions is the leading bankruptcy software product to the bankruptcy industry. It provides software and workflow tools to flawlessly streamline petition preparation and the electronic filing process, while timely incorporating ever-changing court requirements.

ftwilliam.com offers employee benefits professionals the highest quality plan documents (retirement, welfare and non-qualified) and government forms (5500/PBGC, 1099 and IRS) software at highly competitive prices.

MediRegs products provide integrated health care compliance content and software solutions for professionals in healthcare, higher education and life sciences, including professionals in accounting, law and consulting.

Wolters Kluwer Law & Business, a division of Wolters Kluwer, is headquartered in New York. Wolters Kluwer is a market-leading global information services company focused on professionals.

To our wives for their understanding and support.

Summary of Contents

Contents

PART 1: CRIMINAL LAW

PART 2 CRIMINAL PROCEDURE: FROM COMMISSION OF THE OFFENSE TO PLEA BARGAINING AND DIVERSION

CHAPTER 6 ■ DEFENDING THE ACCUSED 161

CHAPTER 7 ■ DISCOVERY AND DISCLOSURE   199

PART 3 CRIMINAL PROCEDURE: TRIALS AND THEIR AFTERMATH

CHAPTER 10 ■ THE NATURE OF CRIMINAL TRIALS   325

List of Illustrations

Preface

This book is designed to be used as a textbook for a paralegal course covering criminal law and procedure. Like most texts on criminal law, it includes general background information on the organization and function of criminal law, it explains the most common types of criminal offenses, and it covers criminal procedures used at the federal and state levels.

Because it is **designed specifically for paralegals**, it describes the various roles played by paralegals and focuses on providing the skills and knowledge students will need to function effectively in jobs related to criminal law. However, the information it covers goes beyond the role that paralegals play in the criminal justice system. It contains discussions of the criminal justice system, the role of police and lawyers, the basic principles of criminal law, constitutional limitations, and trial procedures that **can benefit criminal justice majors, government majors, pre-law students, and anyone wishing to know more about criminal law**.

As with all books of this type, the authors have been faced with the challenge of covering both federal law and variations in state laws. We have tended to focus on federal law because it is relevant to readers in all parts of the country, but we have also discussed how state laws and procedures vary. Because there are so many variations among the states and even between judicial districts within a given state, it is imperative that readers research their own state and local statutes and procedural rules to see how they differ from the ones used as illustrations in this book. This book includes instructions and Application Exercises designed to teach readers how to find and apply the laws and procedures of their own state and/or local area.

Another feature that sets this book apart from many of its competitors is the extent to which we have included discussions of "white-collar" crime. Discussions of criminal codes, the exhibits, and the Application Exercises all include references to these types of crimes. References to juvenile law are also included where relevant.

ORGANIZATION OF THE BOOK

PART 1: CRIMINAL LAW

This book begins with a general overview of the criminal justice system, the major stages of a criminal case, and the roles and responsibilities of the many people who are involved in the day-to-day operation of the system.

Chapter 2 goes on to discuss the underlying principles and concepts reflected in the criminal law, and Chapter 3 provides an overview of the different types of offenses covered by the criminal law. In our discussion of substantive criminal law, we provide a sampling of some of the common offenses included in most criminal codes and examples of charges filed in some highly publicized cases. Special emphasis is placed on learning how to interpret and apply statutory language.

PART 2: CRIMINAL PROCEDURE: FROM COMMISSION OF THE OFFENSE TO PLEA BARGAINING AND DIVERSION

The second section shifts from the substance of the criminal law to criminal procedure. Starting with the discovery and investigation of crimes, we follow the actions of the police, prosecutors, and defense attorneys as the criminal justice system processes those accused of having violated the criminal law. Chapter 4 covers the investigation of crimes and the arrest of the suspected criminals. Chapter 5 focuses on the prosecutor's role and the charging process, and Chapter 6 focuses on the defense attorney's role.

Chapter 7 explores the discovery and disclosure procedures used by both sides to obtain further information about the strengths and weaknesses of their cases. Chapter 8 covers the potential defenses attorneys can assert on their client's behalf.

Chapter 9 includes coverage of pre-trial motions relating to substitution of judges, joinder and severance, competency, and motions to exclude key pieces of evidence. It then goes on to discuss the plea-bargaining process. The chapter ends with a discussion of diversion into specialized treatment programs.

PART 3: CRIMINAL PROCEDURE: TRIALS AND THEIR AFTERMATH

Chapter 10 sets the stage for our coverage of trials, sentencing, and preparation for appeals by reviewing constitutional provisions affecting the conduct of criminal trials and discussing how evidence is presented in trials.

Chapter 11 then discusses the things that attorneys and paralegals do to prepare for a trial. It includes preparation for jury selection and preparation of exhibits, motions, witnesses, and electronic presentations. The actual conduct of the trial itself is covered in Chapter 12, where each stage of the trial is discussed in detail from jury selection to post-verdict motions.

Chapter 13 addresses the sentencing phase of a case. After discussing the various types of punishments courts can impose, it goes on to examine the amount of discretion judges have and the role of sentencing guidelines. From there it goes on to cover sentencing procedures and mechanisms for seeking modification of a sentence.

This section ends with a discussion of appeals in Chapter 14. The focus here is on the process of preparing a case for an appeal rather than on the preparation of the appeal itself. After providing an overview of the appeals process, the chapter discusses the timing of an appeal, the preservation of the record, and alternative methods of challenging criminal convictions.

SPECIAL FEATURES

USE OF LEGAL DOCUMENTS FROM REAL CASES

As in most texts of this type, we will frequently reference statutes and court decisions to explain and illustrate various principles of criminal law and criminal procedure. In addition to including excerpts from featured statutes and cases, we also include arrest reports, mug shots, complaints, and other legal documents from criminal cases that have received national attention.

INTEGRATION OF HYPOTHETICAL CASES

Throughout this text we use four "hypothetical" cases to illustrate how various types of crimes are handled at the various stages of the criminal justice process. One case involves a state reckless homicide charge related to an accident involving a driver who had been drinking alcoholic beverages. The second involves charges related to illegal drugs and weapons. The other two cases involve "white-collar crime." In one a registered securities agent is charged with misappropriation of customer funds; the other involves corporate insider trading.

These cases are integrated in appropriate chapters throughout the book where they are used to illustrate questions of statutory interpretation as well as criminal procedure. They are also incorporated into some of the Discussion Questions and Application Exercises. Initial facts about the nature of the crimes involved in these cases are presented in a separate section following this Preface that should be read in conjunction with Chapter 2 and then referred to again when reading most of the following chapters.

PRACTICAL SKILL DEVELOPMENT

This book incorporates a variety of pedagogical techniques for developing analytical and drafting skills. Most chapters will include excerpts from statutes, court opinions, investigative reports, or court filings.

Discussion Questions raise controversial issues that require legal analysis and argumentation. The Application Exercises involve legal research and the drafting of various reports and legal documents as well as legal analysis.

STUDY AIDS

This book includes standard reader aids such as marginal definitions of key terms, a chapter summary, and Review Questions.

An instructor's manual includes suggested answers for all the Discussion Questions, Review Questions, and Application Exercises. A computerized test bank is also available to help teachers make the most effective use of this book.

SPECIAL THANKS

We would like to thank the staff at Aspen Publishers for the excellent support we have received in the preparation of this book and to the reviewers who gave us such positive feedback and useful suggestions.

We would also like to recognize the contributions of the following research assistants from the Department of Politics and Government at Illinois State University: Anthony Nigliaccio, Theodore Mason, and Renee Prunty.

Finally, we also wish to thank our spouses for their continued support and understanding of our professional activities.

Thomas E. McClure
Thomas E. Eimermann
June, 2011

Acknowledgments

We are grateful to copyright holders for permission to reprint excerpts from the following items:

Model Penal Code, © 1985 by The American Law Institute. Reprinted with permission: All rights reserved.

National Association of Legal Assistants, Code of Ethics and Professional Responsibility. Coypright 2007, NALA, Inc. Reprinted by permission from the National Association of Legal Assistants, 1516 S. Boston, #200, Tulsa, OK 74119, www.nala.org.

NFPA Model Disciplinary Rules. (c) (2006), The National Federation of Paralegal Associations, Inc., www.paralegals.org. Reprinted by permission.

About the Authors

Thomas E. McClure is the Director of Legal Studies and an Assistant Professor of Political Science at Illinois State University. He teaches Introduction to Paralegal Studies, Introduction to Torts, Investigative Techniques & Evidence, Litigation I & II, and a constitutional law course.

He graduated from Illinois State University in 1976 with a B.S. in Political Science. He received his J.D. from DePaul University where he served as an editor of the *DePaul Law Review*. In 2001, he earned his M.S. in Political Science from Illinois State University.

Following law school, Professor McClure served for two years as a law clerk to an Illinois Appellate Court Justice. He then entered private practice as one of the two principals of Elliott & McClure, a Kankakee County, Illinois law firm. Since 2007, he has served as of counsel to the firm. He specializes in personal injury, criminal defense, family law, and civil rights litigation.

He is a member of the Illinois Bar and admitted to practice before three U.S. District Courts, the Seventh Circuit Court of Appeals, and the United States Supreme Court. When the death penalty was in effect, he was a member of the Illinois Capital Litigation Bar.

Professor McClure has published journal articles on the Supreme Court's approach to *ex post facto* law analysis, the constitutional rights of disabled applicants for public employment, and the effectiveness of court-connected parenting classes.

Thomas E. Eimermann is an Emeritus Professor of Political Science at Illinois State University where he started their paralegal program in 1976 and served as its Director until 2004. During those years he taught the Introduction to Paralegal Studies and the Legal Research and Writing courses as well as constitutional law and administrative law.

He received his B.A. in Political Science at North Central College, and then went on to earn an M.A. and a Ph.D. in Political Science from the University of Illinois-Urbana/Champaign.

Professor Eimermann was a member of the American Association for Paralegal Education's Board of Directors from 1986-1993 and served as president of that organization in 1991-1992. He has also served in the Certification Board and Specialty Task Force of the National Association of Legal Assistants; as a member of the Illinois State Bar Association Committee on the Delivery of Legal Services; and as a member of the Hearing Board, the Inquiry Board, and the Oversight Committee of the Illinois Attorney Registration and Disciplinary Commission. As a consultant for the Illinois Department of Corrections, he designed their Uniform Law Clerk Training Program.

Professor Eimermann's other publications include multiple editions of *Fundamentals of Paralegalism, Introduction to Law for Paralegals, Introduction to Paralegal Studies,* and *The Study of Law* (the last three co-authored with Katherine Currier). He has also published journal articles on paralegals, jury behavior, and free speech issues.

Introduction to Hypothetical Cases

At various points in this text, we will be referring to four hypothetical cases that are used as illustrations and in Application Exercises. Take a moment now to read the facts given in each of these cases, and then record this information in a notebook or a word processing file in a way that will allow you to organize and add to it as you learn more about these cases in different chapters.

CASE #1: PEOPLE V. COOK

Bud Cook left a pizzeria at 9:30 P.M. to drive home. He consumed a pitcher of beer with his meal but didn't think it would affect his driving. He drove his pickup truck in the northbound direction in the outermost lane on Sumner Drive.

Several blocks north of the pizza parlor, he came upon a woman wearing a black T-shirt and jeans, riding a black bicycle in the northbound outside lane about two feet from the shoulder of the road. Bud did not notice the bicyclist until the right front fender of his pickup struck the rear of the bike, causing the rider to land on top of the hood and hit the windshield. As she hit the windshield, Bud slammed on his brakes, which in turn threw the rider forward across the pavement.

Bud "panicked" and raced home without stopping. When he told his wife Tammy that he had either struck an animal or a man on a bicycle, she called 911 to report the incident. While driving home, a passerby had called 911 to report that there was a human body on the road. When the police arrived, they found that the victim was dead.

CASE #2: UNITED STATES V. TURNER

At two o'clock in the afternoon, local police officer Steve Milner was on a routine patrol when he saw an automobile run a stop sign. Officer Milner activated his overhead lights on his marked squad car and started to pursue the car.

The driver of the car speeded up and then pulled in front of a sandwich shop. The driver, Brandon Turner, got out of the car and began to walk rapidly toward the restaurant. Officer Milner stepped out of his squad car, blew his horn, and yelled at Turner to halt. Turner did not stop and went into the sandwich shop.

Milner saw the Turner go through the restaurant and then into a restroom. He followed Turner into the restaurant and met him at the restroom door when Turner came out after having been in the restroom for less than a minute.

Through a series of searches, police discovered Turner had hid a loaded handgun in the restroom and that there was a bag of cocaine in Turner's car.

CASE #3: UNITED STATES V. EDWARDS

Bill Edwards is a registered representative for a local broker-dealer. He has many high-net-worth clients and is involved in several local social networks. Many prominent individuals in the community are his clients.

Edwards was also involved in several business ventures outside of his employment as a registered representative. Many of these businesses began having financial troubles and could not maintain their operation without an infusion of capital. He also began having personal problems at home and was having difficulty paying alimony and child support.

To resolve these financial woes, Edwards began diverting customer funds and liquidating customer securities and using the proceeds to help these failing businesses. Edwards did this without permission or authority from customers. To help cover up this misappropriations, he issued promissory notes to these customers.

When customers saw that funds or investments were missing from their accounts and asked Edwards what happened, he told them that he had put them in safe investments with guaranteed returns of 12% to 20%. However, when interest on the promissory notes came due, the entities that issued the notes could not make the payment. To keep these customers from complaining and to cover up the fraud, Edwards began misappropriating funds from other customers to make the interest payments owed to the existing customers.

CASE #4: UNITED STATES V. SCHROEDER

Tom Schroeder was retained by Amalgamated Industries, a publicly traded manufacturing company, to represent it in merger negotiations with ABC Batteries. While working in this capacity he learned that ABC had just got a preliminary patent approval for a new type of process that would revolutionize the industry. Schroeder realized that when news of the pending merger and the new patent would be publicly announced the next month, it would greatly increase the value of Amalgamated's stock.

However, he also knew that it would look suspicious in the eyes of the Securities and Exchange Commission if he bought the stock. So the next time Schroeder was playing golf, he pulled aside his good friend, Jim Stevenson, and told him that he had been doing some work for Amalgamated Industries and that it would be a good time to buy some of their stock. The next day, Stevenson placed a market order to purchase 10,000 shares of Amalgamated's stock. He ended up paying $10 per share.

About a month later, the patent and merger announcements were made on the same day, and a few days after the announcement shares of Amalgamated were selling at $22.00 per share. Later that month, Stevenson sold his entire position for $21.00 per share. Later that year, Stevenson paid Schroeder $60,000 to review his will and set up a simple trust agreement for him.

PART 1

Criminal Law

Chapter 1

The Criminal Justice System

We begin our exploration of criminal law and procedure with an overview of the criminal justice system and the people who work in it. A system is defined as a group of interacting, interrelated, or interdependent elements forming a collective entity. The human digestive system, for example, consists of the various parts of the body that are involved in taking food into the body; extracting the proteins, vitamins, fats, and so on used to fuel the body; and then eliminating waste materials. It includes the esophagus, the stomach, the liver, the pancreas, the intestines, and the rectum.

The **criminal justice system** refers to a collection of different institutions and individuals who are typically involved in the processing of criminal cases. It includes legislators, law enforcement officers, attorneys, paralegals, judges, court clerks, bailiffs, juries, correctional officers, and probation officers.

Criminal justice system
A collection of different institutions and individuals who are typically involved in the processing of criminal cases.

A. PURPOSE OF LAW

A **law** in its most general sense is defined as "a rule of conduct promulgated and enforced by the government."[1] These rules of conduct can be stated in either positive or negative terms. Hence some laws prohibit people from stealing others' property or driving faster than the posted speed limit, while other laws require people to report their income and pay taxes on it.

Law
A rule of conduct promulgated and enforced by the government.

Laws can apply to the behavior of individuals, businesses, and even governments themselves. Thus municipalities may be prohibited from dumping raw sewage into lakes and rivers, and the police are prohibited from conducting unreasonable searches and seizures.

---

[1]K. Currier & T. Eimermann, *Introduction to Paralegal Studies: A Critical Thinking Approach* (4th ed., Aspen Publishers 2009), 42.

Although Americans frequently complain about the specific content of some of the staggering number of laws that have been enacted by federal, state, and local governments, most laws are considered essential to the functioning of a modern industrialized society. Indeed, the development and enforcement of these laws is arguably the most important function of government. As the Task Force on Law and Law Enforcement reported to the National Commission on the Causes and Prevention of Violence:

> Human welfare demands, at a minimum, sufficient order to insure that such basic needs as food production, shelter and child rearing be satisfied, not in a state of constant chaos and conflict, but on a peaceful, orderly basis with a reasonable level of day-to-day security. . . . When a society becomes highly complex, mobile, and pluralistic; the beneficiary, yet also the victim, of extremely rapid technological change; and when at the same time, and partly as a result of these factors, the influence of traditional stabilizing institutions such as family, church, and community wanes, then that society of necessity becomes increasingly dependent on highly structured, formalistic systems of law and government to maintain social order. . . . For better or worse, we are by necessity increasingly committed to our formal legal institutions as the paramount agency of social control.[2]

Some laws, such as restrictions on abortions, pornography, and gambling, are heavily influenced by the religious and moral beliefs of various groups in the society. Others, such as traffic regulations and zoning laws, do not reflect any specific moral code. Drivers on two-lane American roads are required to use the right lane. This permits a greater number of vehicles to travel more safely and efficiently. While it is important that everyone drive in the properly designated lanes, there is no moral principle requiring people to drive in the right lane (as is done in the United States) rather than the left lane (as is done in Great Britain).

As this text proceeds we will discuss the scope of our criminal law and occasionally raise questions about the wisdom of specific laws. For example, in order to save lives and medical costs, many argue that government should require drivers and passengers to wear seat belts and motorcyclists to wear helmets. Others argue that such laws infringe on people's individual rights. But while people often disagree about the application of specific laws, all but a very limited number of anarchists accept the fact that we need laws to establish the type of order and predictability that are essential to the functioning of our modern society.

B. CRIMINAL VERSUS CIVIL LAW

Law can be categorized in a number of different ways. One of the major divisions is between **criminal law** and **civil law**. Both consist of rules of conduct that have been established by the appropriate legal authorities, but they differ in terms of the consequences to the wrongdoer as well as the way in which violations are investigated and prosecuted. (*See* Figure 1.1.) Criminal law has been defined

Criminal law
The body of law defining offenses against the community at large, regulating how suspects are investigated, charged and tried, and establishing punishments for convicted offenders.

Civil law
The body of law defining actions for which individuals can use the courts to seek remedies for violations of their private rights, establishing procedural requirements for using the courts, and establishing remedies for violations of those rights.

---

[2]J. Campbell, J. Sahid, & D. Stang, *Law and Order Reconsidered: Report of the Task Force on Law and Law Enforcement to the National Commission on the Causes and Prevention of Violence* 3, 5 (1970).

	Criminal Law	Civil Law
TYPE OF HARM	Harm to Society	Harm to Individual Interests
PARTIES TO CASE	Government & Defendant	Plaintiff & Defendant
STANDARD OF PROOF	Beyond a Reasonable Doubt	Preponderance of the Evidence
JUDGMENT GIVEN	Guilty or Not Guilty	Liable or Not Liable
SANCTIONS	Fines, Incarceration, Death	Damages, Injunctions

Figure 1.1   Comparison of Civil and Criminal Law

as "the body of law defining offenses against the community at large, regulating how suspects are investigated, charged and tried, and establishing punishments for convicted offenders."[3] On the other hand, civil law concerns private rights and obligations.

The government is the dominant participant in criminal cases. When an individual violates a criminal law, society at large is considered to be the offended party and government agents are responsible for initiating and prosecuting the case. Thus if Peter Jones burglarizes Sam Smith's home, the criminal law views that act as an offense against the state rather than simply as a matter between Smith and Jones. When the case goes to court, it is listed as *People v. Jones* or *State v. Jones* rather than as *Smith v. Jones*. Government attorneys prosecute the accused party, and the victim is relegated to the role of a witness. The victim plays no role in how the case is presented at trial.

In civil cases, on the other hand, the aggrieved party is responsible for filing and prosecuting the claim. Thus when one party defaults on the terms of a contract, for example, the other party must initiate the legal process on an individual basis. Generally, private parties hire their own attorneys to file the suit and present their case in court.

The legal consequences of civil and criminal violations also reflect this difference. Most civil cases are intended to "make whole," or compensate, victims for the losses they suffered. Generally, this is accomplished through awards of money **damages**. In contrast, victims of crimes seldom receive any financial compensation from the perpetrator. Although a negotiated resolution of a criminal case will occasionally contain some provisions for restitution, the fines that are assessed as part of the criminal process are paid to the state rather than the victim. Incarcerating the perpetrator usually reduces the likelihood of that person being able to financially compensate the victim.

Under the civil law, the individual **plaintiff** benefits directly from the outcome. The party who is found to be at fault can be required to directly compensate the victim for various types of injuries sustained. Even when the damages

Damages
The monetary compensation awarded to the wronged party in a civil case.

Plaintiff
The party who initiates a civil lawsuit.

---

[3]B. Garner, ed., *Black's Law Dictionary* 381 (7th ed. 1999).

are punitive (designed to punish the wrongdoer rather than compensate the victim), the plaintiff, rather than the government, receives the damages award. Note, however, there are situations (usually involving antitrust and securities violations) in which the government can seek civil damages rather than criminal penalties for violations of some laws. In these cases, the government takes on the role of the plaintiff and gets any damages that are awarded.

In addition to the contrasting roles of the government and the victim, there are differences in the way trials are conducted. The most significant is the standard of proof that is applied. In criminal cases, the prosecution is required to prove its case "beyond a reasonable doubt," but in civil actions the plaintiff need only meet the "preponderance of the evidence" standard. The "beyond a reasonable doubt" standard is usually explained to jurors as being the degree of doubt that causes a reasonable person to refrain from acting. "Preponderance of the evidence," on the other hand, is usually understood to mean that the facts asserted are more likely to be true than not true.

A study conducted by Rita James Simon and Linda Mahan showed that judges tend to equate "beyond a reasonable doubt" with a median probability of approximately 8.8 out of 10, while jurors averaged approximately 8.6 out of 10. "Preponderance of the evidence" was interpreted by the judges as a median probability of 5.4 out of 10, with 7.1 out of 10 being the median for jurors.[4] While we cannot establish a specific percentage, it is clear that it is more difficult to convict under a "beyond a reasonable doubt" standard than it is to find for the plaintiff under a "preponderance of the evidence" standard.

It is important to note that a single event could become the basis for both a criminal prosecution and a civil action. For example, the victim of a battery could sue the **defendant** for civil damages at the same time the state is prosecuting the defendant on a criminal charge. The driver of an automobile involved in a traffic accident may receive a traffic ticket from the police and at the same time be sued by someone else involved in the accident. In certain types of antitrust cases, the government can choose between seeking criminal charges and civil damages.

Because civil and criminal proceedings involving the same occurrence are conducted independently of each other, a defendant could be unsuccessful before one court and prevail before the other. One of the most publicized cases of the late twentieth century illustrates this point. Former football star and actor O.J. Simpson was prosecuted for the murders of his ex-wife Nicole Brown Simpson and her friend Ronald Goldman. The jury in the criminal case acquitted Simpson but a civil jury found him liable for the victims' wrongful deaths and entered a multimillion dollar verdict against him. The essential facts were the same in the civil and criminal cases, yet the case outcomes were inconsistent.

Defendant

The party who is defending against either a criminal prosecution or a civil lawsuit. In a criminal case, the defendant is the person accused of committing a crime.

DISCUSSION QUESTIONS

1. A jury found O.J. Simpson not guilty of the murders of his ex-wife Nicole Brown Simpson and her friend Ronald Goldman, yet a civil jury found him liable for the victims' wrongful deaths and entered a large monetary verdict against him.

---

[4]R. Simon & L. Mahan, *Quantifying Burdens of Proof*, 5 Law & Soc. Rev. 319 (1971).

The essential facts were the same in the civil and criminal cases. How can these inconsistent outcomes be reconciled?

2. Although the criminal law is designed to protect the interests of the community at large, can a successful criminal prosecution further the interests of a private individual? If so, how?

3. Sometimes, large monetary awards of punitive damages are imposed against wrongdoers in civil cases who act recklessly or in conscious disregard of the safety of other people. How are civil claims for punitive damages similar to criminal prosecutions? How are they different? Should a criminal offender be subject to suit for punitive damages if he was already prosecuted for the crime giving rise to the civil suit?

C. CONFLICTING MODELS OF THE CRIMINAL JUSTICE SYSTEM

Whereas the digestive system is designed to process food, the criminal justice system is designed to process people suspected of having violated the criminal law. The digestive system serves the larger purpose of extracting the nutrients the body needs to survive, but what is the purpose behind processing people who are suspected of having committed crimes?

In a famous law review article published in 1964, a distinguished law professor named Herbert Packer identified two conflicting views as to what the purpose of the criminal justice system should be.[5] He called one the "crime control model" and the other the "due process model." Each presents different criteria for evaluating the criminal justice system. (*See* Figure 1.2.)

	Crime Control	**Due Process**
PURPOSE OF CRIMINAL JUSTICE SYSTEM	Suppress criminal conduct	Preserve the integrity of the process
ANALOGY	Conveyor belt emphasizing speed and efficiency	Obstacle course emphasizing reliability and eliminating errors
UNDERLYING PRESUMPTION	Presumption of guilt	Presumption of innocence
EMPHASIS/FOCUS	Early administrative fact-finding	Integrity of process and adequacy of appeals

Figure 1.2 Comparisons of Crime Control and Due Process Models

---

[5]H.L. Packer, *"Two Models of the Criminal Process,"* 113 U. PA. L. Rev. 1 (1964).

Crime control model
An approach to evaluating the criminal justice system on the basis of how efficiently it suppresses crime.

Due process model
An approach to evaluating the criminal justice system on the basis of how well it protects people from being charged and/or convicted of crimes they didn't commit.

Due process of law
Legal procedures that enforce basic rights that are considered necessary for fairness and justice.

Under the **crime control model**, the purpose of the criminal justice system is to repress criminal conduct in the most efficient way possible. In contrast, the **due process model** asserts that the criminal justice system should focus on protecting innocent people from being falsely convicted. The problem is that actions designed to keep more criminals off the street may increase the number of innocent people who are mistreated by the system, and actions designed to protect the innocent often make it more difficult to convict the guilty.

The application of the due process model raises very important questions about what due process actually involves and how much due process is too much. **Due process** is one of the most ambiguous and difficult-to-explain concepts in our legal system. The term "due process" appears in both the Fifth and Fourteenth Amendments to the U.S. Constitution. The Fifth Amendment states:

> . . . nor shall any person . . . be deprived of life, liberty, or property, without due process of law; . . .

In *Barron v. Baltimore*,[6] the U.S. Supreme Court ruled that the due process protections guaranteed by the Fifth Amendment are only applicable to actions of the federal government and not those of state or local governments. However, the Fourteenth Amendment explicitly expands due process protections to state actions when it declares:

> . . . nor shall any State deprive any person of life, liberty, or property, without due process of law; . . .

However, neither amendment explicitly defines "due process." To find out what it actually means we have to turn to U.S. Supreme Court opinions in which the justices have applied the concept to specific situations.

In a frequently quoted opinion in *Palko v. Connecticut*, U.S. Supreme Court Justice Benjamin Cardozo defined due process as rights that were necessary to protect against practices that subjected defendants to "a hardship so acute and shocking that our polity will not endure it" or which violate those "fundamental principles of liberty and justice which lie at the base of all our civil and political institutions."[7] Other justices have defined due process as being equivalent to "fundamental fairness."

But language like "a hardship so acute and shocking that our polity will not endure it," "fundamental principles of liberty and justice which lie at the base of all our civil and political institutions," and "fundamental fairness" are subjective concepts rather than objective criteria. Therefore, to really be able to determine whether a particular right or practice is an essential part of due process, it is necessary to do a case-by-case review of court decisions that have specifically involved the right or practice in question.

---

[6]32 U.S. 243, 8 L.Ed. 672 (1833).
[7]302 U.S. 319, 328, 58 S.Ct. 149, 82 L.Ed 288 (1937).

In Chapter 2 we will look closer at the role of constitutional law, and in Parts 2 and 4 we will examine what the courts have ruled regarding specific rights and procedures. For now it is sufficient to think of due process as the protections that are provided to people by law when they are involved in legal disputes with the government.

D. STAGES OF THE CRIMINAL JUSTICE PROCESS

Figure 1.3 shows the major stages involved in criminal prosecutions. Although the details of criminal procedure vary among jurisdictions, this diagram should help you understand how the various stages are related to each other.

The process begins when somebody commits an act that has been categorized as a crime by an appropriately authorized lawmaker. In most cases, the criminal act is either discovered by police or reported to them. This information and further investigation usually lead to the arrest and booking of a suspect.

At an initial appearance stage, the suspect is brought before a judge and informed of the nature of the charges that have been made against him or her. **Bail** is set, and a public defender may be appointed if the defendant is unable to afford an attorney.

Depending on the particular **jurisdiction** involved, the defendant's case may either be set for a **preliminary hearing** or sent to a grand jury. In a preliminary hearing the prosecutor must convince a judge that there is probable cause to take the matter to trial. If a grand jury is used, the prosecutor must convince a majority of the people on the grand jury that there is probable cause to take the matter to trial.

At the **arraignment**, the defendant is informed of the official charges and required to enter a formal plea. If a not-guilty plea is entered, the case is set for trial. Plea bargaining usually goes on sometime between the time of the arraignment and the start of the trial.

A sentencing hearing follows either a guilty plea or a conviction at trial, and the defendant is then turned over to correction authorities to serve out the assigned punishment. Meanwhile, appeals are filed and the case proceeds to one or more stages of appellate review. In Parts 2 and 3 of the text we will discuss each of these stages in far greater detail with an emphasis on what paralegals need to know about them and the types of tasks paralegals may be called upon to complete at each stage.

Keep in mind, however, that whereas the digestive system is pretty much a closed system (all food enters at the same point, travels through the same organs, and exits at the same point), the criminal justice system is much more open-ended. Criminal cases can both enter and exit the system at a number of different points. Most cases do not go through all of the stages presented in Figure 1.3.

Bail
Money or something else of value that is pledged to guarantee that the accused will appear in court for scheduled proceedings.

Jurisdiction
The geographic area within which a political entity has the right to exercise authority. Jurisdiction also refers to a court's power to decide a case or issue an order.

Preliminary hearing
The initial hearing by a judge to determine whether there is probable cause for the charge against the defendant.

Arraignment
A court proceeding at which the judge informs the defendant of the charges filed by the government.

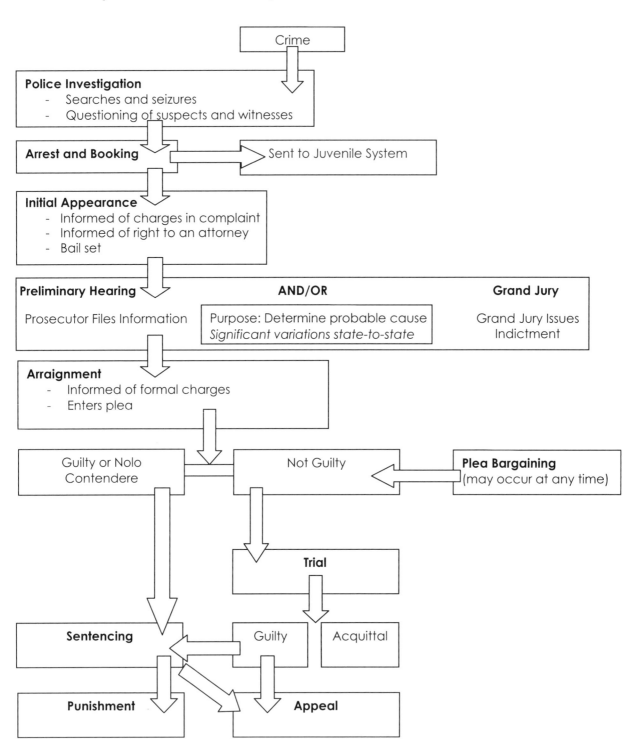

Figure 1.3   The Criminal Process

E. PARTICIPANTS IN THE CRIMINAL JUSTICE SYSTEM

1. THE LAWMAKERS

The United States prides itself on having a government that is based on the **rule of law**. Among other things, the rule of law requires laws to be properly enacted by authorized governmental agencies and officials before they can be enforced. Or, as the Latin maxim *nullum crimen, nulla poena sine lege* declares: "there can be no crime and no punishment without the law."

In Chapter 2, we will explain the differences among constitutional, statutory, administrative, and common law, as well as the differences among federal, state, and local laws. Then in Chapter 3, we will provide an overview of the types of behavior covered in the criminal law and examples of what these laws look like.

For now it is sufficient to point out that most criminal laws are made by state legislatures. The U.S. Congress and local governmental legislative bodies are other common sources of our criminal law. This means that most of our criminal law is made by elected politicians who respond to public opinion within their districts. When constituents express concerns about rising crime rates, the legislators are likely to react by increasing penalties, mandating longer sentences, creating "three strikes and you're out" laws, etc.

Rule of law
A collection of legal principles that all relate to the placement of limitations on the exercise of political power and the operation of government. These principles include (1) government must follow its own rules; (2) government must apply the law impartially; and (3) government must provide due process for those accused of breaking the rules.

2. DEFENDANTS

Criminal defendants are usually involuntary participants in the criminal justice system. While it could be argued that they chose to break the law, they typically do not want to be caught, do not want to spend time in jail prior to the trial, and do not want to be punished after the trial. And the falsely accused defendants certainly don't want to be defendants.

There are numerous examples of criminal defendants who are rich and sometimes famous (e.g., O.J. Simpson, Mel Gibson, Lindsay Lohan, and Winona Ryder), but most defendants are young males with little or no income and are disproportionately from racial and ethnic minority groups. Whereas the rich and famous can usually get out on bail and can hire high-powered lawyers, "average" defendants often remain incarcerated pending their trials and have to rely on public defenders.

3. VICTIMS

As previously mentioned, criminal acts are legally treated as offenses against the state or nation rather than offenses against specific individuals. Thus victims are not formal parties to a criminal action.

Victims are most likely to participate in the criminal process by reporting the existence of the crime to law enforcement personnel and by serving as a witness for the prosecution. However, there are situations in which criminal proceedings are started without any action being taken by the victim. For example, the crime may have been observed by police or by others who were in a position to see it happen. There are also situations in which the victim is either unable or unwilling to testify. In domestic violence cases, it is not unusual for the victim to deny that an offense took place and to refuse to testify against the abuser.

In some cases, victims also have a role in the sentencing process. Indeed, some state victims' rights laws provide for "**victim impact statements**" in which the victim describes how the crime affected his or her life and those of family members.

4. LAW ENFORCEMENT OFFICIALS

Law enforcement officials include local police, sheriff's officers, highway patrol, state police, game wardens, and park rangers. The category also includes Federal Bureau of Investigation (FBI) agents; Bureau of Alcohol, Tobacco, Firearms and Explosives (ATF) agents; Internal Revenue Service (IRS) agents; U.S. Postal Inspection Service agents; and other federal agents assigned to law enforcement duties.

There is wide variation in the nature of the qualifications and training of the various types of law enforcement personnel. Most positions require some minimal level of physical fitness. Some, such as the FBI, have very selective educational background requirements. All have extensive training programs for new agents.

It is the law enforcement agents who usually have the first contact with defendants. Many times they actually see the crime being committed and immediately make an arrest. Other times they are assigned to investigate a crime based on information from either a victim (e.g., business owner reports overnight break-in) or a third party who discovers evidence of a crime (e.g., neighbors find a dead body in their alley). The subsequent investigation then leads law enforcers to question or arrest the defendant.

In lieu of arresting an individual, officials often have the authority to issue a **summons** or a **notice to appear**. These documents inform the individual of an obligation to appear in court on a set date to defend against stated criminal charges. They are most often used for traffic offenses, misdemeanors, and ordinance violations.

When an arrest is made, law enforcement personnel are usually responsible for transporting those who are arrested to a facility (usually a local police station or county jail) where they are booked and often incarcerated pending possible release on bail or on a **personal recognizance bond**. On arriving at the police station, the individual goes through a booking process in which the actual paperwork for the arrest is completed and fingerprints and a picture are taken. If the person is going to be held in custody, the police will also inventory and place in storage the arrestee's personal property.

Law enforcement officers are also responsible for transporting defendants from the lockup to court and for maintaining the security of the courthouse.

Victim impact statement
A written or oral statement made by the victim of the crime (or the family members of a deceased victim) that is presented at the sentencing hearing for the convicted offender.

Summons
An official notice issued under seal of the court informing a party that he or she must appear in court or risk losing the case.

Notice to appear
A notice informing a party that he or she must appear in court or risk losing the matter set for hearing.

Personal recognizance bond (PR) also known as Own recognizance (OR)
A defendant's promise to appear in court without posting cash or other security.

5. ATTORNEYS

Attorneys (also frequently called lawyers) are people who are officially licensed to practice law in a state or federal jurisdiction. In most jurisdictions, they must have attained a bachelor's degree and a graduate degree in law (JD or LLB) and have passed a state bar exam and a morals/character and fitness check.

 The attorney's role in the criminal justice system is to be an advocate for either the governmental unit that is seeking to enforce the law or the defendant who is accused of violating it. The prosecuting attorneys usually carry titles such as District Attorney (or Assistant District Attorney), State's Attorney (or Assistant State's Attorney), or U.S. Attorney (or Assistant U.S. Attorney) and are full-time employees of a unit of the state or federal government.[8] Those representing the defendants are usually in private practice or employees of a government-financed public defender's office.

 In most cases, the prosecuting attorney doesn't get involved in a case until after law enforcement officers have already made an arrest. The attorney then reviews the arrest report and decides what, if any, formal charges should be filed with the court. At other times, prosecuting attorneys become involved prior to an arrest if law enforcement officials need a search warrant or decide that it might be useful to bring a case before a grand jury. Much to the frustration of many defense attorneys, they too seldom get involved in a case prior to the arrest of their client. In most cases, either the defendant doesn't make arrangements to retain an attorney or is unable to have one appointed prior to being arrested. Based on the U.S. Supreme Court's decision in *Miranda v. Arizona*,[9] law enforcement personnel are required to inform criminal suspects of their right to be represented by an attorney (and the right to have one appointed if they cannot afford one on their own) and to remain silent if they are in custody.[10] However, many defendants ignore these warnings and proceed to make incriminating statements prior to having consulted with any attorney.

 Before the start of the trial, attorneys for both sides analyze the evidence, prepare various motions relating to how the trial will be conducted, search for and prepare witnesses, prepare to cross-examine the other side's witnesses, and, when a jury will be used, prepare for jury selection. At the same time, prosecutors and defense attorneys typically engage in **plea bargaining**. This process involves a negotiation in which the defendant agrees to plead guilty to a criminal charge in return for some type of benefit given by the prosecutor to induce the plea. The incentives offered by the government can include reducing the severity of the charge (e.g., settling for a guilty plea on a robbery charge when the original charge was for the more serious offense of armed robbery), dropping related counts (e.g., an original indictment may include three counts of burglary, but the prosecutor may agree to drop two of them in return for a guilty plea to the third), or recommending the minimum sentence or even a suspended sentence rather than going for the maximum sentence authorized by the law.

Attorney
A lawyer; a person licensed by a state to practice law.

Plea bargain
An agreement whereby the defendant pleads guilty to a criminal charge in exchange for a reduction in the charges, the number of counts, or a lesser sentence.

---

[8]In smaller communities these positions may only be part-time and, on occasion, a private attorney may be appointed as a "special prosecutor."

[9]384 U.S. 436, 86 S.Ct. 1602, 16 L.Ed. 2d 694 (1966).

[10]The nature of what constitutes custodial interrogation is discussed in more detail on pp. 101-107.

The prosecutor is willing to make these types of bargains for a variety of reasons. Because most prosecutors' offices are understaffed and overworked, plea bargaining provides a way to both reduce their workload and produce a high conviction rate. Many prosecutors are willing to settle for a sure conviction on the record with at least some jail time for the defendant rather than risk an uncertain conviction for the sake of longer jail time.

If the case proceeds to trial, attorneys for both sides will give opening statements in which they present their respective theories of the case. In other words, the attorneys state what is alleged to have taken place and the anticipated testimony of various witnesses. Then they will begin the process of calling witnesses to testify about what they know of the disputed facts in the case. Each direct examination is followed by a cross-examination by the opposing attorney and then possible re-directs and re-crosses.

It is important to note the degree to which the attorneys, as opposed to the judge, influence the nature of the evidence presented. Unlike the European systems where judges can call witnesses on their own and routinely conduct their own examination of witnesses, witnesses are limited to those called by the parties themselves, and judges are expected to limit themselves to ruling on objections raised by the attorneys.

After all the evidence has been presented, the attorneys get to make their closing arguments. Here they have the opportunity to review and interpret the evidence in its most favorable light and develop emotional appeals on behalf of their clients.

If the judge or jury delivers a guilty verdict, the case will move on to the sentencing stage. Here, attorneys present evidence "in aggravation and mitigation" (testimony designed to influence the judge to give a more severe or less severe sentence). It is also the responsibility of defense attorneys to file post-trial motions and appeals that may follow a conviction. Although many private attorneys handle their own appeals, the federal government and many states have specialized appeals units to take over processing of appeals on behalf of both the prosecutor's office and the public defender's office.

6. PARALEGALS

Paralegal
A person qualified by education, training, or work experience who is employed by a lawyer, law office, corporation, governmental agency, or other entity who performs specifically delegated substantive legal work for which a lawyer is responsible. (American Bar Association definition)

In this text we are particularly interested in the role paralegals play in the criminal justice system. A **paralegal**, sometimes called a legal assistant, is a person with special qualifications who, working under an attorney's supervision, does tasks that, absent the paralegal, the attorney would do. Most have completed at least two years of college and have had specialized paralegal training.[11]

In the criminal law field, you will typically find paralegals working in prosecuting attorneys' offices, for public defenders' offices, and for private defense attorneys. In these offices paralegals are typically involved in reviewing police reports and statements of witnesses, drafting documents such as discovery requests and motions, interviewing potential witnesses, researching legal issues,

---

[11]See Chapter 2 in K. Currier & T. Eimermann, *Introduction to Law for Paralegals: A Critical Thinking Approach* (4th ed., Aspen Publishers 2009).

arranging for expert witnesses, helping to evaluate potential jurors, organizing documents for trial, helping to prepare witnesses, keeping witnesses informed as to when they will be called to testify, and taking notes during the trial. Paralegals are sometimes used by judges to do legal research related to the motions that have been filed and requests for jury instructions. When they work for attorneys doing appellate work, they are frequently called upon to digest the record and help draft appellate briefs.

In later chapters of this book we will go into greater detail regarding the specific tasks paralegals are typically called upon to undertake in the criminal law field. It is also important to keep in mind what paralegals cannot do. They cannot give legal advice and they cannot represent clients in court. It is also important to stress that paralegals must work "under the supervision" of a licensed attorney. Note what the New Jersey Supreme Court had to say about the nature of this supervision.

In Re Opinion No. 24 of the Committee on the Unauthorized Practice of Law
Supreme Court of New Jersey
128 N.J. 114, 607 A.2d 962 (1992)

The opinion of the Court was delivered by JUSTICE GARIBALDI.

The New Jersey Supreme Court Committee on the Unauthorized Practice of Law (the "Committee") concluded in Advisory Opinion No. 24, 126 *N.J.L.J.* 1306, 1338 (1990), that "paralegals functioning outside of the supervision of an attorney-employer are engaged in the unauthorized practice of law." Petitioners are several independent paralegals whom attorneys do not employ but retain on a temporary basis. They ask the Court to disapprove the Advisory Opinion.

Like paralegals employed by attorneys, independent paralegals retained by attorneys do not offer their services directly to the public. Nonetheless, the Committee determined that independent paralegals are engaged in the unauthorized practice of law because they are performing legal services without adequate attorney supervision. We agree with the Committee that the resolution of the issue turns on whether independent paralegals are adequately supervised by attorneys. We disagree with the Committee, however, that the evidence supports a categorical ban on all independent paralegals in New Jersey.

I

The Committee received inquiries from various sources regarding whether independent paralegals were engaged in the unauthorized practice of law. Pursuant to its advisory-opinion powers under *Rule* 1:22-2, the Committee solicited written comments and information from interested persons and organizations.

* * *

The Committee characterized the information that it received in two ways: first, the material expressed positive views on the value of the work performed by paralegals; second, all of the materials expressly or implicitly recognized that the work of paralegals must be performed under attorney supervision. None distinguished between paralegals employed by law firms and those functioning as independent contractors offering services to attorneys. Several recurring themes played throughout the submissions:

1. One need not be a full- or part-time employee of a single attorney to be under the direct supervision of an attorney and independent

paralegals in particular work under the direct supervision of attorneys.

2. Independent paralegals provide necessary services for sole practitioners and small law firms who cannot afford to employ paralegals on a full-time basis.

3. Independent paralegals confer an invaluable benefit on the public in the form of reduced legal fees.

4. Independent paralegals maintain high standards of competence and professionalism.

5. Rather than exacting a *per se* prohibition, the Committee should consider regulations or standards or other alternative forms of guidance, such as licensure and certification.

6. A blanket prohibition on independent paralegals would work a disservice to the paralegals and the general public.

After receiving those submissions, the Committee held a hearing at which four independent paralegals, three employed paralegals, and three attorneys testified. All the independent paralegals testifying before the Committee were well qualified. One independent paralegal noted that as an NALA member she is bound by both the *ABA Model Code of Professional Responsibility* and the ABA *Model Rules of Professional Conduct*. The independent paralegals stated that although they had worked with many attorneys during their careers, they had worked solely for those attorneys and only under their direct supervision.

The independent paralegals gave several reasons for being retained by attorneys. First, attorneys may be understaffed at any time and may need to devote additional resources to one case. Second, attorneys may need paralegal assistance but be unable to afford a full-time paralegal. Third, attorneys may hire independent paralegals who have expertise in a given field.

* * *

II

After the hearing, the Committee issued Advisory Opinion No. 24, 26 *N.J.L.J.* 1306 (1990), in which it compared the amount of supervision attorneys exercise over employed paralegals and retained paralegals. It concluded that attorneys do not adequately supervise retained paralegals.

* * *

Based on those findings, the Committee concluded that attorneys are currently unable to supervise adequately the performance of independent paralegals, and that by performing legal services without such adequate supervision those paralegals are engaging in the unauthorized practice of law. *Ibid.*

We granted petitioners' request for review,— N.J.—(1991), and the Chairperson of the Committee granted their motion to stay the enforcement of Opinion No. 24.

III

No satisfactory, all-inclusive definition of what constitutes the practice of law has ever been devised. None will be attempted here. That has been left, and wisely so, to the courts when parties present them with concrete factual situations. See Milton Lasher, *The Unauthorized Practice of Law*, 72 *N.J.L.J.* 341 (1949) ("What is now considered the practice of law is something which may be described more readily than defined."). Essentially, the Court decides what constitutes the practice of law on a case-by-case basis. *See, e.g., New Jersey State Bar Ass'n v. New Jersey Ass'n of Realtor Bds.*, 93 *N.J.* 470, 461 *A.2d* 1112 (1983) (permitting real-estate brokers to prepare certain residential-sales and lease agreements, subject to right of attorney review); *In re Education Law Center*, 86 *N.J.* 124, 429 *A.2d* 1051 (1981) (exempting non-profit corporations from practice-of-law violations); *Auerbacher v. Wood*, 142 *N.J.Eq.* 484, 59 *A.2d* 863 (E. & A.1948) (holding that services of industrial-relations consultants do not constitute practice of law).

* * *

There is no question that paralegals' work constitutes the practice of law. *N.J.S.A.* 2A:170-78 and 79 deem unauthorized the practice of law by a nonlawyer and make such practice a disorderly-persons offense. However, *N.J.S.A.* 2A:170-81(f) excepts paralegals from being penalized for engaging in tasks that constitute legal practice if their supervising attorney assumes direct responsibility for the work that the paralegals perform. *N.J.S.A.* 2A:170-81(f) states:

> Any person or corporation furnishing to any person lawfully engaged in the practice of law such information or such clerical assistance in and about his professional work as, except for the provisions of this article, may be lawful, but the lawyer receiving such information or service shall at all times maintain full professional and direct responsibility to his client for the information and service so rendered.

Consequently, paralegals who are supervised by attorneys do not engage in the unauthorized practice of law.

IV

Availability of legal services to the public at an affordable cost is a goal to which the Court is committed. The use of paralegals represents a means of achieving that goal while maintaining the quality of legal services. Paralegals enable attorneys to render legal services more economically and efficiently. During the last twenty years the employment of paralegals has greatly expanded, and within the last ten years the number of independent paralegals has increased.

Independent paralegals work either at a "paralegal firm" or freelance. Most are employed by sole practitioners or smaller firms who cannot afford the services of a full-time paralegal. Like large law firms, small firms find that using paralegals helps them provide effective and economical services to their clients. Requiring paralegals to be full-time employees of law firms would thus deny attorneys not associated with large law firms the very valuable services of paralegals.

The United States Supreme Court, in upholding an award of legal fees based on the market value of paralegal services, stated that the use of paralegal services whenever possible "encourages cost-effective legal services * * * by reducing the spiralling cost of * * * litigation." *Missouri v.*

Jenkins, 491 U.S. 274, 288, 109 S.Ct. 2463, 2471, 105 *L.Ed.*2d 229, 243 (1989) (quoting *Cameo Convalescent Center, Inc. v. Senn*, 738 F.2d 836, 846 (7th Cir.1984), *cert. denied*, 469 U.S. 1106, 105 *S.Ct.* 780, 83 *L.Ed.*2d 775 (1985)).

The Court further noted:

> It has frequently been recognized in the lower courts that paralegals are capable of carrying out many tasks, under the supervision of an attorney, that might otherwise be performed by a lawyer and billed at a higher rate. Such work might include locating and interviewing witnesses; assistance with depositions, interrogatories, and document production; compilation of statistical and financial data, checking legal citations, and drafting correspondence. Much such work lies in a gray area of tasks that might appropriately be performed either by an attorney or a paralegal. To the extent that fee applicants under §1988 are not permitted to bill for the work of paralegals at market rates, it would not be surprising to see a greater amount of such work performed by attorneys themselves, thus increasing the overall cost of litigation. [*Id.* at 288 n. 10, 109 *S. Ct.* at 2471-72 n. 10, 105 *L.Ed.*2d at 243 n. 10.]

* * *

We also note that the American Bar Association ("ABA") has long given latitude to attorneys to employ non-lawyers for a variety of tasks. For example, Ethical Consideration 3-6 of the ABA *Model Code of Professional Responsibility* provides as follows:

> A lawyer often delegates tasks to clerks, secretaries, and other lay persons. Such delegation is proper if the lawyer maintains a direct relationship with his/her client, supervises the delegated work, and has complete professional responsibility for the work product. This delegation enables a lawyer to render legal services more economically and efficiently.

The ABA has further stated, in Formal Opinion 316, that "we do not limit the kind of assistance that a lawyer can acquire *in any way* to persons who are admitted to the Bar, so long as the non-lawyers do not do things that lawyers may not do or do the things that [only] lawyers[] may do." (emphasis added)

V

No judicial, legislative, or other rule-making body excludes independent paralegals from its definition of a paralegal. For example, the ABA defines a paralegal as follows:

> A person qualified through education, training or work experience; is employed or *retained* by a lawyer, law office, government agency, or other entity; works under the *ultimate* direction and supervision of an attorney; performs specifically delegated legal work, which, for the most part, requires a sufficient knowledge of legal concepts; and performs such duties that, absent such an assistant, the attorney would perform such tasks. (emphasis added)

The ABA definition expands the role of a legal assistant to include independent paralegals, recognizing that attorneys can and do retain the services of legal assistants who work outside the law office.

* * *

VI

Under both federal law and New Jersey law, and under both the ABA and New Jersey ethics Rules, attorneys may delegate legal tasks to paralegals if they maintain direct relationships with their clients, supervise the paralegal's work and remain responsible for the work product.

Neither case law nor statutes distinguish paralegals employed by an attorney or law firm from independent paralegals retained by an attorney or a law firm. Nor do we. Rather, the important inquiry is whether the paralegal, whether employed or retained, is working directly for the attorney, under that attorney's supervision. Safeguards against the unauthorized practice of law exist through that supervision. Realistically, a paralegal can engage in the unauthorized practice of law whether he or she is an independent paralegal or employed in a law firm. Likewise, regardless of the paralegal's status, an attorney who does not properly supervise a paralegal is in violation of the ethical Rules.

Although fulfilling the ethical requirements of *RPC* 5.3 is primarily the attorney's obligation and responsibility, a paralegal is not relieved from an independent obligation to refrain from illegal conduct and to work directly under the supervision of the attorney. A paralegal who recognizes that the attorney is not directly supervising his or her work or that such supervision is illusory because the attorney knows nothing about the field in which the paralegal is working must understand that he or she is engaged in the unauthorized practice of law. In such a situation an independent paralegal must withdraw from representation of the client. The key is supervision, and that supervision must occur regardless of whether the paralegal is employed by the attorney or retained by the attorney.

We were impressed by the professionalism of the paralegals who testified before the Committee. They all understood the need for direct attorney supervision and were sensitive to potential conflict-of-interest problems. Additionally, they all recognized that as the paralegal profession continues to grow, the need to define clearly the limits of the profession's responsibilities increases.

* * *

We recognize that distance between the independent paralegal and the attorney may create less opportunity for efficient, significant, rigorous supervision. Nonetheless, the site at which the paralegal performs services should not be the determinative factor. In large law firms that have satellite offices, an employed paralegal frequently has less face-to-face contact with the supervising attorney than would a retained paralegal. Moreover, in this age of rapidly-expanding instant communications (including fax tele-transmissions, word processing, computer networks, cellular telephone service and other computer-modem communications), out-of-office paralegals can communicate frequently with their supervising attorneys. Indeed, as technology progresses, there will be more communication between employers and employees located at different sites, even different states. That arrangement will be helpful to both the paralegal and the attorney. Parents and disabled people, particularly, may prefer to work from their homes. Sole practitioners and small law firms will be able to obtain the services of paralegals otherwise available only to large firms.

Moreover, nothing in the record before the Committee suggested that attorneys have found it difficult to supervise independent paralegals. Indeed, the paralegals testified that the use of word processing made an attorney's quick review of their work possible. Most of the independent contractors who testified worked under the supervision of attorneys with whom they had regular communication.

* * *

Nonetheless, we recognize that because independent paralegals are retained by different firms and lawyers, a potential conflict exists. For example, the Advisory Committee on Professional Ethics has noted that "[h]iring a paralegal formerly employed by a firm with which the prospective employer presently is involved in adversarial matters would clearly be improper." In re Opinion No. 546 of the Advisory Committee on Ethics, 114 *N.J.L.J.* 496 (1984). Opinion No. 546 is extremely brief, however, and does not detail the circumstances under which such employment would be improper.

The ABA, however, has also considered whether an employing firm can be disqualified by a change in employment of a non-lawyer employee, specifically a paralegal, in Informal Ethics Opinion 88-1526 (June 22, 1988). The ABA determined that such firms can be disqualified unless they thoroughly screen the paralegal and ensure that the paralegal reveals no information relating to the representation of the client at the former firm to any person in the employing firm. The ABA also noted its concern that paralegals could potentially lose the ability to earn a livelihood if they were prevented from working for different law firms:

> It is important that nonlawyer employees have as much mobility in employment opportunities as possible consistent with the protection of clients' interests. To so limit employment opportunities that some nonlawyers trained to

work with law firms might be required to leave the careers for which they are trained would disserve clients as well as the legal profession. Accordingly, any restrictions on the nonlawyer's employment should be held to the minimum necessary to protect the confidentiality of client information.

We again conclude that regulations and guidelines can be drafted to address adequately the conflict-of-interest problem. For example, as urged by paralegal associations, there could be a requirement that paralegals must keep records of each case, listing the names of the parties and all counsel. Before undertaking new employment, paralegals would check the list. Likewise, attorneys should require the paralegals to furnish them with such a list. The attorney could thus examine whether such matters would conflict with the attorney's representation of a client before retaining that paralegal. Regulation can also remedy any problems resulting from the attendant problem of paralegals sending correspondence directly to clients without the attorney's review and approval.

* * *

VII

Regulation and guidelines represent the proper course of action to address the problems that the work practices of all paralegals may create. Although the paralegal is directly accountable for engaging in the unauthorized practice of law and also has an obligation to avoid conduct that otherwise violates the Rules of Professional Conduct, the attorney is ultimately accountable. Therefore, with great care, the attorney should ensure that the legal assistant is informed of and abides by the provisions of the Rules of Professional Conduct.

Although an attorney must directly supervise a paralegal, no rational basis exists for the disparate way in which the Committee's opinion treats employed and independent paralegals. The testimony overwhelmingly indicates that the independent paralegals were subject to direct supervision by attorneys and were sensitive to potential conflicts of interest. We conclude that given the appropriate instructions and supervision, paralegals, whether as employees or independent contractors, are valuable and necessary members of an attorney's team in the effective and efficient practice of law.

Subsequent to the issuance of the Committee's decision, the State Bar Association forwarded a resolution to this Court requesting the establishment of a standing committee on paralegal education and regulation. We agree that such a committee is necessary, and will shortly establish it to study the practice of paralegals and make recommendations. The committee may consider guidelines from other states, bar associations, and paralegal associations in formulating regulations for New Jersey paralegals. Any such regulations or guidelines should encourage the use of paralegals while providing both attorneys and paralegals with a set of principles that together with the Rules of Professional Conduct can guide their practices. The guidelines drafted will not be static but subject to modification as new issues arise.

We modify Opinion No. 24 in accordance with this opinion.

CASE DISCUSSION QUESTIONS

1. What court decided this case?
2. Who were the petitioners in this case?
3. What were the petitioners asking the court to do?
4. What was the legal issue the court was being asked to decide?
5. What does the court cite as the underlying justification for using paralegals?
6. What is the difference between an "independent paralegal" and a paralegal who is an employee of a law firm?
7. Why did the New Jersey Supreme Court Committee on the Unauthorized Practice of Law consider important the distinction between independent paralegals and paralegals who are employees of law firms?
8. What are the primary reasons for using independent paralegals?
9. What constitutes "the practice of law"?
10. Do paralegals who are supervised by attorneys engage in the unauthorized practice of law? Why or why not?
11. What official action did the New Jersey Supreme Court take?

7. JUDGES

Judge
A governmental official who presides at court proceedings. The judge decides all legal issues presented and determines the facts in non-jury cases.

A **judge** is a public official who presides over various types of legal proceedings and is authorized to take specified types of legal actions. Within the various state and federal court systems, there are different types of judges, serving on different courts, with different types of powers and responsibilities. Some lower-level judges may be called magistrates, justices of the peace, court commissioners, or associate judges. Higher-level judges are appellate judges or Supreme Court Justices.

Judges are either elected or appointed to positions on designated courts. In the federal system they are appointed by the president with the consent of the Senate. At the state level some judges are elected, some are appointed by the governor, and some are appointed by other judges. Although neither the Constitution nor federal statutes require it, standard practice has been to appoint only licensed attorneys to serve as judges. Most states have formal laws establishing a requirement that judges be attorneys.

In the criminal law field, they issue search warrants, determine the terms of any pre-trial release (e.g., set bail or issue personal recognizance bonds), arraign defendants on charges brought by the prosecutor's office, rule on pre-trial motions, preside at criminal trials, empanel and instruct juries, and sentence convicted defendants. In **bench trials**, judges also serve as the sole finder of fact and determine whether a defendant is guilty or not guilty.

Bench trial
A non-jury trial at which the judge decides all questions of fact.

8. OTHER COURT PERSONNEL

There are a number of other people who perform important functions in the court system. They include court clerks, bailiffs, court reporters, sheriffs, and marshals.

Court clerks are responsible for maintaining the court files in proper order as well as ensuring that the various motions submitted by lawyers are properly filed and the actions taken by judges accurately docketed. A head clerk of the courts is usually responsible for running the central records section of the courthouse; his or her assistants may be assigned to sit in on the actual courtroom proceedings.

Bailiffs are responsible for maintaining order in the courtrooms. They are also responsible for watching over the juries when they are in recess or when they have been sequestered. When a jury is sequestered, the members sleep at a hotel and are kept isolated from the public and their families to prevent them from being exposed to prejudicial publicity, threats, bribes, or any other improper influences.

The **court reporter** prepares verbatim transcripts of courtroom proceedings. Most reporters use a stenotype machine rather than shorthand. Because it is expensive, they prepare a written transcript only if the case is being appealed.

Finally, deputy sheriffs and **marshals** also serve as officers of the court. They serve summonses and other court documents, collect money as required by court judgments, and otherwise help in carrying out the court's orders. They also may provide security for the courthouse.

Court clerk
A court employee who is responsible for maintaining the court files in proper order as well as ensuring that the various motions submitted by lawyers are properly filed and the actions taken by judges accurately docketed.

Bailiff
A court employee who is responsible for maintaining order in the courtrooms and watching over juries when they are in recess or when they have been sequestered.

Court reporter
The court employee who prepares verbatim transcripts of courtroom proceedings.

Marshal
A court officer who serves summonses and other court documents, collects money as required by court judgments, provides security for the courthouse, and otherwise helps in carrying out the court's orders.

9. JURORS

The jury system originated in England as a check on the powers of the government and became an important part of the U.S. judicial system. Among other things, the Sixth Amendment to the U.S. Constitution creates a right to a public trial by an impartial jury in federal criminal cases. The U.S. Supreme Court has ruled that the due process clause of the Fourteenth Amendment applies the right to a trial by jury to defendants in state criminal actions when they face possible incarceration of six months or more.

One of the most frequently misunderstood principles of the jury system is the concept of being tried before a jury of one's peers. Contrary to what many people think, this does not mean that the jury must consist of a group of people who are similar to the defendant. Rather, the jury only needs to be broadly representative of the community in which the trial takes place. The focus is not on the characteristics of the people who end up serving on a particular jury, but rather it is on the nature of the general pool from which the jury was chosen.

Grand jury
A court-appointed panel composed of sixteen to twenty-three citizens that considers evidence presented by prosecuters and determines whether there is probable cause to bring formal criminal charges.

There are actually two distinct types of juries. One is called the grand jury and the other is a petit jury. A **grand jury** is supposed to serve as a check on the prosecutor's power to force someone to go through the ordeal of a criminal trial. Grand juries are customarily composed of sixteen to twenty-three members.[12] In situations where they are used, a majority of the members of the grand jury must agree that there is probable cause to believe the defendant committed the crimes the prosecutor wants to charge him or her with.

The Fifth Amendment to the U.S. Constitution requires that "no person shall be held to answer for a capital or otherwise infamous crime, unless on a presentment or indictment of a grand jury." Although this applies only to federal cases, some states also require the use of a grand jury. Other states allow the prosecutor the option of using a grand jury or not using it. There are also states that do not use grand juries at all.

Critics have charged that because the prosecutor suggests who the witnesses should be and also interprets the meaning of the criminal statutes, the laypersons who serve on the grand jury do little more than rubber-stamp the prosecutor's decisions and do not act as an effective check on the prosecutor's use of discretionary powers.

The grand jury also can serve as an investigative arm of the government and can be especially useful when it comes to investigating organized crime or corruption in the government's own bureaucracy. The Watergate grand jury is probably the most famous example of a grand jury used for such investigations. The ability to **subpoena** and give immunity to key witnesses makes the grand jury an effective weapon in the hands of a well-trained prosecutor. When the grand jury takes on this type of role, its investigations frequently include people who are not yet under arrest. If the grand jury decides that those people should be brought to trial, an arrest warrant is issued on the basis of the grand jury's indictment. A defendant arrested in this manner goes directly from the initial appearance stage to the arraignment.

Subpoena
An order issued by the authority of a court that commands an individual to appear to testify or produce documents at a judicial event such as a trial or grand jury proceeding.

The **petit jury** is the type of jury that is used in trials. The U.S. Constitution requires that criminal juries at the federal level consist of twelve members and that their verdicts be unanimous. At the state level, it allows for the use of six-member juries with unanimous verdicts or twelve-person juries with less than unanimous verdicts, as well as for traditional twelve-person unanimous juries. The states themselves select which of these options they wish to use.

Petit jury
A court-appointed panel of citizens who consider the evidence presented by both sides at trial and determine the facts in dispute.

10. CORRECTIONS PERSONNEL

In addition to employing people to serve as prison guards, correctional facilities also employ counselors and therapists, medical staff, and librarians. Probation and parole officers are employed to check up on the whereabouts and activities of people who have been convicted of crimes and have either been placed on probation (rather than being incarcerated) or on parole (after having been conditionally released from their incarceration).

---

[12]At the federal level, "[e]very grand jury impaneled before any district court shall consist of not less than sixteen nor more than twenty-three persons." 18 U.S.C. §3321.

F. THE JUVENILE JUSTICE SYSTEM

A **juvenile** is defined as a young person who has not yet attained the age at which persons are considered to be adults under the criminal law. Under the federal Juvenile Delinquency Act, a person is classified as a juvenile if that person has not attained his or her eighteenth birthday. Some states define it in terms of being under age seventeen.

Juvenile courts are special courts established to deal with juveniles who commit criminal acts or who are adjudged to be abused or neglected. Rather than convicting the juvenile of a crime and punishing the juvenile as they would an adult, juvenile courts adjudicate the individual to be a **juvenile delinquent** and require him or her to take part in various types of treatment options, such as counseling or incarceration.

In cases where older juveniles commit very serious crimes, such as rape or murder, the juvenile court can waive its jurisdiction and authorize adult criminal prosecutions. In *Kent v. United States*[13], the U.S. Supreme Court ruled that juvenile courts could not waive their jurisdiction and authorize adult criminal prosecution without a hearing at which the minor has access to the records on which the juvenile court waived jurisdiction.

Juvenile
A young person who has not yet attained the age at which persons are considered to be adults under the criminal law.

Juvenile courts
Special courts established to deal with juveniles who commit acts that are violations of the criminal law or who are adjudged to be abused or neglected.

Juvenile delinquent
A juvenile who has been adjudicated to have committed acts that are violations of the criminal law.

SUMMARY

This chapter has provided an overview of the criminal justice system. It explained how law prohibits or requires certain types of behaviors in order to protect and improve our society. Criminal law differs from civil law in terms of the types of sanctions imposed and the role of the government in enforcement.

The criminal justice system is a very complex set of people and institutions that make the criminal law, identify and process alleged violators, and punish those who have been found guilty of having violated these laws. It includes legislators and administrative officials, law enforcement authorities (police, FBI, etc.), attorneys (and their staffs), judges (and other court officials), jurors, and corrections officials.

There are, however, two conflicting views as to how the criminal justice system should operate. Those who support the crime control model believe the system should suppress criminal conduct in the most efficient manner possible; supporters of the due process model believe the system should focus on protecting innocent people from being falsely convicted. You should keep these conflicting goals in mind as you learn more about how the criminal justice system operates in the chapters that follow.

In the next two chapters we will explore the substance of our criminal laws. Chapter 2 will discuss how the law is organized and the theoretical principles upon which those laws are based. Chapter 3 will provide examples of the way the law is actually written.

---

[13]383 U.S. 541. 86 S.Ct. 1045, 16 L.Ed. 2d 84 (1966).

Then in Parts 2 and 3 of the book we will go into greater detail about which participants do what at each stage of the criminal justice process. Throughout the book special attention will be given to the roles of paralegals.

INTERNET RESOURCES

General Information on the Criminal Justice System

- National Criminal Justice Reference Service: **http://www.ncjrs.gov**
- National Institute of Justice: **http://www.ojp.usdoj.gov/nij/welcome.html**
- Office of Justice Programs: **http://www.ojp.usdoj.gov/**
- National Center for State Courts: **http://www.ncsc.org/default.aspx**
- U.S. Courts: **http://www.uscourts.gov/Home.aspx**
- Directory of state and local websites: **http://www.statelocalgov.net/**

Participants in the Criminal Justice System

- Attorneys: **http://www.bls.gov/oco/ocos053.htm**
- Corrections Personnel:
  http://www.bls.gov/oco/ocos156.htm
  http://www.bls.gov/oco/ocos265.htm
- Law Enforcement:
  http://legalcareers.about.com/od/careerprofiles/tp/Law-Enforcement-Careers.htm
  http://www.bls.gov/oco/ocos160.htm
  http://www.fbi.gov/
- Paralegals: **http://www.bls.gov/oco/ocos114.htm**

The Juvenile Justice System

- National Center for Juvenile Justice (NCJJ):
  http://www.ncjjservehttp.org/NCJJWebsite/main.html
- Office of Juvenile Justice and Delinquency Prevention (OJJDP):
  http://www.ojjdp.gov/
- National Juvenile Defender Center: **http://njdc.info/state_data.php**

REVIEW QUESTIONS

1. What is a law?
2. Why are laws needed?
3. What are the basic differences between criminal law and civil law?
4. What are the crime control and due process models of the criminal justice system?
5. What governmental bodies are most responsible for the enactment of criminal laws?
6. Because victims of crime are not formal parties to a criminal action, how can they help bring offenders to justice?
7. List the methods that are used to obligate a defendant to make a first appearance in a criminal case.
8. What qualification do attorneys typically possess that enables them to practice law?

9. What rights does the U.S. Supreme Court case of *Miranda v. Arizona* afford to persons taken into custody by law enforcement officers?
10. What are the reasons that prosecutors engage in plea bargaining?
11. What functions do judges carry out in criminal cases?
12. How does the grand jury differ from the petit jury?
13. How does the juvenile justice system differ from the criminal justice system that serves adults?

Chapter 2

Basic Principles of Criminal Law

Before jumping into the details of criminal law and criminal procedure, we need to examine some of the basic concepts upon which our criminal law is based. One of these most basic principles is adherence to the rule of law.

A. RULE OF LAW

As mentioned in Chapter 1, the rule of law is a collection of legal principles that all relate to the placement of limitations on the exercise of political power and the operation of government. These principles include: (1) government must follow its own rules; (2) government must apply the law impartially; and (3) government must provide due process for those accused of breaking the rules.

In order to achieve the rule of law, the laws must:

- Be enacted in accordance with preexisting legal rules (e.g., be constitutionally authorized)
- Be made public
- Be reasonably clear in meaning
- Be capable of being complied with
- Be applied prospectively, not retroactively
- Be applied in an impartial manner consistent with their meaning
- Remain in force for a reasonable period of time

B. SOURCES OF LAW

Law
A rule of conduct promulgated and enforced by the government.

Statutory law
A form of law that is created by legislative bodies in the form of statutes and ordinances.

Statutes
A form of written law that is enacted by federal and state legislative bodies.

Code
A compilation of statues, ordinances, or administrative regulations that is organized by subject matter rather than by the date of its enactment.

Ordinance
A form of law that is created by local legislative bodies such as city councils.

Administrative law
Rules and regulations created by administrative agencies.

Constitutional law
Laws and legal principles derived from constitutions through judicial interpretation.

Court reporters (books)
Books that contain decisions and opinions of courts.

You probably remember something from a high school civics class about the legislature making the law, the executive branch enforcing the law, and the courts applying it. The truth, however, is that the legislative, executive, and judicial branches are all involved in creating the **law**. Their specific roles depend in part upon the type of law that is being promulgated.

When people think about a law, they usually envision what is formally classified as **statutory law**. **Statutes** appear as you would expect a law should appear. They spell out rules that apply to general categories of people, businesses, etc. Statutes are enacted by a majority of an official legislative body, such as the U.S. Congress or a state legislature. These laws are given specific names and citations and are usually incorporated into an official code. (A **code** is a compilation of statutes, ordinances, or regulations that is organized by subject matter rather than by the date of its enactment.) When local governmental units such as county boards, city councils, and sanitary districts pass laws, they are usually called **ordinances** rather than statutes but are still categorized as a type of statutory law.

If all of these statutes were written in such a way that their meaning was clear to everyone, we could apply the conventional wisdom that the legislative branch makes the law, the executive branch enforces it, and the judicial branch applies it. However, statutes and ordinances frequently contain ambiguous language and therefore are not clear to all who read them. In these situations, the executive branch has some degree of discretion over how it chooses to interpret statutes. Similarly, a judge cannot reach a decision as to whether someone is guilty of breaking the law without clarifying what behavior the law actually requires or prohibits. In both these situations, the executive branch and the judicial branch are clearly involved in "making" the law.

Administrative law is similar to statutory law in that it usually consists of fairly specific regulations that are written in a form similar to statutes. In effect, the legislative branch intentionally leaves it to the executive branch and to independent regulatory agencies to "fill in the details" of the law within a general structure set down by the legislature. Through the process of filling in these details, the executive branch, rather than the legislature, is crafting the exact wording of the law. And to the extent that there is some degree of ambiguity in these administrative regulations, the courts are drawn into the lawmaking process when they are called upon to resolve that ambiguity.

A third major category of law is **constitutional law**. This type of law is based on the texts of the constitutions of the United States and of the fifty states. Because constitutions include provisions that speak in general and broad language, the judicial branch has to interpret the meaning of these terms in the context of the facts of the case. Therefore, one cannot understand what a constitution requires without reviewing how it has been applied in the written opinions of the United States Supreme Court and of those of the highest courts of the states. These decisions are published in **court reporters**.

Constitutions define how the government is organized and the powers given to the various governmental institutions. Most also contain a "Bill of Rights" section that enumerates specific rights of the government's citizens. Constitutional law is therefore frequently used to challenge a statute or administrative regulation on the basis that it is prohibited by one or more provisions in the constitution.

While the U.S. Constitution is pretty clear about things like the age requirements for representatives, senators, and the president, it contains many broad, sweeping phrases, such as "interstate commerce," "establishment of religion," "freedom of speech and press," and "unreasonable search and seizure." These somewhat ambiguous phrases open the door for the judicial branch to play a key role in the development of constitutional law. Based on the principle of **judicial review** as it was enunciated by Chief Justice John Marshall in *Marbury v. Madison*,[1] the judicial branch has the power to strike down statutes and void other government actions that are not consistent with the Court's interpretation of the Constitution. State courts also employ judicial review to invalidate statutory and administrative laws that conflict with state constitutions.

A fourth source of law is what is referred to as the common law. **Common law** is the body of law derived from judges' decisions rather than from the other three sources of law. The common law, which originated in England and continues to evolve in the United States, applies to legal disputes involving subjects that are not addressed by the other three types of law. In other words, in the absence of pronouncements from the constitution or a legislative or administrative body, the judge looks to the earlier decisions of other judges in similar circumstances. An earlier judicial decision relied upon in deciding a case is called **judicial precedent**.

Over time, statutory law has superseded much of the common law. This is especially true in the area of criminal law, which is now almost entirely statutory. However, while Section 1.05(1) of the American Law Institute's **Model Penal Code** states: "No conduct constitutes an offense unless it is a crime or violation under this Code or another statute of this State,"[2] there are still a few states that recognize some common law crimes. For instance, as recently as 1999, the Rhode Island Supreme Court upheld convictions on the basis of common law crimes.[3] The common law continues to play its most prominent role in the area of tort law.

In addition to classifying law based on its being found in constitutions, statutes, administrative regulations, or past court decisions, it can also be classified as to whether it is federal, state, or local law. Federal laws consist of laws made by Congress, federal executive agencies, and the rulings of federal courts. State laws are created by state legislatures, state executive agencies, and state court rulings. Local laws are made by local legislative bodies such as city councils and county boards, by local administrative agencies, and by courts interpreting those laws. Whereas federal laws apply nationwide, state laws pertain only to the state in which they were made, and local laws apply only to selected local areas. It is left to the state courts to settle any conflicts between state and local laws and to the federal courts to resolve conflicts between federal and state laws. In some

Judicial review
The legal doctrine that courts have the power to strike down statutes and void other government actions that are not consistent with the court's interpretation of the constitution.

Common law
Legal principles that have evolved over time from the analysis of court decisions made in the absence of constitutional, statutory, and administrative law.

Judicial precedent
An earlier judicial decision that is relied upon by judges in deciding a case.

Model Penal Code
A model criminal code prepared by the American Law Institute (ALI) to promote improvements in and greater consistency among state criminal codes.

---

[1] 5 U.S. (1 Cranch) 137, 2 L. Ed. 60 (1803).

[2] In 1956 the American Law Institute assembled a group of law professors and practicing attorneys to develop a model criminal code to be used to seek legal reform and greater uniformity among the states. While the Model Penal Code has been highly influential, states have not adopted all sections as it was written or as it has been revised in later years.

[3] *State v. Rodriguez*, 731 A.2d 726 (R.I. 1999).

cases, the federal law preempts the state law; in others, both federal and state laws may be enforced simultaneously.

While most criminal law comes from state statutes, certain types of crimes are found only in federal statutes. State and federal regulations can also play a role in criminal prosecutions. Federal and state statutes, regulations, court rules, and constitutional law are also involved in questions of criminal procedure. Constitutional guarantees such as protection against double jeopardy, the right to counsel, the privilege against self-incrimination, the right to confront witnesses, and the right to a jury trial also play a key role in the criminal law.

Although the common law does not play much of a role in criminal law, one frequently needs to refer to case law interpreting constitutional rights and the statutes being applied.

Figure 2.1 summarizes the sources of criminal law; Figure 2.2 lists rights guaranteed to criminal defendants by the U.S. Constitution.

C. CLASSIFICATIONS OF CRIMES

Felony
A major crime that is punishable by a year or more in prison.

Misdemeanor
A minor crime that is punishable by a fine and/ or less than a year in jail.

Crimes are generally classified as either felonies or misdemeanors. **Felonies** are considered to be "major crimes," such as murder, rape, armed robbery, and aggravated assault. The key is that crimes classified as felonies generally carry sentences of a year or more in prison. **Misdemeanors**, on the other hand, involve crimes like disorderly conduct and criminal damage to property. When incarceration is called for in these cases, it usually is for less than one year in a county jail.

In addition to the length and location of incarceration, the consequences of being convicted of a felony versus a misdemeanor often include loss of the right to vote and hold public office. Under federal law, anyone convicted of a felony in any jurisdiction loses the right to possess a firearm.

	Constitutional	**Statutory**	**Administrative**	**Common Law**
FEDERAL GOVERNMENT	U.S. Constitution and federal court decisions interpreting it	U.S. Code (U.S.C.) enacted by Congress and federal court decisions interpreting it	Code of Federal Regulations (C.F.R.) adopted by agencies and federal court decisions interpreting it	None
STATE GOVERNMENT	State constitution and state court decisions interpreting it	State Code enacted by legislature and state court decisions interpreting it	Administrative Code adopted by state agencies and state court decisions interpreting it	State court decisions interpreting common law principles
LOCAL GOVERNMENT	None	Ordinances enacted by municipalities and state court decisions interpreting them	Ordinarily none	None

Figure 2.1 Sources of Criminal Law

Protected Right	Constitutional Provision
Bills of Attainder Prohibited	Article I, §9
No Ex Post Facto Laws	Article I, §10
No Unreasonable Searches & Seizures	Fourth Amendment
Indictment by Grand Jury	Fifth Amendment
No Self-incrimination	Fifth Amendment
No Double Jeopardy	Fifth Amendment
Due Process of Law	Fifth & Fourteenth Amendments
Speedy & Public Trial	Sixth Amendment
Informed of Charge	Sixth Amendment
Confrontation of Witnesses	Sixth Amendment
Compulsory Process of Witnesses	Sixth Amendment
Assistance of Counsel	Sixth Amendment
Jury Trial	Sixth Amendment
No Excessive Bail	Eighth Amendment
No Cruel & Unusual Punishment	Eighth Amendment
Equal Protection of Law	Fourteenth Amendment

Figure 2.2 Rights Guaranteed to Criminal Defendants Under the U.S. Constitution

While there are many similarities from one state to another, there are also many differences. What is treated as a felony in one state may be only a misdemeanor in another. Indeed it may not even be considered a crime in another state. Gun laws provide a good illustration. A failure to register a firearm may be a felony in some states and a misdemeanor in others. In some states it is illegal to carry a concealed weapon without a special permit, while it is perfectly legal in others. Each legislative body decides what will or will not be legal and whether it will be considered a felony or a misdemeanor.

Many states further subdivide felonies and misdemeanors into subcategories on the basis of the degree of harm done and/or the length of the sentence imposed. **Capital offenses** are a special type of felony in which the offense could be punished by death.[4] In addition to having a special category for capital offenses, some states further divide their felonies and misdemeanors to reflect the variations of the punishments that are authorized. For example,

Capital offense
A special type of felony that is punishable by death.

---

[4]See discussion on the death penalty in Chapter 13.

Illinois categorizes felonies as Class X, Class 1, Class 2, Class 3, or Class 4, and misdemeanors as Class A, Class B, Class C, and Petty Offenses. The statute defining the crime also specifies its class.[5] A separate part of the state code lists minimum and maximum sentences for first and second degree murder, habitual criminals, and each of these classes of felonies and misdemeanors.[6]

Petty offense
A violation of the law that is considered less serious than a misdemeanor.

In addition to felonies and misdemeanors, there are some other types of laws that are often called **petty offenses** and are sometimes referred to as being quasi-criminal. Traffic offenses such as speeding or failure to obey a traffic signal are commonly classified as petty offenses and do not carry the same stigma as do violations of the regular criminal law. Nevertheless, the judicial proceedings used to enforce these types of laws are criminal in nature. The state takes it on itself to prosecute offenders, who in turn must be found guilty "beyond a reasonable doubt." Some juvenile proceedings are also criminal in nature. Local ordinances for matters like garbage disposal and barking dogs are additional examples of petty offenses.

Crimes can also be classified on the basis of the nature of the harm done and the type of victim involved. For example, the previously mentioned Model Penal Code is divided into five categories: Offenses Involving Danger to the Person, Offenses Against Property, Offenses Against the Family, Offenses Against Public Administration, and Offenses Against Public Order and Decency. Figure 2.3 provides examples of the types of crimes that fall into each of these categories.

Category	Types of Crimes Included
Offenses Involving Danger to Person	Homicide; Assault; Criminal Endangerment; False Imprisonment; Kidnapping; Sexual Assault
Offenses Against Property	Destruction of Property (i.e., arson); Intrusions of Property (burglary & trespass); Fraud; Forgery
Offenses Against the Family	Bigamy and Incest
Offenses Against Public Administration	Bribery; Obstruction of Government; Perjury; Treason
Offenses Against Public Order and Decency	Alcohol and Drug Offenses; Disorderly Conduct; Obscenity; Prostitution

Figure 2.3   ALI Model Criminal Code Classifications

[5]730 ILCS 5/5-5-1

[6]730 ILCS 5/5-8-1 and 5/5-8-3. See Chapter 13 for a more extended discussion of sentencing.

Crimes can also be categorized on the basis of the nature of the criminal and the context in which they take place. For example, people will sometimes distinguish between **white-collar crime** and **street crime**. The term *white-collar crime* was introduced by a prominent sociologist named Edwin Sutherland in 1939. In his book *White-Collar Crime*, he defined it as "a crime committed by a person of respectability and high social status in the course of his occupation."[7] Sutherland argued that white-collar crime was largely ignored because the press and law enforcement agencies focused on the more violent street crimes carried out by people in the lower economic classes.

Whereas Sutherland focused on the social status of the criminal, the Federal Bureau of Investigation (FBI) defines white-collar crime in terms of the methods used. A 1983 Department of Justice report noted that "white-collar criminals occupy positions of responsibility and trust in government, industry, the professions, and civic organizations."[8] The FBI website provides that "white-collar crimes are categorized by deceit, concealment, or violation of trust and are not dependent on the application or threat of physical force or violence. Such acts are committed by individuals and organizations to obtain money, property, or services, to avoid the payment or loss of money or services, or to secure a personal or business advantage."[9] Typical white-collar crimes involve some type of fraud in the context of business activities, banking, insurance, or the Internet. Other examples include bribery, tax evasion, antitrust violations, and violations of environmental protection regulations.

Whereas state criminal codes are generally very inclusive, the federal criminal law tends to focus on criminal activities that take place in the context of interstate commerce, immigration, national security, and interference with the activities of federal agents and employees. Some of the best-known sections of federal criminal law cover crimes like kidnapping, bank robbery, illegal transportation and sale of drugs and firearms, pornography, and sexual exploitation of children. Thanks to the public attention given to NFL football player Michael Vick, many sports fans also know that federal statutes prohibit "buying, selling, delivering, or transporting animals for participation in animal fighting venture(s)."[10] Less familiar to the layman are federal laws involving bank and securities fraud, bribery, and influence peddling.

D. ELEMENTS OF A CRIME

In order to determine if a crime has taken place, one must analyze not only what the person did but what was going on in that person's mind at the time he or she committed this act and what the results of that act were. The Latin terms *actus reus* (translated as "guilty act" or "wrongful conduct") and *mens rea* (translated as "guilty mind" or "criminal intent") are frequently used in this

White-collar crime
A non-violent crime characterized by deceit, concealment, or violation of trust that is committed by an individual in the course of his or her occupation or by a company in the course of its business.

Street crime
A crime that usually involves violence and is typically carried out by a person considered to be from a low socioeconomic class.

Actus reus
A Latin term referring to a person's wrongful conduct that resulted in an illegal act.

Mens rea
A Latin term referring to what was going on in someone's mind at the time he or she committed an illegal act.

[7]E. Sutherland, *White Collar Crime* (New York, Dryden Press 1949).
[8]E. Podgor & J. Isreal, *White Collar Crime* (2, St. Paul, MN, West Group 1997).
[9]*http://www.fbi.gov/libref/factsfigure/wcc.htm.*
[10]7 U.S.C. §2156(b).

APPLICATION EXERCISES

1. Based on the facts presented in the discussion of the Cook case (*see hypothetical cases information presented on p. xxxvii*):
   a. Identify the types of criminal laws Cook may have violated.
   b. Which of these laws are likely to be federal, state, or local laws?
   c. What, if any, civil actions might also arise out of these facts?

2. Based on the facts presented in the discussion of the Turner case (*see hypothetical case information presented on p. xxxvii*):
   a. Identify the types of criminal laws Turner may have violated.
   b. Which of these laws are likely to be federal, state, or local laws?
   c. What, if any, civil actions might also arise out of these facts?

3. Based on the facts presented in the discussion of the Edwards case (*see hypothetical case information presented on p. xxxviii*):
   a. Identify the types of criminal laws Edwards may have violated.
   b. Which of these laws are likely to be federal, state, or local laws?
   c. What, if any, civil actions might also arise out of these facts?

4. Based on the facts presented in the discussion of the Schroeder case (*see hypothetical case information presented on p. xxxviii*):
   a. Identify the types of criminal laws Schroeder may have violated.
   b. Which of these laws are likely to be federal, state, or local laws?
   c. What, if any, civil actions might also arise out of these facts?
   d. What, if anything, is significant about the fact that Schroeder is an attorney?

context. For example, if Mr. Jones shoots a gun, the existence of a crime will depend upon whether Mr. Jones was authorized to possess the weapon, why he shot it, where he shot it, and the nature of the damage caused by the bullet he fired.

We will focus on *actus reus* first. If Mr. Jones was not authorized to possess or shoot a firearm, he could be guilty of violating a number of possible state and/or federal laws regulating firearms. If the bullet damaged someone's house or automobile, he could be guilty of such crimes as criminal damage to property or disorderly conduct. If the bullet injured someone, the potential crimes could include first degree homicide, second degree homicide, involuntary manslaughter, reckless homicide, assault, aggravated assault, battery, aggravated battery, and reckless conduct.

As previously mentioned, *mens rea* translates as "guilty mind." Here the focus is on what a person's intentions were. Why did Mr. Jones shoot the gun? What did he think was going to happen to the bullet? Although it is difficult to prove what was going on in someone's mind when a crime was committed, the courts allow judges and juries to infer the defendant's state of mind from both statements made and actions undertaken at that time. Furthermore, the law assumes that people know the probable consequences of their acts. A person who strikes another person may be presumed to have intended the infliction of harm in that such a result naturally flows from hitting another.

The defendant's intent is also important in distinguishing one potential crime from another. For example, murder, voluntary manslaughter, involuntary manslaughter, and reckless homicide all involve causing the death of another human being. They differ on the basis of the *mens rea*. Compare the way in which the following offenses are defined in the ALI Model Penal Code. *See* Figure 2.4.

OFFENSES INVOLVING DANGER TO THE PERSON
Article 210. Criminal Homicide

Section 210.1 Criminal Homicide
(1) A person is guilty of criminal homicide if he purposely, knowingly, recklessly or negligently causes the death of another human being.

(2) Criminal homicide is murder, manslaughter or negligent homicide.

Section 210.2 Murder
(1) Except as provided in Section 210.3(1)(b), criminal homicide constitutes murder when

(a) it is committed purposely or knowingly; or

(b) it is committed recklessly under circumstances manifesting extreme indifference to the value of human life. Such recklessness and indifference are presumed if the actor is engaged or is an accomplice in the commission of, or an attempt to commit, or flight after committing or attempting to commit robbery, rape or deviate sexual intercourse by force or threat of force, arson, burglary, kidnapping or felonious escape.

Section 210.3 Manslaughter
(1) Criminal homicide constitutes manslaughter when:

(a) it is committed recklessly; or

(b) a homicide which would otherwise be murder is committed under the influence of extreme mental or emotional disturbance for which there is reasonable explanation or excuse. The reasonableness of such explanation or excuse shall be determined from the viewpoint of a person in the actor's situation under the circumstances as he believes them to be.

(2) Manslaughter is a felony of the second degree.

Offense	Criminal Intent
Murder	Purposely; Knowingly; Reckless Disregard to Human Life
Manslaughter	Recklessly; Influenced by Extreme Mental or Emotional Disturbance
Negligent Homicide	Negligently

Figure 2.4   Model Penal Code *Mens Rea* for Criminal Homicide

Section 210.4 Negligent Homicide

(1) Criminal homicide constitutes negligent homicide when it is committed negligently.

(2) Negligent homicide is a felony of the third degree.

Section 210.5 Causing or Aiding Suicide

(1) A person may be convicted of criminal homicide for causing another to commit suicide only if he purposely causes such suicide by force, duress or deception.

(2) A person who purposely aids or solicits another to commit suicide is guilty of a felony of the second degree if his conduct causes such suicide or an attempted suicide, and otherwise of a misdemeanor.

To constitute the crime of murder, the action that caused the death must have been committed "purposely," "knowingly," or "recklessly under circumstances manifesting extreme indifference to the value of human life." To be considered manslaughter, on the other hand, the action that caused the death must have been committed "recklessly" or "under the influence of extreme mental or emotional disturbance for which there is reasonable explanation or excuse." Negligent homicide requires the action that caused the death to have been committed "negligently." But what do the terms *purposely, knowingly, recklessly,* and *negligently* mean?

Acts are categorized as **purposeful** when the defendant specifically intended to cause the harm that resulted. So, Mr. Jones would meet the purposeful element needed to establish murder if he shot the gun at someone with the intent to kill that person.

He could also be convicted of murder if he acted **knowingly**. This requires a showing that the defendant knew or had reason to know that harm would be caused by the actions taken even if the specific harm was not the objective of the defendant. So, if Mr. Jones fired his gun at a group of people, he could be found guilty of murder even if he did not intend to kill a specific individual.[11]

It could also be murder if Mr. Jones acted **recklessly** "under circumstances manifesting extreme indifference to the value of human life." Acting recklessly is defined in terms of disregarding a substantial and unjustifiable risk that harm will result from the action a person is taking. In Jones's case, the judge or jury would have to consider the number of people in the area and what Jones knew about guns.

The murder section of the Model Penal Code states that recklessness and indifference are presumed "if the actor is engaged or is an accomplice in the commission of, or an attempt to commit, or flight after committing or attempting to commit robbery, rape or deviate sexual intercourse by force or threat of force, arson, burglary, kidnapping or felonious escape." Mr. Jones could be found guilty of murder without proof that he disregarded a known risk if he shot the gun in the context of committing or attempting to commit one of the listed crimes.

Purposeful
Intending to cause a specific harm.

Knowingly
Not intending to cause a specific harm, but being aware that such harm would be caused.

Recklessness
Disregarding a substantial and unjustifiable risk that harm will result.

---

[11]In *United States v. Jewell,* 532 F. 2d 697, 704 (9th Cir. 1976), the court stated that the term knowingly includes a mental state in which the defendant is aware that the fact in question is highly probable but consciously avoids enlightenment.

Notice that recklessness is also a factor in defining the crime of manslaughter. To be convicted of manslaughter, if the defendant's actions must either be reckless or have been committed under the influence of "extreme mental or emotional disturbance for which there is reasonable explanation or excuse."

Negligent homicide occurs when the defendant acted **negligently**. This occurs when one simply fails to be aware of a substantial and unjustifiable risk. To be convicted of negligent homicide, the judge or jury would have to find that Mr. Jones neither knew nor should have known that someone could be killed when he fired his gun.

Negligence
A failure to act reasonably under the circumstances.

So far we have discussed how the law defines a criminal act and different types of criminal intent. But what happens when a person intends to commit a crime but stops short of actually carrying it out? It could be that the person "saw the light" and had a change of heart, or it could be that some intervening event prevented the person from completing the crime. In either case, there would be criminal intent but no criminal act.

A special category of crimes called **inchoate crimes** addresses this situation. *Inchoate* means "imperfect," "partial," or "unfinished." Thus an inchoate crime is one that was planned but not completed. The crimes of attempted murder, attempted robbery, attempted sexual assault, etc., are examples of these inchoate crimes. To satisfy the *actus reus* requirement or an attempted crime, the state must prove that the defendant did some overt act in furtherance of his or her intent that went beyond mere preparation. Other examples are the crimes of solicitation and conspiracy. **Solicitation** involves requesting or encouraging someone to commit a crime. For example, if a wife encourages her boyfriend to kill her husband, she could be found guilty of the crime of solicitation. **Conspiracy** involves an agreement between two or more persons to commit an unlawful act. The state must show that they intended to enter into an agreement and that they had the specific intent to commit some crime. Unlike an attempt, where mere preparation is not enough of an overt act to satisfy the *actus reus* requirement, in many states preparation is sufficient to prove conspiracy. In others, the defendants must take substantial overt steps to be found guilty.

Inchoate crimes
A crime that was planned but not completed.

Solicitation
The crime of encouraging someone to commit a crime.

Conspiracy
An agreement between two or more persons to commit an unlawful act.

APPLICATION EXERCISES

5. How is the concept of *mens rea* relevant to the Cook case (*see hypothetical case on p. xxxvii*)?

6. If you were a prosecuting attorney operating under the Model Penal Code, what charges would you file in Cook's case?

7. In the Turner case (*see hypothetical case on p. xxxvii*), if Turner's actions took place in a non-strict liability state where *mens rea* is required, what would be the *mens rea* and *actus reus* elements for disobeying a stop sign?

8. Why do you think that states have eliminated the *mens rea* requirement for traffic cases?

9. What would be the *mens rea* for the crime of illegal drug possession? What if the vehicle Turner was driving was registered to another person and he denied that the crack cocaine was his? Should the crime of possession of contraband be a strict liability offense? Why or why not?

10. Suppose that when he originally accepted his clients' money, Edwards had every intention to provide a better-than-average rate of return on the money they invested with him. It was only when his personal financial situation deteriorated that he misappropriated their funds. If this is true, how would it affect a potential criminal prosecution?

11. What would be the *actus reus* in any crimes Schroeder may have committed (*see hypothetical case on p. xxxviii*)?

12. Did Schroeder commit an inchoate crime by involving his friend Jim Stevenson in his scheme? Why or why not? What difference would it make if Schroeder only made comments to Jim but never explicitly laid out a plan to take advantage of his inside knowledge?

E. DOUBLE JEOPARDY

In the preceding section you have seen how the same act, such as causing the death of another person, can result in being charged with several different crimes. It is the *mens rea* rather than the act that distinguishes murder from manslaughter or negligent homicide. It is not unusual for a prosecutor to charge a defendant with multiple offenses and then let the jury sort out which one is supported by the evidence presented at the trial. Stop and consider how these types of multiple charges relate to the concept of double jeopardy.

The Fifth Amendment to the U.S. Constitution provides in part: " . . . nor shall any person be subject for the same offence to be twice put in jeopardy of life or limb . . . " But what constitutes an offense and what does it mean to be "put in jeopardy of life or limb"?

Jeopardy is usually defined as a danger or a peril, and *jeopardy of life or limb* refers to being subject to criminal punishment. Being subject to criminal punishment goes beyond being incarcerated or fined, however, and includes being either convicted or acquitted by a court of competent jurisdiction. A defendant is placed in **double jeopardy** when he is prosecuted or punished twice for the same crime.[12] Therefore, the government may not appeal a verdict or institute a second prosecution for the same offense.[13] Jeopardy generally attaches

Double jeopardy
The Fifth Amendment prohibition against prosecuting or punishing a defendant twice for the same crime.

---

[12] "[T]he Double Jeopardy Clause protects against three distinct abuses: a second prosecution for the same offense after acquittal; a second prosecution for the same offense after conviction; and multiple punishments for the same offense." *United States v. Halper*, 490 U.S. 435, 440, 109 S. Ct. 1892, 104 L. Ed. 2d 487 (1989).

[13] The prohibition against government appeals only applies to an initial appeal of the trial court's verdict. It does not prevent the state from appealing an appellate court ruling that overturns the trial court where the appeal was brought by the accused.

once a jury has been selected. However, if the trial ends in a mistrial, due to something like a hung jury, the double jeopardy clause does not prevent the state from prosecuting the defendant in a second trial.[14]

Determining what constitutes the same offense is far more complicated. Take a few minutes to read the following excerpts from *Ashe v. Swenson.*

Ashe v. Swenson
Supreme Court of the United States
397 U.S. 436 (1970)

MR. JUSTICE STEWART delivered the opinion of the Court.

In *Benton v. Maryland,* 395 U.S. 784, the Court held that the *Fifth Amendment* guarantee against double jeopardy is enforceable against the States through the *Fourteenth Amendment.* The question in this case is whether the State of Missouri violated that guarantee when it prosecuted the petitioner a second time for armed robbery in the circumstances here presented.

Sometime in the early hours of the morning of January 10, 1960, six men were engaged in a poker game in the basement of the home of John Gladson at Lee's Summit, Missouri. Suddenly three or four masked men, armed with a shotgun and pistols, broke into the basement and robbed each of the poker players of money and various articles of personal property. The robbers—and it has never been clear whether there were three or four of them—then fled in a car belonging to one of the victims of the robbery. Shortly thereafter the stolen car was discovered in a field, and later that morning three men were arrested by a state trooper while they were walking on a highway not far from where the abandoned car had been found. The petitioner was arrested by another officer some distance away.

The four were subsequently charged with seven separate offenses—the armed robbery of each of the six poker players and the theft of the car. In May 1960 the petitioner went to trial on the charge of robbing Donald Knight, one of the participants in the poker game. At the trial the State called Knight and three of his fellow poker players as prosecution witnesses. Each of them described the circumstances of the holdup and itemized his own individual losses. The proof that an armed robbery had occurred and that personal property had been taken from Knight as well as from each of the others was unassailable. The testimony of the four victims in this regard was consistent both internally and with that of the others. But the State's evidence that the petitioner had been one of the robbers was weak. Two of the witnesses thought that there had been only three robbers altogether, and could not identify the petitioner as one of them. Another of the victims, who was the petitioner's uncle by marriage, said that at the "patrol station" he had positively identified each of the other three men accused of the holdup, but could say only that the petitioner's voice "sounded very much like" that of one of the robbers. The fourth participant in the poker game did identify the petitioner, but only by his "size and height, and his actions."

The cross-examination of these witnesses was brief, and it was aimed primarily at exposing the weakness of their identification testimony. Defense counsel made no attempt to question their testimony regarding the holdup itself or their claims as to their losses. Knight testified without contradiction that the robbers had stolen from him his watch, $250 in cash, and about $500 in checks. His billfold, which had been found by the

---

[14]*United States v. Perez,* 22 U.S. 579, 6 L. Ed. 2d 165, 9 Wheat. 579 (1824).

police in the possession of one of the three other men accused of the robbery, was admitted in evidence. The defense offered no testimony and waived final argument.

The trial judge instructed the jury that if it found that the petitioner was one of the participants in the armed robbery, the theft of "any money" from Knight would sustain a conviction. He also instructed the jury that if the petitioner was one of the robbers, he was guilty under the law even if he had not personally robbed Knight. The jury—though not instructed to elaborate upon its verdict—found the petitioner "not guilty due to insufficient evidence."

Six weeks later the petitioner was brought to trial again, this time for the robbery of another participant in the poker game, a man named Roberts. The petitioner filed a motion to dismiss, based on his previous acquittal. The motion was overruled, and the second trial began. The witnesses were for the most part the same, though this time their testimony was substantially stronger on the issue of the petitioner's identity. For example, two witnesses who at the first trial had been wholly unable to identify the petitioner as one of the robbers, now testified that his features, size, and mannerisms matched those of one of their assailants. Another witness who before had identified the petitioner only by his size and actions now also remembered him by the unusual sound of his voice. The State further refined its case at the second trial by declining to call one of the participants in the poker game whose identification testimony at the first trial had been conspicuously negative. The case went to the jury on instructions virtually identical to those given at the first trial. This time the jury found the petitioner guilty, and he was sentenced to a 35-year term in the state penitentiary.

The Supreme Court of Missouri affirmed the conviction, holding that the "plea of former jeopardy must be denied." *State v. Ashe,* 350 S.W.2d 768, 771. A collateral attack upon the conviction in the state courts five years later was also unsuccessful. *State v. Ashe,* 403 S.W.2d 589. The petitioner then brought the present habeas corpus proceeding in the United States District Court for the Western District of Missouri, claiming that the second prosecution had violated his right not to be twice put in jeopardy.

Considering itself bound by this court's decision in *Hoag v. New Jersey,* 356 U.S. 464, the District Court denied the writ, although apparently finding merit in the petitioner's claim. The Court of Appeals for the Eighth Circuit affirmed, also upon the authority of *Hoag v. New Jersey, supra.* We granted certiorari to consider the important constitutional question this case presents. 393 U.S. 1115.

The question is not whether Missouri could validly charge the petitioner with six separate offenses for the robbery of the six poker players. It is not whether he could have received a total of six punishments if he had been convicted in a single trial of robbing the six victims. It is simply whether, after a jury determined by its verdict that the petitioner was not one of the robbers, the State could constitutionally hale him before a new jury to litigate that issue again.

After the first jury had acquitted the petitioner of robbing Knight, Missouri could certainly not have brought him to trial again upon that charge. Once a jury had determined upon conflicting testimony that there was at least a reasonable doubt that the petitioner was one of the robbers, the State could not present the same or different identification evidence in a second prosecution for the robbery of Knight in the hope that a different jury might find that evidence more convincing. The situation is constitutionally no different here, even though the second trial related to another victim of the same robbery. For the name of the victim, in the circumstances of this case, had no bearing whatever upon the issue of whether the petitioner was one of the robbers.

In this case the State in its brief has frankly conceded that following the petitioner's acquittal, it treated the first trial as no more than a dry run for the second prosecution: "No doubt the prosecutor felt the state had a provable case on the first charge and, when he lost, he did what every good attorney would do—he refined his presentation in light of the turn of events at the first trial." But this is precisely what the constitutional guarantee forbids.

The judgment is reversed, and the case is remanded to the Court of Appeals for the Eighth Circuit for further proceedings consistent with this opinion.

CASE DISCUSSION QUESTIONS

1. What court wrote this opinion?
2. Who is Mr. Ashe and what is he alleged to have done?
3. Who is Mr. Swenson and why is his name part of the title of the case?
4. Is this a civil case or a criminal one? Why?
5. What charges were brought against Mr. Ashe?
6. Who brought these charges and in what court were they filed? Why were they filed in that court?
7. What was the outcome of Ashe's first trial?
8. What happened after Ashe's first trial?
9. What was the outcome of the second trial?
10. How did the case get before the U.S. Supreme Court?
11. Which side won in the U.S. Supreme Court?
12. What, if any, issues of state statutory law were decided in this opinion?
13. What, if any, issues of federal statutory law were decided in this opinion?
14. What, if any, issues of state constitutional law were decided in this opinion?
15. What, if any, issues of federal constitutional law were decided in this opinion?
16. What legal principle (rule of law) did the U.S. Supreme Court use to explain its decision?

It is important to note that in situations where both the state and federal governments criminalize the same act, it does not violate the Double Jeopardy Clause when one government tries the accused after the one has already either acquitted or convicted that person. For example, an act that is prosecuted as a homicide in state court may also be prosecuted as a violation of civil rights in federal court. Furthermore, double jeopardy does not prevent a civil action for damages based on the same set of facts presented in a criminal prosecution. Indeed, the trial in the O.J. Simpson civil case commenced after Simpson was acquitted in the criminal jury trial.

F. PARTIES TO THE CRIME

When more than one person is involved in committing a crime, the people involved can be classified as a principal, an accomplice, or an accessory. The person who commits a criminal act is a **principal** in the first degree. A principal in the second degree, also referred to as an **accomplice**, assists the principal in the first degree during the commission of the crime. That person could literally be standing next to the principal in the first degree or be waiting in a get-away car.

An **accessory**, on the other hand, is someone who assisted in the preparation of the crime but was not present when it was actually carried out. An **accessory after the fact** is someone who first aided the principal after the commission of the crime.

When it comes to punishment, principals of any degree and accessories are all treated the same. However, accessories after the fact are not punished as severely as are principals and accomplices.

Principal
A person who actually commits the crime.

Accomplice
A person who assists the principal with the crime or with the preparation of the crime.

Accessory
A person who assisted in the preparation of the crime but was not present when it was actually carried out.

Accessory after the fact
A person who first aided the principal after the commission of the crime.

G. PUNISHMENTS FOR CRIMES

As pointed out earlier in this chapter, one of the significant differences between criminal law and civil law is the nature of the sanctions involved. Criminal law is enforced through fines, incarceration, and, in some cases, even death.

The range of sanctions for specific crimes is determined by the legislature when it passes the statute or ordinance making certain behavior a crime. In Chapter 13 we will examine how judges determine what the sentences will be in specific cases. In this section we will take a quick look at the alternative justifications that are given for implementing these punishments. The five major justifications for administering punishment are summarized in Figure 2.5. Each provides a different type of justification for punishing criminal offenders.

Deterrence is the most frequently cited justification for punishment. The idea is that fear of punishment will deter people from committing crimes. The difference between general and specific deterrence is that specific deterrence applies to the person who has already committed a crime, and general deterrence is directed at others who might be tempted to commit a similar crime. Both versions of deterrence theory rely on the assumption that, prior to committing a crime, would-be perpetrators will weigh the benefits of committing the crime against the punishment they would receive if they are caught. If the punishment is perceived to outweigh the benefits of the crime, the person will have been successfully deterred.

Under deterrence theory, criminals are sent to prison as punishment. With the incapacitation approach, criminals are incarcerated to prevent them from being able to commit new crimes. As long as criminals are kept behind bars, they will not be in a situation in which they are able to victimize the public. Another application of the incapacitation approach would be in cases where people have argued for castration of rapists.

Rehabilitation involves changing the perpetrators of crime so that they will have no need or desire to commit crimes in the future. This approach usually involves providing offenders with the education and job skills they need to get the kinds of jobs they need to support themselves and their families through legal employment. Rehabilitation programs may also include psychological counseling to help the criminals understand the difference between right and wrong and to appreciate the harm their crimes produce. It is argued that if people are able to legally earn a good income, they will not need to engage in criminal behavior.

Theory of Punishment	Rationale
Specific Deterrence	Perpetrator is punished to deter this individual from committing future crimes.
General Deterrence	Perpetrator is punished to deter others from committing future crimes.
Incapacitation	Perpetrator is prevented from committing future crimes by removing the opportunity or means to commit crime.
Rehabilitation	Treatment is given to perpetrator to eliminate need and/or desire to commit future crimes.
Retribution	Perpetrator is punished to exact revenge on behalf of the victim or the victim's family.

Figure 2.5 Justifications for Punishment

The final theory is called "retribution." It validates people's desire for revenge and cites the biblical admonition that punishment should involve "an eye for an eye, a tooth for a tooth." The theory is that it is better to have the government administer retribution than to leave it up to the victims to seek their own vengeance, thereby starting a cycle of retaliation involving friends and relatives.

Each of these theories of punishment has its critics. Furthermore, the actions suggested by one theory frequently undercut the effectiveness of measures taken on the basis of other theories.

Critics of the deterrence theories are quick to point out that they are based on the assumption that the would-be criminals will stop and think about the punishment before committing the crime. In so-called crimes of passion, however, the perpetrator acts instinctively based on emotion rather than stopping to think through the consequences. Another problem with this approach is that it only works if the potential criminal believes he or she is likely to get caught and to receive a punishment that is severe enough to deter the criminal act. Most criminals expect to get away with their crime and not be caught. If they are caught, they may believe they can "beat the wrap," or get away with "a slap on the wrist." Young "gangbangers" may think their juvenile status will insulate them from serious punishment.

Critics of the incarceration approach point out that the logic behind it could justify lifetime incarceration for relatively minor crimes. Conversely, in situations involving very personal "crimes of passion," no incarceration would be needed. For example, in situations where an abused spouse kills the abusive spouse, there is little reason to believe the perpetrator will kill again.

Critics of rehabilitation argue that it doesn't work and that these programs take away from punishment needed to deter criminals. Critics of retribution point out that the "eye for an eye" concept cannot really be applied in situations involving multiple murders and argue that it is uncivilized to torture the criminal when the criminal tortured the victim.

SUMMARY

This chapter has tried to lay the theoretical and organizational groundwork for a better understanding of what is to come in later chapters. Before jumping into the details of criminal law, it is important to understand the basic concepts behind criminal law and the role it plays in the larger context of our American legal system.

Most laws are created by federal and state legislative bodies as statutes and ordinances. Administrative regulations are enacted by executive agencies and are similar to statutes in form and function. Constitutional law is based on the texts of the constitutions of the United States and of the individual states. The meaning of statutory, administrative, and constitutional law ultimately is determined by the courts interpreting it. Although the common law has been superseded by statutes in most states, there are still a few examples where it has force in criminal matters. Like other forms of the common law, it is found in court decisions and commentaries. In addition to classifying law on the basis of its documentary source, we often break law down into federal, state, and local laws.

Besides classifying law on the basis of its source, it can also be categorized on the basis of the type of the punishment. After splitting criminal law off from civil law, it can be divided into felonies, misdemeanors, and petty crimes. Felonies are often further sub-divided into capital crimes and different classes of felonies on the basis of the type of sentence. Misdemeanors can also be further divided.

Finally, crimes can be classified on the basis of the nature of the harm done and the type of victim involved. Common classifications are: Offenses Against Persons, Offenses Against Property, Offenses Against the Family, Offenses Against Public Administration, and Offenses Against Public Order and Decency.

In order to determine if a crime has taken place, one must analyze not only what the person did but what was going on in that person's mind at the time the act was committed and what the results of that act were. *Actus reus* refers to the nature of the act and *mens rea* relates to what was going on in the criminal's mind when the act was committed. This criminal intent is usually classified as purposeful, knowing, reckless, or negligent. Crimes like attempted murder, solicitation, and conspiracy are called inchoate crimes because they are planned but not completed.

When more than one person is involved in committing a crime, the people involved can be classified as a principal, an accomplice, or an accessory. The person who commits a criminal act is a principal. An accomplice assists during the commission of the crime, and an accessory is someone who assisted in the preparation of the crime but was not present when it was actually carried out. An accessory after the fact is someone who first aided the principal after the commission of the crime.

We ended with a discussion of the theories used to justify various forms of punishment: specific deterrence, general deterrence, incapacitation, rehabilitation, and retribution.

While most criminal law comes from state statutes, certain types of crimes are only found in federal statutes. State and federal regulations can also play a role in criminal prosecutions. Federal and state statutes, regulations, court rules, and constitutional law are also involved in questions of criminal procedure. Constitutional guarantees such as protection against double jeopardy, the right to counsel, privilege against self-incrimination, and the right to a jury trial also play a key role in the criminal law. On rare occasions you might have to consult the common law, but in the federal system and in most states, the common law has been completely superseded by statutory law.

‖‖ INTERNET RESOURCES

General Legal Information

- Legal Information Institute at Cornell University Law School: **http://www.law.cornell.edu/**
- US Law: **http://www.uslaw.com/**

Federal Statutes

- United States Code: **http://www.gpoaccess.gov/uscode/**
  http://www.gpo.gov/fdsys/browse/collectionUScode.action?collectionCode=USCODE
- U.S. Statutes at Large: **http://www.gpoaccess.gov/statutes/index.html**
- Federal Administrative Regulations, Code of Federal Regulations: **http://www.gpoaccess.gov/fr/index.html**
- U.S. Constitution Online: **http://www.usconstitution.net/const.html**

Federal Court Decisions

- http://www.supremecourt.gov/
- http://www.uscourts.gov/FederalCourts.aspx

State and Local Information

- Use these links to find official state websites and then follow links on the state website to find statutes, administrative regulations, etc.
  http://www.usa.gov/Agencies/State_and_Territories.shtml
  http://www.ncsl.org/?tabid=17173

REVIEW QUESTIONS

1. Which branches of government are involved in making the law and what is the branch's respective role?
2. Name and explain the four sources of law.
3. Can a local governing body, such as a city council, pass statutory law? If so, what types of statutory law can a locality enact?
4. What role does case law play in criminal procedure?
5. What are the basic differences between criminal law and civil law?
6. What is the difference between a felony and a misdemeanor?
7. What are the five major categories of crime set forth in the Model Penal Code?
8. What is white-collar crime? How does it differ from street crime?
9. What are the two general elements required of most crimes?
10. Define *inchoate crimes* and give examples of these types of offenses.
11. What is *double jeopardy* and what provision of the U.S. Constitution protects persons from being subjected to double jeopardy?
12. What are the roles of a principal, an accomplice, an accessory, and an accessory after the fact?
13. What are the five major justifications for punishment?

Chapter 3

Types of Offenses

Chapters 1 and 2 covered the nature of the criminal justice system, the people who participate in that system, and basic principles necessary to understand how the criminal law is structured. In this chapter we take a closer look at some of the most common types of criminal offenses and the type of harm they are designed to punish.

There are many similarities among the criminal codes of the different states and that of the federal government, but there are also many differences. Rather than presenting a comparative analysis of the criminal codes of all fifty states or attempting an in-depth analysis of all of the provisions of the Model Penal Code, our goal for this chapter is limited to introducing some of the most common types of offenses included in most criminal codes. You will always need to check your own state's statutes to see how they define these same types of crimes and what additional offenses they may include. This chapter also contains a brief discussion of some of the problems involved in interpreting criminal statutes.

A. OFFENSES INVOLVING DANGER TO THE PERSON

The Model Penal Code and those of many states start with a listing of offenses involving danger to people. They typically include various types of homicides, assaults, rape, kidnapping, and false imprisonment.

1. HOMICIDE

"Thou shalt not kill" is perhaps the most frequently referenced section of the Ten Commandments. But who does it refer to and what does it actually mean? Does it mean slaughterhouses can't kill cattle to provide steaks or hamburgers? Does it mean the police cannot shoot to kill a terrorist trying to drive a tanker truck into a high-rise building? Does it mean that a solder cannot fire a missile at an enemy artillery site? Does it mean a pilot cannot drop a bomb in an area that may include civilians? Does it mean a doctor cannot administer a fatal drug to a prisoner who was convicted of multiple murders? The point is that although it represents a noble ideal, "thou shalt not kill" is too ambiguous to serve as an enforceable criminal statute.

Now contrast the wording of the commandment with that of Section 210.1 (1) of the Model Penal Code, which states: "A person is guilty of criminal **homicide** if he purposely, knowingly, recklessly or negligently causes the death of another human being."

Note first that, unlike the biblical command, it explicitly requires the victim be a "human being." It is thus clear that slaughterhouse employees are not covered by the statute when they kill cattle. But what about a situation in which someone causes the death of a fetus while it is still in the womb? That question is addressed in Section 210.0, in which the Model Code defines a human being as "a person who has been born and is alive." However, some states, such as Illinois, have created special crimes such as intentional homicide of an unborn child,[1] voluntary manslaughter of an unborn child,[2] and involuntary homicide manslaughter and reckless homicide of an unborn child,[3] to fill this gap.

Other questions we raised are also answered by looking at other sections of the Model Code. For example, Section 2.10 states: "It is an affirmative defense that the actor, in engaging in the conduct charged to constitute an offense, does no more than execute an order of his superior in the armed services which he does not know to be unlawful," and Section 3.03(d) relieves people of criminal responsibility when they are following "the law governing the armed services or the lawful conduct of war." Other parts of Section 3.03 relieve police and official executioners of criminal responsibility when their conduct is required or authorized by "(a) the law defining the duties or functions of a public officer or the assistance to be rendered to such officer in the performance of his duties; or (b) the law governing the execution of legal process; or (c) the judgment or order of a competent court or tribunal; . . . or (e) any other provision of law imposing a public duty." We will discuss these and other defenses in greater detail in Chapter 8.

Most criminal codes subdivide homicide into crimes with labels such as murder, manslaughter, and negligent homicide. The primary difference between them is typically related to the state of mind of the perpetrator. (See discussion on *mens rea* in Chapter 2.) **Murder** generally requires that the act has been committed purposefully or knowingly but may also include some situations where it can be shown the person acted recklessly "under circumstances manifesting extreme indifference to the value of human life."[4] **Manslaughter** usually applies where the act was committed recklessly or "under the influence of extreme mental or emotional disturbance for which there is reasonable explanation or excuse."[5] Then, as the name implies, **negligent homicide** involves negligent acts that result in someone's death.

The Model Penal Code also has a crime labeled as "Causing or Aiding Suicide." Section 210.5 creates a felony when a person purposely causes another to commit suicide by "force, duress or deception," and a misdemeanor where "force,

Homicide
An act by one human being that causes the death of another human being. To be considered a crime, the act must have been done purposely, knowingly, recklessly, or negligently.

Murder
A homicide that was committed purposefully, knowingly, or where the person acted recklessly with extreme indifference to the value of human life.

Manslaughter
A homicide where the act was committed recklessly or under the influence of extreme mental or emotional disturbance.

Negligent homicide
A homicide based on a negligent act.

Suicide
The deliberate termination of one's own life.

---

[1] 120 ILCS 5/9-1.2.

[2] 120 ILCS 5/9-2.1.

[3] 120 ILCS 5/9-3.

[4] ALI Model Penal Code, § 210.2(1)(b).

[5] ALI Model Penal Code, § 210.3(1)(b).

duress or deception" were not present. States have taken a variety of approaches to address this issue. For instance, the Illinois law on suicide requires either coercion or "with knowledge that another person intends to commit or attempt to commit suicide, intentionally (i) offers and provides the physical means by which another person commits or attempts to commit suicide, or (ii) participates in a physical act by which another person commits or attempts to commit suicide."[6] In contrast, Oregon became the first state to legalize assisted suicide when voters approved a 1994 referendum enacting the Oregon Death with Dignity Act.[7] This law exempts from civil or criminal liability state-licensed physicians who dispense or prescribe a lethal dose of drugs upon the request of a terminally ill patient.

Throughout this chapter, we will provide you with examples of situations in which people have been charged with violating these types of crimes. Exhibit 3.1 is a copy of the homicide indictment against John Allen Muhammad.

Exhibit 3.1: Homicide Indictment

During October 2002, John Allen Muhammad and Lee Boyd Malvo carried out a series of sniper attacks in the Baltimore-Washington metropolitan area that left ten people killed and three critically wounded. Muhammad's indictment for murdering one of the victims follows. Note that this case was charged in Virginia. The format for indictments may differ in the state where you live.

IN THE CIRCUIT COURT OF SPOTSYLVANIA
AT ITS CRIMINAL TERM COMMENCING

October 28, 2002
Direct Indictment

Commonwealth of Virginia,	)	
	)	**Capital Murder**
v.	)	
	)	
JOHN ALLEN MUHAMMAD,	)	
aka. JOHN ALLEN WILLIAMS	)	
Race: Black Sex: Male DOB: 12/31/60	)	
Hgt: 6'0'' Wgt: 180 Eyes: Brown Hair: Black	)	
SSN: XXX-XX-XXXX.	)	
Defendant	)	
	)	

---

[6]720 ILCS 5/12-31.
[7]Ore. Rev. Stat. § 127.800 *et seq.* (2003).

The Grand Jurors of the Commonwealth of Virginia and of the County of Spotsylvania, attending the Court aforesaid, upon their oaths present that, in this County of Spotsylvania,

JOHN ALLEN MUHAMMAD, aka JOHN ALLEN WILLIAMS

Count I: That on or about the 11th day of October, 2002, did unlawfully and feloniously willfully, deliberately, and with premeditation kill and slay Kenneth Bridges, and did also willfully, deliberately, and with premeditation kill one or more other persons within a three-year period, constituting capital murder, in violation of Section 18.2-31(8) of the Code of Virginia (1950), as amended.

AND/OR:

Count II: That on or about the 11th day of October, 2002 did unlawfully and feloniously willfully, deliberately, and with premeditation kill and slay Kenneth Bridges in the commission or attempted commission of an act of terrorism, pursuant to Code Section 18.2-46.4, constituting capital murder in violation of Section 18.2-31(13) of the Code of Virginia (1950), as amended.

PUNISHMENT: (Class 1 Felony) Death by execution or life imprisonment.

Grand jury witness: Detective J. Cagnina & Detective E.D. Chawning. Spotsylvania County Sheriff's Office	A True Bill	__X__
	Not A True Bill	____

[s]_____

Foreman of the Grand Jury

Malice aforethought
The level of intent shown by the actor's premeditation, the cruelty or conscious disregard for the safety of others, or demonstrated by the intent to commit another felony.

Generally speaking, homicides are prosecuted by local law enforcement officials using state statutes. Federal law enforcement would only get involved if the homicide victims were federal officials or employees, or the killing occurred in the context of a bank robbery, a kidnapping, a civil rights violation, or an act of international terrorism.

Under federal law there are two types of homicide: murder and manslaughter. Murder is defined as the "unlawful killing of a human being with **malice aforethought**,"[8] whereas manslaughter is the "unlawful killing of a human being without malice."[9] This is the same approach that was taken at common law.

---

[8]18 U.S.C. § 1111(a).
[9]18 U.S.C. § 1112(a).

The term *malice aforethought* is a technical legal term. "Malice" does not mean hatred or ill-will towards the victim, but rather it refers to the conscious desire to cause serious injury or death. "Aforethought" includes both a premeditated, planned killing as well as a homicide in which the perpetrator's intent existed immediately prior to the commission of the act. Thus, malice aforethought is the level of intent shown by the actor's premeditation, the cruelty or conscious disregard for the safety of others, or the demonstrated intent to commit another felony. Because term *malice aforethought* appears to be ambiguous, most modern criminal codes do not employ it and instead use an approach similar to that of the Model Penal Code of defining the specific intent element of the first degree murder.

Federal law further subdivides homicides into subcategories. Manslaughter is divided into two different offenses. Voluntary manslaughter is the killing of a human being upon a sudden quarrel or in the heat of passion. Involuntary manslaughter is the killing in "the commission of an unlawful act not amounting to a felony, or in the commission in an unlawful manner, or without due caution and circumspection, of a lawful act which might produce death."[10]

Murder is likewise divided into two degrees. Murder in the first degree is a homicide (a) that is willful, deliberate, malicious, and premeditated; (b) committed in the perpetration of one of a list of other crimes (e.g., arson, escape, murder, kidnapping, treason, espionage, sabotage, aggravated sexual abuse, sexual abuse, child abuse, burglary, robbery, or child torture); or (c) a premeditated design to kill a different human being than the actual victim. Murder in the second degree is "[a]ny murder that is not murder in the first degree."[11]

In essence, first degree murder under federal law is any murder that is either premeditated or a specific type of **felony murder**. Felony murder is the unintended killing of a human being that occurs during the commission of another felony. The intent to commit the felony transfers to the killing, giving rise to the offense of first degree murder. The concept of transferring the *mens rea* from one crime to another is called the **transferred intent doctrine**. Most jurisdictions recognize this doctrine and include felony murder as a basis for first degree murder.

Felony murder
The unintended killing of a human being that occurs during the commission of another felony. The intent to commit the felony transfers to the killing to give rise to first degree murder.

Transferred intent doctrine
The concept that when an actor who intends to injure one victim unintentionally harms another, the *mens rea* from the original offense is transferred to the crime involving the unintended victim.

APPLICATION EXERCISES

After reviewing the facts of the Bud Cook Hypothetical Case (*see p. xxxvii*), answer the following questions:

1. Setting aside questions of drunk driving and leaving the scene of an accident, was Cook guilty of any of the homicide-related provisions in the Model Penal Code?

2. Which, if any, of these crimes would a prosecutor be most likely to file? Why?

3. What additional information would the prosecutor want to have before deciding on the charges?

---

[10]18 U.S.C. § 1112(a).
[11]18 U.S.C. § 1111(a).

> **4.** Locate and read the section of your own state's criminal code that covers these types of crimes.
>   a. What are the citations for these sections?
>   b. How do your state's laws on homicide differ from those of the Model Penal Code?
>   c. How do your state's laws on homicide differ from federal law?

2. ASSAULT AND BATTERY

Assault
An act that causes or attempts to cause serious bodily harm to another individual.

Battery
An act of intentional physical contact that is either offensive or harmful to another person.

A second category of offenses involving danger to the person focuses on bodily harm that doesn't involve death. It includes crimes such as assault, battery, intimidation, stalking, and reckless endangerment.

Although charges of assault and battery often arise from a single incident, assault and battery involves different types of actions. At common law, **assault** was defined as a willful attempt or threat to inflict injury upon another person, while **battery** involved intentional physical contact that was either offensive or harmful. The physical contact can either be direct, person-to-person contact or contact with an object that is held or thrown by another person.

At common law assault and battery were considered both crimes and torts. In other words, the offender could be prosecuted criminally and, if found guilty, be punished by fine or imprisonment. Alternatively, the victim could sue the perpetrator in civil court for damages. Some state criminal codes classify assault and battery as separate crimes, whereas other state codes, federal laws, and the Model Penal Code include battery as a type of assault. For instance, in the State of New York conduct known at common law as a battery is characterized as an assault. See Exhibit 3.2 for a sample of an assault charge brought in New York.

In most states, simple assault and battery are classified as misdemeanors and aggravated assault and battery are felonies. Note how the Model Penal Code defines simple and aggravated assault:

§ 211.1 (1) Simple Assault
A person is guilty of assault if he:

(a) attempts to cause or purposely, knowingly or recklessly causes bodily injury to another, or

(b) negligently causes bodily injury to another with a deadly weapon; or

(c) attempts by fear or menace to put another in fear of imminent serious bodily injury.

§ 211.1(2) Aggravated Assault
A person is guilty of aggravated assault if he:

(a) attempts to cause serious bodily injury to another, or causes such injury purposely, knowingly or recklessly under circumstances manifesting extreme indifference to the value of human life; or

(b) attempts to cause or purposely or knowingly causes bodily injury to another with a deadly weapon.

Under Illinois law, a person is guilty of aggravated battery if he or she intentionally or knowingly causes "great bodily harm, or permanent disability or disfigurement." A person is also guilty of aggravated battery if he uses a deadly

Exhibit 3.2: New York Assault Charge

Actor Russell Crowe was charged with assault for hitting a hotel employee with a telephone and unlawfully possessing a firearm. Crowe pleaded guilty to reduced misdemeanor charges and was fined $160. The judge placed Crowe on conditional discharge, thereby requiring that the actor not be arrested for one year. The criminal complaint follows:

CRIMINAL COURT OF THE CITY OF NEW YORK
COUNTY OF NEW YORK

Page 1 of 1

| THE PEOPLE OF THE STATE OF NEW YORK | FELONY |
| -against- | ADA SJOQUIST |

1. **Russell Crowe (M 41)**

549751

Defendant.

Police Officer Malika Simmons, shield 12871 of the 001 Precinct, states as follows:

On June 6, 2005, at about 04:20 hours at 147 Mercer Street in the County and State of New York, the Defendant committed the offenses of:

1.   PL120.05(2)   Assault in the Second Degree
                   (1 count)
2.   PL265.01(2)   Criminal Possession of a Weapon in the Fourth Degree
                   (1 count)

the defendant, with intent to cause physical injury to another person, caused such injury to another person by means of a dangerous instrument; and the defendant possessed a dangerous or deadly instrument with intent to use it unlawfully against another.

The offenses were committed under the following circumstances:

Deponent states that she is informed by an individual whose name and address are known to the District Attorney's Office that informant is a concierge at the Mercer Hotel and that defendant picked up a telephone and threw it at informant, hitting him in the face and causing a laceration and substantial pain.

Deponent states that she observed informant's injury and that defendant admitted that he picked up the phone and threw it at informant because he was angry.

False statements made herein are punishable as a class A misdemeanor pursuant to section 210.45 of the penal law.

_____   _____
Deponent   Date and Time

weapon, is "hooded, robed or masked in such manner as to conceal his identity," or knows the person harmed to be a peace officer, emergency medical technician, teacher, or other specified types of public service workers.[12] The Illinois statutes go on further to create separate crimes for aggravated battery with a firearm, aggravated battery with a machine gun or a gun with a silencer, aggravated battery of a child, aggravated battery of an unborn child, and aggravated battery of a senior citizen.[13]

3. INTIMIDATION, STALKING, AND ENDANGERMENT

Intimidation
An act which involves putting someone in fear of something bad happening to them, their loved ones, or their property.

Notice that part (c) of the Model Code's definition of simple assault includes "attempts by fear or menace to put another in fear of imminent serious bodily injury." This wording is designed to cover the concept of **intimidation**, which involves putting someone in fear of something bad happening to them, their loved ones, or their property. Synonyms for intimidation are *coercion*, *extortion*, and *duress*.

Many states have a separate statute making intimidation a crime. Take note of how it is defined in the following excerpt from the Illinois Criminal Code:

5/12-6 Intimidation

(a) A person commits intimidation when, with intent to cause another to perform or to omit the performance of any act, he communicates to another, whether in person, by telephone or by mail, a threat to perform without lawful authority any of the following acts:

(1) Inflict physical harm on the person threatened or any other person or on property; or

(2) Subject any person to physical confinement or restraint; or

(3) Commit any criminal offense; or

(4) Accuse any person of an offense; or

(5) Expose any person to hatred, contempt or ridicule; or

(6) Take action as a public official against anyone or anything, or withhold official action, or cause such action or withholding; or

(7) Bring about or continue a strike, boycott or other collective action.

Illinois goes on to define aggravated intimidation as committing the above defined crimes in furtherance of organized gang activities or where the person being intimidated is a peace officer, correctional official, or community policing volunteer.[14]

Stalking
The act of following another person or placing them under surveillance when these actions place that person in reasonable apprehension of bodily harm, sexual assault, confinement, or restraint.

Consider also the crime of **stalking**. This crime in Illinois involves following another person or placing them under surveillance when it places that person "in reasonable apprehension of immediate or future bodily harm, sexual assault, confinement or restraint."[15] It can become aggravated stalking if it violates an order of protection, actual confinement of the victim, or bodily harm to the victim.

---

[12]720 ILSC 5/12-4.

[13]720 ILSC 5/12-4.2, 5/12-4.2-5, 5/12-4.3, 5/12-4.4, & 5/12-4.7.

[14]720 ILSC 5/12-6.2.

[15]720 ILSC 5/12-7.3.

In California, a person is guilty of stalking when he or she harasses another person and "makes a credible threat with the intent to place that person in reasonable fear for his or her safety, or the safety of his or her immediate family."[16] Repeated stalking episodes involving the same victim or violations of a court order result in greater penalties.[17] While many stalking cases involve defendants that have had relationships with their victims, it is not uncommon for the California statute to be enforced against celebrity stalkers. A woman pleaded no contest in 2005 to stalking and threatening actress Catherine Zeta-Jones. That same year, an Idaho man who obsessively followed Mel Gibson claimed that he was on a mission from God to pray with the movie star. He was convicted under the California stalking law. Another type of application of the intimidation concept can be found in Section 211.3 of the Model Penal Code:

§ 211.3 Terroristic Threats

A person is guilty of a felony of the third degree if he threatens to commit any crime of violence with purpose to terrorize another or to cause evacuation of a building, place of assembly, or facility of public transportation, or otherwise to cause serious public inconvenience, or in reckless disregard of the risk of causing such terror or inconvenience.

As was the case with homicides, assault and batteries are usually prosecuted by local law enforcement officials. Federal law enforcement officials would be more likely to get involved where threats were related to federal officials or terrorism and where intimidation was related to organized crime or civil rights activities. Section 245 of Title 18 of the U.S. Code prohibits force or threat of force that injures, intimidates, or interferes with any person exercising their federal civil rights, and the Racketeer Influence and Corrupt Organizations Act (RICO)[18] covers various organized crime activities.

4. KIDNAPPING AND FALSE IMPRISONMENT

Crimes such as kidnapping, unlawful restraint, forcible detention, false imprisonment, and child abduction all involve seizing someone or detaining someone against their will. False imprisonment is also a common law tort. Therefore, the offender may not only be prosecuted in the criminal justice system but also sued for damages in a state court action brought by the victim. Note how the crimes of kidnapping, felonious restraint, and false imprisonment are defined in the Model Penal Code:

§ 212.1 Kidnapping

A person is guilty of kidnapping if he unlawfully removes another from his place of residence or business, or a substantial distance from the vicinity where he is found, or if he unlawfully confines another for a substantial period in a place of isolation, with any of the following purposes:
    (a) to hold for ransom or reward, or as a shield or hostage; or
    (b) to facilitate commission of any felony or flight thereafter; or

---

[16]Cal Pen Code § 646.9(a).

[17]Cal Pen Code § 646.9(b).

[18]18 U.S.C. § § 1961 *et seq.*

(c) to inflict bodily injury on or to terrorize the victim or another; or

(d) to interfere with the performance of any governmental or political function.

§ 212.2 Felonious Restraint

A person commits a felony of the third degree if he knowingly:

(a) restrains another unlawfully in circumstances exposing him to risk of serious bodily injury; or

(b) holds another in a condition of involuntary servitude.

§ 212.3 False Imprisonment

A person commits a misdemeanor if he knowingly restrains another unlawfully so as to interfere substantially with his liberty.

As most people know from newspapers and television, the federal government often gets involved in kidnapping cases where there is reason to believe the victim may have been taken across state lines.

5. SEX OFFENSES

Many criminal codes have a special section on sex-related crimes ranging from rape and sexual assault to prostitution and public indecency and even adultery and bigamy. Although crimes like rape and sexual assault clearly involve danger to the person, it can be argued that crimes such as adultery and bigamy should be classified in the Crimes Against the Family category, while prostitution and public indecency belong in the Public Order and Decency category. Keep in mind that it really doesn't matter how the crime is categorized. As long as it is included someplace in the jurisdiction's statutes, it imposes criminal sanctions, and if it has not been found to be unconstitutional, it is enforceable.

Rape
Traditionally defined as non-consensual sexual intercourse between a male and a female who was not his wife. (Exceptions for forced intercourse with a wife no longer apply in some states.)

Statutory rape
An act of sexual intercourse (even if it was consensual) with a person under a certain age.

Sexual assault and sexual exploitation of children are generally considered the most heinous sex crimes. At common law, **rape** was defined as *non-consensual* sexual intercourse between a male and a female who was not his wife. Later, a crime called **statutory rape** was created to outlaw sexual intercourse with a person under a certain age even if it was *consensual.*

The Model Penal Code follows the common law tradition of defining the crime of rape in terms of males having non-consensual sexual intercourse with females who are not their wives.[19] It then goes on to define a crime called "Deviate Sexual Intercourse by Force or Imposition" that is gender-neutral and does not exclude spouses,[20] and another crime, labeled "Sexual Assault," that covers other forms of non-consensual sexual contact (but still excludes spouses).[21] The concept of statutory rape is incorporated into the Model Code by expanding the definition of rape to include consensual intercourse with a female who is less than ten years old[22] and by creating a crime called "Corruption of Minors and Seduction."[23]

---

[19]ALI Model Penal Code, § 213.1.

[20]ALI Model Penal Code, § 213.2.

[21]ALI Model Penal Code, § 213.4.

[22]ALI Model Penal Code, § 213.1(1(d)).

[23]ALI Model Penal Code, § 213.3.

Note, however, that the Model Code still defines rape in terms of a male having intercourse with a female and that it doesn't apply to a husband forcing himself on his wife. In recent years, many states have revised their rape laws to make them sex-neutral and to remove the exemption for having non-consensual sex with a spouse. Illinois, for example, has replaced the crime of rape with criminal sexual assault and aggravated criminal sexual assault. Notice how it covers female perpetrators as well as males and how it incorporates age limitations found in statutory rape laws.

720 ILCS 5/12-13 Criminal Sexual Assault

(a) The accused commits criminal sexual assault if he or she:

(1) commits an act of sexual penetration by the use of force or threat of force; or

(2) commits an act of sexual penetration and the accused knows that the victim was unable to understand the nature of the act or was unable to give knowing consent; or

(3) commits an act of sexual penetration with a victim who was under 18 years of age when the act was committed and the accused was a family member; or

(3) commits an act of sexual penetration with a victim who was at least 13 years of age but under 18 years of age when the act was committed and the accused was 17 years of age or over and held a position of trust, authority or supervision in relation to the victim.

An act of Criminal Sexual Assault becomes Aggravated Criminal Sexual Assault when a weapon was displayed or use of a weapon was threatened, when the act caused bodily harm, when the victim was age 60 or older, or several other listed factors.[24] Other sex-related crimes in Illinois include predatory criminal sexual assault of a child, criminal sexual abuse, and aggravated criminal sexual abuse.[25]

Pop icon Michael Jackson was charged with and acquitted of statutory rape.[26] The felony complaint against him alleged multiple violations of the following statute:

Cal Pen Code § 288 Lewd or Lascivious Acts Involving Children

Any person who willfully and lewdly commits any lewd or lascivious act, including any of the acts constituting other crimes provided for in Part 1, upon or with the body, or any part or member thereof, of a child who is under the age of 14 years, with the intent of arousing, appealing to, or gratifying the lust, passions, or sexual desires of that person or the child, is guilty of a felony and shall be punished by imprisonment in the state prison for three, six, or eight years.

Whereas crimes against prostitution and obscenity are often classified as crimes against the public order and decency, laws against child pornography are usually justified in terms of protecting children from being harmed in the making and distribution of these materials.

---

[24]720 ILSC 5/12-14.

[25]720 ILSC 5/12-14.1, 5/12-15, and 5/12-16.

[26]*People v. Jackson* (Superior Court of California, Santa Barbara County Case No. 1133603).

6. VIOLATION OF CIVIL RIGHTS AND HATE CRIMES

The federal criminal code includes two key provisions designed to protect people's civil rights. These laws were first passed in 1909 and then revised several times since then. They proved to be very important tools in the civil rights movement in the 1960s and 1970s when some local law enforcement officials turned their back on violent crimes that were being committed against African Americans and civil rights advocates.[27]

18 U.S.C.S. § 241 Conspiracy Against Rights

If two or more persons conspire to injure, oppress, threaten, or intimidate any person in any State, Territory, Commonwealth, Possession, or District in the free exercise or enjoyment of any right or privilege secured to him by the Constitution or laws of the United States, or because of his having so exercised the same; or

If two or more persons go in disguise on the highway, or on the premises of another, with intent to prevent or hinder his free exercise or enjoyment of any right or privilege so secured—They shall be fined under this title or imprisoned not more than ten years, or both; and if death results from the acts committed in violation of this section or if such acts include kidnapping or an attempt to kidnap, aggravated sexual abuse or an attempt to commit aggravated sexual abuse, or an attempt to kill, they shall be fined under this title or imprisoned for any term of years or for life, or both, or may be sentenced to death.

Hate crime
A crime where the selection of the victim is based on that person's membership in a protected category, such as race, sex, or sexual orientation.

So-called **hate crimes** laws are designed to protect groups of people (that are deemed to be in need of special protection) from acts against them or their property that are motivated by hatred toward the group with whom they are perceived to be associated. Examples of such crimes would include the burning of a cross in front of the home of someone thought to be an African American or a group of young men assaulting someone they thought to be a homosexual. Considerable controversy has developed regarding what groups should receive this kind of protection[28] and the extent to which such laws might violate constitutional rights to free expression.[29]

Penalty enhancement statute
A law providing for a stiffer penalty for the violation of a criminal statute due to the presence of an aggravating factor, such as the age or race of the victim, the heinous nature of the offense, etc.

Another form of hate crime legislation involves **penalty enhancement statutes,** which provide for a stiffer penalty if the jury finds the crime victim had been specifically selected on the basis of race, religion, color, disability, sexual orientation, national origin, or ancestry.[30] Penalty enhancement statutes also are

---

[27]The movie *Mississippi Burning* deals with how these laws were used by the Federal Bureau of Investigation and federal prosecutors in Mississippi in the 1960s.

[28]A speech code adopted at the University of Michigan listed twelve different groups that were to receive special protection: race, ethnicity, religion, sex, sexual orientation, creed, national origin, ancestry, age, marital status, handicap, and Vietnam-era veteran status.

[29]While federal courts have struck down "speech codes" that attempt to prohibit the use of certain types of words, they have upheld laws where intimidation was involved. In *Virginia v. Black*, 538 U.S. 343, 123 S. Ct. 1536, 155 L. Ed. 2d 535 (2004), the U.S. Supreme Court ruled that it is not a violation of the First Amendment for a state to prohibit people from burning a cross on public property or the property of another when it is done with the intent to intimidate.

[30]Such statutes were upheld by the U.S. Supreme Court in *Wisconsin v. Mitchell,* 508 U.S. 476, 113 S. Ct. 2194, 124 L. Ed. 2d 436 (1993).

employed in other circumstances besides hate crimes. We will explore the general concept of penalty enhancement when we discuss sentencing in Chapter 13.

DISCUSSION QUESTIONS

1. The Model Penal Code requires proof of some degree of fault in order to convict someone of homicide. Do you think that a person who causes the death of another should be punished even if he or she did not act in a purposeful, knowing, reckless, or negligent manner?

2. The U.S. Supreme Court in *Roe v. Wade*, 410 U.S. 113, 93 S. Ct. 705, 35 L.Ed. 2d 147 (1973) determined that if a fetus were defined as a person for purposes of the Fourteenth Amendment to the Constitution, then the fetus would have a constitutional right to life. However, the *Roe* majority determined that the unborn were not persons under the Constitution. If *Roe v. Wade* is overturned by the Supreme Court, would the killing of an unborn fetus be considered homicide? If so, would the homicide of a pregnant woman be a double homicide even if the killer did not know of the pregnancy?

3. During the Vietnam conflict, President Nixon authorized the "secret" bombing of Cambodia. Critics argued that this action was unconstitutional. Under Section 2.10 of the Model Code, would soldiers carrying out the directives of the President have a defense to homicide charges for the deaths of civilian casualties?

4. If an Illinois physician travels to the state of Oregon for the sole purpose of assisting her terminally ill Illinois patient in suicide, should the physician be held accountable under Illinois criminal law for "causing or aiding suicide"?

5. During the course of a bank robbery, a security guard is killed by one of the robbers. If the robbery takes place in a jurisdiction that recognizes the felony murder doctrine, will the get-away car driver be accountable for the homicide? Could the prosecutor charge the people who harbor the robbers a week after the robbery with homicide?

6. The felony assault charge against Russell Crowe was resolved following an amicable resolution of the victim's tort claim. Do you think that it is appropriate for a crime victim to receive compensation for injuries from the defendant when criminal charges remain pending?

7. Sometimes, both participants in a fight are charged with assault and battery. Should both participants be charged with crimes? If so, how will the prosecution prove its case?

8. A college football team is particularly rough against its rival during a game, thereby causing injuries to several opposing players. Are they guilty of battery? If a fistfight between the teams breaks out after the game, is there a battery?

9. Celebrities seem to be targets for stalkers. Should a star-struck fan be subjected to criminal penalties simply because he wants to get an autograph and photograph of his favorite actor or singer? Should the paparazzi be arrested for doing their job just because a celebrity doesn't appreciate the invasion of privacy? At what point should there be criminal consequences?

10. In the aftermath of the 9/11 terrorist attacks, should all statements suggesting a terroristic threat be criminal? Is this the case even if the statement was made as a joke? Should there be criminal responsibility if an actor makes what appears to be a terroristic threat to the audience during a performance of a play?

B. Crimes Against Property

The second major category of Model Penal Code crimes is "Offenses Against Property." They include offenses such as arson, criminal damage to property, burglary, trespass, robbery, extortion, forgery, and fraud.

1. ARSON AND OTHER TYPES OF DESTRUCTION OF PROPERTY

Arson
An act of starting a fire or causing an explosion with the purpose of destroying or damaging property of another; or to collect insurance for such loss.

Arson occurs when someone "starts a fire or causes an explosion with the purpose of (a) destroying a building or occupied structure of another; or (b) destroying or damaging any property, whether his own or another's to collect insurance for such loss."[31] Lesser, related offenses include reckless burning or exploding,[32] and failure to control or report dangerous fire.[33] The offense of criminal mischief covers damage to property by means that go beyond the use of fire or explosives.[34]

2. TRESPASS AND BURGLARY

Trespass
An unauthorized intrusion onto private land or into a building that belongs to someone else.

In the common law, **trespass** is an unauthorized intrusion onto private land or into a building that belongs to someone else. It is a concept that involves issues of civil liability as well as potential criminal penalties.

The Model Penal Code defines two types of criminal trespass.

§ 221.2 Criminal Trespass

(1) *Buildings and Occupied Structures*. A person commits an offense if, knowing that he is not licensed or privileged to do so, he enters or surreptitiously remains in any building or occupied structure, or a separately secured or occupied portion thereof.

(2) *Defiant Trespasser*. A person commits an offense if, knowing that he is not licensed or privileged to do so, he enters or remains in any place as to which notice against trespass is given by:

(a) actual communication to the actor; or

(b) posting in a manner prescribed by law or reasonably likely to come to the attention of intruders; or

(c) fencing or other enclosure manifestly designed to exclude intruders.

Whereas trespass is treated as a misdemeanor in the Model Penal Code, burglary is a felony. Burglary differs from trespass in that it involves entering for the purpose of committing a crime. Under the common law, the entry had to take place at night and the crime being committed had to be a felony. However, the Model Penal Code and most state statutes are broader than the common law.

---

[31]ALI Model Penal Code, § 220.1(1).
[32]ALI Model Penal Code, § 220.1(2).
[33]ALI Model Penal Code, § 220.1(3).
[34]ALI Model Penal Code, § 220.3.

§ 221.1 Burglary

(1) A person is guilty of burglary if he enters a building or occupied structure, or separately secured or occupied portion thereof, with purpose to commit a crime therein, unless the premises are at the time open to the public or the actor is licensed or privileged to enter. It is an affirmative defense to prosecution for burglary that the building or structure was abandoned.

Note that all of the elements of trespass are included within the offense of burglary. Thus, by definition, a burglar always is a trespasser. A **lesser included offense** is a crime whose elements are all included among the elements of the more serious crime being charged. Under the Model Penal Code, a defendant cannot be convicted of both the serious crime and the lesser included offense for the same conduct.[35]

Burglary
An act of entering into a building for the purpose of committing a crime.

Lesser included offense
A crime whose elements are all included among the elements of the more serious crime being charged.

3. THEFT, LARCENY, ROBBERY, AND FRAUD

Theft is a general term used to refer to a variety of crimes involving what is commonly known as stealing, that is, taking property without the owner's consent. The common law defined the crime of **larceny** as a taking away of the goods or property of another without the consent and against the will of the owner or possessor and with a criminal intent to convert the property to the use of someone other than the owner.

A **robbery** occurs when someone uses force or fear to take something of value from the possession of another against that person's wishes. In the Model Penal Code it is defined as follows:

Theft
A crime involving taking property without the owner's consent.

Larceny
A crime that involves the taking away of the goods or property of another without the consent and against the will of the owner or possessor and with a criminal intent to convert the property to the use of someone other than the owner.

§ 221.1 Robbery

A person is guilty of robbery if, in the course of committing a theft, he:

(a) inflicts serious bodily injury upon another; or

(b) threatens another with or purposely puts him in fear of immediate serious bodily injury; or

(c) commits or threatens immediately to commit any felony of the first or second degree.

An act shall be deemed "in the course of committing a theft" if it occurs in an attempt to commit theft or in flight after the attempt or commission.

Robbery
A crime in which someone uses force or fear to take something of value from the possession of another against that person's wishes.

The Model Penal Code contains separate offenses for theft by unlawful taking or disposition; theft by deception; theft by extortion; theft of property lost, mislaid, or delivered by mistake; and theft of services. Some state statutes list separate offenses for retail theft, library theft, theft of coin-operated machines, unlawful use of recorded sounds or images, and identity theft. There are also laws against falsely reporting a theft, receiving stolen property, and commercial bribery.

A sample retail theft complaint appears in Exhibit 3.3. Note how the format of this complaint differs from the Virginia indictment that appears in Exhibit 3.1 and the New York charging instrument that appears in

---

[35]ALI Model Penal Code, § 1.07(1)(a).

Exhibit 3.3: California Felony Shoplifting Complaint

The Los Angeles County District Attorney charged actress Winona Ryder with several felonies arising from a shoplifting arrest. Investigators claimed that Ryder cut security tags off merchandise valued at more than $4,000. Ryder was convicted of grand theft and felony vandalism and acquitted of commercial burglary. She was originally sentenced to three years' probation, 480 hours community service, and a court-prescribed counseling program. She was ordered to pay more than $10,000 in fines and restitution. Seven months later, the sentencing judge reduced the charges to misdemeanors and placed her on unsupervised probation. The felony complaint reads, in part, as follows:

SUPERIOR COURT OF THE STATE OF CALIFORNIA
FOR THE COUNTY OF LOS ANGELES

THE PEOPLE OF THE STATE OF CALIFORNIA, Plaintiff, v. 01 WINONA RYDER (10/29/1971) Defendant(s).	CASE NO. SA044291 *FELONY COMPLAINT*

The undersigned is informed and believes that:

COUNT 1

On or about December 12, 2001, in the County of Los Angeles, the crime of SECOND DEGREE COMMERCIAL BURGLARY, in violation of PENAL CODE SECTION 459, a Felony, was committed by WINONA RYDER, who did enter a commercial building occupied by SAKS FIFTH AVE with the intent to commit larceny and any felony.

COUNT 2

On or about December 12, 2001, in the County of Los Angeles, the crime of GRAND THEFT OF PERSONAL PROPERTY, in violation of PENAL CODE SECTION 487(a), a Felony, was committed by WINONA RYDER, who did unlawfully take money and personal property of a value exceeding Four Hundred Dollars ($400), to wit merchandise in excess of Four Hundred Dollars ($400.00) the property of SAKS FIFTH AVE.

COUNT 3

On or about December 12, 2001, in the County of Los Angeles, the crime of VANDALISM OVER $400 DAMAGE, in violation of PENAL CODE SECTION 594(a), a Felony, was committed by WINONA RYDER, who did unlawfully and maliciously damage and destroy personal property, to wit, Clothing, not his or her own, belonging to SAKS FIFTH AVE, the amount of said damage being over $400.00.

*****

I DECLARE UNDER PENALTY OF PERJURY THAT THE FOREGOING IS TRUE AND CORRECT AND THAT THIS COMPLAINT, CASE NUMBER SA044291, CONSISTS OF 4 COUNT(S).

Executed at BEVERLY HILLS, County of Los Angeles, on February 1, 2002.

_____

DECLARANT AND COMPLAINANT

Exhibit 3.2. Each state has its own style of drafting charging instruments. Make sure that you check the format of your state when you draft a criminal law document.

Fraud
An act of using deception to commit a theft.

Fraud involves theft through deception. It is an intentional perversion of the truth to induce someone to part with something of value. Rather than physically stealing someone else's property, the offender illegally obtains the victim's property through embezzlement, forgery, false billing, misrepresentation, and other deceptive practices. Fraud is the key component in most forms of white-collar crime.[36] Examples include mail fraud, insurance fraud, identity theft, money laundering, and investment Ponzi schemes like the one run by Bernard Madoff.[37] Like assault and battery, fraud is a common law concept that can be pursued as either a tort or a crime.

---

[36]See distinction between white-color crime and street crime on p. 33.

[37]In 2009, Bernard Madoff pled guilty to orchestrating a massive fraud that bilked investors out of more than $65 billion.

APPLICATION EXERCISES

After reviewing the facts of the Bill Edwards and Tom Schroeder Hypothetical Cases (*see p. xxxviii*), answer the following questions:

5. By diverting customer funds and liquidating customer securities without permission or authority from customers, Edwards appears to be guilty of some form of fraud. He then compounded his crime when he began misappropriating funds from other customers to make the interest payments owed to the existing customers. If Edwards operated in your state, what, if any, statutes might he have violated?

6. Since Edwards was a registered representative for a local broker-securities dealer, he may have violated federal statutes and regulations of the Securities and Exchange Commission. Which, if any, of these regulations might he have violated? Although Schroeder was not a registered securities agent, could he still be subject to federal securities laws by virtue of his representation of Amalgamated Industries?

DISCUSSION QUESTIONS

11. If a camper in a national park causes a fire that develops into a major wildfire, has the camper committed arson? If a firefighter loses his life in combating the fire, is the camper guilty of homicide under the felony murder doctrine?

12. A photographer for a weekly magazine enters the property of a celebrity to take a candid picture. Is the photographer a trespasser? Is the photographer a burglar?

13. Suppose that a private investigator is hired by a celebrity's spouse to check up on his activities. Is the private eye a trespasser? Is the private eye a burglar?

14. Is there a good policy reason not to convict a defendant of the lesser included offense if he or she is convicted of the more serious one? Why shouldn't a burglar also be convicted of trespassing for the same conduct?

15. A shoplifter steals $200 worth of merchandise on Monday, and on Tuesday takes items worth $400 from the same store. The jurisdiction classifies retail theft of $500 or more as a felony and theft of less than $500 as a misdemeanor. If the offender admits she committed both thefts, should she be charged with one felony or two misdemeanors? Why?

C. CRIMES AGAINST THE FAMILY

This section of the criminal code is designed to protect families by criminalizing things such as bigamy, polygamy, incest, and failure to provide child support.

In addition to having general laws for battery and aggravated battery, some states have special laws against domestic battery that apply to actions taken against other family or household members. These types of laws can either be grouped with others involving danger to a person or in the category of those affecting the family. In recent times, states increasingly have relied on assault and battery laws to fight domestic violence. Generally, **domestic violence** means physical abuse, harassment, or intimidation of a victim by a family or household member. The federal government has enacted the Violence Against Women Act. Under this law, it is a crime for anyone to cross state lines with the intent to injure his or her partner or to violate a state **order of protection**.[38] Despite the federal government's involvement in combating domestic violence, the vast majority of assault and battery prosecutions are brought by local authorities under state law. Typically, women are the victims of domestic battery, although there are times when men are the subject of physical abuse (see Exhibit 3.4).

Domestic violence
Physical abuse, harassment, or intimidation of a victim by a family or household member.

Order of protection
A court order entered to forbid an individual from harassing, abusing, or otherwise interfering with the liberty of a particular person. Typically, the order protects a victim from a household or family member.

Exhibit 3.4: Domestic Violence Police Report Excerpt

Men can be victims of domestic violence. This excerpt from a Las Vegas Metropolitan Police Department incident report describes an altercation involving actor Christian Slater and his wife.

Narratives

Entered date/time:	11/12/2003 10:01	Narrative type:	INCIDENT CRIME REPORT
Subject:	BATTERY/DOMESTIC VIOLENCE	Author:	DOSCH, M 7907

CHRISTIAN SLATER AND RYAN SLATER AREA MARRIED, COHABITANTS AND HAVE TWO CHILDREN IN COMMON. CHRISTIAN SLATER WAS THE VICTIM OF BATTERY DOMESTIC VIOLENCE WHEN CHRISTIAN SLATER AND RYAN SLATER WERE INVOLVED IN AN ARGUMENT. DURING THE ARGUMENT, RYAN SLATER STRUCK THE LEFT SIDE AND EAR AREA OF CHRISTIAN SLATER'S HEAD WITH A GLASS WHICH WAS IN HER RIGHT HAND. RYAN SLATER WAS ARRESTED AT 0830 HOURS. THE BATTERY OCCURRED AT APPROXIMATELY 0600 HOURS. THE BATTERY CAUSED A ONE INCH VERTICAL LACERATION TO APPEAR JUST BEHIND THE EAR.

PERSON #1 VISIBLE INJURY
PERSON #2 NERVOUS, CRYING

PERSONS INVOLVED ARE: SPOUSE, COHABITANTS, HAVE CHILD IN COMMON. NO PHOTOS TAKEN. VICTIM DID NOT REQUEST TEMPORARY HOUSING. NO TPO IN EFFECT. VICTIM GIVEN DOMESTIC VIOLENCE INFO CARD. WEAPON: GLASS. EVIDENCE: BROKEN GLASS. 911 CALLED BY SECURITY.

SUSPECT ARRESTED. PRIMARY AGGRESSOR DETERMINED BY SEVERITY OF INJURIES INFLICTED.

---

[38]18 U.S.C. § § 2261(a)(2), 2262(a)(1), (2).

D. CRIMES AGAINST PUBLIC ADMINISTRATION

These types of crimes may also be labeled as offenses affecting governmental functions. They include offenses such as bribery, concealing or aiding a fugitive, obstruction of justice, official misconduct, perjury, tax evasion, treason, espionage, and terrorism.

Treason
An attempt to overthrow the government of one's country or of assisting its enemies in war.

Treason is the offense of attempting to overthrow the government of one's country or of assisting its enemies in war. It is generally considered the most despicable of the crimes in this category and reference to it was specifically included in Article III, Section 3 of the U.S. Constitution.

> Treason against the United States shall consist only in levying War against them, or in adhering to their Enemies, giving them Aid and Comfort. No Person shall be convicted of Treason unless on the Testimony of two Witnesses to the same overt Act, or on Confession in open Court.
>   The Congress shall have power to declare the Punishment of Treason, but no Attainder of Treason shall work Corruption of Blood, or Forfeiture except during the Life of the Person attainted.

Section 2381 of Title 18 of the U.S. Code defines treason as follows:

> Whoever, owing allegiance to the United States, levies war against them or adheres to their enemies, giving them aid and comfort within the United States or elsewhere, is guilty of treason and shall suffer death, or shall be imprisoned not less than five years and fined under this title but not less than $10,000; and shall be incapable of holding any office under the United States.

Related to the offense of treason is espionage. Although this crime is not referenced in the Constitution, it is a serious crime that may be punished by the death penalty. **Espionage** is the act of disclosing information with intent to interfere with the operation or success of the U.S. armed forces or to promote the success of enemies of the United States.

Espionage
The act of disclosing information with intent to interfere with the operation or success of the U.S. armed forces or to promote the success of enemies of the United States.

Section 793 of Title 18 of the U.S. Code prohibits gathering, transmitting, or losing specified types of defense information. Section 794 covers gathering or delivering defense information to aid a foreign government. Exhibit 3.5 displays the criminal complaint against Ronald Hanssen in a highly publicized espionage case. (Notice how the format of the complaint is similar to the state criminal complaints depicted in Exhibits 3.1, 3.2, and 3.3.)

The Hanssen case involved what we think of as the classical spy operation, in which an agent steals secrets and then turns them over to a foreign government. In contrast, the recent WikiLeaks controversy[39] illustrates a situation in which someone who is not working for a foreign government turns over classified government documents to the news media in order to develop political support for policy changes.

The first major example of this type of behavior occurred in 1971 when Daniel Ellsberg leaked a classified military study on the Vietnam War to the *New York Times*, the *Washington Post*, and several other mainstream media outlets.

---

[39]In October 2010, a privately run international website posted almost 400,000 documents called the Iraq War Logs that allowed deaths in Iraq, and across the border in Iran, to be mapped. In November 2010, WikiLeaks began releasing U.S. State Department diplomatic cables.

Exhibit 3.5: Federal Espionage Criminal Complaint

Robert Hanssen is a former FBI agent who was involved in spying against the United States. He was charged with selling American secrets to Moscow for more than $1.4 million in cash and diamonds over a fifteen-year period. In 2001, he pleaded guilty to fifteen counts of espionage.

He was sentenced to life in prison. He is in solitary confinement twenty-three hours each day. The 2007 movie *Breach* starring Chris Cooper is based on Hanssen's story. The criminal complaint initially filed against him follows:

AO 91 (Rev. 5/85) Criminal Complaint

United States District Court

EASTERN   DISTRICT OF   VIRGINIA

FILED

FEB 16

UNITED STATES OF AMERICA

v.

ROBERT PHILIP HANSSEN
9414 TALISMAN DRIVE
VIENNA, VIRGINIA

(Name and Address of Defendant)

CRIMINAL COMPLAINT

CASE NUMBER: 01-185-M

I, the undersigned complainant being duly sworn state the following is true and correct to the best of my knowledge and belief. On or about October 1, 1985 up to the date of this complaint in City of Alexandria and Fairfax County, in the ___Eastern___ District of ___Virginia___, and elsewhere, defendant(s) did, (Track Statutory Language of Offense)

commit a violation of Title 18, United States Code, Section 794(c), that is, with intent and reason to believe that it would be used to the injury of the United States, and the advantage of a foreign nation, ROBERT PHILIP HANSSEN did unlawfully and knowingly conspire with others, to communicate, transmit and deliver to representatives of a foreign government, specifically, the U.S.S.R. and the Russian Federation, information relating to the national defense of the United States, and did overt acts to effect the object of said conspiracy, including, but not limited to, the following: ROBERT PHILIP HANSSEN did on or about March 20, 1989 in Fairfax County, Virginia, deposit at a secret location a package for the KGB, the intelligence service of the Soviet Union, containing multiple classified documents, including a document classified TOP SECRET/SENSITIVE COMPARTMENTED INFORMATION (TS/SCI); and did

commit a violation of Title 18, United States Code, Section 794(a), that is, with intent and reason to believe that it would be used to the injury of the United States, and to the advantage of a foreign nation, ROBERT PHILIP HANSSEN did unlawfully and knowingly communicate, transmit and deliver to representatives and agents of a foreign government, specifically the U.S.S.R., information relating to the national defense of the United States, to wit: On or about October 1, 1985, he disclosed to the KGB the identities of three KGB officers acting as intelligence sources and agents of the United States, and other intelligence sources and methods of the United States, such information constituting classified national defense information.

In violation of Title ___18___ United States Code, Section(s) ___794(a) and (c)___

I further state that I am a(n) ___Special Agent, FBI___ and that this complaint is based on the following facts:
Official Title

See Attached Affidavit

Continued on the attached sheet and made a part hereof: ☒ Yes   ☐ No

_____
Signature of Complainant
Stefan A. Pluta
Special Agent
Federal Bureau of Investigation

Reviewed By: Randy I. Bellows
Justin W. Williams
Assistant United States Attorneys
Laura A. Ingersoll
Senior Trial Attorney, DOJ

Sworn to before me

Feby 16, 2001   at   Alexandria, Virginia
Date   City and State

THOMAS RAWLES JONES, JR.
U.S. MAGISTRATE JUDGE
_____
Name & Title of Judicial Officer

_____
Signature of Judicial Officer

In response, the Nixon administration went to court to stop the press from publishing the so-called Pentagon Papers and brought criminal charges of espionage and theft against Ellsberg. However, the U.S. Supreme Court rejected the government's request for an injunction to prohibit the newspapers from publishing the documents, and the criminal charges against Ellsberg were eventually dropped due to "prosecutorial misconduct."[40] As of the writing of this book, the alleged source of the WikiLeaks documents is still under investigation, no legal actions have yet been taken to prohibit the site from posting the classified documents, and no criminal charges (related to these documents[41]) have been brought against the man who runs the WikiLeaks website.

Other crimes against public administration include perjury and obstruction of justice. Both received a lot of press attention during the presidencies of Bill Clinton and George W. Bush. Charges that President Clinton had perjured himself in a deposition he gave concerning his relationship to a White House intern resulted in one of two articles of impeachment voted by the House of Representatives in 1998. A second article of impeachment alleged obstruction of justice relating to an investigation being conducted by Independent Counsel Kenneth Star.[42]

In 2003, syndicated columnist Robert Novak revealed the cover of a CIA agent in an article designed to discredit a critic of the Bush administration's plans to attack Iraq. A special prosecutor's investigation into the source of the "leak" of this classified information led to an indictment of Lewis (Scooter) Libby, chief of staff to Vice President Dick Cheney, for perjury, obstruction of justice, and making false statements to federal investigators. In 2007, Libby was convicted on one count of obstruction of justice, two counts of perjury, and one count of making false statements to federal investigators. Libby was sentenced to thirty months in federal prison, a fine of $250,000, and two years of supervised release, including 400 hours of community service, but President Bush commuted the thirty-month prison sentence.

Perjury

The act of lying or knowingly making false statements while under oath in court or in affidavits or depositions.

Perjury is the act of lying or knowingly making false statements while under oath in court or in affidavits or depositions. Section 1621 of Title 18 of the U.S. Code states:

Whoever—

(1) having taken an oath before a competent tribunal, officer, or person, in any case in which a law of the United States authorizes an oath to be administered, that he will testify, declare, depose, or certify truly, or that any written testimony, declaration, deposition, or certificate by him subscribed, is true, willfully and contrary to such oath states or subscribes any material matter which he does not believe to be true; or

(2) in any declaration, certificate, verification, or statement under penalty of perjury as permitted under section 1746 of title 28, United States Code,

---

[40]The misconduct involved illegal searches of Ellsberg's psychiatrist's office and attempts to improperly use the information obtained in those searches.

[41]However, at the time of this writing, Julian Assange is out on bail and under house arrest in England pending an extradition hearing related to charges of alleged sex offenses in Sweden. He has denied the allegations and claimed that they were politically motivated.

[42]In the impeachment "trial" in the Senate, fifty-five senators voted "not guilty" and forty-five voted "guilty" on the charge of perjury. The Senate also acquitted Clinton on the obstruction charge with fifty votes cast each way.

willfully subscribes as true any material matter which he does not believe to be true;

... This section is applicable whether the statement or subscription is made within or without the United States.

The crime of **making false statements to federal investigators** is not limited to statements made under oath. Section 1001 of Title 18 of the U.S. Code prohibits lying to or concealing information from a federal official. It is designed to punish those who give false statements meant to pervert or undermine functions of governmental bodies.

Making false statements to federal investigators
The act of lying to or concealing information from a federal official.

§ 1001 Statements or Entries Generally

(a) Except as otherwise provided in this section, whoever, in any matter within the jurisdiction of the executive, legislative, or judicial branch of the Government of the United States, knowingly and willfully—

(1) falsifies, conceals, or covers up by any trick, scheme, or device a material fact;

(2) makes any materially false, fictitious, or fraudulent statement or representation; or

(3) makes or uses any false writing or document knowing the same to contain any materially false, fictitious, or fraudulent statement or entry ...

The crime of **obstruction of justice** involves interference with the work of police, prosecutors, and other government officials. Generally, obstruction charges are levied when it is discovered that a person not considered to be a suspect has lied to the investigating officers. While the Fifth Amendment gives people the right to refuse to answer an investigator's questions based on a claim of self-incrimination, it does not protect anyone from giving false statements to authorities.[43]

Obstruction of justice
An act that intentionally interferes with the work of police, prosecutors, and other government officials.

People can also be prosecuted for obstruction of justice for altering or destroying physical evidence—even if they had no legal obligation to produce the evidence at the time it was destroyed. When Martha Stewart was being investigated for insider trading, she allegedly falsified some documents to create an explanation for a suspicious-looking trade of a pharmaceutical company stock owned by a friend. Although it was ultimately determined that her trades had not violated SEC regulations on insider trading, her falsification of her trading records had made it more difficult for the government to develop its case against the company's CEO.

In addition to criminalizing attempts to obstruct a law enforcement investigation, state and federal laws also make it illegal for government officials to misuse their legal authority. A prime example of this is the following:

18 U.S.C.S. § 242. Deprivation of Rights Under Color of Law

Whoever, under color of any law, statute, ordinance, regulation, or custom, willfully subjects any person in any State, Territory, Commonwealth, Possession, or District to the deprivation of any rights, privileges, or immunities secured or

---

[43] *United States v. Wong*, 431 U.S. 174, 97 S. Ct. 1823, 52 L. Ed. 2d 231 (1977).

protected by the Constitution or laws of the United States, or to different punishments, pains, or penalties, on account of such person being an alien, or by reason of his color, or race, than are prescribed for the punishment of citizens, shall be fined under this title or imprisoned not more than one year, or both; and if bodily injury results from the acts committed in violation of this section or if such acts include the use, attempted use, or threatened use of a dangerous weapon, explosives, or fire, shall be fined under this title or imprisoned not more than ten years, or both; and if death results from the acts committed in violation of this section or if such acts include kidnapping or an attempt to kidnap, aggravated sexual abuse, or an attempt to commit aggravated sexual abuse, or an attempt to kill, shall be fined under this title, or imprisoned for any term of years or for life, or both, or may be sentenced to death.

APPLICATION EXERCISES

7. As mentioned above, the criminal charges brought against Daniel Ellsberg for leaking the Pentagon Papers were dismissed for reasons of prosecutorial misconduct. Identify and report your findings as to what are the relevant provisions of the U.S.C. that deal with espionage and disclosure of classified information.
   a. What types of charges do you think could be brought against whoever was found to have "leaked" the classified documents to WikiLeaks?
   b. Now read *United States v. Morgan*, 604 F. Supp. 655 (D. MD, 1985) and indicate how you think it would affect your response in (a) above.
   c. What types of charges could be brought against Julian Assange for posting these documents on his website?

8. In previous exercises you have been asked to consider the extent to which Bud Cook might be guilty of manslaughter or negligent homicide. What, if any, provisions of your state's motor vehicle code did he violate when he left the scene of the accident without reporting it to police? What other state laws did he disobey?

9. In previous exercises you were asked to consider potential fraud charges against Edwards and Schroeder. What other types of state and/or federal laws might they have violated?

DISCUSSION QUESTIONS

16. Politicians who use their influence to assist their contributors in obtaining governmental contracts are sometimes prosecuted for official misconduct. In response, some critics argue that this is simply business as usual. For instance, former Illinois Governor George Ryan was convicted after a six-month-long jury trial. Should law enforcement use its finite resources to investigate and prosecute government officials simply because political supporters receive a contractual benefit?

17. Illinois requires state employees to take an online ethics exam every year to maintain their governmental employment. Should an employee's failure to take

the exam result in criminal penalties? Should the employee be charged with a crime if he completes the examination in less time than it would take a normal person to simply read all of the questions (based on the assumption that if the person finished the exam that quickly he or she must have cheated)?

18. In most civil lawsuits that go to trial, there is conflicting testimony between the witnesses. Should the prosecuting authorities charge the witnesses whose testimony isn't believed with perjury?

19. In light of the fact that President Bill Clinton, who admitted to giving a false statement under oath, was not impeached, is there any situation in which a perjury prosecution is the appropriate course of action by law enforcement authorities?

20. When a police officer falsely arrests a citizen or physically abuses a suspect, few would claim that the officer should be immune from prosecution for misuse of power. Should the police be prosecuted for helping a friend by "unofficially" running another person's license plates or arrest record?

E. CRIMES AGAINST PUBLIC ORDER AND DECENCY

The final category of crimes is a rather eclectic group of offenses, including prostitution and public indecency, pornography and obscenity, deviant sexual conduct, disturbing the peace, vagrancy, and panhandling. It also includes traffic laws and those involving drugs, alcohol, and firearms.

1. PROTECTING PUBLIC ORDER

The classic offenses related to the protection of public order are rioting and failure to disperse, disorderly conduct, disturbing the peace, public drunkenness, indecent exposure, loitering, and vagrancy and panhandling. Their common thread is that they are designed to preserve peace and quiet in public areas and to protect the general public from being offended by seeing someone exhibiting inappropriate behavior or harassed by someone begging for money. Some examples of the definitions of these crimes in the Model Penal Code are:

§ 250.1 Riot; Failure to Disperse

(1) *Riot.* A person is guilty of riot . . . if he participates with [two] or more others in a course of disorderly conduct;

(a) with purpose to commit or facilitate the commission of a felony or misdemeanor;

(b) with purpose to prevent or coerce official action; or

(c) when the actor or any other participant to the knowledge of the actor uses or plans to use a firearm or other deadly weapon.

(2) *Failure of Disorderly Persons to Disperse Upon Official Order.* Where [three] or more persons are participating in a course of disorderly conduct likely to cause substantial harm or serious inconvenience, annoyance or alarm, a peace officer or other public servant engaged in executing or enforcing the law may order the participants and others in the immediate vicinity to disperse. . . .

§ 250.2 Disorderly Conduct

(1) *Offense Defined.* A person is guilty of disorderly conduct if, with purpose to cause public inconvenience, annoyance or alarm, or recklessly creating a risk thereof, he:

(a) engages in fighting or threatening, or in violent or tumultuous behavior; or

(b) makes unreasonable noise or offensively coarse utterance, gesture or display, or addresses abusive language to any person present; or

(c) creates a hazardous or physically offensive condition by any act which serves no legitimate purpose of the actor.

"Public" means affecting or likely to affect persons in a place to which the public or a substantial group has access; among the places included are highways, transport facilities, schools, prisons, apartment houses, places of business or amusement, or any neighborhood.

§ 250.6 Loitering or Prowling

A person commits a violation if he loiters or prowls in a place, at a time, or in a manner not usual for law-abiding individuals under circumstances that warrant alarm for the safety of persons or property in the vicinity. Among the circumstances which may be considered in determining whether such alarm is warranted is the fact that the actor takes flight upon appearance of a peace officer, refuses to identify himself, or manifestly endeavors to conceal himself or any object . . .

Crimes such as disorderly conduct and loitering typically are not classified as felonies. However, sometimes a conviction for such an offense can have serious ramifications for the offender. For instance, U.S. Senator Larry Craig, a Republican from Idaho, was arrested in the early summer of 2007 by a plainclothes officer as part of a sting directed at homosexual conduct in the Minneapolis–St. Paul International Airport men's restroom. The senator was charged with the misdemeanors of peeping and disorderly conduct. Craig submitted a written guilty plea to the disorderly conduct charge. He was fined $1,000 and sentenced to ten days in the Hennepin County jail. Jail time was stayed as long as Craig did not violate the law for twelve months. Once the senator's plea became public, prominent Republicans and Democrats asked him to resign. Craig announced he would resign but later decided to complete his term.

2. MOTOR VEHICLE CODE AND CONSUMER PROTECTION REGULATIONS

Traffic laws and consumer protection regulations are also designed to protect the general public. Regulating the proper side of the road on which to drive as well as requiring drivers to observe speed limits, stop signs, stop lights, etc., enhance public order by moving traffic more efficiently and more safely.

In addition to laws on speed limits and stop signs, traffic laws also prohibit people from driving while under the influence of alcohol (DUI) or drugs and from leaving the scene of an accident without reporting it to police authorities.

The California Vehicle Code contains the following provisions:

DUI
The offense of driving under the influence of alcoholic beverages. Some states refer to this violation as DWI (driving while intoxicated).

§ 23152. Driving Under the Influence

(a) It is unlawful for any person who is under the influence of any alcoholic beverage or drug, or under the combined influence of any alcoholic beverage and drug, to drive a vehicle.

(b) It is unlawful for any person who has 0.08 percent or more, by weight, of alcohol in his or her blood to drive a vehicle.

§ 20001. Duty to Stop at Scene of Accident

(a) The driver of any vehicle involved in an accident resulting in injury to any person, other than himself or herself, or in the death of any person shall immediately stop the vehicle at the scene of the accident and shall fulfill the requirements of Sections 20003 and 20004.

§ 20003. Duty upon Injury or Death

(a) The driver of any vehicle involved in an accident resulting in injury to or death of any person shall also give his or her name, current residence address, the names and current residence addresses of any occupant of the driver's vehicle injured in the accident, the registration number of the vehicle he or she is driving, and the name and current residence address of the owner to the person struck or the driver or occupants of any vehicle collided with, and shall give the information to any traffic or police officer at the scene of the accident. The driver also shall render to any person injured in the accident reasonable assistance, including transporting, or making arrangements for transporting, any injured person to a physician, surgeon, or hospital for medical or surgical treatment if it is apparent that treatment is necessary or if that transportation is requested by any injured person.

§ 20004. Duty upon Death

In the event of death of any person resulting from an accident, the driver of any vehicle involved after fulfilling the requirements of this division, and if there be no traffic or police officer at the scene of the accident to whom to give the information required by Section 20003, shall, without delay, report the accident to the nearest office of the Department of the California Highway Patrol or office of a duly authorized police authority and submit with the report the information required by Section 20003.

An actual DUI complaint, based upon § 23152 of the California Vehicle Code, is displayed in Exhibit 3.6. Notice how the style of this complaint closely tracks the felony shoplifting complaint set forth in Exhibit 3.3. Contrast the style of these two complaints with the Virginia indictment (Exhibit 3.1), the New York charging instrument (Exhibit 3.2), and the federal criminal charge (Exhibit 3.5).

Exhibit 3.6: California DUI Complaint

Mel Gibson is one of a horde of celebrities who has been charged with driving under the influence. Gibson pleaded no contest to a misdemeanor drunken-driving charge and was sentenced to three years' probation. Counts 1 and 3 of the complaint were dismissed, and Gibson volunteered to do public-service announcements on the hazards of drinking and driving and to immediately enter rehabilitation. The judge ordered Gibson to attend Alcoholics Anonymous meetings five times a week for 4 1/2 months, three AA meetings per week for another 7 1/2 months, and enroll in an alcohol-abuse program for three months. He was fined $1,300 and had his license restricted for 90 days.

SUPERIOR COURT OF THE STATE OF CALIFORNIA
FOR THE COUNTY OF LOS ANGELES

THE PEOPLE OF THE STATE OF CALIFORNIA, Plaintiff, v. MEL C. GIBSON (01/03/1956), Defendant(s).	CASE NO. MAL 6MB01891 *MISDEMEANOR COMPLAINT*

The undersigned is informed and believes that:

COUNT 1

On or about July 28, 2006, in the County of Los Angeles, the crime of DRIVING UNDER THE INFLUENCE OF ALCOHOL OR DRUGS, in violation of VEHICLE CODE SECTION 23152(a), a Misdemeanor, was committed by MEL C. GIBSON, who did unlawfully, while under the influence of an alcoholic beverage, drive a vehicle.

COUNT 2

On or about July 28, 2006, in the County of Los Angeles, the crime of DRIVING WHILE HAVING A 0.08% OR HIGHER BLOOD ALCOHOL, in violation of VEHICLE CODE SECTION 23152(b), a Misdemeanor, was committed by MEL C. GIBSON, who did unlawfully, while having 0.08 percent and more, by weight, of alcohol in the blood, drive a vehicle.

COUNT 3

On or about July 28, 2006, in the County of Los Angeles, the crime of POSSESSION OF OPEN CONTAINER WHILE DRIVING, in violation of VEHICLE CODE SECTION 23223(a), an Infraction, was committed by MEL C. GIBSON, who did unlawfully have in his possession an open alcoholic beverage container while driving in a motor vehicle upon a highway.

* * * * *

I DECLARE UNDER PENALTY OF PERJURY THAT THE FOREGOING IS TRUE AND CORRECT AND THAT THIS COMPLAINT CONSISTS OF 3 COUNT(S).

Executed at MALIBU, County of Los Angeles, on August 2, 2006.

Det. PETE SANZONE
DECLARANT AND COMPLAINANT

DUI charges are generally accompanied by companion minor traffic infractions, such as improper lane usage or speeding. In addition, persons arrested on such charges usually face a **summary suspension** of their driver's license. A summary suspension is the automatic cessation of driving privileges of an individual who has a specified blood alcohol concentration (BAC) in his or her bloodstream as shown by a blood test or a breathalyzer. Summary suspensions come into play when a driver refuses to take the breathalyzer test or if the driver has a BAC over the legal limit.

3. REGULATION OF FIREARMS, DRUGS, AND ALCOHOL

Regulation of who can possess and use firearms is a very controversial issue of public policy in the United States and great variation exist among the states. Since the passage of the National Firearms Act in 1934,[44] the federal government has prohibited the possession and sale of certain types of firearms. In 1993, Congress amended the Gun Control Act of 1968[45] by enacting the Brady Handgun Violence Prevention Act.[46] These acts mandated the establishment of a national system for instant criminal background checks of proposed handgun transferees.

State laws typically regulate how firearms are to be transported, the circumstances under which they can be concealed, and where they can be discharged (e.g., not in urban areas, not within a set number of feet from a public road, etc.). Most states then make unlawful use or possession of weapons a crime, and the level of punishment is often increased when a firearm is used in connection with a crime like robbery or assault.

Some examples include:

720 ILCS 5/24-1.5 Reckless Discharge of a Firearm

(a) A person commits reckless discharge of a firearm by discharging a firearm in a reckless manner which endangers the bodily safety of an individual.

(b) If the conduct described in subsection (a) is committed by a passenger of a moving motor vehicle with the knowledge and consent of the driver of the motor vehicle the driver is accountable for such conduct.

Summary suspension
The automatic cessation of driving privileges of an individual who has a specified blood alcohol (BAC) percentage in his or her bloodstream as shown by a blood test or a breathalyzer. A driver may also have his or her license suspended by refusing to submit to the breathalyzer test.

---

[44] 26 U.S.C. § 1132c
[45] 18 U.S.C. § 921 *et seq.*
[46] 18 U.S.C. § 922.

720 ILCS 5/12-14 Aggravated Criminal Sexual Assault

The accused commits aggravated criminal sexual assault if he or she commits criminal sexual assault and any of the following aggravating circumstances existed during . . . the commission of the offense:

. . .

(8) the accused was armed with a firearm, or

. . .

720 ILCS 5/18-2 Armed Robbery

(a) A person commits armed robbery when he or she violates section 18-1 [Robbery] and

. . .

(1) he or she carries on or about his or her person or is otherwise armed with a firearm; or

(2) he or she, during the commission of the offense personally discharges a firearm; or

. . .

However, the constitutionality of many of these laws was brought into question in 2008 when the U.S. Supreme Court *in District of Columbia v. Heller* struck down two key provisions of a District of Columbia ban on handguns on the basis that they violated the Second Amendment right to bear arms.[47] While the *Heller* decision only applied to federal actions, the Supreme Court followed it up with a ruling in *McDonald v City of Chicago* that the right to bear arms was among those rights protected from state interference by the Fourteenth Amendment due process clause.[48]

It is important to note, however, that the *Heller* and *McDonald* decisions do not, necessarily, preclude all forms of government regulation. The opinion of the court in *Heller* clearly states that the right to bear arms is not unlimited and suggested that laws such as those prohibiting convicted felons and mentally ill persons from possessing firearms would be valid.

Some laws regarding drug and alcohol use can clearly be justified in terms of protecting the public at large, while others are designed more to protect individuals from themselves. Laws that prohibit driving under the influence of drugs or alcohol are a good example of the former, in that they are based on the fact that drug and alcohol use can negatively affect a person's ability to drive safely and that such drivers are a danger to everyone on the road. There are disputes over the methods used for establishing that someone was "under the influence," but there is general agreement that DUI laws are an appropriate exercise of governmental power.

Driving under the influence of drugs or alcohol is frequently treated as a traffic offense for which the penalty may include fines, mandatory substance abuse education or treatment, and suspension or revocation of one's driver's license. Being under the influence of drugs or alcohol can also be an element in other crimes. For example:

---

[47]554 U.S. 570,128 S. Ct. 2783, 171 L. Ed. 2d 637 (2008).
[48]130 S. Ct. 3020, 177 L. Ed. 2d 894 (2010).

720 ILCS 5/9-3 Involuntary Manslaughter and Reckless Homicide

. . .

(b) In cases involving reckless homicide, being under the influence of alcohol or any other drug or drugs at the time of the alleged violation shall be presumed to be evidence of a reckless act unless disproved by evidence to the contrary.

(c) for the purposes of this Section, a person shall be considered to be under the influence of alcohol or other drugs while:

1. The alcohol concentration in the person's blood or breath is 0.08 . . .

2. Under the influence of alcohol to a degree that renders the person incapable of safely driving a motor vehicle or operating a snowmobile, all-terrain vehicle, or watercraft;

3. Under the influence of any other drug or combination of drugs to a degree that renders the person incapable of safely driving a motor vehicle or operating a snowmobile, all-terrain vehicle, or watercraft;

4. Under the influence of alcohol and any other drug or drugs to a degree which renders the person incapable of safely driving a motor vehicle or operating a snowmobile, all-terrain vehicle, or watercraft;

On the other hand, laws prohibiting the use of "recreational drugs" are far more controversial because their focus is more on protecting the user from harming himself or herself than on protecting the public at large. Opponents of these laws cite the philosophical writings of John Stuart Mill and the nation's experience with Prohibition in their arguments against such laws. Mill rejected the concept of paternalism[49] and argued that the government should use the coercive power of the law only to prevent harm to others. He argued that individuals are in a better position to know what is best for them than is the government and that people can develop their intellect best when they learn from their own mistakes. Mill and his followers thus oppose laws designed to prevent people from gambling, smoking, taking drugs, using prostitutes, etc.

The Eighteenth Amendment, passed in 1919, prohibited the manufacture, sale, or transportation of intoxicating liquors within, the importation thereof into, or the exportation thereof from the United States. Its passage was a result of the activities of the Women's Christian Temperance Union and other well-intentioned groups that were motivated by a desire to eliminate the evil effects of drinking alcoholic beverages. However, things did not work out as the supporters had hoped because too many people turned to bootleggers and organized crime as an alternative source of alcoholic beverages. Although Prohibition didn't create organized crime, it did increase its size and scope. Overzealous police and federal agents often violated civil rights while searching for and destroying the paraphernalia of alcohol production.

These negative consequences eventually led to a second political movement to repeal Prohibition. The anti-Prohibition forces argued that it was an affront to personal liberty that had been pushed on the nation by religious moralists. They also argued that legalizing the sale of alcohol could provide a source of revenue for the local and national governments. On February 20, 1933, Congress passed the Twenty-first Amendment (which repealed the Eighteenth) and it was ratified by the states on December 5, 1933.

---

[49]Paternalism is defined as the practice of restricting an individual's liberty for his or her own good.

In recent years, a number of states have significantly loosened the scope of their antigambling laws, but most continue to maintain and enforce laws against recreational drug use. Here are some examples of typical state statutes:

720 ILCS 570/401.1 Controlled Substance Trafficking

(a) Except for purposes as authorized by this Act, any person who knowingly brings or causes to be brought into this State for the purpose of manufacture or delivery or with the intent to manufacture or deliver a controlled or counterfeit substance in this or any other state or country is guilty of controlled substance trafficking.

720 ILCS 570/402 Possession Unauthorized by This Act

Except as otherwise authorized by this Act, it is unlawful for any person knowingly to possess a controlled or counterfeit substance.

The severity of the sentence is usually related to the amount and type of substance involved.

For reasons listed in the following excerpt from the U.S. Code, the federal government has also chosen to criminalize the manufacture and possession of various types of drugs.

21 USCS § 242 Congressional Findings and Declarations: Controlled Substances

The Congress makes the following findings and declarations:

(1) Many of the drugs included within this title have a useful and legitimate medical purpose and are necessary to maintain the health and general welfare of the American people.

(2) The illegal importation, manufacture, distribution, and possession and improper use of controlled substances have a substantial and detrimental effect on the health and general welfare of the American people.

(3) A major portion of the traffic in controlled substances flows through interstate and foreign commerce. Incidents of the traffic which are not an integral part of the interstate or foreign flow, such as manufacture, local distribution, and possession, nonetheless have a substantial and direct effect upon interstate commerce because—

(A) after manufacture, many controlled substances are transported in interstate commerce,

(B) controlled substances distributed locally usually have been transported in interstate commerce immediately before their distribution, and

(C) controlled substances possessed commonly flow through interstate commerce immediately prior to such possession.

(4) Local distribution and possession of controlled substances contribute to swelling the interstate traffic in such substances.

(5) Controlled substances manufactured and distributed intrastate cannot be differentiated from controlled substances manufactured and distributed interstate. Thus, it is not feasible to distinguish, in terms of controls, between controlled substances manufactured and distributed interstate and controlled substances manufactured and distributed intrastate.

(6) Federal control of the intrastate incidents of the traffic in controlled substances is essential to the effective control of the interstate incidents of such traffic.

(7) The United States is a party to the Single Convention on Narcotic Drugs, 1961, and other international conventions designed to establish effective control over international and domestic traffic in controlled substances.

In *Gonzales v. Raich*[50] the Supreme Court held it was not a violation of the Commerce Clause for the federal government to regulate local growth and use of marijuana.

Of special interest is the controversy over the medical use of marijuana (also known as cannabis). Modern research suggests that it is a valuable aid in the treatment of a wide range of clinical applications, including pain relief, nausea, spasticity, glaucoma, and movement disorders. Marijuana is also a powerful appetite stimulant and emerging research suggests that marijuana's medicinal properties may protect the body against some types of malignant tumors and are neuroprotective.[51]

Since 1996, fifteen states and the District of Columbia have adopted legislation exempting patients who use marijuana under a physician's supervision from state criminal penalties.[52] These laws do not legalize marijuana or alter criminal penalties regarding recreational use. Rather, they provide a narrow exemption from state prosecution for defined patients who possess and use marijuana with their doctor's recommendation. However, in *United States v. Oakland Cannabis Buyers Cooperative*,[53] the U.S. Supreme Court rejected claims that the federal penalties for manufacturing and distributing marijuana did not apply to those incidences in which it was being used for medical purposes other than for government-approved research projects. So even though states might grant exemptions from their state laws, the federal regulations still restrict medical use.

It is not uncommon for firearms charges to accompany charges for illegal drug possession. Exhibit 3.7 shows a portion of the felony charges brought by New York prosecutors against singer/songwriter David Crosby. Note how the format of this charge differs from the previous examples from California, Virginia, and the United States. Also notice how this document closely tracks the New York assault charge depicted in Exhibit 3.2.

---

[50]545 U.S. 1, 125 S. Ct. 2195, 162 L. Ed. 2d 1 (2005).

[51]Several books explore this issue in further detail. These include: A. Mack & J. Joy, *Marijuana as Medicine: The Science Beyond the Controversy* (Washington, DC: National Academy Press, 2001); L. Iverson, *The Science of Marijuana* (New York: Oxford University Press, 2000); E. Rosenthal et al., *Marijuana Medical Handbook* (Oakland, CA: Quick American Archives, 1997); and R. Mechoulam. (ed.), *Cannabinoids as Therapeutic Agents* (Boca Raton, FL: CRC Press, 1986).

[52]The states sanctioning the use of marijuana for medical purposes are: Alaska, Arizona, California, Colorado, Hawaii, Maine, Michigan, Montana, Nevada, New Jersey, New Mexico, Oregon, Rhode Island, Vermont, and Washington. *See http://normal.org* for current listing.

[53]532 U.S. 483, 121 S. Ct. 1711, 149 L. Ed. 2d 722 (2001).

Exhibit 3.7: New York Criminal Complaint: Weapons and Drug Charges

David Crosby, from the rock group Crosby, Stills, and Nash, was charged with weapons and drug possession after a New York City hotel employee discovered a pistol, ammunition, a knife, and what appeared to be marijuana in one of the singer's bags. Crosby had encountered other drug and firearms charges in other jurisdictions. Although he was merely fined $5,000 in this case, on other occasions he was sentenced to and actually served penitentiary time. Below is an excerpt of the criminal charges brought against Crosby:

CRIMINAL COURT OF THE CITY OF NEW YORK
COUNTY OF NEW YORK

Page 1 of 2

THE PEOPLE OF THE STATE OF NEW YORK
-against-

1. David Crosby (M 62)

410369

FELONY
ADA MCCARTHY
212-335-3992

Defendant.

Police Officer George Goulart, shield 3522 of the 018 Precinct-Midtown North Precinct, states as follows:

On February 6, 2004, at about 01:00 hours inside of 1568 Broadway Suite 3808 in the County and State of New York, the Defendant committed the offenses of:

1. PL265.02(4)   Criminal Possession of a Weapon in the Third Degree
                     (1 count)
2. AC10.131(i)(3)   Unlawful Possession of Ammunition
                     (1 count)
3. PL221.05   Unlawful Possession of Marijuana
                     (1 count)
4. AC10.133(b)   Possession of Knives or Instruments
                     (1 count)

the defendant possessed a loaded firearm outside of his home and place of business; the defendant possessed pistol and revolver ammunition while not authorized to possess a pistol and revolver within the City of New York; the defendant knowingly and unlawfully possessed marijuana; and the defendant unlawfully possessed in a public place a knife with a blade length of four inches or more.

* * *

APPLICATION EXERCISES

After reviewing the facts of the Brandon Turner case (*see Introduction to Hypothetical Cases, p. xxxvii*), answer the following questions:

10. What additional information is needed to determine which federal and/or state drug statutes Brandon could be charged under. How do the penalties differ?

11. What additional information is needed to determine which federal and/or state firearms statutes Brandon could be charged under? How do the penalties differ?

4. GAMBLING, OBSCENITY, AND DEVIANT SEXUAL CONDUCT

Gambling traditionally has been regulated under state law. At the beginning of the twentieth century, all states outlawed gambling. In 1931, Nevada became the first state in modern times to legalize it. In 1978, New Jersey became the second state to permit casino gambling. Ten years later, the federal government adopted the Indian Gaming Regulatory Act (IGRA),[54] which provides the "statutory basis for the operation of gaming by Indian tribes as a means of promoting tribal economic development, self-sufficiency, and strong tribal governments."[55] A number of states have authorized riverboat casinos, and in the 1960s, New Hampshire and New York started lotteries.[56] Currently, forty-three states have a state-sponsored lottery, and nearly all states have state-sponsored gambling in some form, either casinos, pari-mutuel facilities, or lotteries. Given the popularity of legalized gambling, you might think that law enforcement would legislate against it. However, this has not been the case, although most state criminal codes prohibit some types of gambling and the federal authorities have targeted Internet gambling with several statutes, including RICO, the Wire Act,[57] and the Unlawful Internet Gambling Enforcement Act.[58]

Making offenses such as public indecency and solicitation of a child illegal is clearly designed to protect the public from being confronted by what most consider offensive behavior and to protect children. A few examples are:

720 ILCS 5/11-9 Public Indecency

(a) Any person of the age of 17 years and upwards who performs any of the following acts in a public place commits a public indecency:

(1) An act of sexual penetration or sexual conduct as defined in section 12-12 of this Code; or

---

[54] 25 U.S.C. § 2701 *et seq.*

[55] 25 U.S.C. § 2702.

[56] There is no lottery in the following states: Alabama, Alaska, Mississippi, Nevada, North Dakota, Oklahoma, and Wyoming.

[57] 18 U.S.C. § 1084.

[58] 31 U.S.C. § 5363.

(2) A lewd exposure of the body done with intent to arouse or to satisfy the sexual desire of the person.

Breast feeding of infants is not an act of public indecency.

(b) "Public place" for purposes of this Section means any place where the conduct may reasonably be expected to be viewed by others.

720 ILCS 5/11-21 Harmful Material

(a) *Elements of the Offense.* A person who, with knowledge that a person is a child, that is a person under 18 years of age, or who fails to exercise reasonable care in ascertaining the true age of a child, knowingly distributes to or sends or causes to be sent to, or exhibits to, or offers to distribute or exhibit any harmful material to a child, is guilty of a misdemeanor.

In addition to protecting children, restrictions on "adult-oriented entertainment" are designed to protect property values and community esthetics. While there is strong support for laws against public indecency and for those designed to protect children, laws against prostitution and consensual homosexual activities between adults are far more controversial because they are similar to laws against using alcohol or gambling. Although it may be argued that these crimes victimize people, the "victims" are consciously choosing to participate in these activities. The general trend has been toward loosening restrictions on gambling and liberalizing restrictions on consensual activities, but many statutes remain on the books and continue to be enforced.

Moreover, as society changes, what was once considered highly offensive may no longer even be considered criminal. For example, in 2003 New York Governor George Pataki pardoned comic Lenny Bruce posthumously for his 1960s conviction on the charge of Giving an Obscene Performance. Bruce used more than 100 "obscene" words during the performance. In 2010 Florida Governor Charlie Crist granted a petition to pardon the late Jim Morrison, the lead singer of The Doors, thirty-eight years after he was convicted of indecent exposure and using profanity during a Miami concert. Petitioners claim that under today's standards Morrison would not have been prosecuted.

DISCUSSION QUESTIONS

21. Disorderly conduct under the Model Penal Code makes it a crime for someone to make an "offensively coarse utterance, gesture or display, or [address] abusive language to any person present." Does this mean that swearing in public is a crime? Should it be?

22. In a case that got national news coverage, a carpenter in Oakland, California, was charged with indecent exposure after he was spotted building cabinets in the buff at a home where he had been hired to work. He told the judge that he liked to work in the nude because it was more comfortable and helped him keep his clothes clean. His attorney pointed out that he was not acting lewdly or seeking sexual gratification. How do you think the judge would rule and why?

23. In view of the fact that different people respond to alcohol in different ways, should a driver be conclusively presumed to be in violation of a DUI statute simply because she has a BAC of 0.08? Would a general prohibition of driving under the influence without a set BAC be more appropriate?

24. If paternalism is not good public policy, should recreational drugs be legal? If so, should marijuana be available in vending machines? Should a retailer be allowed to sell heroin through vending machines?

25. If paternalism is good public policy, should the government impose greater criminal sanctions and restrictions on the use of guns?

26. Will the United States ever win the "war on drugs"?

F. INTERPRETING CRIMINAL STATUTES

In Chapter 2 we noted that statutes and ordinances frequently contain ambiguous language that leads to disagreements over how they should be applied. This ambiguity increases the amount of discretion that law enforcement authorities have in choosing how to apply them in different situations. It also opens the door for defense attorneys to mount a judicial challenge to the prosecutor's interpretation of the statute and a possible appeal if the client is convicted. An example of an appeal over the statutory meaning of "use" can be found in the U.S. Supreme Court's opinion in *Smith v. United States*. Take a few minutes to read the Court's decision in the box that follows.

Smith v. United States
Supreme Court of the United States
508 U.S. 223 (1993)

JUSTICE O' CONNOR delivered the opinion of the Court in which REHNQUIST, C.J., and WHITE, BLACKMUN, KENNEDY, and THOMAS, J.J., joined.

We decide today whether the exchange of a gun for narcotics constitutes "use" of a firearm "during and in relation to . . . [a] drug trafficking crime" within the meaning of *18 U.S.C. § 924(c)(1)*. We hold that it does.

I

Petitioner John Angus Smith and his companion went from Tennessee to Florida to buy cocaine; they hoped to resell it at a profit. While in Florida, they met petitioner's acquaintance, Deborah Hoag. Hoag agreed to, and in fact did, purchase cocaine for petitioner. She then accompanied petitioner and his friend to her motel room, where they were joined by a drug dealer. While Hoag listened, petitioner and the dealer discussed petitioner's MAC-10 firearm, which had been modified to operate as an automatic. The MAC-10 apparently is a favorite among criminals. It is small and compact, lightweight, and can be equipped with a silencer. Most important of all, it can be devastating: A fully automatic MAC-10 can fire more than 1,000 rounds per minute. The dealer expressed his interest in becoming the owner of a MAC-10, and petitioner promised that he would discuss selling the gun if his arrangement with another potential buyer fell through.

Unfortunately for petitioner, Hoag had contacts not only with narcotics traffickers but also with law enforcement officials. In fact, she was a confidential informant. Consistent with her post, she informed the Broward County Sheriff's Office of petitioner's activities. The Sheriff's Office responded quickly, sending an undercover officer to Hoag's motel room. Several others were assigned to keep the motel under surveillance. Upon arriving at Hoag's motel room, the undercover officer presented himself to petitioner as a pawnshop dealer. Petitioner, in turn, presented the officer with a proposition: He had an automatic MAC-10 and silencer with which he might be willing to part. Petitioner then pulled the MAC-10 out of a black canvas bag and showed it to the officer. The officer examined the gun and asked petitioner what he wanted for it. Rather than asking for money, however, petitioner asked for drugs. He was willing to trade his MAC-10, he said, for two ounces of cocaine. The officer told petitioner that he was just a pawnshop dealer and did not distribute narcotics. Nonetheless, he indicated that he wanted the MAC-10 and would try to get the cocaine. The officer then left, promising to return within an hour.

Rather than seeking out cocaine as he had promised, the officer returned to the Sheriff's Office to arrange for petitioner's arrest. But petitioner was not content to wait. The officers who were conducting surveillance saw him leave the motel room carrying a gun bag; he then climbed into his van and drove away. The officers reported petitioner's departure and began following him. When law enforcement authorities tried to stop petitioner, he led them on a high-speed chase. Petitioner eventually was apprehended.

Petitioner, it turns out, was well armed. A search of his van revealed the MAC-10 weapon, a silencer, ammunition, and a "fast-feed" mechanism. In addition, the police found a MAC-11 machine gun, a loaded .45 caliber pistol, and a .22 caliber pistol with a scope and homemade silencer. Petitioner also had a loaded 9 millimeter handgun in his waistband.

A grand jury sitting in the District Court for the Southern District of Florida returned an indictment charging petitioner with, among other offenses, two drug trafficking crimes—conspiracy to possess cocaine with intent to distribute and attempt to possess cocaine with intent to distribute in violation of *21 U.S.C. §§ 841(a)(1), 846, and 18 U.S.C. § 2*. App. 3-9. Most important here, the indictment alleged that petitioner knowingly used the MAC-10 and its silencer during and in relation to a drug trafficking crime. *Id.,* at 4-5. Under *18 U.S.C. § 924(c)(1)*, a defendant who so uses a firearm must be sentenced to five years' incarceration. And where, as here, the firearm is a "machinegun" or is fitted with a silencer, the sentence is 30 years. See *§ 924(c)(1)* ("If the firearm is a machinegun, or is equipped with a firearm silencer," the sentence is "thirty years"); *§ 921(a)(23), 26 U.S.C. § 5845(b)* (term "machinegun" includes automatic weapons). The jury convicted petitioner on all counts.

On appeal, petitioner argued that *§ 924(c)(1)*'s penalty for using a firearm during and in relation to a drug trafficking offense covers only situations in which the firearm is used as a weapon. According to petitioner, the provision does not extend to defendants who use a firearm solely as a medium of exchange or for barter. The Court of Appeals for the Eleventh Circuit disagreed. *957 F.2d 835 (1992)*. The plain language of the statute, the court explained, imposes no requirement that the firearm be used as a weapon. Instead, any use of "the weapon to facilitate *in any manner* the commission of the offense" suffices. *Id., at 837* (internal quotation marks omitted).

Shortly before the Eleventh Circuit decided this case, the Court of Appeals for the District of Columbia Circuit arrived at the same conclusion. *United States v. Harris, 294 U.S. App. D.C. 300, 315-316, 959 F.2d 246, 261-262 (per curiam),* cert. denied, *506 U.S. 932 (1992)*. In *United States v. Phelps, 877 F.2d 28 (1989)*, however, the Court of Appeals for the Ninth Circuit held that trading a gun in a drug-related transaction could not constitute use of a firearm during and in relation to a drug trafficking offense within the meaning of *§ 924(c)(1)*. We granted certiorari to resolve the conflict among the Circuits. *506 U.S. 814 (1992)*. We now affirm.

II

Section 924(c)(1) requires the imposition of specified penalties if the defendant, "during and in relation to any crime of violence or drug trafficking crime[,] uses or carries a firearm." By its terms, the statute requires the prosecution to make two showings. First, the prosecution must demonstrate that the defendant "use[d] or carrie[d] a firearm." Second, it must prove that the use or carrying was "during and in relation to" a "crime of violence or drug trafficking crime."

Petitioner argues that exchanging a firearm for drugs does not constitute "use" of the firearm within the meaning of the statute. He points out that nothing in the record indicates that he fired the

MAC-10, threatened anyone with it, or employed it for self-protection. In essence, petitioner argues that he cannot be said to have "use[d]" a firearm unless he used it as a weapon, since that is how firearms most often are used. See *957 F.2d at 837* (firearm often facilitates drug offenses by protecting drugs or protecting or emboldening the defendant). Of course, [HN4] *§ 924(c)(1)* is not limited to those cases in which a gun is used; it applies with equal force whenever a gun is "carrie[d]." In this case, however, the indictment alleged only that petitioner "use[d]" the MAC-10. App. 4. Accordingly, we do not consider whether the evidence might support the conclusion that petitioner carried the MAC-10 within the meaning of *§ 924(c)(1)*. Instead we confine our discussion to what the parties view as the dispositive issue in this case: whether trading a firearm for drugs can constitute "use" of the firearm within the meaning of *§ 924(c)(1)*.

When a word is not defined by statute, we normally construe it in accord with its ordinary or natural meaning. See *Perrin v. United States, 444 U.S. 37, 42, 62 L. Ed. 2d 199, 100 S. Ct. 311 (1979)* (words not defined in statute should be given ordinary or common meaning). . . . ("In the search for statutory meaning, we give nontechnical words and phrases their ordinary meaning"). Surely petitioner's treatment of his MAC-10 can be described as "use" within the everyday meaning of that term. Petitioner "used" his MAC-10 in an attempt to obtain drugs by offering to trade it for cocaine. Webster's [*229] defines "to use" as "to convert to one's service" or "to employ." . . . Black's Law Dictionary contains a similar definition: "to make use of; to convert to one's service; to employ; to avail oneself of; to utilize; to carry out a purpose or action by means of." . . . Petitioner's handling of the MAC-10 in this case falls squarely within those definitions. By attempting to trade his MAC-10 for the drugs, he "used" or "employed" it as an item of barter to obtain cocaine; he "derived service" from it because it was going to bring him the very drugs he sought.

In petitioner's view, *§ 924(c)(1)* should require proof not only that the defendant used the firearm, but also that he used it *as a weapon*. But the words "as a weapon" appear nowhere in the statute. Rather, *§ 924(c)(1)*'s language sweeps broadly, punishing any "use" of a firearm, so long as the use is "during and in relation to" a drug

trafficking offense. See *United States v. Long, 284 U.S. App. D.C. 405, 409-410, 905 F.2d 1572, 1576-1577* (Thomas, J.) . . .

Language, of course, cannot be interpreted apart from context. The meaning of a word that appears ambiguous if viewed in isolation may become clear when the word is analyzed in light of the terms that surround it. Recognizing this, petitioner and the dissent argue that the word "uses" has a somewhat reduced scope in *§ 924(c)(1)* because it appears alongside the word "firearm." Specifically, they contend that the average person on the street would not think immediately of a guns-for-drugs trade as an example of "us[ing] a firearm." Rather, that phrase normally evokes an image of the most familiar use to which a firearm is put—use as a weapon. Petitioner and the dissent therefore argue that the statute excludes uses where the weapon is not fired or otherwise employed for its destructive capacity. . . . Indeed, relying on that argument—and without citation to authority—the dissent announces its own, restrictive definition of "use." "To use an instrumentality," the dissent argues, "ordinarily means to use it for its intended purpose." . . .

There is a significant flaw to this argument. It is one thing to say that the ordinary meaning of "uses a firearm" *includes* using a firearm as a weapon, since that is the intended purpose of a firearm and the example of "use" that most immediately comes to mind. But it is quite another to conclude that, as a result, the phrase also *excludes* any other use. Certainly that conclusion does not follow from the phrase "uses . . . a firearm" itself. As the dictionary definitions and experience make clear, one can use a firearm in a number of ways. That one example of "use" is the first to come to mind when the phrase "uses . . . a firearm" is uttered does not preclude us from recognizing that there are other "uses" that qualify as well. In this case, it is both reasonable and normal to say that petitioner "used" his MAC-10 in his drug trafficking offense by trading it for cocaine; the dissent does not contend otherwise.

The dissent's example of how one might "use" a cane, suffers from a similar flaw. To be sure, "use" as an adornment in a hallway is not the first "use" of a cane that comes to mind. But certainly it does not follow that the *only* "use" to which a cane might be put is assisting one's grandfather in walking. . . . In any event, the only question in this case is whether the phrase "uses . . . a firearm" in *§ 924(c)(1)* is most reasonably read as *excluding* the use of a firearm in a gun-for-drugs trade. The fact that the phrase clearly *includes* using a firearm to shoot someone, as the dissent contends, does not answer it.

* * *

In any event, the "intended purpose" of a firearm is not that it be used in any offensive manner whatever, but rather that it be used in a particular fashion—by firing it. The dissent's contention therefore cannot be that the defendant must use the firearm "as a weapon," but rather that he must fire it or threaten to fire it, "as a gun." Under the dissent's approach, then, even the criminal who pistol-whips his victim has not used a firearm within the meaning of *§ 924(c)(1)*, for firearms are intended to be fired or brandished, not used as bludgeons. It appears that the dissent similarly would limit the scope of the "other use[s]" covered by *USSG § 2B3.1(b) (2)(B)*. The universal view of the courts of appeals, however, is directly to the contrary. . . .

To the extent there is uncertainty about the scope of the phrase "uses . . . a firearm" in *§ 924(c)(1)*, we believe the remainder of *§ 924* appropriately sets it to rest. Just as a single word cannot be read in isolation, nor can a single provision of a statute. . . . Here, Congress employed the words "use" and "firearm" together not only in *§ 924(c) (1)*, but also in *§ 924(d)(1)*, which deals with forfeiture of firearms. . . . Under *§ 924(d)(1)*, any "firearm or ammunition intended to be used" in the various offenses listed in *§ 924(d)(3)* is subject to seizure and forfeiture. Consistent with petitioner's interpretation, *§ 924(d)(3)* lists offenses in which guns might be used as offensive weapons. See *§ § 924(d)(3)(A), (B)* (weapons used in a crime of violence or drug trafficking offense). But it also lists offenses in which the firearm is *not* used as a weapon but instead as an item of barter or commerce. For example, any gun intended to be "used" in an interstate "transfer, sale, trade, gift, transport, or delivery" of a firearm prohibited under *§ 922(a)(5)* where there is a pattern of such activity, see *§ 924(d)(3)(C)*, or in a federal offense involving "the exportation of firearms," *§ 924(d)(3)(F)*, is subject to forfeiture. In fact, none of the offenses listed in four of the six subsections of

§ 924(d)(3) involves the bellicose use of a firearm; each offense involves use as an item in commerce. Thus, it is clear from *§ 924(d)(3)* that one who transports, exports, sells, or trades a firearm "uses" it within the meaning of *§ 924(d)(1)*—even though those actions do not involve using the firearm as a weapon. Unless we are to hold that using a firearm has a different meaning in *§ 924(c)(1)* than it does in *§ 924(d)*—and clearly we should not, . . .—we must reject petitioner's narrow interpretation.

* * *

The dissent suggests that our interpretation produces a "strange dichotomy" between [**2058] "using" a firearm and "carrying" one. *Post*, at 246. We do not see why that is so. Just as a defendant may "use" a firearm within the meaning of *§ 924(c)(1)* by trading it for drugs *or* using it to shoot someone, so too would a defendant "carry" the firearm by keeping it on his person whether he intends to exchange it for cocaine or fire it in self-defense. The dichotomy arises, if at all, only when one tries to extend the phrase "'uses . . . a firearm'" to any use "'for any purpose whatever.'" *Ibid.* For our purposes, it is sufficient to recognize that, because *§ 924(d)(1)* includes both using a firearm for *trade* and using a firearm as a *weapon* as "us[ing]" a firearm," it is most reasonable to construe *§ 924(c)(1)* as encompassing both of those "uses" as well.

* * *

Both a firearm's use as a weapon and its use as an item of barter fall within the plain language of *§ 924(c)(1)*, so long as the use occurs during and in relation to a drug trafficking offense; both must constitute "uses" of a firearm for *§ 924(d)(1)* to make any sense at all; and both create the very dangers and risks that Congress meant *§ 924(c)(1)* to address. We therefore hold that a criminal who trades his firearm for drugs "uses" it during and in relation to a drug trafficking offense within the meaning of *§ 924(c)(1)*. Because the evidence in this case showed that petitioner "used" his MAC-10 machine gun and silencer in precisely such a manner, proposing to trade them for cocaine, petitioner properly was subjected to *§ 924(c)(1)*'s 30-year mandatory minimum sentence. The judgment of the Court of Appeals, accordingly, is affirmed.

CASE DISCUSSION QUESTIONS

1. What did John Smith do that got him arrested?
2. With what crime was he charged? Was it a federal or a state crime?
3. What was the outcome of his trial?
4. What is the basis for Smith's appeal?
5. What, if any, issues of state statutory law were decided in this opinion?
6. What, if any, issues of federal statutory law were decided in this opinion?
7. What, if any, issues of state constitutional law were decided in this opinion?
8. What, if any, issues of federal constitutional law were decided in this opinion?
9. Which side won in the U.S. Supreme Court?
10. What principle of "statutory construction" was utilized in this case?
11. Briefly summarize how this principle was applied in this case.

Now go back and review the Illinois statutes on Public Indecency and Harmful Materials that were reproduced in the preceding section. When does exposure become "lewd," and what constitutes "harmful" materials? Although the indecency statute explicitly exempts breast feeding of infants, questions can be raised as to how long a child is considered an infant. It defines "public place" as "any place where the conduct may reasonably be expected to be viewed by others," but how clear is this definition? Does it apply if the conduct takes place in your backyard at night? What if the backyard is fenced in such a way that something going on there could only be viewed by a neighbor looking out of a second-story window?

To seek answers to these types of questions, an attorney will first look to see if the legislature provided definitions for some of these terms in the statute. (Note that these definitions may be found in a different part of the statute.) The Illinois legislature defined harmful materials as follows:

720 ILCS 5/11-21 Harmful Material

(b)(1) Material is harmful if, to the average person, applying contemporary standards, its predominant appeal, taken as a whole, is to prurient interest, that is a shameful or morbid interest in nudity, sex, or excretion, which goes substantially beyond customary limits of candor in description or representation of such matters, and is material the redeeming social importance of which is substantially less than its prurient appeal.

Do you think they did a good job? Does this section provide reasonable guidelines for determining what is or is not harmful material? It refers to the outlook of the average person, but how do you know what that is? How do you determine what the contemporary standards are? What is a prurient interest? When does an interest in nudity, sex, or excretion become shameful or morbid? How do you identify customary limits of candor or determine if the material has redeeming social importance?

When faced with these kinds of somewhat vague and ambiguous statutory definitions, attorneys will usually look for court cases that have applied the statute to similar types of circumstances. This can be very useful if you find cases that cover identical materials in the same setting, but many times no such cases can be found. When these types of judgments are left to a jury to decide, the outcome may depend on the luck of the draw as to the makeup of the jury in that particular case.

Constitutional challenges can be mounted when criminal statutes are deemed to be either too vague or too broad or when they place unconstitutional restraints on freedom of expression. The **void for vagueness doctrine** is a fundamental part of the Due Process Clause of the U.S. Constitution. It requires that penal statutes fairly inform ordinary people as to what is commanded or prohibited. If a statute is vague, it might also be challenged on the basis of the **chilling effect doctrine** in First Amendment jurisprudence. Under this doctrine, a statute violates rights of free expression if it makes people fearful of engaging in legitimate, constitutionally protected activities.

Another fundamental principle of constitutional law is reflected in the **overbreadth doctrine.** Based on the First Amendment, any regulation of expression must be narrowly tailored to meet the government's legitimate objectives. A law can be struck down as overbroad if it restricts constitutionally protected free expression.

Statutes might also be challenged on the basis that they violate the Equal Protection Clause by discriminating on the basis of race, sex, religion, sexual orientation, etc. A law affecting freedom of expression can be struck down if it discriminates on the basis of viewpoint (e.g., applies to speech activities supporting a war but not those criticizing it).

Void for vagueness doctrine
A principle of constitutional law that requires penal statutes be written so they fairly inform ordinary people as to what is commanded or prohibited.

Chilling effect doctrine
A principle of constitutional law that invalidates statutes that are worded in such a way as to makes people fearful of engaging in legitimate, constitutionally protected First Amendment activities.

Overbreadth doctrine
A principle of constitutional law that any regulation of expression must be narrowly tailored to meet the government's legitimate object.

APPLICATION EXERCISES

12. After reviewing the facts of Bill Edward's case (*see hypothetical case on p. xxxviii*), read Sections 1341 and 1346 of Title 18 of the U.S. Code.
   a. How does the act define "scheme or artifice to defraud"?
   b. What are "honest services"?
   c. Do you think Edwards violated this act? Why or why not?

13. Now read *Skilling v. United States,* 130 S. Ct. 2896 (2010).
   a. What is the relationship of the *Skilling* case and the statute referred to in the previous exercise?
   b. Based on the *Skilling* case, did Edwards violate Section 1341 of Article 18 of the U.S. Code?

SUMMARY

This chapter presented an overview of the scope of criminal law at both the state and federal levels. Most criminal codes are organized into sections that cover topics such as offenses involving danger to people, offenses involving harm to property, offenses against the family, offenses against the government, and offenses against public order and decency.

Since it is not possible to cover every crime and since there are many variations among the states, our goal here was limited to providing a sampling of some of the most common offenses included in most criminal codes. Therefore, we focused on providing a basic understanding of the nature of homicide, assault and battery, intimidation and stalking, kidnapping and false imprisonment, sexual assault, violations of civil rights, arson, trespass, burglary and robbery, fraud, treason, perjury, obstruction of justice, disorderly conduct, drug and alcohol offenses, and gambling and sexual conduct offenses. However, the details of all of these offenses will vary from one state to another, so you will always need to check your own state's statutes to see how they define these same types of crimes and what additional offenses they may include.

Statutes often contain terms that are not part of your everyday language or are open to a wide variety of meanings. When this occurs, you should first check for a listing of definitions that may be included in another section of the code. You also need to research court cases that have applied the statute in similar situations. If the statute is too vague, interferes with First Amendment rights, or discriminates against some classes of people, it might be open to a constitutional challenge.

INTERNET RESOURCES

General Search Engines for Statutes, Cases, and Regulations

- http://lawcrawler.findlaw.com/
- http://www.findlaw.com

Statistical Information on Crimes

- Bureau of Justice Statistics: **http://bjs.ojp.usdoj.gov/**
- Federal Bureau of Investigation (FBI): Uniform Crime Reports: **http://www.fbi.gov/ucr/ucr.htm**

Most state and many local governments have a link to crime statistics for their area posted on their websites.

REVIEW QUESTIONS

1. How does the Model Penal Code define homicide?
2. What jobs or official duties permit individuals to cause the death of another human being without being guilty of homicide?
3. What are the three typical categories of homicide recognized in most criminal codes? How do these categories differ from one another?
4. Define *malice aforethought*.
5. List and define the two different types of manslaughter recognized under federal law.
6. Felony murder is a form of transferred intent. What is felony murder? Can arson be the basis for a felony murder charge? If it can form such a basis, how does it do so?
7. How do criminal assault and criminal battery differ from one another?
8. The offenses of stalking, assault, and terroristic threats are encompassed in a general category of crime. State the name and explain this category of crime.

9. Distinguish common law rape from statutory rape.
10. What are "hate crimes"?
11. For what felony is trespass a lesser included offense? Why is this?
12. How does larceny differ from robbery?
13. What is domestic violence and how does it differ from battery?
14. What classification of crime includes bribery, concealing or aiding a fugitive, obstruction of justice, official misconduct, perjury, tax evasion, treason, espionage, and terrorism?
15. DUI and BAC are abbreviations for what words?
16. What is the concept of paternalism and why did philosopher John Stuart Mill reject it?
17. Is the overbreadth doctrine more like the doctrine of void for vagueness or the chilling effect doctrine? Explain your answer.

PART  2

Criminal Procedure: From Commission of the Offense to Plea Bargaining and Diversion

Chapter 4

Investigation of Criminal Behavior

In the first section of this book we discussed the purpose, the organization, and the major concepts of our criminal law. These topics are typically referred to as "substantive criminal law." In Parts II and III of the text we cover the procedural side of criminal law. Here the focus is on the various stages involved in criminal prosecutions and the roles played by various participants in the criminal justice system.

Back in Chapter 1, we presented a flowchart of the multiple stages of criminal procedure. Take a few minutes to review Figure 1.3 to get the "big picture" view of the all the stages that can be involved in criminal prosecution. Keep in mind, however, that the details of criminal procedure vary greatly among jurisdictions. For example, only about half the states have a grand jury system. Also you should be aware that the stages may be accelerated or even combined in certain types of cases, especially misdemeanors. Also bear in mind the fact that there are many shortcuts and diversions built into the criminal justice system. Charges can be dropped at any time along the way. Many defendants accept plea bargains that move them directly to the corrections stages of the process.

In this chapter we will focus on the role played by police and other law enforcement personnel in identifying the people who commit crimes and in gathering enough evidence to justify their arrest. The other chapters in this section will focus on the roles played by prosecution and defense attorneys in preparing their cases for trial.

A. CONSTITUTIONAL PRINCIPLES RELATED TO PROCEDURAL DUE PROCESS

Before we start our discussion of the investigatory role of law enforcement officers, we need to review or introduce a few key concepts of constitutional law. We begin with due process of law.

1. FIFTH AND FOURTEENTH AMENDMENTS: DUE PROCESS OF LAW

The Fifth Amendment to the U.S. Constitution states: "No person shall . . . be deprived of life, liberty, or property, without due process of law"; and the Fourteenth Amendment states: " . . . nor shall any State deprive any person of life, liberty, or property, without due process of law. . . . " However, since the Constitution does not define what "due process" means, it, like many other terms in the document, is left up to the justices of the U.S. Supreme Court to clarify its meaning.

Because it is beyond the scope of this text to cover the details of the Supreme Court's development of the law on due process, we will instead present a quick "executive summary" of the "bottom line."

Procedural due process
The series of procedures that federal and state government are constitutionally required to follow before they can deny anyone life, liberty, or property.

Substantive due process
The constitutional limitation placed on the federal and state governments barring the deprivation of anyone's life, liberty, or property by means of a law found to be arbitrary and/or unreasonable.

- "Due process" usually refers to the series of procedures that governments have to follow before they can deny anyone life, liberty, or property. (This is called **procedural due process**.)
- However this concept has an *alternative meaning* in which due process refers to the requirement that government cannot deprive anyone of life, liberty, or property where the law being violated is found to be arbitrary and/or unreasonable. (This is called **substantive due process**.)
- Through a process that constitutional scholars call "selective incorporation," the Supreme Court has ruled that most, though not all, provisions of the Bill of Rights are applicable in state criminal prosecutions.[1] They include protections against unreasonable search and seizure, rights against double jeopardy, rights against self-incrimination, rights to a speedy public trial, rights to jury trials, the right to confront accusers, the compulsory process for obtaining witnesses, and assistance of counsel.

---

[1]Throughout the years, various justices have used a variety of different standards for determining whether a particular practice was, or was not, required by the Fourteenth Amendment. The most famous and widely used standard was announced in 1937 in *Palko v. Connecticut,* 302 U.S. 319, 58 S. Ct. 149, 82 L. Ed. 288 (1937), where Justice Benjamin Cardozo announced that the standard for what does or does not violate the Due Process Clause of the Fourteenth Amendment is whether the challenged practice violates "fundamental principles of liberty and justice which lie at the base of all our civil and political institutions." Other tests used by various judges have included "case by case fairness," whether the right was "fundamental to ordered liberty," and whether it reflected the "fundamental principles of liberty and justice which lie at the base of all our civil and political institutions."

2. FOURTH AMENDMENT: NO "UNREASONABLE" SEARCHES AND SEIZURES

The Fourth Amendment to the U.S. Constitution states:

> The right of the people to be secure in their persons, houses, papers, and effects, against unreasonable searches and seizures, shall not be violated, and no Warrants shall issue, but upon probable cause, supported by Oath or affirmation, and particularly describing the place to be searched, and the persons or things to be seized.

As you can see, the entire Amendment consists of only one sentence. The first clause explains that the prohibition against unreasonable searches and seizures is designed to protect a right of the people to be "secure" in their "persons, houses, papers, and effects." The second part limits the circumstances under which warrants can be issued and describes what must be contained in the way they are worded. Warrants can only be issued "upon probable cause" and where they are "supported by oath or affirmation." The content must "particularly describe" the place to be searched and the "persons or things" to be seized.

Although the Amendment doesn't specifically define "unreasonable," the context of its use certainly implies that a search would not be unreasonable if it were based on a warrant that had been issued upon probable cause, where it had been supported by oath or affirmation, and where it particularly described the place to be searched, and/or the persons or things to be seized. Note, however, that this doesn't mean that other types of searches without a warrant are necessarily prohibited by the Fourth Amendment. Indeed, the courts have approved warrantless searches and seizures in a wide variety of situations, including consent searches, searches incident to arrest, inventory searches, searches in "exigent circumstances," and "plain view" seizures. The most fundamental principles of Fourth Amendment jurisprudence are that the search must either be consensual or be based on probable cause to believe that it will lead to the discovery of contraband materials or the collection of evidence that a crime was committed.

Note also that the Amendment doesn't specify the source of the searches or what the penalty for violating this right would be. Based on historical and contextual factors, the courts have ruled that it is a limitation on the actions of governmental agents, not actions of private citizens. The means for enforcing this and other provisions of the Bill of Rights are discussed in Chapter 8.[2]

3. FIFTH AMENDMENT: RIGHT TO GRAND JURY INDICTMENT, NO SELF-INCRIMINATION, AND NO DOUBLE JEOPARDY

The Fifth Amendment to the U.S. Constitution states:

> No person shall be held to answer for a capital, or otherwise infamous crime, unless on a presentment or indictment of a Grand Jury, except in cases arising in the land or naval forces, or in the Militia, when in actual service in time of War or public

---

[2]See discussion of the exclusionary rule on pages 278-281.

danger; nor shall any person be subject for the same offence to be twice put in jeopardy of life or limb, nor shall be compelled in any criminal case to be a witness against himself, nor be deprived of life, liberty, or property, without due process of law; nor shall private property be taken for public use without just compensation.

We have already discussed the meaning of the "due process of law" language in this Amendment. It also contains clauses covering grand juries, double jeopardy, self-incrimination, and just compensation.[3] We will discuss self-incrimination and grand juries later in this chapter. Double jeopardy will be covered in Chapter 8 on legal defenses.[4]

4. SIXTH AMENDMENT: SPEEDY TRIAL, IMPARTIAL JURY, INFORMED OF CHARGES, CONFRONTATION OF WITNESSES, COMPULSORY PROCESS, AND RIGHT TO COUNSEL

The Sixth Amendment to the U.S. Constitution states:

In all criminal prosecutions, the accused shall enjoy the right to a speedy and public trial, by an impartial jury of the State and district wherein the crime shall have been committed, which district shall have been previously ascertained by law, and to be informed of the nature and cause of the accusation; to be confronted with the witnesses against him; to have compulsory process for obtaining witnesses in his favor, and to have the assistance of counsel for his defence.[5]

The provisions in this amendment relate to procedural safeguards available to defendants before and during their trials. We will discuss the right to counsel in Chapter 6. The right to a speedy trial. Impartial juries and compulsory process, as well as the right to confront and cross examine witnesses, will be discussed in Chapter 10.

5. EIGHTH AMENDMENT: RIGHT TO BAIL: NO CRUEL AND UNUSUAL PUNISHMENT

The Eighth Amendment to the U.S. Constitution states: "Excessive bail shall not be required, nor excessive fines imposed, nor cruel and unusual punishments inflicted." While the intent is clear, the clause clearly leaves it up to the courts to determine when the amount of bail or a fine is "excessive" and what constitutes "cruel and unusual" punishment. The issue of bail will be covered in Chapter 5; fines and cruel and unusual punishment will be dealt with in Chapter 13.

---

[3]The "Just Compensation" Clause (or "Takings" Clause) is not relevant to this book because it relates to civil cases rather than to criminal law. It limits the government's power of eminent domain by requiring that "just compensation" be paid if private property is taken for public use.

[4]See discussion of double jeopardy on page 282.

[5]The drafters of the Constitution used the British spelling for defense.

DISCUSSION QUESTION

1. Note the frequent use of inherently ambiguous terms such as *liberty*, *due process*, *unreasonable*, *speedy*, and *cruel and unusual* in the above-mentioned amendments to the Constitution.

  a. Why do you think the drafters used such vague language? Why weren't they more specific?

  b. How should a judge go about determining if a specific search is, or is not, "reasonable"?

  c. How should a judge go about determining if a specific penalty is, or is not, "cruel" or "unusual"?

B. DISCOVERY OF THE CRIME

The criminal process begins when government authorities learn that a crime has been committed. This usually occurs when a law enforcement officer (such as a police officer, a deputy sheriff, an FBI agent, or a state trooper) personally observes a crime being committed. An example would be a situation in which a police officer notices an automobile being driven in a dangerous and erratic manner, pulls the car over, and observes that the driver appears to be drunk. Exhibit 4.1 on page 98 shows a police report of a situation in which the officer discovered evidence of a crime while responding to a motor vehicle accident. One of the drivers involved in the accident, Gary Rossington, turned out not only to be an original member of the southern rock band Lynyrd Skynyrd, but also appeared to be intoxicated. After admitting he was drunk, Rossington was charged with DUI and taken into custody. Alternatively, the victim of a crime, or someone who witnessed the crime, can report it to the police. An example would be where someone calls the police after returning home to find that someone had broken into their house and stolen their new wide-screen television set and the family jewels.

C. QUESTIONING VICTIMS, WITNESSES, AND SUSPECTS

The first stage of a criminal investigation typically involves interviewing victims, witnesses, and suspects to learn more about what happened and who was involved. However, it is not always easy to identify and locate these people. Sometimes potential witnesses turn out to be suspects, and other times the apparent victim may have been involved in criminal activity. Even if the victims, witnesses, and suspects can be identified, they may not be able or willing to cooperate with law enforcement authorities. The victim might be dead or in a coma. Or, the victim or a witness may refuse to cooperate for fear of retribution or of incriminating themselves.

1. THE POWER TO STOP AND QUESTION PEOPLE

Although the police can approach any potential witnesses or suspects to inquire about what they might know about a crime, in most situations, the Fifth Amendment's protection against self-incrimination gives people the right to refuse to answer those questions. Indeed, except for the very limited privilege to briefly detain people and require them to identify themselves, police cannot even

Exhibit 4.1: Report of Incident in Connection with Motor Vehicle Accident

MILTON DEPARTMENT OF PUBLIC SAFETY
GA
MILTON, GA 30004

Printed Date 10/23/2008
Printed Time 9 00 AM
Page 2 of 3

Incident Report

	Incident No
	08-01627

Seq No	Name (Last First Middle)			
	Rossington Gary Robert			

Address		
		MILTON , GA 30004

Race		Age	
WHITE		58	

Height	Weight	Hair	Eyes				Arrest Date
5'08"	185	BLACK	BLUE	☐ Suspect ☐ Warrant	☑ Arrest ☐ Juv. Arrest		09/09/2008

Arrest Charges	Counts	Code
FAILURE TO MAINTAIN LANE	1	40-6-48

Arrest Charges	Counts	Code
DRIVING UNDER THE INFLUENCE-LESS SAFE-ALCOHOL(1ST OFFENSE)	1	40-6-391(A)(1) 1S

Arrest Charges	Counts	Code
DRIVING UNDER THE INFLUENCE .08 GMS. OR MORE(1ST OFFENSE)	1	40-6-391(A)(5) 1S

Vehicle

Year	Make	Model	Vehicle ID No	Color	Type
2005	CADILLAC	CTS	1G6DP567250177755	GOLD	PASSENGER CAR

Insured By	Insurance Policy No	Value	Body Style	Wheels	Axles	Eng
		$0.00				

Cyl	Fuel	Trans	Mileage	Tag No	Tag Yr	State	
				AKG4711	2008	GA	☐ Victim's ☐ Suspect's ☐ Stolen ☐ Recovered ☐ Impounded ☐ Towed

Other Officers

Badge	Name
162	PO BRIAN C KIEL

Comments

GCIC Entry ☐ Requested ☐ Warrant ☐ Missing Person ☐ Vehicle ☐ Article ☐ Boat ☐ Gun ☐ Securities
Additional ☑ A & B ☐ Supplemental ☐ Citation ☐ Accident ☐ Victim Bill of Rights ☐ Vehicle Impound ☐ Inv. Rpt ☐ Evidence Form
Clearance Arrest   Clearance Date: 09/09/2008

Narrative

On 09-09-08, I was on duty and assigned to morning watch. I was dispatched to Birmingham Road at Hopewell Road on an traffic accident. I arrived and and found two vehicles involved. While obtaining licence's and insurance I noticed a odor of an alcoholic beverage coming from the driver that caused the accident. The driver was identified as Gary Rossington. Mr. Rossington was very unsteady on his feet and almost fell over multiple times. Mr. Rossington face was flushed. He also had bloodshot and watery eyes. Mr. Rossington's speech was slurred, thick and slow. I had Mr. Rossington sit in his vehicle so he would not fall. A bystander told me she had to help Mr. Rossington get his licence and insurance. I had Officer Kiel respond to administer field evaluations.

Officer Kiel and myself helped Mr. Rossington to the road way. Officer Kiel asked Mr. Rossington if he would perform the state field evaluations. Mr. Rossington stated "I know I am drunk, I do not want take the evaluations". I placed Mr. Rossington in custody. The handcuffs were checked for fit and double locked. I walked Mr. Rossington to the front of my patrol car. I read Mr. Rossington the Georgia Implies consent notice for suspect age 21 and over and asked for a breath sample. Mr. Rossington stated he would give the breath sample.

I transported Mr. Rossington to the Alpharetta Jail. I performed the intox test. My permit number is 36150. The test was performed on the Georgia Intoxiliyzer 5000 (serial number-68-013385). Mr. Rossington gave two good breath samples. The samples showed .097 and .095. Mr. Rossington was turned over to on duty jail staff and issued citations for DUI Per Sa, DUI Less Safe, and Failure to maintain lane.

make someone stop and listen to their questions. This is because the term *seizure*, as it is used in the Fourth Amendment, has been interpreted as applying to seizing a person as well as a physical object. Therefore, government agents cannot detain people beyond the time it takes to have them identify themselves without having probable cause to believe they were involved in a crime.

Two key U.S. Supreme Court cases have defined what police can and cannot do in these types of situations. In *Terry v. Ohio*,[6] the Justices ruled that police are entitled to stop (detain) an individual for a brief period of time, to ask a few questions where they have a **reasonable suspicion** that the person being stopped has committed, is in the process of committing, or is about to commit a crime. This short detention is referred to as a "*Terry* **stop**." According to *Terry*, that reasonable suspicion must be based on "specific and articulable facts which, taken together with rational inferences from those facts, reasonably warrant that intrusion."[7] In this case, the police officer thought that a group of individuals was hanging around a street corner to plan a "stick-up." He asked the men to identify themselves. (The *Terry* case also involved a "pat-down search," which we will discuss in Section E.)

But what if those individuals do not wish to identify themselves? That question was answered by the Supreme Court in *Hiibel v. Nevada*,[8] where a Nevada police officer was investigating a possible assault. When he asked a man he suspected of having assaulted a woman to identify himself, the rancher refused; and when he refused, the officer arrested him. Based on the fact that the police officer was responding to a call reporting that a man had assaulted a woman, that the officer found the man standing outside a parked truck that matched the description the police had been given, and that a woman was inside the truck, the Court concluded that the officer had reasonable suspicion to stop the defendant and to ask him to identify himself. When the defendant refused to identify himself, the police officer was justified in arresting him. In ruling this way, the Court found that it was not a violation of one's Fifth Amendment rights against self-incrimination to be required to identify oneself to police.[9]

Reasonable suspicion
A reasonable belief in the context of the specific facts of the situation. This standard is greater than a mere hunch but less than a probable cause.

Terry **stop**
A law enforcement officer's stop of a person for a brief period of time to ask a few questions when the officer has "reasonable suspicion" that the person has committed, is in the process of committing, or is about to commit a crime.

2. IDENTIFICATION OF SUSPECTS

One of the most valuable pieces of information a victim or witness can provide is the identification of the person who committed the crime. In cases where they know or recognize someone involved in the crime, they can provide a name, an address, or other information that will help law enforcement officials find the alleged perpetrator.

In situations in which victims and witnesses don't remember having seen the suspect before, they may be asked to look through "mug books" (collections of photos of people who have been arrested in connection with other crimes) or to participate in a police "lineup."[10] (Examples of mug shots of well-known serial killers are displayed in Exhibit 4.2.)

---

[6]392 U.S. 1, 88 S. Ct. 1868, 20 L. Ed. 2d 889 (1968).

[7]392 U.S. at 21.

[8]542 U.S. 177, 124 S. Ct. 2451, 159 L. Ed. 2d 292 (2004).

[9]In many states it is considered obstruction of justice to give police a false identity.

[10]When police place a suspect in a formal lineup they are required to make sure there are other participants of a similar age, race, hair style, etc. as the suspect and to provide an opportunity for the suspect's attorney to be present.

Exhibit 4.2: Mug Shots

These are mug shots of six infamous serial killers. [Clockwise from top left corner: Ted Kaczynski (the "Unabomber"), Jeffrey Dahmer, David Berkowitz (the "Son of Sam"), Charles Manson, John Wayne Gacy, and Richard Speck.]

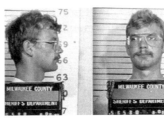
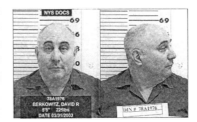

3. INTERROGATING SUSPECTS

a. *Miranda v. Arizona*

Miranda v. Arizona[11] is one of the most frequently referenced decisions in the history of the U.S. Supreme Court. Not only have most people in the United States heard of it, many have seen enough TV cop shows to be able to recite the *Miranda* warnings from memory. The picture on your left is an official "booking photo" of a young man who was actually wearing a T-shirt emblazoned with the *Miranda* warnings when he was arrested. But, in case you need a quick refresher, the essence of *Miranda* warnings are:

■ You have the right to remain silent;

---

[11]384 U.S. 436, 86 S. Ct. 1602, 16 L. Ed. 2d 694 (1966).

- Anything you say can be used against you in a court of law;
- You have the right to have an attorney present during questioning; and
- If you cannot afford an attorney, one will be appointed for you.

After notifying a suspect of these rights, law enforcement personnel are not supposed to question him or her until the suspect waives these rights. In many jurisdictions, the suspect must sign and initial the *Miranda* waiver form before any interrogation begins.

As you read over the following excerpts from the Opinion of the Court in the *Miranda* case, focus on the justifications given for requiring these warnings.

Miranda v. Arizona
Supreme Court of the United States
384 U.S. 436 (1966)

MR. CHIEF JUSTICE WARREN delivered the opinion of the Court.

The cases before us raise questions which go to the roots of our concepts of American criminal jurisprudence: the restraints society must observe consistent with the Federal Constitution in prosecuting individuals for crime. More specifically, we deal with the admissibility of statements obtained from an individual who is subjected to custodial police interrogation and the necessity for procedures which assure that the individual is accorded his privilege under the Fifth Amendment to the Constitution not to be compelled to incriminate himself.

We dealt with certain phases of this problem recently in *Escobedo v. Illinois*, 378 U.S. 478 (1964). There, as in the four cases before us, law enforcement officials took the defendant into custody and interrogated him in a police station for the purpose of obtaining a confession. The police did not effectively advise him of his right to remain silent or of his right to consult with his attorney. Rather, they confronted him with an alleged accomplice who accused him of having perpetrated a murder. When the defendant denied the accusation and said "I didn't shoot Manuel, you did it," they handcuffed him and took him to an interrogation room. There, while handcuffed and standing, he was questioned for four hours until he confessed. During this in-

terrogation, the police denied his request to speak to his attorney, and they prevented his retained attorney, who had come to the police station, from consulting with him. At his trial, the State, over his objection, introduced the confession against him. We held that the statements thus made were constitutionally inadmissible.

* * *

We start here, as we did in *Escobedo*, with the premise that our holding is not an innovation in our jurisprudence, but is an application of principles long recognized and applied in other settings. We have undertaken a thorough reexamination of the *Escobedo* decision and the principles it announced, and we reaffirm it. That case was but an explication of basic rights that are enshrined in our Constitution—that "No person . . . shall be compelled in any criminal case to be a witness against himself," and that "the accused shall . . . have the Assistance of Counsel" — rights which were put in jeopardy in that case through official overbearing. These precious rights were fixed in our Constitution only after centuries of persecution and struggle. . . .

* * *

This was the spirit in which we delineated, in meaningful language, the manner in which the constitutional rights of the individual could be enforced against overzealous police practices. It was necessary in *Escobedo*, as here, to insure that what was proclaimed in the Constitution had not become but a "form of words," *Silverthorne Lumber Co. v. United States*, 251 U.S. 385, 392 (1920), in the hands of government officials. And it is in this spirit, consistent with our role as judges, that we adhere to the principles of *Escobedo* today.

Our holding will be spelled out with some specificity in the pages which follow but briefly stated it is this: the prosecution may not use statements, whether exculpatory or inculpatory, stemming from custodial interrogation of the defendant unless it demonstrates the use of procedural safeguards effective to secure the privilege against self-incrimination. By custodial interrogation, we mean questioning initiated by law enforcement officers after a person has been taken into custody or otherwise deprived of his freedom of action in any significant way. As for the procedural safeguards to be employed, unless other fully effective means are devised to inform accused persons of their right of silence and to assure a continuous opportunity to exercise it, the following measures are required. Prior to any questioning, the person must be warned that he has a right to remain silent, that any statement he does make may be used as evidence against him, and that he has a right to the presence of an attorney, either retained or appointed. The defendant may waive effectuation of these rights, provided the waiver is made voluntarily, knowingly and intelligently. If, however, he indicates in any manner and at any stage of the process that he wishes to consult with an attorney before speaking there can be no questioning. Likewise, if the individual is alone and indicates in any manner that he does not wish to be interrogated, the police may not question him. The mere fact that he may have answered some questions or volunteered some statements on his own does not deprive him of the right to refrain from answering any further inquiries until he has consulted with an attorney and thereafter consents to be questioned.

I

The constitutional issue we decide in each of these cases is the admissibility of statements obtained from a defendant questioned while in custody or otherwise deprived of his freedom of action in any significant way. In each, the defendant was questioned by police officers, detectives, or a prosecuting attorney in a room in which he was cut off from the outside world. In none of these cases was the defendant given a full and effective warning of his rights at the outset of the interrogation process. In all the cases, the questioning elicited oral admissions, and in three of them, signed statements as well which were admitted at their trials. They all thus share salient features—incommunicado interrogation of individuals in a police-dominated atmosphere, resulting in self-incriminating statements without full warnings of constitutional rights.

An understanding of the nature and setting of this in-custody interrogation is essential to our decisions today. The difficulty in depicting what transpires at such interrogations stems from the fact that in this country they have largely taken place incommunicado. From extensive factual studies undertaken in the early 1930's, including the famous Wickersham Report to Congress by a Presidential Commission, it is clear that police violence and the "third degree" flourished at that time. In a series of cases decided by this Court long after these studies, the police resorted to physical brutality—beating, hanging, whipping—and to sustained and protracted questioning incommunicado in order to extort confessions. The Commission on Civil Rights in 1961 found much evidence to indicate that "some policemen still resort to physical force to obtain confessions,". . . .

The examples given above are undoubtedly the exception now, but they are sufficiently widespread to be the object of concern. Unless a proper limitation upon custodial interrogation is achieved—such as these decisions will advance—there can be no assurance that practices of this nature will be eradicated in the foreseeable future. . . . To the contention that the third degree is necessary to get the facts, the reporters aptly reply in the language of the present Lord Chancellor of England (Lord Sankey): "It is not admissible to do a great right by doing a little wrong. . . . It is not sufficient to do justice by obtaining a proper result by irregular or improper means." Not only does the use of the third degree involve a flagrant violation of law by the officers of the law, but it involves also the dangers of false confessions, and it tends to make police and prosecutors less zealous in the search for objective evidence. . . .

Again we stress that the modern practice of in-custody interrogation is psychologically rather than physically oriented.

[*The opinion then quotes at length from police interrogation manuals, to show how police are encouraged to use various psychological pressures and tricks to obtain confessions.*]

* * *

The manuals also contain instructions for police on how to handle the individual who refuses to discuss the matter entirely, or who asks for an attorney or relatives. The examiner is to concede him the right to remain silent. "This usually has a very undermining effect. First of all, he is disappointed in his expectation of an unfavorable reaction on the part of the interrogator. Secondly, a concession of this right to remain silent impresses the subject with the apparent fairness of his interrogator." After this psychological conditioning, however, the officer is told to point out the incriminating significance of the suspect's refusal to talk:

> Joe, you have a right to remain silent. That's your privilege and I'm the last person in the world who'll try to take it away from you. If that's the way you want to leave this, O.K. But let me ask you this. Suppose you were in my shoes and I were in yours and you called me in to ask me about this and I told you, "I don't want to answer any of your questions." You'd think I had something to hide, and you'd probably be right in thinking that. That's exactly what I'll have to think about you, and so will everybody else. So let's sit here and talk this whole thing over.

Few will persist in their initial refusal to talk, it is said, if this monologue is employed correctly. In the event that the subject wishes to speak to a relative or an attorney, the following advice is tendered:

> The interrogator should respond by suggesting that the subject first tell the truth to the interrogator himself rather than get anyone else involved in the matter. If the request is for an attorney, the interrogator may suggest that the subject save himself or his family the expense of any such professional service, particularly if he is innocent of the offense under investigation. The interrogator may also add, "Joe, I'm only looking for the truth, and if you're telling the truth, that's it. You can handle this by yourself."

. . . When normal procedures fail to produce the needed result, the police may resort to deceptive stratagems such as giving false legal advice. It is important to keep the subject off balance, for example, by trading on his insecurity about himself or his surroundings. The police then persuade, trick, or cajole him out of exercising his constitutional rights.

* * *

In these cases, we might not find the defendants' statements to have been involuntary in traditional terms. Our concern for adequate safeguards to protect precious Fifth Amendment rights is, of course, not lessened in the slightest. In each of the cases, the defendant was thrust into an unfamiliar atmosphere and run through menacing police interrogation procedures. The potentiality for compulsion is forcefully apparent, for example, in *Miranda*, where the indigent Mexican defendant was a seriously disturbed individual with pronounced sexual fantasies, and in *Stewart*, in which the defendant was an indigent Los Angeles Negro who had dropped out of school in the sixth grade. To be sure, the records do not evince overt physical coercion or patent psychological ploys. The fact remains that in none of these cases did the officers undertake to afford appropriate safeguards at the outset of the interrogation to insure that the statements were truly the product of free choice.

* * *

From the foregoing, we can readily perceive an intimate connection between the privilege against self-incrimination and police custodial questioning. It is fitting to turn to history and precedent underlying the Self-Incrimination Clause to determine its applicability in this situation.

* * *

III

Today, then, there can be no doubt that the Fifth Amendment privilege is available outside of criminal court proceedings and serves to protect persons in all settings in which their freedom of action is curtailed in any significant way from being compelled to incriminate themselves. We have concluded that without proper safeguards the process of in-custody interrogation of persons suspected or accused of crime contains inherently compelling pressures which work to undermine the individual's will to resist and to compel him to speak where he would not otherwise do so freely. In order to combat these pressures and to permit a full opportunity to exercise the privilege against self-incrimination, the accused must be adequately and effectively apprised of his rights and the exercise of those rights must be fully honored.

* * *

The Fifth Amendment privilege is so fundamental to our system of constitutional rule and the expedient of giving an adequate warning as to the availability of the privilege so simple, we will not pause to inquire in individual cases whether the defendant was aware of his rights without a warning being given. . . .

The circumstances surrounding in-custody interrogation can operate very quickly to overbear the will of one merely made aware of his privilege by his interrogators. Therefore, the right to have counsel present at the interrogation is indispensable to the protection of the Fifth Amendment privilege under the system we delineate today. Our aim is to assure that the individual's right to choose between silence and speech remains unfettered throughout the interrogation process. A once-stated warning, delivered by those who will conduct the interrogation, cannot itself suffice to that end among those who most require knowledge of their rights. . . . Even preliminary advice given to the accused by his own attorney can be swiftly overcome by the secret interrogation process. . . . Thus, the need for counsel to protect the Fifth Amendment privilege comprehends not merely a right to consult with counsel prior to questioning, but also to have counsel present during any questioning if the defendant so desires.

The presence of counsel at the interrogation may serve several significant subsidiary functions as well. If the accused decides to talk to his interrogators, the assistance of counsel can mitigate the dangers of untrustworthiness. With a lawyer present the likelihood that the police will practice coercion is reduced, and if coercion is nevertheless exercised the lawyer can testify to it in court. The presence of a lawyer can also help to guarantee that the accused gives a fully accurate statement to the police and that the statement is rightly reported by the prosecution at trial. . . .

* * *

If the interrogation continues without the presence of an attorney and a statement is taken, a heavy burden rests on the government to demonstrate that the defendant knowingly and intelligently waived his privilege against self-incrimination and his right to retained or appointed counsel. . . .

* * *

IV

A recurrent argument made in these cases is that society's need for interrogation outweighs the privilege. . . .

* * *

Over the years the Federal Bureau of Investigation has compiled an exemplary record of effective law enforcement while advising any suspect or arrested person, at the outset of an interview, that he is not required to make a statement, that any statement may be used against him in court, that the individual may obtain the services of an attorney of his own choice and, more recently, that he has a right to free counsel if he is unable to pay.[54] A letter received from the Solicitor General in response to a question from the Bench makes it clear that the present pattern of warnings and respect for the rights of the individual followed as a practice by the FBI is consistent with the procedure which we delineate today. . . .

The practice of the FBI can readily be emulated by state and local enforcement agencies. The argument that the FBI deals with different crimes than are dealt with by state authorities does not mitigate the significance of the FBI experience. . . .

The experience in some other countries also suggests that the danger to law enforcement in curbs on interrogation is overplayed. . . .

* * *

It is so ordered.

CASE DISCUSSION QUESTIONS

1. Which constitutional rights are involved in this case?
2. How are the *Miranda* warnings related to these constitutional rights?
3. What is the Court's justification for requiring that the *Miranda* warnings be given?
4. What is the Court's response to the argument that society's needs to convict criminals outweighs the enforcement of the defendant's constitutional rights?

As conservative Republican presidents like Nixon, Reagan, and the Bushes replaced liberal Supreme Court Justices with more conservative ones, many observers thought that *Miranda v. Arizona* would eventually be overruled. Although that has not yet occurred,[12] the more conservative Courts that followed rendered several decisions in which they limited the types of situations in which the warnings had to be given. Examples include:

- *Beckwith v. United States.*[13] Court held IRS agents were not required to give *Miranda* rights when they questioned taxpayer in his home,
- *Oregon v. Mathiason.*[14] Court held police were not required to give *Miranda* rights when individual voluntarily came to the station, and
- *Berkemer v. McCarty.*[15] Court held police were not required to give *Miranda* rights when they questioned motorist at the scene of a stop for a traffic offense.

b. Questioning Without Having Given the Miranda Warnings

Miranda v. Arizona established that "the prosecution may not use statements, whether exculpatory or inculpatory, stemming from custodial interrogation of the defendant unless it demonstrates the use of procedural safeguards effective to secure the privilege against self-incrimination." It did not prohibit police from asking general questions of people at the scene of a crime or in circumstances in which a suspect was not "in custody."

Take special note of the fact that the penalty for failure to give the *Miranda* warnings, when they are required, is a ban against using the statements gained in the interrogation against the person in criminal court proceedings. It doesn't mean that the person couldn't still be prosecuted with other evidence that wasn't gained as a result of statements made by the defendant during the interrogation. This means that neither an arrest nor a criminal charge is invalid simply because the officer failed to give the suspect the *Miranda* warnings.

---

[12]In *Dickerson v. United States,* 530 U.S. 428, 120 S Ct. 2326, 147 L. Ed. 2d 405 (2000), the Supreme Court struck down the part of a congressional statute that voluntary confessions were to be admissible even if the warnings required by *Miranda* had not been given.

[13]425 U.S. 341, 96 S. Ct. 1612, 48 L. Ed. 2d 1 (1976).

[14]429 U.S. 492, 97 S. Ct. 711, 50 L. Ed. 2d 714 (1977).

[15]468 U.S. 420, 104 S. Ct. 3138, 82 L. Ed. 2d 317 (1984).

Brewer v. Williams[16] presents an interesting example of how people can be convicted even though police failed to give the appropriate *Miranda* warnings. In this case police attempted to trick a suspect into making incriminating statements while transporting him in the back seat of their squad car. They did so by talking to each other, in front of the suspect, about the need to find the alleged victim's body so she could receive a proper Christian burial. When the suspect eventually told them where it could be found the prosecution used this information and evidence found on the body against the suspect. Although the Supreme Court overturned the conviction on the grounds that *Miranda* warnings had not been given, Williams was again convicted of first degree murder at a second trial. This time, evidence concerning the body's location and condition was admitted on the basis of the doctrine of "inevitable discovery."[17] The Supreme Court affirmed this second conviction.

c. Effectiveness of Interrogations

Movies and television shows often feature dramatic police interrogations that result in suspects either confessing or making surprising admissions that help police make their case. In real life, police interrogations rarely yield these types of results, and in situations where suspects do confess, there is usually sufficient physical and testimonial evidence to convict without the use of the confession.

What is even more surprising to many people is that so many suspects will waive their rights to remain silent and will go ahead and answer police questions without having consulted with an attorney. Part of the answer is that police will often "egg them on" by making comments to the effect that they don't need a lawyer unless they have something to hide. Many times though, it is because the suspects think they can come up with answers that will make police think they didn't commit any crimes.

In the process of trying to talk their way out of their situation, suspects often make the mistake of making inconsistent or contradictory statements that later come back to haunt them when they are used at trial. Exhibit 4.3 contains excerpts of the police interview with basketball star Kobe Bryant when he was being investigated for sexual assault. Notice how Bryant changed his story as the interview progressed.

4. USE OF GRAND JURIES TO INVESTIGATE CRIMES

Since grand juries are most closely associated with the activities of prosecuting attorneys, we wait till the next chapter before we go into more detail about their origin and current use. At this point in the text, we simply wish to mention that at the federal level and in some states, these juries present an additional investigative tool whereby reluctant witnesses can be required to testify in secret about information they may have about criminal activity.

---

[16]430 U.S. 387, 97 S. Ct. 1232, 51 L. Ed. 2d 424 (1977).

[17]A principle that this type of evidence can be admitted if the state proves that it would have been discovered in essentially the same condition even if the defendant had not been improperly induced to reveal its location.

Exhibit 4.3: Excerpts of Transcript of Kobe Bryant Interrogation

235   Detective Winters: Okay. Um, I'll be blunt and ask you. Did you have sexual intercourse with
236   her?

237

238   Bryant: No.

239

240   Detective Winters: Okay. Uh, what, okay, Kobe here's, here's what I'd like to do okay. Um,
241   yet there is an allegation that it was an unconsensual intercourse that occurred last night, okay.
242   All right. Hang on, okay, hang on, I understand you have every right to be upset, okay, but, you
243   know, but, I'm giving you an opportunity to tell the truth if something did happen, because I'm
244   gonna tell you right now, um, we're gonna find out.

* * *

337   Detective Loya: Just be straight up, we're not gonna tell your wife or anything like that. Did you
338   have sexual intercourse with her?

339

340   Bryant: Uh, this is what I need to know because uh, I did have sexual intercourse with her:
341   Cause I was ...(inaudible whisper).

342

343   Detective Winters: And I understand.

344

345   Detective Loya: Okay, was it consensual?

346

347   Bryant: It was totally consensual.

Due to the secretive nature of grand jury proceedings and their power to subpoena witnesses, grand juries are especially useful in investigating governmental corruption, organized crime, and situations involving undercover operatives. Witnesses can be forced to reveal information that incriminates others without the subjects of the inquiry knowing that they are being investigated and without undercover agents having to publicly reveal their identity.

Although grand jury witnesses can still claim the self-incrimination protections of the Fifth Amendment, they do not have the right to have their attorney in the hearing room with them. Furthermore, prosecutors often grant either transactional or use **immunity** to compel a witness's testimony.

Immunity
An exemption from prosecution given to a witness so that the witness can be compelled to give self-incriminating testimony.

Transactional immunity
Prosecutorial immunity that protects a witness from prosecution for the offense revealed in his or her testimony.

Use immunity
Prosecutorial immunity that bars the government from using the testimony in the prosecution of the witness, except on charges of perjury. Use immunity is also known as "derivative use immunity."

Transactional immunity protects a witness from prosecution for the offense revealed in his or her testimony, and **use immunity**, also known as "derivative use immunity," bars the prosecution from using the testimony in any prosecution of the witness, except on charges of perjury.

DISCUSSION QUESTIONS

2. What limits, if any, *should* there be on the right of law enforcement personnel to stop and question individuals to determine if they have any involvement in, or even know anything about, any criminal behavior?

3. Under what circumstances, if any, *should* law enforcement personnel be able to require someone to identify themselves and present proper documentation (such as a driver's license or other form of ID) to prove they are who they claim to be? Should this extend to a requirement to show documentation that the person is not an illegal immigrant?

4. Under what circumstances, if any, *should* law enforcement personnel be able to take a person to another location in order to interrogate that individual?

5. Under what circumstances, if any, *should* law enforcement personnel be required to inform individuals they are questioning about their rights to counsel and their privilege against self-incrimination?

6. Under what circumstances, if any, *should* principals or teachers be required to inform students they are questioning about their rights to counsel and their privilege against self-incrimination?

Arrest warrant
A court order issued at the request of the prosecutor and/or law enforcement that authorizes the arrest and detention of an individual.

Probable cause
The reasonable belief based on specific facts that a person committed a crime or that something will be found in a specific location.

Reasonable force
The amount of force necessary to protect oneself or one's property.

Excessive force
Any force greater than the level of force a reasonable and prudent law enforcement officer would use under the circumstances.

D. ARRESTING SUSPECTS

The difference between a suspect and a defendant is that a suspect is a person that law enforcement officials think may have committed a crime, whereas a defendant is a person that has been formally charged with committing a crime. Since the Fourth Amendment applies to the seizure of people, as well as things, law enforcement officers are either required to have an **arrest warrant** or be able to prove independently that there is **probable cause** to believe the person committed a crime before they can arrest someone. To determine probable cause, the police can rely on their knowledge of the suspect as well as information provided by witnesses and victims.

The process for getting an arrest warrant usually involves the prosecuting attorney's office and will be covered in Chapter 5. In situations in which the police catch the offender in the act of committing the crime or where there is legitimate concern that the offender will flee during the time that it would take to get a warrant, police are allowed to make the arrest without a warrant.

When making an arrest, police are allowed to use "**reasonable force.**" This is the amount of force necessary for the police to protect themselves or their property when they carry out the arrest. Anything beyond that is considered "**excessive force**" and is impermissible. This means, for example, that they cannot purposely bang the arrested person's head on the top of the car door when placing him or her in their squad car, but they can tackle someone who is trying to run away. State laws differ as to the circumstances under which law enforcement personnel can use "deadly force" to effectuate an arrest.

In recent years, the topic of high-speed automobile chases has garnered a great deal of attention, with CNN and other television news outlets broadcasting them live from helicopters flying overhead. The U.S. Supreme Court recently spoke to this issue in *Scott v. Harris*,[18] where the Court ruled that it was not unreasonable for a deputy sheriff to have ended a high-speed chase by applying his "push bumper" to the rear of the fleeing vehicle.

DISCUSSION QUESTION

7. What, if anything, should a law enforcement officer be allowed to do when a person being arrested:
   a. punches the officer;
   b. spits on the officer;
   c. swears at the officer;
   d. sits down or goes limp rather than following the officer's directions?

E. GATHERING OF PHYSICAL AND DOCUMENTARY EVIDENCE

Although victims and witnesses can often provide essential information about what took place and may think they can identify the perpetrator, eyewitness identification has often proved to be quite unreliable. In recent years, there have been several well-publicized cases in which people convicted on the basis of eyewitness testimony were later proven, by DNA testing and/or confessions by others, to have been innocent. For instance, the Northwestern University's Center on Wrongful Convictions reports:

> In the quarter century between restoration of the Illinois death penalty and Governor George Ryan's blanket clemency order, 298 men and women were sentenced to death in Illinois. Of those, 18 have been exonerated—a rate of 6%. . . . [19]

Therefore, much greater weight is now placed on the gathering of physical evidence.

As part of their investigation, the police typically take measurements and pictures of the crime scene, take samples of fluids found at the scene, and do some of the other things you typically see on CSI-type television shows. See examples of these types of photographs in Exhibit 4.4.

In addition to evidence found at the scene of the crime, other incriminating evidence can often be found at a suspect's home, business, or in an automobile. Such searches may locate the fruits of crime (such as stolen property), the instruments of crime (such as burglary tools or weapons), or contraband items (such as illegal drugs or weapons). Letters, notes, e-mails, and financial records can also provide important evidence in criminal trials. This is especially true in cases involving white-collar crimes.

However, in order to assure the admissibility of the evidence they gather, prosecutors must show that it was gathered in a manner that was consistent with

---

[18] 550 U.S. 372, 127 S. Ct. 1769, 167 L. Ed. 2d 686 (2007).

[19] *http://www.law.northwestern.edu/wrongfulconvictions/exonerations/ilIndexdp.html*

Exhibit 4.4: Crime Scene Photographs

Television product spokesman Vince Shlomi (the "ShamWow Guy") and a woman were involved in an altercation in a Miami Beach hotel room in 2009. Crime Scene Unit documented the scene with the following photographs: blood-stained sheets on the bed, a bloody telephone, and an overturned chair. Prosecutors did not charge either party. Excerpts of the police report appear in Exhibit 8.2.

the protections of the Fourth Amendment. In other words, it must either have been authorized by a proper search warrant or be gathered from the type of situation in which a search warrant is not required.

1. SEARCHES THAT DO NOT REQUIRE A WARRANT

While a complete discussion of all exceptions to the warrant requirement is beyond the scope of this chapter, you should become familiar with each of the major types of searches discussed in this section.

a. Consent Searches

Consent is perhaps the most common situation in which law enforcement personnel do not need a search warrant. Defendants cannot claim a violation of their Fourth Amendment rights if they consented to the search. But what are the requirements for a search to be considered consensual and who is authorized to give consent to property that is shared by more than one person?

The courts have ruled that to be a valid consent search, the permission to search must have been given voluntarily and by someone who is authorized to do so. Thus, to be a valid consent, it cannot have been obtained through coercion (actual or threatened) or trickery. In *Bumper v. North Carolina*,[20] for example,

---

[20]391 U.S. 543, 88 S. Ct. 1788, 20 L. Ed. 2d 797 (1968).

the Supreme Court invalidated a search where police claimed to have a search warrant, but in fact did not.

The question of who is authorized to consent to a search is more complicated. If the owner of a house lives in the house, he or she has authority to consent to a search, but if the house or apartment is leased, the consent must be given by the tenant rather then the owner. Where tenants share a dwelling, the general principle is that a single tenant, who is present, can give consent to search the common areas, but not for a search of other tenants' bedrooms, chests, etc. that are used exclusively by the other tenants. However, if other tenants are also present and refuse to consent, police are not allowed to search either the common areas or the personal areas of the others.[21]

b. Exigent Circumstances

Exceptions to the requirement for a search warrant are also made in situations where there are "**exigent circumstances.**" In situations where it is impractical to get a warrant, law enforcement personnel are allowed to conduct limited searches without one. Ordinarily, the conditions that excuse an officer from obtaining a warrant are the protection of life, the preservation of evidence, or the prevention of a suspect's escape.

A common example is a situation in which police are in "hot pursuit," i.e., physically chasing a suspect who they see run into a private residence. Under these circumstances, the police are allowed to enter the residence without a warrant for the purpose of detaining the suspect and preventing him or her from destroying evidence. Though once the suspect has been detained and the premises secured, the police are expected to obtain a warrant before conducting further searches of the area.

A similar type of rationale is used when motor vehicles are involved. Although police cannot search secured areas, such as the trunk of a car, they are allowed to secure the vehicle and move it to a safer location until they can obtain and execute a search warrant.

> **Exigent circumstances**
> Conditions that excuse an officer from obtaining a warrant in order to protect a life, preserve evidence, or prevent a suspect from escaping.

c. Plain View Doctrine

The **plain view doctrine** holds that law enforcement officials have the right to seize contraband items or evidence of a crime when they see such items "in plain view" in public or from a location where there is no reasonable expectation of privacy. It is based on the assumption that Fourth Amendment restrictions apply only to searches that invade spaces for which there is a reasonable expectation of privacy.

For example, if a police officer walking down the sidewalk, or driving down the street, happens to spot what appears to be marijuana plants growing in a window box or in a planter on someone's front porch, he or she can walk up to take a closer look and then seize the plants if they still seem to be marijuana. Similarly, if an officer spots what appears to be an illegal drug in an automobile

> **Plain view doctrine**
> The legal theory that law enforcement officials have the right to seize contraband items or evidence of a crime when they see such items in public or from a location where there is no reasonable expectation of privacy.

---

[21]See *Georgia v. Randolph,* 547 U.S. 103, 126 S. Ct. 1515, 164 L. Ed. 2d 208 (2006).

he or she has stopped for a minor traffic offense, that police officer can seize it and charge the driver with possession of illegal substances he or she observes.[22]

Arizona v. Hicks,[23] provides an example of an overreach of the plain view doctrine. In this case, law enforcement officers entered Hicks's apartment after a bullet was reported as being fired into the apartment below his. Once in the apartment, they noticed two sets of expensive stereo equipment that they thought were inconsistent with the "squalor" of the apartment. They then proceeded to move some of the components in order to read and record their serial numbers. When, after phoning the numbers into headquarters, it was confirmed that the equipment had been taken in an armed robbery, the officers seized the equipment and Hicks was subsequently indicted for robbery. However, the Supreme Court upheld the suppression of the evidence on the basis that the officers' moving of the equipment constituted a separate "search" that was unrelated to the search for the shooter, victims, and weapons that was the lawful objective of their entry and officers lacked probable cause to search for serial numbers.

d. "Stop and Frisk" and Searches Incident to Arrest

In our earlier discussion about the right to stop and question possible suspects (Section C.1), we talked briefly about *Terry v. Ohio*. In addition to authorizing police to stop and question, this case also authorized police to conduct a brief pat-down search for weapons in situations where the officers had legitimate concerns about their personal safety. The officers are not allowed to search the inside clothing or pockets of the suspect unless their initial pat down revealed an object that might be a dangerous weapon.

We need to emphasize that the police cannot stop and frisk individuals whenever they feel like it. Individuals may be stopped only when the officer has a reasonable suspicion that the individual has committed, is in the process of committing, or is about to commit a crime. According to *Terry*, that reasonable suspicion must be based on "specific and articulable facts which, taken together with rational inferences from those facts, reasonably warrant that intrusion."[24]

On the other hand, when police actually arrest someone, as opposed to just questioning a suspect, they are allowed to conduct a more thorough warrantless search of the person and the area immediately surrounding that person. The courts have justified these "searches incident to a valid arrest" on the grounds that they are necessary to protect the safety of the officer (to remove or prevent acquisition of potential weapons) or the destruction of evidence.

As part of the booking process, the police will remove the arrested person's personal items, such as watches, billfolds, notes, etc., and place them in marked, sealed envelopes in order to secure them while the person is incarcerated. Any contraband materials or evidence of a crime that is found during this process would be admissible in court under the in plain view doctrine.

A similar inventory process takes place when a motor vehicle is impounded by police. In order to protect themselves from claims that the vehicle was damaged or that goods were stolen from the vehicle while it was in police cus-

---

[22]Assuming the stop was legitimate and, the drugs were visible to anyone looking in the window.

[23]480 U.S. 321, 107 S. Ct. 1149, 94 L. Ed. 2d 347 (1987).

[24]392 U.S. 1, 21 (1968).

tody, they are allowed to make a detailed inventory of its contents. Whatever they find during this inventory process falls under the in plain view exception.

e. Special Rules Governing Border Searches and Airline Flights

As you probably know, special rules apply to searches conducted at border crossings and when boarding commercial airlines. In these types of situations, authorities do not need to establish probable cause to be able to conduct warrantless searches.

2. APPLICATION FOR A SEARCH WARRANT

Even though it is sometimes possible to conduct legal searches without a formal search warrant having been issued by a judge, the use of warrants is the safest way to ensure that the items seized will eventually be admissible at a trial. Generally, the search warrant application process involves both police and prosecutors. Experienced law enforcement officers may prepare the initial paperwork and then hand it on to the prosecutors to present to the judge. Alternatively, police may supply the information verbally and have attorneys or paralegals prepare the actual court documents.

The **search warrant** is technically a written court order that authorizes law enforcement officers to search a specific place for specific objects. An **application for search warrant** is a motion presented to the court that specifies the reasons that a search warrant should be issued. A judge must determine that the reasons specified in the motion are sufficient to meet the probable cause standard before issuing the warrant.

The application is typically in affidavit form or accompanied by an **affidavit**. An affidavit is a voluntarily written declaration of facts signed under oath or under penalty of perjury. The person who signs the affidavit is referred to as the **affiant**. In some jurisdictions, a notary public, judge, or clerk of the court administers an oath to the affiant. Other states permit an affiant to verify that he or she is telling the truth by signing the affidavit under penalty of perjury. Before you draft an affidavit, research the law of your jurisdiction to determine the proper method of attestation.

An application for a search warrant must make two showings. First, it must demonstrate probable cause that a specific crime was committed. The key to demonstrating this probable cause is to identify the crime at issue along with the evidence that establishes the crime. You should use precise language that fully describes the evidence. Every application for a warrant is unique in that it is based on the particular facts that give rise to the investigation of a specific crime.

Second, the application must give the specific location (street address, apartment number, etc.) and specifically designate the type of physical evidence that is expected to be found at a particular location. This latter requirement, to specifically identify the types of items being sought, is designed to prevent police from just looking to see if they can find anything that might be incriminating. The application must also show probable cause to believe that the items they seek are connected to criminal activity. For example, if police are looking for stolen television sets, the application should list specific brands and model numbers (if they are known).

Although there are boilerplate templates that are routinely used to draft applications, you would be remiss to simply adopt a form without regard to the

Search warrant
A written court order that authorizes an officer to search a specific place for specific objects. A neutral judge must determine that there is probable cause in order to issue a search warrant.

Application for search warrant
A motion presented to the court that specifies the reasons that a search warrant should be issued. The application for search warrant is typically in affidavit form or accompanied by an affidavit.

Affidavit
A voluntarily written declaration of facts signed under oath or under penalty of perjury.

Affiant
The person who signs an affidavit under oath or under penalty of perjury.

peculiarities of your case. Moreover, you should check your jurisdiction's court rules and statutes to see if there is any provision that governs applications for search warrants. Some jurisdictions give detailed instructions as to what should be included in the application. For instance, in Pennsylvania, Rule 206 of the Criminal Code provides:

> Each application for a search warrant shall be supported by written affidavit(s) signed and sworn to or affirmed before an issuing authority, which affidavit(s) shall:
>
> 1. state the name and department, agency, or address of the affiant;
> 2. identify specifically the items or property to be searched for and seized;
> 3. name or describe with particularity the person or place to be searched;
> 4. identify the owner, occupant, or possessor of the place to be searched;
> 5. specify or describe the crime which has been or is being committed;
> 6. set forth specifically the facts and circumstances which form the basis for the affiant's conclusion that there is probable cause to believe that the items or property identified are evidence or the fruit of a crime, or are contraband, or are otherwise unlawfully possessed or subject to seizure, and that these items or property are located on the particular person or at the particular place described;
> 7. if a "nighttime" search is requested (i.e., 10 p.m. to 6 a.m.), state additional reasonable cause for seeking permission to search in nighttime; and
> 8. when the attorney for the Commonwealth is requesting that the affidavit(s) be sealed pursuant to Rule 211, state the facts and circumstances which are alleged to establish good cause for the sealing of the affidavit(s). (234 Pa. Code Rule 206.)

There are a variety of resources available to assist law enforcement officers and prosecutors' offices in drafting these documents. Handbooks for law enforcement officers as well as prosecutor training materials provide helpful instruction on how to prepare the application for a particular type of case. For example, Susan S. Kreston, a senior attorney with the American Prosecutors Research Institute's National Center for Prosecution of Child Abuse, gives a step-by-step approach for preparing warrant applications to retrieve computers on which child pornography is stored:

> Affidavits should contain the following information and be specifically incorporated by reference into the warrant:
>
> 1. Introductory paragraph with a recitation of affiant's training and experience, particularly in this area. * * *
> 2. Identification of the statute that is being alleged to be violated, by both statute number (title and section) and content. * * *
> 3. Description of the premises to be searched, with as much particularity as possible.* * *
> 4. Definition of terms used in the application. * * *
> 5. Background information.* * *
> 6. Description of the investigation in as much detail as possible.* * *
> 7. General description of individuals who are sexually interested in children, including only those characteristics that apply to the suspect in the case. * * *
> 8. Request for search and seizure of computer and computer-related equipment. * * *

9. List of items to be seized. * * *
10. Summary paragraph stating why there is probable cause to believe the items to be seized will be found at the subject premises.[25]

Probably the best guide for preparing applications for warrants are applications prepared by your office that resulted in the issuance of search warrants. These documents should be helpful in understanding what your supervisor and judges expect. An example of a successful application used in a Louisiana terrorism case is depicted in Exhibit 4.5. It appears that the person who prepared the document was using a form. Although some of the language of the second-to-last paragraph does not seem to apply to the facts, the application does set forth with sufficient particularity the pertinent facts that would give the judge a sound basis to conclude that a search warrant should be issued.

The warrant typically incorporates language from the application that identifies the property to be inspected. Thus, the application and the proposed warrant can be prepared at the same time. If the court grants the application for search warrant, it will then sign the warrant. Federal Rules of Criminal Procedure, 41(e)(2)(A) sets forth the required contents of a search warrant for physical property and to seize a person as follows:[26]

> [T]he warrant must identify the person or property to be searched, identify any person or property to be seized, and designate the magistrate judge to whom it must be returned. The warrant must command the officer to:
>
> (i)   execute the warrant within a specified time no longer than 10 days;
> (ii) execute the warrant during the daytime, unless the judge for good cause expressly authorizes execution at another time; and
> (iii) return the warrant to the magistrate judge designated in the warrant.

3. EXECUTING SEARCH WARRANTS

Once the search warrant has been issued, it must be **executed**— that is, the search must actually be carried out—within a specific period of time. In keeping with the underlying Fourth Amendment values of preserving the security and privacy of one's home, police are normally required to announce their presence and, unless the warrant specifically allows other arrangements, execute the warrant during daytime hours.

Under special conditions, the courts will sometimes issue **no-knock warrants**, which allow the police to enter at night without announcing their presence in advance. But, in order to receive one of these special search warrants, the police must convince the judge that evidence is likely to be destroyed or that the police administering the warrant will be in danger.[27]

It is the responsibility of those executing the warrant to prepare an inventory of the items seized in the search. This information is then included in a

Execution of warrant
The carrying out of a search of a person or place.

No-knock warrant
A warrant that allows law enforcement officers to enter a property without knocking and without identifying themselves.

---

[25]S. S. Kreston, Search and Seizure in Cases of Computers and Child Pornography, *www.ndaa.org/publications/newsletters/apri_update_vol_12_no_9_1999.*

[26]The form used for federal search warrants is located online at *http://www.uscourts.gov/forms/AO093.pdf.*

[27]For further discussion of no-knock warrants, see Chapter 8 discussion of *Hudson v. Michigan,* 547 U.S. 586, 126 S. Ct. 2159, 165 L. Ed. 2d 56 (2006) in the section on the exclusionary rule on page 281.

Exhibit 4.5: Application for Search Warrant

In May 2007, Richard Wargo, a Louisiana State college student, was charged with threatening the life of Senator Hillary Clinton. Before he was arrested the university police secured a warrant to search Wargo's dormitory room. The application for the warrant was based upon the statements that Wargo made to another student.

APPLICATION FOR SEARCH WARRANT
050407 005535

STATE OF LOUISIANA
PARISH OF EAST BATON ROUGE

BEFORE ME. The Honorable Michael Irwin, Judge of the Nineteenth Judicial District Court in and for the State and Parish aforesaid, personally appeared Officer Patrick McCarty. LSU Police Officer in and for East Baton Rouge Parish and the state of Louisiana, who, being duly sworn by me, deposed and said:

THAT probable cause does exist for the issuance of a search warrant authorizing the search of the premises at Louisianan State University's Herget Hall, room 233, located in Baton Rouge. LA: further described as a multi-story dormitory with a light tan brick exterior: including Richard Ryan Wargo's personal closet, trash bin, assigned dormitory desk, and common space shared with his roommate located therein where certain fruits of a crime, to wit:

LRS 14:40.1 - Terrorizing

Namely:

> Materials, writings, computers (desktop and/or laptop), any digital audio, video recording devices and vehicle (a 2002 Toyota 4runner, silver in color, Louisiana Lic OXK186, VIN JT3GN87R320240721) that would suggest any intent to execute an arson or any act of terrorism

> Is (are) believed to be secreted or concealed, and such probable cause is based upon the following:

On May 3, 2007, your affiant met with Daniel Demetrios Morgan, a classmate of Richard Ryan Wargo. Morgan stated that on April 20th 2007. Richard Ryan Wargo asked him if he had an interest in committing any arson. According to Morgan, on April 23rd, 2007, Wargo indicated that he was interested in committing an act of terrorism, and that it would be a "national event". Morgan asked "it's political, isn't it?" Morgan stated that Wargo shook his head yes and said "Hillary Clinton". Morgan assumed that Wargo was referencing using a form or arson against Clinton's Headquarters and stated: "You know that that's only going to make her more popular?" to which Morgan stated that Wargo said "True, but have you ever heard of a dead president?" Morgan further advised your affiant that Wargo stated that he would commit this act when Hillary Clinton came to Baton Rouge for the primary, to which Wargo nodded his head yes.

THAT writ to search the aforesaid dormitory room is requested, and when the thing to be searched is a dwelling or other structure, that the writ to search include all other structures. vehicles and places of concealment on the premises where the thing(s) may be found.

THAT it may become necessary to conduct the search during the nighttime or on Sunday. and affiant(s) request(s) that the writ so provide.

SWORN to and subscribed before me on this 3rd day of May 2007

_____
AFFIANT

_____
EX-OFFICIO NOTARY PUBLIC AND DEPUTY CLERK OF COURT

return of the warrant (a court document, signed by the law enforcement officer who conducted the search, specifying when the warrant was executed and lists the items seized). The return of the search warrant served in the Louisiana terrorism case is presented in Exhibit 4.6.

Return of search warrant
A court document that specifies when a search warrant was executed and lists the items of the property seized.

4. SPECIAL RULES FOR ELECTRONIC SURVEILLANCE

Electronic surveillance involves using sophisticated electronic devices to listen in on, view, and record people's activities and messages. These devices include such things as hidden cameras and microphones, parabolic microphones that can hear through walls, thermo-imaging cameras that can see through walls, and devices that can intercept cell phone transmissions and e-mail messages. They are most likely to be used in investigations of organized crime, government corruption, and espionage.

When hidden microphones and cameras were first used for eavesdropping, the courts developed an important distinction between devices that were located within a private building and those that were outside the building. So while a warrant is needed to hide a bug in someone's bedroom, one would not be needed to listen in on telephone calls where the phone lines were "tapped" outside the house.

In *Kyllo v. United States*, the U.S. Supreme Court considered the use of thermo-imaging cameras that allow government agents to "see" through walls. Take a look at the following excerpts to see how the U.S. Supreme Court addressed the use of this new technology.

Although some of the earlier U.S. Supreme Court cases ruled that searches that did not penetrate the walls of a room were not protected by the Fourth Amendment, Congress and many state legislatures have passed anti-eavesdropping statutes that provide much greater protections. Some of these statutes impose stricter standards for obtaining an electronic interception order than for getting a traditional search warrant. Unlike the search warrants application process, which may be initiated by a law enforcement officer, only specifically designated prosecuting attorneys or their designates may apply for orders permitting wiretaps or other electronic surveillance. Moreover, judges may only enter electronic interception orders for the investigation of certain crimes.[28]

At the federal level, the application for the electronic eavesdropping order must be made by the U.S. Attorney General, Associate Attorney General, or specifically designated Assistant Attorneys General in the Criminal Division.[29] Such requests at the state level must be brought by the state or county prosecutor or their authorized representatives.[30] Judges are authorized to enter an interception order only when certain stringent criteria are met. For instance, in federal court there must be a showing that normal investigative procedures have been tried or reasonably appear to be unlikely to succeed if tried or to be too dangerous. Exhibit 4.7 displays an application for an interception order that could

---

[28]For instance, at the state level intercepts are limited to investigations of murder, kidnapping, gambling, robbery, bribery, extortion, drug trafficking, or violent felonies. See 18 U.S.C. §2516(2).

[29]18 U.S.C. § 2516(1).

[30]18 U.S.C. § 2516(2).

Exhibit 4.6: Return of Search Warrant

In addition to seizing items specified in the search warrant, the university police officer also seized suspected illicit drugs and drug paraphernalia. If this contraband were out in the open, the officer had the right to seize it in accordance with the plain view doctrine.

RETURN TO SEARCH WARRANT

To the Honorable Michael Erwin , Judge of the Nineteenth Judicial Court:

I hereby certify that I received the attached Search Warrant on the 3 day of May , 2007 at the hour of 1035 PM, and that I executed the said warrant on the 3 day of May, 2007 at the hour of 1058 PM, and made a diligent search as ordered. The following property was found and seized:

1. Dell Espiron Laptop Computer Model:Ei505 Service Tag #:CB3DKB1
2. Two Sertrolin HCL 50 Mg Pill Bottles containg unknown medication
3. Three Plastic Bags Containing Suspected marijuana
4. Nokia Cell Phone Model 6102j
5. 20GB IPOD
6. Assorted CD's in Black Case
7. Assorted Paperwork
8. Cingular Cell Phone
9. 3 1/2 Black floppy disk
10. Plastic Bottle Containing Suspected marijuana
11. Glass Pipe
12. Dell Computer Bag

A copy of the said search warrant and a receipt (if seizure of property is indicated above) were given to: Richard R. Wargo

Respectfully Submitted.

Patrick McCarty   0589

have been presented to a judge in the Brandon Turner case for drug trafficking. Note that the events cited in the petition are different from the activities giving rise to the sample case.

Kyllo v. United States
Supreme Court of the United States
533 U.S. 27 (2001)

JUSTICE SCALIA delivered the opinion of the Court.

This case presents the question whether the use of a thermal-imaging device aimed at a private home from a public street to detect relative amounts of heat within the home constitutes a "search" within the meaning of the Fourth Amendment.

I

In 1991 Agent William Elliott of the United States Department of the Interior came to suspect that marijuana was being grown in the home belonging to petitioner Danny Kyllo, part of a triplex on Rhododendron Drive in Florence, Oregon. Indoor marijuana growth typically requires high-intensity lamps. In order to determine whether an amount of heat was emanating from petitioner's home consistent with the use of such lamps, at 3:20 a.m. on January 16, 1992, Agent Elliott and Dan Haas used an Agema Thermovision 210 thermal imager to scan the triplex. Thermal imagers detect infrared radiation, which virtually all objects emit but which is not visible to the naked eye. The imager converts radiation into images based on relative warmth—black is cool, white is hot, shades of gray connote relative differences; in that respect, it operates somewhat like a video camera showing heat images. The scan of Kyllo's home took only a few minutes and was performed from the passenger seat of Agent Elliott's vehicle across the street from the front of the house and also from the street in back of the house. The scan showed that the roof over the garage and a side wall of petitioner's home were relatively hot compared to the rest of the home and substantially warmer than neighboring homes in the triplex. Agent

Elliott concluded that petitioner was using halide lights to grow marijuana in his house, which indeed he was. Based on tips from informants, utility bills, and the thermal imaging, a Federal Magistrate Judge issued a warrant authorizing a search of petitioner's home, and the agents found an indoor growing operation involving more than 100 plants. Petitioner was indicted on one count of manufacturing marijuana, in violation of 21 U.S.C. §841(a)(1). He unsuccessfully moved to suppress the evidence seized from his home and then entered a conditional guilty plea.

The Court of Appeals for the Ninth Circuit remanded the case for an evidentiary hearing regarding the intrusiveness of thermal imaging. On remand the District Court found that the Agema 210 "is a non-intrusive device which emits no rays or beams and shows a crude visual image of the heat being radiated from the outside of the house"; it "did not show any people or activity within the walls of the structure"; "the device used cannot penetrate walls or windows to reveal conversations or human activities"; and "no intimate details of the home were observed." Based on these findings, the District Court upheld the validity of the warrant that relied in part upon the thermal imaging, and reaffirmed its denial of the motion to suppress. A divided Court of Appeals initially reversed, but that opinion was withdrawn and the panel (after a change in composition) affirmed, with Judge Noonan dissenting. The court held that petitioner had shown no subjective expectation of privacy because he had made no attempt to conceal the heat escaping from his home, and even if he had, there was no objectively reasonable expectation of privacy because the imager "did not expose any intimate details of Kyllo's life," only "amorphous 'hot spots' on the roof and exterior wall."

II

The Fourth Amendment provides that "the right of the people to be secure in their persons, houses, papers, and effects, against unreasonable searches and seizures, shall not be violated." "At the very core" of the Fourth Amendment "stands the right of a man to retreat into his own home and there be free from unreasonable governmental intrusion." *Silverman v. United States*, (1961). With few exceptions, the question whether a warrantless search of a home is reasonable and hence constitutional must be answered no. . . .

On the other hand, the antecedent question of whether or not a Fourth Amendment "search" has occurred is not so simple under our precedent. The permissibility of ordinary visual surveillance of a home used to be clear because, well into the 20th century, our Fourth Amendment jurisprudence was tied to common-law trespass. . . . Visual surveillance was unquestionably lawful because "the eye cannot by the laws of England be guilty of a trespass. . . . " We have since decoupled violation of a person's Fourth Amendment rights from trespassory violation of his property, . . . but the lawfulness of warrantless visual surveillance of a home has still been preserved. As we observed in *California v. Ciraolo* (1986), "the Fourth Amendment protection of the home has never been extended to require law enforcement officers to shield their eyes when passing by a home on public thoroughfares."

. . . In assessing when a search is not a search, we have applied somewhat in reverse the principle first enunciated in *Katz v. United States* (1967). *Katz* involved eavesdropping by means of an electronic listening device placed on the outside of a telephone booth—a location not within the catalog ("persons, houses, papers, and effects") that the Fourth Amendment protects against unreasonable searches. We held that the Fourth Amendment nonetheless protected Katz from the warrantless eavesdropping because he "justifiably relied" upon the privacy of the telephone booth. As Justice Harlan's oft-quoted concurrence described it, a Fourth Amendment search occurs when the government violates a subjective expectation of privacy that society recognizes as reasonable. We have subsequently applied this principle to hold that a Fourth Amendment search does *not* occur—even when the explicitly protected location of a *house* is concerned—unless "the individual manifested a subjective expectation of privacy in the object of the challenged search," and "society [is] willing to recognize that expectation as reasonable." We have applied this test in holding that it is not a search for the police to use a pen register at the phone company to determine what numbers were dialed in a private home, *Smith v. Maryland*, (1979), and we have applied the test on two different occasions in holding that aerial surveillance of private homes and surrounding areas does not constitute a search, *Ciraolo, supra*; *Florida v. Riley* (1989).

The present case involves officers on a public street engaged in more than naked-eye surveillance of a home. We have previously reserved judgment as to how much technological enhancement of ordinary perception from such a vantage point, if any, is too much. While we upheld enhanced aerial photography of an industrial complex in *Dow Chemical*, we noted that we found "it important that this is *not* an area immediately adjacent to a private home, where privacy expectations are most heightened."

III

It would be foolish to contend that the degree of privacy secured to citizens by the Fourth Amendment has been entirely unaffected by the advance of technology. For example, as the cases discussed above make clear, the technology enabling human flight has exposed to public view (and hence, we have said, to official observation) uncovered portions of the house and its curtilage that once were private. The question we confront today is what limits there are upon this power of technology to shrink the realm of guaranteed privacy.

The *Katz* test—whether the individual has an expectation of privacy that society is prepared to recognize as reasonable—has often been criticized as circular, and hence subjective and unpredictable. . . . While it may be difficult to refine *Katz* when the search of areas such as telephone booths, automobiles, or even the curtilage and uncovered portions of residences are at issue, in the case of the search of the interior of homes—the prototypical and hence most commonly litigated area of protected privacy—there is a ready criterion, with roots deep in the common law, of the minimal expectation of privacy that *exists*, and that is acknowledged to be *reasonable*. To withdraw protection of this minimum expectation would be to permit police technology to erode the privacy guaranteed by the Fourth Amendment. We think that obtaining by sense-enhancing technology any information regarding the interior of the home that could not otherwise have been obtained without physical "intrusion into a constitutionally protected area," *Silverman*, 365 U.S. at 512, constitutes a search—at least where (as here) the technology in question is not in general public use. This assures preservation of that degree of privacy against government that existed when the Fourth Amendment was adopted. On the basis of this criterion, the information obtained by the thermal imager in this case was the product of a search.

The Government maintains, however, that the thermal imaging must be upheld because it detected "only heat radiating from the external surface of the house." The dissent makes this its leading point, contending that there is a fundamental difference between what it calls "off-the-wall" observations and "through-the-wall surveillance." But just as a thermal imager captures only heat emanating from a house, so also a powerful directional microphone picks up only sound emanating from a house and a satellite capable of scanning from many miles away would pick up only visible light emanating from a house. We rejected such a mechanical interpretation of the Fourth Amendment in *Katz*, where the eavesdropping device picked up only sound waves that reached the exterior of the phone booth. Reversing that approach would leave the homeowner at the mercy of advancing technology—including imaging technology that could discern all human activity in the home. While the technology used in the present case was relatively crude, the rule we adopt must take account of more sophisticated systems that are already in use or in development. . . .

* * *

Where, as here, the Government uses a device that is not in general public use, to explore details of the home that would previously have been unknowable without physical intrusion, the surveillance is a "search" and is presumptively unreasonable without a warrant. Since we hold the Thermovision imaging to have been an unlawful search, it will remain for the District Court to determine whether, without the evidence it provided, the search warrant issued in this case was supported by probable cause—and if not, whether there is any other basis for supporting admission of the evidence that the search pursuant to the warrant produced.

The judgment of the Court of Appeals is reversed; the case is remanded for further proceedings consistent with this opinion.

CASE DISCUSSION QUESTIONS

1. What is the holding of this case?
2. Do citizens have a reasonable expectation of privacy as to heat generated in their homes that can be detected on the surface of the home's exterior? Why or why not?
3. How does law enforcement's use of Thermovision imaging differ from officers on a public street conducting naked-eye surveillance of a home?

DISCUSSION QUESTIONS

8. Under what circumstances, if any, do you think a roommate *should* be able to give permission to law enforcement authorities to conduct a search of an apartment that is shared with someone else?

9. Under what circumstances, if any, *should* principals and teachers be able to search students' clothing and personal effects when they are on school property?

10. Under what circumstances, if any, *should* one private person be able to make a video or audio recording of a conversation or an activity with someone else without notifying the other person that it is being recorded?

Exhibit 4.7: Application for Use of Eavesdropping Device

<u>PETITION FOR ORDER AUTHORIZING USE OF EAVESDROPPING DEVICE</u>

Petitioner, D. TRACY, a police officer with the City of Anytown, currently assigned to the Watterson County Drug Enforcement Unit, being duly authorized by the State's Attorney of Watterson County, requests the issuance of an order authorizing the use of an eavesdropping device. In support thereof he states as follows:

1. Petitioner has reasonable cause to believe that a felony has been or is about to be committed as follows: between the months of November 2010 into December 2010, specifically included but not limited to solicitation, conspiracy, unlawful delivery of a controlled substance, unlawful delivery of cocaine, unlawful delivery of a look-alike substance, unlawful possession of a controlled substance with intent to deliver, unlawful possession of cocaine, unlawful possession of cocaine with the intent to deliver, and or possession of a controlled substance and hereby states as follows in support thereof the following under oath:

2. Petitioner is a police officer with the city of Anytown. As a regular part of petitioner's duties, he regularly works with other law enforcement officers investigating sales and distribution of illegal drugs in the Watterson County area. During the course of an ongoing investigation, petitioner has been involved in working with a confidential source regarding illegal drug sales and distribution in the Watterson County area. The confidential source utilized in this investigation has been designated as Confidential Source 857 (hereinafter referred to as "CS 857").

A. On October 30, 2010, petitioner [and affiant] interviewed CS 857 about illegal drug activity in Watterson County involving the sale of crack cocaine. Specifically, CS 857 advised petitioner that CS 857 knows of an African American male who sells crack cocaine who is known to CS 857 as well, "Brandon Turner." CS 857 has bought crack cocaine from "Brandon Turner" a lot of times. CS 857 subsequently positively identified "Brandon Turner" from an EJS photograph. See attached Exhibit 1 incorporated by reference. CS 857 indicated to petitioner that Brandon Turner supplies crack cocaine and that CS 857 could buy any amount of crack cocaine from Brandon Turner but CS 857 usually buys 4 rocks at a time. See attached Exhibit 2 incorporated by reference for the report relating to the October 30, 2010 interview.

B. Specifically, on November 11, 2010, CS 857 made a FIRST CONTROLLED BUY of about 1.1 grams of crack cocaine (5 rocks) directly from Brandon Turner at 999 West First Street in the City of Anytown, Watterson County for the sum of $200.00. A subsequent field test indicated positive for the presence of cocaine. See attached Exhibits 3–6 herein incorporated by reference for the reports containing details relating to said November 11, 2010 FIRST CONTROLLED BUY.

3. CS 857 has agreed to permit the use of an overhear device during in-person and/or telephone conversations with Brandon Turner and/or any unknown others/associates as CS 857 may be directed by said suspects are working with petitioner and the Anytown Police Dept.

4. Petitioner has reasonable cause to believe that a conversation relating to a felony will be overheard as follows: CS 1857 has agreed to participate in arrangements for controlled buys of illegal drugs involving Brandon Turner and any unknown other associates as CS 857 may be directed by said suspects. Said controlled buys with petitioner or the Anytown Police Department will be conducted pursuant to standard law enforcement practice for such buys and in accordance with the aforementioned background, history, and information set forth in this petition.

5. The nature and approximate location of the facilities from which, or the place where the conversation is to take place or to be monitored, is via telephone or in-person conversations

with Brandon Turner and/or any other unknown associates or co-conspirators as CS 857 may be directed in Watterson County and any other locations/individuals as CS 857 may be directed.

6. The type of communication to be monitored is by telephone and/or in person.

7. CS 857 is the party to the expected conversations consenting to the use of the eavesdropping device.

8. The parties and locations, whose conversations are to be overheard by the eavesdropping device requested are as follows: CS 857, Brandon Turner, and/or any possible unknown other associates or co-conspirators as CS 857 may be directed are the parties whose conversations are to be overheard by the eavesdropping device.

9. The time period for the use of the eavesdropping device is from 2:00 p.m. on November 13, 2010 to 2:00 p.m. on December 13, 2010.

10. Petitioner knows of no other previous application requesting permission to use an eavesdropping device involving the same persons or circumstances as in the instant application referred to above by the court.

11. The nature of this investigation is such that any authorization granted pursuant to this petition should not terminate automatically in the event that calls or transactions are necessary in order to obtain needed statements within the 30-day scope of the said order.

_____

D. Tracy, Affiant/Petitioner

11. Under what circumstances, if any, *should* law enforcement officials be able to conduct "no-knock" searches?

5. PRESERVATION OF PHYSICAL EVIDENCE

In addition to collecting physical evidence in a manner that does not violate the Fourth Amendment, law enforcement authorities are also responsible for properly identifying and preserving that evidence. This means that it must be properly "tagged" and stored in a secure location prior to trial. It also means that an appropriate record must be kept of who had access to the evidence from the time it was first collected until the time it is introduced in court. This permits the prosecuting attorney to establish the "chain of custody" of the evidence.

Chain of custody is the chronological documentation of the whereabouts of evidence beginning at the time it comes into the possession of law enforcement authorities. The reason for keeping this record is to show that specific evidence is related to the offense in question. When tight controls are maintained, claims of evidence tampering are less likely to succeed.

Maintaining a proper chain of custody is particularly important in illegal drug cases. Attorneys prosecuting drug cases will present chain of custody documentation and testimony to show that the substance in evidence was indeed in the possession of the defendant. In preparation for trial, paralegals often prepare a synopsis of the chain of evidence to aid the prosecutor in laying the foundation for the admission of exhibits into evidence. The paralegal's synopsis of the chain of evidence in the Brandon Turner sample case is depicted in Exhibit 4.8.

Chain of custody
A record of who possessed an object being presented as evidence from the time it came into possession of government agents until it is presented in court.

Exhibit 4.8: Chain of Evidence Synopsis

MEMORANDUM

To: Grant Manchester, ASA
From: Paula Paralegal

RE: Brandon Turner Chain of Custody

Exhibit #1: (Lab No. M10-0001857) approximately 1.2 grams of purported crack cocaine in plastic sandwich bag:

11/08/10	Steve Milner to locked evidence drop chute at Illinois State Police Department Task Force Fifteen Unit Office
11/08/10	Task Force Fifteen drop chute to Watterson Forensic Science Lab via Special Agent Stevenson
11/18/10	Special Agent Stevenson to Scientist Denise Felmley

Exhibit #2: Vehicle title retrieved from car driven by Brandon Turner:

11/08/10	Steve Milner to locked evidence drop chute at Illinois State Police Department Task Force Fifteen Unit Office

Exhibit #3: Miscellaneous papers retrieved from car driven by Brandon Turner:

11/08/10	Steve Milner to locked evidence drop chute at Illinois State Police Department Task Force Fifteen Unit Office

Exhibit #4: One disc containing photos of the car driven by Brandon Turner:

11/08/10	Detective Gina DeGarmo created Exhibit #4.
11/08/10	Gina DeGarmo to locked evidence drop chute at Illinois State Police Department Task Force Fifteen Unit Office

Exhibit #5: (Lab No. M10-0001858) Smith & Wesson Model 10 revolver 160125, 38 Special:

11/08/10	Detective Gina DeGarmo to locked evidence drop chute at Illinois State Police Department Task Force Fifteen Unit Office
11/08/10	Task Force Fifteen drop chute to Watterson Forensic Science Lab via Special Agent Stevenson
11/18/10	Special Agent Stevenson to Scientist Wesley Horton

Exhibit #6: One disc containing photos of dining area and restroom located at the Normal Eatery, 857 Normal St., Anytown, Illinois:

11/08/10	Detective Gina DeGarmo created Exhibit #6.
11/08/10	Gina DeGarmo to locked evidence drop chute at Illinois State Police Department Task Force Fifteen Unit Office

APPLICATION EXERCISES

1. In the Cook Case (*see Introduction to Hypothetical Cases, p. xxxvii*):
   a. What type of law enforcement official would most likely have been sent out to follow up on the passerby's 911 call?
   b. When authorities arrived at the location at which the phone caller had reported seeing the body, they found that the body was that of someone who appeared to have been struck by a motor vehicle while riding a bicycle. What would typically be done to preserve and investigate the scene of the "accident"?
   c. Police also received a phone call from Cook's wife. What type of law enforcement official would most likely have been sent out to follow up on this call? What do you think that officer would do?

2. In the Turner case (*see Introduction to Hypothetical Cases, p. xxxvii*), a police officer followed Turner into a restaurant and met him at the restroom door when Turner came out after having been in the restroom for less than a minute.
   a. What do you think Officer Milner should do at this point? Why?
   b. Could the officer place Turner under arrest? If so, for what crimes?
   c. What, if any, types of searches could he conduct at this point?
   d. Suppose that Officer Milner had placed Turner under arrest and as he was escorting him out of the restaurant, someone from inside the restaurant called out to him that there was a gun in the restroom. What actions might Officer Milner take in light of this information about a gun being found in the restroom?

3. In the Edwards case (*see Introduction to Hypothetical Cases, p. xxxviii*):
   a. Suppose you were one of Bill Edwards's brokerage clients who began to get suspicious about some of the explanations he was giving you about transactions in your account. Other than simply moving your account to another financial advisor, what actions could you take to follow up on your suspicions?
   b. Now suppose that you are an investigator with the Securities and Exchange Commission. What types of things might you do to follow up on a complaint from one of Edwards's clients?

4. In the Schroeder Case (*see Introduction to Hypothetical Cases, p. xxxviii*):
   a. How might law enforcement authorities become aware of Schroeder's potential violations?
   b. What type of law enforcement personnel would most likely conduct any investigations into Schroeder's activities?
   c. What types of investigative tools would they be likely to use in this type of investigation?

5. Research statutes and court rules in your state to find out if they set out requirements for search warrants. Then provide a brief summary (with citations) of what you found.

6. Using the federal form located online at *http://www.uscourts.gov/forms/AO093.pdf*, prepare a search warrant and return for a federal case based on the information set forth in the Louisiana terrorism case featured in Exhibits 4.5 and 4.6.

SUMMARY

This chapter looked at the role played by police and other law enforcement personnel in identifying the people who commit crimes and in gathering sufficient evidence to warrant their arrest.

Law enforcement officers must carry out their responsibilities in line with the protections guaranteed by the U.S. Constitution. In particular, they must comply with the Fourth Amendment prohibition against unreasonable searches and seizures as well as the Fifth Amendment right of individuals accused of a crime to not be required to incriminate themselves.

Once government authorities learn that a crime has been committed, officers interview victims, witnesses, and suspects to piece together how it occurred. When government investigators question suspects, they must first give the *Miranda* warnings to ensure that the suspect statements are voluntary so that they can be used in court. Grand jury subpoenas are used in a criminal investigation to compel reluctant witnesses to give testimony.

Following the initial investigation, police officers may arrest a suspect. For an arrest to be proper, the officer must either have an arrest warrant or probable cause to believe the suspect committed the offense. Police can use reasonable force to carry out an arrest but are not permitted to use excessive force.

When a search warrant is issued by the court, officers execute it and file a return of the warrant. Law enforcement agents are excused from obtaining a search warrant when the search is consensual, the seized item is in plain view, there are exigent circumstances, or the seized item is discovered during the course of a *Terry* stop and frisk. If prosecutors want to conduct electronic surveillance, they must first apply to the court for the entry of an eavesdropping order.

Once evidence is retrieved from a search, it is inventoried and securely stored so that a chain of evidence can be established at trial.

INTERNET RESOURCES

Government Investigative Agencies

- Federal Bureau of Investigation: **http://www.fbi.gov/**
- Federal Bureau of Alcohol, Tobacco, Firearms, and Explosives: **http://www.atf.gov/**
- Interpol: **http://www.interpol.int/**
- U.S. Border Patrol: **http://www.cbp.gov/xp/cgov/bordersecurity/borderpatrol/**
- U.S. Drug Enforcement Administration: **http://www.justice.gov/dea/index.htm**
- U.S. Immigration and Customs Enforcement: **http://www.ice.gov/**
- U.S. Marshal's Service: **http://www.justice.gov/marshals/**

Crime Scene Investigations

- http://www.crime-scene-investigator.net/csi-photo.html
- http://science.howstuffworks.com/csi.htm
- Investigating child abuse and neglect
- http://www.childwelfare.gov/responding/iia/investigation/

Victim Assistance Services

- http://www.vaonline.org/

REVIEW QUESTIONS

1. How does procedural due process differ from substantive due process?
2. What are the Fourth Amendment requirements for the issuance of warrants?
3. Under what circumstances do government authorities typically learn that a crime has been committed?
4. As used in the Fourth Amendment, to what types of matters does a "seizure" apply?
5. What is a *Terry* stop? Under what set of circumstances can the police carry it out?
6. What constitutional provision gives individuals the right not to identify themselves when asked to do so by the police?
7. What are the *Miranda* warnings?
8. What effect does the failure to give the *Miranda* warnings have on defendant's case?
9. Compare transactional immunity with derivative use immunity.
10. What's the difference between a suspect and a defendant?
11. Name and explain the level of force the police are permitted to use when making an arrest.
12. What are the two alternative bases that law enforcement officers need to make an arrest under the Fourth Amendment?
13. What is a search warrant? How can a prosecutor obtain a search warrant?
14. What are the general showings that must be included in an application for a search warrant?
15. What is the name of the voluntarily written declaration of facts signed under oath or under penalty of perjury? What do you call the person signing this document?
16. What are the required contents for a search warrant issued in federal court?
17. What information would you expect to find in a return of a search warrant?
18. Explain the "plain view" and "exigent circumstances" exceptions to the requirement of a search warrant.
19. Why is maintaining a proper chain of evidence important in an illicit drug prosecution?

Chapter 5

The Prosecutor's Role in Initiating Cases

In the previous chapter we discussed the various ways in which law enforcement personnel become aware of activities that may constitute violations of the criminal law. We also saw how police agencies typically go about gathering the evidence that will be needed to convict the perpetrators of the crimes in court. However, while the police often make the decision to arrest someone for a crime, it falls to the appropriate **prosecuting attorney** ("prosecutor") to make the ultimate decision to initiate formal criminal charges and to manage the government's case in the court system. In this chapter we will focus on the role these prosecuting attorneys play in the preliminary stages of a criminal case. Although we will include some references to **defense attorneys**, we will focus more on their role in Chapter 6.

A. INTRODUCTION TO PROSECUTING ATTORNEYS

Prosecuting attorneys are lawyers who have been authorized to represent a particular unit of government in criminal court. They supervise and advise law enforcement agencies and grand juries in criminal investigations; they decide whether to charge a suspect with a crime and determine the appropriate charge; and they represent the government in court.

Prosecutor
The lawyer authorized to represent a particular unit of government in criminal court.

Defense attorney
The lawyer who represents a criminal defendant in court.

1. FEDERAL, STATE, AND LOCAL PROSECUTORS

U.S. Attorney
The chief federal law enforcement officer of the judicial district to which he or she is assigned. The U.S. Attorney is responsible for prosecuting persons accused of committing federal crimes.

U.S. Attorneys prosecute violations of federal law.[1] They are federal employees of the U.S. Department of Justice who report to the U.S. Attorney General. They are appointed by the President with the advice and consent of the Senate and continue in office at the pleasure of the President. Currently, there are ninety-three U.S. Attorneys who are assigned to specific judicial districts over which they serve as the chief federal law enforcement officer.[2] (The federal judicial districts are presented in Figure 5.1.)

U.S. Attorneys employ Assistant U.S. Attorneys and support staff, including paralegals, to carry out their duties. The number of attorneys in their offices and the scope of their geographic authority vary greatly. For instance, the U.S. Attorney's Office for the Southern District of New York has 170 Assistant U.S. Attorneys in its Criminal Division.[3] It has authority over seven counties plus part of New York City. In contrast, the Criminal Division for the District of Alaska consists of a criminal chief and twelve Assistant U.S. Attorneys.[4] This office is responsible for federal law enforcement for the entire state of Alaska.

The states have a parallel system of enforcing violations of law. However, the job title of the individual who is in charge of criminal prosecutions varies from state to state. They are known as district attorneys,[5] prosecuting attorneys,[6] state's attorneys,[7] state attorneys,[8] county prosecutors,[9] county attorneys,[10] commonwealth's attorneys,[11] solicitors,[12] and attorneys general.[13] In addition, some municipalities have city prosecutors who litigate local ordinance violations. Whereas U.S. Attorneys are appointed officials, attorneys general, district attorneys, and states' attorneys are usually elected officials. They then appoint their

---

[1]The U.S. Attorneys have three statutory responsibilities under 28 U.S.C. § 547: the prosecution of criminal cases brought by the federal government, the prosecution and defense of civil cases in which the United States is a party, and the collection of debts owed the federal government that are administratively uncollectible.

[2]One U.S. Attorney is assigned to each of the judicial districts, with the exception of Guam and the Northern Mariana Islands, where a single U.S. Attorney serves in both districts.

[3]U.S. Department of Justice Southern District of New York website, *www.usdoj.gov/usao/nys/divisions*.

[4]U.S. Department of Justice District of Alaska website, *www.usdoj.gov/usao/ak/criminal*.

[5]The following states designate their chief local prosecutors as district attorneys: Alabama, Alaska, California, Colorado, Georgia, Louisiana, Maine, Massachusetts, Mississippi, Nevada, New Mexico, New York, North Carolina, Oklahoma, Oregon, Pennsylvania, and Wisconsin.

[6]The following states designate their chief local prosecutors as prosecuting attorneys: Arkansas, Hawaii, Idaho, Michigan, Missouri, Ohio, Washington, and West Virginia.

[7]The following states designate their chief local prosecutors as state's attorneys: Connecticut, Illinois, Maryland, North Dakota, South Dakota, and Vermont.

[8]Florida is the only state that designates its chief local prosecutors as "state attorneys."

[9]Indiana and New Jersey use the title of "county prosecutor." Delaware County Prosecutors are part of the Attorney General's Office. Texas refers to its chief local prosecutors as county and/or district attorneys.

[10]The following states designate their chief local prosecutors as county attorneys: Arizona, Iowa, Kansas, Minnesota, Montana, Nebraska, New Hampshire, Utah, and Wyoming.

[11]Kentucky and Virginia refer to their chief local prosecutors as commonwealth's attorneys.

[12]South Carolina is the only state that refers to its chief local prosecuting official as solicitor.

[13]Rhode Island and Tennessee conduct local prosecutions through their attorney general offices.

District	Headquarters City	District	Headquarters City
Alabama, Middle	Montgomery	Montana	Billings
Alabama, Northern	Birmingham	Nebraska	Omaha
Alabama, Southern	Mobile	Nevada	Las Vegas
Alaska	Anchorage	New Jersey	Newark
Arizona	Phoenix	New Hampshire	Concord
Arkansas, Eastern	Little Rock	New Mexico	Albuquerque
Arkansas, Western	Fort Smith	New York, Eastern	Brooklyn
California, Central	Los Angeles	New York, Northern	Syracuse
California, Eastern	Sacramento	New York, Southern	Manhattan
California, Northern	San Francisco	New York, Western	Buffalo
California, Southern	San Diego	North Carolina, Eastern	Raleigh
Colorado	Denver	North Carolina, Middle	Greensboro
Connecticut	New Haven	North Carolina, Western	Asheville
Delaware	Wilmington	North Dakota	Fargo
Florida, Middle	Tampa	Ohio, Northern	Cleveland
Florida, Northern	Pensacola	Ohio, Southern	Cincinnati
Florida, Southern	Miami	Oklahoma, Eastern	Muskogee
Georgia, Middle	Macon	Oklahoma, Northern	Tulsa
Georgia, Northern	Atlanta	Oklahoma, Western	Oklahoma City
Georgia, Southern	Savannah	Oregon	Portland
Hawaii	Honolulu	Pennsylvania, Eastern	Philadelphia
Idaho	Boise	Pennsylvania, Middle	Scranton
Illinois, Central	Springfield	Pennsylvania, Western	Pittsburgh
Illinois, Northern	Chicago	Rhode Island	Providence
Illinois, Southern	East St. Louis	South Carolina	Columbia
Indiana, Northern	South Bend	South Dakota	Sioux Falls
Indiana, Southern	Indianapolis	Tennessee, Eastern	Knoxville
Iowa, Northern	Cedar Rapids	Tennessee, Middle	Nashville
Iowa, Southern	Des Moines	Tennessee, Western	Memphis
Kansas	Topeka	Texas, Eastern	Tyler
Kentucky, Eastern	Lexington	Texas, Northern	Fort Worth
Kentucky, Western	Louisville	Texas, Southern	Houston
Louisiana, Eastern	New Orleans	Texas, Western	San Antonio
Louisiana, Middle	Baton Rouge	Utah	Salt Lake City
Louisiana, Western	Shreveport	Vermont	Burlington
Maine	Portland	Virginia, Eastern	Alexandria
Maryland	Baltimore	Virginia, Western	Roanoke
Massachusetts	Boston	Washington, D.C.	Washington
Michigan, Eastern	Detroit	Washington, Eastern	Spokane
Michigan, Western	Grand Rapids	Washington, Western	Seattle
Minnesota	Minneapolis	West Virginia, Northern	Wheeling
Mississippi, Northern	Oxford	West Virginia, Southern	Charleston
Mississippi, Southern	Jackson	Wisconsin, Eastern	Milwaukee
Missouri, Eastern	St. Louis	Wisconsin, Western	Madison
Missouri, Western	Kansas City	Wyoming	Cheyenne

Districts outside the 50 states: Guam; Northern Mariana Islands; Puerto Rico; Virgin Islands

Figure 5.1   Federal Judicial Districts

Model Rules of Professional Conduct
A set of recommended ethics standards for attorneys promulgated by the American Bar Association. Most of the states have adopted some or all of the model rules.

assistants. Municipal attorneys are usually appointed by local government officials and often hold part-time positions.

Similar to U.S. Attorney offices, state and local prosecutors' offices vary in size and scope of geographic authority. Most state prosecutors' offices have divisions for handling certain types of cases, such as felony, misdemeanor, traffic, and juvenile. Many larger offices have specialized units for such matters as drug prosecutions, high-tech crime, gang activity, asset forfeiture, auto theft, and arson. Small, rural offices are staffed by the supervising public official, a few deputy attorneys, and clerical staff. Because of staffing limitations, these offices typically do not have divisions or specialized units.

Ethical Codes for Lawyers

All attorneys, regardless of the nature of their practice, are subject to ethical rules established and enforced by state supreme courts. Although the format and content of these ethical rules vary from state to state, they typically follow the general principles set out in the American Bar Association's **Model Rules of Professional Conduct**.

In the preface to these model rules, the ABA states that they are designed to ensure the highest standards of professional competence and ethical conduct within the legal profession. They cover topics ranging from how lawyers are suppose to interact with their client and with other lawyers to their responsibility to maintain the integrity of the profession and to see that justice is done. Key areas of concern relate to avoiding conflicts of interest, maintaining client confidentiality, diligently representing the client's interests, and not misusing the client's funds.

Ethical Obligations Specific to Prosecuting Attorneys

All attorneys are expected to be effective advocates for the interests of their clients, but what does that mean when, as in the case of prosecuting attorneys, the client is the people of the state or the people of the United States? Is it necessarily in the people's interest to prosecute every crime,

regardless of the cost, or to seek the maximum sentence for everyone convicted of a crime?

Even if prosecutors had enough budgetary resources to seek as many convictions as possible, the Model Code imposes various ethical limitations on the means by which they can obtain those convictions. Rule 3.8 of the Model Code lists a number of "special responsibilities" that go with being a prosecutor. These ethical duties include:

- Not prosecuting charges that are unsupported by probable cause;
- Making reasonable efforts to assure that defendants have been advised of their constitutional rights;
- Making timely disclosures to the defense of information known to the prosecutor that tends to "negate the guilt of the accused or mitigates the offense";
- Not making extrajudicial comments that are prejudicial to the defendant unless they serve a "legitimate law enforcement purpose."

Section (g), which applies in situations where a prosecutor knows of new, credible, and material evidence creating a reasonable likelihood that a convicted defendant did not commit an offense of which the defendant was convicted, and section

(h) which applies when a prosecutor knows of clear and convincing evidence establishing that a defendant in the prosecutor's jurisdiction was convicted of an offense that the defendant did not commit, will be discussed in Chapter 14 when we cover appeals.

The ABA Model Rules of Professional Conduct can be found on the ABA website at *http://www.americanbar.org/groups/professional_responsibility/publications/model_rules_of_professional_conduct/model_rules_of_professional_conduct_table_of_contents.html*

B. THE INVESTIGATIVE ROLE OF PROSECUTING ATTORNEYS

1. GENERAL INVESTIGATIVE RESPONSIBILITIES

Prosecutors are responsible for the overall coordination of criminal investigations. They must establish good working relationships with local police agencies and give them legal advice as to how they should go about gathering and preserving evidence. When they discover holes or weak points in their cases, prosecutors need to give directions to police or in-house investigators as to the types of additional evidence they need to gather. When physical evidence is sent to crime labs, the prosecutor's office is responsible for making sure the right tests are performed and determining what the results really mean.

2. APPLICATIONS FOR SEARCH WARRANTS

In Chapter 4, we discussed the function of search warrants and how they were prepared. Although there is wide variation as to the roles played by police, prosecutors, and paralegals in drafting some of these documents, it is clear that it is the prosecuting attorney who is ultimately responsible for presenting them to the court.

3. COORDINATION OF GRAND JURY ACTIVITIES

A **grand jury** is a group of citizens, usually consisting of between sixteen and twenty-three laypersons randomly selected from the community, who review the prosecutor's suggestions regarding whether specific individuals should be forced to stand trial for alleged criminal offenses and who initiate independent investigations of criminal activities.

Grand juries are part of our common law tradition. The Fifth Amendment to the U.S. Constitution requires that "[n]o person shall be held to answer for a capital, or otherwise infamous crime, unless on a presentment or indictment of a Grand Jury. . . . " Unlike most other sections of the Bill of Rights, the grand jury provisions of the Fifth Amendment do not apply to the states. About half the

Grand jury
A court-appointed panel composed of sixteen to twenty-three citizens that considers evidence presented by prosecutors and determines whether there is probable cause to bring formal criminal charges.

states use them. Other states allow the prosecutor the option of using or not using a grand jury; some do not use grand juries at all.

Generally, grand jury service is spread out over several months but does not involve meeting on consecutive days. Many grand juries meet once per week or every other week. Their proceedings are conducted in private.

The grand jury serves two basic functions. It was originally developed as a safeguard to prevent citizens from being forced to trial to defend themselves against unjustified criminal charges brought by irresponsible prosecutors. We will explore this part of their role later in this chapter. The second use is to provide assistance in certain types of investigative activities. This aspect of its use was covered in Section E of Chapter 4. The grand jury can theoretically decide on its own who it should investigate and select for itself who should be called as witnesses. In reality, however, grand jurors typically have little legal background, want to get their job over with as soon as possible, and have to rely extensively on the prosecutor's office for direction and assistance. Therefore, it is clearly up to the prosecutor to decide how they will be used.

As a paralegal in a prosecutor's office, you may be asked to prepare a subpoena to compel a witness to appear before a grand jury. This is a relatively simple task to perform. Most subpoenas are fill-in-the-blank forms, which are usually available from the clerk's office and oftentimes available online.[14] Your supervising attorney will give you the name of the witness along with the documents or other items that the witness must bring to the grand jury proceedings. An example of a subpoena issued by an investigative grand jury is depicted in Exhibit 5.1.

These types of grand jury investigations usually, but not always, result in someone being charged with one or more crimes. Sometimes the investigation will be left open until a future grand jury has gathered more information. At times, a grand jury will issue a report without an indictment. For instance, a federal grand jury investigating the deaths of Black Panther leaders in a raid by Chicago police led to the issuance of a public report rather than an indictment.

C. ROLE OF THE PROSECUTOR IN CHARGING THE DEFENDANT

Although law enforcement officers may bring minor charges against offenders, such as traffic citations and municipal code infractions, in most cases it is the prosecutor who determines if formal charges should be filed and what those charges should be.

1. THE DECISION TO CHARGE

As we saw in Chapter 4, most criminal cases begin with a law enforcement officer making an arrest on the basis of criminal activity that the

---

[14]The federal subpoena to appear before a grand jury is available online at *www.uscourts.gov/forms/AO110.pdf*.

Exhibit 5.1: Grand Jury Subpoena

Miss New Jersey for 2007, Amy Polumbo, claimed that she was blackmailed. It was alleged that a group, called "The Committee to Save Miss America," sent photographs from Polumbo's Facebook account to the pageant board. In its investigation, a New Jersey grand jury issued the following subpoena to a Florida radio station that communicated with a caller who claimed to have seen the incriminating photos and the blackmail letter.

Subpoena Duces Tecum
Superior Court of New Jersey

State of New Jersey)
) SS
County of Mercer)

TO: *Clear Channel Inc*
       WXTB, 98 Rock
       4002 West Gandy Blvd.
       Tampa, Fl 33611

           You are commanded to appear at: State Grand Jury
                             Richard J. Hughes Justice Complex
                             4th Floor, West Wing
                             25 Market Street
                             Trenton, NJ 08625

in the City of Trenton on 23   at   09:30 AM to give evidence before the State Grand Jury and you are ordered to appear without prepayment of witness fee and bring with you the following records: Audio tape containing conversation with caller identified as JT to Radio Host on the morning show on July 10, 2007 regarding information on the current Miss New Jersey investigation

       If you fail to appear and produce the said records, a warrant may be issued for your arrest and you may be charged with contempt.

       WITNESS, *the Honorable Linda R. Feinberg, Judge of the Superior Court,*

                 this 12 day of July , 20 07.

officer personally observed or on the basis of information the officer received that gave him or her probable cause to believe the person arrested had committed a crime. In these situations, the "initial charge" is determined by the police.

However, these "initial charges" are usually screened by the prosecutor's office before they are filed with the court. In rural areas prosecutors generally screen all criminal cases before any charges are filed; in large urban areas the police may file misdemeanor charges without prosecutorial review.[15] Screening of misdemeanor cases is typically carried out by a designated attorney in the prosecutor's office; felonies may by screened by either a single prosecutor or a committee. In conducting this review, the screeners examine the reports prepared by the investigating police officer as well as the charge stated when the accused was booked.

Following this screening process, the prosecutor's office can either go with the charge for which the person was arrested, modify the charge to better reflect the facts, or drop charges completely. Based on the police report shown in Exhibit 5.2, the prosecutor's office in Palm Beach County, Florida, chose not to file charges against radio talk show host Rush Limbaugh after he was arrested for allegedly possessing Viagra without a prescription.

2. ROLE OF THE GRAND JURY

Earlier in this chapter we explained the history of the use of grand juries and their role in conducting criminal investigations. Now we turn our attention to their role as a check on prosecutorial discretion.

Grand juries were originally designed to ensure that a person could not be detained for long periods of time and/or put through the ordeal of a trial solely on the discretion of prosecutors and judges appointed by the king or other non-elected public officials. Since most state and local prosecutors and many judges are now elected, it can be argued that there is no longer a need for this kind of democratic check.

Indictment jurisdictions
Jurisdictions in which defendants accused of committing felonies have the right to be indicted by a grand jury.

In federal court, the general rule is that the government must obtain and file an indictment from a grand jury within thirty days of the defendant's arrest unless the court extends the time.[16] The Fifth Amendment to the U.S. Constitution requires a grand jury indictment for all felony cases prosecuted by the federal government. U.S. Attorneys may prosecute misdemeanors by indictment but are not required to do so. Most states, on the other hand, do not require indictment by a grand jury for persons accused of committing felonies.[17] Eighteen states and the District of Columbia, classified as "**indictment jurisdictions**,"

---

[15]W. LaFave, J. Isreal & N. King, *Criminal Procedure* (4th ed., West Publishing 2004) at 13.

[16]18 U.S.C. § 3161(b).

[17]The U.S. Supreme Court has ruled that the grand jury clause of the Fifth Amendment does not apply to the states. *Hurtado v. California*, 110 U.S. 516, 4 S.Ct. 111, 28 L. Ed. 232 (1884).

Exhibit 5.2: Sample Police Report

```
4322                          07/05/06                          EMCH
      P A L M   B E A C H   C O U N T Y   S H E R I F F ' S   O F F I C E   PAGE   2
                 O F F E N S E   R E P O R T          CASE NO. 06082413
```

LATENTS LIFTED ?......... N   SUSPECT'S VEHICLE KNOWN ?.. N
TAG NUMBER KNOWN ?....... N   PROPERTY DAMAGE ?.......... N
EVIDENCE TAKEN BY .... D/S JULIANO #4279

ON JUNE 26TH, 2006, AT APPROXIMATELY 1643 HOURS, THE OFFENSE OF POSSESSION OF DRUGS WITHOUT A PRESCRIPTION OCCURRED, IN UNINCORPORATED WEST PALM BEACH, FLORIDA, PALM BEACH COUNTY, IN CONTRAVENTION OF FSS 499.03.

THE FACTS ARE AS FOLLOWS:

ON JUNE 26TH, 2006, AT APPROXIMATELY 1643 HOURS, I WAS ON DUTY IN MY UNIFORMED ASSIGNMENT PATROLLING PALM BEACH INTERNATIONAL AIRPORT (PBIA). I WAS NOTIFIED VIA POLICE RADIO TO RESPOND TO THE OFFICE OF U.S. CUSTOMS OFFICE, AT PBIA, REGARDING A PASSENGER AT A U.S. CUSTOMS CHECKPOINT IN POSSESSION OF PRESCRIPTION MEDICATION PRESCRIBED TO ANOTHER INDIVIDUAL. I MET WITH U.S. CUSTOMS AGENT ANN ASENIO, WHO STATED THAT SHE WAS ON DUTY PROCESSING SECONDARY INSPECTIONS AT THE U.S. CUSTOMS CHECKPOINT AT THE GENERAL AVIATION FACILITY WHEN SHE OBSERVED A MALE, LATER IDENTIFIED AS RUSH LIMBAUGH, BYPASSING THE INSPECTION AREA, AFTER DEBARKING THE PLANE FROM THE DOMINICAN REPUBLIC. SHE WATCHED AS MR. LIMBAUGH BYPASSED INSPECTION, THEN OPENED THE DOOR TO SPEAK WITH AN INDIVIDUAL STANDING OUTSIDE THE BUILDING. AGENT ASENIO APPROACHED MR. LIMBAUGH AND INFORMED HIM THAT HE HAD NOT BEEN INSPECTED AND WAS NOT CLEARED TO DEPART U.S. CUSTOMS. MR. LIMBAUGH PLACED HIS LUGGAGE ON THE COUNTER. UPON INSPECTION, AGENT ASENIO DISCOVERED A PRESCRITION MEDICATION BOTTLE DEPICTING THE NAME STEPHEN STORMWASSER THAT CONTAINED THE PRESCRIPTION DRUG VIAGRA. WHEN QUESTIONED BY AGENT ASENIO, MR. LIMBAUGH IDENTIFIED STEPHEN STORMWASSER AS HIS PSYCHIATRIST, WHO WAS NOT PRESENT WITH MR. LIMBAUGH. MR. LIMBAUGH TOLD AGENT ASENIO THAT THE PRESCRIPTION VIAGRA WAS GIVEN TO HIM BY HIS PSYCHIATRIST IN AN EFFORT TO PROTECT MR. LIMBAUGH'S PRIVACY. THESE STATEMENTS WERE WITNESSED BY SR. U.S. CUSTOMS AGENT CARL PICERNO. MR. LIMBAUGH WAS COOPERATIVE DURING THE ENCOUTER.

AGENT ASENIO DISCOVERED TWO OTHER PRESCRIPTION MEDICATION BOTTLES IN MR. LIMBAUGH'S LUGGAGE. THE OTHER PRESCRIPTION BOTTLES WERE PROPERLY PRESCRIBED TO MR. LIMBAUGH AND WERE RETURNED TO HIM ON SCENE BY CUSTOMS.

AGENT ASENIO SEIZED 29 PILLS OF VIAGRA 100 MG EACH FROM ONE BOTTLE LABELED VIAGRA IN THE NAME OF STEPHEN STORMWASSER. AGRNT ASENIO SURRENDERED THE EVIDENCE TO D/S JULIANO FOR PROCESSING AND RECEIPT.

I MET WITH MR. LIMBAUGH AT THE OFFICE OF U.S. CUSTOMS. THE MIRANDA RIGHTS WERE READ TO MR. LIMBAUGH FROM A PREPARED PBSO RIGHTS CARD, WHICH WAS SIGNED AND MAINTAINED AS EVIDENCE. MR. LIMBAUGH PROVIDED A SWORN WRITTEN STATEMENT CONSISTENT WITH THE STATEMENTS MADE TO THE U.S. CUSTOMS: TO WIT: "UPON CLEARING CUSTOMS AT PBIA, RETURNING FROM THE DOMINICAN REPUBLIC, CUSTOMS AGENT FOUND A BOTTLE OF VIAGRA PRESCRIBED TO ONE OF MY DOCTORS, NOT ME. I WAS TOLD THIS WAS A POSSIBLE VIOLATION OF THE LAW. WHEN HE ASKED ABOUT THIS, I TOLD THE AGENT THAT MY DOCTOR GOT THE PRESCRIPTION FOR VIAGRA FOR ME IN HIS NAME TO PROTECT MY PRIVACY GIVEN THE POTENTIAL EMBARASSING NATURE OF VIAGRA. THE AGENT CONFISCATED THE BOTTLE AND I ASSUMED AN INVESTIGATION BEGAN."

AFTER A BRIEF PERIOD OF QUESTIONING, MR. LIMBAUGH WAS LEFT IN THE CARE AND CONTROL OF THE U.S. CUSTOMS UNTIL THIS DEPUTY SHERIFF ARRIVED. THE FACTS AS REPORTED WILL BE PREPARED FOR PRESENTATION TO THE PALM BEACH COUNTY STATE ATTORNEY'S OFFICE FOR REVIEW AND CONSIDERATION. THE VIAGRA

Information jurisdictions
Jurisdictions in which prosecutors are authorized to initiate felony charges by either indictment or information.

True bill [of indictment]
The grand jury's determination that the evidence before it constitutes probable cause that an individual committed a crime.

No bill
The grand jury's determination that there is no probable cause that an individual committed a crime.

follow the approach taken in the federal system of justice and require indictments for all felony charges.[18] Four states require indictments only for serious felonies ("limited indictment jurisdictions").[19] The remaining twenty-eight states are categorized as "**information jurisdictions**." In these states, prosecutors are authorized to initiate felony charges by either indictment or information.

In the federal system and where states do use grand juries, there is little evidence that they in fact operate as much more than a rubber stamp for the prosecutor. Since most grand jurors have limited or no knowledge of the law and decisions are reached by a simple majority, they typically go along with whatever the prosecutor suggests. The vast majority of the time, the grand jury issues a "**true bill [of indictment]**," which signifies that the evidence before it constitutes probable cause that an individual committed a crime. On rare occasions, a grand jury votes "**no bill**," which means that it finds there is no probable cause to conclude that the person committed a crime.

In some situations, prosecutors use grand juries to provide cover for politically unpopular decisions.

DISCUSSION QUESTIONS

1. Do you think the grand jury is an effective check on prosecutorial discretion?
2. What are the pros and cons of continuing to use grand juries at either the federal or state levels?

3. TYPES OF CHARGING DOCUMENTS

Once the prosecutor, or the grand jury, has decided to go ahead with a formal prosecution, the prosecutor's office prepares an official charging document to be filed with the court. Depending upon the situation, it will either file a criminal complaint, an indictment, or an information.

Criminal complaint
A charge of the commission of a crime, made under oath.

Complainant
The person who signs a criminal complaint under oath attesting that the allegations of the complaint are true.

Magistrate
A judicial officer vested with limited authority to administer and enforce the law.

The **criminal complaint** is a charge, made under oath, alleging that the defendant committed a crime. Criminal complaints are prepared by the prosecutor's office and signed under oath by the **complainant**. Typically, the investigating officer or the victim is the complainant, although sometimes a prosecutor may sign the complaint. If the complainant does not have first-hand knowledge, he or she will declare the information contained in the document is true "on information and belief." In most cases, the complaint is a fairly brief document that simply alleges the accused committed specific acts in violation of a particular statute at a specified time and place.

In some jurisdictions, a criminal complaint on felony charges must be presented to a judge or **magistrate** before an arrest warrant is issued. In most jurisdictions, a felony complaint will be replaced by an indictment or information before the case goes to trial. Misdemeanor complaints typically remain the

---

[18]The eighteen indictment states are: Alabama, Alaska, Delaware, Georgia, Kentucky, Maine, Massachusetts, Mississippi, New Hampshire, New Jersey, New York, North Carolina, Ohio, South Carolina, Tennessee, Texas, Virginia, and West Virginia. W. LaFave, et al. at 744.

[19]*Id.* at 744.

charging instruments throughout the proceedings. Examples of criminal complaints filed in federal and state courts are depicted in Exhibits 5.3 and 5.4.

Exhibit 5.3: Federal Criminal Complaint

In late 2008, the U.S. Attorney for the Northern District of Illinois charged Illinois Governor Rod Blagojevich with wire fraud and solicitation arising out of an alleged "play to pay" scheme. Even though Blagojevich was the target of a grand jury probe for many months, the United States Attorney cited the importance of expeditiously charging the defendant even though an investigation continued. Although the supporting affidavit is over seventy pages long, the complaint itself is brief.

UNITED STATES DISTRICT COURT

<u>NORTHERN</u>   DISTRICT OF <u>ILLINOIS, EASTERN DIVISION</u>

UNITED STATES OF AMERICA	**UNDER SEAL**
V.	CRIMINAL COMPLAINT
ROD R. BLAGOJEVICH, and	
JOHN HARRIS	

I, the undersigned complainant being duly sworn state the following is true and correct to the best of my knowledge and belief.

Count One

From in or about 2002 to the present, in Cook County, in the Northern District of Illinois, defendants did conspire with each other and with others to devise and participate in a scheme to defraud the State of Illinois and the people of the State of Illinois of the honest services of ROD R. BLAGOJEVICH and JOHN HARRIS, in furtherance of which the mails and interstate wire communications would be used, in violation of Title 18, United States Code, Sections 1341,1343, and 1346; all in violation of Title 18 United States Code, Section 1349.

Count Two

Beginning no later than November 2008 to the present, in Cook County, in the Northern District of Illinois, defendants ROD R. BLAGOJEVICH and JOHN HARRIS, being agents of the State of Illinois, a State government which during a one-year period, beginning January 1, 2008 and continuing to the present, received federal benefits in excess of $10,000, corruptly solicited and demanded a thing of value, namely, the firing of certain Chicago Tribune editorial members responsible for widely-circulated editorials critical of ROD R. BLAGOJEVICH, intending to be influenced and rewarded in connection with business and transactions of the State of Illinois involving a thing of value of $5,000 or more, namely, the provision of millions of dollars in financial assistance by the State of Illinois, including through the Illinois Finance Authority, an agency of the State of Illinois, to the Tribune Company involving the Wrigley Field baseball stadium; in violation of Title 18, United States Code, Sections 666(a)(1)(B) and 2.

I further state that I am a Special Agent of the Federal Bureau of Investigation and that this complaint is based on the following facts:

SEE ATTACHED AFFIDAVIT

Continued on the attached sheet and made a part hereof: __X__ Yes _____ No

_____
Daniel W. Cain, Special Agent
Federal Bureau of Investigation

Sworn to before me and subscribed in my presence,

December 7, 2008   at   Chicago, Illinois
Date   City and State

MICHAEL T. MASON, United States Magistrate Judge
Name & Title of Judicial Officer Signature of Judicial Officer

Indictment
The formal criminal charge against a defendant returned by a grand jury. It is also referred to as "a bill of indictment."

The second type of charging instrument is the **indictment** (or "**bill of indictment**"). It differs from a criminal complaint in that it is technically issued by a grand jury, rather than the prosecutor, and is focused on explaining the charges to the defendant rather than convincing a judge to authorize an arrest. Like the criminal complaint, it alleges that the accused committed specific acts in violation of a particular statute at a specified time and place.

It is not unusual for the federal government to join misdemeanor charges with felony counts in a single indictment. In contrast to federal criminal complaints, federal indictments tend to be lengthy. Unlike state court indictments, federal indictments customarily recite detailed information that chronicles the defendant's alleged criminal conduct. Although an indictment officially comes from the members of the grand jury, the content of the document is prepared by a representative of the prosecutor's office and then presented to the grand jury for its approval. Exhibits 5.5 and 5.6 depict examples of indictments.

Exhibit 5.4: State Criminal Complaint

This is a copy of the first page of a criminal complaint charging the late pop superstar Michael Jackson with multiple counts of child molestation in 2003. After a highly publicized trial, a jury acquitted on all counts.

THE SUPERIOR COURT, STATE OF CALIFORNIA
For the County of Santa Barbara
Santa Maria Division

THE PEOPLE OF THE STATE OF CALIFORNIA

                           Plaintiff,

vs.

MICHAEL JOE JACKSON   DOB: 08/29/1958

                         Defendant.

DA No.   03-12-098996
Court No. 1133603

FELONY COMPLAINT
FILED
SUPERIOR COURT of CALIFORNIA
COUNTY OF SANTA BARBARA

DEC 1 8 2003

GARY M. BLAIR, EXEC. OFFICER
By _Wonda Strand_
WONDA STRAND, Deputy Clerk

The undersigned is informed and believes that:

COUNT 1

On or between February 7, 2003 and March 10, 2003, in the County of Santa Barbara, the crime of LEWD ACT UPON A CHILD, in violation of PENAL CODE SECTION 288(a), a Felony, was committed by MICHAEL JOE JACKSON, who did willfully, unlawfully, and lewdly commit a lewd and lascivious act upon and with the body and certain parts and members thereof of John Doe, a child under the age of fourteen years, with the intent of arousing, appealing to, and gratifying the lust, passions, and sexual desires of the said defendant and the said child.

COUNT 2

On or between February 7, 2003 and March 10, 2003, in the County of Santa Barbara, the crime of LEWD ACT UPON A CHILD, in violation of PENAL CODE SECTION 288(a), a Felony, was committed by MICHAEL JOE JACKSON, who did willfully, unlawfully, and lewdly commit a lewd and lascivious act upon and with the body and certain parts and members thereof of John Doe, a child under the age of fourteen years, with the intent of arousing, appealing to, and gratifying the lust, passions, and sexual desires of the said defendant and the said child.

COUNT 3

On or between February 7, 2003 and March 10, 2003, in the County of Santa Barbara, the crime of LEWD ACT UPON A CHILD, in violation of PENAL CODE SECTION 288(a), a Felony, was committed by MICHAEL JOE JACKSON, who did willfully, unlawfully, and lewdly commit a lewd and lascivious act upon and with the body and certain parts and members thereof of John Doe, a child under the age of fourteen years, with the intent of arousing, appealing to, and gratifying the lust, passions, and sexual desires of the said defendant and the said child.

1

Exhibit 5.5: State Court Indictment for Attempted Homicide

A New York grand jury indicted a woman for attempting to kill Martin Luther King, Jr. The assailant, later determined to be insane, stabbed King. Doctors performed a delicate operation to remove the tip of the letter opener that was pressed against his aorta.

Form 18-4(-5)( )

COURT OF GENERAL SESSIONS
COUNTY OF NEW YORK

- - - - - - - - - - - - - - - - - -X

THE PEOPLE OF THE STATE OF NEW YORK   :

       -against-   :

IZOLA WARE CURRY,   :

         Defendant.   :

- - - - - - - - - - - - - - - - - -X

THE GRAND JURY OF THE COUNTY OF NEW YORK, by this indictment, accuse the defendant of the crime of AN ATTEMPT TO COMMIT THE CRIME OF MURDER IN THE FIRST DEGREE, committed as follows:

The defendant, in the County of New York, on or about September 20, 1958, wilfully, feloniously, intentionally and with a deliberate and premeditated design to effect the death of Martin Luther King, attempted to kill said Martin Luther King by wilfully and wrongfully striking him with a knife.

                        FRANK S. HOGAN
                        District Attorney

Exhibit 5.6: State Court Indictment for Illegal Interception

A grand jury indicted Linda Tripp for recording Monica Lewinsky without her consent in violation of Maryland's wiretapping law. The tapes revealed that President Bill Clinton may have lied in his deposition in a sexual harassment suit. Clinton's alleged perjury was one of the bases for his impeachment. After the judge found that Lewinsky was not a credible witness, the prosecution dismissed the charges.

STATE OF MARYLAND,

     HOWARD COUNTY, TO WIT:

     The Grand Jurors of the State Of Maryland for the body of Howard County, do on their oath present that

          LINDA R. TRIPP,

late of said Howard County, did, on or about 22nd day of December, 1997, at Howard County aforesaid, wilfully and unlawfully intercept a wire communication in violation of Section 10-402(a), *Courts and Judicial Proceedings Article, Annotated Code of Maryland*, to wit: did tape record a telephone conversation between the said LINDA R TRIPP and Monica Lewinsky without the consent of the said Monica Lewinsky, a party to said conversation, contrary to the form of the Act of Assembly in such case made and provided and against the peace, government and dignity of the State.
(Illegal Interception, Section 10-402(a)(1), *Courts and Judicial Proceedings Article, Annotated Code of Maryland*)

SECOND COUNT

     And the Jurors aforesaid, upon their oath aforesaid, do further present that the said

          LINDA R. TRIPP,

did, between on or about 16th day of January, 1998 and on or about the 17th day of January, 1998, at Howard County aforesaid, through her agent, wilfully and unlawfully disclose the contents of the aforesaid wire communication to employees of *Newsweek* magazine and others, knowing and having reason to know that the information was obtained through the interception of a wire communication in violation of the Maryland Wiretapping and Electronic Surveillance Act, Sections 10-401, *et seq.*, *Courts and Judicial Proceedings Article, Annotated Code of Maryland*, to wit: did authorize and instruct her agent and attorney, James Moody, Esquire, to play the contents of said unlawful tape recording for *Newsweek* magazine reporters and others, which was done by the said James Moody, Esquire at the offices of *Newsweek* magazine in Washington, District of Columbia, on or about the 17th day of January, 1998, contrary to the form of the Act of Assembly in such case made and provided and against the peace, government and dignity of the State.
(Illegal Disclosure of Intercepted Communication, Section 10-402(a)(2), *Courts & Judicial Proceedings Article, Annotated Code of Maryland*)

                           Stephen Montanarelli
                           State Prosecutor

Information
The formal written charge presented by the prosecution without a grand jury indictment.

An **information** is the third type of charging instrument. An information is the formal written charge presented by the prosecutor's office without a grand jury indictment. This charging instrument is used in all jurisdictions for most misdemeanor charges. U.S. Attorneys and other indictment jurisdiction prosecutors may not charge felony defendants by information unless the accused waives the right to be indicted. Rule 7(b) of the Federal Rules of Criminal Procedure provides that a defendant may opt to be prosecuted by information by waiving indictment "in open court and after being advised of the nature of the charge and of the defendant's rights." The federal system and eleven of the states in indictment and limited indictment jurisdictions do not permit waiver in capital cases.[20]

The body of an information is virtually identical to the body of an indictment. Thus, federal felony informations tend to be lengthy, reciting the details of the defendant's alleged misconduct. On the other hand, federal misdemeanor informations as well as many state court informations are simply concise recitations of the alleged facts giving rise to an offense along with the citation to the applicable statutes. In this respect, the body portions of many state court informations resemble the bodies of criminal complaints. Exhibit 5.7 depicts an example of a federal misdemeanor information. Most state prosecutors' offices have standard forms that are used for each offense. Although the forms can be a tremendous timesaver, be mindful of the fact that a form may have to be tailored to the circumstances of a particular case. Use the form as an aid; do not feel compelled to follow portions of the form that do not apply to your case. When in doubt, ask your supervising attorney for guidance.

APPLICATION EXERCISE

1. Look up the provision(s) of your state's statutes or court rules that specify the essential requirements of a criminal charge.
   a. What are the essential requirements of a criminal charge in your state? [Include the citations as to where this information was found.]
   b. What types of charging documents are used in your state? (Include the citations to the authority for each document.)
   c. Is your state an indictment jurisdiction, limited indictment jurisdiction, or an information jurisdiction? Cite the statutory (or constitutional) authority that supports your conclusion.

---

4. PREPARATION OF CHARGING DOCUMENTS

The prosecutor's office typically prepares the charging documents, furnishes a copy to the defendant, and files the original with the clerk of the court. Paralegals

---

[20]FRCrP 7; LaFave, W., et al. at 746.

Exhibit 5.7: Federal Misdemeanor Information

The U.S. Attorney for the Eastern District of New York charged a man with the theft of Theodore Roosevelt's Colt revolver that was on display at a federal historical museum. The defendant pleaded guilty. He was fined and sentenced to probation.

CR 06 746

MJL:LTG
F.#2006R01134

UNITED STATES DISTRICT COURT
EASTERN DISTRICT OF NEW YORK

- - - - - - - - - - - - - - - - - -X

UNITED STATES OF AMERICA

   - against -

ANTHONY TULINO,

         Defendant.

- - - - - - - - - - - - - - - - -X

FILED
IN CLERK'S OFFICE
U.S. DISTRICT COURT E.D.N.Y.

★   NOV 1 3 2006   ★

LONG ISLAND OFFICE

MISDEMEANOR
INFORMATION

Cr. No. _____
(T. 16, U.S.C., § 433;
T. 18, U.S.C., §§ 3551 et
seq.)

TOMLINSON, M

THE UNITED STATES ATTORNEY CHARGES:

     In and about April 1990, within the Eastern District of New York, the defendant ANTHONY TULINO knowingly and intentionally, without the permission of the Secretary of the United States Department of the Interior, appropriated an object of antiquity, to wit: an 1895 Colt revolver (the "revolver") bearing serial number 334 and inscriptions stating that the revolver was recovered "from the sunken Battleship Maine," and that on "July 1, 1898, San Juan, [the revolver was] carried and used by Colonel Theodore Roosevelt," which revolver had been situated on lands owned and controlled by the Government of the United States, to wit: Sagamore Hill National Historical Site, Oyster Bay, New York.

     (Title 16, United States Code, Section 433; Title 18, United States Code, Sections 3551 et seq.)

ROSLYNN R. MAUSKOPF
UNITED STATES ATTORNEY
EASTERN DISTRICT OF NEW YORK

are often involved in drafting and filing them. Charging documents, like most other documents filed in a court, typically include the following components:

- Caption
- Introductory paragraph
- Body
- Signature section
- Address block/preparer's data

Refer back to Exhibits 5.3 to 5.7 for illustrations of these different sections.

Caption
The section of a court document containing the names of the parties, case number, name of the court it is being filed in, and a title that identifies the type of document being filed.

The **caption** of a case includes the name of the court, the title of the action with the file number, and the name of the document. Because there are variations from court to court, you should look at other filed documents in your jurisdiction as a guide to local custom and practice.

The name of the court is placed on the line at the top of the page. In federal court, the name of the court includes the district and division. For instance, Chicago is in the Northern District of Illinois, Eastern Division. In state court, the court name includes the name of the state and may include the district or circuit as well as the county or parish. For example, a Chicago suburban court caption may reference the State of Illinois, Twelfth Judicial Circuit, and Will County.

The caption also includes the full names of all of the parties in all capital letters. The title is presented on the left side of the caption. The party initiating the federal criminal prosecution will always be listed as "UNITED STATES OF AMERICA." In state court, the prosecuting authority is oftentimes listed as the "PEOPLE OF THE STATE [or COMMONWEALTH] OF [Name of State]." Following the designation of the prosecuting authority, a line is skipped and the word "versus" or its abbreviation is centered under the government's name. Then the next line is skipped and the name of the person accused of the crime is set forth. The term "Defendant" appears on the next line. This designation is presented in lowercase type.

The case number appears on the right side of the page opposite the title of the action. This number is assigned by the court. The first document filed in a case, such as a complaint, does not have a number when it is initially presented to the clerk of the court. When the clerk accepts the document, the clerk will affix a case number in the caption. Once assigned, the case number must be included in the caption of future documents filed in the case. The case number usually includes a reference to the year in which a document is filed, the type of case, as well as the chronological order of filing. For instance, in a downstate Illinois county, the 150th criminal felony case filed in the year 2005 would be identified as 05 CF 150. Other jurisdictions may include a reference to the division of a court in the case number. A vertical line divides the title. Usually the line is formed by a series of closing parentheses marks—)—placed under each other.

In most jurisdictions, the name for the type of document being filed appears centered below the official title of the court in which it is being filed. In some jurisdictions, the name for the type of document being filed appears in the caption section under the case name. An example of a caption is depicted in Exhibit 5.8.

In most court documents, an introductory paragraph appears directly under the caption. This is ordinarily a one- or two-sentence paragraph that identifies the party who authored the document and succinctly explains the purpose of the

---

Exhibit 5.8: Sample Caption

THE UNITED STATES DISTRICT COURT
FOR THE NORTHERN DISTRICT OF ILLINOIS,
EASTERN DIVISION

UNITED STATES OF AMERICA	)	
	)	
vs.	)	Case No. 10 CR XXX
	)	
BRANDON TURNER,	)	
Defendant.	)	

BILL OF INDICTMENT

---

document. For criminal charges, the introductory paragraph may simply be an attestation by the officer who is verifying the contents of the document, as follows: "I, the undersigned complainant being duly sworn, state the following is true and correct to the best of my knowledge and belief." An introductory paragraph of a bill of indictment might read: "The Grand Jurors of the State of [Name of State] and of the County of [Name of County], attending the Court aforesaid, upon their oaths present the following true bill of indictment against the Defendant [Name]."

The next component of a court document is the body, the most important part. It presents the basis for the relief sought in motions, the information requested in discovery, and the substance of an accusation in a charging document. The body is typically presented in concise, numbered paragraphs. Later in this chapter, we show you how to draft the body of a charging document.

Following the body, there is a place for a signature. This section also references the party's name and designation in the case (e.g., United States of America, Defendant). For bills of indictment, the foreman of the grand jury may provide the signature. In many jurisdictions, the person who signs a charging document must do so under oath or under penalties of perjury.

After the signature section is the **address block**, also know as the preparer's data. The address block identifies the attorney responsible for the preparation of the document, the party that the attorney represents, the address, and the telephone number. In many jurisdictions, the attorney's signature appears on the right side of the page and the address block is on the left side. In other venues, the address block may appear immediately after the attorney's name. A sample of the signature section and address block can be seen in Exhibit 5.9.

For any of the three types of charging documents, the body must set forth information specific enough to adequately apprise the defendant of the offense

Address block
The portion of a court document that identifies the attorney responsible for the preparation of the document, the party that the attorney represents, the address, and the telephone number. The address block is also known as the preparer's data.

Exhibit 5.9: Sample Signature and Address Block

Respectfully submitted,

BRANDON TURNER,
Defendant

By_____

CHARLES HOVEY,
his attorney

CHARLES HOVEY
Attorney for Defendant
1857 Bone Street
Normal, IL 61761
(309) 555-1857

---

being charged against him or her. For example, in Illinois, a criminal charge must include the following information:

- Name of the offense
- Statute alleged to have been violated
- Nature and elements of the charged offense
- Date and county of the offense
- Name or a detailed description of the accused[21]

You should refer to your jurisdiction's statutes to find the requirements for your state.

If the government claims that the defendant committed more than one offense, the body of the charging document should include a separate **count** for each alleged offense. Each count is designated with subtitles, such as "Count I," "Count Two," or "Third Count." If only one charge is alleged, no count subtitle is used. Consult your supervisor to learn the appropriate style for your office. Exhibit 5.6 depicts an indictment charging two separate counts (see Section C.3 of this chapter.)

Most prosecuting attorneys' offices rely on law enforcement agencies to conduct the initial investigation before opening a case file. Accordingly, the prosecutor has the benefit of the investigating officer's reports plus witness

Count
A subsection of the body of a charging document that alleges the defendant's commission of a crime and sets out all of the required elements of an offense.

---

[21]725 ILCS 5/111-3.

statements and summaries when a case is presented. The information contained in these documents is usually sufficient to prepare a charging document.

If you are requested to prepare the charge, you should carefully read the officer's report and materials and make note of the charge that the officer thought was appropriate. Before drafting the charge, you should refer to the criminal code of your jurisdiction to determine whether the conduct reported satisfies all of the elements of the offense suggested by the officer or any other offense. You also should consult charges filed in other cases to familiarize you with the customary drafting style used in your office. Most prosecutors' offices have form books that contain examples of complaints, informations, and indictments for most offenses in their jurisdiction. In addition, most offices keep examples of charging documents they have filed. Use these examples wisely to prepare your assignment. After you have prepared your draft, carefully proofread it for accuracy. Be especially mindful of dates and the spelling of proper names. Careless draftsmanship may result in dismissal of the charge.

Once the court document is in final form, it is filed with the clerk of the court. Traditionally, this has meant that the original of the document was accepted by the clerk and placed in the individual file of the case. At the time of acceptance the clerk's office would have stamp-filed the document to show the date and time of receipt. The filer would also have presented one or more copies of the document to the clerk so that that they could also be date- and time-stamped. The filer would retain the copy to document the filing.

The federal courts and many state courts now require that documents be e-filed. In the federal system, the U.S. District Clerk accepts PDF documents for online filing. Filed documents are available to the public through a service known as Public Access to Court Electronic Records (**PACER**) offered by the Administrative Office of the U.S. Courts. This is an online public-access service that permits users to retrieve case and docket information from the federal courts and the U.S. Party/Case Index.[22]

For both traditional and e-filing jurisdictions, the filer must also present to the court proof of service of a copy of the document to the opposing party. If the document is the first paper filed in the case, the prosecutor typically files a **return of service**. This is a sworn statement from the person who personally served the document on the defendant. For all other documents, the parties file a **proof of service**, sometimes referred to as a "certificate of service." This is a sworn statement by a member of the attorney's office attesting to the service of the document on the opposing side by mail, personal delivery, or other means.[23] You can use the language of proofs of service filed in prior cases as a guide for the format used in your jurisdiction. A sample proof of service is displayed in Exhibit 5.10.

PACER
The acronym for Public Access to Court Electronic Records, an online public-access service that permits users to retrieve case and docket information from the federal courts and the U.S. Party/Case Index.

Return of service
The written verification establishing that a document has been served.

Proof of service
A sworn statement by a member of the attorney's office attesting to the service of the document on the opposing side by mail, personal delivery, or other means.

---

[22]An overview of PACER and information as to registration for this service is available at *http://pacer .psc.uscourts.gov/pacerdesc.html*.

[23]Although service by facsimile is allowed in some circumstances, not all jurisdictions permit it and those that permit it may limit its use.

Exhibit 5.10: Sample Proof of Service

<u>PROOF OF SERVICE</u>

UNDER PENALTIES OF PERJURY and pursuant to the provisions of [citation], the undersigned hereby certifies that he/she served the [name of document] by depositing a copy thereof into a U.S. Post Office mailbox in [city and state] in an envelope, postage fully prepaid, addressed to:

[Name of Opposing Counsel]

[Address of Opposing Counsel]

on the _____ day of_____, 20_____ at or about the hour of _____ p.m.

*[S]*_____

D. ROLE OF THE PROSECUTOR IN ISSUING ARREST WARRANTS AND SUMMONS

When a formal charge is issued against an individual who is not already in police custody, the prosecutor's office will prepare an arrest warrant or a criminal summons to be presented to a judge. Typically, these documents are "fill-in-the-blank forms." Hard copies of forms are usually available at the office of the clerk of the court. Many courts also make forms available online.[24]

An **arrest warrant** is an order issued by a court that authorizes the arrest and detention of an individual. Ordinarily, the court issues the warrant at the request of the prosecutor and/or a law enforcement officer. There must be probable cause in order for the court to have authority to issue the warrant. Many times, an arrest warrant is served on the defendant with the formal criminal charge.

A **bench warrant** is a special type of arrest warrant that authorizes the arrest of someone for failing to show for a court appearance. It can be entered in civil as well as criminal cases and may be issued against parties as well as witnesses. Because a bench warrant is a judicial instrument imposed in response to a person's disobedience to a court order, it need not be accompanied by a criminal charge.

Arrest warrant
A court order issued at the request of the prosecutor and/or law enforcement that authorizes the arrest and detention of an individual.

Bench warrant
A court order that authorizes the arrest of someone for failing to show for a court appearance.

---

[24]The federal warrant for arrest form may be found at *http://www.uscourts.gov/forms/AO442.pdf*. The federal criminal summons is available at *http://www.uscourts.gov/forms/AO083.pdf*.

APPLICATION EXERCISES

2. Prepare a caption, introductory paragraph, signature section, and address block/preparer's data for an indictment that would be filed in the Bill Edwards case (see Introduction to Hypothetical Cases, p. xxxviii). Assume that the case is to be filed in the federal district in which your school is located and that the current U.S. Attorney for the district is the prosecutor. (Do not prepare the body portion of the indictment.)

3. Draft the caption, introductory paragraph, signature section, and address block/preparer's data (not the body) for a state criminal complaint against Bill Edwards (see p. xxxviii of the Introduction to Hypothetical Cases). Assume he is being prosecuted for criminal fraud and embezzlement under the law of your state, that the prosecuting authority for the locality (county, parish, etc.) where your school is located is filing the complaint, and that you are the complainant.

4. Draft the body of a drunk driving criminal complaint to be filed in your state based on the facts given in the Bud Cook sample case (see p. xxxvii). Assume that the incident took place in the community in which your school is located and that the offense occurred on the 5th day of last month.

5. Draft the body of a criminal complaint against Bud Cook for the applicable homicide charge for your state (e.g., reckless homicide, involuntary manslaughter). Assume that the incident took place in the community in which your school is located and that the offense occurred on the 5th day of last month.

6. Prepare a one-count state complaint charging Brandon Turner with the lowest grade of felony for possession of crack cocaine. Assume that the incident took place in the community in which your school is located and that the offense occurred on the 13th day of last month. The top local prosecutor for your community is bringing the charge.

7. Prepare a two-count federal complaint charging Turner with (a) the felony of possession of crack cocaine with intent to deliver and (b) the felony of possession of a firearm by a convicted felon. Assume that the incident took place in the community in which your school is located and that the offense occurred on the 13th day of last month. It will be filed by the U.S. Attorney for the district in which your school is located.

A **criminal summons** is a less intrusive means of obtaining jurisdiction over a person in a criminal case. As part of the arrest process, the individual is taken into custody, where he is searched, fingerprinted, photographed, and interviewed for demographic information. When a criminal summons is used, on the other hand, the accused party is simply directed to appear in court at a set date and time to answer the charges made against him or her. The summons and a copy of the charges are delivered to the accused at the same time.

Criminal summons
A document issued under a court order that directs the accused to appear in court to answer the charges made against him or her.

APPLICATION EXERCISES

8. Use the federal form found at *http://www.uscourts.gov/forms/ AO442.pdf* to prepare an arrest warrant for the defendant in the Tom Schroeder case (see p. xxxviii). Assume that the U.S. Attorney for the district in which your school is located is the prosecutor and that the defendant resides at 123 Main Street in this community.

9. Use the federal form found at *http://www.uscourts.gov/forms/AO083.pdf* to prepare a criminal summons for the defendant in the Tom Schroeder case. Assume the U.S. Attorney for the district in which your school is located is the prosecutor, the defendant resides at 123 Main Street in this community, and the defendant must appear in court on the first Wednesday of next month at 9:30 A.M. on an indictment for securities fraud.

E. THE INITIAL APPEARANCE AND SETTING BAIL

Initial appearance
The first time a person charged with a crime appears before a judge. This is also referred to as a "first appearance."

Within a "reasonable" period of time, persons who have been arrested must be taken before a judge and informed of the charges against them, their right to counsel, and the opportunity to have a reasonable bail set. This hearing is often referred to as the **initial appearance**. Depending on the jurisdiction, the judge will also schedule a date for either an arraignment or a preliminary hearing.

1. TIMING OF THE INITIAL APPEARANCE

The prosecutor has a duty to act in an expedient manner so that the accused can post bond promptly after arrest. But what constitutes a "reasonable" period of time? Read the following U.S. Supreme Court case to see how it interpreted what is meant by "promptly after arrest."

County of Riverside v. McLaughlin
Supreme Court of the United States
500 U.S. 44 (1991)

JUSTICE O'CONNOR delivered the opinion of the Court.

In *Gerstein* v. *Pugh*, 420 U.S. 103, 43 L. Ed. 2d 54, 95 S. Ct. 854 (1975), this Court held that the Fourth Amendment requires a prompt judicial determination of probable cause as a prerequisite to an extended pretrial detention following a warrantless arrest. This case requires us to define what is "prompt" under *Gerstein*.

I

This is a class action brought under 42 U.S.C. § 1983 challenging the manner in which the

County of Riverside, California (County), provides probable cause determinations to persons arrested without a warrant. At issue is the County's policy of combining probable cause determinations with its arraignment procedures. Under County policy, which tracks closely the provisions of Cal. Penal Code Ann. § 825 (West 1985), arraignments must be conducted without unnecessary delay and, in any event, within two days of arrest. This 2-day requirement excludes from computation weekends and holidays. Thus, an individual arrested without a warrant late in the week may in some cases be held for as long as five days before receiving a probable cause determination. Over the Thanksgiving holiday, a 7-day delay is possible.

* * *

In March 1989, plaintiffs asked the District Court to issue a preliminary injunction requiring the County to provide all persons arrested without a warrant a judicial determination of probable cause within 36 hours of arrest. 1 App. 21. The District Court issued the injunction, holding that the County's existing practice violated this Court's decision in *Gerstein*. Without discussion, the District Court adopted a rule that the County provide probable cause determinations within 36 hours of arrest, except in exigent circumstances. The court "retained jurisdiction indefinitely" to ensure that the County established new procedures that complied with the injunction. 2 App. 333-334.

The United States Court of Appeals for the Ninth Circuit * * * determined that the County's policy of providing probable cause determinations at arraignment within 48 hours was "not in accord with *Gerstein*'s requirement of a determination 'promptly after arrest'" because no more than 36 hours were needed "to complete the administrative steps incident to arrest." *Id.*, at 1278.

* * *

In *Gerstein*, this Court held unconstitutional Florida procedures under which persons arrested without a warrant could remain in police custody for 30 days or more without a judicial determination of probable cause. In reaching this conclusion we attempted to reconcile important competing interests. On the one hand, States have a strong

interest in protecting public safety by taking into custody those persons who are reasonably suspected of having engaged in criminal activity, even where there has been no opportunity for a prior judicial determination of probable cause. 420 U.S. at 112. On the other hand, prolonged detention based on incorrect or unfounded suspicion may unjustly "imperil [a] suspect's job, interrupt his source of income, and impair his family relationships." *Id.*, at 114. We sought to balance these competing concerns by holding that States "must provide a fair and reliable determination of probable cause as a condition for any significant pretrial restraint of liberty, and this determination must be made by a judicial officer either before *or promptly after* arrest." *Id.*, at 125 (emphasis added).

The Court thus established a "practical compromise" between the rights of individuals and the realities of law enforcement. *Id.*, at 113. Under *Gerstein*, warrantless arrests are permitted but persons arrested without a warrant must promptly be brought before a neutral magistrate for a judicial determination of probable cause. *Id.*, at 114. Significantly, the Court stopped short of holding that jurisdictions were constitutionally compelled to provide a probable cause hearing immediately upon taking a suspect into custody and completing booking procedures. We acknowledged the burden that proliferation of pretrial proceedings places on the criminal justice system and recognized that the interests of everyone involved, including those persons who are arrested, might be disserved by introducing further procedural complexity into an already intricate system. *Id.*, at 119-123. Accordingly, we left it to the individual States to integrate prompt probable cause determinations into their differing systems of pretrial procedures. *Id.*, at 123-124.

* * *

Given that *Gerstein* permits jurisdictions to incorporate probable cause determinations into other pretrial procedures, some delays are inevitable. For example, where, as in Riverside County, the probable cause determination is combined with arraignment, there will be delays caused by paperwork and logistical problems. Records will have to be reviewed, charging documents drafted, appearance of counsel arranged, and appropriate bail determined. On weekends, when the number of arrests is often higher and available resources tend to be limited, arraignments may get pushed back even further. In our view, the Fourth Amendment permits a reasonable postponement of a probable cause determination while the police cope with the everyday problems of processing suspects through an overly burdened criminal justice system.

But flexibility has its limits; *Gerstein* is not a blank check. A State has no legitimate interest in detaining for extended periods individuals who have been arrested without probable cause. The Court recognized in *Gerstein* that a person arrested without a warrant is entitled to a fair and reliable determination of probable cause and that this determination must be made promptly.

* * *

Our task in this case is to articulate more clearly the boundaries of what is permissible under the Fourth Amendment. Although we hesitate to announce that the Constitution compels a specific time limit, it is important to provide some degree of certainty so that States and counties may establish procedures with confidence that they fall within constitutional bounds. Taking into account the competing interests articulated in *Gerstein*, we believe that a jurisdiction that provides judicial determinations of probable cause within 48 hours of arrest will, as a general matter, comply with the promptness requirement of *Gerstein*. For this reason, such jurisdictions will be immune from systemic challenges.

This is not to say that the probable cause determination in a particular case passes constitutional muster simply because it is provided within 48 hours. Such a hearing may nonetheless violate *Gerstein* if the arrested individual can prove that his or her probable cause determination was delayed unreasonably. Examples of unreasonable delay are delays for the purpose of gathering additional evidence to justify the arrest, a delay motivated by ill will against the arrested individual, or delay for delay's sake. In evaluating whether the delay in a particular case is unreasonable, however, courts must allow a substantial degree of flexibility. Courts cannot ignore the often unavoidable delays in transporting arrested persons from one facility to another, handling late-night bookings where no magistrate is readily available, obtaining the presence of an arresting officer who may be busy processing other suspects or securing the premises of an arrest, and other practical realities.

Where an arrested individual does not receive a probable cause determination within 48 hours, the calculus changes. In such a case, the arrested individual does not bear the burden of proving an unreasonable delay. Rather, the burden shifts to the government to demonstrate the existence of a bona fide emergency or other extraordinary circumstance. The fact that in a particular case it may take longer than 48 hours to consolidate pretrial proceedings does not qualify as an extraordinary circumstance. Nor, for that matter, do intervening weekends. A jurisdiction that chooses to offer combined proceedings must do so as soon as is reasonably feasible, but in no event later than 48 hours after arrest.

* * *

For the reasons we have articulated, we conclude that Riverside County is entitled to combine probable cause determinations with arraignments. The record indicates, however, that the County's current policy and practice do not comport fully with the principles we have outlined. The County's current policy is to offer combined proceedings within two days, exclusive of Saturdays, Sundays, or holidays. As a result, persons arrested on Thursdays may have to wait until the following Monday before they receive a probable cause determination. The delay is even longer if there is an intervening holiday. Thus, the County's regular practice exceeds the 48-hour period we deem constitutionally permissible, meaning that the County is not immune from systemic challenges, such as this class action.

As to arrests that occur early in the week, the County's practice is that "arraignment[s] usually take place on the last day" possible. 1 App. 82. There may well be legitimate reasons for this practice; alternatively, this may constitute delay for delay's sake. We leave it to the Court of Appeals and the District Court, on remand, to make this determination.

The judgment of the Court of Appeals is vacated, and the case is remanded for further proceedings consistent with this opinion.

It is so ordered.

CASE DISCUSSION QUESTIONS

1. Which Supreme Court Justice authored this opinion?
2. What court decided immediately before the U.S. Supreme Court considered the case?
3. In reaching its decision, the Supreme Court interpreted *Gerstein v. Pugh*. What is the holding in *Gerstein*?
4. What did the Supreme Court conclude about propriety of the county's practice of combining probable cause determinations with arraignments?
5. What is the holding of the case?
6. If an individual arrested on state criminal charges does not receive a probable cause determination within 48 hours, what burden of proof does the Supreme Court impose upon the prosecutor?

2. BAIL AND ITS ALTERNATIVES

Bail is security paid on behalf of the accused that is pledged to guarantee that the accused will appear in court for scheduled proceedings. The purpose of bail is not to punish the accused and the Eighth Amendment to the U.S. Constitution prohibits the setting of excessive bail.

Factors that are considered in setting the amount of bail include the seriousness of the crime charged, the strength of the prosecution's evidence, the defendant's prior criminal record, the likelihood the defendant will appear in court, the accused's ties to the community, his or her employment, and the accused's financial circumstances. Sometimes the judge will even agree to release the defendant on his or her **own recognizance** (O.R.). In these situations, the defendants are released on the basis of their simple promise to appear.

Paralegals working for the prosecutor's office and for defense attorneys are often asked to research the defendant's prior record and organize key police reports in anticipation of the hearing. Paralegals employed by defense attorneys often gather information from the accused and family members regarding their family situation and financial resources.

Courts generally give great weight to the prosecution's recommendation in setting bail, and defense attorneys sometimes seek bail agreements with prosecutors prior to the hearing. Depending upon the jurisdiction involved, bail can be posted in the form of cash, a bond posted by a professional bail bondsman, or deeds to real estate property. If the defendant fails to appear, the judge will issue a bench warrant and the prosecutor will petition to revoke bail. If the petition is granted, bail is forfeited. A defendant released on bail or on recognizance may be subject to certain conditions such as non-contact with the alleged victim and witnesses, denial of the right to possess a firearm, prohibition from violating the law, etc.

The federal Bail Reform Act of 1984[25] creates the procedure that the federal courts follow to determine whether the defendant should be released or detained prior to trial. The federal government may keep an accused in custody for three days by seeking detention and a continuance of the detention hearing.[26]

Bail
Money or something else of value that is pledged to guarantee that the accused will appear in court for scheduled proceedings.

Own recognizance (OR) [also known as Personal recognizance bond]
A defendant's promise to appear in court without posting cash or other security.

---

[25] 18 U.S.C. §§ 3141 *et seq.*
[26] 18 U.S.C. § 3142(f).

Under the act, the court initially determines the propriety of pretrial release on the defendant's own recognizance or on an unsecured bond. If these options are inappropriate, then the court decides whether it should release the defendant under restrictions or with conditions. Only if the court concludes after a hearing that no condition or combination of conditions of release will reasonably assure the defendant's appearance in court or protect the safety of others can the court hold the defendant in pretrial detention. In essence, there is a presumption in favor of pretrial release of federal defendants. There also is authority to release a defendant temporarily to the custody of a third person when the court finds that release is necessary for preparation of the defense.[27]

After a defendant is arrested and before the initial court appearance, a pretrial services officer interviews the defendant and attempts to verify the information provided. The Pretrial Services Agency works for the court.[28] Usually, the pretrial services officer contacts persons familiar with the defendant for verification. The officer prepares a report for the court and makes a recommendation as to pretrial release.

In most felony cases, the judge determines the amount of bail at the initial hearing. However, for lesser crimes, some jurisdictions have adopted a fixed schedule and allow defendants to post their bonds immediately after being booked at police headquarters. In traffic cases, it is customary for alleged offenders to post their driver's license in lieu of a predetermined cash amount.

In most states, when a defendant cannot afford bail, a bail bond agent may post the bond. Generally, a bail agent will charge the defendant 10 percent of the bail amount and require the defendant to post collateral. However, if the defendant fails to appear in court, the bail bond agent is responsible for the full amount of the bail. Several years ago, the state of Illinois took steps to eliminate bail bondsmen by only requiring defendants to post 10 percent of the amount of the bail with the court. When the case is concluded, 90 percent of the bond is refunded to the defendant[29] with the court retaining the balance. Hence, if bail is set at $50,000, the defendant must post $5,000. At the conclusion of the case, $4,500 is returned to the defendant and $500 is retained by the court.

DISCUSSION QUESTIONS

3. In 2008, when a nationally prominent financier named Bernard Madoff was arrested for directing a Ponzi scheme that allegedly defrauded investors of somewhere between $13 billion and $65 billion, his bail was set at $10 million. Do you think the amount set for bail was excessive? Why or why not?

4. In addition to posting the $10 million bail, Madoff was placed under house arrest and required to wear an electronic monitoring device. Does this additional information affect your feeling about the appropriateness of the amount of bail?

---

[27]18 U.S.C. § 3142(i).

[28]18 U.S.C. § 3152.

[29]If the defendant is convicted, the defendant's portion of bail is applied to fines, costs, and assessments. The balance, if any, is refunded to the defendant.

F. ARRAIGNMENTS AND PRELIMINARY HEARINGS

The **arraignment** is the court proceeding at which the judge informs the defendant of the charges filed by the government and records the defendant's plea (response) to those charges. In addition to pleading either guilty or not guilty, to each charge, in some jurisdictions defendants can also plead **nolo contendere**.[30] With this plea, the defendant neither admits nor denies the charges but concedes that if the case went to trial, the prosecution would have sufficient evidence to prove its case beyond a reasonable doubt. Because the plea is not considered an admission of guilt, it cannot be used later against the defendant at a civil trial. However, for purposes of the arraignment the case proceeds as though the defendant had pleaded guilty.

If the accused is unable to afford an attorney and the prosecutor is seeking incarceration, the court will appoint a defense lawyer. We will discuss the role of public defenders and other types of appointed counsel in Chapter 6.

In many courts, the judge also enters a scheduling order at this time. The schedule for upcoming steps in the trial process often includes a date for a **preliminary hearing** at which the judge determines whether there is sufficient evidence to show probable cause that the defendant committed the offense charged.[31] If the court concludes that the evidence presented at the preliminary hearing does not establish probable cause, the case is dismissed and the defendant is discharged.

The federal Constitution does not guarantee the right to a preliminary hearing, but a federal felony defendant who has not yet been indicted has a statutory right under FRCrP 5.1(a) to a preliminary hearing. Likewise, states that are classified as indictment jurisdictions have statutes that require preliminary hearings for unindicted defendants who are charged with felonies.[32] Jurisdictions provide almost all of the information for preliminary hearings. In most of these states, the prosecutor can bypass the preliminary examination by indicting the defendant.[33] In many jurisdictions, the defendant's right is premised upon a timely demand for the hearing.[34] Defendants can waive their right to a preliminary hearing, but in many jurisdictions, the prosecutor can insist upon a preliminary hearing even if the defendant waives it.[35]

Under Rule 5.1(a) of the Federal Rules of Criminal Procedure, if the defendant is charged with a crime other than a petty offense, the **U.S. Magistrate Judge** must conduct a preliminary hearing unless the defendant waives the hearing, the defendant is indicted, the defendant waives prosecution by indictment, the government charges the defendant with a misdemeanor, or the defendant is charged with a misdemeanor and consents to a trial by the magistrate. If the magistrate finds that probable cause was not shown and dismisses the case,

Arraignment
A court proceeding at which the judge informs the defendant of the charges filed by the government.

Nolo contendere
A "no contest" plea in which the defendant neither admits nor denies the charges but concedes that if the case went to trial, the prosecution would have sufficient evidence to prove its case beyond a reasonable doubt.

Preliminary hearing
The initial hearing by a judge to determine whether there is probable cause for the charge against the defendant.

U.S. Magistrate Judge
A federal trial judge appointed by the life-tenured federal judges of a district court. Magistrates often try misdemeanor and petty offense cases and handle felony preliminary proceedings.

---

[30]A Latin phrase meaning "no contest."

[31]Probable cause is evidence sufficient to cause a person of ordinary prudence and caution to conscientiously entertain a reasonable belief of the defendant's guilt. *Beck v. Ohio*, 379 U.S. 89, 91, 85 S. Ct. 223, 13 L. Ed. 2d 142 (1964).

[32]W. LaFave, et al. at 721.

[33]*Id.* at 722.

[34]*Id.* at 723.

[35]*Id.* at 724.

the U.S. Attorney can file a complaint or present the case to a grand jury for indictment. This procedure is the same in state court.

Unlike a grand jury proceeding, the accused is afforded a number of significant rights at the preliminary hearing. Procedural protections include the right to an attorney and to challenge the rulings of the magistrate at the time of the hearing. Defendants are also afforded limited rights to cross-examine witnesses and to present defense witnesses. These differences create opportunities for discovering information that will help the attorneys develop their cases and provide both sides an opportunity to assess the credibility of the witnesses. Additionally, both sides can use the statements made by witnesses at this stage for impeachment at trial. From the perspective of the defendant, the preliminary hearing also offers an opportunity to gain insight into the government's theory of the case and its evidence. Moreover, the hearing may permit the perpetuation of testimony of a witness who later becomes unavailable.

At preliminary hearings, paralegals can serve the same functions they do during formal trials. We will discuss these duties in greater detail in Chapter 12. As part of the trial preparation process, paralegals are often called upon to summarize or prepare abstracts of the testimony that was given at the preliminary hearing. These abstracts are helpful in preparing cross-examination questions and impeaching witnesses. Furthermore, it can be used to prepare opening statements.

SUMMARY

This chapter examined the role prosecuting attorneys play in the preliminary stages of a criminal case after the police or other law enforcement agents have begun their investigation. Prosecutors are given different titles and are divided along federal and state jurisdictional lines. Some are elected and some are appointed. Larger offices are usually organized into separate divisions. Although most of the investigative work is typically done by police, prosecutors draft and present applications for search warrants and arrest warrants and direct grand jury investigations.

Prosecutors are the key gatekeepers when it comes to determining who will be brought to trial and with which offenses they will be charged. They, and their paralegals, are also involved in the preparation of various documents that need to be filed with the court. These documents include criminal complaints, indictments, informations, arrest warrants, and summons. In addition to knowing what they contain, paralegals should be able to prepare drafts for attorneys to review. Prosecutors and their paralegals are also involved in initial appearances, bail settings, arraignments, and preliminary hearings.

INTERNET RESOURCES

Participants in the Criminal Justice System
- U.S Attorneys Office: **http://www.justice.gov/usao/**
- Directory of Prosecuting Attorneys in Each State:

http://www.eatoncounty.org/Departments/ProsecutingAttorney/ProsList.htm
- National District Attorneys Association:
  http://www.ndaa.org/
- Handbook for Grand Jurors for Maryland:
  http://www.courts.state.md.us/juryservice/grandjury.pdf
- Legal Ethics:
  http://www.legalethics.com/
  http://www.abanet.org/cpr/mrpc/mrpc_toc.html

REVIEW QUESTIONS

1. How do the basic functions of attorneys employed by the U.S. Attorney's office differ from those of state prosecutors?
2. In what ways are prosecutors involved in the investigation of crimes?
3. What is the original purpose of the grand jury?
4. What is meant by a grand jury issuing a true bill?
5. What are arrest warrants and bench warrants?
6. How does an arrest warrant differ from a criminal summons?
7. What are the five major components of a court document?
8. What information is included in the caption of a case?
9. List and describe the three types of charging documents.
10. What are indictment jurisdictions and information jurisdictions?
11. What is bail? What factors does the court consider in setting bail?
12. How does the arraignment differ from the preliminary hearing?

Chapter 6

Defending the Accused

The previous chapter focused on the activities of prosecuting attorneys and the paralegals who work with them; in this chapter we turn our attention to the attorneys and paralegals working on the defense side of the case. However, before getting into what they actually do, we need to discuss the constitutional right to counsel and the various ways in which this right can be provided.

A. INTRODUCTION TO DEFENSE ATTORNEYS

1. THE NATURE OF OUR ADVERSARIAL SYSTEM

In order to fully understand and appreciate the role of the defense attorney, one must understand the basis for our "adversary system." In the "inquisitorial system" used in many European nations, judges are active participants in the search for truth rather than neutral arbitrators, and it is the responsibility of the judges, rather than the lawyers, to make sure all relevant evidence is heard. The judges determine who will be called as witnesses, and it is the judges, rather than the attorneys, who ask most of the questions of the witnesses. While lawyers are present in the courtroom to assist the judge, their duty to the litigants is clearly secondary to their duty to the court.

The primary criticism of the inquisitorial system is that it puts too much power in the hands of judges, thereby creating an imbalance of power between the individual and the government. In contrast, the adversarial system makes the attorneys responsible for presenting all evidence and arguments relevant to their client's side of the case. The judge's role is limited to enforcing the procedural rules and, when a jury is not involved, rendering a decision based solely on the evidence the attorneys have presented.

Critics of the adversary system argue that it places too much reliance on the quality of the lawyers handling the case. It assumes that the lawyers will use skillful examinations of witnesses and well-researched arguments about the interpretation of the law to present the strongest possible case for their clients. However, if a lawyer is poorly prepared or lacks certain key skills, justice is not necessarily done, and the client will suffer for the lawyer's inadequacies.

One of the most frequent questions asked of lawyers is, "How can you defend a guilty client?" A common response is to point out that guilt is a legal concept that is determined by a judge or a jury rather than by the lawyer. Therefore, a person cannot be considered guilty until after the trial has been completed. The more philosophical justification is that the legitimacy of the adversary system depends upon having lawyers representing the "guilty" as well as the innocent. If criminal defendants cannot find attorneys willing to represent them, "the foundation of the judicial system is eroded and the lawyers become the judges of guilt or innocence by their very decision to accept or reject those criminal clients."[1]

Ethical Considerations Related to Defending the Poor and/or Unpopular Clients

Just as there are specific provisions in the rules of professional conduct that focus on the special role of prosecutors, so too there are certain provisions of the rules that have particular significance for criminal defense attorneys. In this section we highlight ethical obligations related to defending unpopular clients. Other ethical provisions related to defense attorneys are discussed later in this chapter and in succeeding chapters.

Generally, lawyers who work for themselves are free to accept or reject clients on any basis they choose. However, lawyers who work for others, whether it is in a law firm, public agency, corporation, or advocacy group, generally do not have the ability to pick and choose the individuals they wish to represent. Perhaps the most obvious example of this is the lawyer who works for the public defenders' office representing individuals who have been charged with a crime. This type of lawyer is not free to represent only those whom the lawyer believes are innocent.

However, while the general rule is that lawyers cannot be forced to accept specific clients, they do have a professional obligation to provide legal services to those who cannot afford to pay for it. ABA Model Rule 6.1 suggests that attorneys render at least fifty hours a year of pro bono legal services to individuals or charitable organizations. They are also encouraged to provide some legal services at a "substantially reduced fee."

Model Rule 6.2 declares that it is part of an attorney's professional responsibility to represent clients who are assigned to them through judicial appointment. It does, however, contain an exception for a client or cause "so repugnant to the lawyer as to be likely to impair the client-lawyer relationship or the lawyer's ability to represent the client." (See Section A.3 on p. 164 for further discussion of public defenders and judicial appointments.)

Model Rule 1.16 sets out the conditions under which a lawyer can withdraw from a case after the attorney-client relationship has been established. See the ABA website: *http://www .americanbar.org/groups/professional_responsibility /publications/model_rules_of_professional_conduct/ model_rules_of_professional_conduct_table_of_ contents.html*

---

[1]S. Jones, *A Lawyer's Ethical Duty to Represent the Unpopular Client*, 1 Chap. L. Rev. 105, 107 (1998).

2. THE RIGHT TO COUNSEL

Our commitment to the adversary system of justice is reflected in several parts of the Bill of Rights. The adoption of the Sixth Amendment guarantee of the right to counsel recognizes the importance placed on the role of lawyers in our system. The Fourth Amendment prohibition against unreasonable searches and seizures and the Fifth Amendment privilege against self-incrimination demonstrate that constitutional rights take precedence over the government's search for the truth. Although the protection of these rights may result in allowing some guilty persons to go free, they help ensure the innocent are not unjustly convicted.

The Sixth Amendment's guarantee that "in all criminal prosecutions, the accused shall enjoy the right to . . . the assistance of counsel" is critical to the functioning of our adversary system, but its general language leaves us with many important questions. What constitutes "assistance of counsel"? Does it really apply to "all" criminal prosecutions or is it limited to some subset of more "serious" charges? At what stage in a criminal prosecution does this right begin to apply? Does it apply to appeals? Does it require the government to provide you with an attorney if you cannot afford one on your own, or is it simply a provision to prevent the government from consulting the attorney you hired with your own money? Does the assistance of counsel have to be "effective"?

As with other instances involving interpretation of the Constitution, we must look to decisions of the U.S. Supreme Court for the answers to these questions. In various cases involving the Sixth Amendment right to counsel, the Court has ruled that:

- It applies to anyone facing possible federal, state, or local criminal charges[2] as well as to minors involved in juvenile proceedings.[3]
- In prosecutions that could result in a defendant's incarceration where the defendant cannot afford to hire an attorney on his or her own, the government is required to provide an attorney for the defendant's use.[4]
- As soon as a defendant retains a private attorney, that attorney can begin assisting the defendant. When the government is providing an attorney for an indigent defendant, the right to counsel attaches at the initial appearance before a judicial officer. This first time before a court, also known as the preliminary arraignment or arraignment on the complaint, is generally the hearing at which the magistrate informs the defendant of the charge in the complaint and of various rights in further proceedings and determines the conditions for pretrial release.[5]
- While the right to have assistance from a private attorney extends through as many appeals as the defendant is qualified to make, the right to assistance of an appointed counsel applies only to the first level of appeal.[6]
- The effectiveness of counsel is a highly ambiguous concept. It is easy for losing defendants to blame their convictions on having had bad lawyers.

---

[2] *Powell v. Alabama*, 287 U.S. 45, 53 S. Ct. 55, 77 L. Ed. 158 (1932).

[3] *In re Gault*, 387 U.S. 1, 87 S. Ct. 1428, 18 L. Ed. 2d 527 (1967).

[4] *Scott v. Illinois*, 440 U.S. 367, 99 S. Ct. 1158, 59 L. Ed. 2d 383 (1979).

[5] *Rothgery v. Gillespie County*, 554 U.S. 191, 128 S. Ct. 2578, 171 L. Ed. 2d 366 (2008).

[6] *Ross v. Moffitt*, 417 U.S. 600, 94 S. Ct. 2437, 41 L. Ed.2d 341 (1974) & *Halbert v. Michigan*, 545 U.S. 602, 125 S. Ct. 2582; 162 L. Ed. 2d 552 (2005).

But then most of them had in fact committed the crimes for which they were convicted and would have lost their case no matter how good their lawyers were. In order to have one's conviction reversed on the basis of "ineffective assistance of counsel," a defendant must prove both that the defendant's attorney made major errors and that the errors were serious enough to have deprived the defendant of a fair trial.[7]

3. TYPES OF DEFENSE ATTORNEYS

Private counsel ("retained counsel")
A private attorney chosen by the defendant to represent him or her.

Public defender
An attorney paid by the government to represent indigent persons accused of committing crimes.

Contract lawyer
An attorney who enters into an agreement with the government to furnish legal services to indigent clients.

Assigned counsel
A lawyer in private practice appointed by the court to handle a particular indigent criminal case.

Pro bono
The Latin term for "for the good," used to describe legal work that is performed for free as part of the attorney's professional responsibilities.

There are three main types of defense attorneys: private counsel, public defenders, and appointed counsel. **Private counsel** ("retained counsel") are lawyers who contract directly with the defendant to represent them on a fee-for-services basis. The nature of the criminal law practice of private attorneys varies. Some lawyers limit their practice exclusively to criminal cases. As we explain below, these attorneys often accept assignments in state court as appointed counsel and in federal court as CJA (an appointment made under the authority of the Criminal Justice Act) panel attorneys. There are also private attorneys who include criminal defense as part of a more diverse general practice. Furthermore, some criminal defense attorneys have subspecialties, such as white-collar crime, drug offenses, driving while intoxicated, capital crimes, etc.

To meet their constitutional duty to provide attorneys to criminal defendants who cannot afford to hire them on their own, most jurisdictions use some variation of either a public defender's office or an assigned counsel system. Most rely predominantly on either full-time or part-time public defenders.

A **public defender** (commonly referred to as a "PD") is an attorney who is employed by the government to represent indigent persons accused of committing crimes. Cases involving these indigent defendants are referred to the public defender's office where they are delegated by the head public defender to staff lawyers. Although PDs are typically full-time government employees, in many smaller, rural areas they may be either part-time employees or **contract lawyers**.[8] Contract lawyers typically represent PD clients as well as private clients.

Public defender systems are usually the most cost-effective way of providing experienced criminal attorneys. Because PDs get to know the prosecuting attorneys and the judges, they are well situated to plea bargain as well as to try their clients' cases. The major disadvantage is that they are often assigned such large caseloads that they do not have adequate time to prepare their cases or spend much time with their clients.

In an **assigned counsel** system, judges appoint members of the private bar to handle specific cases. In most jurisdictions, the government compensates the attorney on a case-by-case basis, though occasionally members of the local bar are expected to take these cases on a **pro bono** basis.[9] In jurisdictions in which it is common practice to assign indigent cases to all members of the local bar, defendants stand a greater chance of getting a lawyer with little or no experience in criminal law. On the other hand, where attorneys are compensated, there is frequently a pool of experienced criminal attorneys who seek out these appointments to supplement their income from their private practice.

---

[7]*Strickland v. Washington*, 466 U.S. 668, 104 S. Ct. 2052, 80 L. Ed. 2d 674 (1984).

[8]A contract lawyer is technically an independent contractor rather than an employee.

[9]Pro-bono is Latin for "for the good." It is used to describe legal work that is performed for free as part of the attorney's professional responsibilities.

Federal defenders are the federal equivalent of state public defenders. They are the primary representatives for defendants who are unable to afford private counsel in prosecutions initiated by the U.S. Attorney's Office. Like their state counterparts, some federal defender offices are staffed by full-time attorneys; others employ attorneys in private practice on a part-time basis to represent indigent defendants. Additionally, panel attorneys furnish indigent representation in the federal courts. **CJA panel attorneys**[10] are criminal defense lawyers in private practice who are appointed to represent indigent defendants in federal cases for a fixed hourly fee.

When the public defender (or federal defender) has a **conflict of interest**, the judge will appoint another attorney to represent the defendant. This occurs when the public defender's representation of one client either is directly adverse to another client or materially limits the attorney's duties to another client, a former client or third party, or the personal interest of the attorney. So if there are multiple defendants in a case, the public defender can represent only one of them. The remaining defendants are assigned CJA panel attorneys in federal prosecutions or appointed counsel in state cases. A conflict with the federal defender or public defender's office can also exist if it previously represented a material witness or co-defendant.

Over 80 percent of all criminal defendants charged with offenses punishable by incarceration qualify for publicly funded attorneys. As a result, caseloads for indigent defense counsel are heavy and many offices are understaffed. Even recommended maximum caseload levels appear excessive. According to the Federal Law Enforcement Assistance Administration's National Advisory Commission's report, annual public defender caseloads should not exceed: 150 felonies, 400 misdemeanors (excluding traffic), 200 Juvenile cases, 200 Mental Health Act cases,

Federal defender
An attorney appointed to represent persons who are unable to afford private counsel in federal prosecutions.

CJA panel attorney
An attorney in private practice who is appointed in federal cases to represent indigent defendants for a fixed hourly fee.

Conflict of interest
A situation in which an attorney's representation of one client is either directly adverse to another client or materially limits the attorney's duties to another client, a former client or third party, or the personal interest of the attorney.

Ethical Considerations Related to Conflicts of Interest

ABA Model Rule of Professional Conduct Rule 1.7 prohibits most types of "concurrent conflicts of interest." These types of conflicts are defined as situations in which:

- The interests of one current client directly conflict with those of another current client;
- There is a "significant risk" that the attorney's representation will be limited by his or her past or present representation

of another client or by a "personal interest of the lawyer."

ABA Model Rules 1.8–1.10 go into more detail as to what types of situations are considered to be conflicts of interest. See the ABA website: *http://www.americanbar.org/groups/professional_responsibility/publications/model_rules_of_professional_conduct/model_rules_of_professional_conduct_table_of_contents.html*

---

[10]The Criminal Justice Act (CJA), 18 U.S.C. § 3006A, establishes the federal defender and CJA panel attorney models of indigent criminal defense.

> - Public defender offices in the largest 100 counties employed over 12,700 individuals during 1999, including over 6,300 assistant public defenders, 1,200 investigators, 300 social workers, 2,700 support staff, and nearly 400 paralegals.
> - Over 30,700 private attorneys were appointed through assigned counsel programs to represent indigent defendants in the largest 100 counties during 1999.
> - During 1999, over 1,000 contracts for indigent defense services were administered by contract attorney programs.
>
> Source: Bureau of Justice Statistics Indigent Defense Statistics, *http://www.ojp.usdoj.gov/bjs/id .htm#caseload*

Figure 6.1 Public Defender Staffing, Assigned Counsel Participation, and Private Attorney Contracts

or 25 appeals per defender.[11] The Bureau of Justice Statistics website reveals the existence of a caseload problem a decade ago:

- "Indigent criminal defense programs in the largest 100 counties received an estimated 4.2 million cases in 1999. About 80% were criminal cases, 8% juvenile related, 2% civil, and 9% other types of cases dealing with issues such as juvenile dependency, abuse and neglect, and contempt.
- Public defenders handled 82% of the 4.2 million cases in these counties, court appointed private attorneys 15% and contract attorneys 3%."[12]

(Figure 6.1 shows 1999 levels of public defender staffing, assigned counsel participation, and private attorney contracts.) Recently, public defenders' offices in seven states refused to accept new cases or filed suit to limit them, citing overwhelming workloads.[13]

DISCUSSION QUESTIONS

1. List what you think the pros and cons are of each of the different types of defense attorneys. Which type would you want to defend you if you could not afford to hire a private attorney? Why?

2. Model Rule 6.2 allows an attorney to avoid appointment by a tribunal to represent a person when the client or the cause is "so repugnant to the lawyer as to be likely to impair the client-lawyer relationship or the lawyer's ability to represent the client." Do you think it would allow an African American attorney to refuse to represent a member of the Ku Klux Klan accused of placing a burning cross on the front lawn of an integrated church? What other examples can you think of that might fit this exception?

---

[11]Standard 13.12 cited in *Keeping Defender Workloads Manageable,* Bureau of Justice Assistance Monogram prepared by The Spangenberg Group (January 2001) at 8.

[12]*http://www.ojp.usdoj.gov/bjs/id.htm#caseload*

[13]"Citing Workload, Public Lawyers Reject New Cases," *The New York Times,* November 9, 2008.

APPLICATION EXERCISES

1. What type of system is used in the state courts in the area in which you currently reside and what steps does an indigent defendant have to take in order to get an attorney to represent him or her? Where did you find this information?

2. Obtain a copy of the financial affidavit used in your local court system to determine whether a defendant qualifies for a court-appointed defense attorney. Fill in the form as you would if you were the one applying for representation.

B. INITIAL CONTACTS WITH DEFENSE COUNSEL

Whether the defendant is being represented by private counsel, a court-appointed attorney, or a public defender, the role of the defense counsel is the same—to provide the client the opportunity to attain the most favorable resolution of the case. In some cases, this means a negotiated plea agreement. In others, effective representation amounts to zealous advocacy at trial. Representation typically begins when the accused first consults with the attorney. If the defendant is in jail, family members or friends may meet with the lawyer. Paralegals may participate in this initial meeting.

Ethical Considerations Related to the Attorney-Client Relationship

Several of the ABA's Model Rules and the state rules that closely resemble them spell out the nature of an attorney's ethical obligations to clients.

Model Rule 1.3 contains a general admonition that a lawyer should act with "reasonable diligence and promptness" when representing a client. Complaints about lack of diligence and promptness are among the most frequent complaints filed with disciplinary committees by disgruntled clients. Model Rule 1.4 elaborates on Rule 1.3 and adds a requirement that a lawyer "explain a matter to the extent reasonably necessary to permit the client to make informed decisions regarding the representation."

Model Rule 1.2 (d) covers one of the most controversial topics in criminal law by attempting to draw a line between helping a client determine the validity, scope, meaning, or application of the law and assisting a client to engage in conduct that the lawyer knows is criminal or fraudulent. Attorneys have an obligation to fully explain what the law does or does not require and the defenses a defendant might assert but is not suppose to allow a client to present what the attorney knows to be perjured testimony.

See the ABA website: *http://www.american-bar.org/groups/professional_responsibility/ publications/model_rules_of_professional_conduct/ model_rules_of_professional_conduct_table_of_ contents.html*

1. INITIAL ADVICE TO THE CLIENT

The client first contacts the defense counsel because the client is either under investigation or charged with an offense. In either situation, the attorney will give the client the same initial advice—**do not speak to anyone about the case**. If law enforcement officers want to question him or her, the client should decline to speak and request that the attorney be present during questioning.

When interviewed by the police, suspects frequently present a biased account that casts them in the most favorable light. Then, when the officer confronts them with the discrepancies between their version and contradictory facts, suspects typically revise their story. Thus every time a suspect makes a statement, the probability of contradicting a prior statement increases and these internal inconsistencies come back to haunt the defendant's credibility at the trial stage. When placed under the stress of a police interrogation, even innocent persons may become confused.

For example, when NBA star Kobe Bryant was initially interviewed by police about having had sexual relations with a young woman working at the hotel where he was staying, he initially denied having sex with her. Then, after the detective revealed some of the accuser's statements and that they were going to be doing DNA testing of pubic hair and body fluids retrieved from the woman, Bryant acknowledged that he had in fact had sex with her. Later in the interview, the detective told Bryant:

> . . . So, one, you lied to us, okay, that doesn't help. Two, um, then, then we confront this issue and you seemed a little bit skeptical in the details of exactly what happened throughout the entire incident okay. I'm not saying you're a person that would do something like this okay. I agree with you, I agree that you got caught up in the moment. Okay. No doubt about it, you know, no doubt about it whatsoever. What I, what I'm being, what I'm skeptical on is that I don't know how consensual the sexual intercourse was. Okay. I don't , I don't, I guess to be honest with you I'm not sure, I'm not sure, if we're getting all the facts presented to us as far as what exactly happened.[14]

Following the interview, the prosecution charged Bryant with sexual assault.[15]

Even a consistent statement is no guarantee that criminal charges will not be filed. For instance, U.S. Senator Larry Craig was arrested in a sting operation arising out of alleged lewd behavior. Senator Craig gave a statement denying any wrongdoing, yet he was still charged. The first page of the senator's statement to the police appears in Exhibit 6.1.

In addition to advising the client not to speak to anyone about the incident in question, the attorney also should instruct the client to refrain from discussing the facts of the case in a telephone call, fax, or e-mail. Opinions diverge over whether there is an expectation of privacy as to these communication tools. We recommend you err on the side of caution to guard against the disclosure of confidential information. If the client contacts the law firm through any of these

---

[14]Kobe Bryant interview with Eagle County Sheriff's investigators Dan Loya and Doug Winters, Version 8/6/04, p. 33.

[15]The state ultimately dismissed the charges when the accuser declined to participate in the trial.

Exhibit 6.1: Suspect's Statement to Police

In 2007, U.S. Senator Larry Craig was arrested at the Minneapolis–St. Paul International Airport on suspicion of lewd conduct. Craig pleaded guilty to disorderly conduct. His petition to vacate the guilty plea was denied. The first page of the transcript of Craig's interview with the undercover officer follows.

Investigative Sergeant Dave Karsnia #4211 (DK) and Detective Noel Nelson #62 (NN) INTERVIEW WITH Larry Craig (LC)
Case 07002008

DK: You have the right to remain silent. Anything you say can and will be used against you in court of law. You have the right to talk to a lawyer now or have a present, a lawyer present now or anytime during questioning. If you cannot afford a lawyer, one will be appointed to you without cost. Do you understand each of these rights the way I have explained them to you?
LC: I do.

DK: Do you wish to talk to us at this time?
LC: I do.

DK: Okay. Um, I just wanna start off with a your side of the story, okay. So, a
LC: So I go into the bathroom here as I normally do, I'm a commuter too here.

DK: Okay.
LC: I sit down, um, to go to the bathroom and ah, you said our feet bumped. I believe they did, ah, because I reached down and scooted over and um, the next thing I knew, under the bathroom divider comes a card that says Police. Now, um, (sigh) that's about as far as I can take it, I don't know of anything else. Ah, your foot came toward mine, mine came towards yours, was that natural? I don't know. Did we bump? Yes. I think we did. You said so. I don't disagree with that.

DK: Okay. I don't want to get into a pissing match here.
LC: We're not going to.

DK: Good. Um,
LC: I don't, ah, I am not gay, I don't do these kinds of things and...

DK: It doesn't matter, I don't care about sexual preference or anything like that. Here's your stuff back sir. Um, I don't care about sexual preference.
LC: I know you don't. You're out to enforce the law.

DK: Right.
LC: But you shouldn't be out to entrap people either.

DK: This isn't entrapment.
LC: All right.

DK: Um, you you're skipping some parts here, but what, what about your hand?
LC: What about it? I reached down, my foot like this. There was a piece of paper on the floor, I picked it up.

DK: Okay.
LC: What about my hand?

DK: Well, you're not being truthful with me, I'm kinda disappointed in you Senator. I'm real disappointed in you right now. Okay. I'm not, just so you know, just like everybody, I, I, I, treat with dignity, I try to pull them away from the situation
LC: I, I

methods, he or she should limit communication to scheduling and other issues unrelated to the facts of the case. If the client is incarcerated, defense counsel should let the client know that telephone calls are probably being recorded.

2. PRESERVING CONFIDENTIALITY

Maintaining confidentiality is essential to an attorney's ability to become fully informed of the facts of the case. Without the duty to protect confidentiality and recognition of the attorney-client privilege, clients would be likely to withhold key information which the attorney needs to effectively defend the client.

a. Ethical Rules on Confidentiality

As you can see, the Model Rules contain several exceptions to the attorney's ethical obligations to protect a client's confidential information. One of the most controversial exceptions is the one regarding situations in which the attorney has knowledge that the client plans a criminal act. The Model Rules specify a criminal act as one "that the lawyer believes is likely to result in the

Ethical Duties of Attorneys Related to Confidentiality

ABA Model Rule 1.6 and many related state codes prohibit lawyers from revealing confidential information about their clients without the client's consent. There are exceptions however. They include situations in which the disclosure of the confidential information is necessary to:

■ prevent "reasonably certain death or substantial bodily harm";
■ prevent the client from committing a crime that is "reasonably certain" to result in substantial injury to another. Another exception allows the attorney to reveal confidential information when it is related to defending the attorney's actions in cases where the attorney is

facing criminal or civil claims regarding actions taken by the attorney.

ABA Model Rule 4.4 and many related state codes prohibit attorneys from using legal tactics that are designed to "embarrass, delay, or burden a third person" or to obtain evidence by means that violate the legal rights of other parties. They also deal with situations in which a lawyer receives a document relating to the lawyer's client which he or she "knows or reasonably should know" to have been sent by mistake.

See the ABA website: *http://www.american bar.org/groups/professional_responsibility/publications/model_rules_of_professional_conduct/model_rules_of_professional_conduct_table_of_contents.html*

Ethical Duties of Paralegals Related to Confidentiality

The ethical codes of both major national parale-gal organizations speak to the paralegal's ethical duty to maintain confidentiality.

NALA Ethical Canon 7: A paralegal must protect the confidences of a client and must not violate any rule or statute now in effect or hereafter enacted controlling the doctrine of privileged communica-tions between a client and an attorney. (National

Association of Legal Assistants Code of Ethics and Professional Responsibility)

*NFPA® Model Disciplinary Rule 1.5: A paralegal shall preserve all confidential information provided by the client or acquired from other sources before, during, and after the course of the professional relationship. (**National Federation of Paralegal Associations, Inc.**)*

imminent death or substantial bodily harm." This exemption applies only to *future* crimes. In sum, according to the ethical rules, confidences can be revealed only if

1. the client consents after full disclosure or
2. it is necessary to prevent a crime likely to result in imminent death or substantial bodily harm or
3. it is necessary in order for an attorney to collect a fee or defend against charges of attorney misconduct.

The safest course for a paralegal who becomes aware of situations involving any of these exceptions is to notify the supervising attorney so that the attorney can determine the proper course of action.

Meetings with clients should take place at a physical setting that is conducive to open communication and privacy. The law office and a client's home ordinarily provide good settings. In some cases, these meetings take place in special private interview rooms at the jail. In order to maintain client confidentiality and to protect the attorney-client privilege, these meetings should not take place in a public location where other people might overhear the conversation. Neither children nor friends should be present during these client meetings.

It is important to note that this ethical **duty of confidentiality** extends to the attorney's employees and law firm staff, including paralegals. Paralegals regularly receive this type of information and must at all times resist the temptation to disclose it. You must refrain from discussing the particulars of a client's situation as inter-esting gossip with friends or family. Even when names are not used, these con-fidences cannot be revealed if the disclosure violates the client's privacy interests. The duty of confidentiality protects the private information of potential clients and current clients as well as past clients. This obligation even prohibits revealing the identities of the firm's clients. In most jurisdictions, an attorney may reveal confi-dential client information only (1) after full disclosure and with the client's written

Duty of confidentiality
An attorney's ethical duty to maintain the confidences of the client.

consent, or (2) when required by law or court order, or (3) when necessary to prevent the client from committing an act that could result in death or serious bodily harm.[16]

DISCUSSION QUESTION

3. Assume you are an attorney who represents a defendant in a felony matter where the client is charged with pouring acid on a car and repeatedly bashing it with a baseball bat. Based on information you learned from reading his "rap sheet," you have concluded that your client has violent tendencies. What should you do if the defendant's wife approaches you in the courthouse and tells you that your client had threatened to kill her when he gets out of jail?

APPLICATION EXERCISE

3. Your friend Bill Edwards has retained your supervisor, Charles Hovey, to represent him in a state securities fraud case involving the events described on p. xxxviii. When you see Bill at a social function, he takes you off into a corner where no one else can overhear your conversation and then shares some incriminating information about his case with you.
   a. Under the terms of the ABA Model Rules of Professional Conduct, what are your ethical duties regarding the sharing of this information with your supervising attorney?
   b. Under the terms of NALA's Ethical Canon 7, what are your ethical duties regarding the sharing of this information with your supervising attorney?
   c. Under the terms of NFPA's Model Disciplinary Rule 1.5, what are your ethical duties regarding the sharing of this information with your supervising attorney?
   d. Under the terms of the Ethical code adopted by the State Bar or Supreme Court in your state, what are your ethical duties regarding the sharing of this information with your supervising attorney?

---

b. Attorney-Client Privilege

Attorney-client privilege
The rule of evidence that forbids an attorney, or the attorney's employees, from testifying about communications with the client.

Similar to the duty of client confidentiality is the **attorney-client privilege**. This is the rule of evidence that forbids an attorney, or the attorney's staff, from testifying about communications with the client. The privilege exists when the client seeks legal advice from a lawyer in his or her professional capacity and when the communications are made in confidence and relate to the purpose of the legal advice. As in the case of the duty of confidentiality, communications made to paralegals are protected by the privilege.

---

[16]See ABA Model Rule 1.7(b).

There is a four-part test used to determine whether a client disclosure is privileged information: (1) a client's oral or written statement (2) made to the attorney or staff (3) while seeking legal advice (4) given in confidence. The client does not have to pay a fee in order to have the protection of the privilege. A client can waive the attorney-client privilege. Similar to the duty of confidentiality, a third party's presence can waive the privilege. You must make sure that no third party is present when you interview a client. Unlike the duty of confidentiality, the identity of the client is not protected by the privilege. Thus, the duty of confidentiality is much broader in scope than the attorney-client privilege.

In homicide cases, the Montana and Indiana Supreme Courts each were faced with the question of whether the attorney-client privilege protected a statement made to a friend who was a paralegal. In *State v. Ingraham*, the Montana Supreme Court found the privilege did not attach. In *Mayberry v. State*, the Indiana Supreme Court determined the communication was protected.

Montana v. Ingraham
1988 MT 156, 290 Mont. 18; 966 P.2d 103 (1998), appeal after remand,
2000 MT 266, 302 Mont. 39, 22 P.3d 166 (2000)
Supreme Court of Montana

JUSTICE JIM REGNIER delivered the opinion of the Court.

Gregory Lloyd Ingraham appeals from a judgment and commitment of the Twentieth Judicial District Court, Lake County, based on a jury verdict convicting him of negligent homicide, criminal endangerment, and criminal trespass to property. We affirm in part, reverse in part, and remand for further proceedings consistent with this opinion.

* * *

In the early morning hours of October 13, 1995, Ingraham was driving north on Highway 93 near St. Ignatius, in Lake County, Montana. Roughly two miles north of town, Ingraham's vehicle crossed the center line and struck an oncoming Ford Ranger pickup truck, driven by Cynthia Harriman-Larson. Harriman-Larson died in the collision, and her passenger, Delbert Adams, suffered severe injuries.

* * *

Sometime after 5:00 P.M. on the day following the accident, Jeanne Windham, a paralegal and friend of Ingraham's, picked Ingraham up at the hospital. After first stopping at his house to retrieve some clothing, she drove them to the scene of the accident at Ingraham's request. At trial, Windham offered testimony regarding her conversation with Ingraham at the scene of the accident. Windham recollected Ingraham telling her that his dogs began playing in the back seat and that, as he attempted to keep them from jumping into the front seat, his car swerved to the left just prior to colliding with Harriman-Larson's vehicle.

* * *

Did the District Court err in admitting testimony by paralegal Jeanne Windham? Ingraham argues the District Court erred in permitting paralegal Jeanne Windham to testify as to statements Ingraham made to her about the accident. Ingraham asserts that Windham was one of his law firm's employees, and argues the content of his conversations with her about the accident was protected by the attorney-client privilege and constituted privileged work product. Moreover, Ingraham asserts the court erred in admitting rebuttal testimony regarding additional conversations overheard by Windham, but which did not tend to counteract new matter introduced by the defense.

The State, in contrast, argues that neither the attorney-client privilege nor the work product rule apply to protect the content of conversations between Ingraham and Windham in the aftermath of the accident. The State additionally asserts that Windham's testimony on rebuttal was proper, and urges the court did not err in overruling Ingraham's objections to its admission.

* * *

Ingraham first asserts the content of his conversations with Windham was protected by the attorney-client privilege, and that the District Court thus erred in overruling his objections to Windham's proposed testimony. Ingraham argues that, upon making the telephone call to his father on the night of the accident, he became a client of the Ingraham Law Office. Ingraham asserts that, because Windham worked as a paralegal for the Ingraham Law Office at the time of the accident, the attorney-client privilege extends to her and protects any statements he made to her regarding the accident.

In support of his argument, Ingraham points to § 26-1-803(1), MCA, pursuant to which "an attorney cannot, without the consent of his client, be examined as to any communication made by the client to him or his advice given to the client in the course of professional employment." Ingraham asserts his disclosures to Windham were made "in the course of professional employment," and thus fall within the protection afforded by the attorney-client privilege.

Over Ingraham's objection, the District Court permitted Windham to testify, concluding that it did not believe that the communication that took place between the Defendant and Ms. Windham on October 13th, 1995 . . . at approximately six o'clock P.M., can reasonably be construed as communication made by a client to the attorney, as the statute defines in the course of professional employment.

There are several factors that lead me to that conclusion. The first one is that there's no indication that Greg Ingraham had retained Ingraham Law Office as his counsel with regard to this accident. There certainly is no indication, even if that had happened, that Ms. Windham had any reason, whatsoever, to believe that that had happened. And I have no reason to believe that Greg Ingraham believed that that had happened.

Even if it had, Ms. Windham left her professional employment when she left that office at five o'clock that day, on her own volition, to visit the Defendant as a friend. The only reason she received communications from the Defendant that night is because she agreed, as a friend, to transport him to her house so that she could take care of him. And it's inconceivable to me that that can be construed to be in the course of professional employment. The Defendant then requested her, during that visit, to go to the accident scene, apparently, and said certain things to her. That doesn't necessarily become an attorney-client communication just because Ms. Windham happens to have been an independent contractor for the Defendant at that time. I think it's a factor that she wasn't paid for that time that she spent with him. . . . And so I don't believe that this could reasonably have been construed by the Defendant as a conversation by a client with an attorney or a member of his attorney's office. And so I'm going to deny the motion to exclude her testimony.

Windham testified in chambers that, although she worked for Gregory Ingraham as an independent contractor, she performed no paralegal services for Lloyd Ingraham. She also testified that she had done nothing to assist Gregory Ingraham in defending this case, and that to her knowledge, there was no file on this case at the Ingraham Law Firm. Our review of the pertinent testimony indicates that Ingraham's conservations with Windham were purely personal and not in the course of a professional relationship. Having reviewed the record, we conclude the District Court did not abuse its discretion in concluding that the content of Ingraham's conversations with Windham on the day of the accident were not protected by attorney-client privilege and in admitting her testimony.

* * *

Mayberry v. Indiana
670 N.E.2d 1262 (Ind.1996)
Supreme Court of Indiana

SULLIVAN, JUSTICE.

We affirm defendant Elizabeth Mayberry's conviction for the murder of minister Roland Phillips, committed as he concluded his Sunday sermon at the North Salem United Methodist Church.

Background

In May, 1992, defendant met Phillips, a student pastor at the North Salem United Methodist Church, at a singles retreat sponsored by the United Methodist Church. Defendant and Phillips dated for several months after the retreat. During the course of their relationship, defendant, then 35 years old, claims that Phillips encouraged her to allow him to kiss her using his tongue, engage in consensual, mutual, oral sex with him, fondle and kiss her breasts, and digitally penetrate her vagina. Defendant had never before had intimate physical contact with a man. Phillips would later deny to church officials that he had ever engaged in oral sex with defendant. Defendant's relationship with Phillips took a turn for the worse in August of 1992. In an attempt to salvage the relationship, defendant wrote Phillips letters inquiring into the status of their relationship. In one of these letters, she asked Phillips to attend counseling with her. In November, 1992, defendant received a letter from Phillips in which he stated that their relationship was over. This letter deeply hurt defendant and made her angry.

* * *

In a hearing outside the presence of the jury, defense witness Jennie Maretto, a friend of Phillips and a paralegal for a law firm in Fishers, Indiana, testified that Phillips contacted her at work to obtain legal advice regarding a letter he wrote to the UMC in response to the complaint that defendant had filed. Maretto testified that she felt that she was not legally able to give Phillips legal advice but would have to consult with an attorney. Maretto stated that Phillips asked her to consult an attorney. Maretto also testified that she gave a statement regarding her conversations with Phillips to Officer Danny Williams. When defense counsel inquired about the letter Phillips asked Maretto to look over, the State asserted the attorney-client privilege on Maretto's behalf as to any communication between Maretto and the victim. The trial court sustained the State's objection to the admission of Maretto's testimony.

In an offer to prove, the defense introduced into evidence a police report prepared by Officer Williams. In the report, Officer Williams states that when he spoke with Maretto she informed him that Phillips had contacted her to obtain legal advice. The report also states that Maretto advised the officer that Phillips stated that Phillips and defendant had engaged in consensual, mutual oral sex.

Defendant contends that the trial court erroneously determined that the attorney-client privilege attached to comments Phillips made to Maretto because Maretto did not adequately establish that Phillips contacted her in an effort to employ an attorney for professional advice or aid. In *Colman v. Heidenreich*, 269 Ind. 419, 381 N.E.2d 866 (1978), this court made the following observations:

> The attorney-client privilege is a very important provision in our law for the protection of persons in need of professional legal help. It makes provision for a person to give complete and confidential information to an attorney, so that the attorney may be fully advised in his services to the client. At the same time, it assures the client that these confidences will not be violated.

Colman, 269 Ind. at 421, 381 N.E.2d at 868, Indiana Code § 34-1-14-5 (1993) provides that attorneys shall not be competent witnesses "as to confidential communications made to them in the course of their professional business, and as to advice given in such cases." This "attorney-client privilege not only plays a role in our law of evidence but is also fundamental to our rules of professional conduct which forbid attorneys from revealing 'information relating to representation of a client unless the client consents after consultation.' See Ind. Professional Conduct Rule 1.6." *Corll v. Edward D. Jones & Co.*, 646 N.E.2d 721, 724 (Ind. Ct. App. 1995). As long as an attorney is consulted on business within the scope of the attorney's profession, "it is of no moment to the privilege's application that there is no pendency or expectation of litigation. Neither is it of any moment that no fee has been paid." *Colman*, 269 Ind. at 423, 381 N.E.2d at 869 (citations omitted). Rather, the essential prerequisites to invocation of the privilege are to establish by a preponderance of the evidence (i) the existence of an attorney-client relationship and (ii) that a confidential communication was involved. *See Colman*, 269 Ind. at 423, 381 N.E.2d at 869. To meet the burden of showing that an attorney-client relationship existed, the State had to, at the very least, establish that the communication at issue occurred in the course of an effort to obtain legal advice or aid, on the subject of the client's rights or liabilities, from a professional legal advisor acting in his or her capacity as such. *Id.*; *United States v. Demauro*, 581 F.2d 50, 55 (2nd Cir. 1978).

Defendant suggests that Phillips's communications with his friend Maretto are privileged "only if his asking her to have an attorney look over his papers can be construed to be an attempt by Phillips to employ legal counsel." Defendant also states that the State failed to meet its burden of establishing that Maretto's communications with Phillips were privileged because she did not testify that Phillips intended to or sought to employ her firm to represent him concerning his difficulties with the complaint defendant filed with the church. Defendant misstates the State's burden. Although Maretto and Phillips were social friends, the record reveals that Phillips approached Maretto at the law firm where she worked as a paralegal/office manager and asked her to consult an attorney regarding his legal concerns. We believe these facts can be read to establish that the communications at issue occurred in the course of an effort to obtain legal advice or aid from a professional legal advisor in

his capacity as such. *Colman*, 269 Ind. at 423, 381 N.E.2d at 869; *Demauro*, 581 F.2d at 55. Therefore, we cannot say that the trial court erred in determining that the State met its burden of showing the existence of an attorney-client relationship. And if the communications at issue occurred during an attempt to procure professional legal aid, confidential communications were involved here. See *Colman*, 269 Ind. at 423, 381 N.E.2d at 869. Therefore, the trial court did not abuse its discretion in determining that the communications between Maretto and Phillips were subject to the attorney-client privilege.

* * *

[W]e think Williams's testimony was properly excluded because Phillips's statement to Maretto was subject to the attorney-client privilege. Information subject to the attorney-client privilege retains its privileged character until the client has consented to its disclosure. *Key v. State*, 235 Ind. 172, 175, 132, N.E.2d 143, 145 (1956). Phillips did not consent to Maretto's disclosures to Williams. Therefore, the information possessed by Williams was privileged. In short, privileged information does not cease to be privileged merely because it is subject to the statement against interest hearsay exception. We conclude that the trial court properly excluded Williams's testimony.

* * *

CASE DISCUSSION QUESTIONS

1. What are the factual similarities between the *Ingraham* and *Mayberry* cases?
2. What are the factual differences between the *Ingraham* and *Mayberry* cases?
3. Does the application of attorney-client privilege depend on whether the person making the statement is a party to the case? Why or why not?
4. What are the holdings of the courts in *Ingraham* and *Mayberry*?
5. How can you reconcile the *Ingraham* and *Mayberry* holdings?
6. In light of the *Ingraham* and *Mayberry* decisions, what precautions should you take to ensure that the attorney-client privilege protects statements clients make to you?

3. CONDUCTING THE INITIAL INTERVIEW

Defense lawyers approach initial client interviews in a variety of manners. Some require the client to completely disclose all of the pertinent information at the first interview. This method allows the attorney to make a preliminary evaluation of the case and determine how the matter should proceed. The shortcoming of this approach is that the client may not be willing to share all of the relevant information with an attorney at the first visit. Moreover, some clients are unlikely to be truthful if the attorney is not in a position to confront them with the prosecutor's evidence.

On the other hand, other attorneys discourage the client from giving the story at the first interview. Instead, these attorneys elicit the reasons why the client believes law enforcement officers are pursuing him, the names of witnesses, and other information that may be helpful in investigating the case. Once the government's evidence is disclosed, then the attorney conducts a thorough interview during which the client details a full account as to what occurred. This approach permits the lawyer to better understand the case and to assess the client's credibility. The disadvantage of this tactic is that the attorney does not have a full understanding of the merits of the case for a period of time.

Some attorneys use the full disclosure method on some cases but apply the limited disclosure approach for others. You need to check with your supervisor to learn how your office handles first interviews as well as your role in client interviews. Many defense attorneys conduct first interviews themselves whereas others may delegate the task to paralegals.

If you interview clients, you should carry out this responsibility in a professional manner. Meet the client with courtesy, consideration, and warmth but don't be too chummy. Minimize waiting to help the client feel that the case is important and reduce the client's general anxiety. Focus on the client by avoiding interruptions so that you give the client your undivided attention. Treat the client with dignity irrespective of the client's lot in life. Do not be judgmental.

Many attorneys use client information sheets or checklists to assist the interviewer. If you don't have a guide, it is best to start by asking for preliminary information about the client. Then elicit facts underlying the charge. For articulate clients, let them do most of the talking, then ask questions for clarification. For shy clients, you may need to give them more encouragement to help them open up. When you are interviewing overbearing clients, gently lead them back to the matter at hand if they go astray. You should use understandable language but do not speak down to the client. It is unethical to manipulate the answers, so use the interview to find out everything about the occurrence, including the facts harmful to the client's defense. Therefore, it is important to elicit information in an objective, dispassionate manner.

You should make copies of all relevant documents that the client brings to the interview, such as the written charge, bond sheet, police reports, etc. Some offices direct the interviewer to prepare an initial intake memorandum. If the case is accepted, these documents will become part of the client's file.

If the accused is in jail, the initial interview is usually with the defendant's family or friends. Because this meeting occurs before the court sets the bond, the interview can be used to gather information for the bond hearing, such as the defendant's ties to the community, employment, and financial resources.

Exhibit 6.2: Incident Report #1 in *Cook* Case: Case File No. 10-1857

On Sunday evening, 5/15, at approximately 2031 hrs, this officer arrived at Route 185 near Normal Street to assist in the investigation of a serious personal injury accident involving a bicyclist and a motor vehicle. Shortly after arrival to the scene, I learned that the driver had left the scene and the bicyclist had been pronounced dead at Municipal Hospital at 2221 hrs. The driver then called the sheriff's police to report the crash. Local police were dispatched to the location where they then transported him to the local police station. This officer cleared the accident scene at 2252 hrs.

At approximately 2310 hrs this officer met with a Bud Cook in the booking area of the station. As this officer started the interview of Mr. Cook, a strong odor of alcohol could be detected coming from his breath. His eyes were bloodshot and watery. Mr. Cook was given a Miranda warning at 2315 hrs. At first, he became very upset, saying that he should never have reported the accident because he was going to be blamed for getting someone he did not even see. I explained to him that the reason I was reading him the Miranda warning was to protect his rights. He calmed down, and this officer then read him his rights which he advised that he understood and signed the waiver. Mr. Cook had advised that he knew he struck something but did not know what it was. He advised that for all he knew, somebody could have thrown something at his car. Mr. Cook had reported that he drove home, very fast going about 80 to 85 miles an hour. The more he thought about the damage and he started to think that he hit something larger than an animal, and it was probably a person. He arrived home and told his wife to immediately call the police. He was informed of the alcohol odor that I was detecting and asked if he had had anything to drink since the accident occurred. He replied "no, all I did was drive straight home, tell my wife to call the cops and two minutes later the cops were at my house."

This officer requested Mr. Cook to perform a field sobriety test, which he did. The first test requested and performed was a finger to nose test. He was hesitant and touched underneath his nose and above his upper lip. He tried again and completely missed his nose, again touching below the tip of the nose.

The next test requested was the heel to toe test. On this test, he attempted to take his first step and lost his balance. He regained his balance and attempted the second step and again stumbled.

This officer then brought Mr. Cook back to the police department where he was processed—fingerprinting and photographs. At approximately 0225 hrs on 5/16 this officer again gave Mr. Cook his Miranda warnings and told him that I wanted to obtain a typewritten statement from him concerning the events of the evening leading up to the accident. Mr. Cook gave this officer a two page typewritten statement that this officer prepared and Mr. Cook reviewed.

APPLICATION EXERCISES

4. After reviewing the facts of the Cook case (Introduction to Hypothetical Cases, p. xxxvii) and reading the investigating officer's police report in Exhibit 6.2, use the full disclosure model of questioning to prepare a set of questions for the initial client interview. (Be sure to include questions that elicit the defendant's contact information.)

5. After reviewing the facts of the Turner case (Introduction to Hypothetical Cases, p. xxxvii) and reading the investigating officer's police report in Exhibit 6.3, use the limited disclosure model of questioning to prepare a set of questions for the initial client interview. (Be sure to include questions that elicit the defendant's contact information.)

Exhibit 6.3: Incident Report #1 in *Turner* Case: Case File No. 10-0857

At 2:01 P.M. July 29, I was northbound on Bloomington Avenue at Normal Street. I saw a red sedan traveling west on Bloomington Street and fail to stop at the intersection of Bloomington Avenue at Normal Street. I signaled to the driver of the red sedan to pull over and stop. The vehicle began to accelerate and then came to an abrupt stop. The vehicle stopped partially on the roadway at 857 Normal Street. The driver of the vehicle, Brandon Turner, exited the vehicle. I blew the horn of the patrol car three times and then called out to Turner to stop. Turner walked towards the entrance of the business at 857 Normal Street. Turner entered the business and ran into a bathroom in the southwest corner of the business. I removed him from the bathroom and handcuffed him. I patted Turner down and removed him from the business.

As I was securing Turner in my car, I heard someone say, there was a gun under the sink. Located in a sink cabinet in the bathroom was a Taurus 9 mm semi-automatic handgun. The slide of the gun was pulled back and the magazine was loaded with 15 rounds of ammunition. I removed the gun, and locked it in the trunk of the patrol car.

Looking through the front driver's side window of Turner's car, I could see a plastic sandwich bag containing a white granular substance. The substance had the appearance of cocaine. I unlocked Turner's car and retrieved the substance. Upon further examination, I could see that there were two sandwich-type bags. Each bag contained several smaller bags which contained a white substance. The openings of the bags were tied closed. I secured the bag containing the substance in the breast pocket of my jacket. Turner's car was secured by Troopers S. Wright (number 123) and A. Hamilton (number 456). Troopers Wright and Hamilton conducted a search of the Turner car with the assistance of K-9s. Turner was taken to the Municipal Detention Center. A field test on the white substance found in Turner's car was conducted. The substance tested positive for cocaine. The substance was weighed. It weighed 34.5 grams.

4. ACCEPTING THE CASE

Conflicts check
The process of verifying whether the acceptance of a new case would result in a conflict of interest for the attorney.

Before the case is accepted, a **conflicts check** is run on the client to ensure that there is no conflict of interests in representing the client. This check is carried out by verifying whether the client is an adverse party in another case handled by the attorney. Additionally, there may also be a conflict of interest if witnesses against the client are represented by the lawyer. This is accomplished by reviewing a list of clients. Although such lists can be maintained in hard copy, most firms store this data electronically, which may be done on computer software designed for this purpose. In general, a conflict for one lawyer in the firm creates a conflict for other attorneys. Attorneys shifting from defense to prosecution or vice versa must refrain from accepting representation that jeopardizes confidences learned in their prior employment.

Likewise, paralegals must also be careful to avoid their own conflicts of interest. Paralegals are ethically required to disclose to their employers any preexisting client or personal relationship that may conflict with the interests of the employer or prospective clients.[17] The National Federation of Paralegal Associations offers the following advice for preventing conflicts of interests:

- "On your first day of employment (if it has not been done during the interview process), ask the supervising attorney or other appropriate person for a list of legal cases or matters that the firm or employer is handling. Review that list to identify the names of clients, parties in litigation, acquaintances, friends, or family members that you recognize.
- Compare your list of all legal cases or matters on which you have worked against the new employer's list. If you work in litigation, also review the names of attorneys representing the various parties.
- Advise the employer of any matters in which you suspect you may have a conflict of interest. Provide only enough information about the matter for the employer (or a firm or corporation conflicts committee) to determine whether there is a conflict of interest. Usually, the client or matter name is sufficient to assess this.
- As new clients and legal matters come into the office, or if new parties are added to cases already underway, check their names against your list as described above.
- Despite your best efforts, a matter or client in which you have a possible conflict of interest may slip through. If this happens, bring it to the attorney's attention as soon as you become aware of it.
- Maintain your list of matters on which you work throughout your paralegal career."[18]

---

[17]National Association of Legal Assistants (NALA) Code of Ethics and Professional Responsibility, Canon 8; *see also* National Federation of Paralegal Associations (NFPA) Model Code of Ethics and Professional Responsibility and Guidelines for Enforcement, Canon 8.

[18]NFPA website, *http://www.paralegals.org/displaycommon.cfm?an=1&subarticlenbr=390*

APPLICATION EXERCISE

6. Your supervising attorney, Charles Hovey, informs you that he has agreed to represent Brandon Turner in any criminal matters relating to the events reported in Exhibit 6.3. He further informs you that Turner and a Dennis Watterson were co-owners of the car in which the crack cocaine was discovered by the police and that both have been charged with illegal possession of drugs. Draft a memorandum to Mr. Hovey addressing whether the applicable state ethics rules allow him to also represent Mr. Watterson. (Your memorandum should quote your state's statute or rule governing conflicts of interest.)

If there is no conflict of interests in accepting the case, the attorney will discuss the fee with the client. Paralegals are not ethically allowed to set the fee. There are several fee arrangement models used when private counsel is hired in a criminal case. First is the **hourly fee**. Under this approach, the law office bills the client for the time devoted to the case by the attorneys and paralegals. Rates are based on the experience and the local market. Although public defenders are typically salaried, assigned attorneys are usually paid on an hourly basis.

When a private client hires an attorney on an hourly fee basis, the client usually makes an advance payment at the beginning of the representation. This amount is deposited in the **attorney's trust fund**. The trust fund is an account holding money on behalf of an attorney's clients. The rules governing attorney ethics forbid the lawyer from commingling personal or business funds in this account. As the attorneys and paralegals bill for their services, funds from the advance payment are paid to the law office. If any portion of the retainer remains when the case comes to a conclusion, it is refunded to the client. When the funds on deposit are depleted, the lawyer will require that an additional sum be paid into the trust account for payment of future fees.

The second model is the **flat fee**. This is a preestablished amount that the client must pay for representation in the case. Both the client and the attorney

Hourly fee
The rate of compensation earned by an attorney based on the time devoted to the case.

Attorney's trust fund
A special account holding money on behalf of the client.

Flat fee
A preestablished amount that the client must pay for representation in the case.

Ethical Duties of Attorneys Related to Client Trust Accounts

Unfortunately, many attorneys get in trouble by misusing the special trust fund accounts that are established to hold money that belongs to the client but is held by the attorney for specified purposes. The rules governing the use of these client trust funds are spelled out in the ethics codes adopted by state supreme courts and bar associations. Most establish requirements that are similar to those contained **ABA Model Rule of Professional Conduct Rule 1.15**

See *http://www.americanbar.org/groups/professional_responsibility/publications/model_rules_of_professional_conduct/rule_1_15_safe-keeping_priority.html* have the certainty of knowing the amount of the fee before any work is done. The amount of work, however, is not known. A case that languishes in the court system for months or even years will dramatically reduce the attorney's profits. In contrast, the client may be paying an unusually high amount for representation that concludes after a few court appearances.

Contingent fee
The lawyer fee owed by the client if the attorney is successful. There is no fee if the client does not prevail.

Unlike personal injury cases, it is unethical for an attorney to enter into a contingent fee agreement in a criminal case. A **contingent fee** is a lawyer fee owed by the client if the attorney is successful. There is no payment if the client does not prevail.

Criminal attorneys must be mindful of the source of the funds used to pay the fee. If funds were acquired by the client in an illegal transaction, such as the sale of illicit drugs, the government may seize the funds. Payment of the fee in $10,000 cash or more requires the attorney to report the transaction to the federal government.

C. Preliminary Investigation

1. REVIEWING POLICE REPORTS AND WITNESS STATEMENTS

There are three types of documents generated in most criminal cases: charging documents, officer reports, and witness statements. These papers reveal valuable information to the defense team. The charge is provided to the defendant at the arraignment. The other documents are furnished to the defense as discovery documents.

Charging instruments, whether in the form of a citation, criminal charge, information, or bill of indictment, disclose the general factual basis for the complaint as well as the particular law the defendant allegedly violated. If the defendant claims no involvement in the offense, the date alleged in the charging document gives the attorney the starting point for building an alibi defense. The defendant will need to prove his whereabouts on the date in question. Likewise, if the alleged offense involves an adult victim, the charging instrument will reveal the victim's identity.

Law enforcement officer reports provide many details of an investigation. These reports are typically prepared on templates that include fields for witness information, such as DOB, gender, address, etc. Additionally, there is a section containing the officer's narrative. The narrative section presents what the officer did and observed. It may discuss what occurred at the scene or an interview of a witness. A copy of a Miami-Dade police officer's incident report is depicted in Exhibit 6.4. This report includes fill-in-the-blank sections as well as the officer's narrative statement.

Exhibit 6.4: Police Incident Report in Vick Case (Page 1)

In 2007, airport screeners seized a water bottle from NFL star Michael Vick at a security checkpoint. Screeners discovered the bottle included a "concealed compartment" that they believed contained a small amount of marijuana. Laboratory test results revealed no evidence of drugs in the bottle. The State Attorney did not charge Vick. Excerpts of the police incident report follow:

		CIRCLE ONE White Pink Blue Yellow	OFFENSE-INCIDENT REPORT			Juvenile In Report		Juvenile Warn/Claims		1. Original 2. Supplement	1
AGENCY CODE	GANG RELATED										
Date of Supplement			**MIAMI-DADE POLICE DEPARTMENT**		Agency Report Number		PD070117030397				

Original Day Reported	Wed	Date 01-17-07	Time 0715	Time Dispatched 0830		Time Arrived 1100		Time Completed 1100	

Incident Type 1. Felony 2. Traffic Felony	3. Misdemeanor 4. Traffic Misdemeanor	5. Ordinance 6. Other	Incident Day Wed	Date 01-17-07	Time 0715	To	Day	Date	Time

Offense #1	Type 1	Description Found Property		A - Attempted C - Committed	C	7———————————————7		NCIC/UCR Code
Offense #2				A - Attempted C - Committed				

Incident Location (Street, Apt. Number) M.I.A. Concourse "G", TSA screening point	City Miami		District 7	Grid 1154	Area	Zone
Business Name/Area Identifier		Forced Entry 0. N/A 2. No 1. Yes	0		0

Location Type							
01. Residence-Single	06. Gas Station	11. Specialty Store	16. Storage	21. Airport	26. Highway/Roadway	98. Other	
02. Apartment/Condo	07. Liquor Sales	12. Drug Store/Hospital	17. Gov't/Public Bldg.	22. Bus/Rail Terminal	27. Park/Woodlands/Field		21
03. Residence-Other	08. Bar/Nightclub	13. Bank/Financial Inst.	18. School/University	23. Construction Site	28. Lake/Waterway		
04. Hotel/Motel	09. Supermarket	14. Commercial/Office Bldg.	19. Jail/Prison	24. Other Structure	29. Motor Vehicle		
05. Convience Store	10. Dept./Discount Store	15. Industrial Mfg's.	20. Religious Bldg.	25. Parking Lot/Garage	30. Other Mobile		

# Victims 01	# Victims 01	# Offenders 01	# Prem. Ent. 00	# Veh. Recov. 00	Type Weapon 01. N/A 01. Handgun	02. Rifle 03. Shotgun 04. Firearm	05. Knife/Cutting 06. Blunt Object	07. Hands/Fist/Feet 08. Poison 09. Explosive	10. Fire/Incendiary 11. Threat/Intimidation 12. Simulated Weapon	13. Drugs 98. Unknown 99. Other	00

V/W Code V - Victim W - Witness C - Reporting Person	P - Proprietor Z - Other	Victim Type 0. N/A 1. Juvenile 2. L. E. Officer 3. Adult	4. Business 5. Government 6. Church 9. Other	Race N/A/A W-White B-Black	1-American Indian O-Oriental/Asian U-Unknown	Sex N/A/A M-Male F-Female U-Unknown	Residence Status 0. N/A 1. City 2. County	3. Florida 4. Out-of-State	Residence Status 0. N/A 1. Full Year 2. Part Year 3. Non-Resident	Extent of Injury 0. None 1. Minor 2. Serious 3. Fatal

Offense Number 1 #1 3. Both 2 #2	V/W Code 1	V/W Type W	01	N/A Type 3	Name (Last, First, Middle or Business) Joseph, Gertrude					Residence Phone
Address (Street, Apt. Number) 8300 NW 36 St.				City Miami		State FL.	Zip 33172		Business Phone 305-526-2893
Other Contact Info. (Time Available, Hangout, etc.)				Synopsis of Involvement TSA Screener who discovered hidden compartment					

V/W Code V, W, or P	Race B	Sex F	Date of Birth or Age 25	Res. Type 01	Res. Status 01	Extent of Injury 00	Injury Type(s) 00	00	Relationship 01	Ethnicity	Will Victim prefer charges? Yes ☐ No ☐

Offense Indicator 1 #1 3. Both 2 #2	V/W Code 1	V/W Type W	02	N/A Type 03	Name (Last, First, Middle or Business) Rodriguez, Hector					Residence Phone
Address (Street, Apt. Number) 8300 NW 36 St				City Miami		State FL.	Zip 33172		Business Phone 305-526-2893
Other Contact Info. (Time Available, Hangout, etc.)				Synopsis of Involvement "G" Supervisor					

V/W Code V, W, or P	Race W	Sex M	Date of Birth or Age 30	Res. Type 01	Res. Status 01	Extent of Injury 00	Injury Type(s) 00	00	Relationship 01	Witness?	Will Victim prefer charges? Yes ☐ No ☐

OFF-INC Indicator 1 #1 3. Both 2 #2	Suspect Code 1		S	01	Name (Last, First, Middle or Business) Vick, Michael				
Maiden Name		Nickname/Street Name				Place of Birth		Residence Phone	
Last Known Address (Street, Apt. Number)				City		State	Zip	Business Phone	
Occupation		Employer/School			Address			Social Security Number	
Driver's License State/Number		Immigration and Naturalization Number		Other I.D. Number		OBTS Number (Arrest)		FGIC/NCIC	
Clothing (Describe)						Scars/Marks/Tattoos (Location/Description)			

R B	S M	Date of Birth or Age	Height	Weight	Eye Color	Hair Color	Hair Length	Hair Style
Complexion	Build	Facial Hair	Teeth	Speech/Voice	Special Identifiers			

See Narrative

Person/Unit Notified	Time	Related Report Number(s)

Officer(s) Reporting Det. Kevin C. Kozak	ID. Number/Sensor Code 2268	Unit A6222	Date 01-17-07
Officer Reviewing (If Applicable)	ID. Number	Routed To	Referred To	Assigned To Kozak	By Lageyre	Date 01-17-07

Case Status O/P	Clearance Type 1. Arrest 2. Exceptional 3. Unfounded 4. Open Pend.	A - Adult J - Juvenile	Date Cleared	OBTS Number	Page 1 of	Page
Exception Type 1. Extradition Declined	3. Arrest on Primary Offense Secondary Offense Without Prosecution	5. Death of Offender 4. W/W Refused to Cooperate	5. Prosecution Declined 6. Juvenile / No Custody			

CIRCLE ONE Gang		NARRATIVE CONTINUATION			Juvenile In Report	1. Original 2. Supplement		2
Date of Supplement		MIAMI-DADE POLICE DEPARTMENT		Agency Report Number		PD070117-030397		
Original Date Reported 01-17-07	Original Primary Offense Description **Found Property**		Victim #1 Name **State of Fl.**				Original NCIC/UCR Code	
Original OFF/INC Location MIA "G"	Primary Offense Changed To		A - Attempted C - Committed	New Status Violation Number			New NCIC/UCR Code	

I was contacted by **Det. Sgt. R. Lageyre** at approx. 0845 hrs. He advised me that a water bottle with a hidden compartment had been found at Concourse "G" screening point and had been taken to the TSA Operations Center at Miami International Airport. He asked that I impound the bottle and initiate an investigation. Upon arrival at the Ops. Center I made contact with TSA screener **M. Salazar** who signed a property receipt for the bottle. The bottle was a 20 oz. "**Aquafina**" water bottle. The bottle's label concealed a seam which separated the top and the bottom of the bottle. Both ends were sealed by clear partitions and what appeared to be silicone sealant. The concealed compartment contained a small amount of dark particulate and a pungent aroma closely associated with Marijuana. The lower half of the bottle was almost completely full of a clear liquid. The top half contained a small amount of clear liquid. When held upright the bottle appeared to be half full of water.

I next made contact with TSA screening Supervisor for Concourse "G". **Mr. Hector Rodriguez** advised me that a B/M "**AirTran**" airlines passenger had been reluctant to turn over his water bottle during the screening process. Subsequently he surrendered the bottle which was placed in the recycle bin by TSA screener **Gertrude Joseph**. The passenger completed his screening through Concourse "G" and was allowed to go to his gate. The passenger's reluctance to relinquish a simple water bottle aroused the suspicions of TSA screener **Gertrude Joseph**. **Joseph** retrieved the bottle and upon further investigation found the concealed compartment. She notified her supervisor, **Mr. Rodriguez**. The bottle was taken to the TSA Ops center by **M. Salazar**.

I received the written statements from **Joseph** and **Rodriguez** by FAX at approx. 1035 hrs. At approx. 1130 hrs I returned to the "G" Screening point and met with **Joseph**. I asked her specifically how she would have known that the bottle belonged to **Michael Vick**. She advised me that **Mr. Bernard Lee**, another TSA screener had identified the B/M as **Vick**, a Professional football player for the **Atlanta Falcons**. Further, she stated that the "**Aquafina**" bottle was the only item in the recycle bin. I also obtained a written statement from **Mr. Bernard Lee** stating that he had recognized **Vick** as a professional football player. Refer to his written statement for details.

I obtained flight reservation information which indicated that a **Mr. Michael Vick** was a passenger on AirTran flt. 338 to Atlanta, GA.

I later reviewed digital surveillance video of the incident which substantiated the incident as reported by **Rodriguez** and **Joseph**. The bottle will be transported to MDPD lab for analysis.

Officer(s) Reporting **Det. Kevin C. Kozak**			ID. Number(s)/Locator Code **2268**			Unit **A2622**		Date **01-17-07**
Officer Reviewing (if Applicable)	ID. Number	Routed To	Referred To		Assigned To **Kozak**	By **Lageyre**		Date **01-17-07**

| | | | | | | | Page 3 of 3 |

If an officer has first-hand knowledge of the facts asserted in the report, the officer is a potential trial witness. The report may be used to impeach the officer if

> ➢ Challenge capacity to perceive, recall, or relate
> ➢ Show untruthfulness in the following ways:
>   • Bias, prejudice, or self-interest
>   • Prior inconsistent statement (including impeachment by omission)
>   • Reputation for untruthfulness
>   • Prior convictions (felony or misdemeanor involved dishonesty)

Figure 6.2   Basis for Impeaching Witnesses

trial testimony contradicts the statement. **Impeachment** is the challenge of a witness's credibility. Defense attorneys consider not only what is stated in the report but what was omitted. If the officer testifies to matters not contained in his or her report, defense counsel can use **impeachment by omission** to discredit the officer. In other words, the report's omission of important facts can be used to attack the witness's credibility. Through cross-examination the attorney would establish that the officer received training in preparing reports; that if there is anything that is important it would be included in the report; and that a particular matter was not in the report. (An outline of the major ways to impeach a witness is included in Figure 6.2.)

Reports concerning a witness contain the officer's summary of the witness's statement. In addition to the witness summaries, after an interview is conducted police officers prepare a witness statement, which the witness reviews and signs. These statements are a strong indication of the witness's anticipated testimony. They can be used to impeach witnesses who stray from their prior statements.

In addition to helping the defense attorney prepare for trial, police reports and witness statements serve a valuable role in assessing the strength of the prosecution's case. A defendant maintaining his innocence may rethink his position once he is confronted with the compelling evidence against him. Hence these documents are helpful to the defense in determining whether to enter into a plea bargain or to go to trial.

2. INTERVIEWING FACT WITNESSES

There are two types of witnesses in a case: fact witnesses and expert witnesses. A **fact witness** is a person who has first-hand knowledge of the events at issue in a case. **Expert witnesses** are persons with specialized knowledge qualifying them to render an opinion that will be helpful to the trier of fact in deciding the issues of the case. We will discuss expert witnesses in Chapters 10 and 11.

The defense can learn of the identities of fact witnesses through the client, police reports, witness statements disclosed by the prosecution, or from other fact witnesses. The sophistication of fact witnesses varies dramatically. An experienced law enforcement officer who has testified numerous times is typically a strong witness, whereas a child who eyewitnessed an event may not be credible. Fact witnesses' cooperation levels also differ. The defendant's friends and family usually are eager to assist defense counsel. On the other hand, many prosecution witnesses may refuse to speak with the defense.

Impeachment
The challenge to a witness's credibility.

Impeachment by omission
The challenge to a witness's credibility based on what the witness failed to state on a prior occasion.

Fact witness
A person who has first-hand knowledge of the events at issue in a case.

Expert witness
A witness who is called to supply scientific, technical, or other specialized knowledge that will help the jury and/or judge evaluate the facts that have been presented.

a. Methods of Taking Witness Statements

Traditionally, witnesses are interviewed in person. This allows the interviewer to get a sense of how the witness will appear at trial. This also affords the opportunity to have the witness review and sign a statement prepared by the questioner at the time of the interview. This is the approach typically take by investigating law enforcement officers. Statements may be handwritten or typed. Examples of typed and handwritten witness statements about the hunting accident involving former Vice President Dick Cheney appear in Exhibits 6.5 and 6.6.

Exhibit 6.5: Handwritten Witness Statement

In February 2006, U.S. Vice President Dick Cheney accidentally shot Harry Whittington, a 78-year-old Texas attorney, while quail hunting on a Texas ranch. The Kenedy County Sheriff's deputies secured several witness statements during the investigation. The statement of Gerado Medellin, a member of the hunting party, follows.

My name is Gerado Medellin and I live on the Armstrong Ranch, Armstrong, Tx. My mailing address is P.O. Box 395, Armstrong TX 78338 and I am 45 years of age.

On Saturday February 11, 2006 at approximately 5:30 or 5:45 the dog handler's dog found a covey facing west. We flushed the covey and everyone shot and Mr. Whittington had a double. After that I worked the lab dog to find one of the birds of the double shot. Mr. Whittington assisted me in finding the first bird. After finding the first bird, Mr. Whittington asked me if I saw where the second bird had fallen. I told him yes and went to find it. As I was looking for the second bird Mr. Whittington went back to the hunting jeep. It took me approximately 5 minutes to locate the second bird. At that time, I saw Mr. Whittington walking towards the other hunters I yelled to him that I had found his other bird.

Shortly after that the outrider (Oscar) pointing where the other covey was at. At this time I was walking towards them also to you time.

When I was walking towards the hunters a single bird flew behind the Vice President

towards Mr. Whittington. That is when Vice President shot towards the bird and Mr. Whittington was in the line of fire.

Gerado Medellin

Exhibit 6.6: Typewritten Witness Statement

The owner of the ranch where the Cheney accidental shooting incident occurred signed a written statement for the Kenedy County Sheriff's Office.

I, Katharine Armstrong, am one of the owners of the Armstrong Ranch in Kenedy County, Texas and was present and an eye witness to the hunting accident that occurred on Feb. 12th, at approximately 5:30pm in the Comal pasture of the Armstrong Ranch. Although it was late in the afternoon and the sun was low, there was plenty of sunlight. All three shooters were wearing blaze orange gear and to the best of my knowledge there was no alcohol involved.

After being alerted by an outrider our hunting vehicle pulled up to the location where a covey of quail had been found. When the Vice President, Harry Whittington and Pam Willeford got out of the vehicle to work the covey they were told that there was a second covey ahead and to the left. They moved forward on the first covey and Mr. Whittington shot two birds that fell to his right in some tall grass and brush. Mr. Whittington, with the assistance of Gerry Medellin and a Labrador went to the spot where the birds and fallen to find them. The two men and the dog had difficulty finding one of the birds and spent several minutes attempting to find it in the tall grass. While Mr. Whittington stayed behind to look for his bird, the Vice President and Ambassador Willeford moved towards the second covey that was located further ahead and to the left of the first covey. In the meantime, Mr. Whittington returned briefly to the car then went back to look again for his lost bird. A short time later I noticed that Harry was moving forward to rejoin the Vice President and Ambassador Willeford. As he was moving forward I did not hear him announce himself or call to them to let them know he was approaching from behind and to their right. A single bird flushed in front of the Vice President and Ambassador Willeford. The Vice President swung through to his right and shot at the bird. Mr. Whittington fell to the ground about 30 yards away from the Vice President with his head facing towards the hunting vehicle. I saw the Vice President rush towards Mr. Whittington and almost in the same instant the Vice President's security detail was rushing to his side as well. My sister, Sarita Hixon, Ambassador Willeford and I remained out of the way a short distance from Mr. Whittington until the ambulance arrived about 20 to 25 minutes later.

Katharine Armstrong   Feb. 15, 2006

Statements also can be recorded electronically. Recorded statements are the most persuasive means of presenting a prior inconsistent statement in court. There are several methods of recording statements. Audio recordings can be made of in-person and telephone interviews, and video recordings can also be made of in-person and Internet interviews. If you use either of these methods, you need to elicit the witness's consent at the outset of the interview. At the beginning of the recording, introduce yourself and the name of your employer. Then identify the witness by name and ask the witness to acknowledge that the interview is being recorded with his or her consent. You should identify others present, as well as the date and time. You should follow the same protocol at the close of the interview. During the questioning, be careful not to interrupt the witness's answers. Another way of recording a witness's statement is through the use of a court reporter. You either should elicit the witness's consent on the record or have the witness sworn by the court reporter at the outset.

b. Friendly Witnesses

Friendly witness
A fact witness who knows something about the underlying occurrence and holds a favorable impression of the client.

Although this decision is made case-by-case, most defense attorneys question friendly witnesses shortly after the initial client interview. This captures the witness's recollection when it is fresh. A **friendly witness** is a fact witness who knows something about the underlying occurrence and holds a favorable impression of the client. The friendly witness has a relationship with the client besides being present during events involved in the case. Friends, family members, co-workers, and neighbors usually are friendly witnesses. Persons criminally charged in the same occurrence sometimes, but not always, are friendly witnesses. The client should be able to identify the friendly witnesses.

You should prepare before you interview a friendly witness. If the case involves a street crime, visit the location of the alleged crime before you speak to the witness. Try to view the scene at the same time of day as the event and orient yourself with the vantage point of the witness. For white-collar crimes, have the client educate you about the business, the persons involved along with their positions, how the transactions are ordinarily accomplished, and whether the occurrence alleged in the charge was handled in the typical way. Prepare an outline or checklist as a guide for your questioning.

When you carry out the interview, first introduce yourself as a paralegal and let the witness know your supervisor's name. Try to establish rapport with the witness before you begin questioning. Conduct the interview without taking detailed notes. You should only write down specific information such as names, addresses, and dates. At this stage, you should not write down the entire story. Your interview should be used to obtain all relevant information, even if it is unfavorable to the client. You should ask open-ended, non-judgmental questions to ensure the witness states what he or she actually knows rather than what you want said. You also should seek leads to other witnesses and evidence.

Once your questioning has been completed, you should document the interview by preparing a written statement. You should explain that this will be of assistance later on because memories fade over time. The title of the document references the witness by name (e.g., Statement of John Doe or Mary Jones Statement.) The first paragraph should set forth the time, date, and place of the interview along with the name of the person conducting it. The remaining paragraphs should present the witness's story in a chronological order in the first-person narrative format. ("I saw Fred cross the street" rather than "Ms. Witness saw Fred cross the street.") Let the witness assist you as you prepare the chronology. Emphasize the facts personally known to the witness. The witness should initial each correction as well as each page of the statement. Finally, the witness should sign and date the last page of the document. One possible approach is to have the witness sign the following: "I have read this statement of _____ pages, and it is true." This is followed by a signature line. A person other than you should sign as a witness.

After the statement is signed, explain the witness's potential role in the case. Encourage the witness to contact you if he or she remembers something else. Also, give the witness an idea of the time frame of the case. Make sure that you have the witness's contact information.

c. Witnesses Disclosed in Police Reports

Police reports will reveal the identities of witnesses who may be called to testify against the defendant. Many of these individuals are hostile witnesses. A **hostile witness** is one holding a favorable outlook toward the opposing party. Hostility arises from the witness's relationship with the defendant. Hence, the investigating officers and the victim are hostile toward the defendant. Moreover, a large segment of the general public is hostile to persons accused of crimes. Hostile witnesses are not likely to be helpful to the client voluntarily. Not all witnesses identified in police reports are hostile, however. Some may be neutral to the defense. **Neutral witnesses** are witnesses who do not have a relationship with either the defense or the prosecution.

It is best to interview neutral witnesses before speaking to the hostile witnesses. Because they are not aligned with either side, neutral witnesses have the potential to exert great impact on the jury. As these witnesses do not have a relationship with the parties, the events they observed will not have a lasting effect. It is, therefore, important to conduct an interview as soon as possible.

To prepare for an interview with a neutral witness, you should gather background information to determine whether the witness is truly neutral or is connected to the victim or law enforcement. If possible, try to ascertain how this individual came to be a witness. You should also prepare by orienting yourself to the crime scene and creating an outline or interview checklist.

When you contact the witness, identify yourself as a paralegal. Disclose your supervising attorney's name and the name of the client. Let the witness know that you would like to ask him or her about the incident and schedule a time and place for the interview. Some witnesses will not want to come to an attorney's office. A public location or the witness's home may be suitable. You should defer to the witness's choice of locations.

When you conduct the interview, approach it as if you are questioning a friendly witness by asking open-ended questions. If the witness is hesitant to respond, adapt by asking direct questions (e.g., who, what, where, why, when, and how). If this does not work, ask for particular information through short, one-fact-at-a-time inquiries. At the conclusion of your questioning, prepare a written statement for the witness's signature.

After interviewing neutral witnesses identified in the police reports, you should question hostile witnesses. Prepare an interview script outlining specific questions to be posed. When you schedule the interview, identify yourself, your employer, and the name of the client. Some hostile witnesses will refuse to speak with you. Politely let these witnesses know that if they change their mind, they can contact you. When you set up the interview, confirm that the witness was involved in the events in question in the case.

When you start the interview, provide the witness with a time line and place to orient him or her as to the occurrence at issue. Most hostile witnesses will not volunteer information, so you need to ask specific questions about the events. As

Hostile witness
A witness who manifests hostility or prejudice against the side that called him or her testify.

Neutral witness
A witness who has no relationship with either the defense or the prosecution.

APPLICATION EXERCISE

7. After reviewing your notebook materials on the Turner case and reading the Incident Report in Exhibit 6.7, Prepare a set of interview questions to ask Ms. Haney based on the assumption that she is a neutral witness.

Exhibit 6.7: Incident Report #2 in Turner Case: Case File No. 10-0857

On July 31 at 1:10 P.M. Reporting Agent (RA) interviewed RITA HANEY, W/F, DOB 2/29/52, 909 Beauford, Normal. HANEY is currently employed at the Normal Eatery, 857 Normal St. HANEY was interviewed to determine the last time anyone had been inside the cabinet located under the sink of the bathroom inside the restaurant prior to the arrest of Brandon Turner on July 29.

She provided the following information: she worked the evening of July 28 and cleaned the bathroom after she closed the restaurant at 8:00 P.M. HANEY said there was a full roll of toilet paper on the spindle so she did not open the storage cabinet under the sink to obtain a new roll. According to HANEY, there is no reason for any employee to go into the storage cabinet unless there is a need to replace the toilet paper. HANEY said it would be very unlikely that anyone, employee or customer, would have known the contents of the cabinet interior any time prior to Turner's arrest on July 29.

HANEY saw Turner enter the restaurant and enter the bathroom on July 29. HANEY saw Turner enter the bathroom, shut the door, and exit the bathroom within the few seconds. She thought it was unusual that Turner spent only a few seconds in the bathroom.

HANEY said her fellow employee Sue Williams had observed him enter the bathroom with a gun. Williams later found the gun inside the sink's cabinet interior.

---

the witness understands that you are interested in his or her answers, you may be able to shift to open-ended questions. Seek negative as well as favorable information. Following the interview, draft the witness's statement. Although the witness may not sign the statement, he or she may be willing to review, correct, and initial it for mistakes. If you intentionally make a mistake of a routine matter on each page, the witness will in essence verify the accuracy of the statement. If the witness is unwilling to remain with you as you prepare the statement, you should nevertheless prepare it immediately while the witness's oral account is fresh in your mind. Include a variety of non-essential and even unrelated facts, such as age of witness, names and ages of witness's family members, and witness's remarks about the surroundings of the interview location. If the witness's memory fades, these non-essential facts can corroborate the statement in part.

APPLICATION EXERCISE

8. After reviewing the facts of the Cook case and reading the Incident Report in Exhibit 6.8, prepare a set of interview questions to ask Officer Atkin based on the assumption that he will be a hostile witness.

Exhibit 6.8: Incident Report #2 in Cook Case: Case File No. 10-0857

On Sunday, May 15 at 2159 Reporting Officer (R/O) and Ptm Z. Whitten were dispatched to the scene of a personal injury accident on Route 185 and Normal Street. On arrival, north of the intersection, R/O located a bicycle which had been heavily damaged along the east (northbound curb). Farther north, along the same curb, R/O found a white female lying on her back. The body appeared lifeless. R/O observed her left foot to be near completely severed above the ankle. There was blood pooling on the roadway below the victim's head. Her eyes were open and appeared fixed and she made no response to my oral calls. Municipal Ambulance arrived at the scene within seconds off my assessment and elected to transport her in a "load and go" response.

R/O then began to scour the area, looking for witnesses. None of those present witnessed the accident. It was then determined to be an apparent hit and run. Ptm Whitten began photographing the scene. R/O summoned assistance from state investigators and Detective Colby responded to the scene. While conferring with Det. Colby, R/O learned that the driver of the suspect vehicle had contacted the County Sheriff's office from his residence and acknowledged involvement in the accident. R/O asked the sheriff's office to dispatch a unit to pick up the driver and provide transportation to the police station. Jack's Towing was summoned to retrieve and transport the vehicle to the station for processing.

R/O learned that state accident reconstruction officers were on their way and that the scene was to be secured until their arrival. Detective Colby then responded to the police station for follow-up investigation with the driver of the automobile unit.

R/O then gathered information to complete accident report. Items of evidence were secured by both Ptm Whitten and Detective Colby. Those items include the damaged bicycle remains, two pieces of blocked plastic, fragmented window glass, and broken reflector lens.

After completing the evidence recovery, R/O and reconstruction personnel proceeded to the police station to examine the suspect's vehicle. R/O observed the vehicle's plastic wind/bug deflector to be missing a piece which corresponded with the plastic fragments found at the scene. The unit was photographed by Sergeant Walker of the state police. At approximately 0500 R/O and Det. Colby returned to the scene where we secured hair samples which had been found on the roadway along the victim's action path in addition to cloth fiber samples. Det. Colby recovered the hair while R/O secured the cloth fibers. Items were maintained by Det. Colby.

Prepared by Officer Terry Atkin.

d. Witness Interview Summary

After you interview a witness, you should prepare a witness summary. This is a stand-alone document separate from the signed witness statement. The attitudes and background of a witness are almost as important as the statement itself. Therefore, your witness interview summary should evaluate the witness from the standpoint of accuracy, truthfulness, and personal appeal. One style of witness summary contains the following components:

- Preliminary information: name of witness, date of interview, file name, and number.
- Background and personal information.
- Factual information in chronological or topical presentation.
- Evaluation of witness's demeanor and credibility, along with the specific reason for your conclusions.
- List of documents signed by witness.
- List of documents produced by witness along with the location of the originals.
- Conclusions and recommendations for next steps.[19]

D. Defense Preparation for Initial Court Appearances

The first time a criminal defendant appears in court is for the bail hearing. The second court appearance usually is the arraignment. We described these proceedings in Chapter 5. There are specific steps the defense team can perform to prepare for these proceedings.

1. BAIL AND DETENTION HEARINGS

In determining whether a person accused of a crime should be released on bond, the judge will consider factors such as the defendant's prior record, ties to the community, prior failures to appear in court, and employment. If the judge finds the defendant to be a danger to the community or a flight risk, the defendant will remain in jail. In federal court, certain drug-related charges and crimes of violence carry a "presumption of detention." Persons charged with these crimes remain in jail until their trial date unless they convince the judge that there are compelling reasons they should be released.

To prepare for the hearing, the defense attorney needs to gather information about the client's family, employment, financial circumstances, and background. You may be assigned the task of interviewing the client as well as friends and family to gather this information. It is helpful to have an interview sheet to

---

[19]S. Parsons, *Interviewing and Investigating, Essential Skills for the Paralegal* (3d ed., Wolters Kluwer 2008), 322.

collect the important information. In addition, the client will need to identify property that could be used to secure a bond. If witnesses are needed at the hearing, you may need to prepare them. (See Chapter 11 for a discussion of witness preparation.)

In federal cases, a pretrial services officer will ask the client for an interview before the initial appearance. It is the client's choice as to whether he wants to do so. The defense attorney and the client will decide whether it is a wise decision to give the interview. If the client agrees, he must be truthful. Because the judge and the prosecutor will see the pretrial services report, the defense attorney should instruct the client to refuse to answer questions concerning the pending charges or any other illegal activity.

APPLICATION EXERCISE

9. Draft a client questionnaire to gather bond hearing information. The initial questions should elicit the defendant's contact information.

---

2. ARRAIGNMENT

To prepare for the arraignment, the defense attorney will draft an appearance. This is a document filed in court identifying the attorney representing a party in the case. The appearance also identifies the attorney's address and telephone number. In some jurisdictions, an attorney identification number is also included. Exhibit 6.9 depicts an appearance. Some judges require pro se defendants to file an appearance. **Pro se parties** are parties to litigation who are unrepresented by counsel. The original of the appearance is filed with the clerk of the court and a copy is provided to the prosecutor.

Pro se party
A party to litigation who is unrepresented by counsel.

In addition to the appearance, the defense also may file a jury demand or jury waiver, a demand for a speedy trial, and a discovery motion. Under the Sixth Amendment, a criminal defendant has a right to be tried by a jury. In some courts, defendants will be tried by a jury unless there is a waiver by both sides. In other jurisdictions, the defendant must expressly demand trial by jury. The body of a sample jury demand is presented in Exhibit 6.10. In jurisdictions in which the defendant must demand a jury, the defendant also can waive this right, as well. The waiver must be made in writing. An example of the body of a jury waiver is set forth in Exhibit 6.11.

In some states, the defendant may file a demand for a speedy trial at the time of arraignment. The Sixth Amendment and virtually all state constitutions grant defendants the right to a speedy trial. The United States and many states also have adopted statutes specifically granting protections beyond the constitutional guarantees. For instance, the Illinois Speedy Trial Act provides that the trial for defendants not in custody must be commenced within 160 days provided

Exhibit 6.9: Defense Counsel's Appearance

THE UNITED STATES DISTRICT COURT FOR THE NORTHERN DISTRICT OF INDIANA
HAMMOND DIVISION

UNITED STATES OF AMERICA)
    vs.)   Case No. 09 CR XXX
WILLIAM EDWARDS,)
    Defendant.)

APPEARANCE

The undersigned hereby enters his appearance on behalf of the Defendant, WILLIAM
EDWARDS.

Respectfully submitted,
WILLIAM EDWARDS,

Defendant

By_____

CHARLES HOVEY, his attorney

Charles Hovey
Attorney for Defendant
1857 Bone Street
Normal, IL 61617
(309) 555-1857

that they make "a clear and unequivocal" demand for a speedy trial.[20] Thus, a defense attorney files a speedy trial demand to start the clock running. A sample demand for speedy trial is presented in Exhibit 6.12.

In jurisdictions in which the parties must ask the court to order discovery, the defendant may file at arraignment a motion for leave to conduct discovery. Discovery will be discussed in detail in Chapter 7.

[20]725 ILCS 5/103-5(b).

APPLICATION EXERCISES

10. Draft an appearance for defense counsel using the following information:
- Court: state court for the community in which your school is located.
- Defendant: name yourself.
- Case number: fiftieth misdemeanor case of this year.
- Defense attorney: public defender for your community.

To complete the form, you may need to contact the clerk's office or research the court's website for the name, address, and telephone number of the public defender's office.

11. Using the federal form located online at *http://www.ilcd.uscourts.gov/forms/AO458.pdf* and the following information, prepare an appearance for the defendant in the Schroeder case (p. xxxviii):
- Defense attorney: Judith R. Manchester.
- Defense attorney's address and phone number: your school's address and main telephone number; Defense attorney's fax number: same as office number.
- Defense attorney's bar number: 1234.
- Venue: U.S. District and Division for the community in which your school is located.

Exhibit 6.10: Body of Jury Demand

Now comes the Defendant BUD COOK, by CHARLES HOVEY, his attorney, and demands trial by jury.

Exhibit 6.11: Body of Jury Waiver

I, Defendant BUD COOK, hereby waive a jury trial in the above-entitled cause and consent to trial before the court.

APPLICATION EXERCISE

12. Draft a jury demand using the following information:
- Court: state court for the community in which your school is located.
- Defendant: Brandon Turner.
- Case number: Leave blank.
- Defense attorney: Charles Hovey, 1857 Bone Street, Normal, IL 61761, (309)-555-1857.

Exhibit 6.12: Demand for Speedy Trial

IN THE CIRCUIT COURT OF
THE 12th JUDICIAL CIRCUIT
WILL COUNTY, ILLINOIS

PEOPLE OF THE   )
STATE OF ILLINOIS   )
        v.   )   Case No. 09 CF XXXX
BRANDON TURNER,   )
    Defendant.   )

DEMAND FOR SPEEDY TRIAL

The undersigned, as attorney for the Defendant, BRANDON TURNER, pursuant to Section 103-5 (b) of the Code of Criminal Procedure, 725 ILCS 5/103-5(b), hereby demands a speedy trial.

Respectfully submitted,

_____

CHARLES HOVEY,
Attorney for Defendant

CHARLES HOVEY
Attorney for Defendant
1857 Bone Street
Normal, IL 61761
(309)-555-1857

SUMMARY

This chapter examined the role defense attorneys play in the preliminary stages of a criminal case after the prosecutor has brought charges against the defendant. Attorneys defending persons accused of committing crimes may be in private practice, employed in government service as public defenders, or paid by the government as appointed counsel. Private attorneys are paid on an hourly basis, by a flat fee, or by a combination of these two methods.

When the client initially meets with the defense attorney, the client is instructed to refrain from discussing the case with anyone, especially law enforcement officers. Information disclosed to the attorney by the client is protected by the attorney-client privilege and the duty to maintain confidentiality. Before the case is accepted by the attorney, a conflicts check is run to make sure that the representation does not violate the interests of another client.

Paralegals may be involved in the preliminary investigation by interviewing fact witnesses and preparing statements for witnesses to sign. Paralegals also may conduct audio or audio/video witness interviews.

At the preliminary phase of the case, defense attorneys are also involved in the preparation of various documents that need to be filed with the court. These documents include: the appearance, jury demand, jury waiver, demand for speedy trial, and discovery motions. In addition to knowing what they contain, paralegals should be able to prepare drafts for attorneys to review.

REVIEW QUESTIONS

1. What are public defenders? How do they differ from federal defenders?
2. Explain why courts assign private attorneys to represent indigent defendants when public defender offices are available to represent persons who are unable to afford an attorney.
3. What is the primary role of the defense attorney?
4. What is the reason defense attorneys instruct their clients not to give statements to the police?
5. What are appropriate locations for a client interview? Why is a public place inappropriate?
6. When is an attorney permitted to reveal confidential client information?
7. How does attorney-client privilege differ from the duty of confidentiality?
8. What are the full disclosure and limited disclosure models of conducting the initial client interview? What are the advantages of each model?
9. How can you demonstrate professionalism when you carry out a client interview?
10. What is a conflict of interest? What can you do to avoid your own conflicts of interest?
11. List and explain the major fee models used by private criminal defense attorneys.
12. What is impeachment by omission and how is it used to discredit an investigating officer?
13. What is the difference between a fact witness and an expert witness?
14. What steps should you follow when interviewing a hostile witness?
15. What information must be gathered to prepare for a bond hearing?
16. What types of documents do criminal defense attorneys prepare for the defendant's arraignment?

Chapter 7

Discovery and Disclosure

Up to this point, we have covered the actions taken by law enforcement officials (police and prosecutors) as they investigate crimes and prosecute them in the court system. We have also discussed the role of the defense attorney and the responsibilities involved in representing a person accused of a crime. This chapter focuses on the procedures used to acquire and exchange information that is vital to assessing the strength of the case and preparing for trial. It is an aspect of criminal litigation in which paralegals can play a very active role.

To discover something is to uncover that which was previously unknown or hidden. In the legal system, **discovery** is a legal procedure by which a party in the case can obtain information about the case from other sources prior to the start of the trial. **Disclosure** is defined as the revealing of information. As part of the discovery process, parties to the case can be required to disclose relevant information they have regarding matters involved in the litigation.

The discovery process is somewhat analogous to gold mining. Initially, a miner performs an exploratory drilling to find out whether gold is even present at the site. If it is there, the miner taps into this area. He will continue to focus on sites rich with gold ore as long as it is economically feasible to retrieve it. Ultimately, the mineral that is recovered is processed into a polished product. As in gold mining, formal discovery may yield some, much, or no helpful material. A skilled criminal law practitioner will react to the initial disclosures to determine whether it makes sense to seek additional information and what type should be sought. Once all of the raw data are retrieved and organized, the attorney uses this information to design an appropriate approach to the case.

While there are many variations in the rules of criminal procedure among the states and federal government, there are two basic models of formal discovery in criminal cases. Both models will be discussed in this chapter. You will need to check your jurisdiction's criminal procedural rules to see which model applies to your state and the scope of disclosure.

Discovery
A legal procedure by which a party in the case can obtain information about the case from other parties prior to the start of the trial.

Disclosure
The revealing of information.

A. Justifications for Discovery

Discovery is designed to provide both sides of a legal dispute with as much information as possible prior to the start of a trial, on the theory that the availability of this information will encourage out-of-court settlements and make trials fairer and more efficient.

If the defense knows there were several eyewitnesses to the crime or that the defendant's fingerprints were found on the murder weapon, the defendant is far more likely to plead guilty to a lesser crime or in return for a reduced sentence. On the other hand, if the defense knows that the only witness has poor eyesight and a long-standing grudge against the defendant, the defense is more likely to either go to trial or hold out for a better plea bargain. The trial will be more efficient because the information gained through discovery allows the attorneys to fight out various evidentiary issues before the trial begins. By resolving these issues before trial, some potential witnesses may not have to appear or witnesses will spend less time on the stand. Indeed the judge's rulings on some of these pretrial motions may also encourage a plea-bargained alternative to the trial.

Most importantly, discovery should lead to fairer trials by eliminating the element of surprise. Surprise witnesses make for good movies and television shows, but they do not always lead to just results. Through discovery, each side learns the identities of opposition witnesses and their likely testimony. This knowledge gives each side more time to investigate the background of adverse witnesses, find expert witnesses, etc.

B. Constitutional Issues Involved in Discovery

Due process of law
Legal procedures that enforce basic rights that are considered necessary for fairness and justice.

Exculpatory evidence
Evidence that either tends to establish the defendant's innocence or is favorable to the accused on the question of punishment.

Impeachment evidence
Evidence that tends to undermine the credibility of the opponent's witnesses.

Before reading further, go back to pages 94–96 in Chapter 4 to review what we had to say about **due process of law** and the provisions of the U.S. Constitution that protect the rights of criminal defendants. The two main constitutional issues arising in the context of discovery are: (1) whether it is a violation of the Due Process Clause to withhold evidence from the other side, and (2) whether it is a violation of the privilege against self-incrimination to force the defense to turn over materials that may tend to incriminate the accused.

In 1963 in *Brady v. Maryland*[1] the U.S. Supreme Court ruled that the Due Process Clause requires prosecutors to turn over all exculpatory evidence to the defense. **Exculpatory evidence** is evidence that either tends to establish the defendant's innocence or is favorable to the accused on the question of punishment.[2] In *Giglio v. United States*, the U.S. Supreme Court held that the prosecution's *Brady* obligations included the affirmative duty to provide the defense with **impeachment evidence**.[3] In either case, the government's duty to

---

[1]373 U.S. 83, 83 S. Ct. 1194, 10 L. Ed. 2d 215 (1963).

[2]*United States v. Bagley*, 473 U.S. 667, 682, 105 S. Ct. 3375, 87 L. Ed. 2d 481 (1985).

[3]405 U.S. 150, 92 S. Ct. 763, 31 L. Ed. 2d 104 (1972). Impeachment evidence is evidence that tends to undermine the credibility of the government's witnesses.

United States ex rel. Thompson v. Dye
United States Circuit Court of Appeals
221 F.2d 763 (3d Cir., 1955)

OPINION BY: JUSTICE MCLAUGHLIN

A jury sitting in the Court of Oyer and Terminer of Allegheny County, Pennsylvania found relator-appellant guilty of murder in the first degree and recommended the death penalty. The conviction and the death sentence were affirmed by the Pennsylvania Supreme Court.

***On appeal we remanded the case to the district court for a finding of fact whether the court credited the testimony of police officer Heagy or the prosecutor as to what the former told the latter before trial concerning the condition of the accused at or about the time of his arrest. In pursuance of this the district court made further findings of fact, particularly that:

> 2. Mr. Heagy did inform the prosecutor that he participated in the arrest of the relator in a barroom where the latter had been in a brawl and had been disarmed. He further informed Strauss, as the latter admits, that the relator was at that time under the influence of liquor to a quarrelsome degree; that he smelled the odor of alcohol on him; that his shirt and clothes were torn; and that he was perspiring and "messed up."
>
> 3. The prosecuting officers did not communicate to defense counsel or to the State trial judge prior to trial that, at the time of relator's arrest, several police officers detected the odor of alcohol on relator's breath; that he showed signs of having been engaged in a fight; and that at least one officer would say he was under the influence of liquor to a quarrelsome degree.

The court also made an additional conclusion of law, namely:

> The prosecuting officers were not in possession of information or evidence vital to relator's defense which they were obliged to disclose to the defense or to the court.

***

The important question before us is whether the district judge erred in holding as a matter of law that the withheld and suppressed evidence was not vital to the defense of the accused.

The prosecution had alternative theories: (1) that Thompson had committed the killing of Wallace Russell, the bartender at a place called the 'Barbary Coast,' in the course of an armed robbery; or (2) that Thompson willfully and with premeditation killed said Wallace Russell. The defense, while admitting the killing, denied any robbery motivation and contended that Thompson through drink and drugs was in such a mental state that he could not have formulated the necessary intent to raise the killing to first degree murder and that in any event, because of his condition, his offense did not warrant the death penalty. Thompson's testimony was to that effect. One prosecution witness, Mattie Spells, to some extent corroborated him but on a plea of surprise as to another matter the Commonwealth impeached her credibility. One eye witness to the shooting testified that Thompson did not appear intoxicated. The Commonwealth also produced the bartender at the place where Thompson was arrested, and he testified that there was nothing wrong with Thompson, that he was not drunk, and that his eyes were normal and not glassy. The only police witness questioned as to Thompson's condition was the other arresting officer, Dubis. He said Thompson was 'perfectly normal' and 'perfectly all right in every respect.' He said nothing regarding an odor of alcohol on Thompson's breath. . . .

None of the other police officers who were witnesses at the trial said anything about Thompson's condition or relating to an [sic] odor of alcohol on him. Officer Heagy, though subpoenaed by the Commonwealth as a witness and present at most of the trial, was not called to the stand by the prosecutor. He was actually excused by the prosecutor from attendance at the night session of the trial at which Dubis testified. Heagy therefore did not hear that testimony nor, according to him, hear about it until long after the trial. Thompson was arrested within approximately four hours of the shooting. The Common-wealth argues from this that Heagy's testimony is irrelevant because it is too remote. The proofs do not justify that contention.

* * *

. . . In that situation the effect of Heagy's testimony, of Dubis finally revealing that he had smelt alcohol on Thompson, and of the other police witnesses verifying this, might well have induced the jury to believe Thompson's evidence about his physical and mental state. The result could have been a finding of second degree murder, or if first degree, a recommendation of life imprisonment. Admittedly, even with that evidence, the jury might well not have accepted Thompson's testimony, indeed might not have credited Heagy, Dubis and the other policemen. But those conjectures do not permit that evidence to be brushed aside as merely cumulative. Nor can it be held as a matter of law to be unimportant to the defense here. . . .

* * *

The judgment of the district court will be reversed and the case remanded for the issuance of a writ of habeas corpus. . . .

CASE DISCUSSION QUESTIONS

1. What court delivered this opinion?
2. For what crime(s) was Thompson being prosecuted?
3. What was the nature of Thompson's defense?
4. What was the appellate court's ruling in this case?
5. What justification did the court give for reaching its decision in this case?
6. How is this case related to the concept of due process of law?

Material evidence
For purposes of determining the prosecution's disclosure obligations under *Brady*, evidence is material if there is a reasonable probability that had the evidence been disclosed to the defense, the result of the proceeding would have been different.

Fifth Amendment privilege against self-incrimination
An individual's constitutional right to refuse to answer questions or to otherwise provide statements that could be used as evidence against himself.

disclose is limited to **material evidence**. Evidence is material "if there is a reasonable probability that had the evidence been disclosed to the defense, the result of the proceeding would have been different."[4]

The following excerpts from *United States ex rel. Thompson v. Dye* provide an example of the type of factors judges must consider in determining whether the evidence in question was material to the outcome of the case:

A second important constitutional issue revolves around the application of the **Fifth Amendment privilege against self-incrimination**. While pretrial disclosure of information may make the trial fairer and more efficient, it can also be argued that such disclosure may incriminate the defendant. The applicable section of the Fifth Amendment reads: " . . . nor shall any person . . . be compelled in any criminal case to be a witness against himself, . . . "

Take a look at what the U.S. Supreme Court had to say about this issue in the following case containing excerpts from *United States v. Hubbell*. Webster Hubbell and Hillary Clinton were partners in the Rose Law Firm in Little Rock, Arkansas, and Hubbell served as an associate attorney general in the first Clinton administration. The documents involved in this case related to the Clintons' involvement in the "Whitewater" real estate development.

---

[4]*United States v. Bagley*, 473 U.S. 667, 682, 105 S. Ct. 3375, 87 L. Ed. 2d 481 (1985).

United States v. Hubbell
Supreme Court of the United States
530 U.S. 27 (2000)

JUSTICE STEVENS delivered the opinion of the Court.

The two questions presented concern the scope of a witness's protection against compelled self-incrimination: (1) whether the Fifth Amendment privilege protects a witness from being compelled to disclose the existence of incriminating documents that the Government is unable to describe with reasonable particularity; and (2) if the witness produces such documents pursuant to a grant of immunity, whether 18 U.S.C. § 6002 prevents the Government from using them to prepare criminal charges against him.

I

This proceeding arises out of the second prosecution of respondent, Webster Hubbell, commenced by the Independent Counsel appointed in August 1994 to investigate possible violations of federal law relating to the Whitewater Development Corporation. The first prosecution was terminated pursuant to a plea bargain. In December 1994, respondent pleaded guilty to charges of mail fraud and tax evasion arising out of his billing practices as a member of an Arkansas law firm from 1989 to 1992, and was sentenced to 21 months in prison. In the plea agreement, respondent promised to provide the Independent Counsel with "full, complete, accurate, and truthful information" about matters relating to the Whitewater investigation.

The second prosecution resulted from the Independent Counsel's attempt to determine whether respondent had violated that promise. In October 1996, while respondent was incarcerated, the Independent Counsel served him with a subpoena *duces tecum* calling for the production of 11 categories of documents before a grand jury sitting in Little Rock, Arkansas. See Appendix, *infra*. On November 19, he appeared before the grand jury and invoked his Fifth Amendment privilege against self-incrimination. In response to questioning by the prosecutor, respondent initially refused "to state whether there are documents within my possession, custody, or control responsive to the Subpoena." App. 62. Thereafter, the prosecutor produced an order, which had previously been obtained from the District Court pursuant to 18 U.S.C. § 6003(a), directing him to respond to the subpoena and granting him immunity "to the extent allowed by law." Respondent then produced 13,120 pages of documents and records and responded to a series of questions that established that those were all of the documents in his custody or control that were responsive to the commands in the subpoena, with the exception of a few documents he claimed were shielded by the attorney-client and attorney work-product privileges.

The contents of the documents produced by respondent provided the Independent Counsel with the information that led to this second prosecution. On April 30, 1998, a grand jury in the District of Columbia returned a 10-count indictment charging respondent with various tax-related crimes and mail and wire fraud. The District Court dismissed the indictment relying, in part, on the ground that the Independent Counsel's use of the subpoenaed documents violated § 6002 because all of the evidence he would offer against respondent at trial derived either directly or indirectly from the testimonial aspects of respondent's immunized act of producing those documents. 11 F. Supp. 2d 25, 33-37 (DDC 1998). Noting that the Independent Counsel had admitted that he was not investigating tax-related issues when he issued the subpoena, and that he had " 'learned about the unreported income and other crimes from studying the records' contents,' " the District Court characterized the subpoena as "the quintessential fishing expedition." 11 F. Supp. 2d at 37.

The Court of Appeals vacated the judgment and remanded for further proceedings. 167 F.3d 552 (CADC 1999). The majority concluded that the District Court had incorrectly relied on the fact that the Independent Counsel did not have prior knowledge of the contents of the subpoenaed documents. The question the District Court should have addressed was the extent of the Government's independent knowledge of the documents' existence and authenticity, and of respondent's possession or control of them. It explained:

> On remand, the district court should hold a hearing in which it seeks to establish the extent and detail of the Government's knowledge of Hubbell's financial affairs (or of the paperwork documenting it) on the day the subpoena issued. It is only then that the court will be in a position to assess the testimonial value of Hubbell's response to the subpoena. Should the Independent Counsel prove capable of demonstrating with reasonable particularity a prior awareness that the exhaustive litany of documents sought in the subpoena existed and were in Hubbell's possession, then the wide distance evidently traveled from the subpoena to the substantive allegations contained in the indictment would be based upon legitimate intermediate steps. To the extent that the information conveyed through Hubbell's compelled act of production provides the necessary linkage, however, the indictment deriving therefrom is tainted. 167 F.3d at 581.

* * *

On remand, the Independent Counsel acknowledged that he could not satisfy the "reasonable particularity" standard prescribed by the Court of Appeals and entered into a conditional plea agreement with respondent. In essence, the agreement provides for the dismissal of the charges unless this Court's disposition of the case makes it reasonably likely that respondent's "act of production immunity" would pose a significant bar to his prosecution.*** Despite that agreement, we granted the Independent Counsel's petition for a writ of certiorari in order to determine the precise scope of a grant of immunity with respect to the production of documents in response to a subpoena. We now affirm.

II

It is useful to preface our analysis of the constitutional issue with a restatement of certain propositions that are not in dispute.***

It is consistent with the history of and the policies underlying the Self-Incrimination Clause to hold that the privilege may be asserted only to resist compelled explicit or implicit disclosures of incriminating information. Historically, the privilege was intended to prevent the use of legal compulsion to extract from the accused a sworn communication of facts which would incriminate him. Such was the process of the ecclesiastical courts and the Star Chamber—the inquisitorial method of putting the accused upon his oath and compelling him to answer questions designed to uncover uncharged offenses, without evidence from another source.* * * [5]

* * *

More relevant to this case is the settled proposition that a person may be required to produce specific documents even though they contain incriminating assertions of fact or belief because the creation of those documents was not "compelled" within the meaning of the privilege. Our decision in *Fisher v. United States*, 425 U.S. 391, 48 L. Ed. 2d 39, 96 S. Ct. 1569 (1976), dealt with summonses issued by the Internal Revenue Service (IRS) seeking working papers used in the preparation of tax returns. Because the papers had been voluntarily prepared prior to the issuance of the summonses, they could not be "said to contain compelled testimonial evidence, either of the taxpayers or of anyone else." Accordingly, the taxpayer could not "avoid compliance with the subpoena merely by asserting that the item of evidence which he is required to produce contains incriminating writing, whether his own or that of someone else." 425 U.S. at 409-410; see also *United States v. Doe*, 465 U.S. 605, 79 L. Ed. 2d 552, 104 S. Ct. 1237 (1984). It is clear, therefore, that respondent Hubbell could not avoid compliance with the subpoena served on him merely because the demanded documents contained incriminating evidence, whether written by others or voluntarily prepared by himself.

On the other hand, we have also made it clear that the act of producing documents in response to a subpoena may have a compelled testimonial aspect. We have held that "the act of production" itself may implicitly communicate

---

[5]This passage appears in footnote 8 of the Court's decision.

"statements of fact." By "producing documents in compliance with a subpoena, the witness would admit that the papers existed, were in his possession or control, and were authentic." Moreover, as was true in this case, when the custodian of documents responds to a subpoena, he may be compelled to take the witness stand and answer questions designed to determine whether he has produced everything demanded by the subpoena. The answers to those questions, as well as the act of production itself, may certainly communicate information about the existence, custody, and authenticity of the documents. Whether the constitutional privilege protects the answers to such questions, or protects the act of production itself, is a question that is distinct from the question whether the unprotected contents of the documents themselves are incriminating.

Finally, the phrase "in any criminal case" in the text of the Fifth Amendment might have been read to limit its coverage to compelled testimony that is used against the defendant in the trial itself. It has, however, long been settled that its protection encompasses compelled statements that lead to the discovery of incriminating evidence even though the statements themselves are not incriminating and are not introduced into evidence.

* * *

Compelled testimony that communicates information that may "lead to incriminating evidence" is privileged even if the information itself is not inculpatory. *Doe v. United States,* 487 U.S. 201, 208, n.6, 101 L. Ed. 2d 184, 108 S. Ct. 2341 (1988). It is the Fifth Amendment's protection against the prosecutor's use of incriminating information derived directly or indirectly from the compelled testimony of the respondent that is of primary relevance in this case.

III

* * *

The "compelled testimony" that is relevant in this case is not to be found in the contents of the documents produced in response to the subpoena. It is, rather, the testimony inherent in the act of producing those documents. The disagreement between the parties focuses entirely on the significance of that testimonial aspect.

IV

The Government correctly emphasizes that the testimonial aspect of a response to a subpoena *duces tecum* does nothing more than establish the existence, authenticity, and custody of items that are produced. * * *

The question, however, is not whether the response to the subpoena may be introduced into evidence at his criminal trial. That would surely be a prohibited "use" of the immunized act of production. But the fact that the Government intends no such use of the act of production leaves open the separate question whether it has already made "derivative use" of the testimonial aspect of that act in obtaining the indictment against respondent and in preparing its case for trial. It clearly has.

* * *

Indeed, the record makes it clear that that is what happened in this case. The documents were produced before a grand jury sitting in the Eastern District of Arkansas in aid of the Independent Counsel's attempt to determine whether respondent had violated a commitment in his first plea agreement. The use of those sources of information eventually led to the return of an indictment by a grand jury sitting in the District of Columbia for offenses that apparently are unrelated to that plea agreement. * * * It was only through respondent's truthful reply to the subpoena that the Government received the incriminating documents of which it made "substantial use * * * in the investigation that led to the indictment." * * *

* * *

In sum, we have no doubt that the constitutional privilege against self-incrimination protects the target of a grand jury investigation from being compelled to answer questions designed to elicit information about the existence of sources of potentially incriminating evidence. That constitutional privilege has the same application to the testimonial aspect of a response to a subpoena seeking discovery of those sources. . . .

* * *

Given our conclusion that respondent's act of production had a testimonial aspect, at least with respect to the existence and location of the documents sought by the Government's subpoena, respondent could not be compelled to produce those documents without first receiving a grant of immunity under § 6003. As we construed § 6002 in *Kastigar*, such immunity is co-extensive with the constitutional privilege. *Kastigar* requires that respondent's motion to dismiss the indictment on immunity grounds be granted unless the Government proves that the evidence it used in obtaining the indictment and proposed to use at trial was derived from legitimate sources "wholly independent" of the testimonial aspect of respondent's immunized conduct in assembling and producing the documents described in the subpoena. The Government, however, does not claim that it could make such a showing. . . .

Accordingly, the indictment against respondent must be dismissed. The judgment of the Court of Appeals is affirmed.

CASE DISCUSSION QUESTIONS

1. What court delivered this opinion?
2. Who brought this case to this court and what is that party asking the court to do?
3. What constitutes "testimonial" evidence and why is this distinction important?
4. What type of immunity was involved in this case?
5. What was the court's ruling in this case?
6. What justification did the court give for reaching its decision?

Another application of the Fifth Amendment self-incrimination clause arises in situations where the government may be conducting parallel civil and criminal investigations. Consider the situations involved in the Edwards and Schroeder sample cases (Introduction to Hypothetical Cases, p. xxxviii). Bill Edwards and Tom Schroeder both engaged in behaviors that might have violated federal securities regulations as well as state or federal criminal laws. In situations like these it is not unusual for the Securities and Exchange Commission (SEC) to coordinate its investigation with the Department of Justice (DOJ). If, as is often the situation, the underlying facts are relevant to both a civil enforcement suit and a criminal action, materials that are subpoenaed for a civil suit might be incriminating in a criminal trial.

In *United States v. Kordel*[6] the Supreme Court rejected the argument that the government should have to decide whether or not to pursue a criminal prosecution before commencing a civil proceeding. It further stated that the Due Process Clause did not require government agents to inform witnesses in civil litigation that they might also be prosecuted in criminal court. An individual cannot be forced to make incriminating statements in civil proceedings, but if the person does divulge incriminating information, he or she is treated as having the privilege against self-incrimination.

Dicta
Statements made in a court's opinion which go beyond the facts necessary to decide the case and therefore are not binding legal precedent in subsequent cases.

In **dicta**, the *Kordel* opinion suggested that it might reach a different conclusion if it were shown that the civil action was undertaken solely to obtain evidence for a criminal prosecution.[7] SEC policy now mandates that targets of civil enforcement proceedings be made aware of the possibility of criminal prosecution based on information obtained by the SEC from their testimony.[8] In

---

[6]397 U.S. 1, 90 S. Ct. 763, 25 L. Ed. 2d 1 (1970).

[7]*Id.* at 12.

[8]SEC, Division of Enforcement, Enforcement Manual (January 13, 2010), Section 3.2.3.1, Forms 1661 and 1662. *http://www.sec.gov/divisions/enforce/enforcementmanual.pdf* at p. 52.

United States v. Scrushy[9] and *United States v. Stringer*[10] federal district courts ruled that in cases where there was extensive cooperation between the SEC and DOJ, the government had an obligation to inform witnesses that criminal prosecution was "probable" rather than just "possible."

In summary, we have seen that the Due Process Clause requires the prosecution to disclose certain types of information, while the privilege against self-incrimination protects defendants from having to reveal some types of information through discovery. It is important to note, however, that while *Brady* ruled that the Due Process Clause prohibits the prosecution from concealing evidence favorable to the accused, the U.S. Supreme Court has also stated that there is no general constitutional right to discovery in criminal cases[11] and has remarked that "the Due Process Clause has little to say regarding the amount of discovery which the parties must be afforded. . . . "[12]

C. RULES GOVERNING DISCOVERY

Despite the absence of a constitutional mandate, the federal government and all of the states have rules of criminal procedure that provide for significant discovery. We begin with an analysis of the **Federal Rules of Criminal Procedure** (FRCrP) since they apply to all federal courts and illustrate one of the two general approaches to formal discovery that have emerged. The alternative approach will be illustrated by references to the **American Bar Association** (ABA) standards on criminal discovery.

Rule 16 of the Federal Rules of Criminal Procedure provides that *upon the defendant's request*, the government furnish the defense the following information:

(A) *Defendant's Oral Statement* ["the substance of any relevant oral statement made by the defendant, before or after arrest, in response to interrogation by a person the defendant knew was a government agent if the government intends to use the statement at trial"]

(B) *Defendant's Written or Recorded Statement* ["the government must disclose to the defendant, and make available for inspection, copying, or photographing, all of the following: (i) any relevant written or recorded statement by the defendant if: the statement is within the government's possession, custody, or control; and the attorney for the government knows—or through due diligence could know—that the statement exists"][13]

Federal Rules of Criminal Procedure (FRCrP)
The rules that govern the procedure in all criminal proceedings in the U.S. District Courts, the U.S. Courts of Appeals, and the Supreme Court of the United States.

American Bar Association
The largest voluntary association of attorneys in the United States. As the national representative of the legal profession, the ABA's stated mission is to serve the public and the profession by promoting justice, professional excellence and respect for the law.

---

[9]366 F. Supp. 2d 1134 (N.D. Ala. 2005).

[10]408 F, Supp. 2d 1083 (D. Or. 2006).

[11]*Weatherford v. Bursey*, 429 U.S. 545, 97 S. Ct. 837, 51 L. Ed. 2d 30 (1977).

[12]*Wardius v. Oregon*, 412 U.S. 470, 474, 93 S. Ct. 2208; 37 L. Ed. 2d 82 (1973).

[13]In addition, the government must disclose to the defendant: "(ii) the portion of any written record containing the substance of any relevant oral statement made before or after arrest if the defendant made the statement in response to interrogation by a person the defendant knew was a government agent; and (iii) the defendant's recorded testimony before a grand jury relating to the charged offense." FRCrP 16(a)(1)(B).

(C) *Oral Statement Organizational Defendant's Representative* [if the defendant is an organization, the government must disclose to the defendant binding oral, written, or recorded statements made by its representative][14]

(D) *Defendant's Prior Record* ["the defendant's prior criminal record that is within the government's possession, custody, or control if the attorney for the government knows—or through due diligence could know—that the record exists."]

(E) *Documents and Objects* [Under certain specified circumstances, "the government must permit the defendant to inspect and to copy or photograph books, papers, documents, data, photographs, tangible objects, buildings or places, or copies or portions of any of these items"][15]

(F) *Reports of Examinations and Tests* [Under specified circumstances, "the government must permit a defendant to inspect and to copy or photograph the results or reports of any physical or mental examination and of any scientific test or experiment"][16]

(G) *Expert Witnesses* [Under specified circumstances, the government must give to the defendant a written summary of any expert testimony that the government intends to use under Rules 702, 703, or 705 of the **Federal Rules of Evidence (FRE)**.][17]

Federal Rules of Evidence (FRE)

The rules of evidence that govern proof in all civil and criminal proceedings in the U.S. district courts.

Rule 16 discovery is considered restrictive for a number of reasons. It is not self-executing. Unlike federal civil discovery, criminal discovery under Rule 16 must be initiated by the parties. Also in contrast to the federal civil rules, there are no predetermined timelines that establish when disclosures must be made.[18] From the defense point of view, one of the most problematic aspects of Rule 16 is that the government is not required to disclose a list of witnesses or statements of co-defendants prior to trial.[19] About a dozen states take the federal rules approach.[20]

---

[14]FRCrP 16(a)(1)(C) requires disclosure of "any statement described in Rule 16(a)(1)(A) and (B) if the government contends that the person making the statement: (i) was legally able to bind the defendant regarding the subject of the statement because of that person's position as the defendant's director, officer, employee, or agent; or (ii) was personally involved in the alleged conduct constituting the offense and was legally able to bind the defendant regarding that conduct because of that person's position as the defendant's director, officer, employee, or agent."

[15]The item must be "within the government's possession, custody, or control and: (i) the item is material to preparing the defense; (ii) the government intends to use the item in its case-in-chief at trial; or (iii) the item was obtained from or belongs to the defendant." Rule 16(a)(1)(E).

[16]Disclosure is required when "(i) the item is within the government's possession, custody, or control; (ii) the attorney for the government knows—or through due diligence could know—that the item exists; and (iii) the item is material to preparing the defense or the government intends to use the item in its case-in-chief at trial." Rule 16(a)(1)(F).

[17]FRE 702 concerns testimony by experts; FRE 703 relates to basis of opinions by experts; and FRE 705 regards disclosure of facts or data underlying expert opinions.

[18]See Rule 26 of the Federal Rule of Civil Procedure, which imposes mandatory disclosure of information and tangible objects at several stages of a case. The time for each disclosure is referenced to specific events in the case.

[19]FRCrP 26 provides for a method that a party can use to obtain a witness's statement *after* the witness has testified on direct examination.

[20]The Justice Project, *Expanded Discovery in Criminal Cases: A Policy Review* 8 (2007). *http://www.thejusticeproject.org/solution/Discovery/discovery-lr.pdf*

In contrast, the ABA has encouraged greater disclosure of information. In guidelines adopted in 1994 and updated in 1996,[21] it declared that "within a specified and reasonable time prior to trial," the prosecution should disclose the following types of information to the defense:

- written and oral statements of the defendant or of any co-defendant that are within the possession or control of the prosecution;
- the names and addresses of persons known to the prosecution to have information concerning the offense charged;
- written statements of witnesses; the relationship, if any, between the prosecution and any witness it intends to call at trial;
- the nature and circumstances of any agreements between the prosecution and the witness that constitutes an inducement for the cooperation or testimony of the witness;
- reports or written statements of experts made in connection with the case; tangible objects such as books, papers, documents, photographs, and models that pertain to the case; information about prior criminal convictions, pending charges, or probationary status of the defendant, co-defendant, or witness information relating to lineups, showups, and picture or voice identifications;
- any material or information within the prosecutor's possession or control that tends to negate the guilt of the defendant as to the offense charged or that would tend to reduce the punishment of the defendant.

Standard 11-2.1 also requires the government to make additional disclosures to the defense if (1) it intends to use character, reputation, or other act of evidence; (2) the defendant's conversations or premises have been subjected to electronic surveillance in connection with the case; or (3) any tangible object that the object the prosecutor intends to offer at trial was obtained through a search and seizure.[22]

As of 2004, approximately one-third of the states have taken the ABA approach. These jurisdictions include California, New Jersey, Illinois,[23] and Michigan. States that don't fall squarely into either the ABA or the Rule 16 model generally lie somewhere between the two standards.[24] For a comparison of the primary prosecution's pretrial disclosure obligations under the two

---

[21]*ABA Standards for Criminal Justice: Discovery and Trial by Jury* (3d ed., American Bar Association 1996).

[22]Standard 11-2.1 provides in part:

"(b) If the prosecution intends to use character, reputation, or other act of evidence, the prosecution should notify the defense of that intention and of the substance of the evidence to be used.

(c) If the defendant's conversations or premises have been subjected to electronic surveillance (including wiretapping) in connection with the investigation or prosecution of the case, the prosecution should inform the defense of that fact.

(d) If any tangible object which the object which the prosecutor intends to offer at trial was obtained through a search and seizure, the prosecution should disclose to the defense any information, documents, or other material relating to the acquisition of such objects."

[23]Although Illinois has a liberal disclosure policy, the parties must formally move for disclosure. See Illinois Supreme Court Rule 412.

[24]The Justice Project, *Expanded Discovery in Criminal Cases: A Policy Review* 8 (2007). *http://www .thejusticeproject.org/solution/Discovery/discovery-lr.pdf*

Information to Be Disclosed	Rule 16	11-2.1(a)
Defendant's oral, written, or recorded statements	Duty	Duty
Co-defendant statements	No Duty	Duty
Identification of all persons with knowledge	No Duty	Duty
Identities of trial witnesses	No Duty	Duty
Relationship between prosecution and its witness	No Duty	Duty
Expert curriculum vitae, a written description of proposed testimony, expert's opinions, and basis of opinions	Limited Duty	Duty
Reports of examinations and tests	Duty	Duty
Relevant tangible objects and documents	Duty	Duty
Identification of all objects it intends to offer as evidence at trial	No Duty	Duty
Record of prior criminal convictions of defendant	Duty	Duty
Record of prior criminal convictions of co-defendant and any witness a party intends to present at trial	No Duty	Duty
Information relating to lineups, showups, and picture or voice identifications	No Duty	Duty

Figure 7.1 Prosecution Pretrial Disclosure Duties Under Rule 16 of the Federal Rules of Criminal Procedure and ABA Standard 11-2.1(a)

models, see Figure 7.1. Check your own state's rules of criminal procedure to see how they compare. Note also that the *Brady* obligations (see p. 200–202) have not been incorporated into Rule 16 or the rules of criminal procedure for all of the states. Accordingly, in a number of jurisdictions, exculpatory evidence is not defined by rule and there is no established timetable for *Brady* material disclosure. In contrast, some local court rules include the *Brady* requirements as well as disclosure deadlines even though the general rule for the jurisdiction is silent as to these matters. For instance, Local Criminal Rule 16.01(a) for the U.S. District Court for the Middle District of Tennessee provides:

(2) **Standing Discovery Rule.** On or before fourteen (14) days from the date of the arraignment of a defendant, the parties shall confer and the following shall be accomplished:
　　d. The government shall reveal to the defendant and permit inspection and copying of all information and material known to the government which may be favorable to the defendant on the issues of guilt or punishment within the scope of *Brady* . . .

Sometimes the policies regarding *Brady* obligations are set at the local level. For example, the policy of the Los Angeles County District Attorney's Office on the prosecution's duties under *Brady* to provide impeaching evidence states that the prosecution must disclose evidence on witness character for honesty or veracity; bias, interest or other motive; inconsistent statements; and prior convictions of felonies and misdemeanors involving moral turpitude. The district attorney's policy also lists the following examples of possible impeachment evidence of material witnesses:

1. False reports by a prosecution witness;
2. Pending criminal charges against a prosecution witness;
3. Parole or probation status of the witness;
4. Evidence contradicting a prosecution witness's statements or reports;
5. Evidence undermining a prosecution witness's expertise;
6. A finding of misconduct by a Board of Rights or Civil Service Commission, that reflects on the witness's truthfulness, bias or moral turpitude;
7. Evidence that a witness has a reputation for untruthfulness;
8. Evidence that a witness has a racial, religious or personal bias against the defendant individually or as a member of a group; or
9. Promises, offers or inducements to the witnesses, including a grant of immunity.[25]

It is therefore important to carefully check all criminal discovery rules in your jurisdiction. Local rules may establish disclosure requirements that may not be immediately apparent. On the other hand, if there are no rules governing *Brady* evidence, the defense should make a written request for this discovery at the outset of the case.

APPLICATION EXERCISES

1. Find the part of your state's code of criminal procedure or the court rules that govern discovery in criminal cases. What is the citation for where they appear?

2. Under your state's criminal discovery rules, which of the following is the prosecution required to furnish to the defendant?
   - Defendant's oral, written, or recorded statements
   - Co-defendant statements
   - Identification of all persons with knowledge
   - Identities of trial witnesses
   - Relationship between prosecution and its witness

---

[25]Los Angeles District Attorney's Office, Special Directive 02-08 Brady Protocol (Dec. 7, 2002). *http://da.co.la.ca.us/sd02-08.htm* [Citations omitted.]

- Expert curriculum vitae, written description of proposed expert's testimony, opinions, and basis of opinions
- Reports of examinations and tests
- Relevant tangible objects and documents
- Identification of all objects the prosecution intends to offer as evidence at trial
- Record of prior criminal convictions of defendant
- Record of prior criminal convictions of co-defendant and any witness a party intends to present at trial
- Information relating to lineups, showups, and picture or voice identifications

3. What type of duty, if any, is imposed on the prosecution in your state's rules of procedure to provide the defense with exculpatory evidence?

4. Are the rules of criminal procedure in your state more like the federal rules of criminal discovery or the ABA standards? In what ways?

5. Review all rules for criminal discovery for both the state and federal districts where your school is located. How do these rules attempt to implement the requirements of *Brady v. Maryland*? What time limits for discovery compliance are set forth in these rules?

D. DISCOVERY REQUESTS AND RESPONSES

In many jurisdictions, the parties must initiate the request for discovery. Generally, the material that the parties are entitled to receive consists of statements, the defendant's criminal record, the grand jury transcript, documents and tangible items, scientific reports, and *Brady* material. Depending on the jurisdiction, the parties may also get a list of witnesses as well as the witnesses' statements.

In most felony cases, the defense's initial discovery request can be prepared and ready to serve on the prosecution at the time of the defendant's arraignment. Paralegals working for prosecutors and defense attorneys are frequently called upon to draft these discovery requests.

1. PATTERN DISCOVERY REQUESTS

Like most other court documents, discovery requests typically include the following components:

- Caption
- Introductory paragraph
- Body

- Signature
- Address block/preparer's data
- Proof of service

As in the drafting of other types of commonly used court documents, **pattern discovery** requests usually involve customizing **boilerplate language** to reflect the facts of the specific case. See Chapter 5, page 146, for instructions on drafting the **caption** section of court documents. Because there are variations from court to court, you should look at other documents filed in your jurisdiction for guides to the custom and practice used. Exhibit 7.1 on pages 214–215 provides an example of a discovery request for *United States v. Edwards* (one of the sample hypothetical cases).

Notice how the requested material closely tracks FRCrP 16. Although this form includes separate citations to each relevant subparagraph of the rule, most forms simply cite the rule as a whole in the introductory paragraph. This document is specifically drafted for *United States v. Edwards*. If you were to use this form as guide for another case, you should review FRCrP 16 in light of the facts involved in your case and adapt the form accordingly. For instance, if the defendant in your case is an organization, you would seek discovery of statements of agents, officers, and employees.[26] The *United States v. Edwards* form does not include a request for this information because Edwards is an individual defendant rather than an organizational defendant.

In jurisdictions in which court approval is needed to initiate discovery, the parties must file a motion before seeking discovery. As in the case with pattern discovery requests, motions for leave to take discovery contain boilerplate language taken from the jurisdiction's applicable discovery rules. Exhibit 7.2 includes a motion for discovery in an Illinois felony case. The motion closely tracks Illinois Supreme Court Rule 412, which lists the disclosures that the state must make upon motion of the defense.

Pattern discovery
Model discovery requests that use generic, boilerplate language to request all of the information allowable under the applicable criminal discovery rules.

Boilerplate language
Model sentences that include standardized legal terms and phrases.

Caption
The section of a court document containing the names of the parties, case number, name of the court it is being filed in, and a title that identifies the type of document being filed.

2. ELECTRONIC DISCOVERY

Electronic discovery, also known as e-discovery, is the discovery of documents created, disbursed, and stored electronically. Among other things, the types of documents sought and produced in e-discovery include e-mails, word-processed documents, spreadsheets, databases, as well as audio and video files.

Although the Federal Rules of Civil Procedure (FRCP) sets forth standards for electronic discovery,[27] there are no federal discovery rules for criminal cases. Despite this absence, there is no dispute that electronically stored information (ESI) is discoverable in criminal prosecutions. Likewise, most state rules of criminal procedure do not address electronic discovery.

Electronic discovery (e-discovery)
The discovery of documents created, disbursed, and stored electronically.

---

[26]FRCrP 16(a)(1)(C) concerns discovery of oral statements from certain representatives of an organizational defendant.

[27]See FRCP 16(b), 26, 33, 34, 37, & 45.

Exhibit 7.1: Pattern Discovery Request from Defendant in
United States v. Edwards

THE UNITED STATES DISTRICT COURT
FOR THE NORTHERN DISTRICT OF
INDIANA HAMMOND DIVISION

UNITED STATES OF AMERICA

   vs   )   Case No. 09 CR XXX

WILLIAM EDWARDS,   )

   Defendant.   )

DEFENDANT'S INITIAL DISCOVERY REQUEST

Now comes Defendant WILLIAM EDWARDS, by CHARLES HOVEY, his attorney, and as his initial discovery request, brought pursuant to Rule 16 of the Federal Rules of Criminal Procedure and *Brady v. Maryland*, 373 U.S. 83 (1963), asks the UNITED STATES OF AMERICA to disclose and produce the following materials and information:

1. *Defendant's Oral Statements*: The substance of any relevant oral statement made by the defendant, before or after arrest, in response to interrogation by a person the defendant knew was a government agent if the government intends to use the statement at trial. [FRCrP 16(a)(1)(A).] In the event that the government intends to use such an oral statement at trial, Defendant requests that it be reduced in writing and produced. This request includes the substance of the Defendant's response to *Miranda* warnings.
2. *Defendant's Written or Recorded Statements:*
   a. Any relevant written or recorded statement by the defendant if the statement is within the government's possession, custody, or control; and the attorney for the government knows—or through due diligence could know—that the statement exists;
   b. The portion of any written record containing the substance of any relevant oral statement made before or after arrest if the defendant made the statement in response to interrogation by a person the defendant knew was a government agent; and
   c. The defendant's recorded testimony before a grand jury relating to the charged offense. [FRCrP 16(a)(1)(B).]
3. *Defendant's Prior Record*: The defendant's prior criminal record that is within the government's possession, custody, or control if the attorney for the government knows—or through due diligence could know—that the record exists. [FRCrP 16(a)(1)(D).] This request includes the Defendant's entire criminal record, including all arrests along with offenses regardless of conviction or severity. It includes all matters that may affect the Defendant's criminal history score pursuant to the United States Sentencing Guidelines.

4. *Documents and Objects Material to Preparing the Defense:* Inspection and copying or photographing books, papers, documents, data, photographs, tangible objects, buildings or places, or copies or portions of any of these items if they are within the government's possession, custody, or control and the item is material to preparing the defense. [FRCrP 16(a)(1)(E)(i).]

5. *Documents and Objects to be Used in Government's Case-in-Chief:* Inspection and copying or photographing books, papers, documents, data, photographs, tangible objects, buildings or places, or copies or portions of any of these items if they are within the government's possession, custody, or control and the government intends to use the item in its case-in-chief at trial. [FRCrP 16(a)(1)(E)(ii).]

6. *Documents and Objects that Belong to the Defendant:* Inspection and copying or photographing books, papers, documents, data, photographs, tangible objects, buildings or places, or copies or portions of any of these items if they are within the government's possession, custody, or control and the item was obtained from or belongs to the defendant. [FRCrP 16(a)(1)(E)(iii).]

7. *Reports of Examinations and Tests:* Inspection and copying or photographing the results or reports of any physical or mental examination and of any scientific test or experiment when (i) the item is within the government's possession, custody, or control; (ii) the attorney for the government knows—or through due diligence could know—that the item exists; and (iii) the item is material to preparing the defense or the government intends to use the item in its case-in-chief at trial. [FRCrP 16(a)(1)(F).]

8. *Expert Witnesses:* A written summary of any expert testimony that the government intends to use under the Federal Rules of Evidence, the grounds and bases for such opinion testimony, and the qualifications of the expert. [FRCrP 16(a)(1)(G).]

9. *Brady v. Maryland Disclosure*: Any exculpatory evidence material to guilt or punishment, including but not limited to impeachment evidence.

Respectfully submitted,

WILLIAM EDWARDS, Defendant

By_____

CHARLES HOVEY, his attorney

Charles Hovey
Attorney for Defendant
1857 Bone Street
Normal, IL 61617
(309) 555-1857

Certificate of Service

I hereby certify that a true and accurate copy of the foregoing Defendant's Initial Discovery Request was served upon _____, Assistant U.S. Attorney by depositing the same in the U.S. Post Office mailbox in Chicago, Illinois in an envelope, postage fully prepaid, addressed to: Office of the United States Attorney [Address of U.S. Attorney] on the _____ day of _____, 20__ at or about the hour of _____ p.m.

_____

Exhibit 7.2: Pattern Discovery Request from Defendant in *Illinois v. Cook*

IN THE CIRCUIT COURT OF
THE ELEVENTH JUDICIAL CIRCUIT
MCLEAN COUNTY, ILLINOIS

PEOPLE OF THE STATE OF ILLINOIS   )

   v.   )   Case No. 09 CF XXX

)

BUD COOK,   )

   Defendant.   )

Motion for Supreme Court Rule 412 Discovery

Now comes Defendant BUD COOK, by CHARLES HOVEY, his attorney, and moves that the court order the State to provide the defendant with discovery pursuant to Illinois Supreme Court Rule 412. In support of this motion, seeks the following discovery:

1. The names and last known addresses of persons whom the State intends to call as witnesses, together with their relevant written or recorded statements, memoranda containing substantially verbatim reports of their oral statements, and a list of memoranda reporting or summarizing their oral statements. [412(a)(i)]
2. Any written or recorded statements and the substance of any oral statements made by the accused or by a co-defendant, and a list of witnesses to the making and acknowledgment of such statements. [412(a)(ii)]
3. A transcript of those portions of grand jury minutes containing testimony of the accused and relevant testimony of persons whom the prosecuting attorney intends to call as witnesses at the hearing or trial. [412(a)(iii)]
4. Any reports or statements of experts, made in connection with the particular case, including results of physical or mental examinations and of scientific tests, experiments, or comparisons, and a statement of qualifications of the expert. [412(a)(iv)]
5. Any books, papers, documents, photographs or tangible objects which the prosecuting attorney intends to use in the hearing or trial or which were obtained from or belong to the accused. [412(a)(v)]
6. Any record of prior criminal convictions, which may be used for impeachment, of persons whom the State intends to call as witnesses at the hearing or trial. [412(a)(vi)]
7. Disclosure of any electronic surveillance (including wiretapping) of conversations to which the accused was a party, or of his premises. [412(b)]
8. Any material or information within the State's possession or control which tends to negate the guilt of the accused as to the offense charged or which would tend to reduce his punishment therefor. [412(c)]

Respectfully submitted,

WILLIAM EDWARDS, Defendant

By_____

Charles Hovey   CHARLES HOVEY, his attorney
Attorney for Defendant
1857 Bone Street
Normal, IL 61617
(309) 555-1857

APPLICATION EXERCISES

6. Contact a local criminal defense attorney or prosecutor's office to find out what criminal law formbooks are customarily used in the jurisdiction. Make a copy of a form used to seek discovery.

7. Prepare federal and state court requests for discovery directed to the prosecution for the *Brandon Turner* case (discussed in the Introduction to Hypothetical Cases, p. xxxvii and previous chapters). Assume that your instructor is the defense attorney and that the instructor's address and telephone numbers are those of your school.
   a. For the federal prosecution assume that the case was the first case filed this calendar year in the federal district in which your college is located.
   b. For the state prosecution, assume that Brandon Turner was charged with the lowest-class felony for possession of cocaine. If your state requires that the defense must first get leave of court to conduct discovery, also draft a motion for leave to take discovery. This also was the first case filed by the prosecutor this calendar year.

One of the few reported federal cases addressing criminal e-discovery is *United States v. O'Keefe*.[28] In *O'Keefe,* United States Magistrate Judge John Facciola stated:

> In criminal cases, there is unfortunately no rule to which the courts can look for guidance in determining whether the production of documents by the government has been in a form or format that is appropriate. This may be because the "big paper" case is the exception rather than the rule in criminal cases. Be that as it may, Rule 34 of the Federal Rules of Civil Procedure speak[s] specifically to the form of production. . . . It is foolish to disregard them merely because this is a criminal case, particularly where, as is the case here, it is far better to *use* these rules than to reinvent the wheel when the production of documents in criminal and civil cases raises the same problems.[29]

---

[28]521 F. Supp. 2d 14 (D.D.C. 2008).
[29]521 F. Supp. 2d at 18-19.

In the absence of the adoption of e-discovery criminal rules, the prudent way to tackle e-discovery in federal criminal litigation is to use the FRCP as a guide.[30]

FRCP 34 provides that a party may serve a request to produce "electronically stored information—including writings, drawings, graphs, charts, photographs, sound recordings, images, and other data or data compilations—stored in any medium from which information can be obtained either directly or, if necessary, after translation by the responding party into a reasonably usable form."[31] The party seeking the ESI "may specify the form or forms in which electronically stored information is to be produced."[32] Rule 34 addresses responses and objections to e-discovery requests as follows:

> (D) *Responding to a Request for Production of Electronically Stored Information.* The response may state an objection to a requested form for producing electronically stored information. If the responding party objects to a requested form—or if no form was specified in the request—the party must state the form or forms it intends to use.
>
> (E) *Producing the Documents or Electronically Stored Information.* Unless otherwise stipulated or ordered by the court, these procedures apply to producing documents or electronically stored information:
>
> (i) A party must produce documents as they are kept in the usual course of business or must organize and label them to correspond to the categories in the request;
>
> (ii) If a request does not specify a form for producing electronically stored information, a party must produce it in a form or forms in which it is ordinarily maintained or in a reasonably usable form or forms; and
>
> (iii) A party need not produce the same electronically stored information in more than one form.[33]

The typical process of producing electronic discovery is to first obtain the e-documents requested. The prosecution usually retrieves this data from the agency initiating the investigation. The defense attorney will acquire the documents from the client. When the documents are not in a uniformly accepted file format, the legal team will take steps to convert the documents to a format, such as JPEG images, Tagged Image File Format (TIFF), or Portable Document Format (PDF) files. Once converted from their native format, the documents are coded for ease of indexing and organizing. The legal team will then review the data for privileged information. Privileged documents are segregated from the non-privileged. When a document includes both privileged and unprivileged information, the file is redacted. Finally, the documents are numbered. Paralegals

---

[30]Justin P. Murphy, E-Discovery in Criminal Matters—Emerging Trends & the Influence of Civil Litigation Principle: Post-Indictment E-Discovery Jurisprudence, *The Sedona Conference Journal* (2010) 257. http://www.crowell.com/documents/E-Discovery-in-Criminal-Matters-Emerging-Trends-the-Influence-of-Civil-Litigation-Principles.pdf. At least one commentator, however, has criticized the use of civil rules in criminal discovery. See K. Strutin, *Databases, E-Discovery and Criminal Law*, 15 RICH. J.L. & TECH. 6, http://law.richmond.edu/jolt/v15i3/article6.pdf

[31]FRCP 34(a)(1)(A).

[32]FRCP 34(b)(1)(C).

[33]FRCP 34(b)(2).

may play a role in this process. If the amount of data is overwhelming, an outside contractor may be brought in to prepare the discovery production. An example of one prosecuting attorney's office's protocol for responding to e-discovery is presented in Exhibit 7.3.

Exhibit 7.3: Electronic Discovery Working Group Best Practices for Electronic Discovery of Documentary Materials in Large Cases (September 2005) U.S. Attorney's Office, Western District of Washington

In those large cases where the parties agree that electronic discovery of documentary materials is appropriate or the U.S. Attorney's Office already has generated electronic versions of documentary materials prior to the Local Rule 16 discovery conference, the U.S. Attorney's Office will pursue the following best practices:

1. We will provide graphic image files of documentary materials that have been scanned in the industry standard single-page .tif format. Each document page will be identified by a unique Bates or similar identification number.
2. When the parties in a case agree or when, prior to the Local Rule 16 conference, we already have obtained electronic text files for documentary evidence (typically through optical character recognition [OCR] scanning), we will provide those text files in the industry standard .txt format.
3. Absent alternative arrangements agreed upon by the parties in a case, upon request by defense counsel we will provide the .tif files, together with the .txt files in those cases where we have obtained them, in a form that includes free viewer software (e.g., I-Publish) that enables the user to access the files and perform some annotation and/or search functions.
4. When we create an electronic database (using the DOJ-issued database software Concordance), upon request by defense counsel we will provide the "load" files that enable the Concordance database program to link .tif and .txt files with each other and with other associated data fields (e.g., date, author, title of document).
5. To assist counsel with review of electronic discovery of documentary materials, we will provide indexing information that identifies the source and type of the materials, organized by Bates or similar identification numbers. This best practice should not be construed to require the United States Attorney's office to create an exhaustive "index" describing every document produced in electronic form. Rather, what we will provide is in the nature of a discovery letter that allows the defense to identify various types of discovery items within the electronic files produced. For example, the government will identify which electronic files contain reports of defendants' statements or which electronic files represent documents obtained from a particular bank. We reserve the right not to produce any information that we consider to be work product.
6. If, prior to the Local Rule 16 conference, we create an electronic database of discovery materials, we will endeavor to create it in such a manner as to permit us to produce those portions of the database that we do not consider to be our work product.
7. At the Local Rule 16 discovery conference, we will discuss and consider in good faith possible cost-sharing measures in handling voluminous discovery, such as jointly-commissioned Bates numbering, scanning, and/or "objective coding" of

documentary materials by outside vendors; provided, however, that our ability to enter into cost-sharing agreements may be limited by our budget constraints and/or the Department of Justice requirement that we allocate litigation expenditures only for mandatory obligations.

8. In any case where electronic discovery has been generated through the scanning of physical documents in our custody or control, we will make those documents available for inspection in accordance with Local Rule 16 and Rule 16 of the Federal Rules of Criminal Procedure.

9. At the Local Rule 16 discovery conference, we will discuss and consider in good faith alternative arrangements to the above as requested by counsel.

Source: http://www.wawfpd.org/cja/electronic_discovery/usao_best_practices.pdf

3. RESPONSES TO DISCOVERY REQUESTS

When responding to discovery requests, you must first note the date on which the discovery response is due. Failure to comply in a timely manner can prompt a motion from the opposing side and the imposition of sanctions—including the inability to use some types of the evidence at trial.

When gathering the requested documents, be sure to identify all references to any confidential information. For example, prosecutors' offices ordinarily receive reports, statements, and other investigation documents from the law enforcement agency that conducted the investigation. Such materials frequently contain confidential information, such as the identity of an informant or the address of a witness whose safety may be in jeopardy. Paralegals need to bring this information to the attention of their supervisors for direction on how these references should be handled. A paralegal's inadvertent disclosure of privileged information may have serious consequences to law enforcement or to the client. The supervising attorney may either file a formal objection to disclosing the confidential material or **redact** the sensitive information before releasing the documents in question.

After it has been determined how confidential information is to be handled, a paralegal is usually assigned to number and index the materials being turned over. Different offices may use different systems for labeling documents. One of the most common is the **Bates numbering** system. A Bates number is a number that is given to a document to identify it. Ordinarily, sequential Arabic numbers are used to identify each page of the discovery. As additional documents are acquired, each page is given a number. Some offices use labels that are affixed to each page; others use a sequential stamp. Bates numbers typically are placed on the same corner of each document. Paralegals may also prepare a Bates document index that identifies each document. Typically, there is not as much information for the defendant to organize and index at the beginning of a case because most prelitigation information is part of the police investigation.

Materials being sent in response to a formal discovery request should be accompanied by a formal court document identified as a response to a request for

Redaction
The process of masking some part of the content of a document before making it available for inspection.

Bates numbering
An organizational method used to label documents by assigning a number (or alphanumeric designation) to each document (or page), thereby creating a unique identifier for each.

production. This is a captioned document that provides a preview of the information being produced. Like other court documents, it contains a caption, introductory paragraph, body, attorney signature, and preparer's data. A sample face sheet of the response is depicted in Exhibit 7.4.

Exhibit 7.4: Face Sheet of Government Response to Production Request

THE UNITED STATES DISTRICT COURT
FOR THE NORTHERN DISTRICT OF
INDIANA HAMMOND DIVISION

UNITED STATES OF AMERICA

   vs   )   Case No. 09 CR XXX

WILLIAM EDWARDS,   )

   Defendant.   )

GOVERNMENT'S FIRST RESPONSE TO DEFENDANT'S INITIAL DISCOVERY REQUEST

Now comes the UNITED STATES OF AMERICA, by the U.S. ATTORNEY, and as its first response to the defendant's initial discovery request, states as follows:

1. *Defendant's Oral Statements*: The substance of any relevant oral statement made by the defendant, before or after arrest, in response to interrogation by a person the defendant knew was a government agent if the government intends to use the statement at trial. [FRCrP 16 (a)(1)(A).] In the event that the government intends to use such an oral statement at trial, Defendant requests that it be reduced in writing and produced. This request includes the substance of the Defendant's response to *Miranda* warnings.
   Tape recording of November 23, 2008 interview between William Edwards and FBI agent Justin Colby, dated August 3, 2008, is available for inspection at a mutually convenient time during business hours at the office of the United States Attorney. A verbatim transcript of the interview does not exist at this time.

2. *Defendant's Written or Recorded Statements:*
   a. Any relevant written or recorded statement by the defendant if the statement is within the government's possession, custody, or control; and the attorney for the government knows—or through due diligence could know—that the statement exists;
   b. The portion of any written record containing the substance of any relevant oral statement made before or after arrest if the defendant made the statement in response to interrogation by a person the defendant knew was a government agent; and
   c. The defendant's recorded testimony before a grand jury relating to the charged offense. [FRCrP 16 (a)(1)(B).]

Copies of the following documents are produced:

Signed statement of William Edwards prepared by FBI agent Justin Colby on November 23, 2008. [Bates Nos. 1-9]

Form letter to clients from William Edwards, dated August 3, 2008. [Bates No. 10]

Form letter to clients from William Edwards, dated September 13, 2008. [Bates No. 11]

Grand jury transcript [Bates Nos. 11-39]

3. *Defendant's Prior Record:* The defendant's prior criminal record that is within the government's possession, custody, or control if the attorney for the government knows—or through due diligence could know—that the record exists. [FRCrP 16 (a)(1)(D).] This request includes the Defendant's entire criminal record, including all arrests along with offenses regardless of conviction or severity. It includes all matters that may affect the Defendant's criminal history score pursuant to the United States Sentencing Guidelines.

Copies of the following documents are produced: Abstract of criminal record of William Edwards [Bates Nos. 40-43]

* * *

[Attorney Signature]

[Address Block]

The body of this document should reiterate the requests made by the opposing side. Each individual request should then be followed by a response to that specific request. These responses can include:

- a list of the titles of the document(s) being produced;
- the name of the item(s) or document(s) that you are making available for inspection;
- (if required by rule) a narrative answer to the inquiry; or
- an objection to the request.

It is best to use a different type font or boldface for your responsive information for easier reading of the document. Also cite the page number(s) of the document(s).

When a party does not have the information necessary to answer the discovery request, the proper response is "None." If responsive information is later discovered, there is a duty to supplement the response with that information. The prosecution cannot refuse to disclose information simply because the material is in the custody of law enforcement officers but not in the actual physical possession of the prosecutor's office. There is a duty on the part of the various law enforcement agencies to share information with each other. Likewise, the defense is not excused from making a disclosure if the information is the custody of the defendant's employee or agent.

When the information requested should not be disclosed due to an evidentiary privilege or otherwise, the party should object and set forth the basis of the objection in the response to the request. Either side may also file a **motion for a protective order**.[34] There are several bases to object to disclosure. Both parties can claim the information sought is **attorney work product**. Attorney work product consists of trial preparation materials containing the attorney's mental impressions, conclusions, opinions, and legal theories about a case. The government also can object on the basis that disclosure would breach national security or compromise the identity of a confidential informant. The defense may raise attorney-client privilege or the Fifth Amendment privilege against self-incrimination.

The paralegal will provide copies of responsive documents themselves along with the face sheet(s). Originals of the documents will be kept in the office. The paralegal also should prepare a proof of service to accompany the response.

APPLICATION EXERCISE

8. In the *Brandon Turner* case, the police had been provided information by a confidential source before the officer made the traffic stop. The defense is seeking the identity of the source as well as his address. The prosecution does not intend to call the informant as a witness. The police are continuing to use the informant. Draft a motion for a protective order on behalf of the prosecution for the jurisdiction in which your school is located. Assume that your supervising attorney is Terry Law, 123 Main Street, Anytown [555-1234]. This was the first felony case filed by the prosecutor this calendar year.

---

4. INFORMATION ON EXPERT WITNESSES

In addition to producing documentary and tangible items, some criminal rules of procedure impose a duty on the parties to provide a summary of **expert testimony** along with a list of the expert's qualifications.[35] Oftentimes, forensic experts prepare reports that show their findings, bases and reasons for their conclusions, and their opinions. When this is the case, you may satisfy this discovery request by attaching copies of the report along with the expert's **curriculum vitae (CV)**. On the other hand, if the report is not sufficient to meet the obligation imposed under the rules, you may need to draft the summary. Your

---

> **Motion for entry of a protective order**
> A formal request to the court to protect either the opposing party or a third party from an unreasonable or invasive request for discovery.

> **Attorney work product**
> Trial preparation materials consisting of the attorney's mental impressions, conclusions, opinions, and legal theories about a case.

> **Expert testimony**
> Testimony that is given by a witness who the court determines to be expert on the topic upon which the testimony is to be given. Once accepted as an expert witness, the person is allowed to state his or her opinion on relevant matters.

> **Curriculum vitae (CV)**
> A written description of a person's work experience, educational background, and skills. It is also called a CV, or vitae.

---

[34]Motions for protective orders are discussed later in this chapter.

[35]FRCrP 16(a)(1)(G) requires the government to disclose this information upon the defendant's request. Once the defense makes this request, there is a reciprocal obligation on the defense to make the same disclosures. FRCrP 16(b)(1)(C).

draft should fairly and accurately reflect the expert's anticipated testimony. Because the opponent could use the summary to cross-examine the expert, the expert should assist in preparing the statement to prevent any possibility of inconsistency between the statement and the trial testimony. Ask the expert to furnish you with a current CV.

APPLICATION EXERCISE

9. Using the Internet as a resource, locate experts on fingerprints and blood spatter. Provide copies of the experts' curriculum vitaes.

---

5. SUPPLEMENTAL DISCOVERY

It is very important to note that there is a duty to supplement discovery. Therefore, as the defense gathers information during the course of its investigation and law enforcement officers continue to build their case, the attorneys need to furnish supplemental reports to the opposing side. The format of a supplemental discovery response is essentially the same as that of the original.

When supplemental materials are involved, a new face sheet should describe the type of response in the title (e.g., Defendant's First Supplemental Response to the State's Rule 413 Request). The body of the supplemental response should restate the request that you are supplementing. As in the case of the original discovery reply, the description of the supplemental materials being provided should appear after the request in a different font style. You will send copies of the new documents to the opponent along with the face sheet. Another proof of service denoting the date of mailing or delivery should also be prepared and served.

6. WRITTEN DISCOVERY AGREEMENTS

Before we close our discussion of responses to discovery requests, it is worth noting that in federal court the prosecution may react to the defendant's discovery request with a proposal to enter into a written discovery agreement. Typical provisions of this agreement include the following:

- The government will provide a timely response to a Rule 16(a) request on the condition that the defendant produces reciprocal discovery pursuant to Rule 16(b).
- The government will provide statements of prospective witnesses prior to trial on the condition that the defendant produces reciprocal discovery.
- The government will furnish *Brady v. Maryland* material in a timely manner.
- The government will give notice of its intent to use evidence of other crimes or wrong acts of the defendant.

- The government will reserve its right to produce further discovery if the prosecution believes that disclosure presents a security risk to the witness.
- The agreement is void if the defendant files a discovery motion.[36]

If the government has a practice of routinely suggesting the use of an agreement, a paralegal employed by the prosecutor's office may be required to draft the cover letter and the proposed discovery agreement.

Figure 7.2 summarizes the paralegal's role as it relates to these written discovery requests.

Discovery Requests	Discovery Responses

1. Prepare discovery request
   a. Adapt request from other cases
   b. Alternatively, use formbook
	1. Note the due date

2. Arrange for service of request	2. Review documents in file
3. Prepare proof of service	3. Identify sensitive documents
4. Note the due date	4. Obtain direction as to sensitive matters
5. Review response to ascertain compliance	5. Label documents (e.g., Bates)
6. File response	6. Prepare face sheet of response
7. Prepare draft enforcement motion	7. Serve response
	8. Prepare proof of service
	9. Prepare motion for protective order
	10. Prepare supplemental responses

Figure 7.2   Paralegal's Written Discovery Responsibilities

APPLICATION EXERCISE

10. Draft a letter directed to the defense attorney in the *Brandon Turner* case proposing that the United States and the defendant enter into a written discovery agreement.

---

[36]B. Boss & E. R. Marek, *Federal Criminal Practice* (James Publishing 2006) at 10-48 through 10-49.

E. DEPOSITIONS

1. FUNCTIONS OF DEPOSITIONS

Deposition
Testimony taken before trial under oath, subject to cross-examination, and preserved in writing.

Deponent
The witness being questioned under oath at a deposition.

A **deposition** is testimony taken under oath and subject to cross-examination, before the trial begins. It may also be preserved on video or in writing. Those present at the deposition include the parties' attorneys, a court reporter, and the witness being deposed (the **deponent**). The parties themselves have a right to be present but they do not have to be there.

When depositions are used for general discovery, this mechanism can be useful in discovering facts, obtaining leads to other testimony, assessing the strengths and weaknesses of potential trial witnesses, and laying the foundation for impeachment at trial by nailing down a witness's story. A discovery deposition reveals the witness's appearance and demeanor prior to trial. Oftentimes it elicits spontaneous, unanticipated information. It is, however, an expensive and time-consuming method of gathering information. Indeed, a court reporter must be hired to take the deposition and transcribe it. Although depositions are widely used in civil cases, their use is severely restricted in most criminal litigation. Only 20 percent of the states permit depositions as a basic discovery mechanism.[37] The federal courts and the rest of the states only allow **depositions to perpetuate testimony**.[38]

Deposition to perpetuate testimony
A deposition that preserves the witness's statement so that it can be presented at a later time as evidence at trial.

In order to take such a deposition, a party must file a motion with the court for leave to do so. Generally, the party that wishes to take the deposition must make a showing that the deponent is a prospective material witness and is likely not to be available to testify at trial. The deponent's age, sickness, infirmity, or imprisonment are justifications for taking the witness's deposition. In most jurisdictions, the court will permit the deposition when there is a substantial possibility that relevant testimony would be unavailable at the time of trial.

Nevertheless, the presentation of a witness by means of deposition testimony is disfavored by the courts. Federal Rule 15(a)(1) illustrates the reluctance of the federal criminal justice system to permit depositions. The rule provides: "... A party may move that a prospective witness be deposed in order to preserve testimony for trial. The court may grant the motion because of *exceptional circumstances* and in the interest of justice. ..." (Emphasis added.) A judge or jury is in a better position to evaluate the credibility of a witness if the witness appears in person.

2. ROLE OF PARALEGALS

Figure 7.3 lists some of the tasks paralegals perform in the deposition process. Many of these tasks relate to drafting motions and subpoenas. Paralegals often play an important role in contacting the participants and scheduling the room,

---

[37]W. LaFave, J. Isreal & N. King, *Criminal Procedure* 928 (4th ed., West 2004).

[38]In Illinois, depositions to perpetuate testimony are referred to as evidence depositions. Before Illinois abolished the death penalty, Illinois Supreme Court Rule 416(e) permitted general discovery depositions in capital cases upon the court's finding of good cause for doing so.

APPLICATION EXERCISE

11. After reviewing your notebook materials on the *Turner* case (see Introduction to Hypothetical Cases, p. xxxvii along with facts and exhibits included in previous chapters), take note of the following additional facts:

> When the local prosecuting attorneys' office decides to prosecute Turner for the possession of cocaine, Brandon contends that he was unaware of the presence of the narcotic. It turns out that the car in which the cocaine was found was jointly owned by both Turner and a Dennis Watterson. Watterson is a drug dealer who is in the hospital for injuries caused by a gunshot wound and is not expected to be released from the hospital until after Turner's trial. Brandon, who is in custody, has not spoken to Watterson since his arrest, but believes that he will testify that the drugs were his and not Brandon's.

Illinois Supreme Court Rule 414(a) provides as follows:

> If it appears to the court in which a criminal charge is pending that the deposition of any person other than the defendant is necessary for the preservation of relevant testimony because of the substantial possibility it would be unavailable at the time of hearing or trial, the court may, upon motion and notice to both parties and their counsel, order the taking of such person's deposition under oral examination or written questions for use as evidence at a hearing or trial.

> a. What do you think Turner's attorney should do under these circumstances?
> b. Explain why you think this is what the attorney should do.

Although the use of video depositions is becoming more widespread, ordinarily the transcript of the deposition to perpetuate testimony is presented through a public reading of the document. The defense and prosecution attorneys each read their questions aloud while a third person sits on the witness stand and reads the deponent's answers. Paralegals oftentimes play the role of the witness during this presentation. Figure 7.3 presents recommendations as to how a deposition reader can be effective.

- Practice reading the transcript before trial.
- Familiarize yourself with pronunciation of words.
- Become comfortable with the witness's speech pattern.
- Know the script well enough to maintain eye contact with the jury.
- Act as if you actually are the witness.

Figure 7.3   Advice to Deposition Readers

time, etc. Although paralegals cannot actually conduct a deposition, they may be present to take notes and observe the proceedings. Figure 7.4 lists common responsibilities for paralegals involved with depositions.

1. Draft Motion for Leave to Take	7. Prepare Witness, if Appropriate
2. Schedule Motion with Court	8. Prepare Deposition Exhibits
3. Notice Motion for Hearing	9. Confirm Deposition
4. Schedule Deposition	10. Take Notes at Deposition
5. Draft Notice of Deposition	11. Abstract or Summarize Deposition
6. Draft Deposition Subpoena	12. Read Deposed Witnesses' Answers When They Are Not Available at Trial

Figure 7.4   Paralegal's Deposition Responsibilities

3. DRAFTING THE MOTION FOR A DEPOSITION

In most jurisdictions, the party seeking to take a deposition must get leave of the court to do so. This requires preparing a motion and "noticing" it for hearing. A **motion** is an application made to a court for the purpose of getting a ruling on an issue in favor of the moving party.

Motion
An application made to a court for the purpose of getting a ruling on an issue in favor of the moving party.

One approach to preparing a motion is to gather the basic facts first. Ordinarily, your supervising attorney will be able to provide this information. You may be directed to the client or others so that you can gain this knowledge from an interview. Thereafter, you should refer to the criminal code of procedure of the jurisdiction in which the case has been filed. In many cases, this will give you the statutory basis for the relief that you are seeking. Statutory annotations may reveal factual scenarios similar to your case. If the case involves more than procedural matters, then you will also need to research all substantive issues at stake. Once you have completed your legal research, you may need to gather additional facts. Thereafter, you can write the body of the motion.

Your body can be presented as a logical argument. Set forth the facts. Sometimes, you may have to attach documents that are supporting proof of the facts that you cite in the motion, such as affidavits. If there are many facts, you should offer them in multiple paragraphs. Then present the law. If you are relying on a procedural rule, consider quoting the relevant portion. Thereafter, present your analysis. In other words, show the court how the facts warrant the relief that you are seeking under the law.

The body section of a motion differs from the discovery request body. Instead of simply listing information being sought, the body of a motion presents an argument in support of the relief sought. Relevant facts in addition to legal authority are presented in this part of the motion. Although there are many ways to present effective motions, most are organized in concise, consecutively numbered paragraphs. The pertinent facts as well as citations to authorities are set forth to provide a basis for the court to grant the motion.

See Exhibit 7.5 for an example of a motion to take a deposition in the *Turner* case.

4. NOTICING THE DEPOSITION

Once you have drafted your motion for leave to take the deposition, you need to notice it for hearing. "**Noticing a motion**" means sending a written notice to the other party that the motion will be argued in front of the judge on a particular date at a specific time. The party filing the motion is referred to as the **movant**, and the opposing party that receives the motion is called the **respondent**. Motions contain the same components that are included in most court documents plus a **prayer for relief**. The prayer is a short, unnumbered paragraph near the end of a motion in which the moving party presents the relief being sought from the court.

Although there is no requirement that you communicate with the opposing party before scheduling a motion, a professional paralegal will contact the opponent to choose a mutually convenient date. This type of courtesy does not undermine the client's interests and promotes civility in the legal community. Scheduling a motion for a time that the opposing party is unable to attend not only breeds bad will but usually leads to unnecessary court appearances. To notice a hearing, you call the clerk of the judge assigned to the case who will set it in the judge's calendar. Some federal courts do not allow the parties to set motions and instead set the matters themselves. You should consult local rules for guidance.

After you get a court date, send a written notice of hearing to the opposing party. A **notice of hearing** is a court document that states the time, date, and judge who will hear arguments on a particular motion. When both the motion and the notice of hearing are sent at the same time, the notice references a hearing on the "attached" motion. Alternatively, if the motion has already been filed with the clerk, then the notice references the motion by name. There must be written proof of service for the notice of hearing. If the notice and motion are sent together, one proof of service can be used. If the motion is not "noticed up," there will be no ruling on it. In some jurisdictions, you must notice the motion within a set number of days. If the motion is not noticed during this time frame, the motions will be stricken by the court. You should check the local rules. See Exhibit 7.6 for a sample of a notice of hearing.

Both the motion and notice of hearing are filed with the clerk of the court. You should present the original for filing and a copy to be stamp-filed by the court. This is your record that the document has been filed and the date on which it was filed. When the document returns to your office you can include it in a file that should mirror the court's file of the case. If the clerk of the court is located outside of your locale, you can file the document by mail. The best practice for this type of filing is to do so by certified mail, return receipt requested. This should provide your office with proof of filing in the event the document is lost by the clerk's office.

Noticing a motion
The process of sending a written notice to the other party informing the party that the motion will be argued in front of the judge on a particular date at a specific time.

Movant
The party filing a motion with the court.

Respondent
The party who receives the motion from the opposing side of a case.

Prayer for relief
A short, unnumbered paragraph near the end of a motion in which the moving party presents the relief being sought from the court.

Notice of hearing
A court document that states the time, date, and judge who will hear arguments on a particular motion.

Exhibit 7.5: Motion for Order to Take Deposition to Preserve Testimony

Now comes Defendant BRANDON TURNER, by CHARLES HOVEY, his attorney, and pursuant to Illinois Supreme Court Rule 414(a), moves that the court order the taking of Dennis Watterson's deposition under oral examination. In support of this motion, Defendant states as follows:

1. Defendant is charged with unlawful possession of cocaine.
2. The report of the reporting officer disclosed in discovery that a package of a substance believed to be cocaine was found on the front seat of the vehicle that Defendant had been driving. A copy of the report is attached hereto and incorporated herein as Exhibit "A."
3. The car in which the cocaine was found was jointly owned by Defendant and Dennis Watterson. A copy of the vehicle registration is attached hereto and incorporated herein as Exhibit "B."
4. On information and belief, Defendant believes that if called as a witness, Watterson will testify that he sells narcotics and that the drugs found in the car were not Defendant's drugs but were his.
5. The doctrine of constructive possession requires the state to establish the defendant's knowledge of the presence of contraband and his immediate and exclusive control of it. *People v. Williams*, 98 Ill. App. 3d 844, 424 N.E.2d 1234 (3d Dist. 1981).
6. Defense counsel has learned that Dennis Watterson is currently hospitalized at Dunbarton Hospital in Joliet, Illinois for injuries suffered from a gunshot. Watterson is not expected to be released for weeks, well after this case is scheduled to go to jury trial.
7. Supreme Court Rule 414(a) provides as follows:

    > If it appears to the court in which a criminal charge is pending that the deposition of any person other than the defendant is necessary for the preservation of relevant testimony because of the substantial possibility it would be unavailable at the time of hearing or trial, the court may, upon motion and notice to both parties and their counsel, order the taking of such person's deposition under oral examination or written questions for use as evidence at a hearing or trial.

8. The expected testimony of Watterson is relevant to the defense's case. The State's case is based upon the doctrine of constructive possession of cocaine. Indeed, the alleged contraband was not found on Defendant's person but rather in a car to which another person had access. Watterson is expected to testify that he was an owner of the car; that he is a drug dealer; and that the drugs found in the car were his.
9. Because Watterson is not expected to be released from the hospital until after the trial, the court should order the taking of his deposition to preserve relevant testimony.

WHEREFORE, Defendant BRANDON TURNER prays that the court order the taking of Dennis Watterson's deposition under oral examination.

Exhibit 7.6: Notice of Motion with Proof of Service

IN THE CIRCUIT COURT OF
THE 12th JUDICIAL CIRCUIT
WILL COUNTY, ILLINOIS

PEOPLE OF THE STATE OF ILLINOIS	)	
v.	)	Case No. 09 CF XXXX
BRANDON TURNER,	)	
Defendant.	)	

NOTICE OF HEARING

To: [Name and Address of opposing counsel]

On February 1, 20_____ at 9:00 A.M., or as soon after as counsel may be heard, the undersigned will appear before the Honorable Susan Horton, or any judge sitting in her stead, in the courtroom usually occupied by her in the Will County Courthouse located in Joliet, Illinois, and then and there present a Motion for Order to Take Deposition to Preserve Testimony, a copy of which is attached hereto, at which time and place you may appear if you so desire and request an immediate hearing.

_____

CHARLES HOVEY, Attorney for Defendant

CERTIFICATE OF SERVICE

UNDER PENALTIES OF PERJURY and pursuant to the provisions of 735 ILCS 5/1-109, the undersigned, hereby certifies that he/she served the foregoing attached Notice of Motion by depositing a copy thereof into a U.S. Post Office mailbox in Normal, Illinois in an envelope, postage fully prepaid, addressed to:

[Name & Address of Opposing Counsel]

on the _____ day of _____, 20_____ at or about the hour of 5:00 P.M.

_____

CHARLES HOVEY
Attorney for Defendant
1857 Bone Street
Normal, IL 61761
(309)-555-1857

If the court grants the motion for the order to take deposition to preserve testimony, you will need to schedule the deposition. You should contact the opposing party, the witness, and the court reporter before you set the deposition. If you plan a videotaped deposition, you will also need to line up a videographer. Often, the court reporter can refer you to an experienced videographer. Depositions typically take place at the attorney's office or the office of the court reporter. However, circumstances may dictate that they take place at a hotel room, the home of the witness, a hospital room, or a prison.

Noticing the deposition
The process of sending a written notice to the other party informing the opposing party of the time, date, and place of a deposition of a named witness along with the method of recording testimony, such as stenography or audio recording.

After you confirm a date, time, and place, you will be "**noticing the deposition**." The notice of deposition should give reasonable notice to the other party of the date, time, and place for taking the deposition along with the method of recording testimony, such as stenography or audio recording. It also should specify whether the deposition is going to be videotaped. You should direct the notice to the opposing party. Although it is not required, a practice that can eliminate confusion is to also direct the notice to the court reporter who will be taking the deposition. Once you serve a copy of the notice on the opposing side, file the original with the clerk of the court. A sample notice of deposition is depicted in Exhibit 7.7.

Exhibit 7.7: Notice of Deposition

IN THE CIRCUIT COURT OF
THE 12th JUDICIAL CIRCUIT
WILL COUNTY, ILLINOIS

PEOPLE OF THE STATE OF ILLINOIS v. BRANDON TURNER, Defendant.	))) Case No. 09 CF XXXX))

NOTICE OF DEPOSITION

TO: [Opposing Party's Name and Address] [Optional: Court Reporter's Name and Address]

You are hereby notified that pursuant to the provisions of Supreme Court Rules 202 and 414(a), the evidence deposition of Dennis Watterson will be taken by court stenographer for the purpose of preserving evidence for trial, before a Notary Public in the County of Will, State of Illinois, at the hour of 2:00 P.M., on March 15, 20_____, at the Office of Charles Hovey, 185 Bone Street, Normal, IL 61716.

CERTIFICATE OF SERVICE

UNDER PENALTIES OF PERJURY and pursuant to the provisions of 735 ILCS 5/1-109, the undersigned, hereby certifies that he/she served the foregoing attached Notice of Deposition by depositing a copy thereof into a U.S. Post Office mailbox in Normal, Illinois in an envelope, postage fully prepaid, addressed to:

[Name and Address of Opposing Counsel]

on the ____ day of _____, 20____ at or about the hour of 5:00 P.M.

_____

CHARLES HOVEY
Attorney for Defendant
1857 Bone Street
Normal, IL 61761
(309)-555-1857

At the time you prepare the notice of deposition, you also should prepare a deposition subpoena for the deponent. The clerk of the court will provide you with blank subpoena forms that have been issued under seal of the court. You must fill in the blanks and take steps to have the witness served with this document. The subpoena can simply require the witness to appear or to appear and bring documents to the deposition.[39]

APPLICATION EXERCISES

12. Prepare a notice of deposition for the *Bud Cook* sample case (see hypothetical on p. xxxvii). The deposition will take place on the first day of next month at 1:30 P.M. in the conference room of the courthouse closest to your school. The witness is Jeffrey Z. Braden, who lives at 9008 Elm Road, Anytown, USA. You work for the defense attorney, Charles Hovey, 228 Fifteen Ave., Anytown, USA. The opposing counsel is the prosecuting attorney for the district in which your school is located. The deposition will be taken by a court reporter by stenography. It will not be videotaped. Assume that this case was the 55th felony case filed this year.

13. Prepare a notice of hearing (and proof of service) in the *Bud Cook* case on the state's motion to bar deposition of Jeffrey Z. Braden. You work for the local prosecutor. The motion is to be served upon Charles Hovey. The motion should be set for the business day before the deposition of Braden. Judge Susan Bunk will hear the motion at 9 A.M. in courtroom 100 at the state courthouse located closest to your school. Use the information in paragraph 11 to prepare the notice.

---

[39]The methods of serving subpoenas on witnesses will be discussed in Section F of this chapter.

5. PREPARING FOR THE DEPOSITION

In the event that the witness who is going to be deposed is friendly to your side, you may be asked to prepare the witness. This does not mean that you will tell the witness what the substance of his or her testimony is to be. Instead, you will explain to the witness the purpose and format of the deposition. You also should make sure that the witness understands the procedures and tactics of a deposition. Figure 7.5 contains a few simple guidelines that a paralegal can share with witnesses.

- Tell the truth.
- Speak slowly, clearly, and out loud.
- Do not interrupt the questioner.
- Use words to answer; avoid answering with "uh huh" or using body language.
- Bring nothing with you except what you are ordered to bring by the subpoena.
- Listen carefully to the questions.
- If you don't understand a question, let the questioner know.
- Read any documents presented to you carefully.
- Do not guess or speculate.
- Do not volunteer information.

Figure 7.5   Advice to Witnesses

Your supervising attorney may also ask you to go over the anticipated testimony with the witness. If the witness doesn't recall details, your supervisor may have you show the witness his or her previous statements to help refresh memory. Sometimes, you may accompany witnesses to the scene of the place where they originally made their observations. When you meet with a witness, make sure that you identify yourself as a paralegal, give the name of your employer, and state whether you work for the prosecutor or for the defendant.

Exhibit
A tangible item that is marked for identification for purpose of being used as evidence at a trial.

Prior to a deposition, you may be asked to prepare **exhibits**. Exhibits are tangible items that are marked for identification for use in a case. When the deposition is for the purpose of preserving testimony, the exhibits may become "trial exhibits," which ultimately are shown to the jury if the judge admits them into evidence. The preferred approach to preparing exhibits is to mark the original with a label that adheres to the exhibit and copy the exhibit for each party. If the exhibit is non-documentary evidence such as a gun or marked U.S. currency, copies are not produced for the parties. An exhibit is identified by the designation of the party presenting it along with a letter or number. For instance, the defendant's first exhibit may be marked as "Defendant's Exhibit No. 1" or "Defendant's Exhibit A." The next exhibit would then be marked as "Defendant's Exhibit No. 2" or "Defendant's Exhibit B." Exhibits do not have to be presented in the same order as they are marked. Thus, the prosecution may present People's Exhibit 15 first and then present People's Exhibit 2. If you do not have exhibits that your supervising attorney will need for the deposition but have reason to believe that they are in the possession of a third party, your attorney should ask for permission from the court to subpoena the items prior to taking the deposition. We will discuss third-party subpoenas below.

A day or two before the deposition, you should contact the opposing side, the witness, and the court reporter to verify that the deposition will still move forward as scheduled. This will not take much time and will alert you to possible problems. For instance, if you learn that the witness does not speak English, you would have to arrange for a translator to be present. The court reporter can probably refer you to a competent interpreter.

Your supervising attorney may have you sit in on the deposition. Your role will probably be limited to taking notes and assisting with the exhibits. Following the deposition, the attorney may seek your impressions of the witness.

6. DRAFTING SUMMARIES AND ABSTRACTS

Following the deposition, the attorney usually orders a transcript. The party noticing the deposition requests an original and the other party asks for a copy. The transcript contains a verbatim record of the questions and answers presented during the deposition. Each page and line of the transcript is numbered. Transcripts often are lengthy and cumbersome.

In order to increase their effectiveness, attorneys may have their paralegals prepare summaries or abstracts. There are various styles and formats. Your supervising attorney can give you direction as to the way that he or she wants you to lay out the abstract or summary. Generally, these are substantially shorter than the deposition transcript. The rule of thumb is that for every five pages of transcript, there is one page of summary or abstract.

A deposition summary captures the thrust of what the witness said and is prepared as a narrative. One possible format is as follows:

- Caption
- Introductory information (name of witness; persons present; date of deposition)
- Witness personal information (job; relation to defendant or victim)
- Expertise (if expert: education; training; experience)
- Incident
- Conversations with parties
- Credibility issues (bias, etc.)
- Other matters

If the deposition is used to preserve testimony, a summary may be useful in the preparation of the opening statement and closing argument.

If the deposition is a general discovery deposition, an abstract can be helpful to the attorney at trial who may impeach the witness by showing contradictions between trial testimony and deposition testimony. The abstracted testimony captures the essence of the witness's position with pinpoint citations to the line and page of the transcript. This makes the deposition useful at trial. Unlike a summary, which is written as a narrative, the abstract presents the witness's statements as one- or two-sentence bits of information that are accompanied by the page and line reference. The body of the abstract should be organized into segments based upon the type of examination (direct, cross, re-direct, re-cross). The name of the questioner for each examination should be included in the subtitles. A possible format for a deposition abstract follows:

- Caption
- Introductory information (name of witness; persons present; date of deposition)
- Direct examination
- Cross-examination
- Re-direct examination
- Re-cross examination

Although most depositions taken to preserve testimony are presented at trial, sometimes the witness is available and presents live testimony. When this occurs, the deposition can be used for impeachment. Accordingly, an abstract of the deposition may be a useful trial aid. Exhibit 7.8 provides a side-by-side comparison between a deposition transcript and the body of the abstract of that deposition.

Exhibit 7.8: Comparison between Deposition Transcript and Abstract

		Transcript	Body of Abstract
		Page 1	
1		DIRECT EXAMINATION	**DIRECT EXAMINATION**
2		BY MR. HOVEY	**BY MR. HOVEY**
3			**Page, Line**
4	Q	What is your name?	
5	A	Dennis Watterson.	
6	Q	Now, we are at Dunbarton Hospital in Joliet,	
7		Illinois right now?	
8	A	Yes.	**1, 6-10 Witness is patient at Dunbarton Hospital.**
9	Q	And you are a patient here?	
10	A	Yes.	
11	Q	What is your current physical condition?	

12	A	Paralyzed.			
13	Q	You're paralyzed?	**1, 13-14**	**He is paralyzed.**	
14	A	Yes.			
15	Q	And do you expect to remain in the hospital	**1, 15-17**	**He will be in hospital**	
16		throughout the month of April of this year?		**through April, YY.**	
17	A	Yes.			
18	Q	Mr. Watterson, do you know a man by the			
19		name of Brandon Turner?			
20	A	Yes.			
21	Q	How do you know him?			
22	A	Through a relationship; we're friends.	**1,18-22**	**He's friends with defendant.**	
23	Q	All right. How long have you and Mr. Turner			
24		known each other?			

Page 2

1	A	About five years.			
2	Q	Do you and Mr. Turner own any property			
3		together?			
4	A	Yes, a car.	**2, 2-4**	**He owns a car with defendant.**	
5		MR. HOVEY: I'd like to have this marked, Ms. Reporter,			
6		as Defendant's Exhibit No. 1.			
7					
8		(Defendant's Exhibit No. 1 was	**2, 5-22**	**Witness identifies title**	
9		marked for identification as of		**application for car.**	
10		3/15/–)		**[DEFENDANT'S EXHIBIT 1]**	
11					
12	Q	I'm handing you what's been marked as			

13   Defendant 's Exhibit No. 1 and ask you to take a look at

14   that piece of paper. Do you recognize your signature on

15   that piece of paper?

16   A   Yes.

17   Q   Do you recognize any other signatures?

18   A   Yes, the other one in Brandon's.

19   Q   Do you mean Brandon Turner?

20   A   Yes.

21   Q   This document is the title application

22   for the car that you and Brandon own together?

23   A   Yes.

24   Q   What kind of car is it?

Page 3

2, 24-3, 1 Car was 1995 Buick.

1   A   A 1995 Buick.

2   Q   When did you buy it? You can look at

3   the exhibit.

4   A   October 30 of last year.

5   Q   Now after you and Mr. Turner bought the   **3, 1-9   After 10/30/YY, both the witness**

6   car, who used the car?   **and defendant used the car.**

7   A   Me and him.

8   Q   Both of you?

9   A   Yes.

10   Q   Would the car stay at one particular place?

11   A   At Brandon's house.

12	Q	All right. I'd like to direct your attention to		
13		November 29 of last year. Do you remember		
14		that particular day, the day that Brandon was arrested?		
15	A	Not too clearly, but I remember parts of it.		
16	Q	On the morning of November 29 do you	**3, 16-20**	**On morning of 11/29/YY,**
17		remember who had the car?		**witness used the car to take**
18	A	Yeah, I used the car.		**his girlfriend to the grocery**
19	Q	Where did you go?		**store.**
20	A	I took my girlfriend to the grocery store.		
21	Q	Which store?		
22	A	Goodman's in Joliet.		
23	Q	Where is that located?		
24	A	I think it's on Wright Street near Haney.		

Please note that the actual transcript testimony does not appear in the abstract as it is depicted in this figure; only the digested information with pinpoint citations is presented. When you prepare a deposition abstract, you should skip one line between each abstracted piece of information. Additional space appears between each entry here so that you can see the testimony that was digested and compare it to the abstract.

You also can also draft summaries and abstracts of a variety of other documents. If there is a preliminary hearing, the police officers who testify oftentimes are witnesses at trial. An abstract can be helpful from the defense side of the case to impeach the officer's trial testimony. From the government's point of view, a summary of preliminary hearing testimony can assist the prosecutor or the paralegal in preparing the officer for trial. Other relevant transcribed proceedings also can be abstracted or summarized, such as a coroner's inquest for a homicide victim, a civil trial stemming from the circumstances that gave rise to criminal charges, etc.

F. Subpoenas Directed to Third Parties

Subpoena *duces tecum*
A special form of the subpoena used to compel the witness to bring documents or other tangible items to court or to a grand jury proceeding.

A subpoena is a tool that can be used at various stages of a case to assist the parties in procuring evidence. Most laypeople consider a subpoena to be a court order requiring them to appear in court to testify. Although subpoenas are commonly used for this purpose, they are also used to gather non-testamentary information to prepare for trial. A subpoena that seeks the production of documents or other tangible items is referred to as a **subpoena *duces tecum***. Before a case goes to trial, a party may apply to the court for the issuance of a subpoena *duces tecum* directed toward a non-party. Unlike civil pre-trial subpoenas *duces tecum* that are returnable to the party requesting the subpoena, a pre-trial criminal subpoena *duces tecum* is returnable to the court itself. Material procured through the use of a subpoena *duces tecum* that was not sanctioned by and returnable to the court generally is inadmissible at trial.

The first step in obtaining a subpoena for documents is to file a motion with the court. In *United States v. Nixon*,[40] the U.S. Supreme Court held that under FRCrP 17, the movant must show the following:

> (1) that the documents are evidentiary and relevant; (2) that they are not otherwise procurable reasonably in advance of trial by exercise of due diligence; (3) that the party cannot properly prepare for trial without such production and inspection in advance of trial, and that the failure to obtain such inspection may tend unreasonably to delay the trial; and (4) that the application is made in good faith and is not intended as a general 'fishing expedition.'[41]

State court standards may be different. Accordingly, you should research the law of your state before you prepare the motion. An example of a motion for issuance of subpoenas *duces tecum* is set forth in Exhibit 7.9. It is from a widely publicized case in which three Duke University lacrosse players were charged with the rape and kidnapping of an exotic dancer who claimed that she was assaulted at a team party.

If the court allows the motion, your supervisor will direct you to prepare the subpoena. Each court system has preprinted subpoena forms; many are available online.[42] When you draft the subpoena, make sure that you direct the custodian to produce the documents at the courthouse rather than at your office. Otherwise, you simply fill in the blanks of the form. You must have the subpoena issued by the clerk of the court. This means that you must present the subpoenas to the clerk's office before they are served upon the custodian of the documents or other tangible property.

After the subpoena *duces tecum* is prepared and sealed by the court, you need to take steps to have it served. This means that you will have to arrange for a subpoena server. In most jurisdictions, the person serving the subpoena does not have to be a law enforcement officer, although there may be circumstances when an officer is the best choice to deliver the subpoena. In federal cases, any non-party

---

[40]418 U.S. 683, 94 S. Ct. 3090, 41 L. Ed. 2d 1039 (1974).

[41]418 U.S. at 699-700.

[42]The federal form for a subpoena in a criminal case is Form A0 089, located online at *http://www.uscourts.gov/forms/uscforms*.

Exhibit 7.9: Motion for Issuance of Subpoenas *Duces Tecum*

NORTH CAROLINA

DURHAM COUNTY

STATE OF NORTH CAROLINA

vs.

READE WILLIAM SELIGMANN,
                              Defendant.

IN THE GENERAL COURT OF JUSTICE
SUPERIOR COURT DIVISION
FILE NOS. 06 CRS 4334-356

)
)
)
)
)
)
)

RITCHIE MOTION FOR PRODUCTION AND INSPECTION OF RECORDS OF MENTAL DISABILITY, HOSPITAL COMMITMENT, DRUG ABUSE HISTORY EDUCATIONAL HISTORY, DEPARTMENT OF SOCIAL SERVICE RECORDS, JUVENILE RECORDS, PROBATION AND PAROLE RECORDS, CHILD PROTECTIVE SERVICES RECORDS, AND VICTIM'S ADVOCACY RECORDS

NOW COMES the Defendant, READE WILLIAM SELIGMANN, through counsel, and respectfully moves this Honorable Court pursuant to the Fifth, Sixth, Eighth and Fourteenth Amendments to the United States Constitution, Article I, §§ 19, 23 & 27 of the North Carolina Constitution, and *Pennsylvania v. Ritchie*, 480 U.S. 39, 59-61 (1987) and its progeny, for orders directing the appropriate agencies to provide to the Court copies of all records of the complaining witness, ▮▮▮▮▮▮▮▮▮▮▮, regarding Mental Disability, Hospital Commitments, Drug Abuse History, Educational Records, Probation and Parole Record, and Department of Social Service Records. This request is based on the fact that the complaining witness has a history of criminal activity and behavior which includes alcohol abuse, drug abuse, and dishonesty, all conduct which indicate mental, emotional and/or physical problems which affect her credibility as a witness. Since these problems do not occur overnight, they probably began in her teenage years and continue to exist. The Defendant requests that these orders include directing both Hillside High School and North Carolina Central University to provide to this Court her entire educational records including any disciplinary action and that the State make affirmative inquiry of the complaining witness as to any and all hospitalizations, treatment at mental centers, involvement with the Department of Social Services Agencies, Probation and Parole, Juvenile Agencies, Child Protective Services Agencies, Victims' Advocacy Agencies or Organizations, or any other agencies providing services for mental, emotional, drug or alcohol problems.

***

WHEREFORE, Defendant respectfully requests the Court to issue orders to accompany subpoenas to produce documents (subpoena duces tecum) to all hospital, agencies, treatment centers, including the Durham County Office of Probation and Parole, Durham Department of Social Services, Juvenile Agencies, Child Protective Services Agencies, Victims' Advocacy Agencies or Organizations, Hillside High School, North Carolina Central University, and any other institution or agency which may have housed or treated the complaining witness in this matter and any other agency identified by the District Attorney's Office pursuant to an inquiry ordered by this Court.

After this material is produced, counsel for the Defendant request a pretrial "reliability hearing" in which to review the following in addition to the materials provided pursuant to this Motion to determine if the complaining witness is even credible enough to provide reliable testimony:

1.   The complaining witness' complete criminal history;

2.   Any deal, promise, inducement, or benefit the State has made or may make in the future to her;

3.   The time, place, and manner of any specific statements the complaining witness has made in this case;

4.   All other cases in which the complaining witness has testified or offered statements against an individual but was not called;

5.   Whether the complaining witness has recanted testimony or statements in this case or any other case and a transcript or copy of the recantation; and

6.   Any other information relevant to her credibility.

RESPECTFULLY SUBMITTED this the 24th day of April, 2006.

J. KIRK OSBORN
ATTORNEY FOR THE DEFENDANT

CASE DISCUSSION QUESTIONS

1. How significant is "the complaining witness" to this prosecution?
2. What type of subpoena was the defense seeking permission to issue?
3. In what ways could the enumerated items sought at the conclusion of the motion be used to assist the defense in preparing the case for trial?

who is at least eighteen years old is authorized to serve a subpoena. This is the situation in many states; however, you must check the law of the jurisdiction where the case is pending to make sure that your subpoena server is qualified.

Because most adults are qualified, you may be asked to serve the subpoena yourself. If you are the subpoena server, you need to act in a professional manner. Be prepared to let the witness know that he or she is ordered to produce the item(s) specified on the subpoena at a particular time and date. Emphasize that the items are to be delivered to the court, not to the lawyer's office. It is not your role to discuss the facts of the case with this individual. If the person served asks a question that you either are unable to answer or do not feel comfortable answering, direct that person to your supervising attorney.

In some jurisdictions, including federal court, the recipient of the subpoena must be given a fee. FRCrP 17(d) provides that the server must "tender to the witness one day's witness-attendance fee and the legal mileage allowance." On the other hand, Illinois does not require the tender of fees at the time of service of a subpoena in a criminal case. You, therefore, must find out the fee requirements of the jurisdiction. The clerk of the court may be able to direct you to the current fee/mileage schedule. A fee check is typically stapled to the copy of the subpoena that is delivered to the custodian.

After the subpoena is delivered, the server then prepares a proof of service, or affidavit of service. This is a document in which the server attests under penalty of perjury or under oath when he or she served the witness with the subpoena and tendered fees. Most subpoenas provided by the clerk's office have a fill-in-the-blank form as part of the document. The original of the subpoena along with the proof of service is filed with the clerk of the court. You should retain a copy of the subpoena and proof of service to be file-stamped by the clerk of the court.

---

1. Research law
2. Prepare motion to issue subpoena *duces tecum*
3. Draft motion for issuance of subpoena *duces tecum*
4. Obtain subpoena *duces tecum* form from clerk of court or online
5. Complete subpoena *duces tecum* form
6. Have clerk of court issue subpoena *duces tecum*
7. Attach copy of the fee check for the subpoena *duces tecum*
8. Arrange for subpoena server
9. Prepare a proof of service
10. File original along with proof of service with clerk of court

Figure 7.6   Paralegal's Responsibilities for Obtaining Documents or Other Items from Third Parties

APPLICATION EXERCISE

14. Prepare a subpoena *duces tecum* in the Turner case that is directed to Dennis Watterson, 357 Magee Drive, Anytown, USA requiring production of the vehicle title of the 1995 Buick automobile owned by Watterson and Brandon Turner. Use the information contained in Application Exercise 11 above.

   a. For the federal prosecution, have the subpoena returned to the federal court located closest to your college at 9 A.M. on the first business day of next month. Use Form A089 located at *http://www.uscourts.gov/forms/uscforms.*

   b. For the state prosecution, have the subpoena returned to the state court located closest to your college at 9 A.M. on the first business day of next month. Obtain the appropriate form from the Internet or from the clerk's office.

G. DISCLOSURE OF THE PERSON

In addition to disclosing written material, the defendant may be required to present his or her person for discovery. Illinois Supreme Court Rule 413(a) is illustrative of this type of discovery. The rule provides as follows:

[A] judicial officer may require the accused, among other things, to:

(i) Appear in a lineup;

(ii) Speak for identification by witnesses to an offense;

(iii) Be fingerprinted;

(iv) Pose for photographs not involving reenactment of a scene;

(v) Try on articles of clothing;

(vi) Permit the taking of specimens of material under his fingernails;

(vii) Permit the taking of samples of his blood, hair and other materials of his body which involve no unreasonable intrusion thereof;

(viii) Provide a sample of his handwriting; and

(ix) Submit to a reasonable physical or medical inspection of his body.

Usually, the attorney will escort the defendant to this processing, but it is possible that a paralegal might accompany the client instead of or in addition to the attorney. The primary role of the law firm's representatives is to provide support to the client, who is going through an unfamiliar and uncomfortable situation.

Although a criminal defendant may be requested to give basic information such as name and address, the client should not discuss the case with anyone. If you have any doubt about disclosure, contact your supervising attorney. The meeting with the government's representative will be professional.

APPLICATION EXERCISE

15. What type of disclosure of one's body must a defendant make in your state? What is the citation for the authority requiring this production?

H. Other Discovery Tools for the Defense

Defendants can also gain pertinent information through a number of mechanisms that are not specifically designed for discovery. The bail hearing, the preliminary hearing, and hearings on pre-trial motions such as a motion to suppress will reveal some of the prosecution's evidence. Court reporters typically record the proceedings through stenography or audio recordings. Both sides can obtain transcripts of the testimony provided at the hearings through the court's administrator or clerk's office.

The defense can also obtain information by filing a **motion for bill of particulars**. The federal rules, along with many state codes, permit the defendant to file a motion to seek specifics of a charge. Federal Rule 17(f) allows the defendant to file a motion for bill of particulars before arraignment, within ten days after the arraignment, or at a later date with permission of the court. States, such as Illinois, allow the defense to make the motion before or within a reasonable time after arraignment.[43]

The purpose of the bill of particulars is to provide sufficient information so that the defendant is apprised of the nature of the charges and is in a position to prepare for trial. The court may allow the motion when the information, indictment, or charge fails to allege essential information, such as the time, date, or place of the alleged offense. This information is paramount when the defense is claiming an alibi or that the charge was filed after the statute of limitations expired.

Although most criminal law formbooks contain sample motions for a bill of particulars, you should customize the motion to address the specific deficiencies of the charging instrument. In preparing your draft, you should not only point out what information is missing but also explain how the defendant is prejudiced by the omission. Courts have a great deal of discretion in ruling on these motions, so it is important that the motion present particularized reasons for allowing the request.

Finally, the defense can acquire information through means outside of the criminal case itself. Indeed, some cases have parallel proceedings. For example, crime victims may file civil actions against defendants—for battery, wrongful death, sexual assault, driving under the influence, and so on. A coroner's office often convenes a coroner's jury to consider evidence in deciding the cause of a victim's death. Also Freedom of Information requests can be used to obtain documents in the custody of governmental bodies.

Motion for bill of particulars
A defense motion that requests the court to order the prosecution to file a supplementary document that gives the specifics of a charge that were not set forth in the original charge.

---

[43]725 ILCS 5/114-2.

I. Discovery Variations

We have noted throughout this text that specific procedures and formats for documents will vary from one state to another and between state and federal courts. More complex criminal litigation may have a more diverse set of rules than the procedures that are generally applied. In addition, misdemeanor discovery may differ from felony discovery.[44]

1. DISCOVERY IN MISDEMEANOR CASES

An example of differences between discovery procedures for misdemeanor and felony cases can be illustrated by reference to Illinois Supreme Court Rule 411, which defines the scope of the criminal discovery rules is expressly limited to felony prosecutions. There are no rules addressing discovery in other criminal cases. This absence of a parallel procedure for misdemeanor cases gave rise to the Illinois Supreme Court case of *People v. Schmidt.*

Illinois v. Schmidt
Supreme Court of Illinois
56 Ill. 2d 572; 309 N.E.2d 557 (1974)

Mr. Chief Justice Underwood delivered the opinion of the court.

OPINION

The defendant, Alice L. Schmidt, was arrested for driving while under the influence of intoxicating liquor, in violation of the Illinois Vehicle Code, section 11—501 (Ill. Rev. Stat. 1971, ch. 95 1/2, par. 11—501). She sought pretrial discovery of an alcoholic-influence report and any police reports containing observations and statements. The alcoholic-influence report contained results of a breathalyzer test and was furnished to defendant as a chemical test pursuant to section 11—501(g). Also made available to defendant was the video tape of defendant presumably made upon her arrival at the police station following her arrest. The prosecutor, however, refused to disclose, prior to trial, a Driving While Intoxicated Arrest Report, characterizing it as a routine police report of the facts of the arrest and not subject to pretrial dis-

covery in a misdemeanor case, although agreeing to its production at trial for impeachment purposes. The trial court examined the arrest report *in camera*, held it to be "an extension of the visual" and a "supplemental alcoholic influence report" and therefore discoverable. The State refused to comply with the order to furnish the report to defendant prior to trial. The trial court thereupon entered an order excluding all information contained in the report from use at trial. The trial judge's comments indicate he believed this court would ultimately be "forced" to extend application of the discovery rules to misdemeanor cases, and was exercising his discretion in extending them in this case. In reversing the trial court the Appellate Court for the Second District (*People v. Schmidt*, 8 Ill.App.3d 1024) held discovery rules were inapplicable since the charge in this case did not carry with it the possibility of imprisonment in the penitentiary. We allowed leave to appeal.

Defendant contends that while the rules of discovery are mandatory in application to cases

---

[44]The Federal Rules of Criminal Procedure do not distinguish between felonies and misdemeanors. FRCrP 1 states that the "rules govern the procedure in all criminal proceedings in the Unites States district courts. . . . "

where penitentiary imprisonment is possible, discretion remains with the trial courts as to application of those rules to misdemeanors. Our Rule 411 in relevant part provides: "These rules shall be applied in all criminal cases wherein the accused is charged with an offense for which, upon conviction, he might be imprisoned in the penitentiary." 50 Ill.2d R. 411.

Prior to the adoption of these rules, criminal discovery was governed solely by case law and statutory provisions. Substantial variations in the scope of discovery permitted among the several circuits and even among judges in the same circuits prompted this court to appoint a committee of experienced lawyers and judges for the purpose of formulating criminal discovery rules for consideration by us. That committee submitted to us majority and minority reports indicating the views of its members as to the offenses to which the rules should be applicable and the subject matter which should be discoverable. The views of the committee members ranged from recommendations permitting discovery in cases involving violations of "any penal statute" to those where a penitentiary sentence was a possible punishment. After careful consideration of the various factors involved this court adopted Rule 411 as it now reads. Among the factors motivating the decision to restrict application of the rules to cases in which a penitentiary sentence was possible was our awareness of the very substantial volume of less serious cases and the impact upon their expeditious disposition of the expanded discovery provided by the new rules. A second consideration in reaching our conclusion was our desire to eliminate, so far as feasible, substantial variances in the scope of discovery permitted in the courts of this State. To now hold, as defendant urges we do, that the trial judges have discretion to apply our criminal discovery rules to less serious offenses would renew in those cases the very problems we sought to eliminate in the more serious cases.

The State is required to furnish defendants in misdemeanor cases with a list of witnesses (Ill. Rev. Stat. 1971, ch. 38, par. 114—9), any confession of the defendant (Ill. Rev. Stat. 1971, ch. 38, par. 114—10), evidence negating the defendant's guilt (*Brady v. Maryland*, 373 U.S. 83, 10 L. Ed. 2d 215, 83 S. Ct. 1194), and, in this particular case, the results of the breathalyzer test (Ill. Rev. Stat. 1971, ch. 95 1/2, par. 11—501(g)). Additionally, the report which the defendant seeks will be available at trial for use in impeachment of the prosecution witness who prepared it. (*People v. Cagle*, 41 Ill.2d 528.) At the time of adoption of the 1971 rules we believed adequate for the lesser offenses the discovery provided by case law and statute, and we see no reason to depart from that view now.

The judgment of the appellate court is affirmed.

Judgment affirmed.

CASE DISCUSSION QUESTIONS

1. Which Illinois Supreme Court Justice authored this opinion?
2. What court decided immediately before the Illinois Supreme Court considered the case?
3. With what offense(s) was the defendant charged?
4. What information did the trial court order the prosecution to provide to the defense?
5. What, if any, issues of federal constitutional law were relied upon in this opinion?
6. Based upon this decision, what type of information must the state produce to the defendant in misdemeanor cases?
7. Which side won in the Illinois Supreme Court?
8. What is the holding of the case?

You should therefore carefully review the criminal discovery rules of procedure of your jurisdiction to determine whether they apply to misdemeanor and petty offenses. If the rules are inapplicable, research the case law to determine whether there are common law standards that govern discovery for cases other than felonies. Ordinarily, you can use standard forms containing boilerplate language for requests and responses in misdemeanor cases.

2. DISCOVERY IN COMPLEX CRIMINAL CASES

There is a movement toward requiring more extensive discovery in certain types of serious cases. For instance, in federal death penalty cases the government is required to disclose the identities of its witnesses at least three days prior to trial.[45] This responsibility is not conditioned upon the defendant's request. Likewise, during the last ten years when the death penalty was available in Illinois,[46] the Illinois Supreme Court Rules included a series of procedures designed to improve pre-trial procedures in capital cases. Among other things, parties could seek leave of the court to take depositions and the state had to certify that all disclosures required for felony cases were completed.[47]

Discovery has also expanded in non-capital cases. For instance, in Illinois cases in which a party intends to use DNA evidence, there is a mandatory disclosure requirement imposed upon that party to furnish all pertinent information and testing data involving the DNA results.[48]

APPLICATION EXERCISE

16. How does misdemeanor discovery differ from felony discovery in your state? What, if any, differences are there in felony discovery when the defendant faces capital punishment? Give citations to authority for your answer.

J. Discovery Disputes and the Court's Role

There are two general categories of dispute that arise in the course of discovery: (1) one party seeks material that should not be disclosed, and (2) a party does not provide what should be tendered. In both situations, the court may be asked to resolve the dispute. Courts have a great degree of discretion in regulating discovery, so these types of disputes are determined on a case-by-case basis.

Protective order
A court order commonly used to protect a party or witness from unreasonable or invasive discovery requests.

1. PROTECTIVE ORDERS

When a party requests some item or information for which there is a legitimate basis to withhold disclosure, such as attorney work product, the party receiving the request can object to the discovery request. In addition, the party from whom discovery is sought may apply to the court for a **protective order**. A protective

---

[45]18 U.S.C. § 3432.
[46]The Illinois General Assembly abolished capital punishment effective July 1, 2011.
[47]Illinois Supreme Court Rule 416.
[48]Illinois Supreme Court Rule 417.

order is a decree issued by a court that is issued to shield a party or witness from unreasonable or invasive discovery requests. The party filing a motion for entry of a protective order must make a showing of good cause in order to obtain a protective order.

The federal courts, as well as most state courts, have the authority to enter this type of order. FRCrP 16(d)(1) provides that a party may file a motion with the district court for an order to delay, restrict, or deny pretrial discovery. Some jurisdictions require that the parties meet and confer prior to the filing of the motion. Paralegals may be asked to prepare a draft letter asserting the basis for the order and inviting a conference between the attorneys. Sometimes, the motion may ask the court to review materials at issue in the absence of the parties to determine whether the information should be released. This type of proceeding is referred to as an *in camera* **review**. Many times, this procedure is needed to avoid disclosure of the information for which protection is sought. The movant must make a showing of good cause in order to obtain a protective order. In some jurisdictions, the court on its own initiative may enter a protective order. If the motion is granted, the record of the materials that were reviewed *in camera* is sealed and made available to the appellate court on review.

A non-party can also apply to the court for protection against unwarranted discovery. Specifically, the custodian of records who has been served with a subpoena *duces tecum* can seek a protective order. The party making the original discovery request can file a response. In view of the burden of proof obligation faced by the movant, a respondent can argue that the motion must articulate specific facts to justify the entry of the order. Respondents also can argue that the basis enunciated in the motion does not justify non-disclosure. Defendants objecting to the entry of a protective order oftentimes maintain that the information sought is necessary to prepare a defense and that the material should be disclosed under *Brady v. Maryland*.

In camera review
A judge's review of materials in the absence of the parties and the public.

In camera
In a judge's chambers, outside the presence of a jury and the public.

2. DISCOVERY ENFORCEMENT

When discovery is not produced in a timely fashion or is provided in an inadequate manner, the requesting party can appeal to the court in order to obtain discovery. This is accomplished though a motion to compel compliance. The court also can impose sanctions upon a party that fails to abide by a discovery request or a court order.

The first step in response to the opponent's failure to comply is for the attorney to contact the opponent. If you are responsible for tracking the due date of discovery, you will alert your supervisor of the other party's lack of diligence. You may be required to draft the letter alerting the other side of its failure to respond or the inadequacy of the response.

If conferring with opposing counsel does not result in compliance, the matter can be brought before the court through a **motion to compel**, which asks the court to order either the opposing party or a third party to take some action. The motion should give the factual basis for the relief sought. Specifically, the motion should tell the court of the material requested and why your side is entitled to it. If the opponent failed to provide any discovery, attach a copy of the discovery request as an exhibit to the motion. If the opponent declined to fully respond to portions of the request, you should quote the requests in the body of

Motion to compel
A formal request to the court to order either the opposing party or a third party to take some action. Typically, this motion is filed in connection with discovery disputes.

the motion. The body of the motion should also set forth in chronological order the dates of the request and all follow-up contacts with the opponent. You also should cite the authority under which the material is sought. The motion for compliance can seek an order compelling compliance as well as a prayer for sanctions.

If the respondent is objecting to disclosure on a legitimate basis, the respondent may file a response that discusses the basis for no-disclosure. In addition, the respondent may file a motion for a protective order.

FRCrP 16(d)(2) provides that when a party fails to comply with the discovery rules, the court may order the discovery, grant a continuance, prohibit a party from introducing the undisclosed evidence, or enter any other order that is just under the circumstances. State courts have similar authority. When pretrial discovery is incomplete, courts will often compel the offending party to respond and reserve judgment on the request for more severe sanctions to see if there is compliance. Thereafter, if the court order is disobeyed, the judge will impose sanctions. When the discovery violation becomes apparent at trial, the offended party can move for sanctions at that time.

SUMMARY

This chapter presented the two major discovery models along with the principles underlying disclosure in criminal prosecutions. In addition to discovery requirements imposed by various rules of criminal procedure, the government has a constitutional duty under *Brady v. Maryland* to disclose exculpatory evidence to the accused.

As a paralegal, you may be required to draft written discovery requests, respond to the requests tendered by the opposing side, prepare discovery motions, notice depositions and motions, and subpoena documents. We showed you how to prepare these documents. We also presented how to object to a discovery request and seek a protective order to counter an inappropriate request for information.

This chapter also discussed the role of the paralegal with respect to depositions. The deposition to perpetuate testimony can be an important part of a criminal case. The discovery deposition is becoming an increasingly significant discovery tool in a number of jurisdictions. You were shown how to abstract and summarize depositions and how to prepare witnesses for them.

Rules of discovery vary from one jurisdiction to another. Even in the same jurisdiction there may be separate rules for discovery in different types of cases. You will always need to check the applicable court rules to see what rules apply to the cases assigned to you.

REVIEW QUESTIONS

1. What is the difference between discovery and disclosure?
2. What is the purpose of criminal discovery?
3. In *Brady v. Maryland*, the U.S. Supreme Court ruled that the Due Process Clause requires prosecutors to turn over all exculpatory evidence to the defense. What is exculpatory evidence?

4. What is impeachment evidence and when is it considered to be material?
5. Which part of the U.S. Constitution contains the right to be free from self-incrimination? What is the nature of this constitutional right?
6. What are the major criticisms of Rule 16 of the Federal Rules of Criminal Procedure?
7. What are the components of a pattern discovery request?
8. How should a paralegal who is preparing a response to a discovery request address sensitive information that is contained in the documents requested by the other side?
9. What is the face sheet of a discovery response and what are its component parts?
10. What are the types of appropriate responses that can be made on the face sheet of the response in reaction to individual discovery requests?
11. What is attorney work product and what bearing does it have on discovery?
12. List and explain the use of the types of depositions that are used in criminal cases. There are two types of criminal depositions: discovery depositions and depositions to perpetuate testimony.
13. How do you "notice a deposition" and "notice a motion" for hearing?
14. How does a paralegal prepare a witness for a deposition?
15. How do deposition summaries and abstracts differ from one another?
16. What is a subpoena *duces tecum* and how does it differ from other written discovery requests?
17. What is the purpose of a bill of particulars and when can a defendant make a motion to seek it?
18. Why do courts conduct *in camera* reviews when deciding whether to grant a motion for protective order?
19. What remedies are available to a federal judge for sanctioning a party that fails to comply with discovery rules?

Chapter 8

Legal Defenses

In Chapter 6, we discussed the nature of the responsibilities of defense attorneys in our adversarial system of justice and why attorneys are ethically required to defend clients, even after they have admitted to committing criminal acts. In this chapter we will explore the different types of "defenses" a lawyer can raise on the client's behalf.

A **legal defense** is a set of facts or legal arguments that, if accepted by the court, relieves a person of legal liability for having committed an act that is prohibited under the law. Some are **complete defenses** whereby the defendant is absolved of all legal liability, while others are **partial defenses** that, in the criminal context, serve to reduce a crime to a **lesser included offense**.[1]

Although we could have presented these defenses as part of our discussion of criminal offenses in Chapter 3, we deferred this topic until after we covered the various ways in which prosecutors and defense attorneys use discovery to learn more about the strengths and weaknesses of their cases in Chapter 7. Defense attorneys need to have a pretty good idea of what actually happened, why it happened, the specific charges being filed, and the nature of the evidence the prosecutor can present at trial before he or she can evaluate which of the many legal defenses might be appropriate to utilize in the client's case. In analyzing some of the examples used in this chapter, you may find it useful to go back and review the discussions of various offenses in Chapter 3.

A. DENIAL OF THE FACTS

A common criminal defense is to deny that the defendant did what the prosecution claims he or she did. For example, the defendant may dispute he fired the

Legal defense
A set of facts or legal arguments that, if accepted by the court, relieves a person of criminal liability for having committed an act that is defined as a crime.

Complete defense
A defense that, if proven, relieves the defendant of all criminal responsibility.

Partial defense
A defense that reduces a crime to a lesser included offense.

Lesser included offense
A crime that shares some, but not all, of the elements of a more serious criminal offense. Thus, the greater offense cannot be committed without committing the lesser crime.

---

[1]Some states recognize what is called an imperfect defense in homicide prosecutions. It is a type of partial defense used in efforts to reduce the crime from homicide to involuntary manslaughter.

gunshot that killed the victim or may deny ownership of the illegal drugs found in her car.

In Hypothetical Case #1, Bud Cook could deny that he was driving the car at the time it struck the bicyclist or he could admit to having been driving but deny that he caused the accident. Note, however, that admitting he was driving the pickup truck might make it easier for the state to convict him of DUI. In Hypothetical Case #2, there would be no reason to claim that Brandon Turner wasn't driving the car that contained the illegal drugs, but he can certainly claim that the drugs and the gun were not his. Given the number of clients he had and the nature of the paperwork that accompanies securities transactions, it would be pretty hard for Bill Edwards (Hypothetical Case #3) to successfully deny that he was running an illegal Ponzi scheme. On the other hand, in Hypothetical Case #4 if both Tom Schroeder and Jim Stevenson denied that Schroeder passed on insider information to Stevenson, the prosecution's case would have been based on circumstantial evidence.

Alibi defense

A defense requiring proof that the defendant could not have been at the scene of the crime.

An **alibi defense** is a particular type of denial defense in which it is claimed that the defendant could not have committed the crime because he or she was not at the location of the crime when it was committed. For example, a defendant charged with robbery might claim that he was playing poker at a friend's home at the time the robbery was taking place on the other side of town.

Although it seems obvious that a defendant could not have committed a crime in one location while he or she was doing something else in a different part of town, or even in a different state, it is often difficult to prove the validity of an alibi. Most judges and juries will not give any weight to a defendant's claim that he was home sleeping or at a movie if there are no eyewitnesses to back up the alibi. Even when there are alibi witnesses, they are frequently friends or family of the accused and, therefore, appear to have a motive to lie. Because the term *alibi* has such a negative connotation, defense attorneys do not use it when they are before the jury, and sometimes present motions *in limine* to bar the use of this term at the trial. (We will discuss motions *in limine* in Chapter 11.)

Perhaps one of the most well-known successful uses of the alibi defense occurred in the criminal prosecution of O.J. Simpson for the murder of his wife Nicole and her friend Ronald Goldman. At his trial, defense attorney Johnnie Cochran claimed that Simpson never left his house on the evening of the killings and that he was alone in the house packing to fly to Chicago. Cochran also maintained that Simpson went outside to hit some golf balls in his yard. The jury acquitted Simpson of the murder charges.

Another example of a high-profile defendant successfully using an alibi defense involved the prosecution of actor Robert Blake for fatally shooting his wife, Bonnie Lee Bakley, outside a restaurant where they had just eaten dinner. Blake's attorneys claimed that he left his wife at the car when he went back to the restaurant to get a handgun he had forgotten in the booth where they ate and that she was shot while he was gone. Blake was found not guilty of Bakley's murder and of one of two counts of solicitation of murder. A third count was dropped after it was revealed that the jury was deadlocked 11–1 in favor of an acquittal.

In federal court, the defense must disclose its intent to raise an alibi defense and must identify all alibi witnesses during the discovery phase of a criminal prosecution. Rule 12.1(a) requires the defendant to give notice of intent to assert the alibi defense within ten days of the prosecutor's demand. The defense must name the specific place where the defendant claims to have been when the crime was allegedly committed, along with the names, addresses, and telephone numbers of the alibi witnesses. On request, the defendant must also furnish the government with their alibi witnesses' written statements after their direct examination at trial.[2] Once the defendant has served notice on the prosecution, the prosecutor is obligated to furnish the defense with the names, addresses, and telephone numbers of the witnesses who can establish the accused's presence at the scene of the crime in addition to information about other witnesses it intends to call to rebut the alibi witnesses' testimony.[3] The defendant does not need to request the information. Instead, 12.1(b)(1) requires the government to disclose its alibi witness information within ten days of service of the notice of intent to raise the alibi defense.

If either side fails to provide alibi information within their respective ten-day time limits, the court may exclude testimony of undisclosed witnesses.[4] However, courts have discretion to impose less drastic remedies, such as continuing the case so that the surprised party can contact the newly disclosed witnesses and otherwise prepare for their testimony.

More than forty states mandate that the defense give advance notice of the defendant's intent to raise the alibi defense.[5] Most alibi provisions are similar to the federal requirements found in Rule 12.1.[6] You should check the requirements of your state for the procedures for requesting and disclosing alibi information.

Interviewing Alibi Witnesses

If you, as a paralegal, are involved in interviewing alibi witnesses, it is particularly important to pay close attention to details of their stories and to elicit information that can be compared with the defendant's story. For instance, if the accused maintains that he was at a movie, have the witness give a detailed account of everything that took place in the defendant's presence before and after the show. Also have witnesses relate the plot of the movie, actors' names, previews shown, the time the movie ended, etc. If they have any written documents, such as ticket stubs or charge card receipts, request that they produce them for you.

B. IGNORANCE OR MISTAKE

Although it is generally true that "ignorance of the law is no excuse," there are a limited number of circumstances in which ignorance or a mistaken understanding of the facts can be used as a legal defense. The Model Penal Code places the following conditions on the use of the defense of ignorance or mistake:

---

[2]FRCrP 26.2(a).

[3]FRCrP 12.1(b)(1).

[4]FRCrP 12.1(e).

[5]W. LaFave, J. Isreal & N. King, *Criminal Procedure* 953 (4th ed., Thomson West 2004).

[6]*Id.*

Section 2.04 Ignorance or Mistake

(1) Ignorance or mistake as to the matter of fact or law is a defense if:

(a) the ignorance or mistake negatives the purpose, knowledge, belief, recklessness or negligence required to establish a material element of the offense. . . .

(3) A belief that conduct does not legally constitute an offense is a defense to a prosecution for that offense based upon such conduct when:

(a) the statute or other enactment defining the offense is not known to the actor and has not been published or otherwise reasonably made available prior to the conduct alleged; or

(b) he acts in reasonable reliance upon an official statement of the law, afterward determined to be invalid or erroneous. . . .

In utilizing this defense, it must be shown that the defendant's ignorance or mistake negated the *mens rea* element of the crime. You will recall from our discussion in Chapter 2 that *mens rea* means "guilty mind" and refers to the fact that various crimes require different degrees of "criminal intent." Therefore, where homicide requires a mental state of purposely or knowingly causing someone's death, manslaughter requires only that the death result from a reckless or negligent action.

Now, take a couple of minutes to review the Model Penal Code's definition of the crime of criminal trespass as it is stated on page 60 in Chapter 3. Note that it requires proof that the accused entered or occupied someone else's property "knowing" that he was not authorized to do so. Therefore, if a defendant entered your neighbor's house because you had asked him to let your dog out over the lunch hour and he mistook the neighbor's house for your house, he would not be guilty of criminal trespass because he mistakenly thought that he was authorized to enter the property.

At first blush, it would appear that "mistake of age" would fit the conditions necessary to show a mistake of fact. However, this is not so in many jurisdictions. For instance, states differ as to whether mistake of age is a defense to the illegal sale of alcoholic beverages to minors.[7] Likewise, there is a similar divide as to cases involving sexual relations with minors. Indeed, California permits a defendant to assert mistake of age in statutory rape cases, whereas Maryland views this offense as a strict liability crime and thus rejects the defense.[8] A majority of the states do not allow the mistake of age defense to statutory rape.

---

[7]Compare *City of West Allis v. Megna*, 26 Wis. 2d 545, 548, 133 N.W.2d 252 (1965) (finding a bar's good-faith defense irrelevant because providing alcohol to minors is a strict liability crime) with *State v. Niesen*, 415 N.W.2d 326, 329 (Minn. 1987) (holding that bartender did not commit a crime because he acted in good faith by asking a nineteen-year-old woman for identification before serving her).

[8]Compare *People v. Hernandez*, 61 Cal. 2d 529, 536, 39 Cal. Rptr. 361, 365, 393 P.2d 673, 677 (1964) with *Garnett v. Maryland,* 332 Md. 571, 632 A.2d 797 (Md. 1993).

APPLICATION EXERCISES

1. Based on the wording of the Model Penal Code, evaluate the extent to which an ignorance of the law/mistake defense might be used successfully in defending Brandon Turner (see Hypothetical Case #2) against charges that he was in unlawful possession of drugs.

2. Based on the wording of the Model Penal Code, evaluate the extent to which an ignorance of the law/mistake defense might be used successfully in defending Bill Edwards (see Hypotherical Case #3) against charges that he committed fraud.

3. Based on the wording of the Model Penal Code, evaluate the extent to which an ignorance of the law/mistake defense might be used successfully in defending Tom Schroeder (see Hypothetical Case #4) against charges that he engaged in insider trading.

C. STATUS OF DEFENDANT

The status defenses involve excusing people from the criminal consequences of their actions because their status or condition renders them incapable of formulating the required element of *mens rea*.[9] The status defenses include being too young to form a criminal intent, being legally insane, and being intoxicated.

1. INFANCY

Under the common law, children under the age of seven were conclusively presumed to be incapable of forming criminal intent, and there was a rebuttable presumption that those between the ages of seven and fourteen were not capable of forming such intent. The juvenile court system was created to provide a non-criminal alternative for processing juveniles who are accused of acts that are considered crimes if they are committed by adults. In recent years, however, especially with the increase in violent, gang-related crimes, there has been a movement to waive juvenile court jurisdiction and apply adult standards to the criminal prosecution of these juvenile offenders. As illustrated in Figure 8.1, not only does the age at which juveniles are transferred to the adult criminal justice system vary from state to state but also the age often varies within a state based on the type of crime involved.[10]

---

[9]See discussion of *mens rea* in Chapter 2 on pp. 33–35.

[10]Note that some states may have made changes since the table was published by the Department of Justice in 1998, but there is still wide diversity among them.

State	Lower Age	Any Criminal Offense	Certain Felonies	Capitol Crimes	Murder	Person Offenses	Certain Offenses Property Offenses	Drug Offenses	Weapon Offenses
Alabama	14	14	16	16				16	
Alaska	NS	NS			NS	16			
Arizona	NS		NS		15	15			
Arkansas	14		14*	14	14	14			14
California	14	16	16		14	14	14	14	
Colorado	12		12*		12	12	14		14
Connecticut	14		14	14	14				
Delaware	NS	NS/14*	15		NS*	NS	16	16	
D.C.	NS	16*	15		15	15	15		NS
Florida	NS	NS	NS	14	NS*	14		14	
Georgia	NS	15		NS	13	13	15		
Hawaii	NS		14*		NS				
Idaho	NS	14	NS		NS	NS	NS	NS	
Illinois	13	13	15		13*	15		15	15
Indiana	NS	14	NS		10*	16		16	16
Iowa	14	14*	16					16	16
Kansas	10	10	14			14		14	14
Kentucky	14		14	14					
Louisiana	14				14	14	15	15	
Maine	NS		NS		NS				
Maryland	NS	15		NS	16	16			16
Massachusetts	14		14		14	14			14
Michigan	14	14	14		14	14	14	14	
Minnesota	14		14		16				
Mississippi	13	13	13*	13					
Missouri	12		12						
Montana	12				12*	12*	16	16	16
Nebraska	NS	16	NS						

State	Lower Age	Any Criminal Offense	Certain Felonies	Capitol Crimes	Murder	Certain Offenses		
						Person Offenses	Property Offenses	Drug Offenses	Weapon Offenses
Nevada	NS	NS	14		NS	14			14
New Hampshire	13		15		13	13		15	
New Jersey	14	14			14	14	14	14	14
New Mexico	15				15				
New York	13				13*	14	14		
North Carolina	13		13	13					
North Dakota	14	16	14		14	14		14	
Ohio	14	14	14		14*	16	16		
Oklahoma	NS		NS		13	15*	15*	16	15
Oregon	NS		15		NS	NS*	15		
Pennsylvania	NS		14		NS*	15			
Rhode Island	NS		16	NS	17	17			
South Carolina	NS	16	14		NS	NS*		14	14
South Dakota	NS		NS						
Tennessee	NS	16			NS	NS			
Texas	14			14				14	
Utah	14		14		16	16	16		16
Vermont	10	16			10	10	10		
Virginia	14		14		14	14			
Washington	NS	NS			16	16	16		
West Virginia	NS		NS*		NS	NS	NS	NS	
Wisconsin	NS	15	14		10	NS	14	14	
Wyoming	13	13	14						

Note: "NS" indicates "none specified."

*See appendix in original source for more detail on state provisions.

Source: U.S. Department of Justice, Office of Juvenile Delinquency and Juvenile Problems, *Trying Juveniles as Adults in Criminal Court: An Analysis of State Transfer Provisions,* (December 1998). *http://ojjdp.ncjrs.org/pubs/tryingjuvasadult/toc.html*

Figure 8.1   Minimum Age and Offenses for Which a Juvenile Can Be Transferred to Criminal Court

2. INSANITY

Insanity defense
A defense that relieves people who are legally insane from criminal responsibility for their actions.

Although the **insanity defense** has gotten a lot of publicity over the years, it is hard to prove and rarely used. Studies have shown that defendants allege insanity in less than 1 percent of all criminal cases, and of these cases, less than half involve murder charges. When the insanity defense is raised, it proves to be successful in only 1 out of 4 cases. So, out of every 1,000 criminal cases, the insanity defense is raised in approximately 9 and is successful in 2.[11] Further, in a majority of the cases in which insanity was raised and used successfully, it was as the result of an agreement between the prosecution and the defense.

Like the infancy defense, the insanity defense is also based on the assertion that the defendant was incapable of formulating the required element of *mens rea*. Furthermore, many people believe that it is not appropriate to punish someone for actions over which the individual had no control and that insane individuals have no control over their actions. Although the rationale for the insanity defense is relatively clear, the operational standards are not. To begin with, we have to emphasize that *insanity* is a legal term rather than a psychiatric term. Having a mental disorder is not the same as being legally insane.

Over the years, the federal and state courts have developed different tests for determining whether a person was legally insane at the time the crime was committed. The three most common standards are the M'Naghten test, the irresistible impulse test, and the Model Penal Code Substantial Capacity test. These tests are summarized in Figure 8.2.

M'Naghten test
A test that provides that the defendant is not guilty due to insanity if, at the time of the killing, the defendant suffered from a defect or disease of the mind and could not understand whether the act was right or wrong.

The oldest of the standards, the **M'Naghten test**, originated in the 1840s in an English case where Daniel M'Naghten was tried for killing the secretary to the prime minister of England. M'Naghten mistook the secretary for the prime minister, whom M'Naghten thought to be engaged in a plot to kill him. The court found M'Naghten not guilty due to insanity because, at the time of the killing, he suffered from a defect or disease of the mind and could not understand whether the act was right or wrong. This test, or standard, is commonly known as either the M'Naghten test (sometimes also spelled McNaughten, M'Naughten, or M'Naughton) or the "right from wrong" test.

Under this test, a defendant is not considered guilty of the crime if, at the time of committing the *actus reus*,[12] the defendant was suffering from a defect or disease of the mind and could not understand whether the act was right or wrong. However, the court did not define what constituted a disease or defect of the mind. Under the M'Naghten test, a defendant will be found sane if he or she knew that a certain action was wrong but could not stop taking that action.

Irresistible impulse test
A test that provides that the defendant is not guilty due to insanity if, at the time of the killing, the defendant could not control his or her actions.

Therefore, some jurisdictions use both the M'Naghten standard and a variation of what is commonly known as the **irresistible impulse test**. With this test, the focus is on the defendant's ability to control his or her own actions. If a mental disease robs the individual of control over his or her conduct, the person is not guilty by reason of insanity.

The drafters of the American Law Institute's Model Penal Code developed a third test, which combines elements of the other two. This ALI test is known as

---

[11]For a full discussion of this issue, see G.H. Morris, *Placed in Purgatory: Conditional Release of Insanity Acquittees*, 39 Ariz. L. Rev. 1061 (1997).

[12]See discussion of *actus rea* in Chapter 2 on pp. 33–35.

M'Naghten or "Right from Wrong" Test

"[T]o establish insanity sufficient to relieve the defendant of guilt, it must be proved that, at the time of the commission of the act, the defendant was laboring under such a defect of reason, from disease of the mind as not to know the nature and quality of the act he was doing, or if he did know it, that he did not know that what he was doing was wrong." *M'Naghten's Case,* 8 Eng. Rep. 718, 722 (1843).

Irresistible Impulse Test

One is not guilty by reason of insanity if it is determined that the defendant has a mental disease that kept the defendant from controlling his or her conduct.

Substantial Capacity Test (Model Penal Code)

(1) A person is not responsible for criminal conduct if at the time of such conduct, as a result of mental disease or defect, he or she lacks substantial capacity to appreciate the criminality (wrongfulness) of his or her conduct or to conform that conduct to the requirements of law.

(2) The terms *mental disease* and *mental defect* do not include an abnormality manifested only by repeated criminal or otherwise antisocial conduct.

Figure 8.2 Major Insanity Tests

the **substantial capacity test**. It requires that the defendant "appreciate," rather than "know," the wrongfulness of his or her actions. Under the two options provided in this test, defendants can lack either the ability to understand their acts were wrong or the ability to control their behavior.

The 1982 trial of John Hinckley, Jr. for his attempted assassination of then President Ronald Reagan is one of the most highly publicized cases dealing with an insanity plea. The defense presented three psychiatrists who diagnosed Hinckley as psychotic—and legally insane—at the time of the shooting. They told of his obsession with actress Jodie Foster and the wild plans[13] he thought up for getting her attention. One of Hinckley's letters to Foster is shown in Exhibit 8.1. Although he was under the care of a psychiatrist, his mental health continued to deteriorate. After being told he could not return home to live with his wealthy parents, Hinckley flew to Washington, D.C., and wrote a letter to Foster a few hours before his failed assassination attempt.

As in most insanity defense cases, the prosecution found other psychiatrists who testified that although he was psychologically disturbed, Hinckley was legally sane because, at the time of the shooting, he appreciated the wrongfulness of his act. Thus it was left to a jury of laypersons to choose among contradictory psychiatric testimony. In this case, they agreed with the defense experts and found Hinckley not guilty by reason of insanity.

Substantial capacity test
Part of the Model Penal Code, a test that provides that the defendant is not guilty due to insanity if, at the time of the killing, the defendant lacked either the ability to understand the act was wrong or the ability to control the behavior.

---

[13]Hinckley developed plots such as hijacking an airplane and committing suicide in front of her to gain her attention. Eventually, he settled on a scheme to win her over by assassinating the President.

Exhibit 8.1: Transcribed Letter from John Hinckley to Jodie Foster

3/30/81
12:45 P.M.
Dear Jodie,

   There is a definite possibility that I will be killed in my attempt to get Reagan. It is for this very reason that I am writing you this letter now.

   As you well know by now I love you very much. Over the past seven months I've left you dozens of poems, letters and love messages in the faint hope that you could develop an interest in me. Although we talked on the phone a couple of times I never had the nerve to simply approach you and introduce myself. Besides my shyness, I honestly did not wish to bother you with my constant presence. I know the many messages left at your door and in your mailbox were a nuisance, but I felt that it was the most painless way for me to express my love for you.

   I feel very good about the fact that you at least know my name and know how I feel about you. And by hanging around your dormitory, I've come to realize that I'm the topic of more than a little conversation, however full of ridicule it may be. At least you know that I'll always love you.

   Jodie, I would abandon this idea of getting Reagan in a second if I could only win your heart and live out the rest of my life with you, whether it be in total obscurity or whatever.

   I will admit to you that the reason I'm going ahead with this attempt now is because I just cannot wait any longer to impress you. I've got to do something now to make you understand, in no uncertain terms, that I am doing all of this for your sake! By sacrificing my freedom and possibly my life, I hope to change your mind about me. This letter is being written only an hour before I leave for the Hilton Hotel. Jodie, I'm asking you to please look into your heart and at least give me the chance, with this historical deed, to gain your respect and love.

I love you forever,
John Hinckley

This not-guilty verdict aroused so much controversy in some segments of the public that it led Congress and a number of states to rewrite their laws covering the insanity defense. The old Model Penal Code test was replaced by one that shifted the burden of proof of insanity from the prosecution to the defense. In addition to shifting the burden in insanity cases, Congress also narrowed the defense itself. Legislation passed in 1984 states that a person accused of a crime can be judged not guilty by reason of insanity if "the defendant, as a result of a severe mental disease or defect, was unable to appreciate the nature and quality or the wrongfulness of his acts."[14]

Unlike other affirmative defenses, the defendant has the burden of proving the elements of the insanity defense by clear and convincing evidence.[15] The defense must give the prosecution written notice of its intention to raise the insanity defense. In federal court, notice must be provided within the time allotted for filing pretrial motions.[16] Likewise, the defense must also give the government notice that it intends to call expert witnesses to testify to the defendant's mental disease or defect.[17] Upon request, each side must provide the opponent with the identities of their experts along with a written summary of the expert testimony on the issue of the defendant's mental health.[18]

Once the defendant has expressed an intent to raise the insanity defense, the court may order the defendant to submit to a psychiatric or psychological evaluation.[19] When it orders a mental examination, the court has discretion to determine whether the defendant remains free on pre-trial release for an outpatient exam or be committed to the attorney general.[20] The report on the evaluation is filed with the court and provided to the parties.

In federal court, when the defense is asserted there are three possible outcomes at trial: guilty, not guilty, and not guilty only by reason of insanity.[21] If the defendant is found not guilty only by reason of insanity, the court must commit the defendant to a facility for a mental examination and order the preparation of the report prior to a hearing to determine the defendant's eligibility for release. (This is known as a "dangerousness hearing."[22]) The purpose of the hearing is to determine whether the defendant's release poses a substantial risk to another person or serious damage to another's property because of a present mental disease or defect.[23] If the court finds that release poses such risks, the court remands the defendant to the attorney general, who in turn arranges for placement in a hospital or institution.[24]

Within three years after the Hinckley verdict, two-thirds of the states placed the burden on the defense to prove insanity, eight states adopted a separate verdict of "guilty but mentally ill," and one state (Utah) abolished the defense altogether.[25] So while most jurisdictions have some form of an insanity defense available to criminal defendants, there is disagreement among the states and the federal circuits over the standard that should be used for determining when the insanity defense should apply.

---

[14]The Insanity Defense Reform Act of 1984, 18 U.S.C. § 17.

[15]18 U.S.C. § 17(a)(b).

[16]FRCrP 12(2)(a).

[17]FRCrP 12(2).

[18]FRCrP 16(b)(1) & 16(a)(1)(g).

[19]FRCrP 12(2)(c)(1)(b).

[20]18 U.S.C. § 4247(d).

[21]18 U.S.C. § 4242(b).

[22]18 U.S.C. § 4243.

[23]18 U.S.C. § 4242(d).

[24]18 U.S.C. § 4243(n).

[25]D.Linder, *The Trial of John W. Hinckley, Jr.* (2008). *http://www.law.umkc.edu/faculty/projects/ftrials/hinckley/hinckleyaccount.html*

Another highly publicized insanity defense case involved a Texas mother who confessed to drowning her five children in a bathtub because she heard voices telling her to kill her children in order to "save them from Satan."[26] Both the prosecution and the defense agreed that the defendant was mentally ill, but they disagreed as to whether she was aware that what she was doing was wrong. In a three-week-long trial, the defense called psychiatrists, relatives, and friends to testify that Andrea Yates suffered from severe postpartum depression. The prosecution countered by arguing that Yates's prompt action in reporting the drowning to the police established that she did know what she had done was wrong. The jury members apparently agreed with the prosecution and convicted her of murder. She was sentenced to life in prison and then sent to a prison psychiatric ward to receive treatment for her mental illness while serving out her sentence.[27]

A comparison of the Hinckley and Yates cases illustrates the fact that mentally ill defendants typically end up in secured mental institutions regardless of whether they are found "**not guilty by reason of insanity**" or "**guilty but mentally ill**." Even though he was found not guilty, John Hinckley ended up being civilly committed to a large-scale, federally run psychiatric hospital. According to the American Psychiatric Association, "studies show that persons found not guilty by reason of insanity, on average, are held at least as long as—and often longer than—persons found guilty and sent to prison for similar crimes."[28] While a finding of guilt will result in a fixed sentence, a finding of not guilty by reason of insanity can result in defendants being committed for an indefinite term, potentially for life, until they are deemed no longer a threat to themselves or society. In fact, Daniel M'Naghten's trial in 1843, which resulted in the creation of the M'Naghten test, also resulted in his commitment to a mental institution, where he remained until his death.[29]

Another related concept is the notion of temporary insanity. The **temporary insanity** defense asserts that a defendant was insane at the time the criminal act was committed but that the defendant has since recovered from this temporary condition. A famous example involved a U.S. congressman who killed his wife's lover in 1859. If this defense is successful, it relieves the defendant of both criminal penalties and involuntary commitment to a mental institution. However, it is seldom successful because it is extremely difficult to convince a jury of the validity of this defense.

3. INTOXICATION

In some jurisdictions and under limited circumstances, being under the voluntary influence of drugs or alcohol is considered a valid defense. The rationale is that the intoxicating substance interfered with the defendant's ability to form the

Not guilty by reason of insanity
A verdict finding that the defendant carried out the actions constituting a crime but lacked the mental capacity to have intended to commit the crime.

Guilty but mentally ill
A verdict finding that the defendant is guilty of a crime although he or she lacked the mental capacity to commit it.

Temporary insanity
The defense that the accused was momentarily insane when the crime was committed and therefore was incapable of understanding the nature of his or her actions.

---

[26]*Jury to Decide Yates' Sentence*, USA Today 3A (March 14, 2002).

[27]Later, a Texas appeals court reversed Yates's conviction based on improper expert testimony and ordered a retrial. As of this writing, Yates remains in a Texas prison psychiatric ward.

[28]American Psychiatric Association, The Insanity Defense, *www.psych.org/publicinfo/insanity.cfm* (last updated Sept. 2003).

[29]G.H. Morris, *Placed in Purgatory: Conditional Release of Insanity Acquittees*, 39 Ariz. L. Rev. 1062 (1997).

required *mens rea*. This defense is applicable to specific-intent crimes, such as murder or burglary.

Voluntary intoxication is not a defense to general intent or strict liability offenses. For general-intent crimes, the prosecution does not have to show that a defendant intended to violate the law. Instead, the government need only prove the commission of an unlawful act (*actus reus*) and the defendant's intent to carry out that act (*mens rea*). Although voluntary intoxication can generally be used as a defense for major crimes requiring a specific intent, it cannot be used as a defense to charges involving reckless behavior.

In many jurisdictions, **involuntary intoxication** can be raised as a defense to both general- and specific-intent crimes. When it is asserted, the defendant must show intoxication without knowledge or consent. An unwitting victim of a spiked drink could present this as a defense to a general-intent crime.

Voluntary intoxication
The knowing and voluntary consumption of alcohol and/or drugs.

Involuntary intoxication
The consumption of alcohol and/or drugs without knowledge or consent.

4. COMPETENCY AND MITIGATING FACTORS

Whereas infancy, insanity, and intoxication relate to a defendant's condition at the time the alleged criminal act took place, competency focuses on the defendant's condition at the time that charges are filed as well as when the trial is to be held. Whereas the former relates to determining legal responsibility for criminal behavior, the latter relates to whether defendants are able to adequately assist their attorneys in preparing a defense, whether they can make informed decisions about trial strategy, and whether they should plead guilty or accept a plea agreement. Even if someone's mental illness or intoxication does not meet the standards necessary to relieve him or her of criminal responsibility, they may still be used as a mitigating factor for reducing the charge to a less serious offense or getting a more lenient sentence.

D. REACTIVE DEFENSES

This next category of defenses involves circumstances in which people find themselves in unusual situations requiring actions that, while ordinarily considered to be bad, are justified by the special circumstances existing at that particular time.

1. DURESS AND NECESSITY

Duress and necessity both involve situations in which people are forced to violate the law because of the unusual circumstances facing them. Whereas **duress** involves using force or the threat of force to cause someone to commit a criminal act, **necessity** involves situations in which circumstances require people to break the law in order to avert some greater harm from taking place. The rationale for both defenses is that people shouldn't be punished for involuntary acts and that in these situations breaking the law was their only acceptable course of action.

Section 2.09 of the Model Penal Code defines duress as coercion through "the use of, or a threat to use, unlawful force against his person or the person of another, which a person of reasonable firmness in his situation would have been

Duress
A defense requiring proof that force or a threat of force was used to cause a person to commit a criminal act.

Necessity
A defense requiring proof that the defendant was forced to take an action to avoid a greater harm.

unable to resist.'' Therefore, if someone held a gun to your head and forced you to commit a criminal act, you would be entitled to use the defense of duress.

To assert this defense, you must prove that you reasonably believed that you were threatened with your death, the death of another person, or serious injury to yourself or others unless you committed the crime. In a highly publicized case in the mid-1970s, Patty Hearst, the daughter of a millionaire newspaper publisher, was placed on trial for bank robbery. Approximately a year before the robbery took place she had been kidnapped by a radical group calling itself the Symbionese Liberation Army. When members of this same group robbed a bank, Ms. Hearst appeared to be a willing participant. At her trial, attorney F. Lee Bailey argued that Ms. Hearst had been ''brainwashed'' by her Symbionese Liberation Army kidnappers and had been coerced into participating in the robbery. The state countered with evidence showing that Ms. Hearst had passed up opportunities to flee and call police and argued that this showed she was a willing participant who was acting voluntarily. The jury agreed with the prosecution and convicted her of armed robbery.

Whereas duress involves someone else purposely threatening the life of the defendant (or some innocent third party), under the necessity defense, the defendant broke the law in order to avoid a harm (either to himself or others) due to special circumstances resulting from natural causes (like floods) or from the actions of another person that were not specifically intended to affect the defendant. For example, you may be forced to trespass across a neighbor's yard to escape a fire in your home. In addition, this defense may be used in a more general way to exonerate otherwise criminal conduct when a person believes that such conduct is necessary to avoid a greater injury. An example would be a motorist choosing to crash an automobile into a building in order to avoid hitting a child who runs into the street. The necessity defense has been asserted by seriously ill patients charged with the possession of marijuana. In these cases, the defendants have claimed that the medical use of cannabis was a necessity because no other drugs were available to address their symptoms. Although this claim has been successful in a few cases, this application of the necessity defense has been rejected by most courts.[30]

2. SELF-DEFENSE AND THE DEFENSE OF OTHERS

Self-defense
The justified use of force to protect oneself or others.

Actions taken in **self-defense** or in the defense of others are also reactive defenses in that they allow people to do things in reaction to special circumstances that would ordinarily be violations of the law. Here, the special circumstances relate to defending yourself or others from a criminal action by others that put you or someone else in danger of losing your life or suffering serious bodily injury.

Depending upon the law of your state, individuals may also be allowed to use force in defending their dwellings and other property. There is significant variation among the states as to the amount of force that can be used and the circumstances under which one is required to retreat when that is a viable option.

---

[30]See generally, A.J. LeVay, *Urgent Compassion: Medical Marijuana, Prosecutorial Discretion and the Medical Necessity Defense*, 41 B.C.L. REV. 699 (2000). Also available at *http://www.bc.edu/bc_org/avp/law/lwsch/journals/bclawr/41_3/06_FMS.htm*

Generally, however, this right to use force is valid only as long as the following conditions are met:

- The person claiming self-defense must not have been the initiator of the violence.
- The threat of bodily harm must be immediate.
- Once the threatening party ceases the threatening behavior, the right to self-defense disappears.
- The amount of force used must be no more than is reasonably necessary to repel the attack.

This last condition is often especially difficult to determine. The amount of force necessary to repel an attack will depend on the physical characteristics of both the attacker and the person attempting to fend off the attack and the weapons being used by both the attacker and the defender. Furthermore, many state laws attach special conditions to the use of **deadly force**, which is usually defined as a force that would cause serious bodily injury or death and is usually limited to situations in which the danger faced includes fear of serious bodily injury or death.

Deadly force
A force that would cause serious bodily injury or death.

Consider the prosecution of Bernhard Goetz, dubbed the "subway vigilante," in the mid-1980s in New York.

New York v Goetz
Court of Appeals of New York
68 N.Y.2d 96, 497 N.E.2d 41, 506 N.Y.S.2d 18 (1986)

CHIEF JUDGE WACHTLER

A Grand Jury has indicted defendant on attempted murder, assault, and other charges for having shot and wounded four youths on a New York City subway train after one or two of the youths approached him and asked for $5. The lower courts, concluding that the prosecutor's charge to the Grand Jury on the defense of justification was erroneous, have dismissed the attempted murder, assault and weapons possession charges. We now reverse and reinstate all counts of the indictment.

* * *

On Saturday afternoon, December 22, 1984, Troy Canty, Darryl Cabey, James Ramseur, and Barry Allen boarded an IRT express subway train in The Bronx and headed south toward lower Manhattan. The four youths rode together in the rear portion of the seventh car of the train. Two of the four, Ramseur and Cabey, had screwdrivers inside their coats, which they said were to be used to break into the coin boxes of video machines.

Defendant Bernhard Goetz boarded this subway train at 14th Street in Manhattan and sat down on a bench towards the rear section of the same car occupied by the four youths. Goetz was carrying an unlicensed .38 caliber pistol loaded with five rounds of ammunition in a waistband holster. The train left the 14th Street station and headed towards Chambers Street. . . .

According to Goetz's statement, the first contact he had with the four youths came when Canty, sitting or lying on the bench across from him, asked "how are you," to which he replied "fine." Shortly thereafter, Canty, followed by one of the other youths, walked over to the defendant and stood to his left, while the other two youths remained to his right, in the corner of the subway car. Canty then said "give me five dollars." Goetz stated that he knew from the smile on Canty's face that they wanted to "play with me." Although he was certain that none of the youths had a gun, he had a fear, based on prior experiences, of being "maimed." Goetz then established "a pattern of fire," deciding specifically to fire from left to right. His stated intention at that point was to "murder [the four youths], to hurt them, to make them suffer as much as possible." When Canty again requested money, Goetz stood up, drew his weapon, and began firing, aiming for the center of the body of each of the four. Goetz recalled that the first two he shot "tried to run through the crowd [but] they had nowhere to run." Goetz then turned to his right to "go after the other two." One of these two "tried to run through the wall of the train, but . . . he had nowhere to go." The other youth (Cabey) "tried pretending that he wasn't with [the others]" by standing still, holding on to one of the subway hand straps, and not looking at Goetz. Goetz nonetheless fired his fourth shot at him. He then ran back to the first two youths to make sure they had been "taken care of." Seeing that they had both been shot, he spun back to check on the latter two. Goetz noticed that the youth who had been standing still was now sitting on a bench and seemed unhurt. As Goetz told the police, "I said '[you] seem to be all right, here's another,'" and he then fired the shot which severed Cabey's spinal cord. Goetz added that "if I was a little more under self-control . . . I would have put the barrel against his forehead and fired." He also admitted that "if I had had more [bullets], I would have shot them again, and again, and again." . . .

III

Penal Law article 35 recognizes the defense of justification, which "permits the use of force under certain circumstances." One such set of circumstances pertains to the use of force in defense of a person, encompassing both self-defense and defense of a third person. Penal Law § 35.15(1) sets forth the general principles governing all such uses of force: "[a] person may . . . use physical force upon another person when and to the extent he *reasonably believes* such to be necessary to defend

himself or a third person from what he *reasonably believes* to be the use or imminent use of unlawful physical force by such other person" (emphasis added).

Section 35.15(2) sets forth further limitations on these general principles with respect to the use of "deadly physical force": "A person may not use deadly physical force upon another person under circumstances specified in subdivision one unless (a) He *reasonably believes* that such other person is using or about to use deadly physical force . . . or (b) He *reasonably believes* that such other person is committing or attempting to commit a kidnapping, forcible rape, forcible sodomy or robbery" (emphasis added).

Because the evidence before the second Grand Jury included statements by Goetz that he acted to protect himself from being maimed or to avert a robbery, the prosecutor . . . properly instructed the grand jurors to consider whether the use of deadly physical force was justified to prevent either serious physical injury or a robbery, and, in doing so, to separately analyze the defense with respect to each of the charges. . . .

As expressed repeatedly in the Appellate Division's plurality opinion, because section 35.15 uses the term "he reasonably believes," the appropriate test, according to that court, is whether a defendant's beliefs and reactions were "reasonable to him." Under that reading of the statute, a jury which believed a defendant's testimony that he felt that his own actions were warranted and were reasonable would have to acquit him, regardless of what anyone else in defendant's situation might have concluded. Such an interpretation defies the ordinary meaning and significance of the term "reasonably" in a statute, and misconstrues the clear intent of the Legislature, in enacting section 35.15, to retain an objective element as part of any provision authorizing the use of deadly physical force.

Penal statutes in New York have long codified the right recognized at common law to use deadly physical force, under appropriate circumstances, in self-defense. These provisions have never required that an actor's belief as to the intention of another person to inflict serious injury be correct in order for the use of deadly force to be justified, but they have uniformly required that the belief comport with an objective notion of reasonableness. . . .

In 1961 the Legislature established a Commission to undertake a complete revision of the Penal Law and the Criminal Code. The impetus for the decision to update the Penal Law came in part from the drafting of the Model Penal Code by the American Law Institute, as well as from the fact that the existing law was poorly organized and in many aspects antiquated. . . . While using the Model Penal Code provisions on justification as general guidelines, however, the drafters of the new Penal Law did not simply adopt them verbatim.

The provisions of the Model Penal Code with respect to the use of deadly force in self-defense reflect the position of its drafters that any culpability which arises from a mistaken belief in the need to use such force should be no greater than the culpability such a mistake would give rise to if it were made with respect to an element of a crime. Accordingly, under Model Penal Code § 3.04(2)(b), a defendant charged with murder (or attempted murder) need only show that he "[*believed*] that [the use of deadly force] was necessary to protect himself against death, serious bodily injury, kidnapping or [forcible] sexual intercourse" to prevail on a self-defense claim (emphasis added). If the defendant's belief was wrong, and was recklessly, or negligently formed, however, he may be convicted of the type of homicide charge requiring only a reckless or negligent, as the case may be, criminal intent. . . .

New York did not follow the Model Penal Code's equation of a mistake as to the need to use deadly force with a mistake negating an element of a crime, choosing instead to use a single statutory section which would provide either a complete defense or no defense at all to a defendant charged with any crime involving the use of deadly force. The drafters of the new Penal Law adopted in large part the structure and content of Model Penal Code § 3.04, but, crucially, inserted the word "reasonably" before "believes." . . .

We cannot lightly impute to the Legislature an intent to fundamentally alter the principles of justification to allow the perpetrator of a serious crime to go free simply because that person believed his actions were reasonable and necessary to prevent some perceived harm. To completely exonerate such an individual, no matter how aberrational or bizarre his thought patterns, would allow citizens to set their own standards for the permissible use of force.

It would also allow a legally competent defendant suffering from delusions to kill or perform acts of violence with impunity, contrary to fundamental principles of justice and criminal law.

We can only conclude that the Legislature retained a reasonableness requirement to avoid giving a license for such actions. . . .

Goetz also argues that the introduction of an objective element will preclude a jury from considering factors such as the prior experiences of a given actor and thus require it to make a determination of "reasonableness" without regard to the actual circumstances of a particular incident. This argument, however, falsely presupposes that an objective standard means that the background and other relevant characteristics of a particular actor must be ignored. To the contrary, we have frequently noted that a determination of reasonableness must be based on the "circumstances" facing a defendant or his "situation." Such terms encompass more than the physical movements of the potential assailant. As just discussed, these terms include any relevant knowledge the defendant had about that person. They also necessarily bring in the physical attributes of all persons involved, including the defendant. Furthermore, the defendant's circumstances encompass any prior experiences he had which could provide a reasonable basis for a belief that another person's intentions were to injure or rob him or that the use of deadly force was necessary under the circumstances. . . .

Accordingly, the order of the Appellate Division should be reversed, and the dismissed counts of the indictment reinstated.

CASE DISCUSSION QUESTIONS

1. The order of the New York Supreme Court, Appellate Division, was reversed by this opinion. What court rendered this decision?
2. What is the defense of "justification" and how does it does it differ from self-defense?
3. Is the New York defense of justification based on an objective or subjective standard? On what basis do you reach this decision?
4. How does the application of the New York statute differ from the Model Penal Code in determining whether defendant Goetz's use of force was justified?

Retreat exception
The rule that in order to claim self-defense there must have been no possibility of retreat.

To further complicate the doctrine of self-defense, most jurisdictions include a **retreat exception** in their statutes. This exception generally requires a person in danger to get away from the danger, or give up possessions, before resorting to the use of deadly force. If the victim can avoid danger but chooses instead to use deadly force, the victim may be prosecuted for any crime committed. Potential victims need not retreat if they are in their own homes or if retreating would create additional danger for them. Potential victims using non-deadly force need not retreat. Only rarely can deadly force be applied to protect property because the law values human life over property even when the human life in question is trying to steal the property. The key is whether the potential victim of a burglary or robbery can convince a jury that there was reason to believe the thief was attempting to do great bodily harm to the person using the deadly force.

Some states, however, do authorize the use of deadly force to protect property. For instance, § 776.013(1) of the Florida "Stand Your Ground" law provides:

> (1) A person is presumed to have held a reasonable fear of imminent peril of death or great bodily harm to himself or herself or another when using defensive force that is intended or likely to cause death or great bodily harm to another if:
>> (a) The person against whom the defensive force was used was in the process of unlawfully and forcefully entering, or had unlawfully and forcibly entered, a dwelling, a residence, or occupied vehicle, or if that person had removed or was attempting to remove another against that person's will from the dwelling, residence, or occupied vehicle; and
>> (b) The person who uses defensive force knew or had reason to believe that an unlawful and forcible entry or unlawful and forcible act was occurring or had occurred.[31]

Notice that the wording used in (1)(a) not only covers situations in which the force was used against a person who was "*in the process of* unlawfully and forcibly entering . . . " but also applies in situations where the person "*had* unlawfully and forcibly entered a dwelling, a residence, or occupied vehicle." In a recent Florida case, a man who was being prosecuted for having fatally shot a man who had forced his way into a car in which he was a passenger raised a self-defense claim even though the man he shot was retreating from the scene when the shooting took place. A Florida appeals court ruled that the wording of the state statute in question granted the shooter immunity even though the original aggressor had been in retreat at the time he was shot.[32]

---

[31]Fla. Stat. § 776.013(1).
[32]*Hair v. State of Florida*, 17 So.3d 804 (Fla. Dist. Ct. App. 1st Dist., 2009).

One recent change to the self-defense rule in a few jurisdictions is the addition of the **battered woman's or spouse's syndrome**. This defense allows a person who has been the victim of repeated attacks the right to self-defense even when there may not be immediate danger at the exact moment that the right to self-defense is exercised. Experts believe that, especially for battered women, the fear of immediate harm extends beyond individual episodes of violence and becomes a part of everyday life. It is therefore argued that because the fear of immediate harm is always present, the doctrine of self-defense should apply to such situations as killing a spouse while he sleeps.

It is important to note that the application of the battered spouse defense is very problematic. Not all states have been willing to accept this defense—especially when the woman's actions were not taken in the face of "imminent" death or great bodily harm. The effects of the battered woman's syndrome may be used, however, to reduce the charge from murder to manslaughter or as a mitigating factor in sentencing.

Probably the most publicized of the battered woman's cases was the Bobbit case. In 1993, Lorena Bobbit was charged with aggravated assault for cutting off more than half of her husband Jon's penis with a carving knife. At trial, Lorena testified that John sexually, physically, and emotionally abused her during their marriage. Other witnesses corroborated her story. However, rather than make a self-defense argument, Lorena's attorneys presented an insanity defense. They argued that her husband's abuse caused her to "snap" because she was suffering from clinical depression as well as post-traumatic stress disorder caused by the abuse. The jury found Lorena "not guilty" due to insanity causing an irresistible impulse to assault her husband.

Finally, it should be noted that law enforcement and military personnel are given special exemptions from the law to take actions that are required as part of their official duties. The killing of enemy soldiers by soldiers in battle and the killing of escaping felons by police officers both fall under the category of justifiable homicide.

Battered woman's or spouse's syndrome
A syndrome of being the victim of repeated attacks; self-defense is sometimes allowed to the victim even when the victim is not in immediate danger.

Investigative Tips for Paralegals

As a paralegal working for the defense, you need to conduct a thorough investigation if the client is claiming self-defense. Specifically, you should gather information regarding the physical characteristics of the parties, such as height, weight, physical health, and mental condition. You also should explore the parties' cultural backgrounds and possible gang membership.

Additionally, you also should find out the accused's propensity for violence as well as what the client knew about the accuser's violent tendencies before the altercation. Along this line, you should conduct a criminal background search on the accuser and the client. WestLaw and NexisLexis offer criminal background checks as part of their extended software packages. If you do not have access to these services, you can research criminal backgrounds in your venue by conducting a search at the office of the clerk of the court. Likewise, you can use PACER for researching prior federal charges. Don't overlook evidence of the accuser's violent nature that was unknown to the defendant. Some courts permit this evidence to be presented when self-defense is asserted.[33]

---

[33]*People v. Lynch*, 104 Ill. 2d 194, 470 N.E.2d 1018 (1984).

APPLICATION EXERCISE

4. First study the police report in Exhibit 8.2 (a police report detailing the arrest of Vince Shlomi (a TV pitchman for the Sham Wow super towel) for aggravated battery related to an altercation he had with a female prostitute in a Florida hotel room. Then consider how the following provisions of Florida's aggravated battery statute apply to this situation:

A person commits aggravated battery who, in committing battery:

   1. Intentionally or knowingly causes great bodily harm, permanent disability, or permanent disfigurement; or
   2. Uses a deadly weapon.[34]

Under Florida law, a person commits a "simple" battery when he or she:

   1. Actually and intentionally touches or strikes another person against the will of the other; or
   2. Intentionally causes bodily harm to another person.[35]

The Florida self-defense statute in effect at the time of the incident provided:

A person is justified in using force, except deadly force, against another when and to the extent that the person reasonably believes that such conduct is necessary to defend himself or herself or another against the other's imminent use of unlawful force.[36]

   a. Do the facts gathered by the police give the prosecutor a legitimate basis to charge Vince Shlomi with battery? If so, should the charge be aggravated battery or simple battery?
   b. Assuming that he is charged under Florida law with battery, does Vince Shlomi have a justifiable basis to raise self-defense? Why or why not?
   c. Do the facts gathered by the police give the prosecutor a legitimate basis to charge the woman with battery? If so, should the charge be aggravated battery or simple battery?
   d. Assuming that she is charged under Florida law with battery, does the woman have a justifiable basis to raise self-defense? Why or why not?
   e. Draft a single-count information against Vince Shlomi charging him with the commission of aggravated battery in Dade County, Florida.
   f. Using the aggravated battery statute in the jurisdiction in which your college is located, draft a single-count information against Vince Shlomi. Assume that the offense was committed in the community in which your school is located.

---

[34]Fla. Stat. § 784.045 (1)(a).
[35]Fla. Stat. § 784.03 (1)(a).
[36]Fla. Stat. § 776.012.

Exhibit 8.2: Police Arrest Report

COMPLAINT/ARREST AFFIDAVIT

Defendant's Name: Shlomi, Vince
DOB: 04-25-1964 Age: 44 Race: W Sex: M Anglo
Scars/Marks: L. Arm (KSW)
Place of Birth: Israel
Local Address: 1680 Michigan Ave. Suite #700 Miami Bch, FL. 33139   Citizenship: U.S.A
Permanent Address: Same As Above   Occupation: Marketing

Charge: 1. Aggravated Battery (Hands)   784.045

Date: 7th Feb 09 0411 Location: 2001 Collins Ave #512 (Setai Hotel)

Def. and Co-Def. apparently met at luigis nightclub located
at 2377 collins Ave. Def and Co-Def. both went to the Def's
Hotel room located at 2001 collins Ave room #512. While inside
the room Def. stated that he kissed the Co-Def. when all
of a sudden the Co-Def. bit his tongue and would not let
go. Def stated that he punched the Co-Def. several times
until the Co-Def released his tongue. Co-Def sustained

a large laceration to her right side of her lip/mouth, lacerations
all over her face, including several facial fractures. While
further speaking with Def. he stated that he paid the
Co-Def. approx One Thousand dollars in twenties after
the Co-Def propositioned him for straight sex. Def.
stated this after he was read Miranda per Card. Search
incident to Arrest $930.00 U.S. Dollars were discovered
inside Co-Def's purse. Money was impounded into property
per investigatory evidence. Crime Scene #831 photographed
Scene and both Def. & Co-Def.

E. Entrapment

Entrapment
A defense requiring proof that the defendant would not have committed the crime but for police trickery.

The defense of **entrapment** arises when law enforcement personnel trick or encourage the defendant to commit a crime that the defendant would not have committed without the government's enticement. In other words, the government cannot encourage people to break the law and then turn around and prosecute them for having done so. However, it is not considered entrapment when government agents simply provide an opportunity to commit a crime that the person was already contemplating.

So, for example, the entrapment defense would apply to a situation where a sexily dressed undercover police officer approached a man at a bar and offered to have sex with him for money. On the other hand, if that same sexily dressed undercover officer sat down next to the defendant and struck up a conversation about the weather or the music, it would not be entrapment if it was the defendant who first raised the idea of paying to have sex with her. The key factor in using an entrapment defense is the determination of whether the defendant had a predisposition to commit the crime before the government agents contacted the defendant.

However, the entrapment defense is rarely successful because most juries believe that people should be held responsible for their actions because they chose to follow the suggestion even though they knew it was illegal.

F. Constitutional Defenses

Since the defining and enforcement of the criminal law must be consistent with the provisions of the U.S. Constitution and the relevant state constitutions, defense attorneys may be able to challenge both the statute the client is accused of violating and the way in which the evidence was gathered. If a statute is found to be unconstitutional, a defendant cannot be legally convicted or punished for having violated it, and if constitutional rights were violated during the investigative stage, it may be possible to prevent that evidence from being used at the trial.

1. CHALLENGING THE CONSTITUTIONALITY OF THE LAW

a. Ex Post Facto and Bill of Attainder Restrictions

Bill of Attainder
A law that imposes criminal penalties on a single person or small, select group of people.

Ex post facto law
A law that imposes criminal penalties for actions that were taken prior to the passage of the law.

Article I, Section 9 of the U.S. Constitution declares that "No Bill of Attainder or ex post facto law shall be passed." A Bill of Attainder is defined as a law that imposes criminal penalties on a single person or small, select group of people. An ex post facto law is one that imposes criminal penalties for actions that were taken prior to the passage of the law. In *Calder v. Bull*[37] Justice Chase wrote:

1st. Every law that makes an action done before the passing of the law, and which was innocent when done, criminal; and punishes such action. 2d. Every law that aggravates a crime, or makes it greater than it was, when committed. 3d. Every law that changes the punishment, and inflicts a greater punishment, than the law

---

[37]3 U.S. 386, 1 L. Ed. 648 (1798).

annexed to the crime, when committed. 4th. Every law that alters the legal rules of evidence, and receives less, or different, testimony, than the law required at the time of the commission of the offense, in order to convict the offender.

Although this section of the U.S. Constitution is only applicable to laws passed by the U.S. Congress, most states have similar provisions in their state constitutions.

In late 2008, the Illinois legislature adopted legislation, dubbed "Drew's Law," that changed the rules of evidence on the admission of hearsay statements made by a murder victim when the murder was intended to cause the unavailability of the person making the statements.[38] The prosecutor, who was investigating the death of former police officer Drew Peterson's third wife and the disappearance of Peterson's fourth wife, drafted the law. Five months after passage, the same prosecutor secured the indictment of Peterson and announced that he would be using the new hearsay law in his prosecution of Peterson. Peterson's attorney has challenged the hearsay law as being an unconstitutional ex post facto law.[39]

APPLICATION EXERCISES

5. Is Drew's Law an ex post facto law? Why or why not?

6. Does your state's constitution prohibit the passage of ex post facto laws or bills of attainder? If so, what are the citations for these prohibitions?

---

b. Vagueness and Overbreadth

One of the most common challenges to a criminal statute is the claim that it is "void for vagueness" or "overbroad." Both are based on the Due Process Clauses of the Fifth and Fourteen Amendments. The **void for vagueness** concept is based on the principle that "fundamental fairness requires that criminal statutes have to be written in such a way that a person of average intelligence has notice as to what is or is not prohibited by the law."

Consider, for example, a Texas stalking statute that made it illegal to engage in conduct that is "reasonably likely to harass, annoy, alarm, abuse, torment, or embarrass" someone. Because terms such as "annoy," "alarm," and "embarrass" are ambiguous and susceptible to different meanings, the highest Texas criminal appellate court struck down the statute on the basis that it was unconstitutionally vague on its face.[40]

Void for vagueness defense
A claim that a criminal charge should be dismissed because the statute being applied fails to fairly inform ordinary people as to what is commanded or prohibited.

---

[38] 725 ILCS 5/115-10.6.

[39] After the trial judge found the hearsay statements were inadmissible, the prosecution took an interlocutory appeal. At the time this book went to press, the appeal was still pending.

[40] *Long v. State*, 931 S.W.2d 285 (Tex. 1996).

Overbreadth
A reason for invalidating a statute that criminalizes constitutionally protected activities along with those that it can legally prohibit.

The courts also require criminal statutes to be narrowly drawn so that they don't prohibit more than they are constitutionally permitted to limit. Therefore, if a statute goes too far and can reasonably be interpreted as prohibiting some constitutionally protected behavior, it is said to be "**overbroad**." For example, a law designed to prevent destruction of public property cannot include a ban on all protests or mass gatherings, and an obscenity statute must define the type of material it prohibits narrowly enough so that it does not also prohibit sexually explicit materials that are not legally obscene.

Another example of a successful challenge based on vagueness and overbreadth can be found in the federal prosecution of former Enron chief executive Jeffrey Skilling on charges that he defrauded Enron stockholders in violation of the provisions of 18 U.S.C. § 1341 and § 1346. § 1341 declares:

> Whoever, having devised or intending to devise any scheme or artifice to defraud, or for obtaining money or property by means of false or fraudulent pretenses, representations, or promises, or to sell, dispose of, loan, exchange, alter, give away, distribute, supply, or furnish or procure for unlawful use any counterfeit or spurious coin, obligation, security, or other article, or anything represented to be or intimated or held out to be such counterfeit or spurious article, for the purpose of executing such scheme or artifice or attempting so to do, places in any post office or authorized depository for mail matter, any matter or thing whatever to be sent or delivered by the Postal Service, or deposits or causes to be deposited any matter or thing whatever to be sent or delivered by any private or commercial interstate carrier, or takes or receives therefrom, any such matter or thing, or knowingly causes to be delivered by mail or such carrier according to the direction thereon, or at the place at which it is directed to be delivered by the person to whom it is addressed, any such matter or thing, shall be fined under this title or imprisoned not more than 20 years, or both. . . .

§ 1346 states:

> For the purposes of this chapter [18 USCS § § 1341 *et seq.*], the term "scheme or artifice to defraud" includes a scheme or artifice to deprive another of the intangible right of honest services.

But what does "honest services" mean? Skilling's attorneys attacked the law in question as being vague and overbroad and in June of 2010, the U.S. Supreme Court declared:

> Congress intended at least to reach schemes to defraud involving bribes and kickbacks. Construing the honest-services statute to extend beyond that core meaning, . . . would encounter a vagueness shoal. We therefore hold that § 1346 covers only bribery and kickback schemes."[41]

---

[41]*Skilling v. United States*, 130 S. Ct. 2896, 177 L. Ed. 2d 619 (2010). Prior to the Supreme Court's ruling in this case, U.S. Attorneys had convicted dozens of state and local governmental officials for violating this "honest services" provision. The list of convictions included former Illinois governor George Ryan.

Because Skilling's alleged misconduct entailed no bribe or kickback, the Supreme Court ruled that it does not fall within § 1346's proscription.

c. Challenges Based on Violations of Civil Liberties

Criminal statutes can also be challenged on the ground that they violate constitutionally based civil liberties, such as the First Amendment rights of freedom of religion or freedom of speech or the Equal Protection Clause of the Fourteenth Amendment.

When freedom of religion is used as a basis for challenging a statute, the government must show that the law in question is neutral on its face and of general applicability. If this standard is met, the statute is valid even though it may have the incidental effect of burdening a particular religious practice.[42] For example, the U.S. Supreme Court upheld the constitutionality of a statute prohibiting polygamy, even though the Mormon defendant argued that polygamous marriage was part of his religion.[43] However, more recently, the Supreme Court invalidated a city ordinance prohibiting the ritual sacrifice of animals on the grounds that it was neither neutral on its face nor of general applicability.[44] It was not neutral because it was directed at a specific religious group, the Santerias, and it was not of general applicability because it applied only to the killing of animals in the context of a religious service. If the city had been motivated by legitimate public health concerns, the ordinance would have been applicable to all situations in which animals are killed.

The First Amendment protection of freedom of speech can also form the basis for a constitutional challenge. The concept of **content neutrality** plays a critical role in First Amendment cases. For example, in *Texas v. Johnson*,[45] the Supreme Court determined that the State of Texas could not punish someone for symbolic speech, in that case the burning of an American flag, simply because it disagreed with the message being sent. Similarly, the government cannot grant or deny a permit for a rally or parade on the basis of which political party is sponsoring the event. The Court held that the Village of Skokie could not prevent a neo-Nazi group from marching in its town even though their presence would be offensive to the 60 percent of its residents who were Jewish, 10 percent of whom were survivors of the Holocaust.[46]

Content neutrality also plays a role in the Court's treatment of **hate crime** laws. Hate crimes are offenses that are motivated by a hatred of a specific group or category of people, such as racial or religious minorities or homosexuals. In analyzing these types of laws, one needs to distinguish between those prohibiting certain types of **hate speech** and those that enhance the punishment of another, underlying crime.

Content neutrality
Laws may not limit free expression on the basis of whether the speech's content supports or opposes any particular position.

Hate crime
A crime where the selection of the victim is based on that person's membership in a protected category, such as race, sex, or sexual orientation.

Hate speech
Speech directed at a particular group or classification of people that involves expressions of hate or intimidation.

---

[42]*Employment Division, Department of Human Resources of Oregon v. Smith*, 494 U.S. 872, 110 S. Ct. 1595, 108 L. Ed. 2d 876 (1990).

[43]*Reynolds v. United States*, 98 U.S 145, 25 L. Ed. 244 (1879).

[44]*Church of the Lukumi Babalu Aye Inc. v. City of Hialeah*, 508 U.S. 520, 113 S. Ct. 2217, 124 L. Ed. 2d 472 (1993).

[45]*Texas v. Johnson*, 491 U.S. 397, 109 S. Ct. 2533, 105 L. Ed. 2d 342 (1989).

[46]*National Socialist Party v. Skokie*, 432 U.S. 43, 97 S. Ct. 2205, 53 L. Ed. 2d 96 (1977).

The contrast between these two approaches can be seen in two recent Supreme Court cases. In a case dealing with a form of hate speech, the Court was asked to consider whether a state statute that outlawed cross burning unconstitutionally infringed on protected symbolic speech. The Court held that cross burning by itself could be protected speech. However, if the intent behind the cross burning was to intimidate, the state could constitutionally criminalize that behavior.[47] Therefore, the Court reversed the conviction of a man who had led a Ku Klux Klan rally during which a cross was burned but affirmed that the state could prosecute those who used a cross burning to intimidate, as was done by two men who placed a burning cross in the yard of an African American family.

In contrast to hate speech laws, the penalty enhancement statutes simply provide for stiffer penalties in situations where the defendant has been found guilty of another crime, such as robbery, but it is proven that the defendant selected the specific victim because of that person's race, religion, or other specified factors. The Supreme Court upheld the validity of such a statute in *Wisconsin v. Mitchell*.[48]

Criminal statutes can also be challenged on the ground that they violate the Equal Protection Clause by treating people differently on the basis of their race, sex, age, sexual orientation, religion, etc. without having a legally acceptable basis for doing so.[49] For example, several criminal statutes have been challenged on the basis that they discriminated on the basis of sex in the way the offense was defined or the nature of the punishment that was attached to the crime.[50]

2. CHALLENGING THE CONSTITUTIONALITY OF PROCEDURES USED

In this section, we discuss how these procedural rights can be used to advance the defendant's interests in criminal cases. Before continuing, we recommend that you go back and review Section A in Chapter 4 where we highlighted the portions of the Bill of Rights relating to criminal prosecutions. Note that some, such as the Fourth Amendment prohibition against "unreasonable searches and seizures," relate to how evidence is gathered, and others, such as the Sixth Amendment right to confront witnesses, relate to how trials must be conducted.

a. The Exclusionary Rule

Motion to suppress
A request that the court prohibit specified material from being admitted into evidence at a trial because it was gathered in an illegal manner.

Defense attorneys usually address violations of constitutional rights related to the gathering of evidence by filing a **motion to suppress** the evidence involved. We will discuss the mechanics of filing and opposing these motions to suppress in the next chapter; we focus our attention here on the justification for granting them.

---

[47] *Virginia v. Black*, 538 U.S. 343, 123 S. Ct. 1536, 155 L. Ed. 2d 535 (2003).

[48] 508 U.S. 476, 113 S. Ct. 2194, 124 L. Ed. 2d 436 (1993).

[49] The standard for determining what constitutes a legally acceptable basis differs according to the type of group that is being discriminated against.

[50] See *Craig v. Boren*, 429 U.S. 190, 97 S. Ct. 451, 50 L. Ed. 2d 397 (1976) and *Michael M. v. Superior Court of Sonoma County*, 450 U.S. 464, 101 S. Ct. 1200, 67 L. Ed. 2d 437 (1981).

When judges grant motions to suppress based on alleged violations of constitutional rights, they are applying what is commonly referred to as the **exclusionary rule**. If a judge concludes that evidence was collected in a manner that violated the defendant's fundamental constitutional rights, the judge is expected to prevent that evidence from being used at trial.

Use of the exclusionary rule has long been one of the most controversial topics in criminal law because it can sometimes result in a situation in which guilty men and women go free. If the murder weapon was suppressed because there was an illegal search of the defendant's house, or if a confession is thrown out because the defendant wasn't *Mirandized* before the police began a custodial interrogation, prosecutors may no longer have enough evidence to meet the beyond a reasonable doubt standard of the judge or the jury.

A critical part of the operation of the exclusionary rule is what is known as the **fruit of the poisonous tree doctrine**. This doctrine holds that evidence that is spawned by or directly derived from an illegal search or illegal interrogation is inadmissible against the defendant by virtue of being tainted by the original illegality. If the tree (the primary evidence) has been poisoned from the illegal search, then all the fruit (collateral or additional evidence) must also be suppressed. It is important to note, however, that the application of this doctrine does not invalidate the arrest or prevent the defendant from being convicted on the basis of independent evidence. Nor does it prohibit officers from later conducting legal searches and gathering additional evidence as long as that evidence was gathered without the aid of knowledge gained from the tainted evidence that was suppressed.

The following excerpts from *Mapp v. Ohio* explain why the Supreme Court chose to apply the exclusionary rule in both federal and state criminal cases.

Exclusionary rule
A requirement that evidence obtained in violation of a defendant's constitutional rights cannot be used against the defendant in a criminal prosecution.

Fruit of the poisonous tree doctrine
Evidence that is derived from an illegal search or interrogation is inadmissible.

Mapp v. Ohio
Supreme Court of the United States
367 U.S. 643 (1961)

Mr. JUSTICE CLARK delivered the opinion of the Court.

Appellant stands convicted of knowingly having had in her possession and under her control certain lewd and lascivious books, pictures, and photographs in violation of § 2905.34 of Ohio's Revised Code. As officially stated in the syllabus to its opinion, the Supreme Court of Ohio found that her conviction was valid though "based primarily upon the introduction in evidence of lewd and lascivious books and pictures unlawfully seized during an unlawful search of defendant's home. . . ."

On May 23, 1957, three Cleveland police officers arrived at appellant's residence in that city pursuant to information that "a person [was] hiding out in the home, who was wanted for questioning in connection with a recent bombing. . . ." Miss Mapp and her daughter by a former marriage lived on the top floor of the two-family dwelling. . . . When Miss Mapp did not come to the door immediately, at least one of the several doors to the house was forcibly opened and the policemen gained admittance. . . . It appears that Miss Mapp was halfway down the stairs from the upper floor to the front door when the officers, in this highhanded manner, broke into the hall. . . . Running rough-shod over appellant, a policeman "grabbed" her, "twisted [her] hand," and she "yelled [and] pleaded with him" because "it was hurting." Appellant, in handcuffs, was then forcibly taken upstairs to her bedroom where the officers searched a dresser, a chest of drawers, a closet and some suitcases. They also looked into a photo album and through personal papers belonging to the appellant. The search spread to the rest of the second floor including the child's bedroom, the living room, the kitchen and a dinette. The basement of the building and a trunk found therein were also searched. The obscene materials for possession of which she was ultimately convicted were discovered in the course of that widespread search.

At the trial no search warrant was produced by the prosecution, nor was the failure to produce one explained or accounted for. . . .

The State says that even if the search were made without authority, or otherwise unreasonably, it is not prevented from using the unconstitutionally seized evidence at trial, citing *Wolf v. Colorado*, 338 U.S. 25 (1949), in which this Court did indeed hold "that in a prosecution in a State court for a State crime the Fourteenth Amendment does not forbid the admission of evidence obtained by an unreasonable search and seizure." At p. 33. On this appeal, of which we have noted probable jurisdiction, it is urged once again that we review that holding.

I

[T]his Court, in *Weeks v. United States*, 232 U.S. 383 (1914), stated that

> the Fourth Amendment . . . put the courts of the United States and Federal officials, in the exercise of their power and authority, under limitations and restraints [and] . . . forever secure[d] the people, their persons, houses, papers and effects against all unreasonable searches and seizures under the guise of law . . . and the duty of giving to it force and effect is obligatory upon all entrusted under our Federal system with the enforcement of the laws.

Specifically dealing with the use of the evidence unconstitutionally seized, the Court concluded:

> If letters and private documents can thus be seized and held and used in evidence against a citizen accused of an offense, the protection of the Fourth Amendment declaring his right to be secure against such searches and seizures is of no value,

and, so far as those thus placed are concerned, might as well be stricken from the Constitution. The efforts of the courts and their officials to bring the guilty to punishment, praiseworthy as they are, are not to be aided by the sacrifice of those great principles established by years of endeavor and suffering which have resulted in their embodiment in the fundamental law of the land.

Finally, the Court in that case clearly stated that use of the seized evidence involved "a denial of the constitutional rights of the accused." At p. 398. Thus, in the year 1914, in the *Weeks* case, this Court "for the first time" held that "in a federal prosecution the Fourth Amendment barred the use of evidence secured through an illegal search and seizure." . . .

IV

Since the Fourth Amendment's right of privacy has been declared enforceable against the States through the Due Process Clause of the Fourteenth, it is enforceable against them by the same sanction of exclusion as is used against the Federal Government. Were it otherwise, then just as without the *Weeks* rule the assurance against unreasonable federal searches and seizures would be "a form of words," valueless and undeserving of mention in a perpetual charter of inestimable human liberties, so too, without that rule the freedom from state invasions of privacy would be so ephemeral and so neatly severed from its conceptual nexus with the freedom from all brutish means of coercing evidence as not to merit this Court's high regard as a freedom "implicit in the concept of ordered liberty." . . .

Moreover, our holding that the exclusionary rule is an essential part of both the Fourth and Fourteenth Amendments is not only the logical dictate of prior cases, but it also makes very good sense. There is no war between the Constitution and common sense. Presently, a federal prosecutor may make no use of evidence illegally seized, but a State's attorney across the street may, although he supposedly is operating under the enforceable prohibitions of the same Amendment. Thus the State, by admitting evidence unlawfully seized, serves to encourage disobedience to the Federal Constitution which it is bound to uphold. . . .

There are those who say, as did Justice (then Judge) Cardozo, that under our constitutional exclusionary doctrine "the criminal is to go free because the constable has blundered." In some cases this will undoubtedly be the result. But, as was said in *Elkins*, "there is another consideration —the imperative of judicial integrity." 364 U.S. at 222. The criminal goes free, if he must, but it is the law that sets him free. Nothing can destroy a government more quickly than its failure to observe its own laws, or worse, its disregard of the charter of its own existence. As Mr. Justice Brandeis, dissenting, said in *Olmstead v. United States*, 277 U.S. 438, 485 (1928): "Our Government is the potent, the omnipresent teacher. For good or for ill, it teaches the whole people by its example. . . . If the Government becomes a lawbreaker, it breeds contempt for law; it invites every man to become a law unto himself; it invites anarchy." . . .

CASE DISCUSSION QUESTIONS

1. According to the Supreme Court, what is the main justification for the exclusionary rule?

2. What negative consequences arise out of application of the exclusionary rule?

3. What problems would be created by having one set of rules for the federal courts and a separate set of rules for the state courts?

Although *Mapp v. Ohio* has not been overruled, the more conservative Supreme Courts of the last forty years have limited its applicability. In *United States v. Leon*,[51] for example, the Supreme Court carved out a major exception to the exclusionary rule in situations in which the police seized illegal drugs while administering a search warrant that they thought was valid. Later, Leon's defense attorney filed a motion to suppress the drug evidence based on the theory that the affidavit on which the warrant was based was insufficient to establish the probable cause needed to justify its issuance, and the trial judge found that the affidavit had in fact been insufficient. However, the judge rejected the motion to suppress the evidence because the officer who filed it had done so in good faith. In upholding the trial judge's ruling, the Supreme Court cited the "substantial social costs . . . exacted by the exclusionary rule."[52]

Typical of the manner in which the U.S. Supreme Court has been chipping away at many of the most famous precedents of the Warren Court era, a recent Roberts Court ruling held that the Fourth Amendment did not require the exclusion of evidence that was obtained in a search that violated Michigan's "knock-and-announce" rule. Writing for the majority, Justice Scalia stated:

Whether that preliminary misstep had occurred *or not*, the police would have executed the warrant they had obtained, and would have discovered the gun and drugs inside the house. . . . What the knock-and-announce rule has never protected . . . is one's interest in preventing the government from seeing or taking evidence described in a warrant. Since the interests that *were* violated in this case have nothing to do with the seizure of the evidence, the exclusionary rule is inapplicable.[53]

---

[51]468 U.S. 897, 104 S. Ct. 3405, 82 L. Ed. 2d 677 (1984).

[52]*Id.* at 907.

[53]*Hudson v. Michigan*, 547 U.S. 586, 594, 126 S. Ct. 2159, 165 L. Ed. 2d 56 (2006). Note also the discussion of *Brewer v. Williams* on p. 106, where evidence that was excluded on the basis of an unconstitutional interrogation was allowed on the basis of the inevitable discovery doctrine.

APPLICATION EXERCISE

7. Review what you have learned so far about the *Turner* case and then list what, if any, evidence might be challenged based on the exclusionary rule. How do you think the judge would rule on these challenges?

b. Double Jeopardy

Double jeopardy
The Fifth Amendment prohibition against prosecuting or punishing a defendant twice for the same crime.

Double jeopardy is another type of constitutional defense based on the process being used to obtain a criminal conviction. The **Double Jeopardy** Clause of the Fifth Amendment was designed to prevent a situation in which the government could keep retrying the defendant over and over for the same crime until the prosecutor got the conviction and/or the sentence he wanted, but the wording used—"no person shall be subject for the same offense to be twice up in jeopardy of life or limb"—raises some key questions. What constitutes being put "in jeopardy," and when is something considered the "same offense" as opposed to being different offenses related to the same act?

Based on decisions of the U.S. Supreme Court, "jeopardy" attaches once a jury has been selected.[54] If charges are dropped prior to the start of the trial, they can be reinstated at a later date unless they were dismissed "with prejudice." If the trial concludes with either a conviction or acquittal, a defendant cannot be tried again for the same offense. However, if the trial ends in a mistrial because of a hung jury, for example, the double jeopardy clause will not prevent the State from prosecuting the defendant in a second trial.

Although the double jeopardy clause prohibits being tried twice for the same offense, it does not prohibit separate prosecutions for different offenses arising out of the same action. For example, an act that is prosecuted as a homicide in state court may also be prosecuted as a violation of civil rights in federal court. Furthermore, double jeopardy does not prevent a civil action for damages based on the same set of facts presented in a criminal prosecution. Finally, if the defendant successfully appeals a conviction, the appellate court may remand the case for a new trial without violating the double jeopardy clause.

G. STATUTES OF LIMITATIONS AND SPEEDY TRIAL ACTS

Statute of limitations
A law that sets forth a maximum time limit between the occurrence or discovery of a crime and the date at which formal charges must be filed.

Many crimes, like civil actions, are covered by statutes of limitations. Under these statutes the government cannot prosecute an individual after a designated number of years have passed since either the date of the crime or the discovery of the crime. However, there are some crimes, such as murder, for which there usually is no time limit on when charges may be brought.

---

[54]In bench trials it would attach when the trial began with opening statements.

The Speedy Trial Act of 1974[55] requires that defendants in federal court be brought to trial within 100 days of their being charged with a crime. Many state legislatures have also established specific time limits. Defendants can usually waive these time limits if added time is needed to prepare for the trial, but prosecutors cannot claim the same privilege. Speedy trial statutes may require that the charges be dismissed if defendants are not brought to trial within a given number of days. Therefore, as is true with statutes of limitations, failure to comply with these dates can become a basis for having the charges dismissed.

APPLICATION EXERCISE

8. Review the facts of the *Cook* case (referenced on p. xxxvii and in previous chapters) and then read the Traffic Crash Reconstruction Report in Exhibit 8.3. Based on these materials, what defenses might Cook assert?

Exhibit 8.3: Police Report in *Cook* Case

STATE POLICE DISTRICT 18 TRAFFIC CRASH RECONSTRUCTION REPORT

FINDINGS

Route 185 is a four lane asphalt roadway accommodating two lanes northbound and two lanes southbound with 4-foot paved shoulders on both sides.

- The speed limit on Route 185 at the crash site was posted in both directions as 45 mph.
- There is no overhead lighting at the immediate vicinity of the crash.

CONCLUSIONS

Environment

- Visibility for the motorist approaching the rear of the bicycle was limited due to the lack of overhead lighting in the area of the crash.

Unit #1 Schwinn Bicycle

- The Schwinn bicycle was black in color and was not equipped with a headlight or rear taillight as required by state statute. The bicycle was equipped with rear yellow

---

[55]18 U.S.C. § 3161 (2009).

reflectors on both sides of both panels and a white reflector mounted below the seat to the rear.

- The bicyclist was not wearing any type of reflective clothing.
- The bicycle was struck in the rear end approximately 2 feet west of the east side of the northbound driving lane of the roadway.
- At impact, the bicycle struck the left front bumper of the Blazer approximately 8 inches inward from the passenger side of the vehicle.
- The bicyclist struck the front hood area of the Blazer causing the hood to be pushed inward 2 inches.
- The bicyclist continued rearward striking the front passenger side windshield of the Blazer.
- The driver of the Blazer then applied the brakes, without leaving any evidence of skid marks, causing the bicyclist to be thrown forward onto the pavement.
- The bicyclist traveled 82′9″ in a northerly direction on the roadway before coming to final rest.
- County Coroner tests show the bicyclist had a blood alcohol concentration (BOC) of 0.121.

Unit #2 Chevrolet Blazer

- The Chevrolet Blazer was traveling a minimum of 38 mph when it struck the bicyclist.
- The front passenger's side headlamp was pushed inward, causing it to point toward the passenger's side of the vehicle. It is unknown if the headlamp was misaligned prior to the crash.
- Bud Cook, the driver of the Blazer, had a BOC of 0.178.

SUMMARY

The most common defense usually involves denial that the defendant did what he or she is accused of doing. "The light wasn't red when my car entered the intersection" or "I never gave anyone any inside information about our company's plan to introduce a new drug." A specialized version of this denial approach is the alibi defense, which claims that the defendant could not have committed the crime because he or she was someplace else at the time the criminal act took place. In these cases the prosecution has the burden of presenting enough evidence to convince the judge or jury to reject the defendant's denial.

In a limited number of situations, ignorance or mistakes can be raised as a defense, when the ignorance relates to *mens rea* or the defendant relied on incorrect official statements about the application of the law.

Another group of defenses is related to the status of the accused at the time the crime was committed. In situations where the defendant is under a certain age, has certain types of mental disorders, or is under the influence of drugs or alcohol, it may be possible for these individuals to establish that they were incapable of formulating the required *mens rea*. Although the insanity defense receives a lot of attention in the media, the legal defi-nition of insanity is very restrictive and difficult to establish. Whereas a "not guilty by reason of insanity" verdict relieves the defendant of all criminal responsibility, he or she might still be committed to a mental health facility. With a "guilty but mentally ill" verdict, the defendant has a criminal conviction on record but is sent to a mental treatment facility rather than to a regular prison.

Duress, necessity, self-defense, and defense of others are reactive defenses. These defenses are based on the recognition that in some situations the crime committed was justified because it was the "lesser of two evils." Therefore, a person *may* (depending on the state and the circumstances) be able to shoot a home invader without committing a crime.

Entrapment, statutes of limitations, and constitutional defenses are all based on the idea that the agents of the government have done something wrong and that these actions have invalidated some part of the criminal prosecution. So the government cannot prosecute someone when a government agent talked the defendant into taking the illegal action. It cannot prosecute someone after certain time limits have run out, and it cannot use evidence that was illegally obtained. It also cannot prosecute someone for actions that did not constitute a crime until after they were performed or based on laws that were vague and overly broad.

REVIEW QUESTIONS

1. Define the alibi defense and explain the role that alibi witnesses play in a case.
2. In federal court, what duties of disclosure do the defense attorneys owe when the alibi defense is raised?
3. In federal court, what duties of disclosure do the prosecuting attorneys owe when the alibi defense is raised?
4. What defense can be raised when a defendant charged with statutory rape claims the victim lied when she told him that she was eighteen when in fact she was fifteen? Is this defense likely to prevail? Explain why or why not.
5. Explain why the status of a defendant can be raised as a defense. Name three status defenses.
6. List and describe the three major models of the insanity defense.
7. If a federal jury makes a finding of not guilty by reason of insanity, what happens to the defendant?
8. Which intoxication defense is limited to specific-intent crimes? Why is the defense so limited?
9. Compare and contrast the insanity defense and the concept of the defendant's competency to stand trial.
10. What must a defendant show to prove that he or she committed the crime under duress?
11. What potential defense can be raised by a person accused of possession of marijuana when the accused was using it to treat his condition of glaucoma? Explain this defense.
12. What conditions must be met in order to raise self-defense?
13. How does the "retreat exception" affect a person's right to use deadly force to protect property?
14. What defense allows a person who has been the victim of repeated attacks the right to self-defense even when there may not be immediate danger at the exact moment that the right to self-defense is exercised? What is the rationale for this defense?
15. What is the defense based upon government agents simply providing the defendant an opportunity to commit a crime that the person was already contemplating?

16. What constitutional attacks can be raised to challenge a retroactive statute designed to criminalize the conduct of a single individual?
17. Under what circumstances can hate speech, such as cross burning, be criminalized? When would such hate crime legislation be considered unconstitutional?
18. How does the "fruit of the poisonous tree" doctrine relate to the exclusionary rule?
19. What limitations are imposed on the prosecution in retrying a defendant on the same charge after the first trial resulted in a hung jury?
20. How many days do federal prosecutors have to put the defendant on trial? What is the statutory basis for this requirement?

Chapter 9

Pretrial Motions and Plea Bargaining

In Chapters 4 and 5, we followed the development of a criminal case from the commission of the crime through the police investigation and the prosecution's role in filing formal charges. Chapter 6 followed with a discussion of defense attorneys. We focused in Chapter 7 on how both prosecuting attorneys and defense counsel use discovery and disclosure procedures to develop the information they need to evaluate the strengths and weaknesses of their case and gather evidence they may be able to use at trial. Then in Chapter 8, we presented an overview of the legal defenses that might be available to the accused.

In this chapter, we will discuss the types of motions attorneys file to determine what a trial on the matter will involve. These motions are related to who the judge will be, whether there will be co-defendants, competency to stand trial, whether evidence should be suppressed because it was illegally gathered, and when the trial will begin. After these issues have been settled, the prosecutor and the defense attorney typically engage in what is known as "plea bargaining," and in this chapter we will discuss the pros and cons of this practice as well as the procedures used.

Since the discussions held during plea bargaining often include consideration of diversionary programs, we end the chapter with an overview of optional programs designed to reduce taxpayer costs by providing educational and treatment options for selected types of defendants.

A. Pre-Trial Motions

1. MOTIONS RELATING TO DISCOVERY

We have already discussed motions related to discovery in Chapter 7. As more information is revealed, additional discovery motions may be filed.

2. MOTIONS RELATING TO THE FORUM

As we saw in Chapter 6, a criminal case officially begins when the prosecutor's office files formal charges in a particular court. For example, if a violation of the state criminal code took place in Normal, Illinois, the McLean County State Attorney's Office would file charges with the McLean County Circuit Court in Illinois' 11th Judicial Circuit. On the other hand, if there was a violation of federal law, it would be up to the U.S. Attorney's Office to decide to file charges, and the charging document would be filed in the U.S. Clerk's Office for the Peoria Division of the U.S. District Court for the Central District of Illinois.

As pointed out in Chapter 8, the constitutional protection against double jeopardy does not prohibit trial in both a state and a federal court for the same act, when that action violates both state and federal laws. In practice, however, such situations are rare and one jurisdiction will usually hold off on its prosecution until the other is completed. Additionally, state prosecutors sometimes decline to pursue charges against certain types of offenders, such as drug traffickers, to clear the way for the U.S. Attorney's Office to pursue charges because federal offenses carry greater penalties or the federal government may have greater resources at its disposal.

Motion for a change of venue

A formal request to the court to move the trial to a different location.

A **motion for a change of venue** is made when one of the parties wants to change the location of the trial so that the case is heard in some other city, county, or judicial district, rather than where the case originally was filed. (*Venue* is Latin for "a place where people gather.") A change of venue might be requested if one of the parties believes that either the current venue is improper under the court's procedural rules or an alternative location would be more appropriate. These motions for a change of venue are most common in highly publicized cases where the defense argues that the trial must be moved to another community in order to be able to impanel an impartial jury. In order to justify a venue change, the defense must prove that the prejudice against the defendant is so great that the defendant cannot obtain a fair and impartial trial.[1] Newspaper articles, transcripts of radio and television broadcasts, and commissioned public opinion polls are often used as evidence to show the predisposition of potential jurors against the defendant. Paralegals may be called upon to research media coverage to support a motion for change of venue.

An excerpt from a motion for change of venue is displayed in Exhibit 9.1. It was filed by the attorney representing Drew Peterson when the former Bolingbrook, Illinois, police sergeant was charged with drowning his third wife, Kathleen Savio. The bill of indictment was issued five years following her death, after the disappearance of his fourth wife, Stacy. Prior to the indictment, Peterson appeared on CNN's *Larry King Live*, NBC's *Today Show*, Fox News, the *Dr. Phil Show*, and a number of local Chicago media outlets. Peterson moved for a change of venue on the basis of prejudicial pretrial publicity.

---

[1]FRCrP 21(a).

Exhibit 9.1: Excerpts from Motion for Change of Venue

<u>DEFENDANT'S MOTION FOR CHANGE OF VENUE</u>

NOW COMES the above named Defendant, Drew Peterson, and hereby files this Motion for Change of Venue, and further states as follows:

* * *

18.   In the present case, there is no reasonable dispute that this matter has received saturated media attention. For example, but not by way of limitation:

       a.   A Google search for "Drew Peterson" returned about 2,950,000 results.[1] This is almost double the amount of results of a Google search for "Rod Blagojevich."[2]

       b.   An article about Drew Peterson entitled "Ex-cop arrested on murder charges in '04 death of third wife" was the most viewed article on the Chicago Tribune Website for the week of May 3-10, 2009.[3]

19.   In addition, numerous articles have been prejudicial toward the Defendant and have prejudiced the jury pool toward him. For example, but not by way of limitation:

* * *

The judge denied the motion.

In some cases, a motion is brought on the basis that a different venue would be more convenient for the parties and/or the witnesses if the trial were held in an alternative location.

A limited number of states have enacted statutes providing for a **change of venire** to provide defendants an alternative remedy for prejudicial pre-trial publicity. Under this scheme, the trial takes place in the venue where the charge was filed, but the jury is selected from another judicial district.[2]

Change of venire
The process of selecting jurors from a different area than the place of the trial.

---

[2]W. LaFave, J. Isreal & N. King, *Criminal Procedure* 1092 (4th ed., Thomson West 2004).

3. MOTIONS RELATING TO THE PARTICIPANTS

a. Motions for Substitution of Judges

In most state courts, cases are randomly assigned to a pool of judges who hear specialized types of cases, e.g., major felonies, misdemeanors and traffic, juvenile, family law, etc. If more than one judge is assigned to a particular call, the "luck of the draw" usually determines which member of the bench will hear a particular case. However, in smaller jurisdictions, there may be only one judge handling a specific type of case. Therefore, when a case is assigned to a judge who appears to favor the government in criminal cases or has had personal conflicts with the defense attorney, the attorney may file a **motion for substitution of judges.**

Motion for substitution of judges
A formal request to the court to substitute a different judge for the one that is currently assigned to the case.

The circumstances under which such a motion may be granted differ from one jurisdiction to the next. Some states provide a statutory right to change judges at least once, without cause. For instance, in Illinois both the prosecutor and the defendant can move for substitution of judges as a matter of right so long as the motion to substitute is made within ten days of the assignment of the judge to the case. When an Illinois defendant is charged with a Class X felony or a crime punishable by death or life imprisonment, the defendant may name two judges in the motion for substitution.[3] There is no provision in the federal courts for substitution of judges without cause.

Substitution for cause can be for any bias a judge may have in the case, such as an association with a party (family, friendship, or even stock ownership), having made vocal comments in the past on the topic at trial, etc. Ordinarily, the basis for the motion must be set forth with particularity and shown through affidavit or live testimony. The defendant bears the burden of proving bias. Generally, these motions are heard by a different judge since the judge from whom the defendant is seeking a change is not likely to believe that there is bias.

Recusal
The judge's voluntary removal of himself or herself from a case because of bias or the appearance of impropriety if he or she continues to preside over the case.

Sometimes judges will remove themselves from a case without a motion for substitution of judges having been filed. When judges determine on their own that they are biased, they announce that they are **recusing** themselves from the case. The Ethical Code for U.S. Judges (see accompanying box on page 294) lists various circumstances in which recusal is required.

It is important to note that if the motion to substitute judges is granted, the attorney filing the motion does not get to select the new judge. Rather, a random assignment is usually made from among the remaining judges hearing those kinds of cases. If a substitution takes place in a jurisdiction with no other available judges, a retired judge or one from a neighboring jurisdiction may be assigned to the case.

DISCUSSION QUESTIONS

1. Why should it make any difference who the judge is?
2. What factors does an attorney need to evaluate when deciding whether to seek a substitution for a judge?

---

[3]725 ILCS § 114-5.

Canon 3 C (1) of the Ethical Code for United States Judges

A judge shall disqualify himself or herself in a proceeding in which the judge's impartiality might reasonably be questioned, including but not limited to instances in which:

(a) the judge has a personal bias or prejudice concerning a party, or personal knowledge of disputed evidentiary facts concerning the proceeding;

(b) the judge served as a lawyer in the matter in controversy, or a lawyer with whom the judge previously practiced law served during such association as a lawyer concerning the matter, or the judge or lawyer has been a material witness;

(c) the judge knows that the judge, individually or as a fiduciary, or the judge's spouse or minor child residing in the judge's household, has a financial interest in the subject matter in controversy or in a party to the proceeding, or any other interest that could be affected substantially by the outcome of the proceeding;

(d) the judge or the judge's spouse, or a person related to either within the third degree of relationship, or the spouse of such a person is:

(i) a party to the proceeding, or an officer, director, or trustee of a party;

(ii) acting as a lawyer in the proceeding;

(iii) known by the judge to have an interest that could be substantially affected by the outcome of the proceeding; or

(iv) to the judge's knowledge likely to be a material witness in the proceeding;

(e) the judge has served in governmental employment and in that capacity participated as a judge (in a previous judicial position), counsel, advisor, or material witness concerning the proceeding or has expressed an opinion concerning the merits of the particular case in controversy.

The Code of Conduct for United States Judges was initially adopted by the Judicial Conference in 1973 and last revised in 2009. It can be found at http://www.uscourts.gov/Viewer.aspx?doc=/uscourts/RulesAndPolicies/conduct/Vol02A-Ch02.pdf.

b. Joinder and Severance

Rule 8 of the Federal Rules of Criminal Procedure provides for **joinder of offenses and defendants**. Specifically, joinder of offenses is proper when the offenses are "of the same or similar character or are based on the same act or transaction or on two or more acts or transactions connected together or constituting parts of a common scheme or plan."[4] Co-defendants may be charged in the same indictment if they have participated in the same series of acts constituting the offense. "Defendants may be charged in one or more counts together or separately and all of the defendants need not be charged in each count."[5]

An example of the joining of charges would be the government's charging one defendant with a series of separate drug trafficking offenses in a single indictment. A joinder of defendants would occur when the government tries

Joinder of offenses
A process whereby a defendant is tried on multiple charges at the same time.

Joinder of defendants
A process whereby individual defendants who are alleged to have committed the same offense(s) are tried together at the same time.

---

[4]FRCrP 8(a).
[5]FRCrP 8(b).

Motion to sever
A formal request to the court to require separate trials for individual defendants who are scheduled to be tried together, or for individual charges against a specific defendant.

several defendants who had all been charged with conspiracy to distribute illegal drugs, even though some of them had not also been charged with money laundering. Even if initial joinder is proper, Federal Rule of Criminal Procedure 14 authorizes a court to order separate trials of counts if it appears that a defendant is prejudiced by the joinder. In order to seek such an order the defense attorney would file a **motion to sever**. The same procedure is used in state court.

It is important to emphasize that the decision to sever is up to the discretion of the judge. Federal and state law generally favors joint trials of defendants who are charged together and only allows severance upon a showing of real prejudice to an individual defendant.[6] To be successful, a defense motion for severance must show that concerns for the defendant's right to a fair trial outweigh the goals of judicial economy and efficiency. Trial courts are thus reluctant to grant severance, and rarely do appellate courts overturn a lower court decision to refuse severance. One of the most successful grounds for seeking severance arises when a defendant wishes not to testify on all charges in a trial and chooses to claim a Fifth Amendment privilege on one or more counts.

APPLICATION EXERCISE

1. For the Brandon Turner Hypothetical Case, draft the body of a motion to sever Count I (sexual assault) from Count II (possession of crack cocaine with intent to deliver) and Count III (possession of a firearm in connection with a drug trafficking crime). Assume that the sexual assault allegedly occurred on January 1 of last year and that the two other charges were alleged to have taken place September 1 of last year. All occurrences took place in the state where your school is located. The charges were brought in a state court bill of indictment.

DISCUSSION QUESTIONS

After reviewing the facts of the Brandon Turner Hypothetical Case (see Intro-duction to Hypothetical Cases, p. xxxvii), answer the following questions:

3. If both Brandon Turner and Dennis Watterson (co-owner of the car driven by Turner at the time of arrest) were charged with possession of illicit drugs with the intent to distribute, how do you think a judge would rule on Turner's motion to sever the counts against him from the charges against Watterson?

---

[6]*Zafiro v. United States*, 506 U.S. 534, 537, 113 S. Ct. 933, 122 L. Ed. 2d 317 (1993).

4. If Turner was also charged with a sexual assault that allegedly occurred nine months prior to his drug arrest, how successful would a motion be to sever the sexual assault charge from the other charges?

c. Motion for a Competency Hearing

In addition to being important to the determination of a person's legal responsibility for criminal actions, the mental condition of the defendant is also relevant to the government's ability to put the accused on trial and to enter into a plea agreement. (See the discussion of the insanity defense in Chapter 8.) Therefore, if there are serious questions about the defendant's mental ability to adequately assist his or her attorneys in preparing a defense, the defense attorney should consider filing a **motion for a competency hearing**. In some jurisdictions, instead of seeking a competency hearing, the defense moves for a continuance on the ground that the defendant is incompetent.[7] In determining whether the motion should be allowed, the court conducts a competency hearing.

If the motion is granted, a special hearing will be held, prior to the trial, at which evidence will be presented relating to the defendant's ability to make informed decisions about trial strategy. The U.S. Supreme Court has defined competency in this context to mean the defendant has the ability to understand the charges and consult rationally with an attorney to aid in his or her own defense.[8] Customarily, the court relies on psychiatric expert testimony to decide whether the defendant should stand trial. Prior to the hearing, both the government and the defense will have the defendant undergo a psychological assessment. (See Exhibit 9.2 for an excerpt of the government psychiatrist's report on a defendant's competency to stand trial.) Although the statutes addressing competency vary from state to state, they generally reflect these same elements. A judge may also rule a defendant incompetent to stand trial even though neither side files a motion to determine competency.

Motion for a competency hearing
A formal request to the court to hold a hearing to determine if the defendant is competent to stand trial.

4. MOTIONS INVOLVING THE EVIDENCE

a. Motion to Suppress Evidence

One of the most common and perhaps most important pretrial motions filed by the defendant in a criminal case is a **motion to suppress**. This is a formal request to have the judge prohibit the use of certain kinds of evidence on the basis that it was collected in a manner that violated the defendant's constitutional or statutory rights. For example, if the evidence was seized during an illegal search or an incriminating statement was made under conditions that violated the defendant's

Motion to suppress
A request that the court prohibit specified material from being admitted into evidence at a trial because it was gathered in an illegal manner.

---

[7]For instance in Illinois, the judge may allow a motion for continuance based on the defendant's inability to stand trial due to physical or mental incompetency. 725 ILCS 5/114-4(b)(4).

[8]*Dusky v. United States*, 362 U.S. 402, 80 S. Ct. 788, 4 L. Ed. 2d 824 (1960).

Exhibit 9.2: Excerpt of Report of Defendant's Competency to Stand Trial

In 2007 after a jury trial, José Padilla, an alleged Al Qaeda operative, was found guilty of federal terrorism charges and sentenced to seventeen years in prison. Before trial, a federal judge determined that Padilla was competent. Defense counsel contended the defendant was suffering from post-traumatic stress syndrome and therefore incompetent to stand trial. In contrast, the government maintained that Padilla was not suffering from a severe mental disorder. The first page of the government doctor's report appears below.

U.S. DEPARTMENT OF JUSTICE
FEDERAL BUREAU OF PRISONS
FEDERAL DETENTION CENTER
MIAMI, FLORIDA

FORENSIC REPORT

DEFENDANT NAME: Padilla, Jose   REGISTRATION NUMBER: 20796-424
DATE OF BIRTH: October 18, 1970   DATE OF REPORT: February 5, 2007
CASE NUMBER: 04-60001-CR-COOKE/Brown
DATE OF EVALUATION: December, 2006 to February, 2007

IDENTIFICATION AND REASON FOR REFERRAL:

Mr. Jose Padilla, also known as (AKA) Jose Rivera, Julio Rodriguez, Jose Ortiz, Ibrahim, Abu Abdullah the Puerto Rican, and Abu Abdullah Al Mujahir, is a 36-year-old, Caucasian-Hispanic male who has been charged with the following offenses: Conspiracy to Murder, Kidnap, and Maim Persons in a Foreign Country; Conspiracy to Provide Material Support for Terrorists; and Material Support for Terrorists, all in violation of Title 18, United States Code (USC), Sections 956(a)(1), 371, 2339A(a) and 2.

On December 18, 2006, the Court ordered the Federal Bureau of Prisons (BOP) to examine the defendant and determine if he is suffering from a mental disease that would preclude his ability to participate in the court process or assist his attorney. The tests of competency involve determining whether or not the defendant is suffering from a mental illness that precludes his ability to understand the nature and consequences of the proceedings against him, and to properly assist in his own defense.

Mr. Padilla was admitted on January 5, 2006, to the Federal Detention Center (FDC), Miami, Florida as a pre-trial inmate, and designated on December 21, 2006, for the evaluation. This evaluation was conducted under the provisions of Title 18, USC Section 4241.

ASSESSMENT PROCEDURES:

During the initial interview, it was explained to Mr. Padilla that the purpose of the examination was to determine if he is competent to stand trial. He was also informed of the limits of confidentiality and advised that the usual client/doctor privilege would not be in effect. It was explained to him that anything he discussed with the examiner might be relayed to the Court. Mr. Padilla was informed that a written report summarizing test results and clinical findings would be provided to the Court, to his attorney, and to the prosecuting attorney. Mr. Padilla indicated that he understood; however, he indicated that he did not intend to cooperate with the parameters set forth by the examination procedures.

right to counsel, the **exclusionary rule**[9] prohibits this evidence from being used during the trial.

A **motion** *in limine* is another type of motion that is also designed to prohibit the admission of certain types of evidence, but since these motions aren't usually made until the pre-trial conference stage, we will wait until Chapter 11 to discuss them in greater detail.

A defense counsel's first step in determining whether a motion to suppress should be filed is to review the police reports and witness statements furnished by the prosecution in discovery. If there appears to be reason to suspect illegal conduct by law enforcement officers, the defense should immediately launch its own investigation. The next step is for counsel to develop a legal theory for suppressing the evidence. In jurisdictions where state constitutional law is not in lockstep with U.S. constitutional law, there may be dual standards for suppression. If a basis for suppressing the evidence is found, the defense attorney will prepare a written motion to suppress. It must contain specific facts evidencing a constitutional or statutory violation. Boilerplate language that simply asserts conclusions that the government violated statutory or constitutional law is not sufficient. Jurisdiction and/or local rules may require that the motion be supported by affidavit or verified under penalties of perjury. Unless the motion is sufficiently definite, specific, and not based on conjecture, the court may reject it without conducting an evidentiary hearing.

The components of the motion are: caption, introductory paragraph (citing specific statutory and constitutional provisions), body, prayer for relief, attorney's signature, and address block. The body of the motion may be written in narrative format or in numbered paragraphs, depending upon local custom. Oftentimes, the motion is accompanied by a memorandum of law, also known as points and authorities.

When the court conducts a suppression hearing, the defendant has the burden of presenting evidence to support the claim that the government acted illegally. Although the prosecutor generally has to prove by a preponderance of evidence that the government obtained evidence properly, there are a few limited situations in which the defendant has the burden of persuasion.[10] Because the rules of evidence are relaxed at suppression hearings, hearsay testimony is routinely considered by the judge. Although defendants testifying at suppression hearings do not waive their Fifth Amendment right against self-incrimination,[11] their testimony at the hearing may be used to impeach any inconsistent statements they may make at trial.

The success of a motion to suppress often has a great impact on plea bargaining because the exclusion of evidence often makes it more difficult for the prosecution to meet its burden of proving guilt beyond a reasonable doubt. This

Exclusionary rule
The doctrine that evidence obtained in violation of a defendant's constitutional rights cannot be used against the defendant in a criminal prosecution.

Motion *in limine*
A formal request to the court to prohibit mention of specified information because it is not sufficiently relevant to the issues being tried and would have a prejudicial effect on the jury.

---

[9]See discussion in Chapter 8, pp. 278–281.

[10]The defendant has the burden of persuasion on issues such as defendant's standing to assert a constitutional violation (*Rawlings v. Kentucky*, 448 U.S. 98, 104, 100 S. Ct. 2556; 65 L. Ed. 2d 633 (1980)) and due process challenges of suggestive identification of the defendant (*Stovall v. Denno*, 388 U.S. 293, 87 S. Ct. 1967, 18 L. Ed. 2d 1199 (1967)).

[11]*Simmons v. United States*, 390 U.S. 377, 394, 88 S. Ct. 967, 19 L. Ed. 2d 1247 (1968).

APPLICATION EXERCISE

2. After reviewing the facts of the *Turner* case (Hypothetical Case #2 referenced on page xxxvii and previous chapters), take note of the following additional facts, about the case:
   ■ Brandon Turner was pursued by the police for an alleged traffic violation. He traveled one block, left his car and entered a restaurant, and went into the public restroom for less than one minute. A baggie of what appeared to be cocaine was left on the front seat of the car. The police officer recovered a handgun from the restroom.

   After he was arrested for possession of cocaine and use of a firearm during a drug felony, Brandon Turner was taken to the local county jail. During processing, a local drug enforcement unit police officer took information without first advising Turner of his rights. Officer Manfred Chester obtained biographical information from him. Sgt. Hugh Ett, the supervising officer of the drug enforcement unit, then joined the conversation and began talking to Turner. The government's discovery included a police report that stated, in part, as follows:

   > The suspect was interviewed by Sergeant Hugh Ett after his arrest. He told Sgt. Ett that the reason he attempted to hide his gun and not the cocaine was because he had current firearms charges pending against him.

   After researching your jurisdiction's criminal code to locate the provision governing motions to suppress evidence, draft a motion to suppress evidence in Turner's case. Your draft should cite the applicable statutes and constitutional provisions. (Assume that the case is the first felony filed this year by the local prosecuting authority in the jurisdiction in which your school is located. The attorney for the defendant is Charles Hovey. Hovey's address and telephone numbers are those of your school.)

in turn may motivate the prosecution attorney to offer to reduce the charges or request a lighter sentence. Likewise, when the court denies a motion to suppress, a defendant may be more likely to enter into a plea agreement, knowing that the prosecutor will be able to use the contested evidence at the trial. On rare occasions, the prosecution may even dismiss the charges if the court suppresses key evidence. See Exhibit 9.3.

Exhibit 9.3: Dismissal of Charges After Evidence Is Suppressed

After the judge granted the defense motion for suppression of evidence, a Florida prosecutor dropped all twelve counts of possession of child pornography filed against singer R. Kelly. A Chicago jury acquitted him of similar charges several years later. The Florida prosecutor's notice of dismissal of the charges (*nolle prosequi*) is below.

IN THE CIRCUIT COURT OF THE TENTH JUDICIAL CIRCUIT
IN AND FOR POLK COUNTY, FLORIDA

STATE OF FLORIDA,   CASE NO.: 53-2003-CF-000196-01XX-XX
vs   AGENCY CASE # :
ROBERT S. KELLY

CHARGES:

POSSESSION OF CHILD PORNOGRAPHY
(TWELVE COUNTS)

NOTICE OF NOLLE PROSEQUI [NP]

BRADFORD H COPLEY as Assistant State Attorney, gives notice that the above-styled cause is hereby **TERMINATED AND DISMISSED** for the following principal reason, to-wit:

THE DEFENDANT IN THIS CASE IS CHARGED WITH TWELVE COUNTS OF POSSESSION OF CHILD PORNOGRAPHY BASED ON 12 PICTURES OF AN UNDERAGE GIRL INVOLVED IN SEXUAL SITUATIONS WITH THE DEFENDANT, MR. KELLY, AND WITH AN UNIDENTIFIED WOMAN. THESE PICTURES THAT WERE FOUND IN MR. KELLY'S POSSESSION HAVE BEEN SUPPRESSED BY THE COURT AND THE STATE CANNOT PROVE THIS CASE WITHOUT THE EVIDENCE.

CERTIFICATE OF SERVICE

I HEREBY CERTIFY that a true copy of the foregoing has been furnished to MR. RON TOWARD, POST OFFICE BOX 1772, BARTOW FL 33830-1772 AND MS DIANE BUERGER, 766 E MAIN STREET, BARTOW FL 33830-4832 this _19st_ day of March, 2004.

BRADFORD H COPLEY
Assistant State Attorney
Bar Number:0437662
Drawer SA. Box 9000
Bartow, Florida 33831

b. Motion *in Limine*

A motion *in limine* asks the court to limit the issues or evidence presented in the trial. For example, the defendant might ask the court to exclude certain inflammatory allegations that are not related to the charges against him, evidence of a prior conviction that occurred a long time ago, or hearsay statements contained in a police report.

5. MOTION TO DISMISS

Motion to dismiss
A formal request to the court to drop a pending criminal charge against the defendant.

A **motion to dismiss** asks the court to dismiss charges against the defendant. At the federal level, these motions fall under Rule 12, which authorizes parties to raise by motion any defense, objection, or request that the court can determine without a trial of the general issue. It can be used in criminal cases to seek dismissal of charges on the basis that there were procedural defects in the indictment or information.[12] States also authorize defendants to move for dismissal. For example, the Illinois Code of Criminal Procedure lists the following grounds to dismiss charges:

(1)   The defendant has not been placed on trial in compliance with [the Speedy Trial Act].
(2)   The prosecution of the offense is barred by [the statute of limitations or the defendant's double jeopardy rights were violated].
(3)   The defendant has received immunity from prosecution for the offense charged.
(4)   The indictment was returned by a Grand Jury which was improperly selected and which results in substantial injustice to the defendant.
(5)   The indictment was returned by a Grand Jury which acted contrary to [statute] and which results in substantial injustice to the defendant.
(6)   The court in which the charge has been filed does not have jurisdiction.
(7)   The county is an improper place of trial.
(8)   The charge does not state an offense.
(9)   The indictment is based solely upon the testimony of an incompetent witness.
(10) The defendant is misnamed in the charge and the misnomer results in substantial injustice to the defendant.
(11) [The indictment was not returned or a preliminary hearing was not held in a timely manner in accordance with statute.][13]

Statute of limitations
A law that sets forth a maximum time limit between the occurrence or discovery of a crime and the date at which formal charges must be filed.

Although grounds for dismissal vary from state to state, defendants typically can seek dismissal when the charges were filed after the **statute of limitations** expired or when the case is not brought to trial soon enough in violation of the state's **Speedy Trial Act**.

Speedy Trial Act
A law that sets forth a maximum time limit between the time that formal charges are filed and the start of a trial on those charges.

---

[12]FRCrP 12(a)(3)(B).
[13]725 ILSC 5/114-1.

6. MOTION FOR A CONTINUANCE

One of the most common pre-trial motions is a **motion for a continuance**. A **continuance** is the postponement of a scheduled court proceeding, such as a hearing or the trial. Lawyers typically request continuances either because they have a schedule conflict before a different judge or because they need more time to prepare for the scheduled proceeding. Other reasons could include the absence of key witnesses or important pieces of evidence. In rare cases, a judge might grant a continuance where there has recently been a great deal of prejudicial publicity in the local press[14] or when the defendant is not competent to stand trial.[15]

In some jurisdictions, motions for continuance must be accompanied by a supporting affidavit, whereas in others the attorney need only recite the basis for the delay in the motion itself. An example of a federal motion for continuance appears in Exhibit 9.4.

Many times, motions for continuance are unopposed. Sometimes this is due to the exercise of professional courtesy. An attorney may not object to the opposing counsel's request for more time to prepare knowing that he or she may ask for the same accommodation at a later time. Other times, an advocate, in choosing his or her battles, may not challenge a motion that the court will most likely allow. Finally, the attorney may need a continuance, as well.

In response to delays in bringing cases to trial, some states have adopted "fast-track" rules that sharply limit the ability of judges to grant continuances. However, a motion for continuance may be granted when necessitated by unforeseeable events, or where the court deems it necessary and prudent in the "interest of justice."

Under most speedy trial statutes, the granting of a defense motion for a continuance "stops the clock" on the time limits within which the defendant must be brought to trial. Even the delay resulting from a prosecution motion for continuance may be charged to the defense if the defendant fails to object to the motion.

> **Motion for continuance**
> A formal request to the court to postpone the date of an upcoming court proceeding.
>
> **Continuance**
> The postponement of a scheduled court proceeding, such as a hearing or the trial.

B. PLEA BARGAINING

Like it or not, our modern criminal justice system has become dependent upon the widespread use of plea bargaining. A **plea bargain** is an agreement between the prosecutor and the defendant in which the defendant pleads guilty to a criminal charge in exchange for a benefit in the eventual disposition of the case. Typical benefits received by defendants include the dismissal of one or more charges, the reduction of a charge to a lesser offense, and a lesser penalty as part of the sentence. While the numbers vary from one jurisdiction to the next, it is widely accepted that more than 90 percent of all felony convictions are the result of plea-bargaining

> **Plea bargain**
> An agreement whereby the defendant pleads guilty to a criminal charge in exchange for a reduction in the charges, the number of counts, or a lesser sentence.

---

[14]In cases where prejudicial press coverage is involved, attorneys might also file a motion for a change of venue. See pp. 401–403.

[15]For instance, in Illinois, the judge may allow a motion for continuance based on the defendant's inability to stand trial due to physical or mental incompetency. 725 ILCS 5/114-4(b)(4).

Exhibit 9.4: Motion for Continuance in Federal Court

Three weeks prior to his tax evasion trial, actor Wesley Snipes fired his legal team and moved to continue the case. In the order denying this motion, the federal judge stated, "This series of events would lead any reasonable person to suspect that the defendant's dismissal of able counsel is nothing more than a ploy designed to force a continuance of the trial." Here is the motion for continuance.

**UNITED STATES DISTRICT COURT
MIDDLE DISTRICT OF FLORIDA
OCALA DIVISION**

UNITED STATES,	)	
	)	
Plaintiff,	)	
	)	Case No. ___5:06-cr-00022-WTH-GRJ___
v.	)	
	)	
WESLEY SNIPES,	)	
	)	
Defendant.	)	

DEFENDANT'S EMERGENCY MOTION TO CONTINUE TRIAL

Wesley Trent Snipes ("Snipes"), the defendant in the above-captioned matter, by and through counsel of record, Robert G. Bernhoft, hereby respectfully moves this Court to continue the currently scheduled trial date of October 22, 2007, to give new counsel adequate time to prepare for trial. Snipes' fundamental right to the effective assistance of counsel compels a continuance to ensure a fair trial.

Grounds for this motion are two-fold. First, Snipes' concerns over Attorney Meachum's health, which were previously conveyed to the Court, may preclude Attorney Meachum's meaningful involvement in the trial at this time. Second, and most importantly, Snipes' former lead trial counsel, William R. Martin, was responsible for discovery review, pre-trial investigation, and motion practice. It is abundantly apparent, however, from the defense's discovery motion practice and this Court's recent orders relating thereto, that there are fundamental deficiencies in Mr. Martin's pre-trial preparation in this matter, involving lack of diligence in reviewing hundreds of thousands of pages of discovery documents that form the core of this case. It is also undisputed that Attorney Martin failed to timely raise critical issues of venue, and furthermore, failed to seek remedy for serious grand jury abuse of which he should have known with the exercise of reasonable diligence. The scope and prejudicial effect of this pervasive ineffective assistance of counsel only recently came to Snipes' attention, causing an irreparable breach in the attorney-client relationship with his former attorneys, and precipitating their discharge by Snipes, and the hiring of new trial counsel.

Of particular import here, these deficiencies have rendered Snipes wholly unprepared for trial. Consequently, Snipes' fundamental right to effective assistance of counsel is violated, and he is axiomatically prejudiced, without a continuance for new counsel to perform and discharge these tasks. *See Williams v. Taylor*, 529 U.S. 362, 371 (2000); *Wiggins v. Smith*, 539 U.S. 510

* * *

For the foregoing reasons, Snipes respectfully requests a trial continuance so that his new attorneys may obtain the voluminous discovery documents from former counsel; review, index, and incorporate those documents into necessary trial preparation; conduct the necessary pre-trial investigations; protect Mr. Snipes' right to raise all issues concerning venue, including those not previously raised and all issues improperly waived through ineffective assistance of counsel;

* * *

Respectfully submitted on October 3, 2007.

THE BERNHOFT LAW FIRM, S.C.
Attorneys for the Defendant

By: /s/ Robert G. Bernhoft
      Robert G. Bernhoft
      Wisconsin State Bar No. 1032777

207 East Buffalo Street, Suite 600
Milwaukee, Wisconsin 53202
(414) 276-3333 telephone
(414) 276-2822 facsimile
rgbernhoft@bernhoftlaw.com

* * *

At his jury trial, Snipes was convicted of three counts of willfully failing to file income tax returns.

agreements. The discussions and negotiations that are an essential part of the plea-bargaining process are often going on at the same time as the motions discussed above are being filed and argued in court. Therefore, the judge's rulings on these motions typically have a significant impact on the terms of any potential plea bargain.

1. THE BENEFITS OF PLEA BARGAINING

The extent to which the criminal justice system currently uses plea bargaining is probably best explained by noting the cost savings it provides for taxpayers. If everyone (not just the current 5 to 10 percent) had to go to trial, it would require roughly nine times as many judges, prosecutors, public defenders, jurors, bailiffs, court reporters, etc., and the costs of their salaries and fees would have to be paid by the taxpayers. Plea bargaining is a far more efficient and less expensive way of obtaining convictions and ensuring some degree of punishment.

Plea bargaining also reduces the lost productivity that businesses incur and the disruptions in the lives of witnesses and jurors. Both often have to take time off from their jobs and other activities to sit around the courthouse waiting to be called to testify or be selected to serve on a jury. If an individual is selected to serve on a jury, he or she may end up enduring hours (sometimes even weeks and months) of testimony and jury deliberations. In addition to the time witnesses have to spend waiting to be called and the time they spend actually testifying, they often have to spend hours meeting with attorneys and paralegals preparing to give their testimony. Victims are often forced to relive traumatic events and face emotionally unsettling, public examinations by attorneys. This is especially true in cases involving murder, rape, and sexual abuse of minors.

Another advantage of plea bargaining is that it replaces the uncertainty of the trial process with a guarantee that guilty defendants will be punished for their actions. Even when the prosecutor has strong evidence of guilt, it is always possible that key witnesses may not be available at the time of the trial or may change their testimony. Police departments have been known to lose or contaminate evidence, and there is always the possibility that at least one juror will have what he or she considers to be a "reasonable" doubt. Therefore, the prosecutor would rather settle for a guaranteed five-year sentence for manslaughter than risk having the defendant go free on a murder charge.

In some cases, plea bargains secure a defendant's assistance in building a case against other wrongdoers. For instance, Illinois Governor George Ryan's former chief of staff and campaign manager, Scott Fawell, agreed to a plea agreement that reduced the prison time for him and his fiancée in exchange for his testimony against his former boss. Fawell's testimony helped prosecutors convict the ex-governor of multiple counts of political corruption. Likewise, Tony Taylor pleaded guilty to his role in a brutal dog fighting ring and agreed to cooperate with the U.S. Attorney's Office in the prosecution of NFL star Michael Vick. Taylor received a two-month sentence for his role in the conspiracy, whereas Vick was sentenced to twenty-three months in prison.

There are also instances in which prosecutors may negotiate a plea bargain because they sincerely believe there are extenuating circumstances that make the mandatory minimum sentence for the crime more severe than it should be.

2. THE CRITICISMS OF PLEA BARGAINING

Although plea bargaining increases the probability that criminals will end up with a conviction on their record and at least some form of punishment for their crime, it also creates greater inequalities in the system and the possibility of innocent defendants being punished for crimes they did not commit.

One obvious inequity is that those who plead guilty typically end up with a lesser punishment than they would have had if they had been found guilty in a trial. By rewarding those who speed up the process by accepting a plea bargain, the system penalizes those who choose to use their constitutional right to a trial. Thus two people who commit the same crime receive very different punishments.

Even more disturbing is the fact that the plea-bargaining system sometimes pressures innocent men and women to plead guilty to crimes they did not commit. In general, prosecutors with weaker cases are more likely to offer better deals to defendants. Thus defendants with a stronger defense are forced to choose between risking years in prison (perhaps even death) by going to trial or pleading to a crime they didn't commit and serving a relatively short time in jail in order to avoid that risk. The situation is especially tough for indigent defendants who are represented by overworked public defenders and cannot afford bail while their case is pending. In these types of situations, accepting the plea bargain may mean immediate release from jail for time already served as opposed to remaining in jail for many more months waiting for the case to come to trial.

A **plea of convenience,** or "*Alford* plea," involves a situation in which a defendant pleads guilty to a crime the defendant did not commit in order to end the case in a way that the defendant perceives to be in his or her long-term best interests.[16] Authorities are divided as to whether this practice is appropriate. Florida Criminal Procedure expressly recognizes that some defendants plead guilty to crimes they did not commit. Rule 3.172(d) provides:

> Before the trial judge accepts a guilty or nolo contendere plea, the judge must determine that the defendant either (1) acknowledges his or her guilt or (2) acknowledges that he or she feels the plea to be in his or her best interest, while maintaining his or her innocence.

Plea of convenience
A guilty plea for a crime the defendant does not acknowledge committing that is made in order to conclude the case on terms the defendant feels are in his or her best interest.

In contrast, the form used in Minnesota courts to petition for approval of a plea bargain requires the defendant to acknowledge commission of the crime. Exhibit 9.5 displays an example of this petition.

Although he had voluntarily agreed to the plea agreement shown in Exhibit 9.5, Senator Craig later expressed regrets when publicity about the plea had a negative effect on his political career. On the other hand, when "Pee-wee Herman" actor Paul Reubens entered into a plea agreement in a case in which he was charged with exposure of a sexual organ, his attorney declared: "Mr. Reubens continues to insist upon his innocence—it was a plea of convenience. . . . It was a fair resolution for everyone concerned."[17]

---

[16] This type of plea was approved by the U.S. Supreme Court in *North Carolina v. Alford,* 400 U.S. 25, 91 S. Ct. 160, 27 L. Ed. 2d 162 (1970). A defendant asserting an *Alford* plea maintains his or her innocence but admits there is sufficient evidence for a conviction.

[17] *Pee-wee's Big Plea Bargain,* The Free-Lance Star A3 (Nov. 8, 1991). Under the terms of the plea, Reubens agreed to pay a $50 fine plus $85 court costs and produce and pay for a nationally distributed antidrug commercial to fulfill a seventy-five-hour community service requirement. The court placed him on six months of court supervision.

Exhibit 9.5: State Court Plea Agreement

Idaho U.S. Senator Larry Craig was arrested and charged with disorderly conduct arising out of an incident in a Minneapolis–St. Paul International Airport bathroom. Craig petitioned for approval of a written plea agreement under which he pleaded guilty, was fined $1,000, and sentenced to ten days in the Hennepin County lockup with jail time stayed so long as he did not commit similar acts within one year. This is his petition to enter plea of guilty–misdemeanor.

FILED

AUG 6 2007

STATE OF MINNESOTA   DISTRICT COURT

COUNTY OF HENNEPIN   HENNEPIN COUNTY DISTRICT FOURTH JUDICIAL DISTRICT

COURT DEPUTY

Case No. <u>07043231</u>

State of Minnesota.

          Plaintiff,   **PETITION TO ENTER**

vs   **PLEA OF GUILTY-MISDEMEANOR**

Larry Edwin Craig,

          Defendant.

I, Larry Edwin Craig, am the defendant in the above action. My date of birth is July 20, 1945 I state to the court that:

1. I have reviewed the arrest report and/or complaint relating to the charges against me.

2. I understand the charge(s) made against me in this case, which are: Disorderly Conduct, pursuant to Minn. Stat. § 609 72 subd. 1(3), a Misdemeanor; and Interference with Privacy, pursuant to Minn. Stat. § 609.746, subd. 1(c), a Gross Misdemeanor. I am pleading guilty to the offense of Disorderly Conduct as a Misdemeanor.

3. I am pleading guilty to the charge of Disorderly Conduct as alleged because on June 11, 2007, within the property or jurisdiction of the Metropolitan Airports Commission. Hennepin County, specifically in the restroom of the North Star Crossing in the Lindbergh Terminal, I did the following: Engaged in conduct which I knew or should have known tended to arouse alarm or resentment of others which conduct was physical (versus verbal) in nature.

4. I understand that the court will not accept a plea of guilty from anyone who claims to be innocent.

5. I now make no claim that I am innocent of the charge to which I am entering a plea of guilty.

                                                  _____
                                                  Larry Edwin Craig, Defendant

6.   I understand that I am entering a plea of guilty to a misdemeanor charge for which the maximum sentence is a $1000.00 fine and/or 90 days imprisonment.

7   I am/am not represented by an attorney, whose name is

8   I and/or my attorney have reviewed the rights I will be waiving by entering this plea.

9   I understand that I have the following constitutional rights which I knowingly voluntarily and intelligently give up (waive) by entering this plea of guilty:

   a.   the right to a trial, to the court (judge only) or to a jury of six (6) members, at which I am presumed innocent until proven guilty beyond a reasonable doubt, and in which all jurors in a jury trial must agree I am guilty before the jury could find me guilty;
   b.   the right to confront and cross-examine all witnesses against me;
   c.   the right to remain silent or to testify for myself;
   d.   the right to subpoena witnesses to appear on my behalf;
   e.   the right to a pretrial hearing to contest the admissibility of evidence obtained from a search or seizure and/or information I offered to the police in the form of written or oral statement.

10.   Understanding the above I am entering my plea of guilty freely and voluntarily and without any promises except as noted in number 11 below.

11   I am entering my plea of guilty based on the following plea agreement with the prosecutor. Plead guilty to the charge of Disorderly Conduct, pursuant to Minn. Stat. § 609.72, subd. 1(3); sentence is 10 days of jail time and a fine of $1000.00; 10 days of jail and $500.00 of the fine are stayed for 1 year on the conditions that Larry Edwin Craig does not commit any same or similar offenses, Larry Edwin Craig pays the unstayed fine amount of $500.00, plus the surcharge of $75.00 for a total of $575.00.

12   I understand that if the court does not accept any agreement stated in number 11 above, I have the right to withdraw my plea of guilty and have a trial.

13   I am not entering this plea in person. As this plea is being entered via mail or through my attorney I understand that I am giving up my right to be present at the time of sentencing and to exercise my right to speak on my own behalf by making whatever statement or presenting whatever evidence that I wish. If I am not present when this plea is accepted by the court I understand that I am voluntarily waiving (giving up) my right to be present and consent to sentencing in my absence. I understand that the court may impose a sentence that includes probation and I

Larry Edwin Craig, Defendant

3. THE PLEA-BARGAINING PROCESS

a. Timing

In state court, the plea-bargaining process can take place anytime between the arraignment and the start of the trial. In traffic cases, many plea agreements are made at the defendant's first court appearance. Even some misdemeanor cases are resolved by plea bargain at the first appearance. However, in more serious cases, plea negotiations do not usually take place until the government produces discovery and pre-trial conferences are held.

In federal court, plea agreements may be reached at any time during an investigation or prosecution of a case. This means that some defendants reach agreements with the government before charges are even filed against them. Ordinarily, these deals involve the defendant's promise to cooperate in the investigation and prosecution of other persons for criminal activity.

b. Participants

Prosecutors are generally expected to begin the plea-bargaining process by "making an offer." This offer may involve reducing the charges or agreeing to recommend a lighter sentence than would normally be given for the offense in question. For example, the prosecutor can offer to settle for a guilty plea on a robbery charge where the original charge was for the more serious offense of armed robbery. Or, the prosecutor can offer to drop related counts. So, if the original indictment included three counts of burglary, the prosecutor might agree to drop two of them in return for a guilty plea to the third. When it comes to sentencing, the prosecutor can recommend the minimum authorized sentence, probation, or suspending the sentence. Once the prosecutor puts an initial offer "on the table," negotiations involve a series of counteroffers that go on until an agreement is reached between the two attorneys. If an agreement is reached, it will then be up to the defendant and the judge to decide if it will be formalized and implemented.

After having negotiated the best possible deal, the defense attorney must present the offer to the client. The client must then decide whether he or she wants to accept the deal or roll the dice on the outcome of a trial. As mentioned in our discussion of the negative aspects of plea bargaining, there are significant pressures on defendants to accept these bargains, even when they may not have committed the crimes with which they are being charged.

The other key participant in the plea-bargaining process is the judge. The nature of the judge's involvement varies widely among different jurisdictions, though in most the plea agreement must be entered into the record and the judge can reject agreements that are deemed to be against the public interest. In some localities, the defense attorney and the prosecutor can meet with the judge prior to the formal presentation of a plea bargain to find out whether the court will approve the tentative plea agreement.[18] In federal court, the judge is not

---

[18]For example, Illinois Supreme Court Rule 402(d)(2).

permitted to participate in the plea-bargaining discussions.[19] You will need to check your jurisdiction's rules to determine what the practices in your locale are.

4. TYPES OF DEALS

There are three major types of plea agreements: charge bargaining, count bargaining, and sentence bargaining. **Charge bargaining** occurs when the prosecution agrees to dismiss the crime charged, in exchange for the defendant's plea of guilty to a less serious offense. For instance, a defendant might plead guilty to voluntary manslaughter in return for the prosecutor's agreement to dismiss a first degree homicide charge. Although charge bargaining is common in state courts, it is not typically used in federal court.[20]

Count bargaining occurs when the defendant agrees to plead guilty to one or more of the counts for which he or she is charged in exchange for the government's agreement to dismiss the remaining counts charged. For example, where someone is charged with three separate counts of fraud (each involving a different transaction) the prosecutor might agree to dismiss two of the counts in return for the defendant pleading guilty to the third.

In federal court, these agreements are governed by Department of Justice Policy and the Federal Sentencing Guidelines.[21] The federal prosecutor must pursue the most serious, readily provable charge consistent with the nature and extent of the defendant's criminal conduct.[22] Only under limited circumstances may the prosecutor dismiss the most serious provable charge and allow a lesser charge to remain.

The third type of plea negotiations is **sentence bargaining**, in which the defendant pleads guilty in exchange for a lighter sentence. It saves the prosecution the necessity of going through a trial and proving its case. It provides the defendant with an opportunity for a lighter sentence.

Sentencing bargaining can take a number of forms. First, the parties negotiate an agreed-upon sentence. This sentence may take the form of an agreed range of sentences or an agreed-upon sentencing guideline range. Under this scenario, the parties set a "floor" and a "ceiling" defining the perimeters of the eventual sentence. For example, the parties can enter an agreement limiting the sentence to thirty-six to forty-eight months of incarceration. If the court does not accept the agreement, the defendant can withdraw the plea of guilty.[23] Another variation of sentence bargaining focuses on the prosecutor's sentencing recommendation. The prosecutor can agree not to oppose the defendant's request for a particular sentence or to make no recommendation. However, with this type of agreement, the defendant is not permitted to withdraw the plea of guilty if the court imposes a sentence that is not acceptable to the defendant.

Charge bargaining
A plea bargain in which the prosecution dismisses a more serious charge in exchange for the defendant's pleading guilty to a lesser offense.

Count bargaining
A plea bargain in which the prosecution drops one or more related charges in exchange for the defendant's pleading guilty to at least one of the counts originally charged.

Sentence bargaining
A plea bargain in which the defendant enters a plea of guilty in exchange for a lighter sentence.

---

[19]FRCrP 11(c)(1).

[20]FRCrP 11(c)(1) lists the possible approaches the government can take in entering plea agreements. Reduction of charges to less serious offenses is not listed.

[21]The Federal Sentencing Guidelines will be discussed in detail in Chapter 13.

[22]Department of Justice U.S. Attorneys Manual § 9-27.430. *http://www.justice.gov/usao/eousa/foia_reading_room/usam/title9/27mcrm.htm#9-27.430*

[23]FRCrP 11(d)(2)(A).

Open plea

A plea agreement under which the defendant pleads guilty and the judge determines the sentence without a joint recommendation from the parties.

Oftentimes, the negotiated agreement is a combination of charge, count, and/or sentence bargaining. When a count bargain or a charge bargain is not accompanied by a sentence bargain, the guilty plea is known as an **open plea**.[24] In this situation, the judge decides the appropriate sentence without a joint recommendation from the parties.

5. FORMALIZING THE PLEA

When the prosecutor makes an offer, the defense attorney must convey it to the defendant. In doing so, the defense attorney must provide sufficient information for the client to be able to make an intelligent, informed decision. The decision should be based on the potential evidence that both sides will present at trial, the applicable sentencing statutes and/or guidelines, and the sentences imposed historically by the judge. Defense paralegals may be asked to research sentences ordered in cases similar to the client's case.[25]

In federal court, the Assistant U.S. Attorney typically prepares a written plea agreement. Among other things, this document includes the defendant's voluntary waiver of constitutional rights, a plea of guilty to specified charge(s), a recitation of the proposed penalties for such charge(s), the factual basis for the charge(s), and an acceptance of the agreement by the government, defendant, defense counsel, and the court. The practice in state court varies.

Once a bargain is struck, the plea agreement is presented by the prosecution and defense to the judge in open court. At that time, the prosecutor gives the factual basis for the plea. This can either be accomplished through the defendant's admissions in open court or the prosecutor's proffer of the evidence the government expects to present if the case goes to trial. Depending on the jurisdiction, either the prosecutor or the judge will question the defendant to make sure he or she is entering into the plea agreement knowingly and voluntarily. This questioning process is often referred to as a **plea colloquy**. In most state courts, this examination is recorded by a court reporter and documented by a formal order or docket entry. Even in misdemeanor and traffic cases, defendants are examined to assure that they are freely and consciously entering into the plea bargain.

Plea colloquy

The in-court examination of a criminal defendant entering a guilty plea to determine whether the defendant is entering the plea intelligently, knowingly, and voluntarily.

Although it appears tedious, this line of questioning is typical of proceedings on the presentation of pleas. During the colloquy, the court must advise the defendant of the nature of the charge; the potential penalties that might result from the plea, including any mandatory minimum sentence; and the constitutional rights the defendant is waiving by pleading guilty. Exhibit 9.6 is an example of a plea colloquy. In 1977, acclaimed film director Roman Polanski, charged with unlawful sexual intercourse, entered into a plea bargain with the Los Angeles District Attorney's Office. In the passages included in this exhibit,

---

[24]Defendants can also make a "blind plea" in which they plead guilty without any promise of leniency from the prosecution.

[25]Although some courthouses may provide this type of information online, most of the time your investigation must take place at the courthouse.

there are questions designed to make sure the defendant intelligently, knowingly, and voluntarily entered into the plea agreement.[26]

Note that the plea agreement reached in the Polanski case did not cover the nature of the sentence. After presentation of the plea, but before sentencing,

---

Exhibit 9.6: Excerpts from Plea Colloquy in the Roman Polanski Case

"[Prosecutor]: Do you realize that by pleading guilty, you give up your right to a jury trial?

[Defendant]: Yes.

[Prosecutor]: Do you have any questions about your right to a jury trial?

[Defendant]: No.

[Prosecutor]: Do you then give up your right to a jury trial?

[Defendant]: Yes.

[Prosecutor]: Do you realize that by pleading guilty, you give up your right to be confronted by the witnesses against you?

[Defendant]: Yes.

[Prosecutor]: Do you realize that by pleading guilty, you give up your right of cross examination; to have your attorney ask those witnesses questions?

[Defendant]: Yes.

[Prosecutor]: Do you give up your right to confrontation and your right to cross examination of the witnesses?

[Defendant]: Yes.

[Prosecutor]: Do you know that you have a right against self-incrimination? That is, the right to remain silent, and to require the prosecution to prove a case against you beyond a reasonable doubt?

[Defendant]: Yes.

[Prosecutor]: Do you realize that by pleading guilty, you give up this right and admit the commission of the crime charged?

[Defendant]: Yes.

[Prosecutor]: Do you have any questions about your right to remain silent?

[Defendant]: No.

[Prosecutor]: Do you give up your privilege against self-incrimination?

[Defendant]: Yes.

* * *

---

[26]*People of the State of California v. Roman Raymond Polanski*, Case No. A-334139, August 8, 1977 Report of Proceedings, 8-15.

[Prosecutor]: Mr. Polanski, before you can plead guilty, you have to understand the charges against you, and there must be a factual basis for your plea.

[Defendant]: Yes.

[Prosecutor]: Do you know what the charges are against you?

[Defendant]: Yes.

[Prosecutor]: And what is the nature of the charge to which you want to plead guilty?

[Defendant]: Unlawful Sexual Intercourse.

[Prosecutor]: What does the person have to do to be guilty of that charge?

[Defendant]: He has to—the person has to have sexual intercourse with the female person not his wife, under the age of 18.

[Prosecutor]: Are you in fact guilty of this charge?

[Defendant]: Yes.

[Prosecutor]: What did you do in this case?

[Defendant]: I had sexual intercourse with a female person not my wife, under the age of 18.

[Prosecutor]: And was this female person the complaining witness in this case?

[Defendant]: That's correct.

[Prosecutor]: And was it in the evening at 12850 Mulholland Drive?

[Defendant]: Mulholland Drive, yes.

[Prosecutor]: And that was in Los Angeles County?

[Defendant]: Yes.

[Prosecutor]: Mr. Polanski, before you can plead guilty, you must understand the possible direct consequences of your plea. Do you understand you are pleading guilty to a felony?

[Defendant]: Yes.

[Prosecutor]: What is the maximum sentence for unlawful sexual intercourse?

[Defendant]: It's one to fifteen–twenty years in State Prison.

[Prosecutor]: Do you understand it is also possible that you could be placed on probation, with or without being required to serve up to one year in the County Jail?

[Defendant]: Yes.

[Prosecutor]: . . . Mr. Polanski, who do you believe will decide what your sentence will be in this matter?

[The Defendant]: The Judge.

[The Prosecutor]: Who do you think will decide whether or not you will get probation?

[Defendant]: The Judge.

[Prosecutor]: Who do you think will determine whether the sentence will be a felony or a misdemeanor?

[Defendant]: The Judge.

* * *

[Prosecutor]: Do you understand that the Judge has not made any decision?

[Defendant]: Yes.

* * *

> *[Prosecutor]:* Has anyone threatened you or threatened any one near and dear to you, in order to get you to plead guilty?
>
> *[Defendant]:* No.
>
> *[Prosecutor]:* The District Attorney will make a motion to dismiss the remaining pending charges after sentencing. Other than that promise, has anyone made any promises to you, such as a lesser sentence or probation, or reward? Immunity? A Court recommendation to the Immigration and Naturalization Service, or anything else, in order to get you to plead guilty?
>
> *[Defendant]:* No.
>
> *[Prosecutor]:* Do you have any questions about your plea?
>
> *[Defendant]:* No.
>
> *[Prosecutor]:* Are you pleading guilty freely and voluntarily?
>
> *[Defendant]:* Yes."

Polanski reportedly learned that the judge was going to send him to prison. He then fled to Europe to escape incarceration. Thirty-two years later, Polanski was taken into custody in Switzerland on an international arrest warrant. In 2010, the California Superior Court ruled that he must return to the United States to be sentenced.

APPLICATION EXERCISE

3. After reviewing the information you have been given on the Cook Hypothetical Case (Introduction to Hypothetical Cases, p. xxxvii), take note of the following additional information

   Before trial, defense attorney Charles Hovey asked the prosecutor for an offer to conclude the case that did not include incarceration. In support of this position, he pointed out that:

   - The area lacked overhead lighting, making it difficult for any driver to see a bicyclist at 10 P.M.
   - The bicyclist was difficult to see for a number of reasons. First, she was wearing non-reflective clothes. Next, the bicycle did not have a headlamp or rear taillights as required under state law. Finally, the bike itself was black.
   - The bicyclist was riding two feet into the lane of traffic even though there was a two-foot-wide paved shoulder she could have used.
   - The bicyclist was legally intoxicated as shown by a toxicology report reflecting a blood alcohol concentration greater than 0.08.

> ■ The accident reconstruction report indicated that the Cook vehicle was traveling no less than 38 mph in a 45 mph zone and did not conclude that the speed of the Cook vehicle was a contributing cause to the fatality.

Several days later, Hovey received the written offer shown in Exhibit 9.7.

   a. What steps need to be taken to analyze the State's offer?
   b. What type of plea bargain is the State offering to the defendant? Explain your answer.
   c. Based upon defense counsel's original argument and the prosecutor's offer, what disposition do you think is just for the defendant? What is a just result for the prosecutor? What is just for the victim's family? What is just for the public at large?
   d. What do you think the prosecutor's offer would be if the judge had already ruled on the motion to suppress all statements Cook made to the police following his arrest?
   e. What, in your opinion, would be a just outcome in terms of charges Cook would plead guilty to and the type of sentence to be served?

Exhibit 9.7: Prosecution Offer of a Plea Agreement

STATE'S ATTORNEY
1857 Bloomington Street
Normal, Illinois 61761

Mr. Charles Hovey
Attorney at Law
1857 Bone Street
Normal, IL 61761

In re: People v. Bud Cook

Dear Charlie:

   I have reviewed the file, and am prepared to make you the following offer. If your client pleads guilty to either count of reckless homicide, I will offer 5 years in the Illinois Department of Corrections. As you are aware, this is a class 2 felony carrying a prison term of 3-14 years.

```
    If your client is unwilling to accept the above offer, as an alterna-
tive, I will agree to "cap" a sentencing recommendation at 7 years in
exchange for an open plea to one count of reckless homicide.

    If you have questions, please call me.


                                            Yours truly,

                                            Mark O. Union, ASA
```

6. ENFORCEMENT OF PLEA BARGAINS

Because plea bargains are treated as enforceable contracts, it is important to get the terms in writing and documented in court records. If a plea agreement includes provisions requiring the defendant to cooperate in an ongoing investigation or testify against a co-defendant, the prosecutor can cancel the agreement if the defendant does not fulfill these promises. If the prosecutor fails to follow through on his or her promises, the defendant may be able to either withdraw the guilty plea or have the judge force the prosecutor to comply with its terms. Read *Santobello v. New York* to see how the U.S. Supreme Court has approached these issues.

Santobello v. New York
Supreme Court of the United States
404 U.S. 257 (1971)

MR. CHIEF JUSTICE BURGER delivered the opinion of the Court (joined by JUSTICES DOUGLAS, WHITE, and BLACKMUN).

We granted certiorari in this case to determine whether the State's failure to keep a commitment concerning the sentence recommendation on a guilty plea required a new trial.

The facts are not in dispute. The State of New York indicted petitioner in 1969 on two felony counts, Promoting Gambling in the First Degree, and Possession of Gambling Records in the First Degree, N.Y. Penal Law § § 225.10, 225.20. Petitioner first entered a plea of not guilty to both counts. After negotiations, the Assistant District Attorney in charge of the case agreed to permit petitioner to plead guilty to a lesser-included offense, Possession of Gambling Records in the Second Degree, N.Y. Penal Law § 225.15, conviction of which would carry a maximum prison sentence of one year. The prosecutor agreed to make no recommendation as to the sentence.

On June 16, 1969, petitioner accordingly withdrew his plea of not guilty and entered a plea of guilty to the lesser charge. Petitioner represented to the sentencing judge that the plea was voluntary and that the facts of the case, as described by the Assistant District Attorney, were true. The court accepted the plea and set a date for sentencing. A series of delays followed, owing primarily to the absence of a pre-sentence report, so that by September 23, 1969, petitioner had still not been sentenced. By that date petitioner acquired new defense counsel.

Petitioner's new counsel moved immediately to withdraw the guilty plea. In an accompanying affidavit, petitioner alleged that he did not know at the time of his plea that crucial evidence against him had been obtained as a result of an illegal search. The accuracy of this affidavit is subject to challenge since petitioner had filed and withdrawn a motion to suppress, before pleading guilty. In addition to his motion to withdraw his guilty plea, petitioner renewed the motion to suppress and filed a motion to inspect the grand jury minutes.

These three motions in turn caused further delay until November 26, 1969, when the court denied all three and set January 9, 1970, as the date for sentencing. On January 9 petitioner appeared before a different judge, the judge who had presided over the case to this juncture having retired. Petitioner renewed his motions, and the court again rejected them. The court then turned to consideration of the sentence.

At this appearance, another prosecutor had replaced the prosecutor who had negotiated the plea. The new prosecutor recommended the maximum one-year sentence. In making this recommendation, he cited petitioner's criminal record and alleged links with organized crime. Defense counsel immediately objected on the ground that the State had promised petitioner before the plea was entered that there would be no sentence recommendation by the prosecution. He sought to adjourn the sentence hearing in order to have time to prepare proof of the first prosecutor's promise. The second prosecutor, apparently ignorant of his colleague's commitment, argued that there was nothing in the record to support petitioner's claim of a promise, but the State, in subsequent proceedings, has not contested that such a promise was made.

The sentencing judge ended discussion, with the following statement, quoting extensively from the presentence report:

Mr. Aronstein [Defense Counsel], I am not at all influenced by what the District Attorney says, so that there is no need to adjourn the sentence, and there is no need to have any testimony. It doesn't make a particle of difference what the District Attorney says he will do, or what he doesn't do.

I have here, Mr. Aronstein, a probation report. I have here a history of a long, long serious criminal record. I have here a picture of the life history of this man. . . .

'He is unamenable to supervision in the community. He is a professional criminal.' This is in quotes. 'And a recidivist. Institutionalization—'; that means, in plain language, just putting him away, 'is the only means of halting his anti-social activities,' and protecting you, your family, me, my family, protecting society. 'Institutionalization.' Plain language, put him behind bars.

Under the plea, I can only send him to the New York City Correctional Institution for men for one year, which I am hereby doing.

The judge then imposed the maximum sentence of one year.

Petitioner sought and obtained a certificate of reasonable doubt and was admitted to bail pending an appeal. The Supreme Court of the State of New York, Appellate Division, First Department, unanimously affirmed petitioner's conviction, 35 App. Div. 2d 1084, 316 N. Y. S. 2d 194 (1970), and petitioner was denied leave to appeal to the New York Court of Appeals. Petitioner then sought certiorari in this Court. Mr. Justice Harlan granted bail pending our disposition of the case.

This record represents another example of an unfortunate lapse in orderly prosecutorial procedures, in part, no doubt, because of the enormous increase in the workload of the often understaffed prosecutor's offices. The heavy workload may well explain these episodes, but it does not excuse them. The disposition of criminal charges by agreement between the prosecutor and the accused, sometimes loosely called "plea bargaining," is an essential component of the administration of justice. Properly administered, it is to be encouraged. If every criminal charge were subjected to a full-scale trial, the States and the Federal Government would need to multiply by many times the number of judges and court facilities. Disposition of charges after plea discussions is not only an essential part of the process but a highly desirable part for many reasons. It leads to prompt and largely final disposition of most criminal cases; it avoids much of the corrosive impact of enforced idleness during pretrial confinement for those who are denied release pending trial; it protects the public from those accused persons who are prone to continue criminal conduct even while on pretrial release; and, by shortening the time between charge and disposition, it enhances whatever may be the rehabilitative prospects of the guilty when they are ultimately imprisoned. See *Brady v. United States*, 397 U.S. 742, 751-752 (1970).

However, all of these considerations presuppose fairness in securing agreement between an accused and a prosecutor. It is now clear, for example, that the accused pleading guilty must be counseled, absent a waiver. *Moore v. Michigan*, 355 U.S. 155 (1957). Fed. Rule Crim. Proc. 11, governing pleas in federal courts, now makes clear that the sentencing judge must develop, *on the record*, the factual basis for the plea, as, for example, by having the accused describe the conduct that gave rise to the charge. The plea must, of course, be voluntary and knowing and if it was induced by promises, the essence of those promises must in some way be made known. There is, of course, no absolute right to have a guilty plea accepted. *Lynch v. Overholser*, 369 U.S. 705, 719 (1962); Fed. Rule Crim. Proc. 11. A court may reject a plea in exercise of sound judicial discretion.

This phase of the process of criminal justice, and the adjudicative element inherent in accepting a plea of guilty, must be attended by safeguards to insure the defendant what is reasonably due in the circumstances. Those circumstances will vary, but a constant factor is that when a plea rests in any significant degree on a promise or agreement of the prosecutor, so that it can be said to be part of the inducement or consideration, such promise must be fulfilled.

On this record, petitioner "bargained" and negotiated for a particular plea in order to secure dismissal of more serious charges, but also on condition that no sentence recommendation would be made by the prosecutor. It is now conceded that the promise to abstain from a recommendation was made, and at this stage the prosecution is not in a good position to argue that its inadvertent breach of agreement is immaterial. The staff lawyers in a prosecutor's office have the burden of "letting the left hand know what the right hand is doing" or has done. That the breach of agreement was inadvertent does not lessen its impact.

We need not reach the question whether the sentencing judge would or would not have been influenced had he known all the details of the negotiations for the plea. He stated that the prosecutor's recommendation did not influence him and we have no reason to doubt that. Nevertheless, we conclude that the interests of justice and appropriate recognition of the duties of the prosecution in relation to promises made in the negotiation of pleas of guilty will be best served by remanding the case to the state courts for further consideration. The ultimate relief to which petitioner is entitled we leave to the discretion of the state court, which is in a better position to decide whether the circumstances of this case require only that there be specific performance of the agreement on the plea, in which case petitioner should be resentenced by a different judge, or whether, in the view of the state court, the circumstances require granting the relief sought by petitioner, *i.e.*, the opportunity to withdraw his plea of guilty. [If the state court decides to allow withdrawal of the plea, the petitioner will, of course, plead anew to the original charge on two felony counts.] We emphasize that this is in no sense to question the fairness of the sentencing judge; the fault here rests on the prosecutor, not on the sentencing judge.

The judgment is vacated and the case is remanded for reconsideration not inconsistent with this opinion.

MR JUSTICE DOUGLAS, concurring.

I join the opinion of the Court and add only a word. I agree both with THE CHIEF JUSTICE and with MR. JUSTICE MARSHALL that New York did not keep its "plea bargain" with petitioner and that it is no excuse for the default merely because a member of the prosecutor's staff who was not a party to the "plea bargain" was in charge of the case when it came before the New York court. The staff of the prosecution is a unit and each member must be presumed to know the commitments made by any other member. . . .

However important plea bargaining may be in the administration of criminal justice, our opinions have established that a guilty plea is a serious and sobering occasion inasmuch as it constitutes a waiver of the fundamental rights to a jury trial, *Duncan v. Louisiana*, 391 U.S. 145, to confront one's accusers, *Pointer v. Texas*, 380 U.S. 400, to present witnesses in one's defense, *Washington v. Texas*, 388 U.S. 14, to remain silent, *Malloy v. Hogan*, 378 U.S. 1, and to be convicted by proof beyond all reasonable doubt, *In re Winship*, 397 U.S. 358. Since *Kercheval v. United States*, 274 U.S. 220, this Court has recognized that "unfairly obtained" guilty pleas in the federal courts ought to be vacated. . . .

State convictions founded upon coerced or unfairly induced guilty pleas have also received increased scrutiny as more fundamental rights have been applied to the States. After *Powell v. Alabama*, 287 U.S. 45, the Court held that a state defendant was entitled to a lawyer's assistance in choosing whether to plead guilty. *Williams v. Kaiser*, 323 U.S. 471. In *Herman v. Claudy*, 350 U.S. 116, federal habeas corpus was held to lie where a lawyerless and uneducated state prisoner had pleaded guilty to numerous and complex robbery charges. And, a guilty plea obtained without the advice of counsel may not be admitted at a subsequent state prosecution. *White v. Maryland*, 373 U.S. 59. Thus, while plea bargaining is not *per se* unconstitutional, *North Carolina v. Alford*, 400 U.S. 25, 37-38, *Shelton v. United States*, 242 F.2d 101, aff'd *en banc*, 246 F.2d 571 (CA5 1957), a guilty plea is rendered voidable by threatening physical harm, *Waley v. Johnston, supra*, threatening to use false testimony, *ibid.*, threatening to bring additional prosecutions, *Machibroda v. United States, supra*, or by failing to inform a defendant of his right of counsel, *Walker v. Johnston, supra*. Under these circumstances it is clear that a guilty plea must be vacated.

But it is also clear that a prosecutor's promise may deprive a guilty plea of the "character of a voluntary act." *Machibroda v. United States, supra*, at 493. Cf. *Bram v. United States*, 168 U.S. 532, 542-543. The decisions of this Court have not spelled out what sorts of promises by prosecutors tend to be coercive, but in order to assist appellate review in weighing promises in light of all the circumstances, all trial courts are now required to interrogate the defendants who enter guilty pleas so that the waiver of these fundamental rights will affirmatively appear in the record. *McCarthy v. United States*, 394 U.S. 459; *Boykin v. Alabama*, 395 U.S. 238. The lower courts, however, have uniformly held that a prisoner is entitled to some form of relief when he shows that the prosecutor reneged on his sentencing agreement made in connection with a plea bargain, most jurisdictions preferring vacation of the plea on the ground of "involuntariness," while a few permit only specific enforcement. . . .

This is a state case over which we have no "supervisory" jurisdiction; and Rule 11 of the Federal Rules of Criminal Procedure obviously has no relevancy to the problem.

I join the opinion of the Court and favor a constitutional rule for this as well as for other pending or oncoming cases. Where the "plea bargain" is not kept by the prosecutor, the sentence must be vacated and the state court will decide in light of the circumstances of each case whether due process requires (a) that there be specific performance of the plea bargain or (b) that the defendant be given the option to go to trial on the original charges. One alternative may do justice in one case, and the other in a different case. In choosing a remedy, however, a court ought to accord a defendant's preference considerable, if not controlling, weight inasmuch as the fundamental rights flouted by a prosecutor's breach of a plea bargain are those of the defendant, not of the State.

MR. JUSTICE MARSHALL, with whom MR. JUSTICE BRENNAN and MR. JUSTICE STEWART join, concurring in part and dissenting in part.

I agree with much of the majority's opinion, but conclude that petitioner must be permitted to withdraw his guilty plea. This is the relief petitioner requested, and, on the facts set out by the majority, it is a form of relief to which he is entitled.

There is no need to belabor the fact that the Constitution guarantees to all criminal defendants the right to a trial by judge or jury, or, put another way, the "right not to plead guilty," *United States v. Jackson*, 390 U.S. 570, 581 (1968). This and other federal rights may be waived through a guilty plea, but such waivers are not lightly presumed and, in fact, are viewed with the "utmost solicitude." *Boykin v. Alabama*, 395 U.S. 238, 243 (1969). Given this, I believe that where the defendant presents a reason for vacating his plea and the government has not relied on the plea to its disadvantage, the plea may be vacated and the right to trial regained, at least where the motion to vacate is made prior to sentence and judgment. In other words, in such circumstances I would not deem the earlier plea to have irrevocably waived the defendant's federal constitutional right to a trial.

Here, petitioner never claimed any automatic right to withdraw a guilty plea before sentencing. Rather, he tendered a specific reason why, in his case, the plea should be vacated. His reason was that the prosecutor had broken a promise made in return for the agreement to plead guilty. When a prosecutor breaks the bargain, he undercuts the basis for the waiver of constitutional rights implicit in the plea. This, it seems to me, provides the defendant ample justification for rescinding the plea. Where a promise is "unfulfilled," *Brady v. United States*, 397 U.S. 742, 755 (1970) specifically denies that the plea "must stand." Of course, where the prosecutor has broken the plea agreement, it may be appropriate to permit the defendant to enforce the plea bargain. But that is not the remedy sought here. Rather, it seems to me that a breach of the plea bargain provides ample reason to permit the plea to be vacated.

It is worth noting that in the ordinary case where a motion to vacate is made prior to sentencing, the government has taken no action in reliance on the previously entered guilty plea and would suffer no harm from the plea's withdrawal. More pointedly, here the State claims no such harm beyond disappointed expectations about the plea itself. At least where the government itself has broken the plea bargain, this disappointment cannot bar petitioner from withdrawing his guilty plea and reclaiming his right to a trial.

I would remand the case with instructions that the plea be vacated and petitioner given an opportunity to re-plead to the original charges in the indictment.

CASE DISCUSSION QUESTIONS

1. Why does Justice Burger think that plea bargaining is an essential component of the administration of justice?
2. What does Rule 11 of the Federal Rules of Criminal Procedure require, and how is it relevant to this case?
3. Was the breach of the plea agreement intentional, and how does the answer to this question affect the Court's decision?
4. Was the sentencing judge influenced by knowledge of the details of the negotiations for the plea, and to what degree does the answer to this question affect the Court's decision?
5. How would you summarize the issue before the Court, and what was the Court's decision with respect to this issue?
6. With which part of the Opinion of the Court did Justice Douglas agree, and what additional points did he make in his concurring opinion?
7. With which part of the Opinion of the Court did Justice Marshall agree, and what additional points did he make in his concurring opinion?

C. Diversion Programs

Diversion program
An educational and/or social service program operated by public and private agencies outside of the criminal justice system to which criminal defendants are sent as an alternative to getting a criminal conviction on their record and/or serving time in an official government corrections program.

Designed to relieve some of the demands on and reduce the costs of the criminal justice system, **diversion programs** divert certain types of lawbreakers (typically, first offenders involved in lesser crimes) away from the criminal justice system and into alternative educational and social service programs. In jurisdictions where they are available, these programs have become an important option in the plea-bargaining process. A plea bargain is part of the official court proceedings and involves some type of formal criminal conviction, but diversion programs delegate the matter to public and/or private institutions that are not part of the formal criminal justice system. Successful completion of the diversion program's requirements often will lead to a dropping or reduction of the charges, whereas failure may return the matter to the criminal courts.

In addition to reducing the costs associated with criminal prosecutions and incarceration, diversion programs are designed to educate and rehabilitate minor criminals in such a way that they will not repeat the behavior for which they were arrested. Examples of educational programs would include special classes geared to anger management, coping with domestic relations problems, becoming safer drivers, or developing parenting skills. Public service activities can range from picking up trash along a highway to helping underprivileged children learn how to read.

Most diversion programs contain provisions that allow prosecutors to reinstate the original criminal charges if the defendant does not complete all the conditions of the diversionary program or commits another crime within an established time limit. In addition to the requirements for participating in educational programs or performing public service activities, defendants are often also required to compensate any victims of their criminal activity or refrain from having any further contact with the victims.

The Tulsa County, Oklahoma, Drug and DUI Court is a good example of how diversion operates. The Tulsa County District Office's website describes the program as follows:

> Drug Court is designed to last a minimum of eighteen months and a maximum of three years. There are currently five phases the participants must complete prior to graduation from the program. Participants are promoted from one phase to the next after they have completed milestones for that phase. Failure of a participant to follow the rules and conditions of their performance contract results in a sanction imposed by the Drug Court team. Sanctions may include community service, increased urinalysis, increased supervision contacts, increased treatment, increased court appearances, jail time, or phase demotion. Participants who are abiding by the rules and conditions are given incentives such as curfew extensions, gift cards, candy bars, fee waivers, and positive reinforcement from the team. Upon graduation of the program, participants may have their cases dismissed, reduced, or withdrawn by the district attorney's office. To date, Tulsa County has had 2095 participants in Drug Court and 665 participants in DUI Court. Out of those, 823 have graduated from Drug Court and 339 from DUI Court.[27]

The application for the Tulsa County diversion program is displayed in Exhibit 9.8. Paralegals regularly assist clients in completing this type of form.

---

[27]*http://www.doc.state.ok.us/community/tulsaco.htm*

Exhibit 9.8: Diversion Program Application

DRUG/DUI COURT
SCREENING/REFERRAL FORM
Please write legibly

Client Information:

Full Legal Name _____

A/K/A _____

Current in Custody?____Y ____N DLM#_____DOC# _____

DOB:_____Age:_____Race:_____Gender:_____SSN:_____

Client address:_____

_____Street:_____City: _____Zip: _____

Client Phone (home) _____-_____ (cell/other) _____-_____

_____

Criminal Information:

Attorney: _____ Phone: _____

Current Charge(s): _____ Case #: _____

_____ Case #: _____

_____ Case #: _____

_____ Case #: _____

Has client ever been arrested for a violent felony and/or a sex crime? _____Y _____N

Is client subject to a Protective Order? _____Y _____N

If yes, Probation/Parole Officer's Name: _____

_____

BOLDED ITEMS ARE MANDATORY!

Current substance abuse treatment? ___Y ___N If yes, agency: _____

Prior mental health treatment? ___Y ___N If yes, agency: _____

Diagnosis:_____

Have you previously been prescribed medication? ___Y ___N If yes, please list:

1._____   4._____

2._____   5._____

3._____   6._____

Prior substance abuse treatment? _____Y _____N If yes, agency:_____

Client waiver information:

    1. **I wish to apply to the Tulsa County Drug/DUI Court Program.**

_____ **Date:**_____
    Defendant/Client signature

SUMMARY

After studying the information gained from the discovery process, the attorneys select their strategy and file a wide variety of pre-trial motions to clarify the nature of the trial that will be held if a plea bargain cannot be reached. In addition to motions to exclude certain types of evidence, other motions are filed related to who the judge will be, whether there will be co-defendants, competency to stand trial, what can be introduced as evidence, and when the trial will begin. The judge's rulings on motions to suppress evidence are especially important in the plea-bargaining process.

After discussing the pros and cons of plea bargaining, we described how the process works and the types of agreements that are usually reached. We also discussed how they are enforced.

Since the discussions held during plea bargaining often include consideration of diversionary programs, the chapter ended with an overview of optional programs designed to reduce taxpayer costs by providing educational and treatment options for selected types of defendants.

INTERNET RESOURCES

General Information on the Criminal Justice System

- Court Rules and Forms: **http://www.llrx.com/courtrules**
- List of Resources on Plea Bargaining: **http://www.pbs.org/wgbh/pages/frontline/shows/plea/etc/links.html**
- Information on Drug Courts: **http://www.ncjrs.gov/spotlight/drug_courts/Summary.html**
- Diversion Programs for Juveniles: **http://www.ncjrs.gov/html/ojjdp/9909-3/contents.html**

REVIEW QUESTIONS

1. Why would state prosecutors decline to pursue charges against some offenders and allow the U.S. Attorneys' Office to be the prosecuting agency?
2. What steps must a defendant take to change the location of the case to some other city, county, or judicial district from where the case originally was filed?
3. What is the difference between a "change of venue" and a "change of venire"?
4. Under what circumstances is a judge "substituted" out of a case, and in what situations does the judge "recuse" himself or herself from a case?
5. What are the differences and similarities between "joinder of offenses" and "joinder of defendants"?
6. How would a defendant attack an improper joinder of offenses or defendants? What is the likelihood of success?
7. What does the term *competent to stand trial* mean?
8. What is the purpose of a motion to suppress?
9. What are the components of a motion to suppress?

10. What impact does the judge's grant or denial of a motion to suppress have on the progression of the case?
11. What relief is sought in a motion to dismiss?
12. For what reasons would an attorney choose not to object to the opponent's motion for continuance?
13. What benefits do defendants receive from entering into a plea bargain?
14. What benefit does society receive from plea bargains?
15. Why do innocent men and women plead guilty to crimes they did not commit? What is the name of this type of plea?
16. At what stage of a case can the parties enter into a plea bargain?
17. List and define the three major types of plea agreements.
18. What is a plea colloquy?
19. What are the purposes of diversion programs?

PART | 3

Criminal Procedure: Trials and Their Aftermath

Chapter 10

The Nature of Criminal Trials

In Part 2, we followed the development of criminal cases from the detection of a crime through the bringing of formal charges, pre-trial discovery, plea bargaining, and diversion. In this section, we cover trials, sentencing, and appeals.

Our coverage of trials begins in this chapter with a look at their basic functions and the roles played by key participants. We then move on to examine the constitutional principles governing criminal trials and the rules concerning the introduction of evidence at trials. Chapter 11 will discuss the steps taken immediately before trial begins. In Chapter 12, we will go into more detail about what happens at all of the stages in a criminal trial and how paralegals can assist the attorney at each stage. Chapter 13 will cover sentencing, and finally, in Chapter 14, we will show the steps necessary to take the case to an appellate court.

A. FUNCTIONS OF THE COURTS IN CRIMINAL CASES

In Chapter 2, we discussed the importance of the concept of the "rule of law" and noted how it involved three basic principles:

- Government must follow its own rules;
- Government must apply the law impartially; and
- Government must provide due process for those accused of breaking the rules.

In our legal system, it is the responsibility of the courts to ensure that government officials impartially follow the law and that those accused of breaking the law receive "due process of law."

Criminal trials are the mechanism used to determine if the government can prove, beyond a reasonable doubt, that someone has done something that the government has designated a crime.[1] The rules used to conduct the trial must comport with the constitutional protections considered to be essential to the "due process of law," and if the defendant is found guilty, either the judge or sometimes a jury plays a role in determining what the punishment will be.

B. CONSTITUTIONAL RIGHTS RELATED TO THE CONDUCT OF TRIALS

Figure 2.2 (see Chapter 2) listed sixteen constitutional rights that apply to applications of criminal law. Some, such as the right to indictment by a grand jury and the prohibition against unreasonable searches and seizures, were discussed in Part 2 where they related to actions that are taken prior to the start of a criminal trial. In this section, we will focus on the constitutional rights that are directly related to what goes on at the trial itself.

1. RIGHT TO A PUBLIC TRIAL

Public trial

A trial open to the public.

The Sixth Amendment declares: "In all criminal prosecutions, the accused shall enjoy the right to a speedy and **public trial**. . . ."[2] This provision, along with several others in the Bill of Rights, was designed to prevent the type of secret star-chamber proceedings that had taken place in England from the fifteenth into the seventeenth centuries whereby someone was seized in the middle of the night and secretly tried, convicted, and punished without relatives or the general public ever knowing what happened to the person. The provision for public trials was clearly designed to be a check against the abuse of governmental power.

Although the U.S. Supreme Court has allowed judges to close some types of pre-trial hearings to protect privacy rights and to avoid prejudicial publicity, it ruled in *Richmond Newspapers, Inc. v. Virginia* that criminal trials had to be open to the public and that the public included representatives of the press.[3] Note, however, that trials related to juvenile offenses are typically not open to the public. Although the U.S. Supreme Court has ruled that the Due Process Clause required juveniles be given the right to notice of charges, the right to counsel, the privilege against self-incrimination, and the right to confront and cross-examine witnesses, it does not require that trials of juveniles be open to the public.

---

[1] At the federal level and in most states, an action must be formally prohibited by a valid statute or regulation. There are a few states, however, that still recognize common law crimes.

[2] The speedy aspect of the trial was covered in Chapter 8.

[3] 448 U.S. 555, 100 S. Ct. 2814; 65 L. Ed. 2d 973 (1980). In *Presley* v. *Georgia*, 558 U.S.__, 130 S. Ct. 721, 175 L. Ed. 2d 675 (2010) (*per curiam*), the Court ruled that the *voir dire* selection process also had to be open to the public.

2. RIGHT TO A JURY TRIAL

There are three references to jury trials in the U.S. Constitution. The first appears in Article Three, which states in part: "The Trial of all Crimes . . . shall be by Jury; and such Trial shall be held in the State where the said Crimes shall have been committed." The other two references are part of the Bill of Rights: the Sixth Amendment establishes a right to a trial "by an impartial jury of the State and district wherein the crime shall have been committed . . . ," and the Seventh Amendment establishes a right to a jury trial in many types of civil cases.

a. Functions of Juries

The basic function of the jury is to resolve the factual, as opposed to the legal, questions raised in the case. **Factual questions** relate to the determination of who did what and when, where, and how they did it. Was the defendant the person who witnesses claim they saw robbing the gas station; did the blow struck by the defendant cause the victim's death? The resolution of factual issues usually comes down to which witnesses the jurors choose to believe. On the other hand, **legal questions** relate to the procedures used in the trial, the admissibility of different kinds of evidence, and the interpretation of the statutes being applied. These legal issues are handled by the judge, rather than the jury, because they require special legal training and experience. When a case is tried by a judge alone (bench trial), the judge decides both questions of law and questions of fact.

Factual questions
Issues related to the determination of who did what and when, where, and how they did it.

Legal questions
Issues related to the interpretation of the meaning of the law, including procedures used in the trial and the admissibility of different kinds of evidence, as well at the type of behavior that is covered by the terms of the statutes being applied.

b. Justifications for the Use of Juries

Juries are an important part of our English common law heritage. They developed as a means of limiting the powers of the English monarchy and safeguarding citizens against corrupt or biased judges and prosecutors. In addition to serving as a check on potential abuses of power and/or political corruption, an argument in favor of the jury system is that a representative group of common, ordinary people from the local community is better situated to judge the credibility of the witnesses than a single judge would be. This is especially true in smaller communities where jurors may be more apt to have had personal dealings with the defendant and/or the witnesses and may have knowledge of their reputations for truth and veracity.

c. A Jury of One's Peers

All of you have probably heard the phrase "jury of one's peers," but you will not find it in the Constitution. There is no legal requirement that a jury be made up of people like the defendant. The Sixth Amendment does, however, require "an impartial jury of the State and district wherein the crime shall have been committed." Thus it is the demographics of the community, rather than the characteristics of the defendant, that have to be represented in the jury.[4]

---

[4]An exception to this general practice would be a change of venire. See the discussion in the next section on impartial juries.

Jury selection is a two-step process: The first involves identifying people who are eligible to serve on juries in general, and the second involves selection of individuals to be jurors in a specific case. Usually in the first stage, public officials with titles like jury commissioner collect names and addresses from public records, such as lists of registered voters and licensed drivers. Questionnaires are then sent to a random sampling of people on these lists to collect data relating to their age, occupation, citizenship, disabilities, ability to understand the English language, and the existence of any conditions that would excuse them from being a juror.

Local practices vary with respect to exempting certain classes of people from jury duty. Historically, people would be excused if they could convince jury commissioners that jury service would be a personal hardship or a hardship for their employer. In many jurisdictions, mothers of small children were routinely excused; however, that practice is becoming far less common today. Attorneys had also been typically excused, but many jurisdictions are now requiring them to serve as well. People with certain types of physical and mental disabilities may also be excused.

On the basis of the information gathered from questionnaires and other sources, the public officials then develop a list of people they will call for jury duty on specific dates. Typically, individuals are sent a summons that requires them to be available to report for a period of a week. During that period, they are required to call a special phone number or check a special website to learn the specific dates and times at which they will have to report to the courthouse for duty.

d. An Impartial Jury

The Sixth Amendment specifically states that juries should be "impartial." In other words, the members of the jury should not be biased or prejudiced toward either the government or the defendant. Note that this requirement of impartiality may be somewhat at odds with the justifications for the jury system discussed above. The more knowledge jurors have about the reputation of the defendant and key witnesses, the more likely it is that the jurors have already formed opinions that may bias their conclusions about the credibility of the testimony they hear. When these types of situations arise, the impartiality requirement is supposed to supersede the advantages of prior knowledge.

Voir dire
An examination of prospective jurors to see if they are fit to serve on a jury in a specific case.

The court relies on the *voir dire* process to determine if an individual will be considered sufficiently impartial to qualify to serve on the jury in a specific case. Prior to the actual start of the trial, people who were called in for jury duty are brought into the courtroom to be questioned by the judge, and in many cases by the attorneys, about what they know of the case and if there are any factors that might bias their judgment.[5] We will discuss how attorneys prepare for *voir dire* in detail in Chapter 11.

Based on the answers given during *voir dire*, the attorneys may raise one of two types of challenges to keep a potential juror from serving in that specific

---

[5]In order to stop attorneys from using *voir dire* questions to begin indoctrinating the jurors, and to simply reduce the time taken up by *voir dire*, some jurisdictions require the attorneys submit their questions for the judge to ask.

case. The first line of attack is usually a **challenge for cause**. To exercise this challenge, the attorney must convince the judge that something about the juror's background or answers demonstrates that the person has some type of bias. If unsuccessful at removing a juror for cause, an attorney can achieve the same result by using a **peremptory challenge**. Whereas the decision to excuse a juror for cause ultimately rests with the judge, a peremptory challenge is within the sole discretion of the attorney who exercises it. Therefore, the attorney need not even give a reason for having used a peremptory challenge. However, the number of peremptory challenges available to each side is strictly limited.

e. Types of Trials Covered

At the beginning of this section, we identified the provisions of the U.S. Constitution specifically mentioning juries. Although the Bill of Rights was originally interpreted as applying only to the federal government, the Supreme Court has ruled that the Fourteenth Amendment Due Process Clause makes the right to a jury trial in criminal cases applicable to the states.[6] Furthermore, most state constitutions also grant a right to a trial by jury in most criminal matters.

Several key court cases, however, have limited the application of the Sixth Amendment right to a jury trial in cases involving "minor offenses." In *Duncan v. Louisiana*,[7] the U.S. Supreme Court overturned a conviction for simple battery because the state trial court had denied defendant's request for a jury trial. The Court ruled that although the offense was classified as a misdemeanor, it was considered to be serious enough to entitle the defendant to a jury trial because it carried a penalty of up to two years' incarceration. In the majority opinion, the justices stated that a person accused of any crime punishable by more than six months' imprisonment was entitled to demand trial by jury, but that when the punishment involved imprisonment for six months or less, it was up to the states to choose whether or not to permit a defendant to have a jury trial.

In *Apprendi v. New Jersey*[8] and *Blakely v. Washington*,[9] the Supreme Court held that a criminal defendant has a right to a jury trial not only on the question of guilt or innocence but any time facts were used to increase a defendant's sentence beyond the maximum otherwise allowed by statutes or sentencing guidelines. These rulings invalidated the procedures used in many states and the federal courts that allowed sentencing enhancement based on "a preponderance of evidence," where enhancement could be based on the judge's findings alone.

As with most other rights, a legally competent defendant can choose to voluntarily waive the right to be tried by a jury. Defendants typically choose to waive this right in cases that have received a great deal of prejudicial publicity, that involve a community perceived as prejudiced against members of the defendant's racial or ethnic group, or that involve a particularly gruesome crime. In

Challenge for cause
A method of removing a prospective juror based on a finding by the judge that the juror has some sort of bias or other factors that should disqualify him or her from serving on this specific case.

Peremptory challenge
A method an attorney can use to remove a prospective juror without being required to state a reason.

---

[6]See the discussion in Chapter 4 on p. 94 for general background on selective incorporation of the Bill of Rights.

[7]391 U.S. 145, 88 S. Ct. 1444, 20 L. Ed. 2d 491 (1968).

[8]530 U.S. 466, 120 S. Ct. 2348, 147 L. Ed. 2d 435 (2000).

[9]542 U.S. 296, 124 S. Ct. 2531, 159 L. Ed. 2d 403 (2004).

cases where a jury is not used, the judge takes over the jury's function and decides the guilt or innocence of the defendant as well as questions of law.

f. The Number of Jurors Required

Under the common law, a jury consisted of twelve people. However, in order to cut costs and expedite the legal process, federal and state courts have sometimes used smaller juries in civil and sometimes even in criminal cases. The U.S. Supreme Court has ruled that there is nothing that is constitutionally significant about having twelve jurors and has permitted six-person juries in civil cases at both the federal and the state levels. While twelve are required in federal criminal trials,[10] *Williams v. Florida*[11] approved the use of six-person juries in state criminal cases. Then in *Ballew v. Georgia* (presented below), the Court held that criminal juries composed of fewer than six members do not meet Sixth and Fourteenth Amendment standards.[12]

Whatever the number of jurors required to serve on a particular type of jury, it is common practice to select one or two extra jurors as alternates—especially when the trial is expected to last for more than a few days. These alternates sit in the jury box with their fellow jurors throughout the trial and are used as substitutes if regular jurors are unable to continue. An alternate does not participate in the deliberations, however, unless he or she has replaced one of the original jurors.

g. Requirement for a Unanimous Verdict

Just as common law tradition called for twelve jurors, it also required that verdicts be unanimous. If all twelve could not agree with either a guilty or a not-guilty verdict, a mistrial was declared and the prosecution had to either re-try the case or drop the charges against the defendant.

As in cases involving the number of jurors, the Supreme Court has established different standards for federal and state courts. The key case here is *Apodaca v. Oregon*,[13] in which the defendants were convicted of assault with a deadly weapon, burglary in a dwelling, and grand larceny by jury votes of 11 to 1 and 10 to 2. In the process of affirming their convictions, the nation's high court held that that the Sixth and Fourteenth Amendments did not require a conviction by a unanimous verdict in state courts. In federal criminal cases, jury unanimity is required.

---

[10]*Rassmussen v. United States*, 197 U.S. 516, 25 S. Ct. 514, 49 L. Ed. 862 (1905). The Supreme Court invalidated a conviction by a six-man jury in a federal territorial court in Alaska.

[11]399 U.S. 78, 90 S. Ct. 1893, 26 L. Ed. 2d 446 (1970).

[12]435 U.S. 223, 98 S. Ct. 1029, 55 L. Ed. 2d 234 (1978). In this case, the defendant was convicted by a five-person jury of two misdemeanor counts for violating Georgia obscenity statutes.

[13]406 U.S. 404, 92 S. Ct. 1628, 32 L. Ed. 2d 184 (1972).

Ballew v. Georgia
Supreme Court of the United States
435 U.S. 223 (1978)

MR. JUSTICE BLACKMUN announced the judgment of the Court and delivered an opinion in which MR. JUSTICE STEVENS joined.

This case presents the issue whether a state criminal trial to a jury of only five persons deprives the accused of the right to trial by jury guaranteed to him by the Sixth and Fourteenth Amendments. Our resolution of the issue requires an application of principles enunciated in *Williams v. Florida*, 399 U.S. 78 (1970), where the use of a six-person jury in a state criminal trial was upheld against similar constitutional attack.

I

In November 1973 petitioner Claude Davis Ballew was the manager of the Paris Adult Theatre at 320 Peachtree Street, Atlanta, Ga. On November 9 two investigators from the Fulton County Solicitor General's office viewed at the theater a motion picture film entitled "Behind the Green Door." After they had seen the film, they obtained a warrant for its seizure, returned to the theater, viewed the film once again, and seized it. Petitioner and a cashier were arrested. Investigators returned to the theater on November 26, viewed the film in its entirety, secured still another warrant, and on November 27 once again viewed the motion picture and seized a second copy of the film.

On September 14, 1974, petitioner was charged in a two-count misdemeanor accusation . . . (of) . . . "distributing obscene materials." . . .

Petitioner was brought to trial in the Criminal Court of Fulton County. After a jury of 5 persons had been selected and sworn, petitioner moved that the court impanel a jury of 12 persons. That court, however, tried its misdemeanor cases before juries of five persons pursuant to Ga. Const., Art. 6. § 16, P1, codified as Ga. Code § 2-5101 (1975), and to 1890-1891 Ga. Laws, No. 278, pp. 937-938, and 1935 Ga. Laws, No. 38, p. 498. Petitioner contended that for an obscenity trial, a jury of only five was constitutionally inadequate to assess the contemporary standards of the community. He also argued that the Sixth and Fourteenth Amendments required a jury of at least six members in criminal cases.

The motion for a 12-person jury was overruled, and the trial went on to its conclusion before the 5-person jury that had been impaneled. At the conclusion of the trial, the jury deliberated for 38 minutes and returned a verdict of guilty on both counts of the accusation. The court imposed a sentence of one year and a $1,000 fine on each count, the periods of incarceration to run concurrently and to be suspended upon payment of the fines. After a subsequent hearing, the court denied an amended motion for a new trial.

Petitioner took an appeal to the Court of Appeals of the State of Georgia. There he argued: First, the evidence was insufficient. Second, the trial court committed several First Amendment errors, namely, that the film as a matter of law was not obscene, and that the jury instructions incorrectly explained the standard of scienter, the definition of obscenity, and the scope of community standards. Third, the seizures of the films were illegal. Fourth, the convictions on both counts had placed petitioner in double jeopardy because he had shown only one motion picture. Fifth, the use of the five-member jury deprived him of his Sixth and Fourteenth Amendment right to a trial by jury.

The Court of Appeals rejected petitioner's contentions. . . . In its consideration of the five-person-jury issue, the court noted that *Williams v. Florida* had not established a constitutional minimum number of jurors. Absent a holding by this Court that a five-person jury was constitutionally inadequate, the Court of Appeals considered itself bound by *Sanders v. State*, 234 Ga. 586, 216 S.E. 2d 838 (1975), cert. denied, 424 U.S. 931 (1976), over the constitutionality of the five-person jury had been upheld. . . . The Supreme Court of Georgia denied certiorari.

In his petition for certiorari here, petitioner raised three issues: the unconstitutionality of the five-person jury; the constitutional sufficiency of the jury instructions on scienter and constructive, rather than actual, knowledge of the contents of the film; and obscenity vel non. We granted certiorari. Because we now hold that the five-member jury does not satisfy the jury trial guarantee of the Sixth Amendment, as applied to the States through the Fourteenth, we do not reach the other issues.

II

The Fourteenth Amendment guarantees the right of trial by jury in all state nonpetty criminal cases. *Duncan v. Louisiana*, 391 U.S. 145, 159-162 (1968). The Court in *Duncan* applied this Sixth Amendment right to the States because "trial by jury in criminal cases is fundamental to the American scheme of justice." Id., at 149. The right attaches in the present case because the maximum penalty for violating § 26-2101, as it existed at the time of the alleged offenses, exceeded six months' imprisonment.

In *Williams v. Florida*, 399 U.S., at 100, the Court reaffirmed that the "purpose of the jury trial, as we noted in *Duncan*, is to prevent oppression by the Government. 'Providing an accused with the right to be tried by a jury of his peers gave him an inestimable safeguard against the corrupt or overzealous prosecutor and against the compliant, biased, or eccentric judge.' *Duncan v. Louisiana*, [391 U.S.] at 156." ... This purpose is attained by the participation of the community in determinations of guilt and by the application of the common sense of laymen who, as jurors, consider the case. *Williams v. Florida*, 399 U.S., at 100.

Williams held that these functions and this purpose could be fulfilled by a jury of six members. As the Court's opinion in that case explained at some length, common law juries included 12 members by historical accident, "unrelated to the great purposes which gave rise to the jury in the first place." Id., at 89-90. The Court's earlier cases that had assumed the number 12 to be constitutionally compelled were set to one side because they had not considered history and the function of the jury.

Rather than requiring 12 members, then, the Sixth Amendment mandated a jury only of sufficient size to promote group deliberation, to insulate members from outside intimidation, and to provide a representative cross-section of the community. Although recognizing that by 1970 little empirical research had evaluated jury performance, the Court found no evidence that the reliability of jury verdicts diminished with six-member panels. Nor did the Court anticipate significant differences in result, including the frequency of "hung" juries. Because the reduction in size did not threaten exclusion of any particular class from jury roles, concern that the representative or cross-section character of the jury would suffer with a decrease to six members seemed "an unrealistic one." Id., at 102. As a consequence, the six-person jury was held not to violate the Sixth and Fourteenth Amendments.

III

When the Court in *Williams* permitted the reduction in jury size—or, to put it another way, when it held that a jury of six was not unconstitutional—it expressly reserved ruling on the issue whether a number smaller than six passed constitutional scrutiny. See *Johnson v. Louisiana*, 406 U.S. 356, 365-366 (1972) (concurring opinion). The Court refused to speculate when this so-called "slippery slope" would become too steep. We face now, however, the two-fold question whether a further reduction in the size of the state criminal trial jury does make the grade too dangerous, that is, whether it inhibits the functioning of the jury as an institution to a significant degree, and, if so, whether any state interest counterbalances and justifies the disruption so as to preserve its constitutionality.

Williams v. Florida and *Colgrove v. Battin*, 413 U.S. 149 (1973) (where the Court held that a jury of six members did not violate the Seventh Amendment right to a jury trial in a civil case), generated a quantity of scholarly work on jury size. These writings do not draw or identify a bright line below which the number of jurors would not be able to function as required by the standards enunciated in *Williams*. On the other hand, they raise significant questions about the wisdom and constitutionality of a reduction below six. We examine these concerns:

First, recent empirical data suggest that progressively smaller juries are less likely to foster effective group deliberation. At some point, this decline leads to inaccurate fact finding and incorrect application of the common sense of the community to the facts. Generally, a positive correlation exists between group size and the quality of both group performance and group productivity. A variety of explanations have been offered for this conclusion. Several are particularly applicable in the jury setting. The smaller the group, the less likely are members to make critical contributions necessary for the solution of a given problem. Because most juries are not permitted to take notes, . . . memory is important for accurate jury deliberations. As juries decrease in size, then, they are less likely to have members who remember each of the important pieces of evidence or argument. Furthermore, the smaller the group, the less likely it is to overcome the biases of its members to obtain an accurate result. When individual and group decision making were compared, it was seen that groups performed better because prejudices of individuals were frequently counterbalanced, and objectivity resulted. Groups also exhibited increased motivation and self-criticism. All these advantages, except, perhaps, self-motivation, tend to diminish as the size of the group diminishes. Because juries frequently face complex problems laden with value choices, the benefits are important and should be retained. In particular, the counterbalancing of various biases is critical to the accurate application of the common sense of the community to the facts of any given case.

Second, the data now raise doubts about the accuracy of the results achieved by smaller and smaller panels. Statistical studies suggest that the risk of convicting an innocent person (Type I error) rises as the size of the jury diminishes. Because the risk of not convicting a guilty person (Type II error) increases with the size of the panel, an optimal jury size can be selected as a function of the interaction between the two risks. Nagel and Neef concluded that the optimal size, for the purpose of minimizing errors, should vary with the importance attached to the two types of mistakes. After weighting Type I error as 10 times more significant than Type II, perhaps not an unreasonable assumption, they concluded that the optimal jury size was between six and eight. As the size diminished to five and below, the weighted sum of errors increased because of the enlarging risk of the conviction of innocent defendants.

Another doubt about progressively smaller juries arises from the increasing inconsistency that results from the decreases. Saks argued that the "more a jury type fosters consistency, the greater will be the proportion of juries which select the correct (i.e., the same) verdict and the fewer 'errors' will be made." . . .

Third, the data suggest that the verdicts of jury deliberation in criminal cases will vary as juries become smaller, and that the variance amounts to an imbalance to the detriment of one side, the defense. Both Lempert and Zeisel found that the number of hung juries would diminish as the panels decreased in size. . . . Both studies emphasized that juries in criminal cases generally hang with only one, or more likely two, jurors remaining unconvinced of guilt. Also, group theory suggests that a person in the minority will adhere to his position more frequently when he has at least one other person supporting his argument. In the jury setting the significance of this tendency is demonstrated by the following figures: If a minority viewpoint is shared by 10% of the community, 28.2% of 12-member juries may be expected to have no minority representation, but 53.1% of 6-member juries would have none. Thirty-four percent of 12-member panels could be expected to have two minority members, while only 11% of six-member panels would have two. As the numbers diminish below six, even fewer panels would have one member with the minority viewpoint and still fewer would have two. The chance for hung juries would decline accordingly.

Fourth, what has just been said about the presence of minority viewpoint as juries decrease in size foretells problems not only for jury decision making, but also for the representation of minority groups in the community. The Court repeatedly has held that meaningful community participation cannot be attained with the exclusion of minorities or other identifiable groups from jury service. . . . Although the Court in Williams concluded that the six-person jury did not fail to represent adequately a cross-section of the community, the opportunity for meaningful and appropriate representation does decrease with the size of the panels. Thus, if a minority group constitutes 10% of the community, 53.1% of randomly selected six-member juries could be expected to have no minority representative among their members, and 89% not to have two. Further reduction in size will erect additional barriers to representation. . . .

IV

While we adhere to, and reaffirm our holding in *Williams v. Florida*, these studies, most of which have been made since *Williams* was decided in 1970, lead us to conclude that the purpose and functioning of the jury in a criminal trial is seriously impaired, and to a constitutional degree, by a reduction in size to below six members. We readily admit that we do not pretend to discern a clear line between six members and five. But the assembled data raise substantial doubt about the reliability and appropriate representation of panels smaller than six. Because of the fundamental importance of the jury trial to the American system of criminal justice, any further reduction that promotes inaccurate and possibly biased decision making, that causes untoward differences in verdicts, and that prevents juries from truly representing their communities, attains constitutional significance.

Georgia here presents no persuasive argument that a reduction to five does not offend important Sixth Amendment interests. First, its reliance on *Johnson v. Louisiana*, 406 U.S. 356 (1972), for the proposition that the Court previously has approved the five-person jury is misplaced. . . . Because the issue of the constitutionality of the five-member jury was not then before the Court, it did not rule upon it.

Second, Georgia argues that its use of five-member juries does not violate the Sixth and Fourteenth Amendments because they are used only in misdemeanor cases. If six persons may constitutionally assess the felony charge in *Williams*, the State reasons, five persons should be a constitutionally adequate number for a

misdemeanor trial. The problem with this argument is that the purpose and functions of the jury do not vary significantly with the importance of the crime. In *Baldwin v. New York*, 399 U.S. 66 (1970), the Court held that the right to a jury trial attached in both felony and misdemeanor cases. Only in cases concerning truly petty crimes, where the deprivation of liberty was minimal, did the defendant have no constitutional right to trial by jury. In the present case the possible deprivation of liberty is substantial. The State charged petitioner with misdemeanors under Ga. Code Ann. § 26-2101 (1972), and he has been given concurrent sentences of imprisonment, each for one year, and fines totaling $2,000 have been imposed. We cannot conclude that there is less need for the imposition and the direction of the sense of the community in this case than when the State has chosen to label an offense a felony. The need for an effective jury here must be judged by the same standards announced and applied in *Williams v. Florida*.

Third, the retention by Georgia of the unanimity requirement does not solve the Sixth and Fourteenth Amendment problem. Our concern has to do with the ability of the smaller group to perform the functions mandated by the Amendments. That a five-person jury may return a unanimous decision does not speak to the questions whether the group engaged in meaningful deliberation, could remember all the important facts and arguments, and truly represented the sense of the entire community. Despite the presence of the unanimity requirement, then, we cannot conclude that "the interest of the defendant in having the judgment of his peers interposed between himself and the officers of the State who prosecute and judge him is equally well served" by the five-person panel.

Fourth, Georgia submits that the five-person jury adequately represents the community because there is no arbitrary exclusion of any particular class. We agree that it has not been demonstrated that the Georgia system violates the Equal Protection Clause by discriminating on the basis of race or some other improper classification. But the data outlined above raise substantial doubt about the ability of juries truly to represent the community as membership decreases below six. . . . Even though the facts of this case would not establish a jury discrimination claim under the Equal Protection Clause, the question of representation does constitute one factor of several that, when combined, create a problem of constitutional significance under the Sixth and Fourteenth Amendments.

Fifth, the empirical data cited by Georgia do not relieve our doubts. . . .

V

With the reduction in the number of jurors below six creating a substantial threat to Sixth and Fourteenth Amendment guarantees, we must consider whether any interest of the State justifies the reduction. We find no significant State advantage in reducing the number of jurors from six to five.

The States utilize juries of less than 12 primarily for administrative reasons. Savings in court time and in financial costs are claimed to justify the reductions. The financial benefits of the reduction from 12 to 6 are substantial; this is mainly because fewer jurors draw daily allowances as they hear cases. On the other hand, the asserted saving in judicial time is not so clear. Pabst in his study found little reduction in the time for voir dire with the six-person jury because many questions were directed at the veniremen as a group. Total trial time did not diminish, and court delays and backlogs improved very little. The point that is to be made, of course, is that a reduction in size from six to five or four or even three would save the States little. . . .

Petitioner, therefore, has established that his trial on criminal charges before a five-member jury deprived him of the right to trial by jury guaranteed by the Sixth and Fourteenth Amendments.

VI

The judgment of the Court of Appeals is reversed, and the case is remanded for further proceedings not inconsistent with this opinion.

It is so ordered.

MR. JUSTICE POWELL, with whom THE CHIEF JUSTICE and MR. JUSTICE REHNQUIST join, concurring in the judgment.

I concur in the judgment, as I agree that use of a jury as small as five members, with authority to convict for serious offenses, involves grave questions of fairness. As the opinion of MR. JUSTICE BLACKMUN indicates, the line between five- and six-member juries is difficult to justify, but a line has to be drawn somewhere if the substance of jury trial is to be preserved.

I do not agree, however, that every feature of jury trial practice must be the same in both federal and state courts. *Apodaca v. Oregon*, 406 U.S. 404, 414 (1972) (POWELL, J., concurring). Because the opinion of MR. JUSTICE BLACKMUN today assumes full incorporation of the Sixth Amendment by the Fourteenth Amendment contrary to my view in Apodaca, I do not join it. Also, I have reservations as to the wisdom—as well as the necessity—of MR. JUSTICE BLACKMUN's heavy reliance on numerology derived from statistical studies. Moreover, neither the validity nor the methodology employed by the studies cited was subjected to the traditional testing mechanisms of the adversary process. The studies relied on merely represent unexamined findings of persons interested in the jury system.

For these reasons I concur only in the judgment.

MR. JUSTICE BRENNAN, with whom MR. JUSTICE STEWART and MR JUSTICE MARSHALL join.

I join MR. JUSTICE BLACKMUN's opinion insofar as it holds that the Sixth and Fourteenth Amendments require juries in criminal trials to contain more than five persons. However, I cannot agree that petitioner can be subjected to a new trial, since I continue to adhere to my belief that Ga. Code Ann. § 26-2101 (1972) is overbroad and therefore facially unconstitutional. See *Sanders v. Georgia*, 424 U.S. 931 (1976) (dissent from denial of certiorari). See also *Paris Adult Theatre I v. Slaton*, 413 U.S. 49, 73 (1973) (BRENNAN, J., dissenting).

CASE DISCUSSION QUESTIONS

1. Note the multiple bases upon which the case was appealed. Identify the issues raised on appeal and explain why the appellant raised more than one issue.
2. What justification did the Georgia Court of Appeals give for rejecting Ballew's assertion that he had a right to a jury with more than five jurors? Do you think its

decision was correctly based on the precedents that existed at the time it decided the case?

3. What is the holding of this case?

4. What are the four main reasons given by Justice Blackmun to justify the Supreme Court's holding? Which, if any, did you agree with?

5. What arguments were raised by the state of Georgia, and what reasons did Justice Blackmun give for rejecting these arguments? Which, if any, did you agree with?

6. In what way is the requirement for a unanimous verdict related to the number of people on a jury?

7. What part(s) of the Opinion of the Court did Chief Justice Burger and Justices Powell and Rehnquist agree with, and what part did they specifically disagree with?

8. What part(s) of the Opinion of the Court did Justices Brennan, Stewart, and Marshall agree with, and what did they add to their concurring opinion that was not covered in Blackmun's opinion?

h. Jury Nullification

Jury nullification
A term used to describe a situation in which a jury votes to acquit a defendant even though the facts clearly establish a violation of the letter of the law.

Jury nullification refers to a situation in which a jury votes to acquit a defendant even though the facts clearly establish a violation of the letter of the law. In these types of cases, the jury is in effect refusing to apply a law because the jurors believe the law itself is unjust or because they believe it is unjust to apply it to the defendant in the specific circumstances presented in the case they are deciding. An example might be where an elderly spouse assists in the suicide of a partner who is suffering from terminal cancer.

In some situations, nullification can become a means by which the public expresses its opposition to an unwanted legislative enactment. When such a pattern of verdicts exists, it can have the de facto effect of invalidating the statute, because prosecutors decide not to use it. An historical example of nullification would be the American revolutionaries' refusal to convict under English laws. Although the legal system permits jury nullification, legal ethics do not permit defense attorneys to explicitly ask the jurors to disregard the law.

DISCUSSION QUESTIONS

1. What is the justification for requiring a public trial? Should public trials also be required in juvenile cases or those involving rape or incest?

2. On what basis should authorities decide who gets to be present at a trial where there is more demand for seats than there are seats available in the courtroom?

3. What are the pros and cons of allowing video cameras in the courtroom? Do you think they should be allowed? Why or why not?

4. What are the pros and cons of having lawyers serve as jurors?

5. Under what circumstances, if any, should there be a requirement that minorities be represented on the jury when the defendant is a member of a racial minority? Should the minority jurors be from the same racial group as the defendant? Should the same principles apply to sex and religion?

6. In the 2010 federal trial of former Illinois governor Rod Blagojevich, the jury found him guilty of lying to the FBI but could not persuade the single holdout

juror to vote for any of the other twenty-three counts of corruption and fraud. Since federal criminal juries are required to reach unanimous verdicts, the judge declared a mistrial on these remaining twenty-three counts.

   a. Do you think it is right that a single juror should be able to stand in the way of a conviction? Why?

   b. If you were the U.S. Attorney in this situation, what factors would you consider in deciding whether to re-try Blagojevich on some or all of the other twenty-three counts?

7. Should judges have the authority to throw out jury verdicts when they reflect a form of jury nullification?

APPLICATION EXERCISES

1. Look through the archive files of a newspaper in the area of your college/university and identify a local criminal case that received a lot of publicity in that paper. Then, make a list of the information disclosed in the newspaper that might be prejudicial to the defendant(s).

2. In the clerk's office, review the file(s) that apply to the case you used in Exercise 1. Did the defense attorney file any motions to either delay or move the trial? If so, how did the judge rule on those motions?

3. Were there any motions or orders in the case that were designed to limit what the attorneys could say to the press?

4. Based on your review, do you think the press account of the defendant and the crime could have prevented the defendant from receiving a fair trial? What is the basis for your opinion?

---

3. PRESUMPTION OF INNOCENCE

The presumption of innocence is one of the most basic elements of due process. It is reflected in the fact that the prosecution is assigned the burden of proving the defendant's guilt beyond a reasonable doubt.[14] Furthermore, the defense is not required to put the defendant, or any other witnesses, on the stand, and if the defendant chooses not to testify, the prosecution cannot comment or otherwise draw attention to it during any part of the trial.

Judges usually explain the **beyond a reasonable doubt** standard to jurors as the degree of doubt that causes a reasonable person to refrain from acting. The proof must be so conclusive and complete that all reasonable doubts regarding the facts are removed from the jurors' minds.

Beyond a reasonable doubt
The standard of proof used in criminal trials. The evidence presented must be so conclusive and complete that all reasonable doubts regarding the facts are removed from the jurors' minds.

---

[14]In contrast to the preponderance of the evidence and the clear and convincing standards used in civil cases.

It should be noted, however, that even though the prosecution must meet this high standard of proof, it does not have to establish guilt beyond *any* doubt or beyond a *shadow of a doubt.*

4. PRIVILEGE AGAINST SELF-INCRIMINATION

The presumption of innocence is enhanced by the privilege against self-incrimination. Not only does the prosecution bear the burden of proving a defendant's guilt but it must be able to do so without requiring the defendant to incriminate himself or herself. Specifically, the Fifth Amendment declares: "No person shall be . . . compelled in any criminal case to be a witness against himself. . . ." Back in Chapter 4 we discussed how this privilege against self-incrimination applies to police investigations, and in Chapter 9 we pointed out how violations of this right can result in the suppression of evidence that was illegally gathered. At the trial stage it means that the prosecution cannot call the defendant as a witness as part of its "case in chief."[15]

Defendants can, of course, choose to waive this privilege and testify as a defense witness on their own behalf. However, if defendants do testify, the prosecution has the right to cross-examine them. They cannot pick and choose which questions they wish to respond to or refuse to discuss topics, such as a criminal record, if the judge rules that it is relevant.

5. RIGHT TO CONFRONT AND CROSS-EXAMINE WITNESSES

You can probably relate to the frustration that comes from having false or misleading rumors spread, in a way that allows you neither to know what exactly is being alleged nor to explain why they are false or misleading. In order to prevent this happening in criminal trials, the Sixth Amendment includes the following: "In all criminal prosecutions, the accused shall enjoy the right . . . to be confronted with the witnesses against him. . . ."

Although it isn't specifically stated in the Sixth Amendment, the right to confront witnesses includes the right to cross-examine them. After the prosecuting attorney has elicited the witness's testimony, the defense has the opportunity to elicit further testimony that may bring out additional information either in support of the defendant's position or challenging the witness's credibility.

6. RIGHT TO COMPEL WITNESSES TO TESTIFY

In addition to the right to confront the prosecution's witnesses, the Sixth Amendment also gives the defendant the right to compel the testimony of other witnesses who may have information relevant to the trial. It declares: "In all criminal prosecutions, the accused shall enjoy the right . . . to have compulsory process for obtaining witnesses in his favor. . . ." In order to enforce this right, the defense must place the name of the persons on the official witness list and have the court issue subpoenas requiring the witnesses' attendance.

---

[15]The part of the trial during which the prosecution presents evidence to prove its case.

It is important to note, however, that although witnesses can be compelled to appear, they may be able to claim their own privilege against self-incrimination as a legitimate reason for not answering all the questions that are asked. In some cases, this problem can be overcome by a grant of immunity, but in others it cannot.[16]

7. RIGHT TO COUNSEL

In order to help the defendant take advantage of all these rights, the Sixth Amendment also includes a provision creating a right to counsel. It declares: "In all criminal prosecutions, the accused shall enjoy the right . . . to have the Assistance of Counsel for his defense."[17]

Back in Chapter 4, we discussed how the right to counsel has been interpreted to apply to the criminal investigation stage, and in Chapter 6 we discussed the appointment of counsel for people who couldn't afford to hire an attorney on their own. Chapters 6 through 9 covered various activities defense attorneys undertake to prepare a defense and attempt to negotiate favorable plea agreements. In the remaining chapters of this section, we will cover their roles in the trial process, sentencing, and appeals.

DISCUSSION QUESTIONS

8. If your client chose not to testify at the criminal trial, would you want the judge to give the jury an instruction about there being a constitutional right not to testify and that the jury should not allow its verdict to be influenced by the defendant's failure to testify? Why or why not?

9. Even though he had made frequent public statements about how he looked forward to telling his side of the story at his trial, and his attorney had declared in his opening statement that his client would testify on his own behalf, former Illinois Governor Rod Blagojevich chose not to testify at his federal criminal trial on corruption charges. What factors do you think went into this decision? Given the fact that the jury found him guilty on one of twenty-four counts and failed to reach a unanimous verdict on the other twenty-three counts, what can you conclude about the wisdom of this decision?

10. Should someone on trial for child molestation have the right to be in the courtroom when the victim is testifying about the alleged molestation? Why or why not?

C. THE USE OF EVIDENCE

In the previous section, we discussed how the presumption of innocence makes the prosecution responsible for proving the defendant's guilt beyond a reasonable doubt. It must meet this burden of proof by presenting legally admissible **evidence** at the trial. This evidence can take the form of testimony by witnesses,

Evidence
Witness testimony, documents, physical objects, and stipulations that are presented in court for the purpose of determining the facts of the case.

---

[16]See discussion on severance and joinder on pp. 291–292 in Chapter 9.

[17]The drafters of the Constitution used the British spelling for *defense*.

Stipulation
An agreement by both sides to accept something as being true so as to simplify and expedite the trial by dispensing with the need to present formal proof.

Testimonial evidence
Verbal statements that are given under oath at a trial for the purpose of helping the jury and/or judge to understand the facts of the case.

Physical evidence
Tangible physical objects that can be picked up and handled.

Demonstrative evidence
Physical objects, such as photos, maps, x-rays, and diagrams, used to illustrate or aid in the understanding of verbal testimony.

Documentary evidence
Legal instruments such as contracts, leases, wills, and deeds and other written documents used to support claims made in court.

Competency
The ability of a witness to testify; generally, the witness must be capable of being understood by the jury; must understand the duty to tell the truth; and have knowledge of the facts to which he or she is testifying.

relevant documents, physical objects, **stipulations**, and what is referred to as judicial notice.

The specific rules governing the presentation of evidence in federal courts are set forth in the Federal Rules of Evidence. Each state has a similar set of rules that apply to trials in their courts. The sources of state rules of evidence may include case law, statutory enactments, and court rules. Figure 10.1 presents an overview of the organization and topics covered in the federal rules of evidence.

ARTICLE I. GENERAL PROVISIONS
ARTICLE II. JUDICIAL NOTICE
ARTICLE III. PRESUMPTIONS IN CIVIL ACTIONS AND PROCEEDINGS
ARTICLE IV. RELEVANCY AND ITS LIMITS
ARTICLE V. PRIVILEGES
ARTICLE VI. WITNESSES
ARTICLE VII. OPINIONS AND EXPERT TESTIMONY
ARTICLE VIII. HEARSAY
ARTICLE IX. AUTHENTICATION AND IDENTIFICATION
ARTICLE X. CONTENTS OF WRITINGS, RECORDINGS, AND PHOTOGRAPHS
ARTICLE XI: MISCELLANEOUS RULES

Figure 10.1   Federal Rules of Evidence

1. TYPES OF EVIDENCE

Evidence is often categorized as being either testimonial or physical. **Testimonial evidence** consists of verbal statements that witnesses give under oath at a trial in response to appropriate questions from the attorneys or the judge; **physical evidence** involves tangible physical items. Examples include items such as guns, knives, shell casings, drugs, stolen jewelry, counterfeit money, etc. Examples of physical evidence are shown in Exhibit 10.1. Physical evidence can also take the form of **demonstrative evidence,** such as visual aids (e.g., photos, maps, x-rays, and diagrams), or **documentary evidence,** which includes legal instruments (e.g., contracts, leases, wills, and deeds) and other written documents (e.g., estimates, letters, and e-mails).

2. QUALIFICATIONS OF WITNESSES

In order to be able to present testimonial evidence, witnesses must first be sworn and determined to be **competent** to give testimony on the issues involved in the case. Rule 603 states:

Before testifying, every witness shall be required to declare that the witness will testify truthfully, by oath or affirmation administered in a form calculated to awaken the witness' conscience and impress the witness' mind with the duty to do so.

Exhibit 10.1: Photographs of Explosive Materials

Below are FBI evidence photographs of copper tubing, wiring, various chemicals, electrical components, and other bomb-making materials recovered from the home of Theodore Kaczynski, the "Unabomber." The items themselves are physical evidence. The photographs are demonstrative evidence.

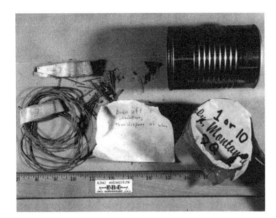 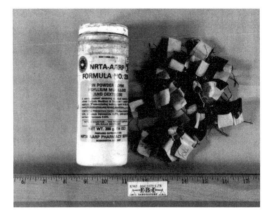

According to the Advisory Committee on the Federal Rules, this requirement is designed to afford the flexibility required in dealing with religious adults, atheists, conscientious objectors, mental defectives, and children. Affirmation is simply a solemn undertaking to tell the truth and no special formula is required. Witnesses must be old enough and have enough mental competency to understand the questions and the duty to tell the truth. Where language might be a barrier, the court will provide an interpreter.

3. TYPES OF WITNESSES

Fact witnesses (often called **lay witnesses**) are limited to testifying about events they personally observed and/or statements they heard with their own ears. They are not allowed to speculate about things for which they lack personal knowledge. On the other hand, **expert witnesses** are brought in to supply scientific, technical, or other specialized knowledge that will help the jury and/or judge evaluate the facts that have been presented. In this capacity, they are allowed to speculate as to the probability of certain things having occurred if they have

Lay witness
A witness who is called to testify about things personally observed through his or her senses.

Expert witness
A witness who is called to supply scientific, technical, or other specialized knowledge that will help the jury and/or judge evaluate the facts that have been presented.

properly been recognized as experts[18] on the subject and limit their opinions to their area of recognized expertise. Prior to having someone be recognized as an expert witness, the examining attorney must ask preliminary questions designed to qualify the witness as an expert in the field that witness is going to give testimony on.

Article VII of the Federal Rules of Evidence is devoted to sorting out when different types of witnesses can give opinions and what it means to be an "expert witness." Rule 701 states:

> If the witness is not testifying as an expert, the witness' testimony in the form of opinions or inferences is limited to those opinions or inferences which are (a) rationally based on the perception of the witness, and (b) helpful to a clear understanding of the witness' testimony or the determination of a fact in issue, and (c) not based on scientific, technical, or other specialized knowledge within the scope of Rule 702.

This rule allows witnesses who have not been qualified as experts to give opinions on matters such as the similarity of a person's voice or handwriting to that of someone's with whom they are familiar or whether a person appeared to be angry or intoxicated. Most courts have permitted the owner or officer of a business to testify to the value or projected profits of the business without the necessity of qualifying the witness as an accountant, appraiser, or similar expert. Such opinion testimony is admitted not because of experience, training or specialized knowledge within the realm of an expert, but because of the particularized knowledge that the witness has by virtue of his or her position in the business.

Rule 702 spells out the role of expert testimony:

> If scientific, technical, or other specialized knowledge will assist the trier of fact to understand the evidence or to determine a fact in issue, a witness qualified as an expert by knowledge, skill, experience, training, or education may testify thereto in the form of an opinion or otherwise, if (1) the testimony is based upon sufficient facts or data, (2) the testimony is the product of reliable principles and methods, and (3) the witness has applied the principles and methods reliably to the facts of the case.

While expert witnesses are allowed to give their opinions and are frequently asked "hypothetical questions," they are not limited only to giving opinions. Rule 702 recognizes that an expert witness may also testify about scientific facts and theories relevant to the case. It leaves it up to the judge to decide whether the opinion evidence is reasonably reliable, whether it will substantially assist the trier of fact, and whether the proposed witness has sufficient expertise to express such opinions in court.[19]

---

[18]To be recognized as an expert, the judge must find that the witness has special skills or knowledge that exceed those of the average person.

[19]In *Daubert v. Merrell Dow Pharmaceuticals, Inc.*, 509 U.S. 579, 113 S. Ct. 2786, 125 L. Ed. 2d 469 (1993), the Court charged trial judges with the responsibility of acting as gatekeepers to exclude unreliable expert testimony, and the Court in *Kumho Tire Co. v. Carmichael*, 526 U.S. 137, 119 S. Ct. 1167, 143 L. Ed. 2d 238 (1999) clarified that this gatekeeper function applies to all expert testimony, not just testimony based in science.

Although witnesses are not permitted to express their opinions as to the guilt or innocence of the defendant, Rule 704 does permit experts to give opinions that embrace ultimate issues. However, this rule explicitly prohibits opinion testimony as to whether the defendant was legally insane at the time the crime was committed. The Rule provides:

(b) No expert witness testifying with respect to the mental state or condition of a defendant in a criminal case may state an opinion or inference as to whether the defendant did or did not have the mental state or condition constituting an element of the crime charged or of a defense thereto. Such ultimate issues are matters for the trier of fact alone.

APPLICATION EXERCISES

5. Based on the Federal Rules of Evidence, should a judge allow a lay witness to testify that a substance appeared to be a narcotic?

6. Locate and read what the U.S. Supreme Court has said about assessing the reliability of scientific expert testimony in *Daubert v. Merrell Dow Pharmaceuticals, Inc.*, 509 U.S. 579 113 S. Ct. 2786, 125 L. Ed 469 (1993) and *Kumho Tire Co. v. Carmichael*, 526 U.S. 137, 119 S. Ct. 1167, 143 L. Ed. 2d 238 (1999).
   a. Based on the *Daubert* opinion, make a checklist of factors a judge should use in assessing the reliability of scientific expert testimony.
   b. How does the *Kumho Tire Co.* opinion affect the *Daubert* decision?

4. HEARSAY EVIDENCE

One of the most important limitations on the presentation of evidence is the rule against **hearsay evidence (the hearsay rule)**. Rule 801(c) defines hearsay as "a statement, other than one made by the declarant while testifying at the trial or hearing, offered in evidence to prove the truth of the matter asserted." Rule 801(a) defines a statement as "(1) an oral or written assertion or (2) nonverbal conduct of a person, if it is intended by the person as an assertion." Rule 801(b) defines a **declarant** as "a person who makes a statement." In nontechnical terms, hearsay is secondhand information about an event that the witness got from someone else, rather than having observed it with his or her own senses. For example, it would be hearsay for a witness to testify that a friend had told him that the friend had seen the defendant near the scene of the crime or that the friend had overheard the defendant bragging about having robbed a liquor store Tuesday night.

The general principle, stated in Rule 802, is: "Hearsay is not admissible except as provided by these rules or by other rules prescribed by the Supreme Court pursuant to statutory authority or by Act of Congress." Hearsay is generally excluded because the witnesses cannot personally attest that what someone else told them had actually occurred and because the original source of the information is not there to be cross-examined. In the examples given above, the witness has personal knowledge of what somebody else claimed to have seen

Hearsay evidence
A statement, other than one made by the declarant while testifying at the trial or hearing, offered in evidence to prove the truth of the matter asserted.

Hearsay rule
The general rule of evidence providing that hearsay evidence is not admissible at trial or hearing.

Declarant
The person who made the out-of-court statement.

or heard but cannot offer proof the defendant had in fact been at the scene of the crime or that the defendant had in fact bragged about having committed the robbery.

Two types of out-of-court statements routinely permitted into evidence are (1) admissions by party opponents and prior statements by a witness. Under Federal Rule 801(d), these types of statements are considered as non-hearsay and therefore are not barred by the hearsay rule. In most states, however, prior witness statements and admissions by party opponents are admissible as exceptions to the hearsay rule. Although the underlying legal theories differ, the practical effect is the same—these types of out-of-court statements are admitted into evidence.

Prior statements can be used to impeach the credibility of a witness. If a key witness testifies at the trial that the robber drove off in a red car but had previously told someone that it had been a white car, the defendant could have that person testify as to what the witness had previously told her about the color of the getaway vehicle in order to create doubt about the reliability of the prosecution witness's identification. Admissions by a party opponent can be particularly important to the prosecution. Virtually anything the defendant tells the police, his friends, his girlfriend, or his cellmate potentially can be presented at trial by the prosecutor. For example, when a defendant brags to someone that he robbed a liquor store, the people who heard this admission can testify as to what the defendant had said. Furthermore, a statement by a co-conspirator made in furtherance of the conspiracy can be used against everyone in the conspiracy.

Rules 803 and 804 list twenty-four general exceptions and five that apply only when the declarant is not available. See Figure 10.2 for a listing of these exceptions.

Rule 803: Hearsay Exceptions; Availability of Declarant Immaterial

The following are not excluded by the hearsay rule, even though the declarant is available as a witness:

(1) Present sense impression.

(2) Excited utterance.

(3) Then existing mental, emotional, or physical condition.

(4) Statements for purposes of medical diagnosis or treatment.

(5) Recorded recollection.

(6) Records of regularly conducted activity.

(7) Absence of entry in records kept in accordance with the provision (6).

(8) Public records and reports.

(9) Records of vital statistics.

(10) Absence of public record or entry.

(11) Records of religious organizations.

(12) Marriage, baptismal, and similar certificates.

(13) Family records.

(14) Records of documents affecting an interest in property.

(15) Statements in documents affecting an interest in property.

(16) Statements in ancient documents.

(17) Market reports, commercial publications.

(18) Learned treatises.

(19) Reputation concerning personal or family history.

(20) Reputation concerning boundaries or general history.

(21) Reputation as to character.

(22) Judgment of previous conviction.

(23) Judgment as to personal, family or general history, or boundaries.

(24) Other exceptions covered in Rule 807.

Rule 804. Hearsay Exceptions; Declarant Unavailable

The following are not excluded by the hearsay rule if the declarant is unavailable as a witness:

(1) Former testimony.

(2) Statement under belief of impending death.

(3) Statement against interest.

(4) Statement of personal or family history.

(5) Other exceptions covered in Rule 807.

(6) Forfeiture by wrongdoing.

Figure 10.2   Federal Rules of Criminal Procedure Rules 803 and 804 on Hearsay Exceptions

According to Rule 804, a declarant is considered to be "unavailable as a witness" if he or she:

(1) is exempted by ruling of the court . . . ; or
(2) persists in refusing to testify . . . despite an order of the court to do so; or
(3) testifies to a lack of memory. . . . or
(4) is unable to be present or to testify at the hearing because of death or then existing physical or mental illness or infirmity; or

(5) is absent from the hearing and the proponent of a statement has been unable to procure the declarant's attendance . . . by process or other reasonable means.

A declarant is not unavailable as a witness if exemption, refusal, claim of lack of memory, inability, or absence is due to the procurement or wrongdoing of the proponent of a statement for the purpose of preventing the witness from attending or testifying.

Although many states follow the federal rules of evidence, in many situations there are differences. You should check the case law, statutes, and court rules for your jurisdiction when you research an evidentiary issue.

5. ROLE OF EVIDENCE IN PROVING THE CASE

Direct evidence

Evidence that establishes a direct link to the fact or event that a party seeks to prove.

Circumstantial evidence

Evidence that permits the inference of the existence or nonexistence of a fact or event that a party seeks to prove.

Cumulative evidence

Evidence that does not add any new information but confirms facts that already have been established.

Corroborative evidence

Evidence supporting other evidence that has already been admitted but that is presented in a different form.

Authentication of evidence

The process of establishing that the objects being introduced into evidence are what they are claimed to be.

Evidence can also be classified on the basis of how it contributes to proving the case. **Direct evidence** establishes a direct link to a fact or event that a party seeks to prove. For example, a witness's testimony that "I saw the defendant shoot the victim" would be direct evidence of a key event in a homicide case. **Circumstantial evidence**, on the other hand, provides information that permits the inference of the existence or nonexistence of a fact or event that a party seeks to prove. An example would be testimony given by a police officer who did not witness the crime, but who testifies that the defendant was found at the scene with powder burns on his hands consistent with having recently fired a handgun. Although the powder burns do not directly prove the defendant shot the victim in question, this information is logically consistent with a conclusion that the defendant did. This bit of information by itself would be insufficient to gain a criminal conviction, but it could be combined with other pieces of circumstantial evidence that together might be sufficient to meet the prosecution's burden of proof.

Cumulative evidence is evidence that confirms facts that already have been established by previously admitted evidence. For example, if two people both testify that they saw the defendant fire a handgun at the victim, the second witness would be providing cumulative evidence. Such evidence may be excluded if the judge believes that the facts it proves have already been sufficiently established. This is especially true if the other party is not contesting the particular fact in question.

The concept of **corroborative evidence** is very similar in that this evidence also supports previous testimony, but it comes in a different form. For example, if a second person testified that he had seen the defendant make a phone call shortly before leaving the scene of an accident, that would be classified as cumulative evidence. On the other hand, the introduction of telephone company records showing the defendant made a call to a certain party on a certain date and time would be corroborative evidence.

6. AUTHENTICATION AND IDENTIFICATION

Although physical and documentary evidence is supposed to speak for itself, witnesses are needed to **authenticate** it before it can be introduced. Before a business record can be introduced, an appropriate official of the company must take the witness stand to identify the document, explain what it is, and tell how it is used in the ordinary course of the business. Before an alleged weapon can be used as evidence, appropriate law enforcement officials have to take the witness stand to identify the object as being one that was found at the scene of the crime or in the defendant's possession and establish the "**chain of custody**."

Articles IX and X of the Federal Rules of Evidence lay out specific guidelines for authenticating different types of evidence. Certain types of official public documents can be "self-authenticated"; other types of evidence require specific types of testimony. Authentication is accomplished through a practice commonly referred to as "**laying a foundation**," in which attorneys ask witnesses a series of preliminary questions designed to identify the evidence they want to introduce and explain how it relates to the issues involved in the trial. Prior to giving testimonial evidence about what he or she saw or heard, the attorney must ask preliminary questions designed to establish where the witness was and who else may have been present at the time of the witness's observations.

Proper testimony must establish that a document being presented is in fact what it is purported to be. Under some circumstances, however, a copy may be considered admissible. Public records (official governmental documents as well as private deeds and mortgages that are officially recorded with the government) can be presented by means of certified copies. In addition to an official seal and signature, an affidavit from the record's custodian usually is presented explaining what the record shows and attesting that it is an accurate copy of the one on file. In terms of other documents, according to the **best evidence rule**, usually an original document must be produced at the trial. However, copies of documents may be allowed when the original has been lost or destroyed, is in the hands of an adverse party who has refused to produce it, or is in the hands of a third party who is outside the jurisdiction of the court's subpoena power. In cases where the original is so voluminous that it is impractical to produce it in its entirety, the litigant is usually allowed to produce a summary.

The rules governing the authentication of photographs differ from one jurisdiction to the next. Most courts simply require that a witness who is familiar with an object or a scene in the photograph testify that it is an accurate representation of that object or scene as it appeared at the time of the incident. On the other hand, a few courts require that the person who actually took the photograph testify about the type of camera and the settings used. Some require testimony relating to the chain of possession of the photograph.

There is a trend in the federal courts to require the parties to address issues of authenticity of exhibits prior to trial. Under this practice, the parties list all of the exhibits in a joint pre-trial memorandum. Any objections to authenticity are included in the document. This approach streamlines the trial of the case.

7. JUDICIAL NOTICE

As an alternative to providing witness testimony to introduce information into evidence, attorneys can request that the judge take **judicial notice** of certain types of adjudicative facts. For example, a judge could take judicial notice that a city lies within a particular county or that May 1, 2010 fell on a Saturday. In effect, the judge acknowledges that the information is so well known that specific proof is not required.

Judicial notice is covered in Article II of the Federal Rules of Evidence. Rule 201 declares: "A judicially noticed fact must be one not subject to reasonable

Chain of custody
A record of who possessed an object being presented as evidence from the time it came into the possession of government agents until it is presented in court.

Laying a foundation
A process by which an attorney asks a witness a series of preliminary questions designed to identify potential evidence and explain how it relates to the issues involved in the trial.

Best evidence rule
An evidentiary rule requiring that the original document be produced at trial.

Judicial notice
An action taken by a judge to formally recognize something as being a fact without requiring the attorneys to prove it through the introduction of other evidence.

dispute in that it is either (1) generally known within the territorial jurisdiction of the trial court or (2) capable of accurate and ready determination by resort to sources whose accuracy cannot reasonably be questioned." It also states: "In a criminal case, the court shall instruct the jury that it may, but is not required to, accept as conclusive any fact judicially noticed."

8. RELEVANCE AND MATERIALITY

In order for physical evidence to be accepted as an exhibit, or for witness testimony to become part of the record, it must be both relevant and material. Relevance refers to the "probative value" of the evidence. **Relevant evidence** is defined in Rule 401 as: "[E]vidence having any tendency to make the existence of any fact that is of consequence to the determination of the action more probable or less probable than it would be without the evidence." For example, the fact that the defendant had a tattoo on his shoulder would be relevant if the store clerk had testified that because the robber had been wearing a sleeveless tank top, she had noticed that he had a tattoo on his shoulder. However, if the clerk had reported that the robber was wearing a long-sleeved hoodie, the existence of the defendant's tattoo would not be relevant to determining if the defendant had been the robber.

Materiality is usually thought of as either a subcategory of relevancy or simply another word for relevancy. Often it is stated as requiring that the evidence be more probative than prejudicial. This concern is reflected in Rule 403.

> Although relevant, evidence may be excluded if its probative value is substantially outweighed by the danger of unfair prejudice, confusion of the issues, or misleading the jury, or by considerations of undue delay, waste of time, or needless presentation of cumulative evidence.

Thus a gruesome photograph of the condition of the victim of a mutilation murder may be relevant yet be excluded because of the probability that it would inflame the jury.

One of the most complex areas of evidence law involves the handling of "character evidence." This area of the law involves the admissibility of information about a person's reputation within the community for moral behavior. Rule 404 states:

> (a) Evidence of a person's character or a trait of character is not admissible for the purpose of proving action in conformity therewith on a particular occasion, except:
>
> (1) Character of accused—*In a criminal case, evidence* of a pertinent trait of character offered by an accused, or by the prosecution to rebut the same, or if evidence of a trait of character of the alleged victim of the crime is offered by an accused and admitted under Rule 404 (a)(2), evidence of the same trait of character of the accused offered by the prosecution;
>
> (2) Character of alleged victim—*In a criminal case, and subject to the limitations imposed by Rule 412, evidence* of a pertinent trait of character of the alleged victim of the crime offered by an accused, or by the prosecution to rebut the same, or evidence of a character trait of

Relevant evidence
Evidence that leads one to logically conclude that an asserted fact is either more or less probable.

Materiality
A requirement that the evidence be more probative than prejudicial.

Character evidence
Evidence of a person's reputation in the community as to a particular trait, such as honesty or chastity.

peacefulness of the alleged victim offered by the prosecution in a homicide case to rebut evidence that the alleged victim was the first aggressor;

(b) Evidence of other crimes, wrongs, or acts is not admissible to prove the character of a person in order to show action in conformity therewith. It may, however, be admissible for other purposes, such as proof of motive, opportunity, intent, preparation, plan, knowledge, identity, or absence of mistake or accident, provided that upon request by the accused, the prosecution in a criminal case shall provide reasonable notice in advance of trial, or during trial if the court excuses pretrial notice on good cause shown, of the general nature of any such evidence it intends to introduce at trial.

Other rules relating to the admissibility of various types of character evidence include:

- Rule 410: Inadmissibility of Pleas, Plea Discussions, and Related Statements
- Rule 412: Sex Offense Cases; Relevance of Alleged Victim's Past Sexual Behavior or Alleged Sexual Predisposition
- Rule 413: Evidence of Similar Crimes in Sexual Assault Cases
- Rule 414: Evidence of Similar Crimes in Child Molestation Cases
- Rule 415: Evidence of Similar Acts in Civil Cases Concerning Sexual Assault or Child Molestation and
- Rules 608 and 609: Evidence related to the character of witnesses

DISCUSSION QUESTION

11. Can you think of a situation in which circumstantial evidence alone would be sufficient to justify returning a guilty verdict in a murder case? If so, what would that evidence have to be?

SUMMARY

Criminal trials are the mechanism used to determine if the government can prove, beyond a reasonable doubt, that someone has done something that the government has designated a crime. The rules used to conduct the trial must comport with the constitutional protections considered to be essential to the "due process of law."

The most important constitutional rights impacting the conduct of criminal trials are: the right to a public trial, the right to a jury trial, the presumption of innocence, the privilege against self-incrimination, the right to confront and cross-examine witnesses, the right to compel witnesses to testify, and the right to counsel. The nature of each of these rights was explained in this chapter.

At the end of the trial, the judge or jury is supposed to decide the guilt or innocence of the defendant based on the evidence that was presented during the trial. This evidence can take the form of witness testimony, documents, physical objects, and stipulations. Lay witnesses can testify as to what they personally observed, and expert witnesses are called upon to provide specialized knowledge (usually scientific/technical information) relevant to a better understanding of the facts being presented.

One of the most confusing parts of the rules of evidence involves the hearsay rule. Not only is the definition of hearsay (a statement, other than one made by the declarant while testifying at the trial or hearing, offered in evidence to prove the truth of the matter asserted) hard to grasp, Rules 803 and 804 list a total of thirty exceptions to the basic rule.

Finally, there are also the concepts of relevance and materiality. Relevance refers to the "probative value" of the evidence and materiality requires that it be more probative than prejudicial. In order for physical evidence to be accepted as an exhibit, or for witness testimony to become part of the record, it must be both relevant and material.

INTERNET RESOURCES

Handbooks for Jurors

- Judicial Conference of the United States: **http://www.ksd.uscourts.gov/jury/hand-book.php**
- Texas Universal Juror Handbook: **http://www.sugarlandtx.gov/municipal_court/services/jury_summons/documents/jury_handbook_e.pdf**
- Websites on Jury Nullification:
  http://www.caught.net/juror.htm
  http://fija.org/

REVIEW QUESTIONS

1. What does the Sixth Amendment right to a public trial encompass?
2. What are the three references to jury trials in the U.S. Constitution?
3. In a jury trial, who decides factual questions? Who decides legal questions?
4. What is the difference between legal questions and factual questions?
5. What are the two steps of jury selection?
6. Name and describe the two types of challenges attorneys can assert during the *voir dire* process.
7. What is the minimum potential sentence of incarceration that gives rise to the Sixth Amendment right to trial by jury?
8. In what types of situations would criminal defendants ordinarily choose to waive their right to be tried by a jury?
9. What is the minimum number of jurors required in federal and in state felony cases?
10. What is jury nullification?
11. How does the presumption of innocence affect each side's obligations at trial?
12. What part of the Sixth Amendment gives criminal defendants the right to cross-examine witnesses against them?
13. Besides witness testimony, what are the typical forms of evidence used to prove facts at trial?
14. What is the difference between testimonial and physical evidence?
15. What evidence can expert witnesses present that fact witnesses cannot?
16. What is hearsay, and is it ever admissible in a criminal trial?

17. How are cumulative evidence and corroborative evidence similar? How are they different?
18. Before an exhibit is introduced into evidence, identify and explain the process that the attorney must follow.
19. Other than the parties' stipulation of facts, what other method authorizes a judge to inform the jury that certain facts are to be accepted as true without any proof?
20. According to the Federal Rules of Evidence, under what circumstances can relevant evidence be inadmissible because it is not material?

Chapter 11

Preparation for the Trial

In one sense, pre-trial preparation begins as soon as the government receives the police reports or when the defense attorney begins representation of the client. From the very beginning, both sides are taking actions that will prepare them for an eventual trial. For example, the discovery process discussed in Chapter 7 is designed to gather information that will minimize surprises at the trial.

In this chapter, we will discuss the preparations that generally don't take place until after the initial plea-bargaining attempts have failed and the case has been formally set for trial. At this stage of a case, the parties must notify the opposition as to who will be called to testify and what exhibits will be offered as evidence. Activities taking place during this period usually include preparing for *voir dire*, meeting with witnesses, preparing trial subpoenas, conducting further factual research, preparing exhibits, creating slide presentations, organizing the file for trial, and preparing motions and briefs on evidentiary issues.

A. PREPARATION FOR JURY TRIALS

1. THE DECISION TO USE A JURY

As discussed in Chapter 10, the right to be tried by a jury differs between the federal and the state courts and depends upon the severity of the crimes being charged. In those situations in which the right to a jury trial does apply, in state court it is ultimately up to the defendant to decide whether to exercise this right or to waive it and leave the verdict in the hands of the judge. Although the decision ultimately rests with the defendant, it is the defense attorney's obligation to carefully discuss the pros and cons associated with this decision. As a general rule, defendants typically choose to use a jury because they think at least some of the jurors will be more sympathetic and more likely to identify with their situation than a judge would. Since jury verdicts typically have to be either unanimous or require a "super majority" to convict, the defendant's odds of avoiding a conviction usually seem better with a jury. On the other hand, in cases where there has been a great deal of prejudicial publicity, where the community is perceived as being prejudiced against members of the defendant's racial or ethnic group, or where the crime was particularly gruesome, some believe they are better off having the case decided by a professional who is committed to following the letter of the law and is less likely to be influenced by these prejudicial factors.

2. PREPARATION FOR *VOIR DIRE*

Once it has been determined that a jury will hear the case, both prosecution and defense must begin preparation for the *voir dire* examinations that will occur during the process of seating the jury. These examinations are supposed to uncover factors that might prevent the person being questioned from being a fair and impartial juror. The combination of challenges for cause and peremptory challenges that we discussed in Chapter 10 is designed to eliminate jurors who are not deemed to be impartial. However, there is no guarantee that these challenges will successfully achieve that result, and much depends on the extent to which each side has researched the background of the potential jurors, how skillful their questioning is, how carefully they listen to inflections in the answers, and how well they read the potential juror's body language.

The preparation for this questioning typically begins by examining the list of people who have been summoned for jury duty during the time that the trial is expected to begin. In addition to names and addresses, the potential jurors' birthdates may also be listed. If juror questionnaires are available, the attorneys can also learn other information about jury candidates, including educational and employment background; marital and family status; whether they have been victims of a crime; and whether they have friends or relatives who are crime victims, police officers, or attorneys.

If the financial resources are available, attorneys for both sides may have paralegal employees or outside investigators do further research to find out as much as they can about the people on the list. Public records frequently give indications of the potential jurors' attitudes: Voter registration lists may reveal party affiliation; real estate and vehicle ownership records may indicate financial wherewithal and self-image; court documents often show detailed information about financial status, criminal background, and relationships with others. Sources such as the *Haines Directory*, city directories, and *Who's Who* are available in most public libraries. These reference books provide information about occupation, neighborhood income level, and family members.

The Internet is also an excellent source of information. These days, people seem to be less guarded in communicating on the Internet than in person, and social networking sites like Facebook, LinkedIn, Twitter, and MySpace contain personal data and provide insight into the personality, emotions, interests, and attitudes of the author. Blogs and personal websites can also be productive sources of information. Search engines like Google can yield fruitful information, as well. When conducting this type of research, investigators should use more than one search engine. Bing, for instance, may yield different results from

Google or Dogpile. Over 100 free websites can be used to acquire information about people.[1]

When entering search terms, consider putting the person's first and last names in quotes. If this generates too many results, add the city in which the person lives or the person's occupation. If the search is not productive, consider variations of the person's first name (e.g., Bill or Billy or Will for William).

In high-profile cases, either or both sides may contract with jury consultants to collect and review this background information. Jury consultants may even organize and evaluate focus groups and mock trials to identify characteristics that are correlated with different types of views about the type of crimes or the type of defendants involved. Although this type of information is unlikely to convince a judge to remove a juror for cause, it may well become the basis for exercising peremptory challenges.

In addition to collecting background information, paralegals can help attorneys draft questions either to be submitted to the judge or for the attorneys to ask themselves. Good *voir dire* questions should be designed to uncover potential conflicts of interest or biases that might work against the client's interests. Sample *voir dire* questions appear in Figure 11.1.

---

1. As the Court has just stated, my client is an African American Chicago Police Department patrolman. Is there anything about him being an African American male that would prejudice you for or against him in connection with your obligation to hear all of the evidence, listen to all arguments given by counsel, and carefully consider all of the instructions and law provided by the Court before making a decision as to whether my client, Officer Isaac Berry Innocent, is guilty of the crimes charged?
2. Is there anything about my client's status as a Chicago police officer that would unfairly bias or prejudice your own opinion concerning the Defendant's guilt or innocence based on his occupational status?
3. Have you ever been involved in any law enforcement work whatsoever?
4. Do you have any family members or close friends who are currently or who have been previously involved in law enforcement?
5. Have you had any adverse encounters with African American males under any circumstances whatsoever? If so, describe those experiences.
6. Have you had any adverse encounters with any African American law enforcement personnel on any level whatsoever? If so, describe those experiences.

Source: William H. Hooks, *Trial Issues: Defending Illinois Criminal Cases* (IICLE 2003, Supp. 2007) at 11S-65.

Figure 11.1 Proposed *Voir Dire* Questions from the Defense

DISCUSSION QUESTIONS

1. If you were an attorney for the defense, in what types of situations would you recommend having a bench trial rather than a jury trial?
2. Do you think attorneys should be allowed to ask their own questions during *voir dire* as opposed to having the judge read the attorney's questions to the jurors? Why?

APPLICATION EXERCISES

1. List five biographical resources or community directories available at your school's library.

2. Conduct an Internet search about your instructor for this course and then prepare a list of all facts about the instructor's professional life along with the web address for the source of each fact.

3. Conduct an Internet search about the mayor of your community and list four of the mayor's attitudes and/or beliefs and cite the web addresses for this information.

4. Prepare six *voir dire* questions concerning alcoholic beverages that would be appropriate to use in *People v. Bud Cook* (Hypothetical Case #1).

5. Prepare six *voir dire* questions concerning "experiencing financial troubles" in *United States v. William Edwards* (Hypothetical Case #3).

B. PREPARATION OF EXHIBITS

Exhibit
A tangible item presented by the parties at trial.

Physical evidence
Material objects related to the case.

Documentary evidence
Legal instruments such as contracts, leases, wills and deeds, or other written documents used to support claims made in court.

Demonstrative evidence
Physical objects, such as photos, maps, x-rays, and diagrams, used to illustrate or aid in the understanding of verbal testimony.

Exhibits are tangible items presented by the parties at the trial to supplement the testimony of witnesses. They can include **physical evidence** such as a murder weapon or blood-stained clothes, as well as relevant **documentary evidence** and **demonstrative evidence** such as photos, diagrams, etc.

Regardless of the type of evidence, each exhibit must be marked by the side that presents it. For instance, the knife used as a weapon in an aggravated battery case may be designated "People's Exhibit 1"; a ticket stub corroborating the defendant's alibi could be "Defendant's Exhibit 3." Paralegals are often charged with organizing and compiling the exhibits their supervising attorneys plan to submit at trial.

The parties should determine the exhibits they plan to present before the case goes to trial. In some courts, the parties prepare a formal exhibit list, which is attached to the final pretrial memorandum. The format of this exhibit list is usually set forth in the local court rules governing pre-trial memoranda. Often-times, the rules require the parties to state whether there are foundation objections to the exhibits.

A less formal procedure is followed in many state courts. In these jurisdictions, parties still organize exhibit lists for trial but are not required to share them with the opponent. Because the other side does not share its list, one of the functions of a paralegal assisting trial counsel is to keep an ongoing list of the opposing side's trial exhibits. The paralegal also may track the court's ruling on admission into evidence of both side's exhibits.

Once the trial attorney has finalized the exhibit list, defense paralegals may be asked to compile and mark the exhibits, using one of a number of methods. The labeler may affix stickers to the exhibits, and documents may be marked by hand, stamped, or imprinted with computer-generated labels. Each item has a separate identifier. Examples of stickered and stamped/handwritten labeled trial exhibits are shown in Exhibits 11.1 and 11.2. If an exhibit is comprised of multiple parts, it may be presented as a **group exhibit**. For instance, a package containing a number of bullet casings found at the scene of the crime could be labeled "Government's Group Exhibit 19." For multipaged documentary exhibits, each page may have a label (e.g., "Exhibit _____, page _____ of _____ pages."). In addition to preparing and properly labeling each potential exhibit, it is also important to identify which witnesses will be used to properly authenticate the evidence contained in the exhibit[2] and to prepare relevant witnesses to discuss these exhibits.

If the court holds that a portion of a documentary exhibit is inadmissible, it may order that the exhibit be redacted. **Redaction** is the deletion of the objectionable portion of an exhibit. Although blackening out the objectionable work does eliminate objectionable material, it also draws attention to the objection. Therefore, the problematic portion may have to be whited out and the document copied so that the exhibit looks clean and unaltered. There are software programs that permit the electronic redaction of documents. These programs make clean erasures. An example of a redacted document appears in Exhibit 11.3.

Demonstrative evidence is used to illustrate a key point. Demonstratives include videotapes, DVDs, photographs, blowups, charts, scale models, and diagrams. Juries appreciate visual aids. There is no reason for a witness to go without the aid of a diagram, photographs, DVD, or computer-assisted blueprint when describing the layout of a building. When these exhibits are used, the jury is less likely to be confused or misunderstand the testimony. Exhibit 11.4 depicts contraband recovered at a crime scene.

Before the computer age, litigators used large art boards as the primary mode of presenting demonstrative evidence. Typically, these boards were used to display enlargements of photographs or other trial exhibits and time lines as well as brief commentaries. Today, demonstrative exhibits are presented more often in electronic format, although printed demonstratives, hard-copy charts, and models are still commonly used. Ordinarily, enlargements are outsourced to specialty shops. However, a paralegal can prepare a text-based demonstrative by pasting passages printed in an extremely large typeface onto art boards.

Group exhibit
A trial exhibit comprised of multiple components.

Redaction
The process of masking some part of the content of a document before making it available for inspection.

C. PREPARATION FOR EVIDENTIARY DISPUTES

In addition to preparing the exhibits, attorneys must also prepare to both defend their admissibility and to attack the admissibility of evidence that may be presented by the other side. Indeed, the outcome of a case is often determined

---

[2]See Chapter 10 at pp. 346–347.

Exhibit 11.1: Transcript of Cockpit Voice Recorder

The exhibit below, presented in *United States v. Zacarias Moussaoui*, is marked by a sticker. Government Exhibit 01-455-A is the transcript of the last half hour of United Airlines Flight 93, as captured by the cockpit voice recorder on September 11, 2001.

```
GOVERNMENT
EXHIBIT
P200056T
01-455-A (ID)
```

United Airlines Flight #93 Cockpit Voice Recorder Transcript

Key:
Bolded text = English translation from Arabic

Time (EDT)	Transcript
09:31:57	*Ladies and Gentlemen: Here the captain, please sit down keep remaining seating. We have a bomb on board. So sit.*
09:32:09	*Er, uh . . . Calling Cleveland Center . . . You're unreadable. Say again slowly.*
09:32:10	*Don't move. Shut up.*
09:32:13	*Come on, come.*
09:32:16	*Shut up.*
09:32:17	*Don't move.*
09:32:18	*Stop.*
09:32:34	*Sit, sit, sit down.*
09:32:39	*Sit down.*
09:32:41	Unintelligible . . . **the brother.**
09:32:54	*Stop.*
09:33:09	*No more. Sit down.*
09:33:10	**That's it, that's it, that's it,** *down, down.*
09:33:14	*Shut up.*
09:33:20	Unintelligible.
09:33:20	*We just, we didn't get it clear . . . Is that United Ninety Three calling?*
09:33:30	**Jassim.**
09:33:34	**In the name of Allah, the Most Merciful, the Most Compassionate.**
09:33:41	Unintelligible.
09:33:43	*Finish, no more. No more.*
09:33:49	*No. No, no, no, no.*
09:33:53	*No, no, no, no.*

1

Exhibit 11.2: Evidence Envelope and Bullet

This exhibit shows the marked evidence envelope and the mangled bullet that killed Malcolm X. The state presented the bullet as Exhibit 68 in the murder prosecution of the assailants. This exhibit is marked by an ink stamp and handwriting.

JUDGES' CHAMBERS, 17TH FLOOR
COURT OF GENERAL SESSIONS
100 CENTRE STREET, NEW YORK 13, N. Y.

BULLET MARKED "J"

Joe

68 ___ EXHIBIT *FOR ID*

N Y SUPREME CT.

FEB 16 1966

MURRAY DEUTSCH
OFFICIAL STENOGRAPHER

Exhibit 11.3: Redacted Transcript of Witness Statement

Sexual assault victims' statements are often redacted to protect their privacy. Below is the redacted statement of the resort employee who claimed she was sexually assaulted by NBA star Kobe Bryant.

FINAL COPY
Kobe Bryant S03-1169 Videotape transcribed

Detective Winters
Deputy Marsha Rich
Nicole Shanor – victim advocate

Det. W: This is Detective Winters of the Eagle County Sheriff's office in Eagle, Colorado. Present with me is Deputy Marsha Rich, the Eagle County Sheriff's Office.

N: Nicole Shanor of the advocates against assault and resource center of Eagle County.

Det W: Ok. Go ahead and state your name, spell your last name and give your date of birth.

████████████████████

Det W: 6/18/84. With the air conditioner going here its kinda loud so when I'm talking to you, we are video taping the interview, I'll need you to speak up, you have kinda of a soft voice.

██ Ok.

Det W: ██████ how do spell your first name?

████████████

Det W: Ok. Can you kinda of explain to me um, why we're here and what happened last night?

██ Last night I was at work and I was sexually assaulted.

Det W: Ok. And when you mean, well where do you work at?

██ Cordillera Lodge and Spa.

Exhibit 11.4: Photograph of Contraband

During a traffic stop, Louisiana State Police recovered baggies of cannabis and a bag of mushrooms during a search of singer Willie Nelson's tour bus. An officer photographed the drugs on the hood of a police cruiser. This photo could be used by the government in the prosecution of an illegal possession charge.

by the evidentiary rulings of the judge. References to items seized during an unreasonable search or information about prior acts of the defendant can influence an individual juror's verdict. Some of these evidentiary issues may have already been decided in pre-trial hearings, but others may not be settled until the trial is actually underway. Therefore, good litigators try to anticipate these issues in advance of the trial and draft motions *in limine* or pocket briefs to address them.

Motion to suppress
A request that the court prohibit specified materials from being admitted into evidence at a trial because it was gathered in an illegal manner.

1. MOTIONS TO SUPPRESS EVIDENCE

Back in Chapter 8, we discussed the nature of the exclusionary rule and how it could be invoked by defendants to prevent evidence that was obtained in violation of the Constitution from being used in criminal prosecutions. Chapter 9 went into great detail regarding the drafting and filing of motions to suppress. Typically, judges set a cutoff date for the filing of motions to suppress before setting the case for trial.

2. MOTIONS *IN LIMINE*

Motion *in limine*
A formal request to the court to prohibit mention of specified information because it is not sufficiently relevant to the issues being tried and would have a prejudicial effect on the jury.

Unlike motions to suppress, which ask for the exclusion of evidence that was illegally collected, **motions *in limine*** typically seek to exclude lawfully gathered evidence that violates the rules of admissibility. Motions *in limine* seek not only to prohibit the admission of specified evidence but also to prohibit any verbal references to the information in question in the presence of the jury. Motions *in limine* are usually used to bar evidence, but they also can be used to obtain a formal pre-trial ruling from the court that certain evidence will be admissible. For example, the defendant might ask the court to exclude certain inflammatory allegations that are not related to the charges against him, evidence of a prior conviction that occurred a long time ago, or hearsay statements contained in a police report. In reaching a decision on the motion, the judge must determine if the material in question is admissible under the rules of evidence. If the judge decides that it is inadmissible, the motion is granted.

The motion is made and acted upon either before the trial or during a recess when the jury is not present because it is designed to head off the possibility of the jury learning about the challenged material. It is based on the well-founded assumption that once jurors are exposed to the prejudicial information, they will be influenced by it even though the judge instructs them not to be. A violation of an order not to mention prejudicial material can result in the court declaring a mistrial and/or finding the attorney who violated it in contempt.

There are numerous approaches to drafting motions *in limine*. Some attorneys draft one comprehensive motion addressing all potentially objectionable matters (see Exhibit 11.5). Other litigators prepare individual motions for each objectionable matter. Sometimes, motions *in limine* merely ask the court to exclude the evidence without giving the basis for the exclusion (see Exhibit 11.6). These motions are supported by memoranda of law that cite law and analysis in support of the motion (see Exhibit 11.7). If you are asked to draft a motion *in limine*, find out the preference of your supervising attorney. Your supervisor may also be able to refer you to the appropriate formbook.

Exhibit 11.5: Motion *in Limine* in State Reckless Homicide Prosecution

IN THE CIRCUIT COURT OF THE 11th JUDICIAL CIRCUIT
McLEAN COUNTY, ILLINOIS

PEOPLE OF THE	)	
STATE OF ILLINOIS	)	
v.	)	Case No. 10 CF XXXX
BUD COOK,	)	
Defendant.	)	

<u>MOTION IN LIMINE</u>

Now comes Defendant, BUD COOK, by CHARLES HOVEY, his attorney, and prior to the selection of the jury in this case, respectfully moves this court *in limine* to enter an order directing the McLean County State's Attorney, her assistants, and any witnesses called by the prosecution to refrain from making any direct or indirect mention, whatsoever, at the trial, before the jury or potential jurors, of the matters hereinafter set forth without first obtaining the express permission from this court, outside the presence and hearing of the jury:

1. Numerous photographs of the alleged victim.
    a. The Defendant does not dispute the cause of death or the identity of the victim.
    b. It is error to admit gruesome photographs of a corpse when it is not relevant to any fact in issue and has no real purpose other than to horrify the jurors and arouse their emotions against the Defendant. *People v. Coleman*, 116 Ill. App. 3d 28, 451 N.E.2d 973, 978 (3d Dist. 1983).
2. Any statement that either the Defendant's attorney advised him not to make a statement or that the Defendant himself exercised his right to remain silent.
    a. The 5th Amendment to the U.S. Constitution grants the right to remain silent.
    b. The right of the accused to remain silent is violated when a police officer is permitted to testify that, after advising the accused of his rights, the accused stated that he did not want to speak to the officer any further. *People v. Hughes*, 11 Ill. App. 3d 224, 296 N.E.2d 643, 649 (2d Dist. 1973).
3. Statements or opinions made by the State's accident reconstruction expert that the Defendant's alleged intoxication was a cause of the alleged victim's death.
    a. Expert accident reconstruction testimony should be permitted where it is needed to rely on knowledge and application of principles of physics, engineering, and other sciences beyond the ken of the average juror. *People v. Rushtin*, 254 Ill. App. 3d 156, 626 N.E.2d 1378, 1385 (2d Dist. 1993).
    b. Expert opinions on matters of common knowledge are not admissible unless the subject is difficult to comprehend or explain. *Thacker v. UNR Industries, Inc.*, 151 Ill. 2d 343, 603 N.E.2d 449, 460 (1992).

c. Opinion testimony by the State's accident reconstruction expert in a reckless homicide case, that alcohol consumption by the Defendant was a contributing cause of a fatal accident, is inadmissible. *People v. Reding,* 191 Il. App. 3d 424, 547 N.E.2d 1310, 1320-21 (2d Dist. 1989).

4. Any statement directly or indirectly suggesting that the Defendant's alleged intoxication alone establishes recklessness. *People v. Pomkala,* 203 Ill. 2d 198, 784 N.E.2d 784, 787 (2003).

5. The Defendant's convictions for driving while suspended and other minor traffic offenses.

a. The only purpose for which a prior criminal conviction can be used is to attack the credibility of the witness. *People v. Williams,* 72 Ill. App. 2d 96, 218 N.E.2d 771, 774 (1st Dist.1996).

b. Convictions are not admissible to impeach a defendant unless the crime is punishable by death or more than one year imprisonment or under a law involving dishonesty or false statement. *People v. Montgomery,* 47 Ill. 2d 510, 268 N.E.2d 695, 698 (1971).

WHEREFORE, Defendant BUD COOK, respectfully requests this court to enter an order directing the People of the State of Illinois, through its counsel, not to mention, refer to or interrogate concerning, or voluntarily answer or attempt to convey before the jury, at any time during these proceedings, in any manner, either directly or indirectly, the subject matters as stated above without first informing the court and obtaining permission of the court, outside the presence and hearing of the jury; and further, to instruct the People, through its counsel, not to make and reference or inference to the fact that this motion has been filed, argued or ruled upon by this court, and further, that each respective counsel be instructed to warn and caution each and every witness appearing in their phase of this litigation to strictly comply with this rule of the court.

Respectfully submitted,

BUD COOK, Defendant

By_____

CHARLES HOVEY, his attorney

CHARLES HOVEY
Attorney for Defendant
1857 Bone Street
Normal, IL 61761
(309)-555-1857

Exhibit 11.6: Excerpts from a Motion *in Limine* in Federal Court

This is an excerpt of a motion in limine filed by the U.S. Attorney in an antitrust case. The motion sought exclusion of a number of items of evidence. The motion was supported by a separate memorandum of law, which appears in Exhibit 11.7.

UNITED STATES DISTRICT COURT
SOUTHERN DISTRICT OF TEXAS
HOUSTON DIVISION

UNITED STATES OF AMERICA,	)	
v.	)	Criminal No.: H-97-93
MARK ALBERT MALOOF,	)	15 U.S.C. § 1
Defendant.	)	18 U.S.C. § 371
	)	FILED 6/11/97

UNITED STATES' MOTION IN LIMINE

Pursuant to Fed. R. Crim. P. 12(b), and for the reasons set forth in the accompanying Memorandum, the United States hereby moves that the Court enter an Order:

Prohibiting the defendant from offering or commenting on the following evidence on the grounds that it is irrelevant to the charges against him and the fact-finding duties of the jury:

a. Evidence related to the punishment that may be provided by law for a violation of the Sherman Act (15 U.S.C. § 1); and conspiracy to commit wire fraud (18 U.S.C. § 371); and

b. Evidence of the potential direct or indirect effects of a conviction of the defendant.

* * *

Respectfully submitted,

_____

MARK R. ROSMAN
Attorney-in-Charge
Florida State Bar No. 0964387
U.S. Department of Justice
Antitrust Division
1601 Elm Street, Suite 4950
Dallas, Texas 75201-4717
(214) 880-9401

Exhibit 11.7: Excerpts from a Memorandum in Support of a Motion *in Limine*

UNITED STATES DISTRICT COURT
SOUTHERN DISTRICT OF TEXAS
HOUSTON DIVISION

UNITED STATES OF AMERICA,)	
v.)	
)	Criminal No.: H-97-93
MARK ALBERT MALOOF,)	
Defendant.)	15 U.S.C. § 1
)	18 U.S.C. § 371
)	
)	

MEMORANDUM IN SUPPORT OF <u>UNITED STATES' MOTION IN LIMINE</u>

Pursuant to Rule 12(b) of the Federal Rules of Criminal Procedure, the United States has filed a Motion *in limine* with the Court that addresses certain matters that are capable of resolution prior to trial. This Memorandum sets forth the reasons for the relief sought and the supporting legal authority.

I

INADMISSIBILITY OF EVIDENCE REGARDING PUNISHMENT OR COLLATERAL CONSEQUENCES OF CONVICTION

In a federal criminal prosecution, the jury's sole function is to determine guilt or innocence. Evidence regarding punishment or the effects of conviction is thus irrelevant and inadmissible before the jury. The punishment provided by law upon conviction of a criminal violation is a matter exclusively in the province of the Court and should never be considered by the jury in any manner in arriving at their verdict as to guilt or innocence. *See, e.g., Beavers v. Lockhart*, 755 F.2d 657, 662 (8th Cir. 1985) ("Historically, the duty of imposing sentence has been vested in trial judges. . . .") (citing *United States v. Hartford*, 489 F.2d 652, 654 (5th Cir. 1974)); *United States v. Brown*, 744 F.2d 905, 909 (2d Cir.), *cert. denied*, 469 U.S. 1089 (1984) ("[T]he fact finding necessary for sentencing is the responsibility of the sentencing judge. . . ."); *Turnbough v. Wyrick*, 551 F.2d 202, 203 (8th Cir.), *cert. denied*, 431 U.S. 941 (1977) (defendant has no constitutional right to have punishment assessed by a jury). *See also* Pattern Jury Instr., Crim., 5th Cir., Instruction No. 1.21 (1990).

It is recognized that, when the pertinent statute does not vest responsibility for sentencing in the jury, the jury's duty is to find facts without consideration of the potential punishment:

The authorities are unequivocal in holding that presenting information to the jury about possible sentencing is prejudicial. Breach of this standard has often been grounds for reversal. A jury is obligated to "reach its verdict without regard to what sentence might be imposed." [Citations omitted.] Absent a statutory requirement that the jury participate in the sentencing decision, nothing is left "for jury determination beyond the guilt or innocence of an accused." *United States v. Greer*, 620 F.2d 1383, 1385 (10th Cir. 1980). *Accord United States v. McCracken*, 488 F.2d 406, 423 (5th Cir. 1974); *United States v. Davidson*, 367 F.2d 60, 63 (6th Cir. 1966); *Lyles v. United States*, 254 F.2d 725, 728 (D.C. Cir. 1957), *cert. denied*, 356 U.S. 961 (1958).

Evidence that relates to the issue of punishment upon conviction of a criminal offense has no bearing on the only question the jury in this case will be called upon to decide—that of the guilt or innocence of the defendant. As the Fifth Circuit held in *McCracken*, "[e]xcept where a special statutory provision mandates a jury role in assessment or determination of penalty, the punishment provided by law for offenses charged is a matter exclusively for the court and should not be considered by the jury in arriving at a verdict as to guilt or innocence." 488 F.2d at 423. Evidence dealing with possible fines or other collateral consequences of conviction is not probative of the issue of guilt or innocence. Since such evidence would not tend to prove or disprove any fact of consequence to the jury's determination of guilt or innocence, such evidence is not "relevant," as that term is defined by Fed. R. Evid. 401. Such evidence should, therefore, be excluded under Fed. R. Evid. 402, which specifically provides that evidence which is not relevant is inadmissible.

Punishment evidence is inadmissible not only during the parties' examination of witnesses, but also in closing argument. If the issue of punishment is raised during closing argument, the trial court should instruct the jury not to consider the matter of punishment in arriving at their verdict. *Gretter v. United States*, 422 F.2d 315, 319 (10th Cir. 1970). It is error to tell the jury the probable or potential consequences resulting from a particular verdict. *United States v. McCracken*, 488 F.2d at 424-25. The disposition of the defendant is "not a matter for the jury's concern." *Pope v. United States*, 372 F.2d 710, 731 (8th Cir. 1967), *cert. denied*, 401 U.S. 949 (1971).

Therefore, for the reasons discussed above, the United States respectfully requests that this Court enter an order that any evidence or argument relating to possible punishment upon, or collateral consequences of, conviction be excluded from the trial of this case.

* * *

The first part of the motion is the caption, including the title, "Motion *in Limine*." Next is an introductory paragraph that identifies the party bringing the motion and the authority under which it is brought and that a motion *in limine* is being presented. This is followed by the body of the motion. In many courts, the body is presented in a series of short numbered paragraphs. Approaches to drafting the body vary from court to court and from lawyer to lawyer. One approach to drafting the body of a motion *in limine* seeking to exclude evidence follows:

- Identify the potentially prejudicial fact expected to be presented by the opponent.

■ State the rule of evidence that bars the prejudicial fact. If the legal principle is embodied in a statute or court rule, quote the relevant rule. If the principle is part of the common law, cite case law along with the applicable **black letter law** rule.

■ Present your analysis by applying the rule of evidence to the facts in the case at bar.

■ If a court of review has decided a closely analogous case, then present the facts of the analogous case and compare them to the facts of the case at hand.

■ Conclude that under the rule of evidence the prejudicial fact is inadmissible.

Black Letter Law
Widely used, generally accepted, basic legal principles.

The prayer for relief, attorney's signature, and address block follow the body of the motion.

The following excerpts from *United States v. Harper* illustrate the manner in which judges go about reaching decisions as to whether they will grant motions *in limine*.

United States v. Harper
United States District Court, for the Eastern District of Wisconsin
2010 WL 1507869

DECISION AND ORDER

LYNN ADELMAN, District Judge.

The government charged defendant Adrian Harper with possessing a firearm as a felon, contrary to 18 U.S.C. § 922(g)(1), and the case is currently scheduled for trial. Before me is the government's motion in limine seeking a ruling on the admissibility of certain evidence. First, the government seeks permission to introduce the hearsay statement of an unidentified bystander-witness. Second, if defendant testifies, the government seeks permission to impeach him with his prior felony convictions. Defendant opposes both requests.

I. BYSTANDER STATEMENT

A. Background

According to the government, on September 17, 2008, at about 1:50 a.m., two Milwaukee police officers conducting surveillance outside a nightclub heard multiple gunshots. One of the officers saw smoke emanating from the window of a truck about fifteen feet away. The truck took off

at a high rate of speed, and as the officers made a u-turn to follow, a woman yelled at the officers, "There they go right there; that's the one," as she pointed to the truck. The woman was walking in the middle of the street, right behind where the truck was stopped when the shots were fired.

The government seeks admission of the woman's statement as either a present sense impression, Fed.R.Evid. 803(1), or an excited utterance, Fed.R.Evid. 803(2). Defendant responds that the statement is not relevant, qualifies as neither a present sense impression nor an excited utterance, and that its admission would violate his confrontation rights.

B. Analysis

1. Relevance

Defendant argues that the bystander's statement is not relevant because the purpose of the trial is not to determine whether the police had grounds to stop the truck. He indicates that he will stipulate that a firearm was found in the truck; the only issue for trial is whether he possessed that gun; and the bystander's statement has no tendency to make the existence of that disputed fact more or less probable. See Fed.R.Evid. 401 ("'Relevant evidence' means evidence having any tendency to make the existence of any fact that is of consequence to the determination of the action more probable or less probable than it would be without the evidence.").

The government indicates that its theory in this case is that defendant possessed the gun when he fired shots out the window of the truck. The government does not intend to prove its case simply by establishing that the gun was in the truck. The bystander's statement helps to prove, not that there was a firearm in the truck, but that someone (defendant or the driver) fired shots from the truck. This, in turn, helps to establish that defendant actually possessed the firearm.

To be relevant, evidence need not conclusively decide the ultimate issue in a case, nor make the proposition appear more probable; it need only to some degree advance the inquiry. *Thompson v. City of Chicago,* 472 F.3d 444, 453 (7th Cir.2006). "This is not a difficult standard to meet." *United States v. Brisk,* 171 F.3d 514, 525 (7th Cir.1999). I find that the bystander's statement has a tendency to prove that defendant possessed the gun by firing it from the truck. *Cf. United States v. Canady,* 578 F.3d 665, 671 (7th Cir.2009) ("[I]f the parties contest whether Canady possessed the gun in the SUV, evidence that he was seen with (and may have used) the gun minutes beforehand increases the likelihood that he possessed the gun in the car.").

2. Hearsay Exceptions

a. Present Sense Impression

Federal Rule of Evidence 803(1) permits the introduction of a hearsay statement "describing or explaining an event or condition made while the declarant was perceiving the event or condition, or immediately thereafter." A statement may be admitted under this Rule if: (1) the statement describes an event or condition without calculated narration; (2) the speaker personally perceived the event or condition described; and (3) the statement was made while the speaker was perceiving the event or condition, or immediately thereafter. *United States v. Ruiz,* 249 F.3d 643, 646 (7th Cir.2001).

The bystander's statement may be admitted under this Rule. The proffered facts indicate that the woman, who was standing right behind the truck, made the statement immediately after she observed the shots being fired, and her brief statement contains no "calculated narration." Defendant argues that the statement does not describe "the event," i.e. the shots being fired, but rather pertained to what happened afterward. But the woman described her present perception of the shots by stating "that's the one," and her perception of the truck from which they came by stating "there they go right there" as she observed the vehicle driving away.

In any event, courts have not demanded the sort of strict contemporaneousness defendant would require. For example, in *United States v. Thomas,* 453 F.3d 838 (7th Cir.2006), the court admitted under Rule 803(1) a 911 call, in which the caller stated "[t]here's a dude that just got shot," and "the guy who shot him is still out there." Later in the call, the caller stated that "[t]here is somebody shot outside, somebody needs to be sent over here, and there's somebody runnin' around with a gun, somewhere." *Id.* at 844. In *United States v. Campbell,* 782 F.Supp. 1258 (N.D.Ill.1991), a 911 caller told a police dispatcher that a shooting just occurred in a drug store and described the general appearance and clothing of the alleged assailant. The court admitted the statement, even though it occurred after the shooting was complete. The court noted that "precise contemporaneity" often is impossible and that a slight time lapse between the event and the statement is allowable. *Id.* at 1260-61; *see also United States v. Mejia-Valez,* 855 F. Supp. 607, 613 (E.D.N.Y.1994) (admitting two 911 calls indicating that there had been a shooting and providing the location and a description of the alleged assailant).

b. Excited Utterance

Federal Rule of Evidence 803(2) permits the introduction of a hearsay statement "relating to a startling event or condition made while the declarant was under the stress of excitement caused by the event or condition." A statement may be admitted under this Rule if: (1) a startling event occurred; (2) the declarant made the statement while under the stress of excitement caused by the startling event; and (3) the declarant's statement relates to the startling event. *United States v. Wesela*, 223 F.3d 656, 663 (7th Cir.2000).

The bystander's statement may also be admitted under this Rule. The shots fired from the truck on a public street qualify as a startling event. The government indicates that the officer will testify that the woman gestured excitably towards the truck, spoke in an almost frantic tone, and her facial expression was one of surprise and fear. Defendant again argues that the statement does not relate to the event (the shots) but rather to what occurred thereafter. His analysis is again too cramped. The woman's statement "that's the one" relates to the shooting, and her statements "there they go right there" relates to the truck from which the shots emanated.

It is also worth noting in this regard that the "excited utterance exception allows a broader scope of subject matter coverage than does the present sense impression exception." *United States v. Moore*, 791 F.2d 566, 572 (7th Cir.1986). Under Rule 803(2), if the subject matter of the statement would likely be evoked by the event, the statement may be admitted, even if it goes beyond a mere description of the event. *Id.* Courts have admitted similar statements under the excited utterance exception. *See, e.g., Thomas*, 453 F.3d at 844 (admitting as an excited utterance a 911 call indicating that someone had been shot and that the shooter was outside running around with a gun); *Reid v. Fischer*, No. 00-CV-3054, 2003 WL 23185754, at *13 (E.D.N.Y. Oct. 24, 2003 (Weinstein, J.) (holding that the trial court properly admitted as an excited utterance a witness statement implicating the defendant in a shooting made immediately after the shooting and virtually while the witness was fleeing the scene of the shooting); *Mejia-Valez*, 855 F.Supp. at 614 (admitting as excited utterances 911 calls reporting shooting and describing assailant); *Campbell*, 782 F.Supp. at 1262 (admitting under the excited utterance exception a tape recording of a police officer's statements to the dispatcher during his attempt to apprehend shooting suspect); *see also United States v. Harper*, No. 05-CR-6068L, 2009 WL

140125, at *3 (W.D.N.Y. Jan.20, 2009) (collecting cases).

3. Confrontation Clause

Having concluded, based on the government's proffer, that the bystander's statement is relevant and admissible, I turn to the issue of whether admission of the statement would nevertheless violate defendant's rights under the Sixth Amendment's Confrontation Clause. The Clause forbids admission of out-of-court, testimonial statements, unless the declarant is unavailable and the defendant had a prior opportunity for cross-examination. *Crawford v. Washington*, 541 U.S. 36, 53-54, 124 S. Ct. 1354, 158 L. Ed.2d 177 (2004). The crucial issue here is whether the bystander's statement is "testimonial."

In *Davis v. Washington*, 547 U.S. 813, 822, 126 S. Ct. 2266, 165 L.Ed.2d 224 (2006), the Court explained that:

> Statements are non-testimonial when made in the course of police interrogation under circumstances objectively indicating that the primary purpose of the interrogation is to enable police assistance to meet an ongoing emergency. They are testimonial when the circumstances objectively indicate that there is no such ongoing emergency, and that the primary purpose of the interrogation is to establish or prove past events potentially relevant to later criminal prosecution.

Under this test, the bystander's statement is non-testimonial. She made the statement spontaneously, rather than in response to police questioning, and it appears that her purpose in making the statement was to assist the officers responding to the ongoing emergency presented by a fleeing suspect who just fired shots on a crowded public street.

Defendant contends that the emergency situation presented by the shots being fired had ended when the bystander identified the truck containing the shooter; he argues that her statement instead proved a past event relevant to a later criminal prosecution. I disagree. At the time the bystander spoke, the shooter was still on the scene; it was certainly possible that he might fire again; and the truck then started to flee at a high rate of speed, creating further danger. Further, the statement—"there they go right there"— pertained to events as they were happening. *See Davis*, 547 U.S. at 827 (finding non-testimonial statements to a 911 operator describing events as they were actually happening, rather than describing past events).

Defendant cites no case finding similar statements testimonial, and I have found none. *See, e.g., United States v. Dodds*, 569 F.3d 336, 340-41 (7th Cir.) ("In this case, the police were responding to a 911 call reporting 'shots fired' and had an urgent need to identify the person with the gun and to stop the shooting. The witness's description of the man with a gun was given in that context, and we believe it falls within the scope of *Davis*."), *cert. denied*, _____ U.S. _____ , 130 S. Ct. 523, _____ L.Ed.2d _____ (2009); *Thomas*, 453 F.3d at 844 (finding non-testimonial a 911 call reporting a shooting and indicating that the shooter "was still out there"); *see also United States v. Clemmons*, 461 F.3d 1057, 1060-61 (8th Cir.2006) (holding that shooting victim's statements to police officer that the defendant had shot him were non-testimonial). Therefore, I will grant the government's motion pertaining to the bystander statement.

II. DEFENDANT'S PRIOR CONVICTIONS

Under Fed.R.Evid. 609(a)(1), a defendant may be impeached by evidence of his prior felony convictions "if the court determines that the probative value of admitting this evidence outweighs its prejudicial effect to the accused." Rule 609(b) generally imposes a ten-year time limit on such convictions, measured from the date of the conviction or of the release of the defendant from the confinement imposed for that conviction, whichever is later, to the start of the trial. *See United States v. Watler*, 461 F.3d 1005, 1008-09 (8th Cir.2006) (collecting cases).

In the present case, the parties stipulate that defendant has four prior felony convictions: (1) battery by a prisoner on August 23, 1995, for which he was sentenced to five years in prison and released on May 11, 1999; (2) manufacture/ delivery of cocaine on August 30, 2001; (3)

vehicle operator flee/elude police officer on September 25, 2006; and (4) possession of THC-second offense on November 23, 2006. If defendant testifies, the government indicates that it wishes to attack his credibility with evidence of these convictions. I first note that, according to the parties' stipulation, defendant was released from the battery sentence more than ten years prior to the commencement of this trial. Thus, absent the presentation of specific facts and circumstances demonstrating that the probative value of this conviction "substantially outweighs its prejudicial effect," Fed.R.Evid. 609(b); *see United States v. Redditt*, 381 F.3d 597, 601 (7th Cir.2004) (explaining that the purpose of Rule 609(b) is to ensure that convictions over ten years old will be admitted very rarely and only in exceptional circumstances), this conviction will not be admitted. However, I will permit the government to impeach defendant with evidence of the other three felony convictions.

The Seventh Circuit has established a five-part test to guide the district court in the exercise of its discretion in determining whether the probative value of a conviction outweighs its prejudicial effect: (1) the impeachment value of the prior crime; (2) the point in time of the conviction and the defendant's subsequent history; (3) the similarity between the past crime and the charged crime; (4) the importance of the defendant's testimony; and (5) the centrality of the credibility issue. *United States v. Montgomery*, 390 F.3d 1013, 1015 (7th Cir.2004) (citing *United States v. Mahone*, 537 F.2d 922 (7th Cir.1976)). Although none of defendant's prior convictions go directly to his truthfulness (e.g., they do not involve fraud or false statements), the remaining *Mahone* factors favor admission.

The convictions are all fairly recent in time, occurring in 2001 and 2006. None are similar to the charged crime; thus, admission of defendant's prior convictions for drug possession and delivery, and fleeing an officer will not suggest to the jury that defendant has a propensity to possess firearms. Further, it appears that defendant's credibility will be a significant issue in this case. Presumably, he will testify that he never possessed the firearm found in the truck, which is the ultimate issue for the jury to decide. Thus, the value of impeachment evidence is increased.

Finally, I note that the prejudice to defendant is decreased by the nature of the charge; because he is charged with being a felon-in-possession of a firearm, the jury will learn that he is a felon whether or not the government impeaches him with his prior convictions. *See Montgomery*, 390 F.3d at 1015. It is true that this case involves three prior convictions, which may increase the possibility of prejudice. However, given the importance of the credibility issue, the probative value outweighs the prejudicial effect. I will, in order to reduce the possibility of prejudice, give an appropriate limiting instruction to the jury. *See id.* at 1015-16 (affirming use of six prior convictions to impeach the defendant in a felon-in-possession case where credibility was important and the district court gave a limiting instruction); *United States v. Nururdin*, 8 F.3d 1187, 1192 (7th Cir.1993) (admitting four prior convictions for impeachment purposes in a felon-in-possession case given the importance of the defendant's testimony and the centrality of the credibility issue, where the court gave a limiting jury instruction); *see also United States v. Smith*, 131 F.3d 685, 687 (7th Cir.1997) (admitting evidence of prior convictions for robbery, armed robbery, kidnapping and attempted sexual assault in a bank robbery case).

Defendant argues that his prior convictions did not involve acts of dishonesty and thus say little about his veracity. The nature of the prior conviction is just one factor for the court to consider; Rule 609(a)(1) allows the introduction of any prior felony conviction so long as the probative value outweighs the prejudicial effect; it is not limited to crimes involving dishonesty or deceit. *See United States v. Wolf*, 561 F.2d 1376, 1381 (10th Cir.1977). Defendant further argues that admission of his 2006 fleeing conviction would be prejudicial because it is similar to the facts of this case. But defendant is charged here with possessing a firearm, not fleeing from the police. And, based on the proffered facts, the government will not argue that defendant operated the truck and fled from the police; rather, he

was the passenger. Thus, I see no significant similarity between that case and this one. Finally, defendant argues that admitting his 2006 marijuana conviction would be prejudicial because one of the AUSA's assigned to this case sentenced him in that case while serving as a state court trial judge. The identity of the sentencing judge will not be presented to the jury, so there is no danger that the jury will come to believe that this prosecution carries a judicial imprimatur. See *United States v. Smith*, 454 F.3d 707, 716 (7th Cir.2006) (indicating that the government should limit its inquiry to the name, the date and the disposition of the prior felony).

III. CONCLUSION

THEREFORE, IT IS ORDERED that the government's motion in limine is granted.

CASE DISCUSSION QUESTIONS

1. What was the government attempting to accomplish through its motion *in limine*?
2. What hearsay statement made by a bystander did the prosecutor seek to admit into evidence?
3. Identify and explain the exceptions to the hearsay rule the court discussed as its bases for the admission of the bystander's statement.
4. The district judge held that the bystander's statement was "non-testimonial" and therefore admissible under the confrontation clause. What is meant by the term *non-testimonial statement*?
5. Which provision of the U.S. Constitution gives a defendant the right to confront his or her accusers?
6. On what basis did the court rule that some of the defendant's convictions may be presented but one was inadmissible?
7. Which of the Federal Rules of Evidence did the court rely on in its decision and order?

3. POCKET BRIEFS

Just as your side will attempt to prevent prejudicial evidence from being heard by the jury, the opposing side will try to keep facts harmful to its client from being admitted into evidence. In anticipation of the opponent's challenge, your litigation team can prepare a **pocket brief**. This document is a short legal memorandum used to advise the court on a discreet point of law. Often the opposing side will not prepare pocket briefs, so your litigation team's brief may be the only argument shown to the judge. It is, therefore, extremely important to use an objective tone in drafting this document. Although motions *in limine* are the preferred method of seeking exclusion of evidence, pocket briefs may also be used to support an argument against the admission of evidence. Pocket brief may also be used to address procedural matters arising at trial.

Typically, a pocket brief addressing an evidentiary question begins with a caption, including a title headlining the application of the rule of evidence at issue. After an introductory paragraph, the body of the document should present pertinent facts, the rule of evidence, and the application of the rule to the facts. You can use the pocket brief to give support for the admission of evidence favoring your side or in opposition to unfavorable evidence. A possible approach to the body of a pocket brief seeking to admit evidence is as follows:

- Identify the facts your side wants admitted into evidence.
- State the applicable rule of evidence. If the legal principle is embodied in a statute or court rule, quote the relevant rule. If the principle is part of the common law, cite case law along with the applicable black letter rule.
- Present your analysis by applying the rule of evidence to the facts in the case at bar.
- If a court of review has decided a closely analogous case, then present and compare the facts of the analogous case to the facts of the case at hand.
- Conclude that under the rule of evidence the facts are admissible.

The prayer for relief, attorney's signature, and address block follow the body of the motion.

Pocket brief
A short memorandum of law used to advise the court on a discreet point of law.

APPLICATION EXERCISES

6. Prepare a motion *in limine* on behalf of the defense in Hypothetical Case #2, *United States v. Brandon Turner,* to exclude evidence of the defendant's nine-year-old felony conviction for aggravated driving under the influence of alcohol. The case is filed in the U.S. District Court in which your school is located and docketed as case number [CURRENT YEAR]-666. List your instructor as the attorney representing the defendant. Use your instructor's professional address.

7. Prepare a motion *in limine* on behalf of the prosecutor in Hypothetical Case #4, *United States v. Thomas Schroeder,* to exclude evidence of $250,000 in medical bills the defendant owes for cancer treatment for his

nine-year-old child. The case is filed in the U.S. District Court in which your school is located and docketed as case number [CURRENT YEAR]-987. List the U.S. Attorney for the federal district as the person subpoenaing the witness on behalf of the government.

8. Prepare a pocket brief on behalf of the United States Attorney for Hypothetical Case #4, *United States v. Thomas Schroeder*, on the admissibility of evidence as to witness Jim Stevenson's reputation in the community of telling lies. The case is filed in the U.S. District Court in which your school is located and docketed as case number [CURRENT YEAR]-987. List the U.S. Attorney for the federal district as the person subpoenaing the witness on behalf of the government.

D. PREPARATION OF WITNESSES

1. PREPARING LAY WITNESSES

Although favorable witnesses are usually interviewed early in the life of a case, final witness preparation typically takes place within a few weeks of the starting date. This preparation is designed to put the witness at ease and to help make the testimony as effective as possible. Many times, the paralegal may participate in witness preparation.

In order to make the witnesses feel more comfortable, they should be educated about the trial proceeding. Begin by describing the general format of a trial. Although most witnesses think they are familiar with courtroom procedures, you need to walk them through what will happen at trial. Explain that once a jury is seated, the trial begins with the attorneys' opening statements, followed by the presentation of witnesses and exhibits by each party, and then closing arguments. Let them know how direct, cross, and re-direct examination works. Explain objections and that the witness must stop talking when an objection is made and wait until the judge rules before continuing. Define the terms *sustained* and *overruled*. Discuss the setup of the courtroom, the exclusion of witnesses from the courtroom when they are not testifying, and the importance of following the directions of the judge. If possible, witnesses should visit the courtroom where the trial will take place so they can become comfortable with the courtroom environment.

You should also preview the types of questions they will be asked on direct and cross examinations. If the witnesses will be used to discuss a particular exhibit, make sure they understand the nature of the questions they will be asked about it. Also emphasize the importance of telling the truth. While it is unethical to put your words into the witness's mouth, it is acceptable to refresh the witness's recollection. This is usually accomplished by showing witnesses their police statements. If they gave prior testimony, transcripts of what was said are also excellent ways to help them remember what took place.

Witnesses should be forewarned that the opposing side may ask whether they have discussed their testimony with anyone. Let them know that there is nothing wrong with talking to the lawyer's staff about their testimony. Let them

Objection
A request to the judge to disallow either (1) specific questions or comments by another attorney or (2) certain responses from witnesses.

Sustained objection
The judge's favorable ruling on an evidentiary objection.

Overruled objection
The judge's unfavorable ruling on an evidentiary objection.

know they should acknowledge talking to you if they are asked about discussing their testimony with anyone.

Third, teach them how to respond to questions. Emphasize that they should not volunteer information. Their role is to answer the questions presented, not to offer information not elicited. They should be especially careful not to speculate or offer testimony not within their personal knowledge. Explain that the witness will be answering questions posed by both sides and to listen carefully to the whole question, regardless of which lawyer is asking the question. Instruct the witness to ask for the question to be rephrased if he or she truly does not understand it. Remind witnesses that this is not a test to see how smooth they are, but rather an opportunity to make an accurate record of the testimony. Finally, advise the witness to speak to the jury when testifying.

It is also important to discuss how they should act during cross-examination. Sometimes witnesses who are identified with one side of a case tend to respond in a confrontational or sarcastic manner on cross-examination. Instruct witnesses to treat the cross-examiner in the same manner that they treat the favorable attorney on direct examination and not to get angry or act discourteously toward the opposing attorney. Alert witnesses that if they are impeached by use of their prior statements, they must be able to explain the inconsistency. A string of "I don't remember" answers on cross-examination diminishes the witness's credibility. Furthermore, tell the witness not to look at your attorney during cross-examination, as it gives the impression answers are being fed to the witness.

Finally, good witness preparation covers not only what they say and how they say it but their appearance and dress as well. One size does not fit all and the clothes worn should fit the personality and occupation of the witness. Think of it in the way a director would dress an actor for a performance. The witness should look the part because a landscaper dressed like an attorney will be less credible than one dressed like the public image of a landscaper. If the witness doesn't feel comfortable with the outfit, the witness will appear uneasy to the jury.

Local customs vary, but there are a still a few universal guidelines. The witness should wear clean clothes—not ones they have been wearing all day on the job. A witness, such as a police officer or nurse, may wear a uniform if it is customary dress. A person who works with his hands all day, for example, probably would not be comfortable wearing a suit and tie. Emphasize the need for the witness to act appropriately at the courthouse, to respond to questions respectfully, and to not chew gum.

At the close of your meeting, you will give the witness a trial subpoena and the required fees. Let the witness see where his or her testimony fits into the trial schedule and tell him or her about the uncertainty of maintaining a rigid timetable. The trial attorney will probably conduct a dress rehearsal of the direct examination of the witness. If you have done your job in witness preparation, this should go smoothly.

2. PREPARING EXPERT WITNESSES

Expert witnesses are familiar with the subject matter of their area of expertise, but they may not be familiar with the courtroom and trial procedure. If they have testified extensively in other cases, they may already be familiar with court proceedings and how to handle cross-examination; if they haven't, it is important to give them the same type of orientation given to non-expert witnesses.

Make sure that the experts have copies of all relevant documents, including their reports and statements containing facts on which their opinions are based. If they have given sworn statements, such as testimony in a prior hearing or in a deposition, you should provide them with a copy. Likewise, make sure that the expert has given you an up-to-date résumé or curriculum vitae (CV).

If the expert witness is rehearsing testimony with you, pay attention to the witness's manner and word choice. If the expert comes off as a know-it-all, the jury may not want to believe the testimony. In a non-judgmental tone, let the expert know that some of the jurors may not be high school graduates, so the expert will be more effective if he or she addresses these jurors. If technical terms are used, the expert needs to explain them in a non-condescending manner.

Often experts use demonstrative exhibits to explain their testimony. Make sure the rehearsal includes the staging of this part of the testimony. An unrehearsed use of a demonstrative aid or item of physical evidence may lead to unanticipated disastrous results. For instance, in the O.J. Simpson murder trial, one of the prosecutors asked the defendant to put on a glove that was presumably worn by the murderer. When it became obvious that the glove was too small and did not fit, the prosecution lost tremendous credibility with the jury.

3. PREPARING TRIAL SUBPOENAS

Trial subpoena
A document prepared under the authority of the court that commands a witness to appear at trial to give testimony.

In order to ensure a witness will appear in court, the party who intends to call the witness must subpoena that individual. **Trial subpoenas** are often prepared by a paralegal employed by the attorney seeking the attendance of the witness. In federal court as well as a growing number of state courts, the attorney can issue the subpoena by signing it. In more traditional jurisdictions, the clerk of the court must impress the seal of the court on the document before it is issued under authority of law. Exhibit 11.8 is the subpoena form used in South Carolina criminal cases.

Although a law office can generate its own subpoenas, most criminal litigators use the standard forms provided by the clerk of the court. The forms are generally available at the clerk's office in hard copy and online at the clerk's website. The subpoena must be accompanied by the payment of a witness fee and mileage in order to be enforceable. Although some jurisdictions may not require this payment, most do. Check the applicable rules in your court to find out what is required along with the amount of payment to be tendered. The subpoena must be served on the witness prior to the date he or she is to appear in court. Unlike a summons, in most jurisdictions any competent person who is not a party to the action may serve the witness. When a witness resides a great distance from the place of trial, the subpoenaing party must pay for the witness's travel expenses. For instance, in the sexual assault prosecution of the late Michael Jackson, the California District Attorney's office subpoenaed the New York City journalist whose documentary movie led to the criminal investigation of the defendant. The proof of payment of these expenses is presented in Exhibit 11.9.

Return of service
The written verification establishing that a document has been served.

The person serving the subpoena must complete under oath a **return of service**. The return documents that the witness was served with the subpoena along with the applicable witness fee and mileage. Often, the return of service appears on the reverse side of the subpoena. Exhibit 11.10 is the return of service appearing on the back of the South Carolina criminal subpoena form. As noted above, in the case of "friendly witnesses," the attorney or paralegal may serve the trial subpoena when meeting with witnesses to prepare them for trial.

Exhibit 11.8: South Carolina Trial Subpoena

SUBPOENA IN A CRIMINAL CASE SOUTH CAROLINA _____ COURT	COUNTY

	CASE NO.
V.	SUBPOENA FOR PERSON
	DOCUMENT(S) OR OBJECT(S)

TO:

YOU ARE HEREBY COMMANDED to appear in the above-named court at the place, date, and time specified below to testify in the above-entitled case.

PLACE	COURTROOM
	DATE AND TIME

YOU ARE ALSO COMMANDED to bring with you the following document(s) or object(s).

LIST DOCUMENT(S) OR OBJECT(S)

This subpoena shall remain in effect until you are granted leave to depart by the court or by an officer acting on behalf of the court.

CLERK OF COURT	DATE
(BY) DEPUTY CLERK	
THIS SUBPOENA IS ISSUED UPON APPLICATION OF THE: SOLICITOR DEFENDANT	ATTORNEY'S NAME AND ADDRESS
SCCA 253 (JULY 1, 1993)	

Exhibit 11.9: Proof of Travel Expenses for Subpoenaed Witness

By: Patrick J. McKinley
    Assistant District Attorney
State Bar #44297
1105 Santa Barbara Street
Santa Barbara, CA 93101
Telephone: (805) 568-2300
Attorneys for Plaintiff

DEC 2 1 2004

GARY M. BLAIR, Executive Officer
ᴮʸ *Carrie L Wagner*
CARRIE L WAGNER, Deputy Clerk

SUPERIOR COURT OF THE STATE OF CALIFORNIA

FOR THE COUNTY OF SANTA BARBARA

COOK STREET DIVISION FILED UNDER SEAL

Unsealed per order
dated 1/10/05

PEOPLE OF THE STATE OF CALIFORNIA,	)	Case No. 1133603
Plaintiff,	)	
vs.	)	DECLARATION OF VICTIM/WITNESS ASSISTANT
MICHAEL JOE JACKSON,	)	
Defendant.	)	

I, SHAMRA LIMON, am employed by the Santa Barbara County District Attorney's Office.

In accordance with the California Penal Code section 1434.3, I shall make the following travel arrangements in the name of MARTIN BASHIR, for the date of March 1, 2005, and to return when his testimony is complete, plane reservations (for which tickets are prepaid) from a convenient airport in New York to Santa Maria and back; lodging reservations (which are to be billed to Santa Barbara County District Attorney's Office) for the above-stated dates at an appropriate hotel in Santa Maria.

Ground transportation between airport, place of lodging, and courthouse while in Santa Maria, will be provided by this office. Reimbursement for ground transportation between a convenient airport in New York and place of residence in New York City is enclosed (at twenty cents per mile x miles round trip). I am informed and believe that the cost of a taxi ride to either of the New York City airports is approximately $50.00 from Manhattan.

Witness fees of $20.00 per day for 10 days of travel and days of testimony, have also been enclosed.

A check in the total amount is being forwarded. This is the total amount of the above-listed expenditures.

I declare under penalty of perjury that the foregoing is true and correct.

Executed _December 20, 2004_, at Santa Maria, California.

Victim Witness Assistant

Exhibit 11.10: South Carolina Criminal Subpoena Return of Service

PROOF OF SERVICE

SERVED	DATE	PLACE
SERVED ON (PRINT NAME)		MANNER OF SERVICE
SERVED BY (PRINT NAME)		TITLE

DECLARATION OF SERVER

I certify that the foregoing information contained in the Proof of Service is true and correct.

Executed on _____ _____
DATE SIGNATURE OF THE SERVER

_____
ADDRESS OF THE SERVER

_____

Sometimes subpoenas are served by certified or registered mail, return receipt requested. This type of service is spelled out in the criminal rules or code. There are express time limits governing this service by mail. If service is accomplished this way, the server must furnish an affidavit showing that the mailing was prepaid and was addressed to the witness, restricted delivery, with a check or money order for the fee and mileage enclosed.

When the party wants the witness to bring objects, documents, or other tangible items to court, the party serves the witness with a subpoena *duces tecum*. As you will recall from our discussion of this document in Chapter 7, a **subpoena** *duces tecum* is a special form of the subpoena used to compel the witness to bring documents or other tangible items to court. Other than the requirement that the witness bring something to court, the rules regarding trial subpoenas and subpoenas *duces tecum* are the same.

Subpoena *duces tecum*
A special form of the subpoena used to compel the witness to bring documents or other tangible items to court or to a grand jury proceeding.

You should be mindful that most people do not want to be witnesses in criminal cases. The experience can be stressful for many and downright frightening for others. Moreover, participation in court proceedings disrupts work, school, or other obligations. Seasoned litigators are careful not to alienate their witnesses. They send witnesses a cover letter with the subpoena to explain the expected timetable for the case and ask the witnesses to call at specified times to learn exactly when they need to show up in court. Generally, these attorneys subpoena all of the witnesses to appear on the first day of trial and ask the court to continue the subpoenas from day-to-day.

4. PREPARING THE DEFENDANT

Although the Fifth Amendment privilege against self-incrimination protects defendants from being forced to testify, there are several potentially negative consequences that can accompany the use of that right. Despite a judicial admonition to the contrary, many jurors expect defendants to assert their innocence and are more inclined to convict them if they don't. However, if defendants do choose to take the stand, they become subject to cross-examination and their past criminal activities may be brought out. Although defense attorneys must inform and should advise their clients with respect to their testifying, it is ultimately up to the defendant to make this critical decision.

If the defendant chooses to testify, the defense team has to go through the same type of preparation as it does for other witnesses it will call. Additionally, the attorney may take a greater role in directing the client's courtroom appearance. Excessive jewelry or makeup should be avoided. Both women and men should avoid overtly sexually suggestive apparel. In conservative communities, clients should cover their tattoos. In these venues, other than ear piercings, body piercings should likewise not be on display. If the defendant's dress or hairstyle is distracting, consider toning them down, without turning the witness into a phony. A California attorney who represented Richard Rodriguez, a gang member allegedly attacked by a California police officer at the end of a televised high-speed chase, had his client undergo a significant transformation for trial. Rodriguez's attorney instructed him to grow a moustache to cover the name of his street gang, which is inked on his upper lip, and to grow out the hair on his shaved head to hide the tattoos on his scalp. He also directed Rodriguez to wear a conservative suit at trial.[3] An extreme makeover strategy can present the client in a better light, but it can also backfire if jurors believe they are being deceived.

Last, in order to be effective, the defendant must maintain self-control and show respect for the prosecutor.

5. PREPARING FOR OPPOSING WITNESSES

In addition to preparing the witnesses their side plans to call, the attorneys and paralegals must also prepare to cross-examine the witnesses called by the other side. This is usually done by reading witness statements and police reports, conducting background checks, and, when possible, interviewing the witnesses.

---

[3]*Makeover advised for gang member kicked by El Monte officer*, Los Angeles Times (July 24, 2009). *http://articles.latimes.com/2009/jul/24/local/me-elmonte24*

Prosecutors have access to this information and routinely run criminal background checks. The defense bar has access to a variety of online services that enable subscribers to conduct criminal background checks. If your employer has not purchased one of these subscriptions, you may investigate a witness by reviewing the criminal file index maintained by the clerk of the court. This information is often available on public-access computer terminals. Cases in which a witness is a party may reveal criminal convictions and/or relationships of the witness with others. This is the most cost-effective way to obtain background information.

In addition, you can interview witnesses. Law enforcement officers and agents typically perform this task for the government. Private investigators do this on behalf of the defense. Sometimes, however, paralegals may conduct these interviews for the defense team. If you are given this assignment, identify yourself, your supervising attorney, and the defendant. If the witness declines to talk to you, leave a business card so that he or she can contact you later if there is a change of heart. Write down your favorable and unfavorable impressions of the witness. Even if a witness is against the defendant, that does not mean the witness is an adversary. Try to place yourself in the witness's position and reenact the situation from the witness's point of view to assist in objectively evaluating the witness. Your report will be helpful to your supervising attorney in developing cross-examination.

APPLICATION EXERCISES

9. Use the Internet to find a curriculum vitae of an accident reconstruction expert and a forensic pathologist located in your state.

10. Prepare a trial subpoena directed to the president of your school in Hypothetical Case #4, *United States v. Thomas Schroeder*. Assume that (a) the trial will take place the first Tuesday of next month, beginning at 10:00 A.M. in courtroom 201 at the federal courthouse for the U.S. District and division in which your school is located, (b) the case number is [CURRENT YEAR]-1857, (c) the witness is to bring all educational records concerning the defendant to court, and (d) the president will be served at his or her office at the school. List the U.S. Attorney for the federal district as the person subpoenaing the witness on behalf of the government. Use U.S. Courts form AO89 found at: http://www.uscourts.gov/FormsAndFees/Forms/Viewer.aspx?doc=/uscourts/FormsAndFees/Forms/AO089.pdf.

11. Prepare a trial subpoena on behalf of the defense directed to the president of your school in Hypothetical Case #1, *People v. Bud Cook*. Assume that (a) the trial will take place the last Thursday of next month, beginning at 9:30 A.M. in courtroom 400 at the state courthouse exercising jurisdiction over events occurring in the community where your school is located, (b) the case number is [CURRENT YEAR]-123, and (c) the president will be served at his or her office at the school. List your instructor as the attorney representing the defendant along with the instructor's professional address.

12. Cite the court rule or statute applicable to the state where your school is located that sets the amount of the witness fee and the rate of mileage to which a subpoenaed witness is entitled in a criminal case.

E. Organizing File Materials for the Trial

Trial notebook

A three-ring notebook with appropriately tabbed sections containing materials required for a specific trial.

In order to be an effective member of the litigation team, one must be able to review and produce critical documents during various stages of the trial. These documents can include charging instruments, police reports, witness statements, and lab reports. Prior to the use of laptop computers in courtrooms, many attorneys used **trial notebooks** to organize these types of materials. Others simply brought in expandable accordion-style organizers filled with manila folders. Today, however, increasing numbers of attorneys keep this kind of information on laptop computers and in flash drives. They use software programs, such as Summation or Concordance, to manage high volumes of documents, and CaseMap to organize the facts, witnesses, and issues of the case. Regardless of which method is used, paralegals typically play a key role in collecting, organizing, and retrieving these trial materials.

The three basic components of any trial file are: a court filings folder, witness folders, and discovery folders. The court filings folder contains copies of the documents filed with the clerk of the court for the case. These filings should be organized in either forward or reverse chronological order. An index should be prepared to make it possible to identify each document by title and the date it was filed with the clerk.[4]

The largest part of the case file is the witness section. It contains individual subfiles for each witness expected to testify. The first step in preparing witness folders is to outline the evidence to be presented by both sides at trial. The outline initially should list all of the witnesses for the prosecution along with a brief statement of the witness's direct testimony and the exhibits expected to be introduced through the witness. Next, the same information should be included for the defense's witnesses. Similarly, witness and exhibit information should be included for the government's rebuttal and the defendant's surrebuttal.

The outline should also include references to the pertinent documents on which direct and cross-examination are based. Typically, this means citation to police reports, witness statements, or transcripts. Once the basic information is compiled for the direct examination for each witness, the treatment of each witness should be expanded with cross-examination topics and documents required for cross-examination.

In addition to this summary information, the subfiles for each witness should include copies of all documents related to that witness. It also should have an outline of the particular facts expected to be discussed during the witness's testimony, accompanied by references to exhibits or other documents. There should be pinpoint citations to the page, paragraph, and line number of the document. If witness files are voluminous, an individual index should be prepared for each file. If a computer program is not being used to manage documents, many witness files will include copies of documents already included in other witness files.

The third component of the case file is the discovery section. The discovery file contains separate subfiles for the government's discovery as well as the discovery tendered by the defense. The discovery file duplicates documents already

---

[4]Often the court's docket sheet can be used as the index. If you are using a hard-copy organizer, make sure that each document is separately stapled. The documents should be collected in a binder or attached to each other with a paper fastener.

included in the witness subfiles; the redundancy aids the attorney in reacting to the unexpected.

F. Preparation of Computer-Based Presentation

U.S. district courtrooms are now wired for electronic presentations, and most of the attorneys who regularly practice in these courtrooms routinely use this technology to present their case. Technology use in state courts varies from state to state and from county to county within a state. Where the technology is available, witnesses will usually handle hard copies of documentary exhibits while the judge and the jury view electronic copies on courtroom monitors.

Attorneys are also more frequently making use of presentation software in opening statements and closing arguments. The attorney's speaking skills continue to play a key role, but the integration of visual images can increase their effectiveness. Slide presentations during opening statements may include photographs of witnesses, and closing arguments often include visual presentations of documents used to impeach the witness, such as written statements and transcripts of testimony given on prior occasions.

Because many litigators, even though skilled in crafting a theme of the case based upon a legitimate legal theory, do not have the technical expertise to create slides, they generally turn to the paralegal to produce slide presentations. The software requires scanning documents and saving the scans to a laptop computer hard drive, flash drive, or a removable disk prior to the trial. (The PDF file format is preferred for use in federal courts.) The electronic information can then be incorporated into slide presentations with the aid of such software as Power-Point, Sanction, or Trial Director, so the attorney can reference the exhibits during the opening statement or closing argument. In addition to scanning the exhibits, paralegals can assist attorneys in selecting materials to be included.

The slide presentations may be linear or non-linear. Linear presentations move in a fixed chronological order from slide to slide. Once the slide show begins, the order of the slides cannot change. PowerPoint is an example of software that requires a linear presentation. Non-linear presentations allow users to jump from exhibit to exhibit as the needs of a trial develop without having to follow a predetermined order. Sanction and Trial Director are examples of non-linear software. Each slide prepared for an opening statement should be designed not only to educate the jury but also to promote the theme of the case. (See Figure 11.2 for preparation guidelines.) The text should be kept to a minimum so as not to distract the viewer from listening to what the attorney is saying. Long quotes on the slides should be avoided and, wherever possible, each slide should be limited to one point.

Slides should be as attractive as possible, and pictures are better than words. Photographs of witnesses and scenes can be shown, as well as Google Map images, simple time lines, and easy-to-follow charts. If there is video footage of the event, concise video clips may be included. The slides should have visually appealing backgrounds with contrasting lettering. Red and green lettering should be avoided because some jurors may not be able to differentiate between the lettering and the background. Glitzy transitions from slide to slide should also be avoided.

1. Concise: Each slide should be concise; presentation is not repetitive.
2. Educational: Each slide must inform; every slide must present important information; the presentation as a whole tells a story; the theme is well thought out and drives the entire slide show.
3. Attractive: Variety of visuals is used; appropriate slide backgrounds; wise color choices; readable text.

Figure 11.2 Guidelines for Preparing PowerPoint Slides for Opening Statements and Closing Arguments

Exhibit 11.11 shows slides used in the opening statement of a tax evasion prosecution of Joseph Francis, the founder of Girls Gone Wild. The slides promote the message that the defendant operates a legitimate business by comparing his company to Playboy Enterprises and showing the parallels between the two businesses. Notice how the array of photographs tells the story without identifying Playboy founder Hugh Hefner by name. Text is used sparingly. Although the two slides are somewhat busy, they do educate the viewer in an attractive fashion.

A computer-based slide program, such as PowerPoint, planned for use during the opening statement or closing argument, should include photographs of the target of the investigation, the suspects, the witnesses, the victim, and the defendant. Photos are often part of the investigation files. If not, the Freedom of Information Act can be used to get government photographs, such as those displayed on driver's licenses or state identification cards, and photographs can be gathered from social networking websites, such as Facebook or MySpace. It is best to capture images that are not flattering to opposing witnesses. The type of photograph that could be presented as part of a computer-based slide presentation is depicted in Exhibit 11.12.

Proper setup and operation of the electronic equipment is another important task often assigned to paralegals. Courthouse equipment should be checked out in advance to make sure there are no compatibility problems with the program or operating systems being used. The paralegal given this responsibility should make sure to get permission from the court personnel before inspecting their equipment.

If the case is being tried in a courtroom that is not set up for computer-based presentations, the paralegal will need to bring a laptop computer, projector, and projection screen to court. Again, the courtroom will need to be visited in advance to determine where to set up the equipment and to make sure it performs adequately in that courtroom. The paralegal should experiment with the placement of the equipment and the cart, and use duct tape to indicate where to place the equipment. Court personnel need to be informed so that they know not to remove the tape. Cables should also be taped down with duct tape so that people will not trip over them. The monitor/projection screen should be placed where the jury, judge, and both sides can see.

Exhibit 11.11: Opening Statement Presentation Slides

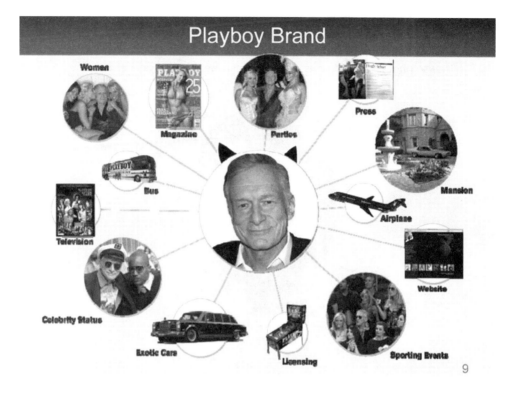

Exhibit 11.12: Jailhouse Photo of Witness for the Prosecution

The first Mafia member to publicly turn against his gangster associates, Joseph Valachi, is shown here in a jailhouse photograph. He died in prison of a heart attack in 1971.

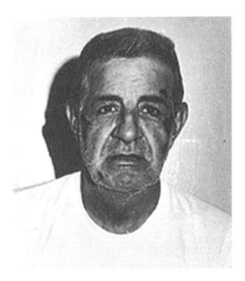

APPLICATION EXERCISES

13. Using the Internet, make copies of unflattering photographs of three members of the faculty of the school you attend.

14. Make a copy of a recent newspaper article in which the U.S. President is quoted. Redact the last name of the President wherever it appears in the article.

15. Exhibit 11.13 shows the narrative portions of the police reports detailing the arrest of Harvard University Professor Henry Gates, Jr. for disorderly conduct. After reading the reports, review the following elements of the Massachusetts statute on disorderly conduct:

    A person is guilty of disorderly conduct if, with purpose to cause public inconvenience, annoyance or alarm, or recklessly creating a risk thereof, he:

(a) engages in fighting or threatening, or in violent or tumultuous behavior; or
(b) * * *
(c) creates a hazardous or physically offensive condition by any act which serves no legitimate purpose of the actor.[5]

Now answer the following questions:

(a) What theme could the government use for this criminal prosecution?
(b) What theme could the defense use for this case?
(c) What story would each side tell to fit its favorable facts within its theme?
(d) What photographs should each side collect to prepare a slide presentation to accompany their opening statements?
(e) Other than pictures of persons, what other photographs would be helpful components of a slide presentation?

Based on your answers, prepare the following presentations:

A. A PowerPoint slideshow of seven to nine slides to accompany the prosecutor's opening statement in a criminal prosecution for disorderly conduct against Professor Gates.
B. A PowerPoint slideshow of seven to nine slides to accompany the defendant's opening statement in a criminal prosecution for disorderly conduct against Professor Gates.

---

[5]In *Alegata v. Commonwealth,* 353 Mass. 287, 231 N.E.2d 201, 211 (1967), the Massachusetts Supreme Judicial Court adopted the Model Penal Code's offense of disorderly conduct. The court struck down subsection (b) of the MPC version as unconstitutionally overbroad and held that subsections (a) and (c) must only be construed as covering conduct, not activities involving the "lawful exercise of a First Amendment right." *See Commonwealth v. A Juvenile, 368 Mass. 580, 334 N.E.2d 617, 628 (1975).*

Exhibit 11.13: Incident Reports Documenting Disorderly Conduct Arrest

CAMBRIDGE POLICE DEPARTMENT
CAMBRIDGE, MA

Incident Report #9005127
Report Entered: 07/16/2009 13:21:34

Narrative

On Thursday July 16, 2009, Henry Gates, Jr. (▬▬▬▬, of ●Ware Street, Cambridge, MA) was placed under arrest at ●Ware Street, after being observed exhibiting loud and tumultuous behavior, in a public place, directed at a uniformed police officer who was present investigating a report of a crime in progress. These actions on the behalf of Gates served no legitimate purpose and caused citizens passing by this location to stop and take notice while appearing surprised and alarmed.

On the above time and date, I was on uniformed duty in an unmarked police cruiser assigned to the Administration Section, working from 7:00 AM-3:30 PM. At approximately 12:44 PM, I was operating my cruiser on Harvard Street near Ware Street. At that time, I overheard an ECC broadcast for a possible break in progress at ● Ware Street. Due to my proximity, I responded.

When I arrived at ● Ware Street I radioed ECC and asked that they have the caller meet me at the front door to this residence. I was told that the caller was already outside. As I was getting this information, I climbed the porch stairs toward the front door. As I reached the door, a female voice called out to me. I turned and looked in the direction of the voice and observed a white female, later identified as Lucia Whalen. Whalen, who was standing on the sidewalk in front of the residence, held a wireless telephone in her hand and told me that it was she who called. She went on to tell me that she observed what appeared to be two black males with backpacks on the porch of ● Ware Street. She told me that her suspicions were aroused when she observed one of the men wedging his shoulder into the door as if he was trying to force entry. Since I was the only police officer on location and had my back to the front door as I spoke with her, I asked that she wait for other responding officers while I investigated further.

As I turned and faced the door, I could see an older black male standing in the foyer of ● Ware Street. I made this observation through the glass paned front door. As I stood in plain view of this man, later identified as Gates, I asked if he would step out onto the porch and speak with me. He replied "no I will not". He then demanded to know who I was. I told him that I was "Sgt. Crowley from the Cambridge Police" and that I was "investigating a report of a break in progress" at the residence. While I was making this statement, Gates opened the front door and exclaimed "why, because I'm a black man in America?". I then asked Gates if there was anyone else in the residence. While yelling, he told me that it was none of my business and accused me of being a racist police officer. I assured Gates that I was responding to a citizen's call to the Cambridge Police and that the caller was outside as we spoke. Gates seemed to ignore me and picked up a cordless telephone and dialed an unknown telephone number. As he did so, I radioed on channel 1 that I was off in the residence with someone who appeared to be a resident but very uncooperative. I then overheard Gates asking the person on the other end of his telephone call to "get the chief" and "what's the chief's name?". Gates was telling the person on the other end of the call that he was dealing with a racist police officer in his home. Gates then turned to me and told me that I had no idea who I was "messing" with and that I had not heard the last of it. While I was led to believe that Gates was lawfully in the residence, I was quite surprised and confused with the behavior he exhibited toward me. I asked Gates to provide me with photo identification so that I could verify that he resided at ● Ware Street and so that I could radio my findings to ECC. Gates initially refused, demanding that I show him identification but then did supply me with a Harvard University identification card. Upon learning that Gates was affiliated with Harvard, I radioed and requested the presence of the Harvard University Police.

With the Harvard University identification in hand, I radioed my findings to ECC on channel two and prepared to leave. Gates again asked for my name which I began to provide. Gates began to yell over my spoken words by accusing me of being a racist police officer and leveling threats that he wasn't someone to mess with. At some point during this exchange, I became aware that Off. Carlos Figueroa was standing behind me. When Gates asked a third time for my name, I explained to him that I had provided it at his request two separate times. Gates continued to yell at me. I told Gates that I was leaving his residence and that if he had any other questions regarding the matter, I would speak with him outside of the residence.

As I began walking through the foyer toward the front door, I could hear Gates again demanding my name. I again told Gates that I would speak with him outside. My reason for wanting to leave the residence was that Gates was yelling very loud and the acoustics of the kitchen and foyer were making it difficult for me to transmit pertinent information to ECC or other responding units. His reply was "ya, I'll speak with your mama outside". When I left the residence, I noted that there were several Cambridge and Harvard University police officers assembled on the sidewalk in front of the residence. Additionally, the caller, Ms. Walen and at least seven unidentified passers-by were looking in the direction of Gates, who had followed me outside of the residence.

As I descended the stairs to the sidewalk, Gates continued to yell at me, accusing me of racial bias and continued to tell me that I had not heard the last of him. Due to the tumultuous manner Gates had exhibited in his residence as well as his continued tumultuous behavior outside the residence, in view of the public, I warned Gates that he was becoming disorderly. Gates ignored my warning and continued to yell, which drew the attention of both the police officers and citizens, who appeared surprised and alarmed by Gates's outburst. For a second time I warned Gates to calm down while I withdrew my department issued handcuffs from their carrying case. Gates again ignored my warning and continued to yell at me. It was at this time that I informed Gates that he was under arrest. I then stepped up the stairs, onto the porch and attempted to place handcuffs on Gates. Gates initially resisted my attempt to handcuff him, yelling that he was "disabled" and would fall without his cane. After the handcuffs were properly applied, Gates complained that they were too tight. I ordered Off. Ivey, who was among the responding officers, to handcuff Gates with his arms in front of him for his comfort while I secured a cane for Gates from within the residence. I then asked Gates if he would like an officer to take possession of his house key and secure his front door, which he left wide open. Gates told me that the door was un securable due to a previous break attempt at the residence. Shortly thereafter, a Harvard University maintenance person arrived on scene and appeared familiar with Gates. I asked Gates if he was comfortable with this Harvard University maintenance person securing his residence. He told me that he was.

After a brief consultation with Sgt. Lashley and upon Gates's request, he was transported to 125 6th. Street in a police cruiser (Car 1, Off's Graham and Ivey) where he was booked and processed by Off. J. P. Crowley.

CAMBRIDGE POLICE DEPARTMENT
CAMBRIDGE, MA

Incident Supplement #9005127 - 1
Report Entered: 07/16/2009 13:52:50

Narrative

On July 16, 2009 at approximately 12:44 PM, I Officer Figueroa#509 responded to an ECC broadcast for a possible break at ⬤ Ware St. When I arrived, I stepped into the residence and Sgt. Crowley had already entered and was speaking to a black male.
As I stepped in, I heard Sgt. Crowley ask for the gentleman's information which he stated "NO I WILL NOT!".
The gentleman was shouting out to the Sgt. that the Sgt.. was a racist and yelled that "THIS IS WHAT HAPPENS TO BLACK MEN IN AMERICA!" As the Sgt. was trying to calm the gentleman, the gentleman shouted " You don't know who your messing with!"
I stepped out to gather the information from the reporting person, WHALEN, LUCIA. Ms. Whalen stated to me that she saw a man wedging his shoulder into the front door as to pry the door open. As I returned to the residence, a group of onlookers were now on scene. The Sgt., along with the gentleman, were now on the porch of ⬤ Ware St. and again he was shouting, now to the onlookers (about seven) ,"THIS IS WHAT HAPPENS TO BLACK MEN IN AMERICA"! The gentleman refused to listen to as to why the Cambridge Police were there.
While on the porch, the gentleman refused to be cooperative and continued shouting that the Sgt. is racist police officer.

SUMMARY

If it appears that a case will not be concluded through plea bargaining, each side must prepare to actually try the case in court. This preparation involves making decisions as to whether to use a jury and what witnesses should be called. Both decisions depend upon the nature of the charges, the nature of the evidence, and the nature of the defendant. Preparation also involves the development of a coherent theory of the case around which the attorneys will organize their opening statements, the questions they will ask the witnesses, and the arguments they will make to the judge and/or jury.

If it is going to be a jury trial, the attorneys and their support staffs should research the backgrounds of the potential jurors and prepare appropriate questions to ask during the *voir dire.*

Regardless of which type of trial it is, the attorneys need to determine who they wish to call as witnesses and to prepare the exhibits they want to introduce. In an attempt to exclude certain types of evidence, the attorneys frequently file additional motions to suppress and motions *in limine.*

In addition to lining up expert witnesses and subpoenaing lay witnesses, the attorneys and their staffs should meet with the witnesses to explain their role and discuss the types of questions they are likely to be asked during both direct and cross-examinations.

Pre-trial preparation also involves the numbering of exhibits and the development of trial notebooks. As courts continue to expand their use of technology, paralegals have begun to play increasingly important roles in organizing databases of documents and developing slide show presentations to enhance opening statements and closing arguments.

INTERNET RESOURCES

General Search Information

- Jury verdict, comparative analysis services: **http://www.juryverdictresearch.com/**
- Address, phone directories/regular and reverse:
  http://www.reversephonedirectory.com/
  http://www.addresses.com/
  http://www.anywho.com/
- Searching public records:
  http://publicrecordsources.com/
  http://www.publicrecordcenter.com/
  http://www.inmatelocater.com/dtzsch/TSK1/-FW2/13208/criminal_public_records
  http://www.peoplefinder.com/
  http://www.peoplefinders.com/
  http://publicrecordsfinder.com/
  http://www.firstinc.com/
  http://www.criminal-info.com/courtrecord/
- Finding someone when you know what school they attended: **http://www.reunion.com/**
- Information about age and relatives: **http://www.intelius.com/**

REVIEW QUESTIONS

1. In a broad sense, when does pre-trial preparation begin?
2. What type of information does the clerk's office collect on prospective jurors?
3. What public records are helpful in gaining insight on prospective jurors' attitudes?
4. What private sources of information are available to conduct background searches on jurors?
5. Why do trial attorneys prepare their own *voir dire* questions?
6. What are the three types of trial exhibits?
7. What methods are used to mark trial exhibits?
8. Give examples of demonstrative exhibits.
9. What are the two documents that are prepared in advance of trial to address evidentiary questions?
10. What are the basic components of a motion *in limine*?
11. What is the purpose of a pocket brief?
12. What are the guidelines for a witness's appearance at trial?
13. How can you refresh a witness's recollection during pretrial preparation?
14. What does it mean when an objection is sustained or overruled?
15. What must accompany a trial subpoena when it is served on the witness?
16. What is the purpose of a subpoena *duces tecum*?
17. What is the risk of having a client undergo an extreme makeover to make a better impression at trial?
18. What are the basic components of the trial file?
19. What is the difference between linear and non-linear slide presentations?
20. What three qualities make individual slides effective in an opening statement presentation?
21. What sources are available for photographs of opposing witnesses?
22. If the courtroom is not designed for computer-based presentations, what advance work must be carried out to prepare for the presentation?

Chapter 12

The Conduct of the Trial

Although paralegals are not authorized to represent clients at trial, they can be instrumental members of the litigation team by providing various types of assistance during the course of a trial. In this chapter, we will walk through the various stages of a criminal trial, from the case being called for trial to verdict. In the course of this journey, we will emphasize the roles played by paralegals.

A. THE ORDER OF EVENTS

A criminal trial is made up of several parts. An overview of the various stages of a typical jury trial of a criminal case is presented in Figure 12.1. Look it over now and then refer back to it as you read through this chapter. Note that items related solely to jury trials are in italics. The non-italicized items apply to both jury and non-jury criminal trials.

B. RULES OF CRIMINAL PROCEDURE

The procedures used in federal criminal trials are spelled out in Section VI of the Federal Rules of Criminal Procedure. Each state has its own, similar rules governing criminal trials. Both federal and state rules can generally be found online and are often supplemented by "local" rules. At both the federal and state levels, it is the trial judge's responsibility to see that they are enforced.

Items that only occur in jury trials are in italic

Case called for trial: Initial hearing before judge
    Scheduling decisions made
    Judge rules on pre-trial motions
Selection of the jury
    Judge's welcome to jurors and swearing in
    Voir dire
    Rulings on challenges for cause
    Exercise of peremptory challenges
    Seating of jurors and alternates
Opening statements
    Prosecution's opening
    Defense's opening
Presentation of the prosecution's case-in-chief
    Prosecution's first witness takes the stand and is sworn in
        Direct examination of prosecution witness #1
        Cross-examination of prosecution witness #1
        Re-direct examination of prosecution witness #1
        Re-cross examination of prosecution witness #1
    Additional prosecution witnesses called and examined.
Consideration of defense's motion for judgment of acquittal/motion for directed verdict
Presentation of defense's case-in-chief
    Defense's first witness takes the stand and is sworn in
        Direct examination of defense witness #1
        Cross-examination of defense witness #1
        Re-direct examination of defense witness #1
        Re-cross examination of defense witness #1
    Additional defense witnesses called, sworn, and examined.
Presentation of rebuttal witnesses (following same format)
Presentation of surrebuttal witnesses (following same format)
Consideration of renewal of defense motion for judgment of acquittal/motion for directed verdict
Jury instructions conference
Closing arguments
    Prosecution's closing argument
    Defense's closing argument
    Prosecution's rebuttal argument
Judge's instructions to the jury
Jury deliberations
Announcement of verdict
Post-verdict actions
    Filing of post-trial motions
    Preparation and filing of pre-sentence investigation report
    Sentencing hearing
    Imposition of sentence
Filing of notice of appeal

Figure 12-1 Stages in a Typical Criminal Trial

APPLICATION EXERCISE

1. Using the Federal Rules of Criminal Procedure and those of your state, develop a table that:
   a. Compares and contrasts the portions of these two sets of rules that apply to the conduct of criminal trials.
   b. Compares and contrasts the portions of these two sets of rules that apply to the conduct of juvenile court proceedings.

C. CALLING THE CASE FOR TRIAL

We begin our discussion of trial procedures at the point at which the case is formally called for trial. At this juncture, the judge takes up preliminary matters, such as scheduling and ruling on pre-trial motions. Neither witnesses nor prospective jurors are present.

The prosecutor, defense counsel, and the defendant typically report to the courtroom on the day and time the case is scheduled. Once the judge calls the case for trial, the judge will address preliminary matters, including the trial schedule. Because paralegals are often the liaison between the attorney and the witnesses, the day-to-day trial schedule the judge sets at this court date is of particular importance for paralegals. If they haven't already done so, the parties provide the judge with their lists of witnesses, any stipulation of facts not in dispute, and exhibit lists.[1] Paralegals are often involved in the preparation of these documents.

Exhibit and witness lists are relatively easy to prepare. Usually, a case caption appears at the top of each document. The document title next appears (e.g., Defendant's Exhibits, Government's List of Witnesses), and a short introductory sentence follows. The body of the exhibit list is a chronological listing of the numbered trial exhibits along with a description of each (see Exhibit 12.1). The witness list consists of an alphabetical listing of the witnesses (see Exhibit 12.2). The attorney's signature and the address block follow the body in both types of lists.

The stipulations lists vary in format. When the stipulation is presented at the time the case is called for hearing, it is usually formatted as a standard captioned document (see Exhibit 12.3). When the parties reach a stipulation after testimony has begun, it may be handwritten on a sheet from a legal pad. In either instance, attorneys from each side typically sign the document.

---

[1] In some jurisdictions, including federal court, many of these documents may have already been submitted prior to the case being called for trial.

Exhibit 12.1: Exhibit List

IN THE CIRCUIT COURT OF THE ELEVENTH JUDICIAL CIRCUIT
MCLEAN COUNTY, ILLINOIS

PEOPLE OF THE STATE OF ILLINOIS)
)
v.)   Case No. 09 CF XXX
)
)
BUD COOK)
    Defendant.)

EXHIBIT LIST

    Now comes the Defendant BUD COOK, by CHARLES HOVEY, his attorney, and states that he will present the following exhibits at trial in his case-in-chief:

Defendant's Exhibit No. 1	Coroner's Inquest Report
Defendant's Exhibit No. 2	Toxicology Report
Defendant's Exhibit No. 3	State Police Accident Reconstruction Report (redacted)
Defendant's Exhibit No. 4	Aerial map of Sumner Drive
Defendant's Group Exhibit No. 5	Photographs of scene of automobile/ bicycle accident
Defendant's Group Exhibit No. 6	Photographs of decedent's clothing
Defendant's Group Exhibit No. 7	Photographs of decedent's bicycle

Respectfully submitted,

BUD COOK, Defendant

By_____

CHARLES HOVEY, his attorney

Charles Hovey
Attorney for Defendant
1857 Bone Street
Normal, IL 61617
(309) 555-1857

Exhibit 12.2: Excerpt from Prosecution Witness List

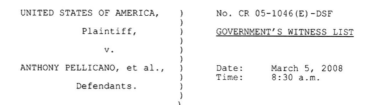

```
UNITED STATES OF AMERICA,      )    No. CR 05-1046(E)-DSF
                               )
           Plaintiff,          )    GOVERNMENT'S WITNESS LIST
                               )
              v.               )
                               )
ANTHONY PELLICANO, et al.,     )    Date:    March 5, 2008
                               )    Time:    8:30 a.m.
           Defendants.         )
                               )
_____)
```

Plaintiff United States of America intends to call the following witnesses in its case-in-chief at trial of the above-captioned matter:

1. Pedro Tenoch Aguilar
2. Thomas Ashley
3. R.T. Ballard III
4. Heidi Binford
5. Laura Buddine
6. Diane Burns
7. Anita Busch
8. Richard Campau
9. Sandra Carradine
10. Keith Carradine
11. Ricardo Cestero
12. Wayne Chen
13. Patrick Coffin
14. Kissandra Cohen
15. Mark Cohn
16. Stephen Corso
17. Jill Cossman
18. Daniel Davis
19. Frederick DeMann
20. Pilar DeMann
21. Jane Doe #2
22. Jane Doe #8
23. Linda Doucett
24. Gregory Dovel
25. Jeffrey Edwards
26. Robert Ellis
27. Elizabeth Eurich
28. Farrah Fawcett

Exhibit 12.3: Stipulation of Undisputed Facts

IN THE CIRCUIT COURT OF THE 12th JUDICIAL CIRCUIT
WILL COUNTY, ILLINOIS

PEOPLE OF THE)
STATE OF ILLINOIS)
      v.)   Case No. 09 CF XXXX
BRANDON TURNER,)
    Defendant.)

STIPULATION

Now come the parties by their respective attorneys and enter into the following stipulation of undisputed fact:

When the Defendant, Brandon Turner, was stopped by Officer Steve Milner, he was driving a 1995 Buick automobile registered to Brandon Turner and Dennis Watterson as co-owners.

_____   _____

CHARLES HOVEY   Will County State's Attorney
Attorney for Defendant   Attorney for the People of the State of Illinois
1857 Bone Street   First Illinois University Plaza
Normal, IL 61761   Joliet, IL 60089
(309)-555-1857   (815)-123-4567

Motions *in limine* may also be presented and decided at this juncture.[2] Once the court rules on the motions *in limine* and addresses any other preliminary matters needing attention, the jury selection process begins.

APPLICATION EXERCISES

2. Prepare a list of prosecution witnesses for the *Brandon Turner* hypothetical case. Assume that (1) all the faculty members of your instructor's department are the government's witnesses; (2) the case is the thirtieth felony case of the year filed in the federal district in which your school is located; and (3) the U.S. Attorney for your federal district is the prosecutor.

---

[2]See Chapter 11, pp. 362–368, for a discussion on how to prepare motions *in limine*.

> **3.** Draft the body of a stipulation of facts in the Vince Shlomi battery case based on the police report displayed in Exhibit 8.2 (Chapter 8, page 273). The stipulation should be based on the undisputed facts found in the statements attributed to defendant Shlomi in the report along with the following hypothetical remarks made by the co-defendant: (a) The defendant kissed me and inserted his tongue in my mouth without my consent; (b) I bit his tongue in self-defense and let go of it as he was beating me up; (c) after he French kissed me, I did not want him to touch me or to have sex with him; (d) the defendant beat me in the face with his fists as soon as I bit his unwelcome tongue; and (e) I had over $900 in my purse when the police showed up.

D. Jury Selection

Prior to the date on which the trial is scheduled to begin, the jury commission will summon people who passed the jury commissioner's standards for service to report to the courthouse on specific dates. Many jurisdictions now use the Internet and telephone call-in numbers to inform jurors as to the specific days and times they need to report within a week or two-week period. The entire array of prospective jurors called during a specific court calendar is known as the **venire**.

Once they arrive at the courthouse, they are sent to a jury assembly room where a judge swears them in and gives them general instructions about their role in the process. Court officials distribute badges or name tags to the jurors that identify them by juror number. Depending on the number of jury trials taking place, some or all of these individuals are then taken to the courtroom being used for a specific trial that is about to begin.

Venire
The group of potential jurors from which the jury for a specific case is selected.

1. THE *VOIR DIRE* PROCESS

When the prospective jurors arrive in the courtroom, they are usually seated in the "audience section" while the judge gives a brief welcoming speech and explains how the questioning will be done. Although the process varies from one courtroom to the next, the judge frequently starts out by using a show-of-hands procedure to obtain responses to some very general questions. After this general introduction, the judge will usually call out the numbers of a smaller group that will then take seats in the **jury box**.

There are two primary methods employed for selecting a jury: the "jury box system" and the "struck jury" method. When courts use the **jury box system**, the initial members of the array are placed in the jury box and then questioned by the judge. Then when jurors are excused, they are individually replaced by other members of the venire also chosen by lot. In this system, prospective jurors are often interviewed in panels of four. After a juror is stricken, another juror in the jury box moves seats and becomes a member of the four-person panel under consideration. The prosecutor initially is given the opportunity to pose challenges for cause or peremptory challenges. The prosecutor may also accept the panel as constituted. If the prosecution removes jurors from the panel, the court then

Jury box
The specific location in the courtroom where the jury sits during the trial.

Jury box system
The method of jury selection in which prospective jurors fill the jury box and are replaced as they are stricken by other prospective jurors, until everyone left in the box is acceptable to both sides or all peremptory challenges are exhausted.

Back strike
The practice of a party's exercise of a peremptory challenge to dismiss a juror who was part of a panel that it had previously accepted.

Struck jury method
The jury selection process in which the judge randomly selects the number of jurors required for the case plus those numbering the total of peremptory challenges and a few extras. After the lawyers exercise all of their challenges, those remaining in the jury box are the jurors and alternates.

questions the replacements. The prosecution again has the opportunity to challenge the new members of the panel. Once the panel is accepted by the government, it is tendered to the defense. The defense can exercise peremptory challenges, ask that juror to be removed for cause, or accept the panel. If the defense replaces a prospective juror, the panel is tendered to the prosecution.

In some courts if a panel is tendered back, a party can exercise a **back strike**, which is the practice of a party's exercise of a peremptory challenge to dismiss a juror who was part of a panel that it had previously accepted. Many courts, however, do not permit back strikes. Once a panel is accepted by both sides, it is then sworn and seated as jurors by the court. The same process is followed until the entire jury is chosen.

An alternative procedure for selecting jurors is called the **struck jury method**. In this system, the judge randomly selects a subgroup of the venire in a number equal to the sum of the total number of jurors required, the total number of peremptory challenges, the number of alternates, and a few extras. After the lawyers exercise all of their challenges, those remaining in the box are the jurors and alternates. Because the parties know the sequence in which the members of the jury pool are seated, they strike jurors knowing the identities of those remaining. The manner in which the struck method is carried out varies. Some judges have the attorneys alternate exercising peremptory challenges until challenges are exhausted. Other judges have the parties submit a list of unacceptable jurors without revealing their selections to the other side. In either situation, the jurors remaining in the box become the jury in the order in which they were seated. The next two usually are named alternate jurors. The remaining prospective jurors are discharged by the court.

In both systems, the judge oversees the process and does much of the actual questioning. However, there is a great deal of variation in the extent to which attorneys participate in the *voir dire* process. In federal court, attorney participation is typically limited to follow-up questions after the venire men and women answer the questions posed by the court. Some federal judges allow the lawyers to ask these questions, whereas other judges require the attorneys to submit written questions which in turn are asked by the judge.[3] In some state courts, attorneys get a chance to ask their own questions; in others, the judge will read questions submitted by the attorneys in advance. Attorneys prefer asking their own questions because it gives them more flexibility and a chance to start "connecting" with the jurors. It also gives them a chance to word the questions in a way that begins to subtly indoctrinate the jury with either the prosecution or defense point of view. Courts exercise broad discretion to modify or decline supplemental *voir dire* or questionnaire inquires. If an attorney's question is rejected, the attorney can make an **objection on the record** along with the basis for the objection.

Objection on the record
A challenge to the judge's ruling that is memorialized either by the electronic or stenographic capture of a verbal objection or a written notation of the objection by docket entry or otherwise.

While this questioning is going on, paralegals working as trial assistants take notes on the potential juror's responses. When professional jury consultants are involved, they will carefully observe the body language the potential jurors exhibit during *voir dire*.

---

[3]FRCrP 24(a)(2)(B) provides that the attorneys may submit proposed *voir dire* questions.

2. EXERCISING CHALLENGES

The point at which the prosecution and defense attorneys get to raise their **challenges for cause** and peremptory challenges depends on which of the above-mentioned *voir dire* systems is being used. Since the number of peremptory challenges available to each side is limited, attorneys prefer to remove potential jurors by using challenges for cause, for which there is no limit. If an attorney is unsuccessful at disqualifying a juror for cause, he or she can still remove the juror with a peremptory challenge.

A challenge for cause is used to excuse a juror after showing good reason that he or she will not or cannot serve in a satisfactory manner. Ordinarily, this means that the candidate expresses a bias that would prevent him or her from fairly and impartially hearing the case. Factors such as present professional relationships with one of the attorneys, racial or ethnic bias, preconceived attitudes about the case, or rigid attitudes about the death penalty in capital cases are among the causes that warrant discharge of a prospective juror. Sometimes, jurors are disqualified for cause when they do not meet the statutory qualifications for jury service, such as age and citizenship.

Sometimes judges act on their own initiative to remove a juror, and sometimes they wait for one of the attorneys to raise a challenge. Although potential jurors sometimes give responses that clearly show a prejudice toward one side or the other, it is usually necessary to show some potential conflict of interest based on occupation or past experiences with the law. If the judge agrees, the person will not be seated. Some examples of situations in which a potential juror would probably be disqualified are a personal relationship with a party in the case or with one of the attorneys involved, having been a victim of a similar crime, or answers indicating prejudice based on race, religion, or some other characteristic relevant to the trial.

The attorneys exercise challenges for cause by asking for a hearing outside the presence of the jurors, known as a **sidebar conference**, and presenting the specific reason they believe the prospective juror should not serve. If the judge is persuaded that the juror should not serve, the juror will be excused following the sidebar. There is no limit to the number of challenges for cause available to both sides.[4] The party asserting the challenge bears a heavy burden to convince the court that either the juror is unqualified to serve or cannot be fair and impartial.

Another basis for dismissal for cause would be a situation in which the potential jurors' answers indicated that they had been influenced by what they had read in newspapers or seen on television about the case. In cases where there has been extensive pre-trial publicity, the defense attorney may have filed a pre-trial motion seeking either a **change of venue** or **change of venire**.[5] However, since either alternative involves additional costs and greater inconvenience for some of the participants, judges are reluctant to grant these requests and instead rely on *voir dire* to eliminate individuals who might be affected by such coverage. In high-profile cases, a public opinion pollster may be employed to determine the

Challenge for cause
A method for removing a prospective juror based on a finding by the judge that the juror has some sort of bias or other factors that should disqualify him or her from serving on this specific case.

Sidebar conference
The discussion between the judge and the attorneys that takes place during the trial outside of the hearing of the jury. (Usually the attorneys stand in front of the bench.)

Change of venue
An action taken by the judge to move a trial to an alternative location.

Change of venire
The process of selecting jurors from a different area than the place of trial.

---

[4]See 28 U.S.C. § 1866(c)(2).
[5]See discussion in Chapter 9 on pp. 288–289.

effect of pre-trial publicity on potential jurors. Exhibit 12.4 displays an excerpt of a pollster's report that was appended to a motion for change of venue.

Exhibit 12.4: Public Opinion Report in Support of Venue Change

The Justice Department filed income tax evasion charges against actor Wesley Snipes in the Middle District of Florida. Snipes filed a motion to change venue to the Southern District of New York. His motion was supported by the report of a public opinion pollster. The court denied the motion. A central Florida jury found Snipes guilty of income tax evasion. Here are excerpts of the report.

Methodology and Data

Overview

The Bernhoft Law Survey project obtained telephone interviews with 353 registered voters in the Ocala Division of the Middle District of Florida, and 226 in the Southern District of New York. The survey was conducted by the Public Opinion Research Laboratory at the University of North Florida. The interviews were done in English and Spanish from October 23 to October 31, 2007. Analysis is not weighted in Ocala or the Southern District of New York since demographic discrepancies do not exist between the sample and the known population of registered voters. (On the Southern District of new York sample, it is slightly low on African Americans (about 3%). Further data collection may correct that. The margin of sampling error for the Ocala set of data is ±5.2%. The margin of sampling error for the Southern District of New York set of data is ±6.5%. A further 147 responses in the Ocala Division and 124 in the Southern District of New York are being collected beginning November 1 and will appear in a supplemental report.

Sample Design

The telephone samples were provided by Survey Sampling International, LLC (SSI). These samples were drawn using standard list-assisted random digit dialing (RDD) methodology. The Ocala Division of the Middle District of Florida covers four counties (Marion, Lake, Sumter, and Citrus). The Ocala sample covers these four counties. The Southern District of New York covers eight counties (New York, Bronx, Westchester, Putnam, Dutchess, Sullivan, Orange, and Rockland). The Southern District sample covers these eight counties.

* * *

When challenging for cause in cases involving prejudicial publicity, a juror's merely having read about the crime in a newspaper or seen something about it on television is usually not sufficient to get someone dismissed for cause. As long as the jurors state that they have not made up their mind and will only consider the evidence presented in the courtroom, most judges will not remove them.

If an attorney is unsuccessful in getting someone removed for cause, that person can be removed by using a **peremptory challenge** *if the attorney has not already exhausted the number authorized for the case.* The number of peremptory challenges each party can exercise is defined by statute and is based on the nature of the offense charged. In federal court, each side receives twenty in capital felonies. In non-capital felonies, the government has six and the defendants collectively have ten. Each side has three in misdemeanors.[6]

Similarly in state court, more peremptory challenges are provided as the severity of the offense increases. For example in Illinois, each side is afforded ten peremptory strikes in felonies with a guarantee of six for each defendant if there are multiple defendants. Each side has five in all other cases, with three for each defendant in multiple defendant cases.[7]

Because the number of peremptory challenges is limited, attorneys are faced with having to decide between accepting a "questionable" juror in order to preserve a peremptory challenge for later use on what may turn out to be a "worse" juror. To help them decide when to use their peremptory challenges, attorneys often rely on generalized stereotypes. Prosecutors generally look for persons who place a high value on the enforcement of the laws and protecting the status quo. The defense favors non-judgmental, sympathetic persons who may be skeptical of the police. Jury consulting firms can be used to create desirable and undesirable juror profiles for specific types of cases. In some cases, these experts may be present during *voir dire* to observe and interpret body language and voice stressors.

The general rule is that attorneys do not need to give a justification for exercising a peremptory challenge, but they cannot be used to strike a juror on the basis of race or sex. The U.S. Supreme Court first wrestled with this dilemma in *Batson v. Kentucky* where it held that the systematic exclusion of jurors on the basis of race is unconstitutional.[8] In *J.E.B. v. Alabama*, it extended the ruling to also apply to exclusions based on gender.[9] The defendant and the struck juror do not have to be of the same race or gender to raise this objection. The procedure for *Batson* objections is initiated by one side making the objection in a sidebar. The opponent then must justify every peremptory challenge exercised against jurors who possess the characteristic on which the objection is based. In other words, the opponent must show that the jurors were struck for a reason other than race or sex. Although this is done in a sidebar or in chambers, a court reporter usually is present so that there is a record of the discussion.

Peremptory challenge
A method whereby an attorney can remove a prospective juror without being required to state a reason.

---

[6]FRCrP 24(b).

[7]725 ILCS 5/115-4.

[8]476 U.S. 79, 96-99, 106 S. Ct. 1712, 90 L. Ed. 2d 69 (1986).

[9]511 U.S. 127, 128-129, 114 S. Ct. 1419, 128 L. Ed. 2d 89 (1994).

Batson v. Kentucky
Supreme Court of the United States
476 U.S. 79 (1986)

Justice POWELL delivered the opinion of the Court, in which BRENNAN, WHITE, MARSHALL, BLACKMUN, STEVENS, and O'CONNOR, JJ. joined.

This case requires us to reexamine that portion of *Swain v. Alabama*, 380 U.S. 202 (1965), concerning the evidentiary burden placed on a criminal defendant who claims that he has been denied equal protection through the State's use of peremptory challenges to exclude members of his race from the petit jury.

I

Petitioner, a black man, was indicted in Kentucky on charges of second-degree burglary and receipt of stolen goods. On the first day of trial in Jefferson Circuit Court, the judge conducted *voir dire* examination of the venire, excused certain jurors for cause, and permitted the parties to exercise peremptory challenges. The prosecutor used his peremptory challenges to strike all four black persons on the venire, and a jury composed only of white persons was selected. Defense counsel moved to discharge the jury before it was sworn on the ground that the prosecutor's removal of the black veniremen violated petitioner's rights under the Sixth and Fourteenth Amendments to a jury drawn from a cross section of the community, and under the Fourteenth Amendment to equal protection of the laws. Counsel requested a hearing on his motion. Without expressly ruling on the request for a hearing, the trial judge observed that the parties were entitled to use their peremptory challenges to "strike anybody they want to." The judge then denied petitioner's motion, reasoning that the cross-section requirement applies only to selection of the venire and not to selection of the petit jury itself.

The jury convicted petitioner on both counts. On appeal to the Supreme Court of Kentucky, petitioner pressed, among other claims, the argument concerning the prosecutor's use of peremptory challenges. . . . The Supreme Court of Kentucky affirmed. . . . We granted certiorari, and now reverse.

II

In *Swain v. Alabama*, this Court recognized that a "State's purposeful or deliberate denial to Negroes on account of race of participation as jurors in the administration of justice violates the Equal Protection Clause." This principle has been "consistently and repeatedly" reaffirmed, in numerous decisions of this Court both preceding and following *Swain*. We reaffirm the principle today.

More than a century ago, the Court decided that the State denies a black defendant equal protection of the laws when it puts him on trial before a jury from which members of his race have been purposefully excluded. *Strauder v. West Virginia*, 100 U.S. 303 (1880). That decision laid the foundation for the Court's unceasing efforts to eradicate racial discrimination in the procedures used to select the venire from which individual jurors are drawn. In *Strauder*, the Court explained that the central concern of the recently ratified Fourteenth Amendment was to put an end to governmental discrimination on account of race. Exclusion of black citizens from service as jurors constitutes a primary example of the evil the Fourteenth Amendment was designed to cure.

In holding that racial discrimination in jury selection offends the Equal Protection Clause, the Court in *Strauder* recognized, however, that a defendant has no right to a "petit jury composed in whole or in part of persons of his own race." . . . But the defendant does have the right to be tried by a jury whose members are selected pursuant to nondiscriminatory criteria. *Martin v. Texas*, 200 U.S. 316, 321 (1906); *Ex parte Virginia*, 100 U.S. 339, 345 (1880). The Equal Protection Clause guarantees the defendant that the State will not exclude members of his race from the jury venire on account of race, or on the false assumption that members of his race as a group are not qualified to serve as jurors, see *Norris v. Alabama*, 294 U.S. 587, 599 (1935); *Neal v. Delaware*, 103 U.S. 370, 397 (1881).

* * *

Accordingly, the component of the jury selection process at issue here, the State's privilege to strike individual jurors through peremptory challenges, is subject to the commands of the Equal Protection Clause. Although a prosecutor ordinarily is entitled to exercise permitted peremptory challenges "for any reason at all, as long as that reason is related to his view concerning the outcome" of the case to be tried, *United States v. Robinson*, 421 F. Supp. 467, 473 (Conn. 1976), . . . the Equal Protection Clause forbids the prosecutor to challenge potential jurors solely on account of their race or on the assumption that black jurors as a group will be unable impartially to consider the State's case against a black defendant.

III

The principles announced in *Strauder* never have been questioned in any subsequent decision of this Court. Rather, the Court has been called upon repeatedly to review the application of those principles to particular facts. A recurring question in these cases, as in any case alleging a violation of the Equal Protection Clause, was whether the defendant had met his burden of proving purposeful discrimination on the part of the State. . . .

Swain required the Court to decide, among other issues, whether a black defendant was denied equal protection by the State's exercise of peremptory challenges to exclude members of his race from the petit jury. The record in Swain showed that the prosecutor had used the State's peremptory challenges to strike the six black persons included on the petit jury venire. While rejecting the defendant's claim for failure to prove purposeful discrimination, the Court nonetheless indicated that the Equal Protection Clause placed some limits on the State's exercise of peremptory challenges.

. . . While the Constitution does not confer a right to peremptory challenges, those challenges traditionally have been viewed as one means of assuring the selection of a qualified and unbiased jury. To preserve the peremptory nature of the prosecutor's challenge, the Court in *Swain* declined to scrutinize his actions in a particular case by relying on a presumption that he properly exercised the State's challenges.

The Court went on to observe, however, that a State may not exercise its challenges in contravention of the Equal Protection Clause. It was impermissible for a prosecutor to use his challenges to exclude blacks from the jury "for reasons wholly unrelated to the outcome of the particular case on trial" or to deny to blacks "the same right and opportunity to participate in the administration of justice enjoyed by the white population." Accordingly, a black defendant could make out a prima facie case of purposeful discrimination on proof that the peremptory challenge system was "being perverted" in that manner. For example, an inference of purposeful discrimination would be raised on evidence that a prosecutor, "in case after case, whatever the circumstances, whatever the crime and whoever the defendant or the victim may be, is responsible for the removal of Negroes who have been selected as qualified jurors by the jury commissioners and who have survived challenges for cause, with the result that no Negroes ever serve on petit juries." Evidence offered by the defendant in *Swain* did not meet that standard. While the defendant showed that prosecutors in the jurisdiction had exercised their strikes to exclude blacks from the jury, he offered no proof of the circumstances under which prosecutors were responsible for striking black jurors beyond the facts of his own case.

A number of lower courts following the teaching of *Swain* reasoned that proof of repeated striking of blacks over a number of cases was necessary to establish a violation of the Equal Protection Clause. Since this interpretation of *Swain* has placed on defendants a crippling burden of proof, prosecutors' peremptory challenges are now largely immune from constitutional scrutiny. For reasons that follow, we reject this evidentiary formulation as inconsistent with standards that have been developed since *Swain* for assessing a prima facie case under the Equal Protection Clause.

* * *

The standards for assessing a prima facie case in the context of discriminatory selection of the venire have been fully articulated since *Swain*. See *Castaneda v. Partida, Washington v. Davis, Alexander v. Louisiana.* . . . To establish such a case, the defendant first must show that he is a member of a cognizable racial group, and that the prosecutor has exercised peremptory challenges to remove from the venire members of the defendant's race. Second, the defendant is entitled to rely on the fact, as to which there can be no dispute, that peremptory challenges constitute a jury selection practice that permits "those to discriminate who are of a mind to discriminate." Finally, the defendant must show that these facts and any other relevant circumstances raise an inference that the prosecutor used that practice to exclude the veniremen from the petit jury on account of their race. This combination of factors in the empaneling of the petit jury, as in the selection of the venire, raises the necessary inference of purposeful discrimination.

In deciding whether the defendant has made the requisite showing, the trial court should consider all relevant circumstances. For example, a "pattern" of strikes against black jurors included in the particular venire might give rise to an inference of discrimination. Similarly, the prosecutor's questions and statements during *voir dire* examination and in exercising his challenges may support or refute an inference of discriminatory purpose. These examples are merely illustrative. We have confidence that trial judges, experienced in supervising *voir dire*, will be able to decide if the circumstances concerning the prosecutor's use of peremptory challenges creates a prima facie case of discrimination against black jurors.

Once the defendant makes a prima facie showing, the burden shifts to the State to come forward with a neutral explanation for challenging black jurors. Though this requirement imposes a limitation in some cases on the full peremptory character of the historic challenge, we emphasize that the prosecutor's explanation need not rise to the level justifying exercise of a challenge for cause. But the prosecutor may not rebut the defendant's prima facie case of discrimination by stating merely that he challenged jurors of the defendant's race on the assumption —or his intuitive judgment—that they would be partial to the defendant because of their shared race. Just as the Equal Protection Clause forbids the States to exclude black persons from the venire on the assumption that blacks as a group are unqualified to serve as jurors, supra, so it forbids the States to strike black veniremen on the assumption that they will be biased in a particular case simply because the defendant is black. The core guarantee of equal protection, ensuring citizens that their State will not discriminate on account of race, would be meaningless were we to approve the exclusion of jurors on the basis of such assumptions, which arise solely from the jurors' race. Nor may the prosecutor rebut the defendant's case merely by denying that he had a discriminatory motive or "affirm[ing] [his] good faith in making individual selections." If these general assertions were accepted as rebutting a defendant's prima facie case, the Equal Protection Clause "would be but a vain and illusory requirement." The prosecutor therefore must articulate a neutral explanation related to the particular case to be tried. The trial court then will have the duty to determine if the defendant has established purposeful discrimination.

IV

The State contends that our holding will eviscerate the fair trial values served by the peremptory challenge. Conceding that the Constitution does not guarantee a right to peremptory challenges and that *Swain* did state that their use ultimately is subject to the strictures of equal protection, the State argues that the privilege of unfettered exercise of the challenge is of vital importance to the criminal justice system.

While we recognize, of course, that the peremptory challenge occupies an important position in our trial procedures, we do not agree that our decision today will undermine the contribution the challenge generally makes to the administration of justice. The reality of practice, amply reflected in many state- and federal-court opinions, shows that the challenge may be, and unfortunately at times has been, used to discriminate against black jurors. By requiring trial courts to be sensitive to the racially discriminatory use of peremptory challenges, our decision enforces the mandate of equal protection and furthers the ends of justice. In view of the heterogeneous population of our Nation, public respect for our criminal justice system and the rule of law will be strengthened if we ensure that no citizen is disqualified from jury service because of his race.

Nor are we persuaded by the State's suggestion that our holding will create serious administrative difficulties. In those States applying a version of the evidentiary standard we recognize today, courts have not experienced serious administrative burdens, and the peremptory challenge system has survived. We decline, however, to formulate particular procedures to be followed upon a defendant's timely objection to a prosecutor's challenges.

V

In this case, petitioner made a timely objection to the prosecutor's removal of all black persons on the venire. Because the trial court flatly rejected the objection without requiring the prosecutor to give an explanation for his action, we remand this case for further proceedings. If the trial court decides that the facts establish, prima facie, purposeful discrimination and the prosecutor does not come forward with a neutral explanation for his action, our precedents require that petitioner's conviction be reversed.

It is so ordered.

CHIEF JUSTICE BURGER, joined by JUSTICE REHNQUIST, dissenting.

I

Today the Court sets aside the peremptory challenge, a procedure which has been part of the common law for many centuries and part of our jury system for nearly 200 years.

* * *

Permitting unexplained peremptories has long been regarded as a means to strengthen our jury system in other ways as well. One commentator has recognized:

> The peremptory, made without giving any reason, avoids trafficking in the core of truth in most common stereotypes. . . . Common human experience, common sense, psychosociological studies, and public opinion polls tell us that it is likely that certain classes of people statistically have predispositions that would make them inappropriate jurors for particular kinds of cases. But to allow this knowledge to be expressed in the evaluative terms necessary for challenges for cause would undercut our desire for a society in which all people are judged as individuals and in which each is held reasonable and open to compromise. . . . [For example,] [although] experience reveals that black males as a class can be biased against young alienated blacks who have not tried to join the middle class, to enunciate this in the concrete expression required of a challenge for cause is societally divisive. Instead we have evolved in the peremptory challenge a system that allows the covert expression of what we dare not say but know is true more often than not." Babcock, Voir Dire: Preserving "Its Wonderful Power," 27 Stan. L. Rev. 545, 553-554 (1975).

* * *

Instead of even considering the history or function of the peremptory challenge, the bulk of the Court's opinion is spent recounting the well-established principle that intentional exclusion of racial groups from jury venires is a violation of the Equal Protection Clause. I too reaffirm that principle, which has been a part of our constitutional tradition since at least *Strauder v. West Virginia*. But if today's decision is nothing more than mere "application" of the "principles announced in *Strauder*," as the Court maintains, some will consider it curious that the application went unrecognized for over a century. The Court in *Swain* had no difficulty in unanimously concluding that cases such as *Strauder* did not require inquiry into the basis for a peremptory challenge. See (REHNQUIST, J., dissenting). More recently we held that "[defendants] are not entitled to a jury of any particular composition. . . . " *Taylor* v. *Louisiana*, 419 U.S., at 538.

A moment's reflection quickly reveals the vast differences between the racial exclusions involved in *Strauder* and the allegations before us today:

> "Exclusion from the venire summons process implies that the government (usually the legislative

or judicial branch) . . . has made the general determination that those excluded are unfit to try *any* case. Exercise of the peremptory challenge, by contrast, represents the discrete decision, made by one of two or more opposed *litigants* in the trial phase of our adversary system of justice, that the challenged venireperson will likely be more unfavorable to that litigant in that *particular case* than others on the same venire.

"Thus, excluding a particular cognizable group from all venire pools is stigmatizing and discriminatory in several interrelated ways that the peremptory challenge is not. The former singles out the excluded group, while individuals of all groups are equally subject to peremptory challenge on any basis, including their group affiliation. Further, venire-pool exclusion bespeaks *a priori* across-the-board total unfitness, while peremptory-strike exclusion merely suggests potential partiality in a particular isolated case. Exclusion from venires focuses on the inherent attributes of the excluded group and infers its *inferiority*, but the peremptory does not. To suggest that a particular race is unfit to judge in any case necessarily is racially insulting. To suggest that each race may have its own special concerns, or even may tend to favor its own, is not." *United States v. Leslie*, 783 F.2d 541, 554 (CA5 1986) (en banc).

* * *

The Court also purports to express "no views on whether the Constitution imposes any limit on the exercise of peremptory challenges by *defense* counsel." But the clear and inescapable import of this novel holding will inevitably be to limit the use of this valuable tool to both prosecutors and defense attorneys alike. Once the Court has held that *prosecutors* are limited in their use of peremptory challenges, could we rationally hold that defendants are not? "Our criminal justice system 'requires not only freedom from any bias against the accused, but also from any prejudice against his prosecution.'" . . .

Rather than applying straightforward equal protection analysis, the Court substitutes for the holding in *Swain* a curious hybrid. The defendant must first establish a "prima facie case," of invidious discrimination, then the "burden shifts to the State to come forward with a neutral explanation for challenging black jurors." . . .

While undoubtedly these rules are well suited to other contexts, particularly where (as with Title VII) they are required by an Act of Congress, they seem curiously out of place when applied to peremptory challenges in criminal cases. Our system permits two types of challenges: challenges for cause and peremptory challenges. Challenges for cause obviously have to be explained; by definition, peremptory challenges do not. "It is called a peremptory challenge, because the prisoner may challenge peremptorily, on his own dislike, *without showing of any cause.*" Analytically, there is no middle ground: A challenge either has to be explained or it does not. . . .

Confronted with the dilemma it created, the Court today attempts to decree a middle ground. To rebut a prima facie case, the Court requires a "neutral explanation" for the challenge, but is at pains to "emphasize" that the "explanation need not rise to the level justifying exercise of a challenge for cause." I am at a loss to discern the governing principles here. A "clear and reasonably specific" explanation of "legitimate reasons" for exercising the challenge will be difficult to distinguish from a challenge for cause. Anything short of a challenge for cause may well be seen as an "arbitrary and capricious" challenge, ... Apparently the Court envisions permissible challenges short of a challenge for cause that are just a little bit arbitrary—but not too much. . . .

An example will quickly demonstrate how today's holding, while purporting to "further the ends of justice," will not have that effect. Assume an Asian defendant, on trial for the capital murder of a white victim, asks prospective jury members, most of whom are white, whether they harbor racial prejudice against Asians. The basis for such a question is to flush out any "juror who believes that [Asians] are violence-prone or morally inferior. . . ." Assume further that all white jurors deny harboring racial prejudice but that the defendant, on trial for his life, remains unconvinced by these protestations. Instead, he continues to harbor a hunch, an "assumption," or "intuitive judgment," that these white jurors will be prejudiced against him, presumably based in part on race. The time-honored rule before today was that peremptory challenges could be exercised on such a basis. . . .

The effect of the Court's decision, however, will be to force the defendant to come forward and "articulate a neutral explanation" for his peremptory challenge, a burden he probably cannot meet. This example demonstrates that today's holding will produce juries that the parties do not believe are truly impartial. This will surely do more than "disconcert" litigants; it will diminish confidence in the jury system.

* * *

JUSTICE REHNQUIST, with whom THE CHIEF JUSTICE joins, dissenting.

* * *

I cannot subscribe to the Court's unprecedented use of the Equal Protection Clause to restrict the historic scope of the peremptory challenge, which has been described as "a necessary part of trial by jury." *Swain*. In my view, there is simply nothing "unequal" about the State's using its peremptory challenges to strike blacks from the jury in cases involving black defendants, so long as such challenges are also used to exclude whites in cases involving white defendants, Hispanics in cases involving Hispanic defendants, Asians in cases involving Asian defendants, and so on. This case-specific use of peremptory challenges by the State does not single out blacks, or members of any other race for that matter, for discriminatory treatment. Such use of peremptories is at best based upon seat-of-the-pants instincts, which are undoubtedly crudely stereotypical and may in many cases be hopelessly mistaken. But as long as they are applied across-the-board to jurors of all races and nationalities, I do not see—and the Court most certainly has not explained—how their use violates the Equal Protection Clause.

* * *

The use of group affiliations, such as age, race, or occupation, as a "proxy" for potential juror partiality, based on the assumption or belief that members of one group are more likely to favor defendants who belong to the same group, has long been accepted as a legitimate basis for the State's exercise of peremptory challenges. See *Swain, supra; United States v. Leslie*, 783 F.2d 541 (CA5 1986) (en banc); *United States v. Carter*, 528 F.2d 844 (CA8 1975), cert. denied, 425 U.S. 961 (1976). Indeed, given the need for reasonable limitations on the time devoted to *voir dire*, the use of such "proxies" by both the State and the defendant may be extremely useful in eliminating from the jury persons who might be biased in one way or another. . . .

CASE DISCUSSION QUESTIONS

1. To what extent does this decision alter the definition we gave for a peremptory challenge? How would you modify the definition to take this decision into account?
2. What procedure is the trial judge supposed to use to determine if the prosecutor's peremptory challenge was based on race? Do you think this procedure is appropriate? Can you think of a better way for the judge to determine if a peremptory challenge was based on race?
3. What negative consequences do Chief Justice Burger and Justice Rehnquist think will occur as a result of this decision? Do you think they were right?
4. This case was limited to the use of peremptory challenges by the prosecution to eliminate black jurors in a black defendant's trial. Should the holding be extended to the exercise of peremptory challenges by a defense attorney? Why or why not? Should it extend to jurors' religious affiliation? Why or why not?

3. SELECTION OF ALTERNATE JURORS

In trials that are expected to go on for more than a day or two, it is common practice to select a few alternate jurors to be ready to step in if one of the regular jurors gets sick or is unable to continue for some other reason.[10] In federal court, the judge may empanel up to six alternates.[11] Alternate jurors sit in the jury box with the regular jurors and listen to all the same testimony. However, they do not participate in jury deliberations unless they have been chosen to replace one of the original jurors.

4. INSTRUCTIONS TO JURORS AND SEQUESTERING JURIES

Once the jurors, and any alternates, have been chosen, the judge will instruct them not to discuss the case, either among themselves or with anyone else—family and friends. The judge will usually also instruct them not to read any newspaper articles or watch/listen to any news broadcasts about the trial. During lunch breaks, the jurors eat together under the watch of a bailiff or other court officer.

Sequestering a jury
A procedure for protecting jurors from outside influences by having them stay in hotel rooms where bailiffs can monitor their activities and block access to newspaper, television, radio, and Internet news related to the trial.

In highly publicized cases, the court may **sequester the jury**. This means that, collectively, the jurors will be isolated so that they will not be subject to outside influences during the course of the proceedings. Generally, this means that the court houses the jury members in a hotel and blocks access to newspaper, television, radio, and Internet news related to the trial. However, due to the added expense and to the resentment it evokes in the jurors, judges are reluctant to use this option.

APPLICATION EXERCISES

4. Research the number of peremptory challenges given to each side in non-capital felony and misdemeanor cases in the state in which your school is located. Give the citation to the statute or rule.

5. Visit a local court during jury selection in a criminal case. Write a report to your instructor that includes your observations of the following:
   a. The system used to select a jury (jury box or back strike),
   b. The extent to which the attorneys got to directly question jurors,
   c. Whether prospective jurors were dismissed,
   d. If jurors were dismissed for cause, what the reason was for their dismissal, and
   e. If jurors were dismissed through a peremptory challenge, what you speculate the reason was for their dismissal.

   Include the names of the judge, attorneys, and defendant in your report along with the date and time you visited court.

---

[10]Other reasons could include situations in which a juror has a family emergency, is shown to have withheld or lied about key information during *voir dire*, or has acted improperly during the course of the trial.

[11]FRCrP 24(c)(1).

E. OPENING STATEMENTS

Most criminal trials begin with "opening statements" from the attorneys representing the prosecution and the defense. The prosecuting attorney speaks first, because it was the government's decision to file the charges and it carries the burden of proving them. The prosecution's **opening statement** provides a framework that explains the nature of the alleged crimes and helps the decision maker (either a jury or the judge) understand how the evidence to be presented will prove the elements of the crimes being charged. After describing how the prosecutor thinks the crime happened, he or she will usually highlight some of the key witnesses that will be called and what their testimony is expected to contribute to the prosecution's case.

> **Opening statement**
> The speech each side presents to the jury before testimony is presented outlining what the attorney expects the evidence will show.

The prosecution's presentation is typically followed by a defense opening that explains the defense theory of the case, highlights what key defense witnesses are expected to contribute, and encourages the jurors to keep an open mind until the defense has had a chance to present its witnesses.[12]

Note that these remarks are called opening "statements," while the speeches they give at the end of the trial are referred to as closing "arguments." This distinction in terminology reflects the fact that attorneys are not supposed to be able to argue the guilt or innocence of the defendant(s) at this stage of the trial. These opening remarks are supposed to be limited to providing a framework or context in which to place the evidence that will be presented during the trial. The attorneys can describe what a specific witness will be testifying about but cannot argue that some witnesses are more credible than others. Many litigators use their opening statements to introduce the theme of their case. Exhibit 12.5 includes excerpts of the opening remarks made by both sides in the criminal sexual abuse trial of the late pop icon Michael Jackson.

Exhibit 12.5: Excerpts from Opening Statements

Prosecution

"On February 3, 2003, the defendant, Michael Jackson's, world was rocked. Not in the musical sense but in the real world sense," District Attorney Tom Sneddon told Santa Barbara jurors this morning. On that date, Sneddon explained, Martin Bashir's documentary "Living with Michael Jackson" aired in England, immediately creating a firestorm over the pop singer's admission that he shared his bed with boys to whom he was unrelated. Jackson's world was so rocked, Sneddon reported, that an associate, Marc Schaffel, described the fallout from the Bashir production as a "train wreck."

---

[12]In some jurisdictions the defense has the choice of deferring their opening statement until after the prosecution has finished its case-in-chief. However, most prefer to begin to raise doubts from the very beginning of the trial.

Defense

After noting that it was an honor to represent Jackson, Thomas Mesereau told jurors, "I'm here to tell you these charges are fictitious and bogus." He then bellowed, "These charges are fake, silly, ridiculous." After Melville sustained an objection from Sneddon, Mesereau described what he said were attempts by the accuser's mother to weasel money from several celebrities while her son was ill. The woman, Mesereau said, tried to score cash from Jay Leno, comedian George Lopez, and an actress who appeared on "The Fresh Prince of Bel Air."

F. PRESENTATION OF THE EVIDENCE

The heart of the trial process involves putting people on the stand to provide testimonial evidence about what took place and lay the foundation for the admission of written documents, test results, and various types of physical objects like weapons, illicit drugs, stolen goods, etc.[13]

1. PROSECUTION'S CASE-IN-CHIEF

Just as the prosecution side gets to make the first opening statement, it also gets to present its witnesses and exhibits first.[14] This section of the trial is referred to as being the prosecution's case-in-chief. For each witness called, whether that witness is called as part of the prosecution's case-in-chief, the defense's case-in-chief, or as a rebuttal witness, the questioning will follow the pattern of direct, cross, re-direct, re-cross, re-re-direct, re-re-cross, etc.

The complexity of the case will determine the number of witnesses called, the exhibits presented, and the length of the trial itself. In a traffic case, the prosecutor may only need to call the police officer operating the radar gun to prove beyond a reasonable doubt that the defendant was speeding. In contrast, in the illegal wiretapping trial of Los Angeles celebrity private investigator Anthony Pellicano, U.S. Attorneys listed 127 witnesses they intended to call, including actors Keith Carradine and Farrah Fawcett. (See Exhibit 12.2 on page 397 for the first part of the prosecution's witness list.)

Direct examination
The initial questioning conducted by attorneys for the side that called the witnesses.

a. Direct Examinations

Direct examinations begin with a brief ceremony in which witnesses raise their hand and take an oath to answer the questions truthfully.[15] This procedure

---

[13]See Chapter 10 discussion of evidence (pp. 339–349) and Chapter 11 discussion on selection and preparation of witnesses (pp. 374–376).

[14]As was the case with the opening statements, the prosecution goes first because it has the burden of proof.

[15]Because some people have religious objections to "solemnly swearing," they are given the alternative of "affirming" or "declaring."

is designed to impress upon the witnesses the importance of telling the truth while they are on the stand. Failure to tell the truth can, but seldom does, result in perjury charges being brought against the witness.

Direct examinations are usually pretty much scripted and rehearsed[16] because the witnesses are usually cooperative and supportive of the side that called them. After some introductory questions designed to put the witness at ease and to provide relevant background information about the witness, the prosecuting attorney will ask questions designed to bring out the facts needed to describe the nature of the crime and establish the nature of the defendant's involvement.

Perhaps the most important thing to keep in mind about direct examination is that the attorney conducting the examination is generally prohibited from using **leading questions**. These are questions worded in such a way as to suggest what the answer should be. An obvious example would be a prosecutor asking: "Wouldn't you say the defendant appeared to be very angry at that point in time?" The form of the question in effect suggests what the attorney wants the witness to say. A slightly less obviously leading question is: "Is it true that you saw the defendant pull a knife and stab the victim with that knife?" Instead of using these types of leading questions, the attorney must ask such questions as: "Where were you when the victim was attacked?" "Please describe to the court what you saw." "Can you identify the man you saw?"

There are, however, some important exceptions to the general prohibition against asking leading questions on direct. For example, attorneys are allowed to lead witnesses through background information about where they live or what their educational background is. Leading questions are also allowed in situations where the witness may be very young or be mentally disabled. These exceptions are justified in terms of saving time in situations where such questioning isn't expected to disadvantage the other side.

Perhaps one of the most important exceptions involves examinations of **adverse and hostile witnesses**. An adverse witness is either the opposing party in the case or a witness closely affiliated with the opposing party, whereas a hostile witness is a witness who shows great hostility of prejudice against the side calling him or her to testify. In the criminal context, the arresting officer is an adverse witness to the defendant. The defendant's family members or someone who was also involved in criminal endeavors are hostile witnesses when called by the government. By allowing leading questions in these situations, the attorney can prevent the witness from wasting the court's time and giving overly ambiguous answers.

At this point we also want to remind you about the differential treatment given to those accepted as "expert" witnesses.[17] Attorneys are allowed to pose hypothetical questions to expert witnesses that they could not ask of regular witnesses. Although expert witnesses were not present at the scene of the crime or have not seen the defendant, they can give an informed opinion as to the probability of something occurring in a situation similar to that of the defendant.

Leading questions
Questions worded in such a way as to suggest what the answer should be.

Adverse witness
A witness who is either the opposing party in the case or a witness who is closely affiliated with the opposing party.

Hostile witness
A witness who manifests great hostility or prejudice against the side that called him or her to testify.

---

[16]The attorneys and/or their paralegals have often gone over the questions and answers with the witness in advance of their appearance in court.

[17]See Chapter 10, pp. 341–343.

1. Mark exhibits before testimony begins.
2. Chart the use of exhibits at trial:
   a. Marked for identification
   b. Motion to admit
   c. Admit/deny
3. Before resting, verify all exhibits are offered and the court has ruled.
4. Before case goes to the jury, make sure the court has all exhibits.

Figure 12.2 Handling Exhibits at Trial

b. Introduction of Exhibits

Although testimonial evidence is extremely important in most criminal cases, the physical and documentary evidence is often critical. In order to get things like weapons, test results, medical records, and photographs admitted into evidence, attorneys need to use witness testimony to lay a proper foundation.[18]

As mentioned in Chapter 11, paralegals are often assigned the task of organizing and labeling each exhibit so that each is associated with the witness needed to lay the proper foundation. The attorney doing the direct is responsible for seeing that the right questions are asked. For example, to properly authenticate physical evidence, law enforcement officers are typically called to testify that they (1) kept the object in their exclusive personal control from the time it was found until the time it is presented in court, (2) maintained a complete record of everyone involved in the chain of custody (i.e., everyone who handled the object from the time it was found to the time it was presented in court), or (3) marked the object in a way that will make it easily distinguishable at a later time.

Once the proper foundation has been laid, the party calling the witness who identified the exhibit will move for its admission into evidence. The opposing side may object to its admission on the basis of one of the rules of evidence. If the objection is overruled, the exhibit is admitted. Conversely, if the objection is sustained, the exhibit is not admitted into evidence.

APPLICATION EXERCISE

6. Create a five-column Excel spreadsheet to display defense trial exhibits by number and description, along with whether they were offered into evidence, subject to objection, and admitted by the judge. Insert the number and description of the exhibits referenced in Exhibit 12.1 in the *Bud Cook* case.

---

[18]See Chapter 10, pp. 346–347.

c. Objections

During direct examination, opposing attorneys are limited to taking notes and making **objections**. The ability to make effective objections is one of the greatest skills an attorney can have, because the timely use of appropriate objections can keep damaging evidence out and throw opposing attorneys "off their game."

When it comes to making objections, timing is critical. Rule 103(1) of the Federal Rules of Evidence states:

> In case the ruling is one admitting evidence, a timely objection or motion to strike appears of record, stating the specific ground of objection, if the specific ground was not apparent from the context.

Thus, if the objection comes too late, it will be rejected on that basis alone. If the objection is to the type of question being asked or the way in which it is worded, it must be raised as soon as the question is asked rather than waiting until after the witness has answered. If the objection is to something the witness said in response to a legitimate question, the objection must be raised as soon as it is clear that the answer being given is objectionable. Then if the objection is sustained, the attorney must request to have the witness's answer stricken from the record. When the judge sustains an objection to a question, the attorney conducting the examination must either reword the question to make the inquiry in a less objectionable way or get the same information from another witness.

d. Preserving the Record

Attorneys will make objections even when they do not expect the trial judge to sustain them. This "objecting for the record" is sometimes called protecting the record or making a record for appeal. Not only are attorneys required to raise appropriate objections at the proper times during the trial, they are also expected to preserve a proper record for a possible appeal. When attorneys fail to object during trial, they cannot complain later to an appellate court about something that was admitted into evidence during the trial. Additionally, the judge must overrule the objection in order for the error to be preserved on review. If the judge does not rule on an objection, the objection is waived.

When the judge sustains an objection to the admission of testimonial evidence, the attorney who sought to have the testimony admitted should make an **offer of proof** to make a record for appeal. This is a procedure whereby the attorney either (1) tells the judge what the witness would have testified to if the judge had not sustained the objection to admitting it or (2) elicits the challenged testimony from the witness. In either event, the court reporter records the offer of proof. The contested testimony is taken outside the presence of the jury, so the jury won't be influenced by what the judge excluded.

e. Cross-examinations

After the attorney who called the witness finishes a direct examination, the opposing attorney gets an opportunity to **cross-examine** that witness. It is a very

Objection
A request to the judge to disallow either (1) specific questions or comments by another attorney or (2) certain responses from witnesses.

Offer of proof
A procedure whereby excluded testimony is placed into the record for possible appellate review of the judge's decision to exclude it.

Cross-examination
The questioning of a witness called by the opposing side.

important right guaranteed by the Sixth and Fourteenth Amendments to the U.S. Constitution.[19] It provides the opportunity to clarify potentially misleading statements and "half-truths" as well as to bring out additional favorable information not touched on by the opponent's attorney. Although cross is limited to the scope of the topics considered on direct examination, judges give cross-examiners broad latitude in exploring these topics as well as any potential bias or prejudice of the witness.

An important objective in many cross-examinations is to attack the credibility of the witness. In most trials there are conflicts between the testimonies of different witnesses. One says the defendant was at the scene of the crime; another says the defendant was across town playing poker with his buddies. One says the robber had dark hair; another says it was blond. To help jurors resolve these conflicts in their favor, attorneys attempt to bring out possible biases or the inability of the witness to have seen clearly what he or she claims to have seen.

Another key way to attack credibility is to confront the witnesses with inconsistencies between their trial testimony and their written statements. In most states, written statements are provided to the opposing side through discovery. In the federal courts and some states, there is no requirement to furnish witness statements until after direct examination. FRCrP 26.2(a) states:

> After a witness other than the defendant has testified on direct examination, the court, on motion of a party who did not call the witness, must order an attorney for the government or the defendant and the defendant's attorney to produce, for the examination and use of the moving party, any statement of the witness that is in their possession and that relates to the subject matter of the witness's testimony.

You should check your jurisdiction's requirements for witness statement production. Impeachment is usually more effective when the prior statements are available prior to trial.

The process of drawing potentially negative information out of the other side's witnesses is made much easier by the fact that leading questions are allowed in cross-examinations. So, on cross, the attorney can dramatically ask: "Isn't it true that you used to date . . . ," or "Isn't it true that you recently were fired by. . . . "

APPLICATION EXERCISE

7. Research when witness statements must be provided in the state in which your school is located.
   a. Give the citation to the statute or rule.
   b. Is the rule more liberal or more restrictive than FRCrP 26.2?

---

[19]See Chapter 10, p. 338.

f. Re-direct and Re-cross

After the defense has taken its best shot at undercutting the impact of the prosecution's witness, the prosecution gets a chance to rehabilitate its witness's credibility during the **re-direct** phase of the testimony. However, re-direct questions are limited to issues that were raised by the cross-examination of that witness. They cannot be used to raise new issues or to explore subjects that were not covered as part of the cross.

Although the questioning of the witness usually ends with the re-direct, there are occasions in which a re-direct will be followed by a **re-cross**. Re-crosses are limited to issues that were raised in the re-direct. In very rare cases, there could be a re-redirect and a re-re-cross, etc., but in each case the questions must be within the scope of the examination that preceded it.

g. Resting the Case-in-Chief

After the prosecution has finished with all of its planned witnesses, it **rests its case**. This signals the end of the first stage of the presentation of the evidence and leads to the start of the defendant's case-in-chief. The prosecution still retains the right to present additional evidence at the rebuttal stage of the trial.

2. DEFENDANT'S CASE-IN-CHIEF

The presentation of the defendant's case-in-chief generally follows the same pattern and rules as that of the prosecution. Witnesses are called to give testimonial evidence and lay the foundation for documentary and physical evidence. The defendant's direct examinations are followed by prosecution cross-examinations, defendant re-directs, and prosecution re-crosses.

The defendant can use this opportunity to offer evidence in support of a defense or in opposition to the prosecution's evidence. The most effective theory that the defendant can present is one that completely explains all of the facts supporting the hypothesis of innocence. Under this approach, the defendant will explain, impeach, or refute every fact that may contradict the theory of innocence.

The defense can also present character witnesses to establish that the defendant possesses qualities that are inconsistent with the commission of the crime charged. Although the defendant cannot be forced to testify, if the defendant takes the stand, on cross the prosecutor may ask questions beyond the scope of direct and explore facts surrounding the offense(s) for which the defendant is charged.

3. REBUTTAL CASE AND SURREBUTTAL

After both sides have presented their case-in-chief, the prosecution gets a chance to present a rebuttal, also known as the **prosecutor's rebuttal case**. During this phase the prosecutor may call additional witnesses or recall witnesses who have already testified in order to give **rebuttal evidence** to counter evidence presented in the defense's case-in-chief. Following the rebuttal case, the defense may present

---

Re-direct
The portion of a witness's testimony during which the side that conducted the initial direct examination has an opportunity to ask additional questions designed to clarify issues raised during cross-examination.

Re-cross
The portion of a witness's testimony during which the side that conducted the initial cross-examination has an opportunity to ask additional questions designed to clarify issues raised during the re-direct.

Resting the case
A phrase used by attorneys to announce that they have presented all of the evidence they intend to present at the current stage of the trial.

Prosecutor's rebuttal case
The phase of the trial in which the prosecution calls witnesses to dispute the evidence presented by the defense in its case-in-chief. This is also referred to as "the rebuttal."

Rebuttal evidence
Evidence presented to explain, repel, counteract, or disprove facts given in evidence after a party had rested its case.

1. Preparing witnesses and trial exhibits (pre-trial)
2. Preparing witness list (pre-trial)
3. Preparing witness files with impeachment material (pre-trial)
4. Preparing draft *motions in limine* (pre-trial)
5. Preparing pocket briefs on questions of evidence (pre-trial)
6. Preparing stipulations (pre-trial)
7. Preparing stipulations, exhibit list (pre-trial)
8. Preparing list of witnesses (pre-trial)
9. Exhibit management
   a. Charting both sides' exhibits
   b. Acting as custodian of exhibits
   c. Reminding trial attorney of rulings under advisement
   d. Reminding attorney of exhibits not offered into evidence
10. Keeping track of evidentiary rulings taken under advisement
11. Keeping witnesses updated as to when they are expected to testify
12. Taking notes during direct and cross-examinations
13. Highlighting opposition witnesses' statements for use against them on cross-examination.

Figure 12.3 Paralegals' Roles in the Evidence Phase of Trials

Surrebuttal
The phase of the trial in which the defense calls witnesses to dispute the rebuttal evidence offered by the prosecution.

Motion for judgment of acquittal/motion for directed verdict
A request to have the judge enter a verdict of not guilty on the basis that the prosecution failed to present enough evidence to establish a *prima facie* case of guilt.

***Prima facie* case**
Evidence that, if not contradicted by other evidence, is sufficient to meet the burden of proof required for that type of case.

surrebuttal witnesses. In this part of the trial, the defense recalls witnesses who previously testified or calls new witnesses to rebut evidence presented during the prosecution's rebuttal.

G. Motion for Judgment of Acquittal/Motion for Directed Verdict

A **motion for judgment of acquittal** is a request to the judge to enter a verdict of not guilty on the basis that the prosecution failed to present enough evidence to establish a *prima facie* case of guilt. In many state courts, this motion is referred to as a **motion for directed verdict**.[20] Although it is rarely granted, defense attorneys have nothing to lose by making this motion immediately after the prosecution rests its case-in-chief. If the judge agrees that the prosecution has not met its burden of presenting a *prima facie* case that the defendant committed the crime charged, the judge must enter a not-guilty verdict and there is no need for the defense to call any further witnesses. In federal court, the judge may enter a judgment of acquittal on his or her own motion.[21] Although the motion typically is presented orally, it may be written and supported by a legal memorandum.

After all the evidence has been presented, the defendant may renew the motion. In this context, the defense attorney is arguing that all of the evidence taken in the light most favorable to the prosecution, resolving all the credibility

---

[20]A motion for directed verdict brought in a bench trial is referred to as a "motion for directed finding."
[21]FRCrP 29(a).

issues in favor of the government, is insufficient to establish the defendant's guilt beyond a reasonable doubt. However, this motion is rarely granted at this stage of the case, either. The government cannot appeal the granting of the motion. This would place the defendant in double jeopardy in violation of the Fifth Amendment.[22]

APPLICATION EXERCISE

8. For the state in which your school is located, research the type of motion filed when the prosecution does not meet its burden of establishing a *prima facie* case.
   a. Where did you find the answer?
   b. How do the requirements of the motion compare to motions brought pursuant to FRCrP 29(a)?

H. DEVELOPMENT OF JURY INSTRUCTIONS

It is the role of the jury to apply the law to the facts that were presented in the trial and then determine whether the prosecution proved, beyond a reasonable doubt, that the defendant violated specific statute(s). However, the statutes and court rules they are supposed to apply are written in "legalese" and are often very confusing to lay jurors. Therefore, instructions are given to the jurors on the laws they are supposed to apply as well as the procedures they should follow in their deliberations.

Jury instructions are written directions given by the judge to the jury pertaining to the controlling principles of law in the case. They also let the jury know the theories of the case proposed by each party and advise them of the standards they must apply to make their decision.

Jury instructions
Written directions given by the judge to the jury pertaining to the controlling principles of law in the case.

1. PATTERN JURY INSTRUCTIONS

Since it is grounds for reversal if a judge fails to give the proper instructions, judges usually rely on **pattern jury instructions**. These are a set of basic instructions that have been prepared by committees of judges, lawyers, and scholars for use by the trial courts in their jurisdictions. Forty-eight states and many federal circuits[23] make pattern criminal jury instructions available. Although trial courts are not required to use them, most judges do so because they generally are upheld by appellate courts in their jurisdiction.

Pattern jury instructions
Uniform basic jury instructions typically prepared by committees of judges, lawyers, and scholars for use by the trial courts in a specific jurisdiction.

---

[22]See *Smalis v. Pennsylvania*, 476 U.S. 140, 145, 106 S. Ct. 1745, 90 L. Ed. 2d 116 (1986).

[23]Pattern criminal jury instructions are available in the Fifth, Sixth, Seventh, Eighth, Ninth, and Eleventh Circuits.

Examples of pattern jury instructions are given in Exhibit 12.6. The first six relate to general issues that arise in almost all criminal cases, the next four are examples of instructions on issues that would only apply in cases involving certain types of criminal actions. The last two relate specifically to how the jury should proceed in selecting a foreman and communicating with the judge.

Exhibit 12.6: Selected Pattern Jury Instructions*

1.01 THE FUNCTIONS OF THE COURT AND THE JURY

Members of the jury, you have seen and heard all the evidence and the arguments of the attorneys. Now I will instruct you on the law.

You have two duties as a jury. Your first duty is to decide the facts from the evidence in the case. This is your job, and yours alone.

Your second duty is to apply the law that I give you to the facts. You must follow these instructions, even if you disagree with them. Each of the instructions is important, and you must follow all of them.

Perform these duties fairly and impartially. Do not allow sympathy, prejudice, fear, or public opinion to influence you. You should not be influenced by any person's race, color, religion, national ancestry, or sex.

Nothing I say now, and nothing I said or did during the trial, is meant to indicate any opinion on my part about what the facts are or about what your verdict should be.

1.06 WHAT IS NOT EVIDENCE

Certain things are not evidence. I will list them for you:

First, testimony [and exhibits] that I struck from the record, or that I told you to disregard, is [are] not evidence and must not be considered.

Second, anything that you may have seen or heard outside the courtroom is not evidence and must be entirely disregarded. This includes any press, radio, or television reports you may have seen or heard. Such reports are not evidence and your verdict must not be influenced in any way by such publicity.

Third, questions and objections by the lawyers are not evidence. Attorneys have a duty to object when they believe a question is improper. You should not be influenced by any objection or by my ruling on it.

Fourth, the lawyers' statements to you are not evidence. The purpose of these statements is to discuss the issues and the evidence. If the evidence as you remember it differs from what the lawyers said, your memory is what counts.

1.03 TESTIMONY OF WITNESSES (DECIDING WHAT TO BELIEVE)

You are to decide whether the testimony of each of the witnesses is truthful and accurate, in part, in whole, or not at all, as well as what weight, if any, you give to the testimony of each witness. In evaluating the testimony of any witness, you may consider, among other things:

- ■ the witness's age;
- ■ the witness's intelligence;

- the ability and opportunity the witness had to see, hear, or know the things that the witness testified about;
- the witness's memory;
- any interest, bias, or prejudice the witness may have;
- the manner of the witness while testifying; and
- the reasonableness of the witness's testimony in light of all the evidence in the case.

[You should judge the defendant's testimony in the same way that you judge the testimony of any other witness.]

3.07 WEIGHING EXPERT TESTIMONY

You have heard a witness [witnesses] give opinions about matters requiring special knowledge or skill. You should judge this testimony in the same way that you judge the testimony of any other witness. The fact that such a person has given an opinion does not mean that you are required to accept it. Give the testimony whatever weight you think it deserves, considering the reasons given for the opinion, the witness' qualifications, and all of the other evidence in the case.

3.01 FAILURE OF DEFENDANT TO TESTIFY

The [A] defendant has an absolute right not to testify. The fact that the [a] defendant did not testify should not be considered by you in any way in arriving at your verdict.

3.05 IMPEACHMENT OF DEFENDANT—CONVICTIONS

You have heard evidence that the defendant has been convicted of a crime. You may consider this evidence only in deciding whether the defendant's testimony is truthful in whole, in part, or not at all. You may not consider it for any other purpose. A conviction of another crime is not evidence of the defendant's guilt of any crime for which the defendant is now charged.

4.06 "KNOWINGLY"—DEFINITION

When the word "knowingly" [the phrase "the defendant knew"] is used in these instructions, it means that the defendant realized what he was doing and was aware of the nature of his conduct, and did not act through ignorance, mistake or accident. [Knowledge may be proved by the defendant's conduct, and by all the facts and circumstances surrounding the case.]

[You may infer knowledge from a combination of suspicion and indifference to the truth. If you find that a person had a strong suspicion that things were not what they seemed or that someone had withheld some important facts, yet shut his eyes for fear of what he would learn, you may conclude that he acted knowingly, as I have used that word. {You may not conclude that the defendant had knowledge if he was merely negligent in not discovering the truth.}]

3.14 POSSESSION OF STOLEN PROPERTY—INFERENCE

You may reasonably infer that a person who possesses recently stolen property knew it had been stolen. You are never required to make this inference.

The term "recently" is a relative term that has no fixed meaning. The longer the period of time since the property was stolen, the more doubtful the inference of knowledge becomes.

Possession may be explained satisfactorily by facts and circumstances independent of any testimony by the defendant. In considering whether possession has been explained satisfactorily, you are reminded that a defendant has an absolute right not to testify and need not call any witnesses or produce any evidence.

6.04 ENTRAPMENT—ELEMENTS

The government must prove beyond a reasonable doubt that the defendant was not entrapped. Thus, the government must prove beyond a reasonable doubt either (1) that, before contact with law enforcement, the defendant was ready and willing or had a predisposition or prior intent to commit the offense, or (2) that the defendant was not induced or persuaded to commit the offense by law enforcement officers or their agents.

6.05 ENTRAPMENT—FACTORS

In determining whether the defendant was entrapped, you may consider:

(1) The background [or character or reputation] of the defendant [including] [prior criminal history] [or economic status];
(2) Whether it was law enforcement officers or their agents that first suggested the criminal activity;
(3) Whether the defendant performed criminal activity for profit;
(4) Whether the defendant showed reluctance to perform criminal activity;
(5) Whether law enforcement officers or their agents repeatedly induced or persuaded the defendant to perform criminal activity;
(6) Whether law enforcement officers or their agents offered an ordinary opportunity to commit a crime; and
(7) Whether law enforcement officers or their agents offered exceptional profits or persuasion or merely solicited commission of the crime.

While no single factor necessarily indicates by itself that a defendant was or was not entrapped, the central question is whether the defendant showed reluctance to engage in criminal activity that was overcome by inducement or persuasion.

7.01 SELECTION OF FOREPERSON—GENERAL VERDICT

Upon retiring to the jury room, select one of your number as your foreperson. The foreperson will preside over your deliberations and will be your representative here in court.

* * *

7.05 COMMUNICATION WITH COURT

I do not anticipate that you will need to communicate with me. If you do, however, the only proper way is in writing, signed by the foreperson, or if he or she is unwilling to do so, by some other juror, and given to the marshal.

*These instructions come from the Pattern Criminal Federal Jury Instructions for the Federal Seventh Circuit.

2. NON-PATTERN JURY INSTRUCTIONS

When a case presents facts or circumstances that are not covered by the pattern jury instructions for the jurisdiction, the court may present **non-pattern instructions** to the jury. For instance, when a defendant is prosecuted under a newly enacted statute, there typically is no pattern instruction to fit the case, so a non-pattern jury instruction must be produced. Often, attorneys and paralegals draft their non-pattern jury instructions using formbooks for guidance.[24] Other times, non-pattern instructions are created for a particular case by the attorneys based on legal authority, such as a statute or appellate case.

While jury instructions are designed to give greater direction to jurors as to the meaning of the law, there are some concepts that the courts prefer to leave undefined. Perhaps the most controversial of these is "reasonable doubt." In a long line of cases, the courts have repeatedly avoided attempts to instruct jurors how they should define it, because such definitions are likely to "confuse juries more than the simple words themselves."[25]

Non-pattern jury instructions
Jury instructions that were not created as part of the uniform pattern instructions for the jurisdiction.

3. JURY INSTRUCTIONS CONFERENCE

After both sides have rested and before closing arguments, in many courts the judge conducts a **jury instructions conference**. This may take place in the courtroom or in the judge's chambers. During the conference, the judge and each attorney will review the proposed instructions, which are usually numbered and marked with the name of the party offering them. Each pattern instruction lists the pattern instruction number. Non-pattern instructions are referenced to legal authority, such as case law or statutes. In some courts, the judge prepares the proposed instructions; in others, the attorneys draft them. In either event, the attorneys for each side are given an opportunity to raise objections, offer additional instructions, and propose modifications.

Usually, the judge goes through each proposed instruction one at a time. The attorneys will either accept or object to the instruction. The objections and bases for the objections generally are presented "**on the record**," that is, before a court reporter and/or recorded on the court's docket sheet. If neither side's submission is acceptable, the judge may order the preparation of an alternate version of an instruction. By the end of the conference, the judge will have approved a complete set of jury instructions as well as the order in which the instructions will be given. The judge also approves the verdict forms to be distributed to the jury. Before the instructions are presented to the jury, a "clean" set is prepared. This set is not marked with pattern instruction numbers, case or statute citations, or the name of a party. Sample pattern and non-pattern instructions appear in Exhibits 12.7 and 12.8.

Jury instructions conference
The meeting of the parties with the judge following the close of the evidence for the purpose of determining the appropriate instructions to be given to the jury.

On the record
Statements made in court that are recorded by either a court reporter or by the clerk of the court as a written entry in the case file.

---

[24]Among the jury instruction formbooks used in the U.S. District Court are: E. Devitt, C. Blackmar & K. O'Malley, *Federal Jury Practice & Instructions* (West Publishing, 5th ed., 2000); L. Sands et al., *Modern Federal Jury Instructions* (Matthew Bender, 2003).

[25]*United States v. Blackburn*, 992 F.2d 666, 668 (7th Cir.), cert. denied, 510 U.S. 949 (1993).

Exhibit 12.7: Marked Pattern Jury Instruction

The format of proposed jury instructions varies from court to court. The following is a pattern instruction in a format used in many federal courts. Notice the instruction number at the top and the Seventh Circuit Pattern Instruction Number at the bottom. These features are deleted from the "clean copy" which goes to the jury.

JURY INSTRUCTION NO. 31

The verdict must represent the considered judgment of each juror. Your verdict must be unanimous.

You should make every reasonable effort to reach a verdict. In doing so, you should consult with one another, express your own views, and listen to the opinions of your fellow jurors. Discuss your differences with an open mind. Don't hesitate to reexamine your own views and change your opinion if you come to believe it is wrong. But you should not surrender your honest beliefs about the weight or effect of evidence solely because of the opinion of your fellow jurors or for the purpose of returning a unanimous verdict.

You should consider all the evidence fairly and equally and deliberate with the goal of reaching an agreement which is consistent with the individual judgment of each juror. You are impartial judges of the facts.

7th Cir. 1.34

Exhibit 12.8: Marked Non-Pattern Jury Instruction

The following is a hypothetical non-pattern instruction based on a format used in some state courts. The bottom right corner includes the name of the tendering party, the instruction number, and the legal authority for the instruction. Like the pattern instruction depicted in Exhibit 12.7, these references are deleted from the "clean copy."

"Agent" means any officer, director, servant or employee of the corporation or any other person authorized to act on behalf of the corporation.

Prosecution Instruction No. 13

Non-Pattern: *State v. Jenny*, 867 N.E.2d 53 (2009)

In federal court and some state courts, judges may dispense with an instruction conference. When this happens, the judge may ask the attorneys to submit proposed instructions before the trial begins or at a certain stage of the trial, such as the close of the government's case-in-chief. Even when this procedure is used, an attorney may request a jury instruction conference.

APPLICATION EXERCISES

9. Determine whether there are pattern jury instructions in the state in which your school is located.
   a. In what form and where are they published?
   b. Who (occupations, organizations) drafted and approved these instructions?

10. Prepare a marked copy of your state's pattern criminal jury instruction concerning the reasonable doubt burden of proof. (Assume that this will be the prosecution's tenth proposed instruction.) If there is more than one reasonable doubt instruction, prepare all of them and continue the numbering (10, 11, 12, etc.).

11. Prepare a non-pattern instruction for the defendant based on a hypothetical Union Supreme Court case of *Union v. Accused*, 800 Union Rpts. 3d 12 (2010) in which the Court, in overruling a conviction, ruled that "under the Due Process Clause of the State of Union Constitution, persons accused of crimes cannot be convicted of a crime unless the prosecution disproves beyond a reasonable doubt any legitimate hypothesis of innocence."

12. Is there a pattern jury instruction in the jurisdiction in which your school is located that is used to encourage a jury to break its deadlock? If so, provide a copy of this instruction and a citation as to where you found it.

13. In the *Brandon Turner* case (see Preface and your notebook), the defendant was charged with the felony offense of possession of crack cocaine with the intent to deliver.
   a. Under your state's criminal code, what are the lesser included offenses of drug possession?
   b. List the quantity of illicit drugs for each lesser offense along with a citation to the appropriate statute(s).

I. CLOSING ARGUMENTS

Opening statements are supposed to create a framework for viewing the case, whereas **closing arguments** are designed to convince jurors to either convict (the prosecution side) or acquit (the defendant's side).

Closing argument
An oral presentation made to the jury, after all of the evidence has been presented, for the purpose of convincing the jury to find in favor of the side that is presenting the argument.

As with opening statements, the prosecution gets to make its presentation first. In this segment of the closing arguments, the prosecution seeks to show how the evidence presented was sufficient to prove each of the various counts that were included in the complaint. The prosecutor will highlight the testimony of specific witnesses, documents, test results, etc. and explain how each helps provide a basis for a guilty verdict.

The defense's closing argument usually begins with a reminder that it is the prosecution's obligation to prove the defendant guilty, rather than the defense's duty to prove innocence. The presentation will then go on to respond to points made by the prosecution, attack the credibility of the prosecution's evidence, and attempt to show why it was insufficient to prove the defendant committed the alleged crimes. The defense attorney will emphasize the testimony of particular witnesses, documents, and other exhibits that support the defendant's version of what is supposed to have taken place. The attorney will usually end with a discussion of the meaning of "beyond a reasonable doubt" and an emotional appeal to avoid a potential miscarriage of justice.

If the defense presents a closing argument, the prosecutor is then given the opportunity to present a rebuttal argument. This gives the prosecution the chance to counter key points made in the defense close and also allows the prosecutor to have the last word.[26] The rebuttal usually ends with an emotional appeal for justice to be served by punishing the defendant for the harm done to the victim(s).

J. Charging the Jury

Traditionally, the judge reads the instructions to the jury immediately following closing arguments. However, U.S. District Court judges and many state judges have discretion to charge the jury prior to the closings. In federal court, the judge may give selected instructions throughout the course of the trial to fit the individual circumstances of the case.

Charging the jury
A process in which the judge instructs the jurors as to the meaning of the laws they are supposed to apply.

Before sending them to a special conference room to begin their deliberations, judges instruct the jury on the meaning of the laws they are supposed to apply as well as the procedures they should follow in their deliberations. The process of delivering these instructions is called **charging the jury**. The judge accomplishes this task by reading to the jury the instructions approved at the jury instruction conference. The jury is given a set of the instructions before it is dismissed from the courtroom to begin its deliberations.

K. Jury Deliberations

Once the jury gets settled in the deliberations room, the first item of business is the selection of a foreperson to preside over the deliberations and serve as the

---

[26]Unlike witness examinations where there are multiple opportunities for each side to come back with rebuttals and surrebuttals, the defense only gets one closing argument and no rebuttal.

official spokesperson for the jury in communications to the judge and, in some courtrooms, to announce the verdict. Since this selection, like the deliberations over guilt, are held in secret, there is no systematic empirical data regarding how criminal juries actually reach their decisions.[27] Based on scattered tales of juror's self-reported experiences, there is reason to believe that many are chosen simply because they were the first to volunteer for the job.

Perhaps the most famous of all jury deliberations was that portrayed in *Twelve Angry Men*. In this classic movie, the juror's initial vote is 11–1 in favor of conviction, but as they discuss the evidence in greater detail, the lone dissenting juror gradually wins over all the others and the jury returns with a verdict of not guilty. While this made for a great movie, Hollywood's vision of a single juror being so persuasive is not consistent with the experience of most courthouse observers. Indeed, Professors Kalven and Zeisel's research conducted as part of the University of Chicago Jury Project showed that whichever side has the majority on the first vote usually ends up winning over the minority. Furthermore, they found that people in the minority on the first vote were only successful in winning over their fellow jurors when there was a core group of at least three or four jurors dissenting on the first round of votes.[28]

There is no set length of time that a jury can deliberate, and when juries report that they are deadlocked, the judge will often give the following type of instruction:

> The verdict must represent the considered judgment of each juror. Your verdict, whether it be guilty or not guilty, must be unanimous.
>
> You should make every reasonable effort to reach a verdict. In doing so, you should consult with one another, express your own views, and listen to the opinions of your fellow jurors. Discuss your differences with an open mind. Do not hesitate to re-examine your own views and change your opinion if you come to believe it is wrong. But you should not surrender your honest beliefs about the weight or effect of evidence solely because of the opinions of your fellow jurors or for the purpose of returning a unanimous verdict. The twelve of you should give fair and equal consideration to all the evidence and deliberate with the goal of reaching an agreement which is consistent with the individual judgment of each juror.
>
> You are impartial judges of the facts. Your sole interest is to determine whether the government has proved its case beyond a reasonable doubt.[29]

In federal court, this type of jury instruction is referred to as an "*Allen* charge," named for the 1896 U.S. Supreme Court case of *Allen v. United States*.[30]

---

[27]There is, however, empirical data that examines the deliberative process in civil cases. The Arizona Supreme Court sanctioned a study in Pima County in which all phases of fifty civil jury trials, including deliberations, were videotaped and studied. See Supreme Court of Arizona Administrative Order 98-10. The results of the study were published in S. Diamond & N. Vidmar, *Juror Discussions During Civil Trials: A Study of Arizona's Rule 39(f) Innovation* (April 2002).(A report prepared for The Arizona Superior Court in Pima County, The Supreme Court of Arizona, and The State Justice Institute.) *http://www.law.northwestern.edu/faculty/fulltime/diamond/papers/arizona_civil_discussions.pdf*

[28]H. Kalven, Jr. & H. Zeisel, *The American Jury*, 488 (Little, Brown, 1966).

[29]Seventh Circuit Pattern Criminal Jury Instruction 7.06—Disagreement Among Jurors.

[30]*Allen v. United States*, 164 U.S. 492, 501-502, 17 S. Ct. 154, 41 L. Ed. 528 (1896).

If this type of instruction doesn't produce a verdict, it is common practice for the judge to send a stern message to the effect that the jurors have to try harder because they will not go home until they do. If the hour is late at night, they will be required to return early the next morning and to continue to deliberate "for as long as it takes." This type of direction obviously places great social pressure on the hold-out jurors to get on board with the majority so they can resume their normal lives. On occasion, the judge will even sequester the jurors during deliberations so that they will be denied outside contact until they achieve a verdict.

In most cases, the social pressures to go along with the crowd and to get back to one's regular life activities are sufficient to lead to some sort of compromise verdict. The potential for compromise arises when there is more than one simple guilty or not-guilty verdict to be reached for a single crime. As we saw in earlier chapters, there are often multiple counts related to the same basic event. After having concluded that the defendant caused someone else's death, the jurors often have to go on to make a determination as to the defendant's intent at the time the act was committed. So, for example, they are required to decide if the defendant was guilty of homicide, voluntary manslaughter, or involuntary manslaughter. The existence of these types of multiple options opens the door for possible compromise verdicts where a group of jurors that favors a guilty verdict for first degree murder agrees to a guilty verdict on voluntary manslaughter, while jurors who were holding out for a not-guilty verdict agree to go along with a conviction on the lesser charge.

Lesser included offense
A crime that shares some, but not all, of the elements of a more serious criminal offense. Thus, the greater offense cannot be committed without committing the lesser crime.

Sometimes, the defense will ask the judge to give the jury an instruction on a **lesser included offense** when some, but not all, of the elements of the crime charged against the defendant are a separate crime. This allows the jury to enter a guilty verdict on the lesser crime but find the defendant not guilty of the more serious crime. For instance, the jury can reject an aggravated battery charge but convict on simple battery. Many criminal defense attorneys view the conviction on the lesser included defense as a victory because the defendant will receive a lighter sentence. Moreover, the conviction may be for a misdemeanor rather than for a felony. When the jury is deadlocked, a conviction on the lesser included defense often forms the basis of a compromise.

L. ANNOUNCEMENT OF THE VERDICT

When the jury reaches its verdict, the foreperson will fill out a verdict form that reflects the jury's decision as to all charges. A sample jury verdict form appears in Exhibit 12.9. The foreperson then notifies the bailiff, who in turn notifies the judge. Calls then go out to the attorneys so that they and the defendant can assemble for the public reading of the verdict.

Polling the jury
After a jury's verdict has been announced, the procedure in which the judge asks each juror to confirm his or her vote.

Once the court has re-convened, the judge asks if the jury has reached a verdict and the foreperson responds that they have. The verdict form is then given to the judge for review. In some courtrooms, the judge will then read the verdict; in others, the judge will direct the foreperson to read it. In some cases, the parties will request the judge to **poll the jury**. This requires each juror to publicly acknowledge his or her agreement or disagreement with the verdict that was read.

Exhibit 12.9: Jury Verdict Form

A jury convicted entrepreneur and media personality Martha Stewart of conspiracy, obstruction of an agency proceeding, and giving false statements to federal investigators arising from her use of insider information that she received from Peter Bacanovic, her broker. The completed jury verdict form appears below.

UNITED STATES OF AMERICA v. MARTHA STEWART AND PETER BACANOVIC

03 Cr. 717 (MGC)

JURY VERDICT FORM

DEFENDANT MARTHA STEWART

COUNT ONE: Guilty __✓__   or   Not Guilty _____

If and only if you find the defendant guilty on Count One, please check the objects of the conspiracy which you found:

Obstruction of an Agency Proceeding	__✓__
False Statements	__✓__
Perjury	__✓__

COUNT THREE: Guilty __✓__   or   Not Guilty _____

If and only if you find the defendant guilty on Count Three, please check each of the specifications which you found:

Specification One:	_____
Specification Two:	__✓__
Specification Three:	__✓__
Specification Four:	__✓__
Specification Five:	__✓__
Specification Six:	__✓__
Specification Seven:	__✓__

If the defendant is found not guilty on all charges, the defendant and the defense attorneys celebrate while the prosecutors try to quickly and quietly exit the courtroom. On the other hand, in many cases if the jury returns at least one guilty verdict, the defense attorneys try to console the defendant and emphasize that they have prepared for the sentencing and potential appeals. In cases in which a compromise verdict is struck, neither side has cause to celebrate.

M. Mistrials

Mistrial
The early termination of a trial because of extraordinary circumstances such as a deadlocked jury, prejudicial trial error, or the illness or death of a trial participant.

In extraordinary circumstances, the judge may declare a **mistrial**, which requires the trial to begin again. In deciding whether to declare a mistrial, the court must determine whether a trial error is so prejudicial and fundamental that the continuation of the proceedings would be pointless. Some of the reasons for declaring a mistrial include significant misconduct by one of the parties, the judge, or a witness; improper juror selection; outside influence on the jury; significant procedural error; illness or death of a juror, judge, or attorney; and a hopelessly deadlocked jury. A mistrial can be declared up until the jury reaches a verdict.

Hung jury
A jury that is unable to reach a verdict after lengthy deliberations.

A mistrial may be declared by the judge on his or her own motion or on the motion of one of the parties. Probably the most common reason for declaring a mistrial is a jury deadlocked without reaching a verdict after lengthy deliberation, known as a **hung jury**. If the judge declares a mistrial, the jury is dismissed and the case is reset for trial. The trial process starts again with jury selection.

N. Post-Verdict/Post-Trial Motions

Post-verdict motion (also known as post-trial motion)
A defense motion filed after a guilty verdict that seeks court action on various case-related matters.

After a finding of guilt, the defendant has the right to file various types of **post-verdict motions**. In some jurisdictions, they are called **post-trial motions**. Since the Fifth Amendment Double Jeopardy Clause prohibits a retrial once the defendant has been acquitted, the prosecution does not have the right to file post-trial motions where there was a finding of not guilty. The prosecutor does, of course, have the opportunity to respond to arguments made by the defense in support of these types of motions. Note that some of these motions are filed before or during the sentencing phase of the trial and that they are filed with the court that tried the case rather than in an appellate court.

Motion for judgment of acquittal
A formal request to have the judge acquit the defendant notwithstanding the jury's verdict to the contrary.

One common post-verdict motion is a **motion for judgment of acquittal**. It is a request to have the judge acquit the defendant even though the jury returned a guilty verdict. Although it is routinely filed, it is rarely granted.

Motion for a new trial
A request to have the judge order a new trial on the basis of errors that were made in the pre-trial and trial stages.

Another type of post-verdict motion is a **motion for a new trial**. This motion ordinarily lists what the defense believes to be errors and mistakes that occurred at the pre-trial and trial stages of the case. Often, the defense will point to evidentiary rulings, prosecutorial misconduct, or the denial of a motion to suppress in support of the prayer for a new trial. In some jurisdictions, the defendant does not file a motion for judgment of acquittal and instead seeks a judgment of acquittal as part of the motion for a new trial. In federal court, the defendant may file a motion for a new trial if is required in the "interest of justice." In most jurisdictions, a motion for a new trial must be filed within seven days of the verdict or within any longer period the court establishes during the seven-day period.[31]

But what happens if the error isn't discovered until after the deadline for filing a motion for a new trial has passed? When this occurs, the defense is allowed to file a **delayed motion for new trial**. In federal court, FRCrP 33 sets a three-year deadline for filing this type of motion. Time limits in state courts vary significantly across the nation. If the motion is premised upon the government's failure to disclose exculpatory evidence pursuant to *Brady v. Maryland*,[32] the defense must show that there is a reasonable probability that, had the evidence been disclosed to the defendant, the outcome of the trial would have been different.[33] If the motion is not based on the prosecution's failure to comply with *Brady*, the defense must show that the evidence was discovered after trial, it could not have been discovered early through the use of due diligence, the evidence is material and not merely cumulative and impeaching, and the evidence would likely produce an acquittal if the case were retried.[34]

With the obvious exception of the delayed motion for a new trial, the judge will ordinarily rule on defendant's post-verdict motions before proceeding to sentencing. If the motion is allowed, there is, of course, no need for a sentencing hearing. Most of the time, however, the judge denies the motion and sentences the defendant at the same court hearing.

Delayed motion for a new trial
A request to have the judge order a new trial on the basis of errors that were discovered long after the trial ended.

SUMMARY

In this chapter, we walked through the various stages of a typical criminal jury trial from the judge's call of the case for trial through post-trial motions. Although attorneys are the most visible members of the prosecution and defense teams, paralegals can play important roles during the course of these trials,

Given the requirement for unanimous verdicts in most criminal cases, the selection of the jury can be one of the most important parts of the trial. In addition to doing background research on potential jurors, paralegals can help evaluate the nature of people's answers to the *voir dire* questions and the body language they exhibit during the process.

As the trial progresses, paralegals can assist their attorneys by keeping witnesses informed of schedule changes and updating them as to the time at which they are expected to be called to testify.

During direct and cross-examinations, paralegals are often asked to take notes about the answers given and to organize the exhibits their attorneys will be referring to. They can also highlight parts of the opposition witnesses' statements that can be used against them on cross.

---

[31]FRCrP 33(b)(2).

[32]373 U.S. 83, 83 S. Ct. 1194, 10 L. Ed. 2d 215 (1963). See Chapter 7 for a discussion of *Brady v. Maryland*.

[33]*United States v. Bagley*, 473 U.S. 667, 682, 105 S. Ct. 3375, 87 L. Ed. 2d 481 (1985).

[34]See *United States v. Barlow* 693 F.3d 954, 966 (6th Cir. 1982).

Once the judge has ruled on the jury instructions, the paralegal can assist the attorney in putting together PowerPoint presentations to be used during the closing arguments.

Jury deliberations can result in convictions, acquittals, or a mistrial on each count. If the case is a bench trial, the judge must choose among the same three verdicts. When the defendant is convicted, paralegals may assist in drafting post-verdict motions and memoranda in support (for the defense) or opposition (for the prosecution.)

REVIEW QUESTIONS

1. What typically takes place at the time the judge calls a jury case for trial?
2. Who is present in court when the case is called?
3. What documents are presented to the judge?
4. What is the difference between venire and *voir dire*?
5. Describe the two primary methods employed by the courts for jury selection.
6. Describe the two types of challenges used during jury selection to eliminate jurors.
7. What relief is sought when a defendant moves for a change of venue?
8. What relief is sought when a defendant moves for a change of venire?
9. What is the holding of *Batson v. Kentucky*?
10. Why are alternate jurors selected?
11. Which side gives the first opening statement? Why?
12. What limitations are placed on the content of opening statements?
13. State the evidentiary stages of the case, beginning with the prosecution's case-in-chief.
14. State the progression of the examination phases of a witness's testimony, beginning with direct examination.
15. What is the difference between adverse witnesses and hostile witnesses? What benefit does the examiner gain during the direct examination of these types of witnesses?
16. What type of testimony must a law enforcement officer give to properly authenticate physical evidence?
17. What is an offer of proof and why is it made?
18. What is the purpose of a motion for a directed verdict in a criminal case, and how does this motion differ from a motion for judgment of acquittal?
19. What is the purpose of jury instructions?
20. Who creates pattern jury instructions?
21. Which side gets the last opportunity to argue its position to the jury? Why?
22. How long may a jury deliberate?
23. What happens when a jury is deadlocked?
24. What is a lesser included offense? Give an example of a lesser included offense of the felony of theft in excess of $500.
25. What circumstances may prompt a judge to declare a mistrial?
26. What term describes a hopelessly deadlocked jury?
27. What is the difference between a post-verdict motion and a post-trial motion?
28. What are the three most common types of post-verdict motions?

Chapter 13

Sentencing

The previous chapter, which covered the various stages of a trial and discussed what judges, attorneys, and paralegals do at each stage, ended with a discussion of post-verdict motions. If found not guilty on all counts, the defendant will be released from custody (if he or she was in jail at the time of the trial) and funds that were posted for bail will be refunded. The Fifth Amendment Double Jeopardy Clause prevents the prosecutor from re-prosecuting the defendant on those same charges.[1] In those relatively rare cases in which the jury could not agree on a verdict for one or more of the counts, the prosecutor has the option of either re-trying the defendant on some or all of the charges related to those counts or dismissing the charges.[2]

On the other hand, when a defendant is found guilty, the case will move on to the sentencing and appeals stages. In this chapter, we will focus on the sentencing process; Chapter 14 will cover the preliminary procedures involved in commencing appeals.

The formality of the procedure and the severity of the punishment generally vary in proportion to the seriousness of the offense. For minor infractions, such as simple traffic citations, ordinance violations, and lesser misdemeanors, the judge typically imposes a small fine immediately after the finding of guilt. In cases involving more serious crimes, the judge orders a presentence investigation and conducts a more formal sentencing hearing at a later date.

---

[1]See Chapter 12, p. 430.

[2]In the Rod Blagojevich political corruption trial, the jury was unable to reach a decision on 23 of 24 charges against the former Illinois governor and all four of the charges against his brother Robert. The U.S. Attorney chose to drop three charges against Rod and all charges against Robert. The ex-governor was retried on the remaining 19 charges. There was no verdict at the time this book was printed.

A. Types of Punishment

Sentence
A judgment formally pronouncing the punishment to be imposed on a person who has been convicted of a crime.

A **sentence** is a judgment formally pronouncing the punishment to be imposed on a person who has been convicted of a crime. There is a wide array of punishments that can be imposed. They can involve financial penalties, incarceration, and even death. They can also include making restitution to victims and rehabilitative measures such as drug or alcohol addiction counseling. Before going on, it would be a good idea to go back and review the discussion of the justifications for criminal punishments found in Chapter 2.[3] In the federal system, the sentencing judge is authorized to impose fines, restitution, imprisonment, and probation.[4] State court judges have these options as well as a variety of additional sentencing alternatives, such as court supervision, traffic school, and substance abuse treatment.

1. FINES, RESTITUTION, ASSESSMENTS, SURCHARGES, AND COSTS

Fine
The monetary penalty imposed upon a defendant as punishment for committing an illegal act.

All jurisdictions authorize judges to impose fines in misdemeanor cases and most felonies.[5] **Fines** often are the only penalty available for ordinance violations, minor traffic offenses, and insignificant misdemeanors.

The statute or local ordinance creating the offense usually establishes an upper limit for the fine, but leaves the actual dollar amount up to the judge's discretion. Sometimes the amount of the fine is defined in terms of multipliers of the amount of the defendant's financial gain or the victim's loss. Judges will often take the defendant's financial resources into account before imposing large fines, so someone who is wealthy may be ordered to pay a much larger fine than an indigent defendant. For instance, Vice President Dick Cheney's former chief of staff Scooter Libby was ordered to pay the maximum fine of $250,000 as part of his sentence for perjury and obstruction of justice.[6]

Restitution
A component of a sentence entered against a defendant to be used to compensate the victims of the crime for their losses.

Restitution is money paid to the victims of the crime to compensate them for their losses. Judges consider several factors in deciding whether to order restitution, such as the amount of the victim's loss resulting from the crime, the defendant's financial resources, and the defendant's earning ability and financial needs.[7] In the federal system, the judge must order restitution when the defendant is convicted of certain offenses, such as violent crimes, crimes against property, drug offenses, consumer product offenses, sexual abuse of children, and telemarketing fraud.[8]

The restitution amount can be staggering in some white-collar crime cases. For instance, the district judge ordered ex-congressional aid Michael Scanlon to

---

[3]See pp. 42–43.

[4]Federal judges may impose several types of sentences: fines [18 U.S.C. § 3571]; restitution [18 U.S.C. § 3663]; imprisonment [18 U.S.C. § 3581]; and probation [18 U.S.C. § 3561].

[5]W. LaFave, J. Israel & N. King, *Criminal Procedure* 1216 (4th ed., West 2004).

[6]He paid the fine in full by check shortly after he was sentenced.

[7]See 18 U.S.C. § 3663(A)(1)(b).

[8]18 U.S.C. § 3663(A).

pay his victims over $19 million as part of a plea agreement in a fraud and corruption case. New York financier Bernard Madoff agreed to make restitution in the sum of $171 billion dollars to the victims of his Ponzi scheme. Unfortunately, the victims don't always receive all the money that the judge orders. Despite the U.S. District Judge's forfeiture order requiring Madoff to turn over all of his assets, the victims probably will never be fully compensated for their losses.

In addition to fines and restitution orders, the sentencing judge usually orders the defendant to pay court costs and various assessments.[9] The **court costs** are monetary reimbursements for such things as the expenses of subpoenaing witnesses, providing probation services, conducting drug testing, etc. **Assessments** are payments to fund court-connected programs related to the crime.

2. INCARCERATION

Incarceration, mandatory confinement in a facility that limits the ability to move around as the person wishes, is the penalty that comes to most people's minds when they think of a criminal sentence. **Jails** are facilities controlled by a county or other local governmental authority to hold criminal defendants awaiting trial and offenders convicted in state court of misdemeanors. **Prisons**, also known as **penitentiaries**, are facilities controlled by the state or federal government to house convicted felons. Federal misdemeanor offenders also may be sentenced to prison.

In order to protect them from being molested or otherwise negatively influenced by adult criminals, juveniles typically are held either in separate juvenile detention facilities or in special, separate sections of local jails. In some jurisdictions, younger adults may be sentenced to serve their time in a "boot camp" in lieu of prison. These boot camps are frequently set up in remote rural areas, housing their residents in tents or cabins, and maintain a military type of training and atmosphere. This sentence is usually imposed on first-time offenders who are physically capable of withstanding the rigors of the program. In jurisdictions where this option is offered, it is in high demand because the duration of incarceration is significantly shorter than the prison term the offender would likely receive.

3. SUPERVISION

When criminal offenders are not incarcerated, a sentence of supervision involves placing special limitations on what they are allowed to do.

a. Court Supervision

For less serious offenses and infractions, such as traffic tickets and minor offenses, the violators may be eligible for **court supervision**. With court supervi-

Court costs
Fees, charged to the defendant, that are designed to pay for operating expenses of the court system.

Assessment
The charge imposed upon a specified group (i.e., users of the court system) for the purpose of funding specified services (e.g., women's shelters or legal aid programs).

Incarceration
Mandatory confinement in a facility that limits the ability to move around as the person wishes.

Jail
A facility controlled by a local governmental authority to hold criminal defendants awaiting trial and offenders convicted in state court of misdemeanors.

Prison (also known as a penitentiary)
A facility controlled by the state or federal government to house convicted state court felons and federal offenders.

Court supervision
A sentencing option used for minor offenses in which the defendant is not convicted if he or she complies with the judge's conditions during a specific period of time.

---

[9]Defendants are not required to pay costs if they are indigent.

Taking case under advisement
The judge's deferral of a decision on a case or issue raised in a case.

sion, the judge imposes conditions on the defendant and **takes the case under advisement** for a fixed period of time. If the conditions are satisfied, the case is dismissed and the defendant is not convicted. Typical conditions include refraining from committing other offenses while on supervision, payment of fines and costs, performing public service work, undergoing substance abuse treatment, and completing traffic school. Courts do not give court supervision for felonies or to chronic offenders, and the supervision period usually ranges from three to twenty-four months.

b. Probation

Probation
A criminal sentence discharging the defendant to the community subject to conditions, which may include reporting to a probation officer.

Probation is a sentencing alternative to incarceration in which the convicted criminal is allowed to continue to live in the community but must abide by certain conditions set by the judge. Unlike court supervision, probation is used for an offender who has been first convicted of a crime. Furthermore, the conditions of probation are much more restrictive than those of court supervision. The defendant may be ordered to stay away from the victim, consent to random drug testing, and refrain from possessing a firearm. The individual is also required to regularly report to a probation officer. An example of a state court probation order appears in Exhibit 13.1.

Petition to revoke (also called PTR)
A motion filed by the prosecutor seeking to revoke probation and re-sentence the offender.

If a defendant either commits another crime or violates one of the conditions of probation, the prosecutor will file a **petition to revoke** probation (PTR). Usually, the government takes this action when the offender commits a crime, flunks a random drug test, or chronically fails to report to the probation officer. If this petition is granted, the judge may revoke probation and re-sentence the defendant.

c. Periodic Imprisonment

Periodic imprisonment
A probation option that permits a defendant sentenced to imprisonment to leave custody for work or school.

Sometimes, probation is combined with incarceration in what is known as **periodic imprisonment**. In this situation, the convicted criminal is sentenced to jail but is then permitted to leave the jail during specified hours or days to work at their job or attend school. Other conditions of confinement may include halfway houses and home detention.

d. Parole

Parole
A conditional release from incarceration after actually serving part of the sentence.

The other major category involving supervision is parole. This option also allows the conditional release of prisoners, who are then subject to specified conditions and monitoring for a specified period. After a certain percentage of their sentence has been served, and often dependent upon both their "good behavior" and the degree of overcrowding in the prison system, they are released to serve the balance of their sentence on **parole**, a conditional release under which the prisoner is monitored to ensure he or she abides by special conditions for a specified period. Among other things, the parolee must report to a public official, maintain employment, and submit to random drug tests. The major difference between probation and parole is that parole occurs after a set amount of time has already been served in prison, whereas probation is a substitute for incarceration. There is no parole at the federal level, but U.S. District Judges typically impose a term of supervised release when the defendant is sentenced to at least a year of imprisonment.

Exhibit 13.1: Order of Probation

Wisconsin college student Anthony Scholfield was convicted of felony burglary after a search of his apartment uncovered more than 850 pairs of stolen women's underwear. The judge sentenced him to ninety days' periodic jail incarceration so he could attend school and work. He also was ordered to stay away from his female victims and pay $8,873.04 in restitution. Released after two years' probation, Scholfield committed a similar offense two years later. The court's judgment of conviction and sentencing order appears below.

STATE OF WISCONSIN	CIRCUIT COURT BRANCH 2		DUNN COUNTY	For Official Use Only
State of Wisconsin vs. Anthony Allen Scholfield	**Judgment of Conviction** Sentence Withheld, Probation Ordered			**FILED** DEC 2 6 2003
Date of Birth: 02-15-1981	Case No.: 2003CF000099			DUNN COUNTY CLERK OF COURT

The defendant was found guilty of the following crime(s):

Ct. Description	Violation	Plea	Severity	Date(s) Committed	Trial To	Date(s) Convicted
1 Burglary-Building or Dwelling	943.10(1)(a)	No Contest	Felony C	11-01-2002		12-22-2003

IT IS ADJUDGED that the defendant is guilty as convicted and sentenced as follows:

Ct.	Sent. Date	Sentence	Length	Concurrent with/Consecutive to/Comments	Agency
1	12-22-2003	Probation, Sent Withheld	3 YR		Department of Corrections

Conditions of Sentence or Probation

Obligations: (Total amounts only)

Fine	Court Costs	Attorney Fees	Restitution	Other	Mandatory Victim/Wit. Surcharge	5% Rest. Surcharge	DNA Anal. Surcharge
	20.00		8873.04		70.00		

Conditions:

Ct.	Condition	Length	Agency/Program	Begin Date	Begin Time	Comments
1	Jail Time	90 DA	County	12-22-2003	05:00 pm	huber allowed for work and school

Ct.	Condition		Agency/Program	Comments
1	Restitution			Restitution Hearing at 01/21/04 at 10:15am
1	Costs			Defend to pay through Prob.
1	Prohibitions			No contact with any victims- Jessica M, Sara K, Lindsey H, Kristina B, Katie L

IT IS ADJUDGED that 1 days sentence credit are due pursuant to § 973.155, Wisconsin Statutes.

IT IS ORDERED that the Sheriff execute this sentence.

BY THE COURT:

Rod Smeltzer, Judge
Kristina A Cusick, District Attorney
Julie Smith, Defense Attorney

Vera m Beij — Deputy Clerk
Court Official

12-26-2003
Date

4. THE DEATH PENALTY

Capital punishment
Punishment by death. It is also referred to as the death penalty.

The most severe punishment the government can impose on a convicted criminal is the death penalty. Both the use of **capital punishment** and the means of execution are issues of continuing controversy in the United States. Some of the most common arguments raised in the capital punishment debate are summarized in Figure 13.1.

Arguments Used to Support Use of Capital Punishment	Arguments Used to Counter Support's Arguments
Fear of the death penalty deters potential criminals.	The death penalty is not an effective deterrent because the potential criminal either doesn't stop to think about the consequences or doesn't expect to get caught.
Justice demands the killer be killed based on the biblical command of "an eye for an eye. . . ."	Retribution is not a valid justification because the Bible stresses forgiveness rather than revenge.
It gives closure to the victim's families.	Life imprisonment also gives closure.
It ensures that the criminal won't commit any future crimes.	Life imprisonment with adequate security can achieve the same result.
It saves taxpayers' money.	Not true when additional legal costs are considered, and even if it were true the negative aspects of capital punishment out-weigh any added costs.
It gives prosecutors a "bargaining chip" in the plea-bargaining process.	This may be true, but this tactic is not "fair" to the defense.
Capital punishment leads to innocent people being killed for things they didn't do.	More use of modern DNA testing and a better system of defense representation will avoid mistakes.
Life imprisonment adequately protects the public from being harmed by keeping the prisoner away from any contact with the public.	As long as the criminal lives there is a chance he or she might escape and harm the public or harm prison employees or other prisoners.
Many prisoners "suffer" more from life imprisonment than from a quick painless death.	Being executed is worse than life imprisonment.
It violates the Eighth Amendment prohibition against "cruel and unusual punishment" and the Fourteenth Amendment Equal Protection Clause.	A majority of the Supreme Court has rejected these interpretations.
It shows that the United States is "out of step" with the standards of human dignity accepted by the majority of the world's countries.	It is not appropriate for the United States to base its public policy on the views of other countries.
It brings added suffering to innocent members of the criminal's family.	This may be true, but it doesn't outweigh the perceived advantages of having capital punishment.

See Balanced Politics.Org at *http://www.balancedpolitics.org/death_penalty.htm* for a listing of more arguments for and against capital punishment.

Figure 13.1 Arguments Relating to the Imposition of Capital Punishment

DISCUSSION QUESTIONS

1. Which of the arguments in support of capital punishment included in Figure 13.1 do you find most convincing? Why?
2. Which of the arguments against capital punishment included in Figure 13.1 do you find most convincing? Why?
3. Can you think of any persuasive arguments, either for or against capital punishment, that are not included in Figure 13.1? If so what are these arguments?

As noted in the arguments listed in Figure 13.1, the death penalty has been challenged in courts as a violation of both the Eighth Amendment prohibition against "cruel and unusual punishment" and the Fourteenth Amendment Equal Protection Clause. In 1972, the U.S. Supreme Court ruled in *Furman v. Georgia*[10] that the Georgia capital punishment statute *that existed at that time* violated the Eighth and Fourteenth Amendments to the U.S. Constitution. However, four years later, in *Gregg v. Georgia*,[11] it held that a new revised death penalty statute in the state did not violate the U.S. Constitution because the new law had been written in such a way as to reduce the chance for "wanton and freakish" punishment. This isn't a constitutional law text, so we won't get into the details of the statutes in question or the reasoning of the various justices. It is important to note, though, that on the same day the Court upheld Georgia's "guided discretion" death penalty statute, it also struck down several "mandatory" death penalty statutes in other states. Figure 13.2 lists the states (more than two-thirds of them) that, along with the federal government, currently allow capital punishment.

Since 1976, the U.S. Supreme Court has continued to uphold the constitutionality of the death penalty when it is used in situations involving homicides committed by mentally competent adults as long as the statutes contain what the Court considers to be adequate safeguards. In 2002, it held that the execution of mentally retarded criminals violated the Eight Amendment,[12] and in 2005, the Court ruled that it is unconstitutional to sentence anyone to death for a crime he or she committed while younger than age eighteen.[13] Then in 2008, the majority overturned a death sentence for someone who had been convicted of the rape of a child.[14] In recent years, there has been a troubling number of instances in which DNA evidence has established the innocence of people who had been convicted of murder and in some cases sentenced to death. The widespread publicity some of these cases have received has led to states like New Jersey, New Mexico, and Illinois abolishing the death penalty. Eight years prior to the abolition of the death penalty in Illinois, former Governor George Ryan commuted the sentences of 142 death row inmates and imposed a moratorium on capital punishment that has been continued by his successors. During this eight-year-period, the state

---

[10]408 U.S. 238, 92 S. Ct. 2726, 33 L. Ed. 2d 346 (1972).

[11]428 U.S. 153, 96 S. Ct. 2909; 49 L. Ed. 2d 859 (1976)

[12]*Atkins v. Virginia* , 536 U.S. 304, 122 S. Ct. 2242, 153 L. Ed. 2d 335 (2002).

[13]*Roper v. Simmons*, 543 U.S. 551, 125 S. Ct. 1183, 161 L. Ed. 2d 1 (2005).

[14]*Kennedy v. Louisiana*, 554 U.S. 407, 128 S. Ct. 2641, 171 L. Ed. 2d 525 (2008).

The following states currently authorize the use of the death penalty:

Alabama	Arizona	Arkansas
California	Colorado	Connecticut
Delaware	Florida	Georgia
Idaho	Indiana	Kansas
Kentucky	Louisiana	Maryland
Mississippi	Missouri	Montana
Nebraska	Nevada	New Hampshire
North Carolina	North Dakota	Ohio
Oklahoma	Oregon	Pennsylvania
South Carolina	South Dakota	Tennessee
Texas	Utah	Virginia
Washington	Wyoming	

Figure 13.2 States Authorizing Capital Punishment

crafted procedural safeguards for capital defendants. For instance, the legislature created the Capital Litigation Trust Fund to pay defense costs for investigators and forensic experts.[15] The Illinois Supreme Court adopted rules that required special training for judges assigned to try death penalty cases, established minimum qualifications for attorneys representing capital defendants, and set up ethical standards for prosecutors in capital cases.[16] The rules also imposed a deadline for the prosecution's declaration of intent to seek or decline the death penalty, provided for the appointment of two qualified attorneys to represent indigent capital defendants, and allowed for the taking of discovery depositions in capital cases.

B. DISCRETION IN SENTENCING

One of the major controversies in the field of criminal law involves the amount of discretion judges should have in determining the sentences to be given to those convicted of criminal offenses. Traditionally, federal, state, and local legislatures have established broad ranges within which judges were to exercise their own discretion in designating a sentence that would best serve the interests of justice. Within the broad range of options established by the criminal code, judges could select from various fines, types of supervision, and jail/prison terms.

---

[15] 30 ILCS 105/5.519.

[16] Illinois Supreme Court Rules 3.8(a); 43, & 714.

1. DETERMINATE AND INDETERMINATE SENTENCING

There are two general types of sentencing: indeterminate and determinate. **Indeterminate sentencing** is the sentencing of a defendant to a range of imprisonment with the actual release date determined by a parole board. When offenders are released into the community on parole, they continue to serve a sentence under the supervision of the parole authorities. **Determinate sentencing** involves the imposition of a specific sentence. In the Sentencing Reform Act of 1984, Congress abolished the use of parole in federal sentences as a means of attaining uniform determinate sentencing.[17] Most states continue to punish felons with indeterminate sentencing and maintain parole boards to decide whether offenders should be released from prison into the community.

Whether determinate or indeterminate sentencing is employed, the statute creating the offense ordinarily specifies the minimum and maximum terms of incarceration. Often, the statute will state only the class of the offense instead of spelling out the particular range of sentence. Another statute must be referred to to find out the sentence for that class of crime. The minimum and maximum Illinois prison terms by offense classification are displayed in Figure 13.3.

Indeterminate sentencing
A form of punishment in which the defendant is sentenced to a range of imprisonment with the actual release date determined by a parole board.

Determinate sentencing
A form of punishment in which the defendant is sentenced to a specific term of imprisonment.

2. EXTENDED TERM SENTENCES

Under certain circumstances, the judge can subject an offender to an **extended term sentence** (sometimes called an enhanced sentence), which is a sentence beyond the statutory maximum of the basic range of penalties that otherwise could be imposed for the crime charged. A common circumstance is the fact of a prior conviction. Representative circumstances include brutal or heinous behavior;

Extended term sentence (also known as an enhanced sentence)
A sentence beyond the statutory maximum of the basic range of penalties that otherwise could be imposed for the crime charged.

Offense Class	Basic Range
1st degree murder	20–60 years
Class X	6–30 years
Class 1	4–15 years
Class 2	3–7 years
Class 3	2–5 years
Class 4	1–3 years

Note: These basic ranges do not apply to all crimes within each class. Illinois sentencing law is extremely complex and filled with enhancements, add-ons, extended terms, and other exceptions.

Figure 13.3 Illinois Felony Incarceration Terms

---

[17] 18 U.S.C § 3500 *et seq.*

commission of a felony against a senior citizen, disabled person, or young child; torture of a victim as part of a gang ceremony or rite; and participation in a gang rape of a single victim.

However, in *Apprendi v. New Jersey*,[18] the U.S. Supreme Court held that any fact (other than a prior conviction) that increases the defendant's sentence above the otherwise applicable statutory maximum must be submitted to a jury and proven beyond a reasonable doubt. Following this ruling, states reacted by modifying their extended term sentencing statutes. For instance, in Illinois extended sentences are not permitted (except when based on prior convictions) unless the sentence-enhancing facts "are included in the charging instrument or otherwise provided to the defendant through a written notification before trial," submitted to the trier of fact as an aggravating factor, and proven beyond a reasonable doubt.[19] Often the use of a firearm during the commission of the offense is an enhancement that can extend the standard term of the sentence. Other times, it is merely an aggravating factor that can serve as the basis of a longer term within the basic sentencing range for the offense.

3. CONCURRENT VERSUS CONSECUTIVE SENTENCES

Concurrent sentences
Sentences that are served simultaneously rather than one after the other.

Consecutive sentences
Sentences that must be served one after the other rather than simultaneously.

Another type of discretion a judge can exercise arises when an offender is convicted of multiple counts. When this situation occurs, the judge can order either concurrent or consecutive sentences. **Concurrent sentences** are served simultaneously so that the total duration of the sentence is the longest sentence. So, for example, if the judge orders John Offender to serve concurrent sentences of three years, five years, and another five years, Offender would serve a total of five years. In contrast, **consecutive sentences** are served one after the other. In this situation, the defendant does not begin serving the second sentence until the first sentence is completed. Thus, if the judge orders John Offender to serve his three sentences consecutively, the term would be thirteen years (3 + 5 + 5).

Some statutes specifically state that the judge is required to impose consecutive sentencing for certain crimes. In others, the judge is granted discretion to impose consecutive sentences. In this instance, the judge considers the seriousness and circumstances of the crimes along with the history, character, and the prospect for rehabilitation of the defendant to decide whether to order consecutive sentences.

Unless a statute specifically provides for either mandatory or discretionary consecutive sentencing, the judge will order concurrent sentences. The approach taken in North Carolina is typical. N.C.G.S. § 15A-1354(a) provides:

> (a) Authority of Court.—When multiple sentences of imprisonment are imposed on a person at the same time or when a term of imprisonment is imposed on a person who is already subject to an undischarged term of imprisonment, including a term of imprisonment in another jurisdiction, the sentences may run either concurrently or consecutively, as determined by the court. *If not specified or not required by statute to run consecutively, sentences shall run concurrently.* (Emphasis added.)

---

[18]530 U.S. 466, 120 S. Ct. 2348, 147 L. Ed. 2d 435 (2000).
[19]725 ILCS 5/111-3.

4. MANDATORY VERSUS DISCRETIONARY SENTENCING

In response to the perception that the judiciary was "soft on crime," many legislatures have enacted statutes that mandated certain sentences for specific crimes. Proponents contend that **mandatory sentences** deter certain crimes, while opponents argue that judicial discretion is needed to account for the particular circumstances of the crime and of the offender. They further claim that mandatory sentences unnecessarily crowd the prisons.

Among the most controversial mandatory sentencing schemes are **habitual offender laws**, which require judges to give extended terms of imprisonment to persons the third time they are convicted of a serious criminal offense without the possibility of parole for life or an extended period of time. Figure 13.4 lists the states that, along with the federal government, have enacted these "three strikes and you're out" statutes. The U.S. Supreme Court held in *Ewing v. California* that habitual offender sentences do not violate the constitutional Eighth Amendment prohibition against cruel and unusual punishment.[20]

5. SENTENCING GUIDELINES

While some complained that judges weren't being tough enough, others raised concerns about the inequality that resulted from allowing judges to choose between rather open-ended minimum and maximum sentences. Defendants who had committed similar crimes and had similar records of previous convictions often ended up getting very different sentences. In order to make the system "more equitable," courts have been encouraged to create and apply sentencing guidelines.

Mandatory sentence
A requirement, by the legislature, that the judge impose a minimum prison term for a specified crime.

Habitual offender laws (also known as "three strikes and you're out" laws)
Mandatory sentencing laws that require judges to give extended terms of imprisonment to persons the third time they are convicted of a serious criminal offense, without the possibility of parole for life or an extended period of time.

States that have enacted habitual offender statutes:

Alabama	Arkansas	California
Colorado	Connecticut	Florida
Georgia	Illinois	Indiana
Iowa	Kansas	Louisiana
Maryland	Montana	New Jersey
Nevada	New Mexico	North Carolina
North Dakota	Oregon	Pennsylvania
South Carolina	Tennessee	Texas
Vermont	Virginia	Washington
Wisconsin	Wyoming	

Figure 13.4 Habitual Offender Sentencing Laws

---

[20]538 U.S. 11, 123 S. Ct. 1179, 155 L. Ed. 2d 108 (2003).

a. Creation and Role of Federal Sentencing Guidelines

At the federal level, concerns about disparities prompted the creation of the United States Sentencing Commission, an independent agency in the judicial branch. Congress charged the commission with "formulating national sentencing guidelines to define the parameters for federal trial judges to follow in their sentencing decisions."[21] The commission was designed to respond to the lack of uniform structure in sentencing, the need for certainty in administering punishment, and the necessity to target specific offenders with more serious penalties.

Federal Sentencing Guidelines

The uniform sentencing standards used to calculate the sentencing range for federal defendants convicted of felonies or Class A misdemeanors.

The **Federal Sentencing Guidelines** created by this commission went into effect November 1, 1987. They apply to federal defendants convicted of felonies or Class A misdemeanors—not to lesser misdemeanors. They attempt to ensure that sentences are uniformly based on the seriousness of the criminal activity and the defendant's criminal history by establishing mandatory sentencing ranges based on these two factors. Although the guidelines do include a procedure for departing from the range, such departures are rare.

Shortly after the guidelines went into effect, defense attorneys challenged the constitutionality of the act creating the commission. In *Mistretta v. United States*, the Supreme Court held that Congress did not violate the separation of powers by the creation of the commission as a judicial branch agency.[22] A challenge to the constitutionality of the guidelines themselves made it the Supreme Court in *United States v. Booker*,[23] and in 2005, the Supreme Court held that the mandatory nature of the guidelines violated the Sixth Amendment right to trial by jury. The Court struck two specific provisions of the act creating the guidelines but left the remainder in place. As a result, federal judges were expected to take the guidelines into consideration in setting the sentence but were not required to impose stay within the range specified in the guidelines. (Excerpts from the *Booker* decision appear below.)

United States v. Booker
Supreme Court of the United States
543 U.S. 220 (2005)

JUSTICE STEVENS delivered the opinion of the Court in part. [JUSTICE SCALIA, JUSTICE SOUTER, JUSTICE THOMAS, and JUSTICE GINSBURG join this opinion.]

The question presented in each of these cases is whether an application of the Federal Sentencing Guidelines violated the Sixth Amendment. In each case, the courts below held that binding rules set forth in the Guidelines limited the severity of the sentence that the judge could lawfully impose on the defendant based on the facts found by the jury at his trial. In both cases the courts rejected, on the basis of our decision in *Blakely v. Washington*, 296(2004), the

---

[21]An Overview of the United States Sentencing Commission, p. 2. *http://www.ussc.gov/general/ USSC_Overview_200906.pdf*

[22]488 U.S. 361, 109 S. Ct. 647, 102 L. Ed. 2d 714 (1989).

[23]543 U.S. 220, 125 S. Ct. 738, 160 L. Ed. 2d 621 (2005).

Government's recommended application of the Sentencing Guidelines because the proposed sentences were based on additional facts that the sentencing judge found by a preponderance of the evidence. We hold that both courts correctly concluded that the Sixth Amendment as construed in *Blakely* does apply to the Sentencing Guidelines. In a separate opinion authored by Justice Breyer, the Court concludes that in light of this holding, two provisions of the Sentencing Reform Act of 1984 (SRA) that have the effect of making the Guidelines mandatory must be invalidated in order to allow the statute to operate in a manner consistent with congressional intent.

I

Respondent Booker was charged with possession with intent to distribute at least 50 grams of cocaine base (crack). Having heard evidence that he had 92.5 grams in his duffel bag, the jury found him guilty of violating 21 U.S.C. § 841(a)(1). That statute prescribes a minimum sentence of 10 years in prison and a maximum sentence of life for that offense. § 841(b)(1)(A)(iii).

Based upon Booker's criminal history and the quantity of drugs found by the jury, the Sentencing Guidelines required the District Court Judge to select a "base" sentence of not less than 210 nor more than 262 months in prison. See United States Sentencing Commission, Guidelines Manual §§ 2D1.1(c)(4), 4A1.1 (Nov. 2003) (hereinafter USSG). The judge, however, held a post-trial sentencing proceeding and concluded by a preponderance of the evidence that Booker had possessed an additional 566 grams of crack and that he was guilty of obstructing justice. Those findings mandated that the judge select a sentence between 360 months and life imprisonment; the judge imposed a sentence at the low end of the range. Thus, instead of the sentence of 21 years and 10 months that the judge could have imposed on the basis of the facts proved to the jury beyond a reasonable doubt, Booker received a 30-year sentence.

Over the dissent of Judge Easterbrook, the Court of Appeals for the Seventh Circuit held that this application of the Sentencing Guidelines conflicted with our holding in *Apprendi v. New Jersey*,

530 U.S. 466, 490 (2000), that "[o]ther than the fact of a prior conviction, any fact that increases the penalty for a crime beyond the prescribed statutory maximum must be submitted to a jury, and proved beyond a reasonable doubt." . . .

Respondent Fanfan was charged with conspiracy to distribute and to possess with intent to distribute at least 500 grams of cocaine in violation of 21 U.S.C. § 846 841(a)(1), and 841(b)(1)(B)(ii). He was convicted by the jury after it answered "Yes" to the question "Was the amount of cocaine 500 or more grams?" Under the Guidelines, without additional findings of fact, the maximum sentence authorized by the jury verdict was imprisonment for 78 months.

A few days after our decision in *Blakely*, the trial judge conducted a sentencing hearing at which he found additional facts that, under the Guidelines, would have authorized a sentence in the 188-to-235 month range. Specifically, he found that respondent Fanfan was responsible for 2.5 kilograms of cocaine powder, and 261.6 grams of crack. He also concluded that respondent had been an organizer, leader, manager, or supervisor in the criminal activity. Both findings were made by a preponderance of the evidence. Under the Guidelines, these additional findings would have required an enhanced sentence of 15 or 16 years instead of the 5 or 6 years authorized by the jury verdict alone. Relying not only on the majority opinion in *Blakely*, but also on the categorical statements in the dissenting opinions and in the Solicitor General's brief in *Blakely*, the judge concluded that he could not follow the particular provisions of the Sentencing Guidelines "which involve drug quantity and role enhancement." Expressly refusing to make "any blanket decision about the federal guidelines," he followed the provisions of the Guidelines that did not implicate the Sixth Amendment by imposing a sentence on respondent "based solely upon the guilty verdict in this case."

Following the denial of its motion to correct the sentence in Fanfan's case, the Government filed a notice of appeal in the Court of Appeals for the First Circuit, and a petition in this Court for a writ of certiorari before judgment. Because of the importance of the questions presented, we granted that petition, as well as a similar petition filed by the Government in

Booker's case. In both petitions, the Government asks us to determine whether our *Apprendi* line of cases applies to the Sentencing Guidelines, and if so, what portions of the Guidelines remain in effect.

In this opinion, we explain why we agree with the lower courts' answer to the first question. In a separate opinion for the Court, Justice Breyer explains the Court's answer to the second question.

II

* * *

In *Apprendi v. New Jersey*, 530 U.S. 466 (2000), the defendant pleaded guilty to second-degree possession of a firearm for an unlawful purpose, which carried a prison term of 5-to-10 years. Thereafter, the trial court found that his conduct had violated New Jersey's "hate crime" law because it was racially motivated, and imposed a 12-year sentence. This Court set aside the enhanced sentence. We held: "Other than the fact of a prior conviction, any fact that increases the penalty for a crime beyond the prescribed statutory maximum must be submitted to a jury, and proved beyond a reasonable doubt."

The fact that New Jersey labeled the hate crime a "sentence enhancement" rather than a separate criminal act was irrelevant for constitutional purposes. As a matter of simple justice, it seemed obvious that the procedural safeguards designed to protect Apprendi from punishment for the possession of a firearm should apply equally to his violation of the hate crime statute. Merely using the label "sentence enhancement" to describe the latter did not provide a principled basis for treating the two crimes differently.

* * *

In *Blakely v. Washington*, 542 U.S. 296(2004), we dealt with a determinate sentencing scheme similar to the Federal Sentencing Guidelines. There the defendant pleaded guilty to kidnapping, a class B felony punishable by a term of not more than 10 years. Other provisions of Washington law, comparable to the Federal Sentencing Guidelines, mandated a "standard" sentence of 49-to-53 months, unless the judge found aggravating facts justifying an exceptional

sentence. Although the prosecutor recommended a sentence in the standard range, the judge found that the defendant had acted with "'deliberate cruelty'" and sentenced him to 90 months.

For reasons explained in *Jones*, *Apprendi*, and *Ring*, the requirements of the Sixth Amendment were clear. The application of Washington's sentencing scheme violated the defendant's right to have the jury find the existence of "'any particular fact'" that the law makes essential to his punishment. That right is implicated whenever a judge seeks to impose a sentence that is not solely based on "facts reflected in the jury verdict or admitted by the defendant." We rejected the State's argument that the jury verdict was sufficient to authorize a sentence within the general 10-year sentence for class B felonies, noting that under Washington law, the judge was *required* to find additional facts in order to impose the greater 90-month sentence. Our precedents, we explained, make clear "that the 'statutory maximum' for *Apprendi* purposes is the maximum sentence a judge may impose *solely on the basis of the facts reflected in the jury verdict or admitted by the defendant*" (emphasis in original). The determination that the defendant acted with deliberate cruelty, like the determination in *Apprendi* that the defendant acted with racial malice, increased the sentence that the defendant could have otherwise received. Since this fact was found by a judge using a preponderance of the evidence standard, the sentence violated Blakely's Sixth Amendment rights.

* * *

If the Guidelines as currently written could be read as merely advisory provisions that recommended, rather than required, the selection of particular sentences in response to differing sets of facts, their use would not implicate the Sixth Amendment.

* * *

The Guidelines as written, however, are not advisory; they are mandatory and binding on all judges. While subsection (a) of § 3553 of the sentencing statute lists the Sentencing Guidelines as one factor to be considered in imposing a sentence, subsection (b) directs that the court "*shall* impose a sentence of the kind, and within the range" established by the Guidelines, subject to departures in specific, limited cases. Because they are binding on judges, we have consistently held that the Guidelines have the force and effect of laws. See, *e.g., Mistretta v. United States,* 488 U.S. 361, 391 (1989); *Stinson v. United States,* 508 U.S. 36, 42 (1993).

* * *

Booker's case illustrates the mandatory nature of the Guidelines. The jury convicted him of possessing at least 50 grams of crack in violation of 21 U.S.C. § 841(b)(1)(A)(iii) based on evidence that he had 92.5 grams of crack in his duffel bag. Under these facts, the Guidelines specified an offense level of 32, which, given the defendant's criminal history category, authorized a sentence of 210-to-262 months. See USSG § 2D1.1(c)(4). Booker's is a run-of-the-mill drug case, and does not present any factors that were inadequately considered by the Commission. The sentencing judge would therefore have been reversed had he not imposed a sentence within the level 32 Guidelines range.

Booker's actual sentence, however, was 360 months, almost 10 years longer than the Guidelines range supported by the jury verdict alone. To reach this sentence, the judge found facts beyond those found by the jury: namely, that Booker possessed 566 grams of crack in addition to the 92.5 grams in his duffel bag. The jury never heard any evidence of the additional drug quantity, and the judge found it true by a preponderance of the evidence. Thus, just as in *Blakely,* "the jury's verdict alone does not authorize the sentence. The judge acquires that authority only upon finding some additional fact." There is no relevant distinction between the sentence imposed pursuant to the Washington statutes in *Blakely* and the sentences imposed pursuant to the Federal Sentencing Guidelines in these cases.

* * *

The effect of the increasing emphasis on facts that enhanced sentencing ranges, however, was to increase the judge's power and diminish that of the jury. It became the judge, not the jury, that determined the upper limits of sentencing, and the facts determined were not required to be raised before trial or proved by more than a preponderance.

As the enhancements became greater, the jury's finding of the underlying crime became less significant. And the enhancements became very serious indeed. See, *e.g., Jones,* . . . (judge's finding increased the maximum sentence from 15 to 25 years); respondent Booker (from 262 months to a life sentence); respondent Fanfan (from 78 to 235 months); *United States v. Rodriguez,* . . . (from approximately 54 months to a life sentence); *United States v. Hammoud,* . . . (actual sentence increased from 57 months to 155 years).

* * *

IV

All of the foregoing support our conclusion that our holding in *Blakely* applies to the Sentencing Guidelines. We recognize, as we did in *Jones, Apprendi,* and *Blakely,* that in some cases jury factfinding may impair the most expedient and efficient sentencing of defendants. But the interest in fairness and reliability protected by the right to a jury trial—a common-law right that defendants enjoyed for centuries and that is now enshrined in the Sixth Amendment—has always outweighed the interest in concluding trials swiftly. . . . Accordingly, we reaffirm our holding in *Apprendi:* Any fact (other than a prior conviction) which is necessary to support a sentence exceeding the maximum authorized by the facts established by a plea of guilty or a jury verdict must be admitted by the defendant or proved to a jury beyond a reasonable doubt.

JUSTICE BREYER delivered the opinion of the Court in part. [CHIEF JUSTICE REHNQUIST, AND JUSTICES O'CONNOR, KENNEDY, and GINSBURG joined this opinion.]

* * *

We here turn to the second question presented, a question that concerns the remedy. We must decide whether or to what extent, "as a matter of severability analysis," the Guidelines "as a whole" are "inapplicable . . . such that the sentencing court must exercise its discretion to sentence the defendant within the maximum and minimum set by statute for the offense of conviction." We answer the question of remedy by finding the provision of the federal sentencing statute that makes the Guidelines mandatory, 18 U.S.C.A. § 3553(b)(1) (Supp. 2004), incompatible with today's constitutional holding. We conclude that this provision must be severed and excised, as must one other statutory section, § 3742(e) (main ed. and Supp. 2004), which depends upon the Guidelines' mandatory nature. So modified, the Federal Sentencing Act, see Sentencing Reform Act of 1984, as amended, 18 U.S.C. § 3551 *et seq.*, 28 U.S.C. § 991 *et seq.*, makes the Guidelines effectively advisory. It requires a sentencing court to consider Guidelines ranges, see 18 U.S.C.A. § 3553 (a)(4) (Supp. 2004), but it permits the court to tailor the sentence in light of other statutory concerns as well, see § 3553(a) (Supp. 2004).

I

We answer the remedial question by looking to legislative intent. See, *e.g.*, *Minnesota v. Mille Lacs Band of Chippewa Indians*, 526 U.S. 172, 191 (1999); *Alaska Airlines, Inc. v. Brock*, 480 U.S. 678, 684 (1987); *Regan v. Time, Inc.*, 468 U.S. 641, 653 (1984) (plurality opinion). We seek to determine what "Congress would have intended" in light of the Court's constitutional holding. . . . In this instance, we must determine which of the two following remedial approaches is the more compatible with the legislature's intent as embodied in the 1984 Sentencing Act.

One approach, that of Justice Stevens' dissent, would retain the Sentencing Act (and the Guidelines) as written, but would engraft onto the existing system today's Sixth Amendment "jury trial" requirement. The addition would change the Guidelines by preventing the sentencing court from increasing a sentence on the basis of a fact that the jury did not find (or that the offender did not admit).

The other approach, which we now adopt, would (through severance and excision of two provisions) make the Guidelines system advisory while maintaining a strong connection between the sentence imposed and the offender's real conduct—a connection important to the increased uniformity of sentencing that Congress intended its Guidelines system to achieve.

Both approaches would significantly alter the system that Congress designed. But today's constitutional holding means that it is no longer possible to maintain the judicial factfinding that Congress thought would underpin the mandatory Guidelines system that it sought to create and that Congress wrote into the Act in 18 U.S.C.A. §§ 3553(a) and 3661 (main ed. and Supp. 2004). Hence we must decide whether we would deviate less radically from Congress' intended system (1) by superimposing the constitutional requirement announced today or (2) through elimination of some provisions of the statute.

* * *

While reasonable minds can, and do, differ about the outcome, we conclude that the constitutional jury trial requirement is not compatible with the Act as written and that some severance and excision are necessary. . . .

II

Several considerations convince us that, were the Court's constitutional requirement added onto the Sentencing Act as currently written, the requirement would so transform the scheme that Congress created that Congress likely would not have intended the Act as so modified to stand.

* * *

This point is critically important. Congress' basic goal in passing the Sentencing Act was to move the sentencing system in the direction of increased uniformity. See 28 U.S.C. § 991(b)(1) (B); see also § 994(f). That uniformity does not consist simply of similar sentences for those convicted of violations of the same statute—a uniformity consistent with the dissenters' remedial approach. It consists, more importantly, of similar relationships between sentences and real conduct, relationships that Congress' sentencing statutes helped to advance and that Justice Stevens' approach would undermine. Compare *post*, at 18 (dissenting opinion) (conceding that the Sixth Amendment requirement would "undoubtedly affect 'real conduct' sentencing in certain cases," but minimizing the significance of that circumstance). In significant part, it is the weakening of this real-conduct/uniformity-in-sentencing relationship, and not any "inexplicabl[e]" concerns for the "*manner* of achieving uniform sentences," (Scalia, J., dissenting), that leads us to conclude that Congress would have preferred *no* mandatory system to the system the dissenters envisage.

Third, the sentencing statutes, read to include the Court's Sixth Amendment requirement, would create a system far more complex than Congress could have intended. . . .

Fourth, plea bargaining would not significantly diminish the consequences of the Court's constitutional holding for the operation of the Guidelines. Compare *post*, at 3 (Stevens, J., dissenting). Rather, plea bargaining would make matters worse. Congress enacted the sentencing statutes in major part to achieve greater uniformity in sentencing, *i.e.*, to increase the likelihood that offenders who engage in similar real conduct would receive similar sentences. The statutes reasonably assume that their efforts to move the trial-based sentencing process in the direction of greater sentencing uniformity would have a similar positive impact upon plea-bargained sentences, for plea bargaining takes place *in the shadow of* (*i.e.*, with an eye towards the hypothetical result of) a potential trial.

* * *

The Court's constitutional jury trial requirement, however, if patched onto the present Sentencing Act, would move the system backwards in respect both to tried and to plea-bargained cases. In respect to tried cases, it would effectively deprive the judge of the ability to use post-verdict-acquired real-conduct information; it would prohibit the judge from basing a sentence upon any conduct other than the conduct the prosecutor chose to charge; and it would put a defendant to a set of difficult strategic choices as to which prosecutorial claims he would contest. The sentence that would emerge in a case tried under such a system would likely reflect real conduct less completely, less accurately, and less often than did a pre-Guidelines, as well as a Guidelines, trial.

Because plea bargaining inevitably reflects estimates of what would happen at trial, plea bargaining too under such a system would move in the wrong direction. That is to say, in a sentencing system modified by the Court's constitutional requirement, plea bargaining would likely lead to sentences that gave greater weight, not to real conduct, but rather to the skill of counsel, the policies of the prosecutor, the caseload, and other factors that vary from place to place, defendant to defendant, and crime to crime. Compared to pre-Guidelines plea bargaining, plea bargaining of this kind would necessarily move federal sentencing in the direction of diminished, not increased, uniformity in sentencing. It would tend to defeat, not to further, Congress' basic statutory goal.

Such a system would have particularly troubling consequences with respect to prosecutorial power. Until now, sentencing factors have come before the judge in the presentence report. But in a sentencing system with the Court's constitutional requirement engrafted onto it, any factor that a prosecutor chose not to charge at the plea negotiation would be placed beyond the reach of the judge entirely. Prosecutors would thus exercise a power the Sentencing Act vested in judges: the power to decide, based on relevant information about the offense and the offender, which defendants merit heavier punishment.

In respondent Booker's case, for example, the jury heard evidence that the crime had involved 92.5 grams of crack cocaine, and convicted Booker of possessing more than 50 grams. But the judge, at sentencing, found that the crime had involved an additional 566 grams, for a total of 658.5 grams. A system that would require the jury, not the judge, to make the additional "566 grams" finding is a system in which the prosecutor, not the judge, would control the sentence. That is because it is the prosecutor who would have to decide what drug amount to charge. He could choose to charge 658.5 grams, or 92.5, or less. It is the prosecutor who, through such a charging decision, would control the sentencing range. And it is different prosecutors who, in different cases—say, in two cases involving 566 grams—would potentially insist upon different punishments for similar defendants who engaged in similar criminal conduct involving similar amounts of unlawful drugs—say, by charging one of them with the full 566 grams, and the other with 10. As long as different prosecutors react differently, a system with a patched-on jury factfinding requirement would mean different sentences for otherwise similar conduct, whether in the context of trials or that of plea bargaining.

Fifth, Congress would not have enacted sentencing statutes that make it more difficult to adjust sentences *upward* than to adjust them *downward*. . . . For all these reasons, Congress, had it been faced with the constitutional jury trial requirement, likely would not have passed the same Sentencing Act. It likely would have found the requirement incompatible with the Act as written. Hence the Act cannot remain valid in its entirety. Severance and excision are necessary.

III

We now turn to the question of *which* portions of the sentencing statute we must sever and excise as inconsistent with the Court's constitutional requirement. Although, as we have explained, see Part II, *supra,* we believe that Congress would have preferred the total invalidation of the statute to the dissenters' remedial approach, we nevertheless do not believe that the entire statute must be invalidated. Most of the statute is perfectly valid. See, *e.g.,* 18 U.S.C. A. § 3551 (main ed. and Supp. 2004) (describing authorized sentences as probation, fine, or imprisonment); § 3552 (presentence reports); § 3554 (forfeiture); § 3555 (notification to the victims); § 3583 (supervised release). And we must "refrain from invalidating more of the statute than is necessary." *Regan.* Indeed, we must retain those portions of the Act that are (1) constitutionally valid, (2) capable of "functioning independently," and (3) consistent with Congress' basic objectives in enacting the statute.

Application of these criteria indicates that we must sever and excise two specific statutory provisions: the provision that requires sentencing courts to impose a sentence within the applicable Guidelines range (in the absence of circumstances that justify a departure), see 18 U.S.C. § 3553(b)(1) (Supp. 2004), and the provision that sets forth standards of review on appeal,

including *de novo* review of departures from the applicable Guidelines range, see § 3742(e) (main ed. and Supp. 2004) (see Appendix, *infra,* for text of both provisions). With these two sections excised (and statutory cross-references to the two sections consequently invalidated), the remainder of the Act satisfies the Court's constitutional requirements.

* * *

V

In respondent Booker's case, the District Court applied the Guidelines as written and imposed a sentence higher than the maximum authorized solely by the jury's verdict. The Court of Appeals held *Blakely* applicable to the Guidelines, concluded that Booker's sentence violated the Sixth Amendment, vacated the judgment of the District Court, and remanded for resentencing. We affirm the judgment of the Court of Appeals and remand the case. On remand, the District Court should impose a sentence in accordance with today's opinions, and, if the sentence comes before the Court of Appeals for review, the Court of Appeals should apply the review standards set forth in this opinion.

In respondent Fanfan's case, the District Court held *Blakely* applicable to the Guidelines. It then imposed a sentence that was authorized by the jury's verdict—a sentence lower than the sentence authorized by the Guidelines as written. Thus, Fanfan's sentence does not violate the Sixth Amendment. Nonetheless, the Government (and the defendant should he so choose) may seek resentencing under the system set forth in today's opinions. Hence we vacate the judgment of the District Court and remand the case for further proceedings consistent with this opinion.

As these dispositions indicate, we must apply today's holdings—both the Sixth Amendment holding and our remedial interpretation of the Sentencing Act—to all cases on direct review. See *Griffith v. Kentucky,* 479 U.S. 314, 328 (1987) ("[A] new rule for the conduct of criminal prosecutions is to be applied retroactively to all cases . . . pending on direct review or not yet final, with no exception for cases in which the new rule constitutes a 'clear break' with the past").... That fact does not mean that we believe that every sentence gives rise to a Sixth Amendment violation. Nor do we believe that every appeal will lead to a new sentencing hearing. That is because we expect reviewing courts to apply ordinary prudential doctrines, determining, for example, whether the issue was raised below and whether it fails the "plain-error" test. It is also because, in cases not involving a Sixth Amendment violation, whether resentencing is warranted or whether it will instead be sufficient to review a sentence for reasonableness may depend upon application of the harmless-error doctrine.

It is so ordered.

CASE DISCUSSION QUESTIONS

1. What sentences did the trial judges originally impose on each of the two defendants?
2. What questions did the government ask the Supreme Court to decide?
3. Which justice authored the opinion answering each of the questions posed by the government?
4. Which constitutional provision did the Court hold was violated by the mandatory nature of the sentencing guidelines?
5. Which parts of the act setting up the guidelines were found unconstitutional?
6. Which Supreme Court Justice joined in both opinions of the court?

In 2007, the Supreme Court returned two more decisions dealing with the now advisory federal sentencing guidelines. In *Kimbrough v. United States*, the Court ruled that judges were not bound by federal sentencing guidelines that punished crack cocaine crimes more harshly than similar crimes involving powdered cocaine.[24] Three months later, the U.S. Sentencing Commission amended its guidelines to retroactively reduce the penalties for crack cocaine crimes.

In *Gall v. United States*, the Court considered how much deference should be given under the "abuse of discretions standard." The defendant had been a second-year college student at the University of Iowa when he joined an ongoing enterprise distributing a controlled substance popularly known as "Ecstasy." A month or two later he stopped using ecstasy and withdrew from the conspiracy. He had not sold illegal drugs of any kind since then and had, in the words of the district court, "self-rehabilitated." After graduating from the University of Iowa in 2002, he obtained a job in the construction industry and later became a master carpenter. Federal drug agents learned of his earlier involvement with ecstasy and brought charges against him. He entered into a plea agreement. The pre-sentence report recommended a sentencing range of thirty to thirty-seven months of imprisonment, but the district judge sentenced Gall to probation for a term of thirty-six months. The court of appeals reversed and remanded for re-sentencing. The Supreme Court ruled, however, that the court of appeals should have given due deference to the district court's reasoned and reasonable sentencing decision.[25]

b. Application of Federal Guidelines

Even though the federal guidelines are no longer binding, the sentencing judge still must determine the range specified by the guidelines before imposing a sentence. Figure 13.5 displays the guidelines chart pertaining to the length of

---

[24]552 U.S. 85, 128 S. Ct. 558, 169 L. Ed. 2d 481 (2007).
[25]552 U.S. 38, 128 S. Ct. 586, 169 L. Ed. 2d 445 (2007).

Offense level	Criminal History Category (Criminal History Points)					
	I (0 or 1)	II (2 or 3)	III (4, 5, 6)	IV (7, 8, 9)	V (10, 11, 12)	VI (13 or more)
ZONE A 1	0–6	0–6	0–6	0–6	0–6	0–6
2	0–6	0–6	0–6	0–6	0–6	1–7
3	0–6	0–6	0–6	0–6	2–8	3–9
4	0–6	0–6	0–6	2–8	4–10	6–12
5	0–6	0–6	1–7	4–10	6–12	9–15
6	0–6	1–7	2–8	6–12	9–15	12–18
7	0–6	2–8	4–10	8–14	12–18	15–21
8	0–6	4–10	6–12	10–16	15–21	18–24
ZONE B 9	4–10	6–12	8–14	12–18	18–24	21–27
10	6–12	8–14	10–16	15–21	21–27	24–30
ZONE C 11	8–14	10–16	12–18	18–24	24–30	27–33
12	10–16	12–18	15–21	21–27	27–33	30–37
ZONE D 13	12–18	15–21	18–24	24–30	30–37	33–41
14	15–21	18–24	21–27	27–33	33–41	37–46
15	18–24	21–27	24–30	30–37	37–46	41–51
16	21–27	24–30	27–33	33–41	41–51	46–57
17	24–30	27–33	30–37	37–46	46–57	51–63
18	27–33	30–37	33–41	41–51	51–63	57–71
19	30–37	33–41	37–46	46–57	57–71	63–78
20	33–41	37–46	41–51	51–63	63–78	70–87
21	37–46	41–51	46–57	57–71	70–87	77–96
22	41–51	46–57	51–63	63–78	77–96	84–105
23	46–57	51–63	57–71	70–87	84–105	92–115
24	51–63	57–71	63–78	77–96	92–115	100–125
25	57–71	63–78	70–87	84–105	100–125	110–137

continued

26	63–78	70–87	78–97	92–115	110–137	120–150
27	70–87	78–97	87–108	100–125	120–150	130–162
28	78–97	87–108	97–121	110–137	130–162	140–175
29	87–108	97–121	108–135	121–151	140–175	151–188
30	97–121	108–135	121–151	135–168	151–188	168–210
31	108–135	121–151	135–168	151–188	168–210	188–235
32	121–151	135–168	151–188	168–210	188–235	210–262
33	135–168	151–188	168–210	188–235	210–262	235–293
34	151–188	168–210	188–235	210–262	235–293	262–327
35	168–210	188–235	210–262	235–293	262–327	292–365
36	188–235	210–262	235–293	262–327	292–365	324–405
37	210–262	235–293	262–327	292–365	324–405	360–life
38	235–293	262–327	292–365	324–405	360–life	360–life
39	262–327	292–365	324–405	360–life	360–life	360–life
40	292–365	324–405	360–life	360–life	360–life	360–life
41	324–405	360–life	360–life	360–life	360–life	360–life
42	360–life	360–life	360–life	360–life	360–life	360–life
43	life	life	life	life	life	life

Figure 13.5 Federal Sentencing Guidelines

incarceration.[26] The left side of the chart is the offense level, and the top of the sentencing chart is the criminal history.

There are forty-three levels of offense. The *Federal Sentencing Guidelines Manual* provides the base offense level for every federal crime.[27] The greater the seriousness of the crime, the greater the offense score. The base level offense entails more than the crime of which the defendant was convicted. Relevant conduct consists of acquitted acts, all activity committed or aided and abetted by the defendant;[28] and all reasonably foreseeable acts of others in furtherance of jointly taken criminal conduct. The base level is adjusted up or down in

---

[26]There is also a guidelines chart for the range of fines to be levied.

[27]*http://www.ussc.gov/2009guid/GL2009.pdf*

[28]*United States v. Watts*, 519 US 148, 149, 117 S. Ct. 633, 136 L. Ed. 2d 554 (1997).

accordance with other factors listed in the manual that affect the sentencing levels depending on the facts of the crime. The level may be raised by factors such as the amount of harm inflicted or the use of weapons, and it can be lowered when, for instance, the defendant accepts responsibility for the crime or if the defendant's participation in the offense was minimal. To aid in calculating the guidelines sentence, the Sentencing Commission has produced a worksheet.

The sentencing range is determined by locating the intersection of the offense level (row) with the six criminal history categories (column). There are 258 sentence ranges displayed on the chart. Most are shown in months, starting at 0–6 months. However, several go up to life imprisonment. Each of the 258 ranges appears in one of four sentencing zones, labeled A, B, C, and D. The 23 sentences appearing in Zone A include ranges of 0–6 months. The 19 sentences in Zone B consist of ranges greater than those of Zone A but do not exceed 12 months. Zone C consists of 10 sentences harsher than Zone B's but with a minimum incarceration period of less than 12 months. The remaining 206 sentences are included in Zone D.

Under the advisory guidelines, Zone A defendants are eligible for probation without a term of imprisonment. Defendants in Zone B are also probation-eligible if the court also imposes a condition or combination of conditions requiring intermittent confinement, community confinement, or home detention so long as the defendant serves at least one month of the sentence in prison. Zone C defendants qualify for similar treatment but must serve at least half of their sentence in prison.

Prior to the sentencing hearing, a probation officer provides the U.S. Attorney and the defense counsel with the **Presentence Investigation Report,** which includes a calculation of the appropriate guidelines range for presentation to the judge. The parties advise the judge whether they agree with the probation officer's guidelines calculations. Excerpts from the government's sentencing memorandum appear in Exhibit 13.2. Take a look at the guidelines chart (Figure 13.5) to see if you can follow how the government reached its conclusion as to the guidelines sentencing range.

c. Departures from the Guidelines

The advisory guidelines provide for departure from the sentencing ranges. However, the circumstances warranting departure are extremely limited. The most common reason is the prosecutor's recommendation for a lesser sentence based on the defendant's "substantial assistance to authorities."[29] Another basis for departure is an early disposition program ("fast track") authorized by the Justice Department.[30] This program is employed in the border states for drug

Presentence Investigation Report (PSR)

The document which reports the results of the probation officer's post-trial investigation of a convicted defendant, including all factors the court should take into account when determining the sentence.

---

[29]Federal Sentencing Guidelines Manual § 5K1.1 (2009) provides: "Upon motion of the Government stating that the defendant has provided substantial assistance in the investigation or prosecution of another person who has committed an offense, the court may depart from the guidelines."

[30]Federal Sentencing Guidelines Manual § 5K3.1 (2009) provides: "Upon motion of the Government, the court may depart downward not more than 4 levels pursuant to an early disposition program authorized by the Attorney General of the United States and the United States Attorney for the district in which the court resides.

Exhibit 13.2: Excerpts from Prosecution Sentencing Memorandum

Michael Barrett was convicted in federal court of stalking ESPN reporter Erin Andrews. Barrett removed the peephole device from her hotel room doors on three separate occasions without Andrews' knowledge, videotaped her naked in her room, and posted ten nude videos of her on the Internet. The judge sentenced him to thirty months in federal prison. Excerpts of the Government's Sentencing Memorandum appear below.

* * *

6	**ARGUMENT**
7	A. THE GOVERNMENT CONCURS IN THE ADVISORY GUIDELINES
8	CALCULATIONS SET FORTH IN DEFENDANT'S PSR
9	With respect to the presentence investigation report
10	("PSR"), the government requests that the Court adopt its
11	advisory Sentencing Guidelines calculation. This calculation is
12	as follows: a base offense level of 18 (U.S.S.G. § 2A6.2(a)); +2
13	for a pattern of activity involving stalking, threatening,
14	harassing or assaulting the same victim (U.S.S.G.
15	§ 2A6.2(b)(1)(D)); and -3 for acceptance of responsibility--for a
16	total adjusted offense level of 17. The parties stipulated to
17	this calculation in the plea agreement. (Plea Agt. ¶ 13.)
18	The government also respectfully submits that the PSR
19	correctly calculated defendant's criminal history to be Category
20	I and asks that the Court adopt that calculation. Thus, the
21	government requests that the Court adopt an advisory Guidelines
22	range of 24 to 30 months.

and immigration cases. The prosecutor must request "substantial assistance" and "fast-track" departures and the judge determines whether to grant the request. The defendant cannot request either departure.

Although they are not as common, there are also other bases for departure based on policy rationales. For example, there may be justification for a downward departure when the victim contributed significantly to the defendant's conduct. Conversely, there may be an upward departure when the victim suffered extreme psychological injury or the crime significantly disrupted governmental functions.

APPLICATION EXERCISES

Apply the Federal Sentencing Guidelines to each of the following examples. State the offense level, crime history, and sentencing range.

1. A jury convicted Jane Doe, a first-time offender, of kidnapping, level 32. Because the defendant injured the victim through the use of a dangerous weapon, the offense level increased by 4.

2. Joe Smith was found guilty of a minor assault, level 7. During the assault, Smith hit the 21-year-old victim in the face, causing severe bruising and injuries. The nature of the victim's injuries increased the offense level by 2. This is Joe Smith's third offense.

3. Owen Black was convicted of trespass, a level 4 offense. He was found guilty of an invasion of a protected computer with a loss of $3,000, an increase of 1. This is Black's third conviction of this nature, so there are 2 criminal history points for each prior conviction.

4. A jury found Vivian White guilty of obstructing or impeding officers, a level 10 offense. She has five previous convictions of sixty days or more, 2 criminal history points for each offense.

5. John Roe was found to have committed involuntary manslaughter involving criminally negligent conduct, a level 12 offense. He is currently on probation, which gives him 2 criminal history points. He also has six previous convictions with sentences of incarceration over sixty days, which amount to 2 criminal history points each.

6. Seth Owen was found guilty of burglary of a residence, a level 17 offense. The judge determined the property loss to be $10,000, a level increase of 2, and found Owen to have clearly demonstrated acceptance of responsibility, an offense level decrease of 2. This is the first time Seth Owen got into trouble with the law.

7. Jean Green was convicted of robbery, level 20. Because she robbed a financial institution, the offense level increased by 2. During the robbery, she shot the security guards, who sustained life-threatening injuries, thereby increasing the offense level by 6 and 7. Although authorities apprehended Green, they never recovered the $5 million she stole, which increased the offense level by 7. Jean Green had five prior criminal convictions; four did not involve incarceration (1 criminal history point each) and the other resulted in a three-year sentence (3 criminal history points).

8. Hannah Brown was found guilty of robbery, a level 20 offense. No weapons were used and no one was hurt. She stole $250,000, which was never recovered (add 2 levels). The judge found that the defendant was only a minor participant in the robbery, which decreased the offense level by 2. Hannah Brown has two other criminal convictions, neither involving incarceration.

d. Requirements of 18 U.S.C. § 3553

In the aftermath of *Booker*, Congress enacted 18 U.S.C. § 3553. U.S. district court judges now must consider a number of factors, including the range in the guidelines. Section 3553(a) provides that the sentencing judge consider:

(1) the nature and circumstances of the offense and the history and characteristics of the defendant;

(2) the need for the sentence imposed—
   (A) to reflect the seriousness of the offense, to promote respect for the law, and to provide just punishment for the offense;
   (B) to afford adequate deterrence to criminal conduct;
   (C) to protect the public from further crimes of the defendant; and
   (D) to provide the defendant with needed educational or vocational training, medical care, or other correctional treatment in the most effective manner;

(3) the kinds of sentences available;

(4) the kinds of sentence and the sentencing range established [by the Sentencing Guidelines];

(5) any pertinent policy statement [issued by the Sentencing Commission];

(6) the need to avoid unwarranted sentence disparities among defendants with similar records who have been found guilty of similar conduct; and

(7) the need to provide restitution to any victims of the offense.

In light of *Booker* and § 3553, most sentencing courts apply a three-step approach to determining the sentence. First, the judge must determine the appropriate guideline sentencing range. Second, the judge decides whether to depart from the guidelines. If so, the judge must specifically state the reasons for departure. Third, the judge considers the § 3553 factors to determine whether the defendant should be given a non-guideline sentence, referred to as a **variance**. In the appropriate case, defendants can argue for both a guidelines departure and a variance.

> **Variance**
> A federal sentence that is not within the guidelines or based on a departure from the guidelines.

Following *Booker*, a growing minority of federal judges started imposing sentences below the guidelines range. Figure 13.6 illustrates a modest trend toward more lenient sentencing.

It is anticipated that this trend will continue in certain types of cases. A recent survey of federal district court judges reveals that more than two-thirds of the respondents believed the guidelines were too strict with regard to the trafficking of crack cocaine, receipt of child pornography, and possession of child pornography. Although most respondents believed that the guideline ranges should be broadened, they also held the opinion that the guidelines were generally appropriate for most offenses.[31]

---

[31]Results of Survey of United States District Judges, January 2010 through March 2010, United States Sentencing Commission, June 2010. *http://www.ussc.gov/Judge_Survey/2010/JudgeSurvey_201006 .pdf*

Year	Total Cases	Within Guidelines	Gov't Sponsored Below Range	Non-Gov't Sponsored Below Range	Above Range
2006	79,153	61.7%	24.6%	12.0%	1.6%
2007	74,493	60.8%	25.6%	12.0%	1.5%
2008	69,893	59.4%	25.6%	13.4%	1.5%
2009	70,187	56.8%	25.3%	15.8%	2.0%

Source: U. S. Sentencing Commission's *Sourcebook of Federal Sentencing Statistics*
http://www.ussc.gov/ANNRPT/2009/TableN.pdf
http://www.ussc.gov/ANNRPT/2008/TableN.pdf
http://www.ussc.gov/ANNRPT/2007/TableN.pdf
http://www.ussc.gov/ANNRPT/2006/TableN.pdf

Figure 13.6 Federal Sentences Within Guidelines Range

APPLICATION EXERCISES

9. Develop a chart that shows the range of fines associated with different types of drug possession felonies and misdemeanors in your state.

10. Report whether the statutes in your state authorize the death penalty. If so:
   a. For what crimes is it authorized?
   b. What, if any, special rules apply to capital cases in your state?

11. Report whether your state utilizes determinate or indeterminate sentencing.

12. Report whether your state has any habitual offender statutes. If so, how is *habitual offender* defined and what sentence is required?

13. Develop a chart that shows the range of incarceration times associated with different types of illegal drug offenses in your state.

14. Report whether your state has a parole board. If it does, how many members does it have and how are they selected? How often do they meet?

15. Report whether your state uses any type of sentencing guidelines. If it does, who developed them and how do they differ from the federal guidelines?

C. SENTENCING PROCEDURES

Except in capital cases, the judge rather than the jury sentences the defendant.[32] For minor misdemeanors and traffic citations, the judge ordinarily will sentence the defendant immediately after trial. At that time, the prosecutor will let the court know the offender's prior record. Both sides will offer sentencing proposals. The judge will then impose a sentence. In more serious cases, the judge directs the probation department to prepare a pre-sentence investigation report. After the parties have an opportunity to review the report, the judge conducts a sentencing hearing.

1. PRE-SENTENCE INVESTIGATION AND REPORT

The pre-sentence investigation report is the most important document in the sentencing of the defendant. The judge uses it to identify and limit issues decided at a sentencing hearing. The report contains information about the offender's social background, criminal history, and financial circumstances. In federal court and in states that have sentencing guidelines, the probation officer also includes in the report a calculation of the sentencing range. In states in which aggravating and mitigating circumstances are to be taken into account, the report will discuss the applicable circumstances.

The probation officer usually begins the pre-sentence investigation by conducting an extensive interview with the defendant. The defense attorney often attends the interview to advise the client concerning responses to questions, counsel the client not to discuss certain topics, or aid the probation officer in the disclosure of accurate information. A defense paralegal may accompany the attorney.

Under the Fifth Amendment privilege against self-incrimination, the defendant does not have to submit to the interview with the probation officer.[33] In the federal system, the main reason for a defendant to talk about the offense after a guilty plea is to get the offense level reduced two or three levels in the guideline calculation by clearly demonstrating acceptance of responsibility for the offense. However, even if the defendant limits comments to the offense of conviction, there may be a risk in being open with the probation department. For instance, if the defendant admits to taking a leadership role in commission of the crime, the guidelines offense level may increase. There are other reasons for the defendant to cooperate, such as making a record of the defendant's substance abuse when the defense plans to seek treatment as part of the sentence. If the defendant tells the probation officer about a drug or alcohol problem, this issue will be included in the pre-sentence report.

In addition to speaking to the defendant, the probation officer will contact the prosecutor and the investigating law enforcement agents to get their versions of the defendant's conduct. The probation officer may also contact members of the defendant's family, past and present employers, the victims of the crimes at

---

[32]There are a few jurisdictions in which the jury determines the sentence in non-capital cases.

[33]The defendant retains the privilege against self-incrimination prior to sentencing after a guilty plea or jury verdict. *Mitchell v. United States*, 526 U.S. 314, 326, 119 S. Ct. 1307. 143 L. Ed. 2d 424 (1999).

issue, and institutions having had contact with the defendant, such as medical, military, and financial entities.

In federal court, both sides are entitled to know in advance the grounds on which the judge plans to rely to depart upward or downward from the sentencing guideline range, including variances. This means that the attorneys must provide the probation officer with information to support a guidelines departure or variance so that the other party is aware of this possible ground before the sentencing hearing.

Following the investigation, a pre-sentence report is prepared and shared with the parties. The pre-sentence investigation report (PSR) discusses the defendant's background, criminal history, and personal characteristics. The report will include an analysis of the relevant statutory factors.[34] In sentencing guidelines jurisdictions, the PSR will include a calculation of the sentencing range. In non-guidelines jurisdictions, the pre-sentence investigation report will discuss each of the aggravating and mitigating statutory factors pertinent to the offense.

The report will present the range of possible sentences as well as the probation officer's recommended sentence. If a departure from or variance to the guidelines range is proposed, the report will state the applicable guidelines sentence as well as the extent of the departure or variance. The PSR may recommend imprisonment, fines, restitution, costs and assessments, supervised release, or a combination of these options. Typically, terms and conditions of the proposed sentence are set forth in detail.

2. OBJECTIONS AND MEMORANDA

Most jurisdictions require the probation officer to provide the report to the attorneys prior to the sentencing hearing. In federal cases, disclosure must be made no later than thirty-five days before the hearing.[35] Under FRCrP 32, the parties must submit written objections or additions to the PSR to the probation officer within fourteen days after their receipt of the report. They also have to send their objections to the opposing side. The probation officer then must submit a revised PSR to the judge and the parties within seven days before sentencing. The revised report will include an addendum listing the unresolved objections, the grounds for the objections, and the probation officer's analysis of the objections.

After reviewing the PSR and the prosecution's objections and additions, defense counsel may renew their *Brady* request for exculpatory evidence. At this time, the request will specifically seek information pertaining to sentencing. If either side intends to request a departure from the guidelines not mentioned in the PSR, a letter must be sent to the opposing counsel and the probation officer. The letter should give the grounds for the departure or variance and ask that the proposed departure or variance be included in the report. Without advance notice of intent to depart from the sentencing range, the court may lack the authority to deviate from the guidelines.[36]

---

[34]For example, 18 U.S.C. § 3553.

[35]FRCrP 32.

[36]*Burns v. United States*, 501 US 129, 111 S. Ct. 2182, 115 L. Ed. 2d 123 (1991).

In addition to submitting objections and proposed additions to the PSR, parties may also file a sentencing memorandum with the court. The memorandum discusses each relevant factor and explains how the factors justify the sentence the party is proposing. In federal cases, the parties will analyze the § 3553 factors, including the guidelines calculation. The memo should be drafted to help the judge prepare written findings of fact in support of the sentence. If the judge finds the attorney's memorandum persuasive, the judge may use this language in the court's written findings. It is, therefore, important that the memo systematically analyze all of the § 3553 factors.

3. THE HEARING

Often, the judge will rule on the post-verdict motion and then proceed to sentencing if the motion is denied. The judge will give great weight to the PSR. If the probation officer has not resolved objections to the report, the judge will have to come to a decision on the controversy. In federal court, the judge must make written findings as to disputed guidelines factors.

Although the parties may or may not have the opportunity to present live witnesses at a sentencing hearing, both sides have the right to state their positions. Ordinarily, the parties can present evidence regarding objections to the PSR and to disputed sentencing factors. Moreover, the defendant will have the opportunity to rebut hearsay information offered at sentencing. Many states and the federal criminal justice systems allow the victim of an offense to provide a statement at sentencing. Some jurisdictions permit the submission of written statements only; others give the victim the right to speak at the sentencing hearing.[37]

The prosecution bears the burden of proving factors that enhance the sentence, including aggravating factors. The defendant has the burden of proving mitigating factors. Usually the standard of proof for both sides is a showing by a preponderance of the evidence. Hearsay evidence is generally admissible at sentencing so long as there is a minimal indication that the information is reliable.

Before entering a sentence, the judge will give the defendant the opportunity to make a statement and present information in mitigation of the sentence. The defendant's statement at sentencing is known as the right of **allocution**. After the defendant makes this statement, the judge announces the sentence. The judge then advises the defendant of the right to appeal both the judgment of conviction as well as the sentence. The court also will let the defendant know of the right to be represented by counsel on appeal and that if the defendant is unable to pay the cost of an attorney on appeal he has the right to be provided counsel at public expense.

Read the transcript of the sentencing of convicted investment advisor Bernard Madoff (Exhibit 13.3), and answer the Discussion Questions that follow it.

Allocution
The defendant's personal statement in mitigation of the sentence.

---

[37]See, e.g., 18 U.S.C. § 3771.

Exhibit 13.3: Excerpts of Transcript of Sentencing in a White-Collar Crime

The judge in *United States v. Madoff* conducted a sentencing hearing. He considered victim statements and testimony as well as arguments made by counsel. At the conclusion of the hearing, the judge discussed the relevant factors and announced the sentence. Excerpts of the judge's statements follow.

I take into account what I have read in the presentence report, the parties' sentencing submissions, and the e-mails and letters from victims. I take into account what I have heard today. I also consider the statutory factors as well as all the facts and circumstances in the case.

***

Objectively speaking, the fraud here was staggering. It spanned more than 20 years.

***

The fraud reached thousands of victims.

***

As for the amount of the monetary loss, there appears to be some disagreement. Mr. Madoff disputes that the loss amount is $65 billion or even $13 billion. But Mr. Madoff has now acknowledged, however, that some $170 billion flowed into his business as a result of his fraudulent scheme.

***

Moreover, the offense level of 52 is calculated by using a chart for loss amount that only goes up to $400 million. By any of these measures, the loss figure here is many times that amount. It's off the chart by many fold.

Moreover, as many of the victims have pointed out, this is not just a matter of money. The breach of trust was massive. Investors -- individuals, charities, pension funds, institutional clients -- were repeatedly lied to, as they were told their moneys would be invested in stocks when they were not. Clients were sent these millions of pages of account statements that the government just alluded to confirming trades that were never made, attesting to balances that did not exist. As the victims' letters and e-mails demonstrate, as the statements today demonstrate, investors made important life decisions based on these fictitious account statements -- when to retire, how to care for elderly parents, whether to buy a car or sell a house, how to save for their children's college tuition. Charitable organizations and pension funds made important decisions based on false information about fictitious accounts. Mr. Madoff also repeatedly lied to the SEC and the regulators, in writing and in sworn testimony, by withholding material information, by creating false documents to cover up his scheme.

***

Mr. Madoff argues a number of mitigating factors but they are less than compelling. It is true that he essentially turned himself in and confessed to the FBI. But the fact is that with the turn in the economy, he was not able to keep up with the requests of customers to withdraw their funds, and it is apparent that he knew that he was going to be caught soon.

***

largely, if not entirely, symbolic.

But the symbolism is important, for at least three reasons. First, retribution. One of the traditional notions of punishment is that an offender should be punished in proportion to his blameworthiness.

***

The symbolism is important because

the message must be sent that in a society governed by the rule of law, Mr. Madoff will get what he deserves, and that he will be punished according to his moral culpability.

Second, deterrence. Another important goal of punishment is deterrence, and the symbolism is important here because the strongest possible message must be sent to those who would engage in similar conduct that they will be caught and that they will be punished to the fullest extent of the law.

Finally, the symbolism is also important for the victims.

***

A substantial sentence will not give the victims back their retirement funds or the moneys they saved to send their children or grandchildren to college. It will not give them back their financial security or the freedom from financial worry. But more is at stake than money, as we have heard. The victims put their trust in Mr. Madoff. That trust was broken in a way that has left many -- victims as well as others -- doubting our financial institutions, our financial system, our government's ability to regulate and protect, and sadly, even themselves.

I do not agree that the victims are succumbing to the temptation of mob vengeance. Rather, they are doing what they are supposed to be doing -- placing their trust in our system of justice. A substantial sentence, the knowledge that

Mr. Madoff has been punished to the fullest extent of the law, may, in some small measure, help these victims in their healing process.

Mr. Madoff, please stand.

It is the judgment of this Court that the defendant, Bernard L. Madoff, shall be and hereby is sentenced to a term of imprisonment of 150 years, consisting of 20 years on each of Counts 1, 3, 4, 5, 6, and 10, 5 years on each of Counts 2, 8, 9, and 11, and 10 years on Count 7, all to run consecutively to each other. As a technical matter, the sentence must be expressed on the judgment in months. 150 years is equivalent to 1,800 months.

Although it is academic, for technical reasons, I must also impose supervised release. I impose a term of supervised release of 3 years on each count, all to run concurrently.

***

I will not impose a fine, as whatever assets Mr. Madoff has, as to whatever assets may be found, they shall be applied to restitution for the victims.

As previously ordered, I will defer the issue of restitution for 90 days.

Finally, I will impose the mandatory special assessment of $1,100, $100 for each count.

DISCUSSION QUESTIONS

4. What conclusions does the judge reach as to the nature of Madoff's crime?

5. What is it about the nature of the crime, besides the amount of money victims lost, that the judge focuses on in this statement?

6. Where does Madoff's crime fall on the federal sentencing guidelines chart? Why should this matter?

7. What did the judge have to say about the impact of Madoff's having turned himself in to the FBI?

8. How did Madoff's crime compare to similar white-collar crimes?

9. What did the judge note to be lacking from the evidence submitted in mitigation?

10. How did Madoff's age affect the judge's sentencing decision?

11. What is the judge's response to Madoff's attorneys' plea that he (the judge) not succumb to "mob vengeance"?

12. How many separate counts was Madoff sentenced on, and did the judge order that the sentences on those counts be served concurrently or consecutively? All told, how many years was Madoff sentenced to serve?

13. What fine did the judge impose, and what was his justification for his decision?

14. What actions did the judge take at this hearing with regard to supervised release, restitution, and assessments?

15. To what extent do you agree or disagree with the judge's decision in this case?

D. MODIFICATION OF SENTENCES

1. POST-SENTENCE MOTIONS TO CORRECT ERRORS

If the judge enters an erroneous sentence, there are several ways to challenge it. First, either party may move to correct clear error in the sentence. FRCrP 35(a) authorizes the judge to correct a sentence imposed as a result of arithmetic, technical or other clear error. The U.S. district judge must act within seven days of the imposition of the sentence. Second, either side can file a motion to correct a clerical mistake. FRCrP 36 permits the court to modify the record so that it reflects the actual rulings of the judge. Third, in most jurisdictions a party can appeal the sentence to a higher court. (We will discuss the steps needed to perfect the appeal in Chapter 14.) Finally, a defendant may make a collateral attack on a sentence through a post-conviction relief petition.[38]

---

[38]See, e.g., 28 U.S.C. § 2255.

2. REDUCTION OF A SENTENCE BY A JUDGE

There are a few additional circumstances where the trial judge may reduce the original sentence of imprisonment. The most common occurs when the appellate court reverses a sentence and remands the case back to the trial court to modify the sentence or to conduct a new sentencing hearing.

In federal court, the Bureau of Prisons can move for a reduction in hardship cases involving elderly persons serving life terms for serious, violent felonies. Also, the U.S. Attorney may move for a reduction when the defendant assists the government in the investigation or prosecution of another person. The federal district court also is authorized to modify a fine at the request of the prosecution and terminate probation or supervised release after one year. Circumstances for reduction under state law vary from jurisdiction to jurisdiction.

3. REDUCTION OF A SENTENCE BY CORRECTIONS OFFICIALS

A defendant's sentence of imprisonment may be reduced due to a variety of factors outside of the court system. Many jurisdictions release prisoners for "good-time" served. Depending on the nature of the crime, this reduction can be substantial or minimal. For instance, in Illinois many prisoners are given day-for-day credit for good-time served. In contrast, federal prisoners are given only 54 days at the end of each year of a prison term.[39] Federal and state prisoners may get a reduction of time for residential drug treatment. Successful completion of boot camp can also reduce the length of a sentence.

SUMMARY

The criminal justice system provides a variety of options for punishing individuals convicted of violations of the law. These punishments include various types of financial penalties (such as fines, court-ordered restitution, assessments, surcharges, and court costs), incarceration (in local jails, state prisons, boot camps or special juvenile detention facilities), and, in a limited number of cases, even death.

There are also situations in which offenders are not incarcerated as long as they abide by special limitations that don't apply to ordinary citizens. These limitations are imposed as part of court supervision, probation, or parole and can include such things as

---

[39]In *Barber v. Thomas,* 130 S. Ct. 2499, 177 L. Ed. 2d 1 (2010), federal prisoners' contended that federal statutes required a straightforward calculation based upon the length of the term of imprisonment that the sentencing judge imposed, rather than on the length of time that the prisoner actually served. The U.S. Supreme Court interpreted the language of § 3624(b) as supporting the practice of awarding a specific number of days of credit at the end of each full year of imprisonment. The Justices noted that basing the award of credit on the sentence imposed rather than served, as the prisoners suggested, would have resulted in the prisoners receiving good-time credit for a portion of the sentence that was not actually served with good behavior. Further, the government's method of calculation served as a proper incentive for the prisoners to comply with institutional disciplinary rules by awarding credit at the end of the year, after good behavior was demonstrated for a readily identifiable period.

having to attend special classes, not associating with specific types of people, or not consuming alcohol or drugs.

One of the most controversial topics in sentencing involves the amount of discretion judges should have in determining the nature of the sentences given out. Should the offender receive the minimum or the maximum sentence allowed; should the sentence be for a predetermined length of time or left to a parole board to determine when the prisoner will actually be released? When someone is convicted on more than one charge, should the offender serve multiple sentences consecutively or concurrently? How strictly do judges have to apply "sentencing guidelines"?

For minor misdemeanors and traffic citations, the judge ordinarily will sentence the defendant immediately after trial, but in more serious cases, the judge directs the probation department to prepare a pre-sentence investigation report. After the parties have an opportunity to review the report, the judge conducts a sentencing hearing that usually focuses on aggravating and mitigating circumstances that should be taken into consideration in determining what the proper sentence should be.

INTERNET RESOURCES

Criminal Justice System

- U.S. Sentencing Guidelines:
  http://www.ussc.gov/
  http://www.sentencing.us/
- Federal Bureau of Prisons:
  http://www.bop.gov/

REVIEW QUESTIONS

1. In the federal system, what types of sentences is the judge authorized to impose?
2. Generally, what punishment is imposed by the courts for ordinance violations, minor traffic offenses, and insignificant misdemeanors?
3. What types of factors are taken into account by the judge in imposing a large fine?
4. In what types of cases must federal judges order a convicted defendant to pay restitution?
5. What is the difference between court costs and assessments?
6. What governmental bodies typically operate jails, prisons, and penitentiaries?
7. What are typical conditions attached to court supervision?
8. What circumstances would prompt a prosecutor to file a PTR?
9. What is the major difference between probation and parole?
10. What are the main arguments in favor of and against the death penalty?
11. What is the difference between determinate and indeterminate sentencing?
12. How does an enhanced sentence differ from an extended term sentence?
13. How long is an offender's total sentence when sentences of eight years, six years, and five years are to be served concurrently? How long is the total sentence when they are to be served consecutively?
14. What are the main arguments in favor of and against mandatory sentences?
15. Why did Congress create the United States Sentencing Commission?

16. What are the two variables shown in the guidelines chart that come into play in determining the appropriate sentence range when applying the Federal Sentencing Guidelines?

17. What is the most common basis for justifying a departure from the Federal Sentencing Guidelines?

18. What factors does 18 U.S.C. § 3553 require a federal judge to take into account when imposing a sentence?

19. What is the three-step-approach most sentencing courts apply to determining the sentence?

20. What type of information typically appears in a pre-sentence investigation report?

21. In federal court, what is the time frame given to the parties to submit objections or additions to the pre-sentence investigation report?

22. In federal court, what means are available to the defendant, in addition to filing an appeal, to challenge an improper sentence?

23. What length of time is given to federal defendants for "good-time served"?

Chapter 14

Appeals

We end our coverage of criminal procedure with an overview of the appeals process, an analysis of the decision to appeal, and a discussion of the steps that should be taken to prepare for an appeal. In this book, we will not get into the details of the preparation of appellate briefs, motions prepared for the courts of review, or the nature of oral arguments made in appellate courts. We will focus on steps you must take to file an appeal, the preservation of issues for review, the types of errors presented to the appellate court, the standard of review, and collateral remedies.

A. AN OVERVIEW OF THE APPEALS PROCESS

The term *appeal* is most commonly used to refer to a request to reconsider a decision or intended action. Thus a student may appeal to an instructor to raise a grade on a paper or a test.[1] In the legal context, it is an attempt to have a legal decision reviewed and overturned by a higher-ranking legal authority. Most criminal appeals involve lower-level state appellate courts reviewing decisions of trial court judges in their state, or in the case of the federal courts, a U.S. Circuit Court of Appeals reviewing decisions of U.S. District Court judges within their circuit. There are also criminal appeals in which decisions of lower-level state appellate courts are reviewed by higher-level appellate courts (usually, but not always, called supreme courts) and the decisions of the U.S. Circuit Courts of Appeals are reviewed by the U.S. Supreme Court. Finally, there are a limited number of situations in which decisions by the highest state court are reviewed

---

[1]The term *appeal* can also be used to refer to the basis upon which the decision should be made. For example, in asking for a favor, one might *appeal* to the decision maker's sense of fairness, morality, loyalty, etc.

Appeal
A formal request for review of an order or judgment entered by another court, seeking to reverse or modify the other court's decision.

Appellant
The party initiating the appeal.

Appellee
The party defending the trial court's decision on appeal.

Cross appeal
An appeal filed by the appellee of an existing appeal.

Appellant-cross appellee
The party defending the trial court's decision on appeal and initiating the cross appeal.

Appellee-cross appellant
The party initiating the appeal and defending the trial court's decision on appeal.

by the U.S. Supreme Court. In the context of this chapter, we will limit the term **appeal** to refer to a formal request for review of an order or judgment entered by a court, that seeks to reverse or modify another lower court's decision.[2]

When most people think about appeals, they imagine a case where the defendant was convicted after a trial, sentenced to prison, and then looks to a higher court for relief. While this may be a common scenario, there are other cases that end up in the appellate courts. For instance, defendants sometimes appeal orders approving plea agreements. In many jurisdictions, defendants may appeal misdemeanor convictions that did not result in a prison term.

The party initiating the appeal is called the **appellant**, and the party defending the trial court's decision on appeal is called the **appellee**. In some jurisdictions, the appealing party is known as the "petitioner" or "applicant" and the defending party is known as the "respondent." The procedures governing appeals are found in court rules or statutes.

There is no constitutional right to an appeal in a criminal case.[3] However, all states and the federal government provide some type of appellate review for defendants. At both the state and federal levels, convicted felons have a right to appeal to a higher court. Once there is a right to appeal, certain constitutional protections come into play so that defendants can effectively assert this right. For instance, indigent convicted felons are entitled to a free transcript[4] and appointed counsel for their first appeal.[5] In misdemeanor cases, defendants commonly have a right of review in the general trial court, followed by discretionary appellate review.[6]

In some cases, both sides may be unhappy with the outcome of a trial. The defense may contend that guilt was not proved while the government may object to the sentence given to the defendant. When the second party also asks for appellate review, its request is called a **cross appeal**. The parties are then referred to as the "**appellant-cross appellee**" and the "**appellee-cross appellant**."

After ruling on the post-trial motions and sentencing the defendant, the trial court judge will inform the defendant as to the right of appeal. The judge will also instruct the defendant about the rights to counsel and to be furnished with a free transcript if the defendant cannot afford them.[7] The defendant then has a narrow window of time within which to decide whether to appeal the case to a higher court. The specific filing requirements for each court can be found on their websites as well as in the published rules of the pertinent court of review.

After a notice of appeal has been filed, the trial court may take only ministerial actions,[8] such as approving a bystander's report or staying the sentence.

---

[2]Collateral proceedings, initiated through petitions for post-conviction relief or for habeas corpus, are not technically considered "appeals." However, since these remedies are used by defendants to challenge their convictions, we will discuss these actions later in the chapter. See pp. 489–493.

[3]*See McKane v. Durston*, 153 U.S. 684, 14 S. Ct. 913, 38 L. Ed. 867 (1894).

[4]*Griffin v. Illinois*, 351 U.S. 12, 76 S. Ct. 585, 100 L. Ed. 891 (1956).

[5]*Douglas v. California*, 372 U.S. 353, 83 S. Ct. 814, 9 L. Ed. 2d 811 (1963).

[6]W. LaFave, J. Isreal & N. King, *Criminal Procedure* 1273 (4th ed., West 2004).

[7]If the defendant lacks the financial resources to appeal, the court will either assign the case to a state or federal appellate defender's office or appoint counsel to represent the indigent defendant. Except in cases involving the death penalty, the constitutional right to an appeal applies only to a single appeal to the lowest-level appellate court.

[8]Procedural actions mandated by law that do not involve the exercise of discretion.

For the most part, the trial court loses jurisdiction and the appellate court is the only court with authority to act on the merits of the case. Although a trial court may not modify a judgment or otherwise make a decision on the merits of the case once a notice of appeal has been filed, it may correct the record to reflect the judgment actually entered. For instance, the trial judge is authorized to correct typographical mistakes by modifying the record *nunc pro tunc*.

Generally, the court reviewing a judicial decision is made up of at least three judges from a higher court for a particular geographic area. The reviewing court does not conduct a new trial. There are no new witnesses or additional evidence presented. Instead, the appellate panel simply reviews the record of the proceedings at the trial court and the legal arguments raised in the briefs that are filed as part of the appeals process. The outcome of the appeal is then determined by a majority vote of the judges who were assigned to review the case.

At the federal level, appeals from the U.S. district courts are decided by three-judge panels from the circuit in which the district court is located. For example, ex-Governor George Ryan appealed his public corruption conviction entered by the U.S. District Court for the Northern District of Illinois to the Seventh Circuit Court of Appeals. The appellate jurisdiction of each U.S. circuit is displayed in Figure 14.1.

The Federal Rules of Appellate Procedure (FRAP) govern the filing and processing of appeals taken from the U.S. district courts. Appeals to the decisions

Nunc pro tunc
A Latin term meaning "now for then." In the courts, this refers to the modification of an order or record retroactively to show what actually happened at the time.

Circuit	States and Territories Within Circuit's Jurisdiction
First	Maine, Massachusetts, New Hampshire, Rhode Island, and Puerto Rico
Second	Connecticut, New York, and Vermont
Third	Delaware, New Jersey, Pennsylvania, and U.S. Virgin Islands
Fourth	Maryland, North Carolina, South Carolina, Virginia, and West Virginia
Fifth	Louisiana, Mississippi, and Texas
Sixth	Kentucky, Michigan, Ohio, and Tennessee
Seventh	Illinois, Indiana, and Wisconsin
Eighth	Arkansas, Iowa, Minnesota, Missouri, Nebraska, North Dakota, and South Dakota
Ninth	Alaska, Arizona, California, Hawaii, Idaho, Nevada, Montana, Oregon, Washington, Northern Mariana Islands, and Guam
Tenth	Colorado, Kansas, New Mexico, Oklahoma, Utah, and Wyoming
Eleventh	Alabama, Florida, and Georgia
D.C.	District of Columbia

Note: There is also a United States Court of Appeals for the Federal Circuit that has nationwide jurisdiction in a number of subject areas, such as international trade, government contracts, intellectual property, veterans' benefits, and public safety officers' benefits claims.

Figure 14.1   Regional U.S. Circuit Courts of Appeals

of the federal circuit courts of appeal go to the U.S. Supreme Court and are governed by the Rules of the Supreme Court of the United States.

Most, but not all, states have a similar three-tiered judicial system, consisting of trial courts, intermediate appeals courts, and then a single state "Supreme Court."[9] The procedural rules governing the use of these courts of review usually contain the words "Rules of Appellate Procedure" somewhere in their title. Ordinarily, review of intermediate appellate court decisions is discretionary, that is, the state supreme court does not have to accept appeals from the appellate court.[10] If an appeal involves a "federal issue," the party losing in the state's highest court may petition for review in the U.S. Supreme Court. Figure 14.2 displays the path of an appeal through the state and federal court systems.

Because there are variations among the states, appellants should check the jurisdiction's statutes and rules of appellate procedure to determine the proper court for reviewing an adverse decision. Sometimes, a defendant convicted in a capital case may appeal directly to the state's highest court rather than appealing to an intermediate court.

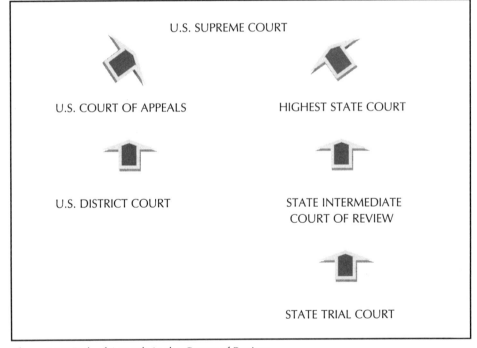

Figure 14.2 Path of Appeals in the Courts of Review

---

[9] Most states call their highest appeals court the Supreme Court, but in New York, trial courts are called "Supreme Courts," the first level of appellate courts is the "Appellate Division of the Supreme Court," and the highest-level appellate court is simply the "Court of Appeals."

[10] The one major exception is when the defendant is sentenced to death.

Once an appeal is filed, the appellant is responsible for having the clerk of the trial court and the court reporters prepare the record for transmittal to the appellate court. Typically, the clerk of the reviewing court will notify the parties of the deadlines for filing the record. There is also a time limit within which the appellant must file a written brief with the court of review. This brief presents arguments, based on facts disclosed in the record and relevant law, as to why the trial court's decision should be overturned.

The opposing side then has a specified amount of time within which to file the appellee's brief that counters the arguments contained in the appellant's brief. It will typically suggest different interpretations of the case law and often include additional cases that contradict, or at least undercut, the cases referenced by the appellant. Following the submission of the appellee's brief, the appellant gets a specified amount of time within which to file a reply brief that responds to the arguments and cases included in the appellee's brief.

Ordinarily, the reviewing court will give the attorneys an opportunity to present oral argument. Following oral argument, the court takes the case under advisement and later renders a written decision or order. The reviewing court's decision usually is subject to discretionary review by a higher court. However, the U.S. Supreme Court is extremely selective when it comes to reviewing cases and declines more than 80 percent of all appeals directed its way.[11]

APPLICATION EXERCISE

1. Based on where your school is located, find and report on the following:
   a. Where would you file an appeal for a criminal case that was tried in your local state court? (Include both the name of the court and the address of the clerk's office.)
   b. What are the time limits within which the appealing party has to file its case?
   c. What, if any, provisions are made for extending any of these deadlines?
   d. What is the time line for both the appellant and the appellee for filing copies of the record, briefs, etc.?
   e. Where would you file an appeal for a criminal case that was tried in your local federal court? (Include both the name of the court and the address of the clerk's office.)
   f. What are the time limits within which the appealing party has to file its case?
   g. What is the time line for both the appellant and the appellee for filing copies of the record, briefs, etc.?
   h. What, if any, provisions are made for extending any of these deadlines?

---

[11]Even prominent political figures like former Illinois Governor George Ryan have their appeals rejected by the U.S. Supreme Court. When Ryan lost his appeal in the Seventh Circuit by a 2–1 vote of the panel, the U.S. Supreme Court declined to review his case.

B. Timing of an Appeal

The general rule is that only final decisions can be appealed. That is, there can be no appeal from any order until the case has been completed in the trial court. For instance, if the trial judge sustains a hearsay objection to a question asked by the defense attorney, this ruling cannot be immediately appealed. Instead, the defendant must wait to appeal the ruling until the judge denies the post-trial motion and sentences the defendant. This approach promotes efficiency by requiring a party to raise all trial errors in one appeal without disrupting the completion of the trial.

Interlocutory appeal
An appeal from an order by a trial court that does not conclude the case.

In many jurisdictions, the appellate rules of procedure permit an exception to the final decision rule and provide for **interlocutory appeals** from non-final orders. For instance, in Illinois the prosecution may appeal an order suppressing evidence even though the case has not been concluded.[12] In some jurisdictions, defendants are permitted to bring interlocutory appeals to challenge a bail order.

Procedures vary from state to state, but the types of orders that the government can appeal are limited. Many jurisdictions permit the prosecution to appeal dismissals of indictments and informations, orders quashing arrests, and sentencing orders. The Fifth Amendment Double Jeopardy Clause forbids the government to appeal the defendant's acquittal. On the other hand, the defense in most jurisdictions can assert on appeal pre-trial rulings, trial errors, and the sentence imposed.

C. Steps Taken to Start the Appeals Process

After having been properly informed of their right to appeal, defendants have a narrow window of time within which to file notice of their intent to appeal the case to a higher court. If an appeal is taken, the defendant's attorney will typically petition for a stay of execution of the sentence at the time the appeal is filed. The judge may issue the stay with or without bond. If the trial judge denies the request, the defense can apply to the reviewing court for the stay. When the prosecution takes an interlocutory appeal, an incarcerated defendant will request release from custody while the appeal is pending. The judge has discretion to determine whether to issue the stay. Even in situations when release from jail is the usual practice, the judge is not required to discharge the defendant.

---

[12]Illinois Supreme Court Rule 604(a)(1) provides:

When State May Appeal. In criminal cases the State may appeal only from an order or judgment the substantive effect of which results in dismissing a charge for any of the grounds enumerated in section 114-1 of the Code of Criminal Procedure of 1963; arresting judgment because of a defective indictment, information or complaint; quashing an arrest or search warrant; suppressing evidence; decertifying a prosecution as a capital case on the grounds enumerated in section 9-1 (h-5) of the Criminal Code of 1961; or finding that the defendant is mentally retarded after a hearing conducted pursuant to section 114-15(b) of the Code of Criminal Procedure.

Paralegals are often involved in taking the steps in the trial court to have the case reviewed by an appellate court. We will now discuss the paperwork used to initiate an appeal.

1. FILING THE NOTICE OF APPEAL

The first step in starting the appellate process is the filing of a document known as a **notice of appeal** with the clerk of the trial court, who will then transmit the notice of appeal to the clerk of the appellate court. The notice is a relatively simple form to draft. In many jurisdictions, the clerk of the court provides notice of appeal forms.[13] Exhibit 14.1 displays the official form used by defendants in Colorado criminal cases. Notice of appeal templates also appear in formbooks. (Exhibit 14.2 is the template for the U.S. Attorney's notice of appeal form used in criminal cases.)

Notice of appeal
A formal document filed with the clerk of the trial court stating that a party is appealing the decision of the trial court.

Exhibit 14.1: State Court Notice of Appeal Form for Defendant

☐ County Court   ☐ District Court

_____ County, Colorado

Court Address:

_____

State of Colorado/Appellee:

v.

▲   ▲

Defendant/Appellant: **COURT USE ONLY**

---

[13]*See, e.g.,* Illinois Supreme Court Rule 606(a).

Attorney or Party Without Attorney (Name and Address):	Case Number:
Phone Number: E-mail: FAX Number: Atty. Reg. #:	Division Courtroom

NOTICE OF APPEAL AND DESIGNATION OF RECORD - CRIMINAL

The Defendant hereby files an appeal in _____ (County Court case number) for the following reason(s):

_____

_____

_____

☐ At this time, I request a stay of execution. I understand that as a condition of the stay of execution, I may be required to post a bond or deposit the amount of fines and costs assessed.

Current information about the Appellant/Defendant:

Full Name: _____

Mailing Address:_____

City & Zip:_____

Home Phone #: _____ Work Phone #: _____ Cell#: _____

Designation of Record:

The clerk of court will prepare the record on appeal, pursuant to Rule 37, Rules of Criminal Procedure and will include the following items:

    ☐ The county court case file, including all pleadings, motions, reports, exhibits, orders of the court, and jury instructions, if applicable.
    ☐ The original transcript: (identify proceedings).

    _____

    _____

Date: _____

_____   _____
Signature of Defendant/Appellant   Signature of Attorney for Defendant/Appellant, if applicable

Exhibit 14.2: Federal Notice of Appeal Form for Government

UNITED STATES DISTRICT COURT FOR THE

DISTRICT OF _____

UNITED STATES OF AMERICA,	)	
Plaintiff	)	
v.	)	Case No. _____
[NAME OF DEFENDANT],	)	
Defendant.	)	

NOTICE OF APPEAL

Notice is hereby given that the United States of America, plaintiff in the above-captioned case, hereby appeals to the United States Court of Appeals for the Circuit from the order of this Court [*describe order appealed from*], entered on [*date order was entered*]. [If the order appealed from is an order suppressing or excluding evidence or requiring the return of seized property, include the following language: "I hereby certify that the appeal is not taken for purpose of delay and that the evidence is a substantial proof of a fact material in the proceeding."].

[SIGNATURE BLOCK]

Source: United States Attorneys' Manual (USAM), Title 9 Criminal Resource Manual 22 Notice of Appeal Form *http://www.justice.gov/usao/eousa/foia_reading_room/usam/title9/crm00022.htm*

The party filing the notice of appeal must send a copy of the notice to the other party in the case. Customarily, the appellant will also send the appellee "a notice of filing notice of appeal." The notice of filing will inform the opposing party of the date on which the notice of appeal was filed. An example of a notice of filing notice of appeal is displayed in Exhibit 14.3.

Notice of filing notice of appeal
A document filed with the clerk and served on the opposing party stating the date on which the appellant filed a notice of appeal.

Exhibit 14.3: Notice of Filing Notice of Appeal

THE UNITED STATES DISTRICT COURT

FOR THE NORTHERN DISTRICT OF INDIANA

HAMMOND DIVISION

UNITED STATES OF AMERICA	)	
vs.	)	Case No. 09 CR XXX
WILLIAM EDWARDS,	)	
Defendant.	)	

NOTICE OF FILING NOTICE OF APPEAL

Now comes Defendant WILLIAM EDWARDS, by CHARLES HOVEY, his attorney, and hereby gives notice that on the XXth day of XXXXXXXX, 20XX, he filed a notice of appeal with the office of the U.S. District Clerk before the hour of 4:30 p.m.

Respectfully submitted,

WILLIAM EDWARDS, Defendant

By_____

CHARLES HOVEY, his attorney

Charles Hovey

Attorney for Defendant

1857 Bone Street

Normal, IL 61617

(309) 555-1857

Certificate of Service

I hereby certify that a true and accurate copy of the foregoing Defendant's Initial Discovery Request was served upon _____, Assistant U.S. Attorney by depositing the same in the U.S. Post Office mailbox in Chicago, Illinois in an envelope, postage fully prepaid, addressed to: Office of the United States Attorney [Address of U.S. Attorney] on the _____ day of _____, 20____ at or about the hour of _____ p.m.

_____

APPLICATION EXERCISES

2. Prepare a notice of appeal in the *Brandon Turner* case using the appropriate form for the state in which your school is located. Assume the following: The trial court's decision became final five days before your assignment is due; the basis of the appeal is that the government presented evidence of a domestic violence order of protection entered against the defendant fifteen years ago over the objection of the defense; the case was heard by the felony judge who customarily decides cases stemming from crimes committed in the place where your school is located; the defense attorney is Charles Hovey and his contact information is listed in the above exhibit; and the defendant currently lives at your address.

3. Prepare a notice of filing notice of appeal in the *Brandon Turner* case using the appropriate form for the state in which your school is located. Assume the facts set forth in the preceding exercise.

The deadline for filing a notice of appeal varies from jurisdiction to jurisdiction. In some states, parties may have as long as sixty days in which to file their appeal. The federal deadlines are much shorter. FRAP 4 (b)(1) provides:

> (A) In a criminal case, a defendant's notice of appeal must be filed in the district court within 14 days after the later of:
> (i) the entry of either the judgment or the order being appealed; or
> (ii) the filing of the government's notice of appeal.
> (B) When the government is entitled to appeal, its notice of appeal must be filed in the district court within 30 days after the later of:
> (i) the entry of the judgment or order being appealed; or
> (ii) the filing of a notice of appeal by any defendant.

Generally, the time for filing the notice of appeal is computed from the date on which the trial judge rules on any post-trial motion. It is extremely important to check a state's filing deadline because the reviewing court may not acquire jurisdiction if the notice is filed late. In some jurisdictions, there are safety net provisions for extreme circumstances when the notice of appeal was not filed by the deadline. For instance, Illinois Supreme Court Rule 606(c) creates thirty-day and six-month safety nets. On the other hand, failure to file the notice of appeal on time may result in a dismissal of the appeal. This, in turn, will eliminate the client's prospects for overturning the trial court's decision and may lead to a legal malpractice case against the lawyer who failed to act diligently. The Texas appellate court's decision in *Strange v. Texas* is typical of the way in which these deadlines are enforced.

Strange v. Texas
Appellate Court of Texas
258 S.W.3d 184 (1ˢᵗ Dist. Tex. App., 2007)

OPINION BY: CHIEF JUSTICE RADACK, joined by JUSTICES ALCALA and BLAND.

On November 6, 2007, this Court considered the State's motions to dismiss these appeals for lack of jurisdiction. The State contends that appellant, Mark Allen Strange, did not timely perfect his appeals. Appellant does not dispute that his notices of appeal were file-marked beyond the deadline imposed by the Rules of Appellate Procedure, but contends that the late filing resulted from clerical error. We grant the State's motions and dismiss the appeals for lack of jurisdiction.

Background

Appellant, Mark Allen Strange, waived a jury trial and was convicted of two first-degree felony offenses of misapplication of fiduciary property. *See* TEX. PEN. CODE ANN. § 32.45(c) (7) (Vernon Supp. 2006). The trial court assessed punishment at 15 years' confinement for each offense, to run concurrently, and signed the judgments on November 10, 2005. No party filed a motion for new trial.

Jurisdiction

Ascertaining whether this Court has jurisdiction is a threshold issue in every case. . . . We have no authority to dispose of a pending controversy unless our jurisdiction has been invoked. . . .
Article 44.02 of the Code of Criminal Procedure codifies a convicted defendant's right to appeal his criminal conviction. . . . Rule 25.2 of the Rules of Appellate Procedure restricts a defendant's right of appeal in certain cases, none of which applies here. . . .
Our jurisdiction over a criminal appeal derives from Article V, section 1 of the Texas Constitution and the Code of Criminal Procedure. . . .

A. Prerequisites to Invoking This Court's Jurisdiction

Rules 25.2 and 26.2 impose the procedural prerequisites by which a defendant may invoke the criminal appellate jurisdiction vested in this Court by the Texas Constitution and the Code of Criminal Procedure. . . .

1. Deadline to File Notices of Appeal—Rules 25.2(b), (c)(1), 26.2(a)

Rule 25.2(b) applies to all non-death-penalty cases. TEX. R. APP. P. 25.2(b). Pursuant to this rule, appellant had to perfect his appeals by "timely filing a sufficient notice of appeal" for each trial-court cause. . . . A notice of appeal must be in writing and must be filed with the clerk of the trial court. . . .
No motion for new trial was filed in either trial-court cause. Therefore, to meet rule 25.2(b)'s timeliness requirement and to invoke this Court's jurisdiction, appellant had to file his notices of appeal with the clerk of the trial court within the 30 days after the trial court signed the judgments. . . .
In this case, the trial court signed the judgments in both causes on Thursday, November 10, 2005. Accordingly, appellant's notices of appeal were due to be filed by Monday, December 12, 2005. . . .

2. Alternative Deadline to File Motion to Extend Deadline—Rule 26.3

This Court may extend a deadline for filing a notice of appeal, provided an appellant complies with rule 26.3. . . . But this rule, too, imposes a time limit. . . . To have invoked our rule 26.3 authority, appellant had to (1) file notices of appeal for both trial-court causes in the trial court and (2) file motions requesting an extension of time with this Court within the 15 days after the notices of appeal were due. . . . Because the notices of appeal were due on Monday, December 12, 2005, appellant had to invoke our rule 26.3 authority by Tuesday, December 27, 2005. The limited, 15-day extended time period applies to both the notice and the motion for extension; both must be filed within the 15-day time period.

B. Prerequisites to Exercise of Jurisdiction Not Met

Appellant directs our attention to the preliminary steps he took to appeal his convictions on November 30, 2005, when the trial court signed the judgments. On that day, appellant filed and presented to the trial court a single-page document pertaining to both trial-court cause numbers. This document contained (1) appellant's pauper's oath, in which (2) he also requested that counsel be appointed for appeal and (3) that the reporter's record be prepared. On that same day, November 30, 2005, the trial court endorsed appellant's oath and signed orders that appointed counsel for appeal and ordered the court reporter to prepare the reporter's record.

Appellant did nothing further to perfect his appeal until January 10, 2006, when the district clerk filed appellant's notices of appeal. Appellant neither filed his notices of appeal by the December 12, 2005 deadline, nor moved to extend the December 12, 2005 deadline pursuant to rule 26.3. Appellant did not, therefore, comply with rule 26.2's mandate that the "written notice of appeal must be filed with the clerk's office within thirty days of sentencing" in a case in which no motion for new trial has been filed. . . . Accordingly, this Court never acquired jurisdiction over the appeals.

Appellant does not dispute the January 10, 2006 filing dates stamped on his notices of appeal by the Harris County District Clerk. January 10, 2006 was 29 days after December 12, 2005, when the notices were initially due to be filed, pursuant to rule 26.2(a), and 14 days after December 27, 2005, the last possible date for a timely rule 26.3 motion in this Court.

C. Filing Error by District Clerk?

Appellant's response to the State's motion to dismiss his appeals acknowledges that his notices of appeal were not marked "filed" until January 10, 2006, but he contends that the file mark constitutes a "clerical error" by the district clerk. Appellant explains the late file marking on the face of the notice as a mere "discrepancy" between actual *presentment* of the notice to the trial court, which occurred on November 30, 2005, and *receipt* of the notice by the district clerk, which did not occur until January 10, 2006.

Appellant's contentions disregard that he had to invoke this Court's jurisdiction by *filing* his notice of appeal *timely* with the clerk of the trial court. *See Few v. State,* 230 S.W.3d 184, 189 (Tex. Crim. App. 2007). ("In a criminal case, appeal is perfected by timely filing a sufficient notice of appeal.") (quoting TEX. R. APP. P. 25.2(b)); . . . . Appellant has not provided us any authority—and we know of none—on which we may rely to support exercise of our appellate jurisdiction based solely on timely "presentment" of a notice of appeal to a trial court, despite late filing with the clerk.

Appellant relies on the following recital in the late-filed notices of appeal: "On *November 30, 2005,* [appellant] *gives* NOTICE OF APPEAL of his conviction." (Emphasis added.) But rules 25.2(b) and (c)(1) do not address either "giving" or "presenting" the notice of appeal, but, rather, unequivocally require that notices be "*filed*" with the clerk in order to perfect an appeal and vest jurisdiction with this Court". . . . A document is "filed" "when it is placed in the custody or control of the clerk.". . . As filed with this Court, the record on appeal shows that appellant's notices were not marked as filed until January 10, 2006 and, thus, too late.

In addition to reaffirming the filing requirement in *Stansberry v. State,* No. PD-0867-06, 239 S.W.3d 260, 2007 Tex. Crim. App. LEXIS 861, 2007 WL 1828901, the Court of Criminal Appeals also recognized that "a litigant who properly pursues his right to appeal should not be prejudiced by a clerk's error that prevents the timely filing of a notice of appeal. . . . " Accordingly, "[i]f a document would have been timely filed but for an error by an employee of the court, then the document is considered to be timely filed." The exception to the filing requirement recognized in *Stansberry* does not apply.

In this case, the notices of appeal appear in the record and were undisputedly filed late. In

Stansberry, the record did not contain a "tangible, written notice of appeal" from which a filing date might be determined. . . . In this case, appellant contends that clerical error is the only possible means of explaining the late file-marking on the notices of appeal. But in *Stansberry,* in contrast to this case, the claim of clerical error was well-founded in the record, not disputed by the State, and supported by express findings by the trial court that the notice had been filed, all of which circumstances compelled the conclusion that clerical error had occurred. In this case, appellant's claim lacks any evidentiary support in the record. Indeed, the record contravenes appellant's claim.

At Stansberry's plea hearing, his trial counsel stated on the record that he would be filing a notice of appeal, and that the notice would be filed as soon as the hearing concluded. . . . There are no similar oral pronouncements in this case. When Stansberry's newly appointed appellate counsel could not locate a notice of appeal in the clerk's file, he filed a motion asking to amend any notice that might exist and also contacted Stansberry's trial counsel, who provided affidavits attesting that the notice had been timely filed. Appellate counsel filed these affidavits with the trial court, which conducted a hearing on the timeliness issue, during which the State did not challenge either the affidavits or appellate counsel's assertions. The hearing concluded with "an express finding" by the trial court that Stansberry had timely filed his notice of appeal. . . .

Though acknowledging the significance of lack of a "tangible, written notice of appeal" in the clerk's record, the Court of Criminal Appeals held that the "circumstances demonstrated by the record" compelled holding that (1) "a clerical error occurred at some point in time between the moment the notice was tendered to the clerk['s] custody and the moment the omission was discovered" and, therefore, (2) that Stansberry had satisfied rule 25.2. . . .

In this case, we have neither findings by the trial court that would support a claim of clerical error, nor any proof that would have supported such findings and, thus, no circumstances like those in *Stansberry* that would warrant our holding that clerical error thwarted appellant's compliance with rule 25.2(b). In contrast to the lack of a "tangible, written" and filed notice of appeal in *Stansberry*, the clerk's records in both of appellant's attempted appeals contain tangible, written, and filed notices of appeal, each of which demonstrates on its face that appellant did not comply timely with rule 25.2(b) and (c)(1) when the notices were "placed in the custody or control of the clerk" on January 10, 2006.

By arguing that clerical error occurred without offering evidence to support that argument, appellant seemingly contends that the notices of appeal he "presented" to the trial court on November 30, 2005 were either lost, overlooked, or somehow misplaced, in dereliction of the clerk's duties imposed by TEX. R. APP. P. 25.2(e), until they were discovered and marked as filed on January 10, 2006. We disagree, because appellant's notices of appeal contain additional, adverse information that precludes applying *Stansberry*'s rule of clerical error to this case.

Based solely on the file stamps placed on the notices of appeal by the district clerk, the notices of appeal were not "tendered" to and thus not "filed" until January 10, 2006. . . . In addition, however, each notice contains a paragraph by appellant's "undersigned attorney," in which appellant's counsel reported to the trial court that (1) he would continue to represent appellant on appeal and that (2) appellant was indigent. In addition to signing this portion of the notices of appeal, appellant's counsel recorded the date on which he made these representations to the trial court. The date counsel provided is January 10, 2006, specifically, the same date on which the district clerk marked the notices filed.

Because the date on which appellant's counsel provided the additional information in the notices is the same date on which the clerk marked the notices as filed, the record of this case compels the conclusion that appellant's counsel did not tender the notices for filing any earlier than January 10, 2006. In contrast to the record in *Stansberry*, which compelled a conclusion of clerical error, the record of this case negates that claim.

We also reject appellant's reliance on the trial court's having certified appellant's right to appeal both causes, as required by rule 25.2(e). . . . Appellant contends that, by certifying his right to appeal, the trial court "clearly recognized" the clerk's clerical error. Nothing in the certification by the trial court supports this contention. In certifying appellant's right to appeal, the trial court stated only that, appellant's case "is not a plea-bargain case, and [appellant] has the right of appeal."

For the reasons stated in this opinion, we grant the State's motions to dismiss the appeals.

Conclusion

We dismiss the appeals for lack of jurisdiction.

CASE DISCUSSION QUESTIONS

1. What actions did Strange take to appeal his case, and why weren't they considered adequate?

2. What does it take to "file" an appeal in the Texas courts? How does "filing" differ from "giving notice"?

3. What was the *Stansberry* case about and why didn't it apply to Strange's situation?

4. What was the significance of the fact that the trial court "certified" appellant's right to appeal?

5. To what extent do you think Strange, rather than his appointed attorney, should be held responsible for the late filing?

Once the reviewing court receives the notice of appeal from the trial court, it will notify the parties of the appellate case number. From that point forward, all documents concerning the appeal, such as docketing statements and briefs, are filed with the clerk of the court of review. The trial court usually will only handle motions to stay enforcement of the sentence and other ministerial matters until the reviewing court makes its decision.

2. ORDERING THE RECORD

The appellant is charged with the responsibility of requesting the clerk of the trial court to prepare the record. Usually the clerk must be asked to prepare the common law record and the court reporter to prepare the report of proceedings. Some courts provide fill-in-the-blank forms for this purpose. The Colorado notice of appeal form (reproduced in Exhibit 14.1) includes a section in which the appealing party makes this request. In other jurisdictions, the appellants do not submit standard forms but must certify to the appellate court that the record has been ordered.[14] It is best to make the requests in writing even if the attorney has a trusting relationship with the clerk and the court reporters. Indeed, if the attorney needs to file a motion for extension of time to file the record, the written request for the record is helpful documentation.

If no court reporter was present and the docket sheet does not completely reflect what took place in court, the attorney may need to reconstruct what occurred so that the appellate court has a sufficient record to consider all of the issues. This can be accomplished through a **bystander's report**. The procedure for obtaining the bystander's report varies from jurisdiction to jurisdiction. Customarily, the appellant's attorney prepares a proposed report that reflects what he or she recalls took place in court on specified date(s). The appellant then notices a motion for approval of the proposed report. Sometimes, the appellee will present an alternative proposed report. The trial judge conducts a hearing to determine what should be included in the bystander's report. The report approved by the judge is forwarded to the appellate court as part of the record on appeal.

Bystander's report
A statement approved by the trial judge as to what happened in court.

---

[14]For example, Illinois Supreme Court Rule 606(g).

D. THE RECORD ON APPEAL

In addition to alleging that errors have been made, the appellant must be able to provide documentation that the alleged errors did indeed occur. This is done by referencing specific parts of the official court records for the case.

Appellants are required to provide the appellate court with what is commonly referred to as the **record on appeal** (commonly referred to as "the record"). It consists of three parts:

- the original papers and exhibits filed in the trial court;
- the docketing sheet accompanying the court file; and
- the transcripts of court proceedings.

Record on appeal ("the record")
The common law record and the report of proceedings.

The first two parts are collectively referred to as the **common law record**, whereas the transcripts of witness testimony as well as the statements made by the judge or lawyers about the case in court are called the **report of proceedings**. (See Figure 14.3 for a listing of the typical components of the record on appeal.)

Common law record
All documents contained in the case file in the trial court, including the docketing statement, exhibits, jury instructions, etc.

Report of proceedings
The transcripts of testimony as well as any other oral statements made in the trial court.

APPLICATION EXERCISES

4. Prepare a letter directed to the official court reporter in the *Brandon Turner* case requesting the preparation of the transcripts of all proceedings. Assume the following: The case was heard by the felony judge who customarily decides cases stemming from crimes committed in the place where your school is located; your supervisor is the prosecutor for the state court jurisdiction in which your school is located; the case was the first felony case filed last year in that jurisdiction; and the court reporter Lee Eastgate's office is located at the local courthouse.

5. Prepare a letter directed to the clerk of the court in the *Brandon Turner* case requesting the preparation of the common law record for all proceedings. Assume the following: Your supervisor is the prosecutor for the state court jurisdiction in which your school is located and the case was the first felony case filed last year in that jurisdiction.

On the record
Statements made in court that are recorded by either a court reporter or by the clerk of the court as a written entry in the case file.

As discussed in Chapter 12, attorneys must make sure the record reflects the various motions and objections made, even if they don't expect the judge to grant them. If they fail to file their motions or make their objections at the appropriate times, they lose their chance to raise these issues on appeal. All objections must be made "**on the record,**" that is, either stenographically recorded by a court reporter or written on the docket sheet. If the error is not on the record, the appellate court will not be able to determine whether the trial court made a mistake. This is because appellate courts do not hear from witnesses but instead examine the documents before them.

Illinois Supreme Court Rule 608(a) lists the required parts of the record on appeal as follows:

(1) a cover sheet showing the title of the case;

(2) a certificate of the clerk showing the impaneling of the grand jury if the prosecution was commenced by indictment;

(3) the indictment, information, or complaint;

(4) a transcript of the proceedings at the defendant's arraignment and plea;

(5) all motions, transcript of motion proceedings, and orders entered thereon;

(6) all arrest warrants, search warrants, consent to search forms, eavesdropping orders, and any similar documents;

(7) a transcript of proceedings regarding waiver of counsel and waiver of jury trial, if any;

(8) the report of proceedings, including opening statements by counsel, testimony offered at trial, and objections thereto, offers of proof, arguments and rulings thereon, the instructions offered and given, and the objections and rulings thereon, closing argument of counsel, communications from the jury during deliberations, and responses and supplemental instructions to the jury and objections, arguments and rulings thereon;

(9) in cases in which a sentence of death is imposed, a transcript of all proceedings regarding the selection of the jury, . . .;

(10) exhibits offered at trial and sentencing, along with objections, offers of proof, arguments, and rulings thereon; except that physical and demonstrative evidence, other than photographs, which do not fit on a standard size record page shall not be included in the record on appeal unless ordered by a court upon motion of a party or upon the court's own motion;

(11) the verdict of the jury or finding of the court;

(12) post-trial motions, including motions for a new trial, motions in arrest of judgment, motions for judgment notwithstanding the verdict and the testimony, arguments and rulings thereon;

(13) a transcript of proceedings at sentencing, including the presentence investigation report, testimony offered and objections thereto, offers of proof, argument, and rulings thereon, arguments of counsel, and statements by the defendant and the court;

(14) the judgment and sentence; and

(15) the notice of appeal, if any.

Figure 14.3 Components of Record on Appeal

For example, in order to make a successful *Batson* claim of systematic exclusion of African Americans from a jury,[15] the record must reveal the races of

---

[15]See discussion in Chapter 12, pp. 404–409, of *Batson v. Kentucky*, 476 U.S. 79, 106 S. Ct. 1712, 90 L. Ed. 2d 69 (1986).

Offer of proof
A procedure whereby excluded testimony is placed into the record for possible appellate review of the judge's decision to exclude it.

Waiver rule
The rule of appellate procedure that an issue not presented in the trial court is waived and cannot be argued on appeal.

Plain error
The exception to the waiver rule that permits an appellant to raise on appeal a mistake that was not preserved in the trial court because it was a highly prejudicial error affecting the fundamental rights of the defendant.

Harmless error
A mistake that is not considered prejudicial enough to justify overturning the court's decision/action.

Reversible error
A mistake that is considered sufficiently prejudicial to warrant reversing the trial court's decision/action.

Cumulative error
The prejudicial impact of a series of two or more trial errors that do not warrant reversal of a case when viewed separately but collectively amount to reversible error.

the jurors selected as well as the races of the prospective jurors who were subject to the prosecution's peremptory challenges. If this information is absent, the appellate court cannot conclude that African Americans were systematically excluded from the jury. Similarly, if the trial judge sustains an objection to a question asked of a witness, the attorney must make an **offer of proof** in order to show the expected testimony. This is a procedure whereby the attorney either (1) tells the judge what the witness would have testified to if the judge had not sustained the objection to admitting it or (2) elicits the challenged testimony from the witness. In either event, the court reporter records the offer of proof. The contested testimony is taken outside the presence of the jury so the jury won't be influenced by what the judge excluded. This procedure allows the appellate court to decide whether the absence of the testimony harmed the appellant's case. Without the offer of proof, the reviewing court cannot conclude that the trial judge's ruling prejudiced the appellant.

As we noted in Chapter 13, following the trial, attorneys present all trial and pre-trial errors in the post-trial motion. Although redundant, this action not only protects the record but also gives the trial judge one last opportunity to review and correct mistakes in a less pressured environment than the heat of trial. If an issue is not presented in the trial court or is omitted from the post-trial motion, it is considered to have been waived and cannot be argued on appeal. This policy is known as the "**waiver rule**."

There is, however, an exception to the waiver rule when the mistake at trial is a highly prejudicial error affecting the fundamental rights of the defendant. These types of errors are referred to as "**plain error**." Since courts of review are reluctant to characterize an error as "plain error," careful litigators will present the issue in pre-trial motions, make timely objections at trial, and include all issues for a second time in their post-trial motions.

E. IDENTIFICATION OF MATTERS THAT CAN BE APPEALED

An appeal of a judge or jury's decision cannot be successfully made solely on the basis of not liking the outcome. The appeal must allege that one or more legally significant errors were made at trial. Furthermore, these mistakes must be sufficiently serious to have affected the outcome of the case.

Errors that do not meet this standard are classified as **harmless errors** and cannot be used as a basis for overturning a lower court's action. Examples of harmless errors include (1) a mistake in the pleadings if the facts can be determined at trial; (2) errors in jury instructions unless there is reason to believe that they actually misled the jury; and (3) the failure to strictly follow the rules of evidence in a bench trial, as it is assumed a judge is unlikely to be affected by incompetent evidence. In contrast, errors that could have changed the result in the case are classified as **reversible errors**. Examples of these reversible errors would include failure to exclude evidence that was illegally obtained or failure to allow testimony from a competent witness when the testimony was relevant and material.

Sometimes several errors occur in the trial of a case but none is sufficient by itself to warrant reversal. However, when the errors are viewed together, the appellate court may conclude that **cumulative error** prevented the defendant from receiving a fair trial. In these circumstances, the court of review will reverse the verdict and remand the case to the lower court to conduct a new trial.

F. STANDARDS USED IN APPELLATE REVIEW

At the trial court level, the defendant is presumed to be innocent and the prosecution has the burden of proving guilt beyond a reasonable doubt. But when the case proceeds to the appellate level, the burdens and standards of proof change. At the appellate level, the appellant carries the burden of proving that a reversible error occurred at the trial court level. Furthermore, the standard of proof used in appellate courts depends on whether the decision being reviewed involves the facts of the case or the interpretation and application of the law.

Appellate judges will generally defer to the findings made by trial judges and juries with regard to factual issues. Unless the appellant can prove that the trial court's findings of fact were **clearly erroneous**, they will not overturn them. This deference is based on the fact that the judge and jury were in the better position to reach these judgments about the facts by virtue of their having been able to personally observe the demeanor, body language, etc. of the witnesses.

Clearly erroneous
The standard used by appellate courts when reviewing a trial court's findings of fact in which appellate judges defer to conclusions reached by the trial judge or jurors unless appellant demonstrates that those findings were clearly unreasonable.

Appellate judges also give great deference to the trial judge's case management decisions, such as permission to amend a complaint or a denial of a request for a continuance. They will only reverse in these types of situations if the appellant can prove the judge committed a clear error of judgment, lacked the authority to act, or acted with prejudice or malice.

On the other hand, if it is reviewing a decision involving the interpretation or application of a statute or court decision, such as a trial judge's ruling on the admissibility of evidence, the appropriateness of a line of questioning, or the nature of the jury instructions, the appellate judges will make their own independent review without any deference being given to the trial judge's decision.

Situations can also arise where the resolution of a legal issue requires the court to review the facts. For example, when a party appeals based on the trial judge's decision to deny a motion for a directed verdict, the appellant is arguing that the evidence was so one-sided it could support only one conclusion. Because the appellate judges are ruling on a motion, it is a legal question. However, before they can reach a decision on this issue, they must make their own judgment about the strength of the evidence itself. In these mixed fact/law situations, the appellate court judges may end up making an independent review of the facts.

It is important to remember that even where the appellant has met the stiff burden of convincing an appellate court that legal errors were made, the previously convicted defendant may still wind up with the same, or even a worse, sentence. Not only can a lower-level appellate court be reversed by a higher-level appellate court, but an appellate reversal may lead to a "re-do" in which the conviction or sentence is reinstated after the remaining "appropriate evidence" is reheard.

G. ALTERNATIVE WAYS OF CHALLENGING TRIAL COURT DECISIONS

As we have seen, direct appeals must take place within specific, limited time periods after the completion of the trial. But what about the situation in which new evidence of the defendant's innocence (such as DNA test results that weren't available at the time of the trial, or a confession from the real killer) doesn't come to light until after this limited time frame has expired? Although there appears to be a strong national consensus that the execution of innocent convicts should be prohibited, whether that innocence is proved before or after trial, there is still much controversy over how that is to be accomplished.

One approach is to seek executive clemency by asking for a pardon or commutation of sentence. Federal defendants petition the President, and state defendants petition the governor of the state. More often, those who believe they have been unjustly convicted return to the courts to seek collateral remedies, such as petitioning for a writ of habeas corpus or for post-conviction relief to gain their release from incarceration.

Collateral remedies
Actions designed to challenge judgments of conviction that have otherwise become final in the normal appellate review process.

A **collateral remedy** is an action designed to challenge a judgment of conviction that has become final in the normal appellate review process. It is commonly used in situations in which new evidence has come to light. A **writ of habeas corpus** is a court document ordering public officials to produce the person named so that a neutral judge can determine if there is a lawful basis for detaining that person. It was designed to protect against authorities incarcerating someone for indefinite periods of time without legal authority to do so, but it can also be used as a way of challenging a prisoner's conviction or sentence. Most jurisdictions have enacted statutes that offer convicted persons the opportunity to petition for **post-conviction relief**. Both habeas corpus and post-conviction relief proceedings are highly technical. Unless you work for a criminal attorney specializing in this area of practice, you probably will not encounter these types of proceeding often.

Writ of habeas corpus
A court document ordering public officials to produce the person named so that a neutral judge can determine if there is a lawful basis for detaining that person.

Because a petition for a writ of habeas corpus is technically not an appeal of a conviction, but a new civil action by the individual against the government, the first step usually involves filing for a writ in the state trial court. In a sense, this action is like a new trial, so if it is unsuccessful, the individual appeals the rejection through the state appellate system. After exhausting habeas appeals in the state system, the inmate can seek a writ in the federal system. This federal petition is somewhat akin to yet another, separate trial, and starts in the U.S. district court. If the inmate is unsuccessful there, he or she can appeal to the U.S. Circuit Court of Appeals, and then to the U.S. Supreme Court.

Post-conviction relief
A statutory collateral challenge to a judgment of conviction.

In the 1990s, there were numerous attempts to streamline the habeas process because of criticisms that it provided death row inmates with endless opportunities to delay their day of reckoning. In 1995, the Supreme Court ruled that, under most circumstances, inmates could file only one petition for a writ of habeas corpus.[16] Instead of being able to spend years developing new petitions on different issues, the petitioner was required to place every argument possible in one petition. That same year, Congress eliminated funding for Post-Conviction Capital Defender Organizations that did the research necessary for many inmates' lawyers to adequately develop habeas claims. Then in 1966, Congress passed the Antiterrorism and Effective Death Penalty Act,[17] which attempted to curb the number of death row inmates' habeas petitions by strengthening the prohibition against multiple petitions, limiting the time in which a federal or state

---

[16]*Schlup v. Delo*, 513 U.S. 298, 115 S. Ct. 851, 130 L. Ed. 2d 808 (1995).

[17]28 U.S.C. § 509.

inmate can file a habeas petition in federal court,[18] and directing federal courts to presume that state courts' habeas decisions are constitutional.[19]

Critics of this legislation argue that most inmates are unable to meet either the six-month or the one-year deadline for filing a federal habeas petition because such deadlines fail to recognize that proper preparation for such a proceeding requires, among other things, a complete reinvestigation of the entire case, which includes a review of the crime itself and factors not presented at trial that might have led to a non-death sentence.[20] Critics also argue that the presumption of constitutionality that the federal courts must now give state court procedures in habeas petitions will make it very difficult for errors in state courts to be rectified.[21]

The Supreme Court upheld the Antiterrorism Act's limits on federal habeas petitions in *Felker v. Turpin*.[22] The Opinion of the Court declared that although the Act did affect the standards governing the granting of such relief, it did not preclude the Court from entertaining an application for habeas corpus relief. Therefore, the provisions in question did not violate Article I, Section 9, of the U.S. Constitution's declaration that "the privilege of the Writ of Habeas Corpus shall not be suspended, unless when in Cases of Rebellion or Invasion the public Safety may require it."

The *In re Davis* case[23] illustrates not only the difficulty of getting a court to review a conviction but also the length of time a case can remain in the court system. In a 1991 trial in the Georgia criminal courts, Troy Davis was convicted of murder and sentenced to death for the 1989 killing of a police officer in Savannah. Troy continued to insist he was innocent and began a long process of appeals that eventually attracted international attention when he received support from former President Jimmy Carter and Pope Benedict XVI. After his motion for new trial was denied, Davis appealed directly to the Georgia Supreme Court, which unanimously affirmed his convictions and the capital sentence. In November 1993, the U.S. Supreme Court denied his petition for a writ of certiorari.

In March of 1994, Davis filed a petition for a writ of habeas corpus in the Georgia Superior Court. It held an evidentiary hearing in December 1996 in

---

[18]If an inmate did not have counsel for any post-conviction proceeding, then he or she has one year from the date the conviction becomes final to file a federal habeas petition. In other words, the inmate has one year from the final appeal of the conviction to file that petition. If the inmate had counsel for any post-conviction proceeding, then he or she has six months to file a federal habeas petition.

[19]"[P]rovided these determinations are neither 'contrary to' nor an 'unreasonable' application of' clearly established Federal law as determined by the Supreme Court." Previously, federal courts could consider the federal constitutional issues raised in a habeas petition without deferring to state court holdings on that petitioner's earlier (and rejected) state habeas petition.

[20]This deadline is particularly difficult to meet given the demise of the post-conviction defendant resource centers.

[21]For example, Ronald J. Tabak argues "the 'reform' legislation would make it far more difficult to secure a federal evidentiary hearing, even where crucial facts were not developed in state court through no fault of the death row inmate." See *Capital Punishment: Is There Any Habeas Left in This Corpus?* 27 Loy. U. Chi. L.J. 523.

[22]518 U.S. 651, 116 S. Ct. 2333, 135 L. Ed. 2d 827 (1996).

[23]2010 U.S. Dist. LEXIS 87340 (S.D. Ga August 24, 2010), *appeal dismissed*, 625 F.3d 716 (11th Cir. 2010), *writ denied* 2011 U.S. LEXIS 2433 (U.S. Mar. 28, 2011).

which Davis submitted six affidavits purporting to establish his innocence.[24] However, the court did not find these affidavits to be a sufficient basis for reviewing the case and, in September 1997, denied his petition. Davis unsuccessfully appealed this denial to the Georgia Supreme Court and then to the U.S. Supreme Court.

In December 2001, Davis filed a habeas corpus petition in the federal district court. As part of this petition, his lawyers included sixteen new innocence affidavits along with the six they had submitted as part of his state habeas petition. In March 2003, the district court denied Davis's request for an evidentiary hearing to receive live testimony from the affiants, and in May 2004, the district court denied the petition.[25] In September 2006, the Eleventh Circuit Court of Appeals affirmed the district court's decision.[26] And in June 2007, the U.S. Supreme Court denied Mr. Davis's petition for writ of certiorari.

The next stage in this very drawn out process involved the filing of a motion for a new trial in Chatham County Superior Court in July 2007. In this motion, Davis directly argued that he was innocent and that new evidence showed a man named Coles had murdered the policeman. In support of his claim, twenty-six innocence affidavits were presented, the bulk of which were the same affidavits Mr. Davis presented in his state and federal habeas petitions. When this motion was denied, a divided Georgia Supreme Court affirmed the denial. The three justices in the minority reasoned that the trial court should at least "conduct a hearing, to weigh the credibility of Davis's new evidence, and to exercise its discretion in determining if the new evidence would create the probability of a different outcome if a new trial were held."[27]

Following the denial of this latest motion for a new trial, Davis submitted an application for executive clemency to the Georgia State Board of Pardons and Paroles. In reviewing his case, the board allowed Davis's attorneys "to present every witness they desired to support their allegation that there is doubt as to Davis' guilt." The board also reviewed the trial transcript, the police investigation report, and the initial statements of all witnesses. Following its review, the board concluded that Davis's showing was insufficient to warrant clemency.

After all of these reviews, Davis's lawyers filed a second habeas petition to the Eleventh Circuit in October 2008. When a divided Eleventh Circuit panel denied this request, the lawyers filed a Petition for Writ of Habeas Corpus *within the original jurisdiction* of the U.S. Supreme Court in May 2009. In August, the Supreme Court transferred Davis's petition to the federal District Court for the Southern District of Georgia with instructions to "receive testimony and make

---

[24]The six affidavits were from several of the state's key witnesses in which they recanted their testimony about the events on the night of the murder. Twenty-seven additional affidavits were submitted relating to his other claims, such as ineffective assistance of counsel and the unconstitutionality of the death penalty.

[25]The district court denied the petition on the basis that Davis's claims of constitutional error were without merit and did not directly address his claims of innocence.

[26]The Eleventh Circuit did not recognize Davis's claim as a substantive one based on actual innocence. Rather, that court characterized Davis as "argu[ing] that his constitutional claims of an unfair trial must be considered, even though they are otherwise procedurally defaulted, because he has made the requisite showing of actual innocence."

[27]The U.S. Supreme Court denied Davis's petition for writ of certiorari in October 2008.

findings of fact as to whether evidence that could not have been obtained at the time of trial clearly establishes [Mr. Davis's] innocence."[28]

Prior to reaching a decision on the merits of Davis's claims, the judge had to determine the standard of review that should be applied. Davis's lawyers argued that case law established that they had a burden of proving "a clear probability that any *reasonable juror* would have reasonable doubt about [Davis's] guilt." However, the presiding judge read the case law differently and ruled that they were required to show "it is *more likely than not* that no *reasonable juror* would have convicted him in the light of the new evidence."[29] After carefully examining both the evidence presented at the trial, as well as the new evidence presented by Davis, the judge concluded:

> Mr. Davis's new evidence does not change the balance of proof from trial. Of his seven "recantations," only one is a meaningful, credible recantation. The value of that recantation is diminished because it only confirms that which was obvious at trial—that its author was testifying falsely. . . . Four of the remaining six recantations are either not credible or not true recantations and would be disregarded. . . . The remaining two recantations were presented under the most suspicious of circumstances, with Mr. Davis intentionally preventing the validity of the recantation from being challenged in open court through cross-examination. . . .
>
> Mr. Davis's additional, non-recantation evidence also does not change the balance of proof from trial. . . . The hearsay confessions carry little weight because the underlying confessions are uncorroborated and there is good reason to believe that they were false. . . .
>
> Ultimately, while Mr. Davis's new evidence casts some additional, minimal doubt on his conviction, it is largely smoke and mirrors. The vast majority of the evidence at trial remains intact, and the new evidence is largely not credible or lacking in probative value. After careful consideration, the Court finds that Mr. Davis has failed to make a showing of actual innocence that would entitle him to habeas relief in federal court.[30]

So, after nineteen years of trying to get the case back before a jury, the reviewing judge ruled that Davis's new evidence was not strong enough to justify a re-trial.

DISCUSSION QUESTIONS

1. How should the interests of justice be balanced against the needs for finality and closure when it comes to limiting the number and types of criminal appeals? Should different rules apply when someone has been sentenced to death?

2. Do you approve of the provisions of the Antiterrorism and Effective Death Penalty Act that were listed in this text? Why or why not?

3. Do you think Davis received adequate representation at his trial?

---

[28]*In re Davis*, 130 S.Ct. 1, 174 L.Ed. 2d 614 (2009).

[29]*In re Davis*, No. CV409-130, slip op. at 145 (SD Ga. Aug. 24, 2010).

[30]*In re Davis*, No. CV409-130, slip op. at 213-217.

4. How should appellate judges go about determining if an attorney chose a reasonable legal strategy that just didn't work or if the attorney failed to provide a competent defense?

5. Do you think it would make a difference in the outcome of an appeal if the defense attorney at the trial or sentencing level had had an ethics complaint filed against him or her for misuse of a different client's funds? Should it make a difference?

6. What do you think the standard of review should be when judges are considering appeals based on claims of new evidence? Why?

SUMMARY

In the context of this chapter, appeals are formal legal requests for review of an order or judgment entered by a trial court that are designed to reverse or modify the trial court's decision. While they most frequently occur after the defendant has been convicted and sentenced, there are some situations in which an interlocutory appeal can be made on the basis of such things as an order suppressing evidence or a challenge to a bail order.

Appeals from state criminal court decisions must proceed through that state's appellate court system; federal convictions are appealed to the regionally designated circuit of the U.S. Circuit Court of Appeals. Where an issue of federal law is involved, state court decisions may be brought to the federal courts after the state appeals have been exhausted. Appeals must be filed within strict time limits, and there are also limits on the number of times habeas corpus petitions can be brought to the federal courts.

It is particularly important to remember that, to be successful, appeals must identify and document "reversible errors" in the official court record. Furthermore, the standard of review utilized by appellate courts depends upon whether the court is dealing with questions of fact or questions of law. Appellate judges are much more likely to defer to the judgment of the trial court judges on factual issues and much more likely to make an independent judgment as to the way in which the law should be applied to those facts.

In addition to direct appeals, in some cases criminal defendants may challenge their convictions by filing collateral actions. These remedies include requests for issuance of a writ of habeas corpus and a petition for post-conviction relief. Paralegals are most likely to be involved in drafting the notice of appeal, ordering the record, tracking the filing deadlines for appeal documents, and researching supporting case law.

INTERNET RESOURCES

■ U.S. Court of Appeals:
http://www.uscourts.gov/FederalCourts/UnderstandingtheFederalCourts/HowCourtsWork/CriminalCases.aspx

REVIEW QUESTIONS

1. What are the designations for the parties initiating an appeal and defending an appeal?
2. When there is a right to appeal, what constitutional rights are afforded to indigent criminal defendants?
3. After a notice of appeal is filed, what type of authority remains in the trial court?
4. In federal non-capital cases, what court of review considers the appeal of a trial court's decision?
5. In what federal circuit is the state in which your school is located?
6. What is the three-tiered judicial system?
7. What types of tasks associated with appealing a case have deadlines?
8. How do interlocutory appeals differ from other appeals in criminal cases?
9. What is the first step in the appellate process?
10. When a defendant decides to appeal the decision of the trial court, in which courts will the parties file documents?
11. What is the purpose of a bystander's report?
12. What are the components of the record?
13. Why is it important that objections be made on the record?
14. What are the two ways in which an attorney can make an offer of proof?
15. Generally, what is the consequence of a party's failure to raise an objection or other issue to the trial judge?
16. Explain the difference between plain error and harmless error.
17. What is the relationship between reversible errors and cumulative errors?
18. How are the concepts of "proving guilt beyond a reasonable doubt" and showing that findings of fact were "clearly erroneous" related to each other?
19. Identify and define two major alternatives to a direct appeal from conviction.
20. What are the steps involved in petitioning for a writ of habeas corpus?

Table of Cases

Featured cases are in **bold**. *Page number followed by "N" and number indicate a footnote at bottom of that page.*

Glossary

Accessory A person who assisted in the preparation of the crime but was not present when it was actually carried out.

Accessory after the fact A person who first aided the principal after the commission of the crime.

Accomplice A person who assists the principal with the crime or with the preparation of the crime.

Actus reus A Latin term referring to a person's wrongful conduct that resulted in an illegal act.

Address block The portion of a court document that identifies the attorney responsible for the preparation of the document, the party that the attorney represents, the address, and the telephone number. The address block is also known as the preparer's data.

Administrative law Rules and regulations created by administrative agencies.

Adverse witness A witness who is either the opposing party in the case or a witness who is closely affiliated with the opposing party.

Affiant The person who signs an affidavit under oath or under penalty of perjury.

Affidavit A voluntarily written declaration of facts signed under oath or under penalty of perjury.

Alibi defense A criminal defense requiring proof that the defendant could not have been at the scene of the crime.

Allocution The defendant's personal statement in mitigation of the sentence.

American Bar Association The largest voluntary association of attorneys in the United States. As the national representative of the legal profession, the ABA's stated mission is to serve the public and the profession by promoting justice, professional excellence, and respect for the law.

Appeal A formal request for review of an order or judgment entered by another court, seeking to reverse or modify the other court's decision.

Appellant The party initiating the appeal.

Appellant-cross appellee The party defending the trial court's decision on appeal and initiating the cross appeal.

Appellee The party defending the trial court's decision on appeal.

Appellee-cross appellant The party initiating the appeal and defending the trial court's decision on appeal.

Application for search warrant A motion presented to the court that specifies the reasons that a search warrant should be issued. The application for search warrant is typically in affidavit form or accompanied by an affidavit.

Arraignment The court proceeding at which the judge informs the defendant of the charges filed by the government.

Arrest warrant A court order issued at the request of the prosecutor and/or law enforcement that authorizes the arrest and detention of an individual.

Arson An act of starting a fire or causing an explosion with the purpose of destroying or damaging property of another, or to collect insurance for such loss.

Assault An act that causes or attempts to cause serious bodily harm to another individual.

Assessment The charge imposed upon a specified group (i.e., users of the court system) for the purpose of funding specified services (e.g., women's shelters or legal aid programs).

Assigned counsel A lawyer in private practice appointed by the court to handle a particular indigent criminal case.

Attorney A lawyer; a person licensed by a state to practice law.

Attorney-client privilege The rule of evidence that forbids an attorney, or the attorney's employees, from testifying about communications with the client.

Attorney work product Trial preparation materials consisting of the attorney's mental impressions, conclusions, opinions, and legal theories about a case.

Attorney's trust fund A special account holding money on behalf of the client.

Authentication of evidence The process of establishing that the objects being introduced into evidence are what they are claimed to be.

Bail Money or something else of value that is pledged to guarantee that the accused will appear in court for scheduled proceedings.

Bailiff A court employee who is responsible for maintaining order in the courtrooms and watching over juries when they are in recess or when they have been sequestered.

Back strike The practice of a party's exercise of a peremptory challenge to dismiss a juror who was part of a panel that it had previously accepted.

Bates numbering An organizational method used to label documents by assigning a number (or alpha-numeric designation) to each document (or page), thereby creating a unique identifier for each.

Battered woman's or spouse's syndrome A syndrome of being the victim of repeated attacks; self-defense is sometimes allowed to the victim even when the victim is not in immediate danger.

Battery An act of intentional physical contact that is either offensive or harmful to another person.

Bench trial A non-jury trial at which the judge decides all questions of fact.

Bench warrant A court order that authorizes the arrest of someone for failing to show for a court appearance.

Best evidence rule An evidentiary rule requiring that the original document be produced at trial.

Beyond a reasonable doubt The standard of proof used in criminal trials. The evidence presented must be so conclusive and complete that all reasonable doubts regarding the facts are removed from the jurors' minds.

Bill of Attainder A law that imposes criminal penalties on a single person or small, select group of people.

Bill of particulars A supplementary document that gives the specifics of a charge that were not set forth in the original charge.

Black Letter Law Widely used, generally accepted, basic legal principles.

Boilerplate language Model sentences that include standardized legal terms and phrases.

Burglary An act of entering into a building for the purpose of committing a crime.

Bystander's report A statement approved by the trial judge as to what happened in court.

Capital crimes Crimes for which the death penalty is an authorized punishment.

Capital offense A special type of felony that is punishable by death.

Capital punishment Punishment by death. It is also referred to as the death penalty.

Caption The section of a court document containing the names of the parties, case number, name of the court it is being filed in, and a title that identifies the type of document being filed.

Chain of custody A record of who possessed an object being presented as evidence from the time it came into possession of government agents until it is presented in court.

Challenge for cause A method of removing a prospective juror based on a finding by the judge that the juror has some sort of bias or other factors that should disqualify him or her from serving on this specific case.

Change of venire The process of selecting jurors from a different location than the place of the trial.

Change of venue An action taken by the judge to move a trial to an alternative location.

Character evidence Evidence of a person's reputation in the community as to a particular trait, such as honesty or chastity.

Charge bargaining A plea bargain in which the prosecution dismisses a more serious charge in exchange for the defendant's pleading guilty to the lesser offense.

Charging the jury A process in which the judge instructs the jurors as to the meaning of the laws they are supposed to apply.

Chilling effect doctrine A principle of constitutional law that invalidates statutes that are worded in such a way as to make people fearful of engaging in legitimate, constitutionally protected First Amendment activities.

Circumstantial evidence Evidence that permits the inference of the existence or nonexistence of a fact or event that a party seeks to prove.

Civil law The body of law defining actions for which individuals can use the courts to seek remedies for violations of their private rights, establishing procedural requirements for using the courts, and establishing remedies for violations of those rights.

CJA panel attorney An attorney in private practice who is appointed in federal cases to represent indigent defendants for a fixed hourly fee.

Clearly erroneous The standard used by appellate courts when reviewing a trial court's findings of fact in which appellate judges defer to conclusions reached by the trial judge or jurors unless appellant demonstrates that those findings were clearly unreasonable.

Closing argument An oral presentation made to the jury, after all of the evidence has been presented, for the purpose of convincing the jury to find in favor of the side that is presenting the argument.

Code A compilation of statues, ordinances, or administrative regulations that is organized by subject matter rather than by the date of its enactment.

Collateral remedies Actions designed to challenge judgments of conviction that have otherwise become final in the normal appellate review process.

Common law Legal principles that have evolved over time from the analysis of court decisions made in the absence of constitutional, statutory, and administrative law.

Common law record All documents contained in the case file in the trial court, including the docketing statement, exhibits, jury instructions, etc.

Competency The ability of a witness to testify; generally, the witness must be capable of being understood by the jury; must understand the duty to tell the truth; and have knowledge of the facts to which he or she is testifying.

Complainant The person who signs a criminal complaint under oath attesting that the allegations of the complaint are true.

Complete defense A defense that, if proven, relieves the defendant of all criminal responsibility. [Contrast with partial defense]

Concurrent sentences Sentences that are served simultaneously rather than one after the other.

Conflict of interest A situation in which an attorney's representation of one client is either directly adverse to another client or materially limits the attorney's duties to another client, a former client or third party, or the personal interest of the attorney.

Conflicts check The process of verifying whether the acceptance of a new case would result in a conflict of interest for the attorney.

Consecutive sentences Sentences that must be served one after the other rather than simultaneously.

Conspiracy An agreement between two or more persons to commit an unlawful act.

Constitutional law Laws and legal principles derived from constitutions through judicial interpretation.

Content neutrality Laws may not limit free expression on the basis of whether the speech's content supports or opposes any particular position.

Contingent fee The lawyer fee owed by the client if the attorney is successful. There is no fee if the client does not prevail.

Continuance The postponement of a scheduled court proceeding, such as a hearing or the trial.

Contract lawyer An attorney who enters into an agreement with the government to furnish legal services to indigent clients.

Corroborative evidence Evidence supporting other evidence that has already been admitted but that is presented in a different form.

Count A subsection of the body of a charging document that alleges the defendant's commission of a crime and sets out all of the required elements of an offense.

Count bargaining A plea bargain in which the prosecution drops one or more related charges in exchange for the defendant's pleading guilty to at least one of the counts originally charged.

Court clerk A court employee who is responsible for maintaining the court files in proper order as well as ensuring that the various motions submitted by lawyers are properly filed and the actions taken by judges accurately docketed.

Court costs   Fees, charged to the defendant, that are designed to pay for operating expenses of the court system.

Court reporter (person)   The court employee who prepares verbatim transcripts of courtroom proceedings.

Court reporters (books)   Books that contain decisions and opinions of courts.

Court supervision   A sentencing option used for minor offenses in which the defendant is not convicted if he or she complies with the judge's conditions during a specific period of time.

Crime control model   An approach to evaluating the criminal justice system on the basis of how efficiently it suppresses crime.

Criminal complaint   A charge of the commission of a crime, made under oath.

Criminal justice system   A collection of different institutions and individuals who are typically involved in the processing of criminal cases.

Criminal law   The body of law defining offenses against the community at large, regulating how suspects are investigated, charged and tried, and establishing punishments for convicted offenders.

Criminal summons   A document issued under a court order that directs the accused to appear in court to answer the charges made against him or her.

Cross appeal   An appeal filed by the appellee of an existing appeal.

Cross-examination   The questioning of a witness called by the opposing side.

Cumulative error   The prejudicial impact of a series of two or more trial errors that do not warrant reversal of a case when viewed separately but collectively amount to reversible error.

Cumulative evidence   Evidence that does not add any new information but confirms facts that already have been established.

Curriculum vitae (CV)   A written description of a person's work experience, educational background, and skills. It is also called a CV, or vitae.

Damages   The monetary compensation awarded to the wronged party in a civil case.

Deadly force   A force that would cause serious bodily injury or death.

Declarant   The person who made the out-of-court statement.

Defendant   The party who is defending against either a criminal prosecution or a civil lawsuit. In a criminal case, the defendant is the person accused of committing a crime.

Defense attorney   The lawyer who represents a criminal defendant in court.

Delayed motion for a new trial   A request to have the judge order a new trial on the basis of errors that were discovered long after the trial ended.

Demonstrative evidence   Physical objects, such as photos, maps, x-rays, and diagrams, used to illustrate or aid in the understanding of verbal testimony.

Deponent   A witness being questioned under oath at a deposition.

Deposition   Testimony taken before trial under oath that is subject to cross-examination and preserved in writing.

Deposition to perpetuate testimony   A deposition that preserves the witness's statement so that it can be presented at a later time as evidence at trial.

Determinate sentencing   A form of punishment in which the defendant is sentenced to a specific term of imprisonment.

Dicta   Statements made in a court's opinion which go beyond the facts necessary to decide the case and therefore are not binding legal precedent in subsequent cases.

Direct evidence   Evidence that establishes a direct link to the fact or event that a party seeks to prove.

Direct examination   The initial questioning conducted by attorneys for the side that called the witnesses.

Disclosure   The revealing of information.

Discovery   A legal procedure by which a party in the case can obtain information about the case from other parties prior to the start of the trial.

Diversion program   An educational and/or social service program operated by public and private agencies outside of the criminal justice system to which criminal defendants are sent as an alternative to getting a criminal conviction on their record and/or serving time in an official government corrections program.

Documentary evidence Legal instruments such as contracts, leases, wills and deeds, and other written documents used to support claims made in court.

Domestic violence Physical abuse, harassment, or intimidation of a victim by a family or household member.

Double jeopardy The Fifth Amendment prohibition against prosecuting or punishing a defendant twice for the same crime.

Due process model An approach to evaluating the criminal justice system on the basis of how well it protects people from being charged and/or convicted of crimes they didn't commit.

Due process of law Legal procedures that enforce basic rights that are considered necessary for fairness and justice.

DUI The offense of driving under the influence of alcoholic beverages.

Duress A defense requiring proof that force or a threat of force was used to cause a person to commit a criminal act.

Duty of confidentiality An attorney's ethical duty to maintain the confidences of the client.

DWI Driving while intoxicated.

Electronic discovery (e-discovery) The discovery of documents created, disbursed, and stored electronically.

Entrapment A defense requiring proof that the defendant would not have committed the crime but for police trickery.

Espionage The act of disclosing information with intent to interfere with the operation or success of the U.S. armed forces or to promote the success of enemies of the United States.

Evidence Witness testimony, documents, physical objects, and stipulations that are presented in court for the purpose of determining the facts of the case.

Excessive force Any force greater than the level of force a reasonable and prudent law enforcement officer would use under the circumstances.

Exclusionary rule The doctrine that evidence obtained in violation of a defendant's constitutional rights cannot be used against the defendant in a criminal prosecution.

Exculpatory evidence Evidence that either tends to establish the defendant's innocence or is favorable to the accused on the question of punishment.

Execution of warrant The carrying out of a search of a person or place.

Exhibit A tangible item that is marked for identification for purpose of being used as evidence at a trial.

Exigent circumstances Conditions that excuse an officer from obtaining a warrant in order to protect a life, preserve evidence, or prevent a suspect from escaping.

Expert testimony Testimony that is given by a witness who the court determines to be expert on the topic upon which the testimony is to be given. Once accepted as an expert witness, the person is allowed to state his or her opinion on relevant matters.

Expert witness A witness who is called to supply scientific, technical, or other specialized knowledge that will help the jury and/or judge evaluate the facts that have been presented.

Ex post facto law A law that imposes criminal penalties for actions that were taken prior to the passage of the law.

Extended term sentence (also known as an enhanced sentence) A sentence beyond the statutory maximum of the basic range of penalties that otherwise could be imposed for the crime charged.

Fact witness A person who has first-hand knowledge of the events at issue in a case.

Factual questions Issues related to the determination of who did what and when, where, and how they did it.

Federal defender An attorney appointed to represent persons who are unable to afford private counsel in federal prosecutions.

Federal Rules of Criminal Procedure (FRCrP) The rules that govern the procedure in all criminal proceedings in the U.S. District Courts, the U.S. Courts of Appeals, and the Supreme Court of the United States.

Federal Rules of Evidence (FRE) The rules of evidence that govern proof in all civil and criminal proceedings in the U.S. district courts.

Federal Sentencing Guidelines The uniform sentencing standards used to calculate the sentencing range for federal defendants convicted of felonies or Class A misdemeanors.

Felony A major crime that is punishable by a year or more in a state prison.

Felony murder The unintended killing of a human being that occurs during the commission of another felony. The intent to commit the felony transfers to the killing to give rise to first degree murder.

Fifth Amendment privillege against self-incrimination An individual's constitutional right to refuse to answer questions or to otherwise provide statements that could be used as evidence against himself.

Fine The monetary penalty imposed upon a defendant as punishment for committing an illegal act.

Flat fee A pre-established amount that the client must pay for representation in the case.

Fraud An act of using deception to commit a theft.

Friendly witness A fact witness who knows something about the underlying occurrence and holds a favorable impression of the client.

Fruit of the poisonous tree doctrine Evidence that is derived from an illegal search or interrogation is inadmissible.

Grand jury A court-appointed panel composed of sixteen to twenty-three citizens that considers evidence presented by prosecutors and determines whether there is probable cause to bring formal criminal charges.

Group exhibit A trial exhibit comprised of multiple components.

Guilty but mentally ill A verdict finding that the defendant is guilty of a crime although he or she lacked the mental capacity to commit it.

Habitual offender laws (also known as "three strikes and you're out" laws) Mandatory sentencing laws that require judges to give extended terms of imprisonment to persons the third time they are convicted of a serious criminal offense, without the possibility of parole for life or an extended period of time.

Harmless error A mistake that is not considered prejudicial enough to justify overturning the court's decision/action.

Hate crime A crime where the selection of the victim is based on that person's membership in a protected category, such as race, sex, or sexual orientation.

Hate speech Speech directed at a particular group or classification of people that involves expressions of hate or intimidation.

Hearsay evidence A statement, other than one made by the declarant while testifying at the trial or hearing, offered in evidence to prove the truth of the matter asserted.

Hearsay rule The general rule of evidence providing that hearsay evidence is not admissible at trial or hearing.

Homicide An act by one human being that causes the death of another human being. To be considered a crime, the act must have been done purposely, knowingly, recklessly, or negligently.

Hostile witness A witness who manifests great hostility or prejudice against the side that called him or her to testify.

Hourly fee The rate of compensation earned by an attorney based on the time devoted to the case.

Hung jury A jury that is unable to reach a verdict after lengthy deliberations.

Immunity An exemption from prosecution given to a witness so that the witness can be compelled to give self-incriminating testimony.

Impeachment The challenge to a witness's credibility.

Impeachment by omission The challenge to a witness's credibility based on what the witness failed to state on a prior occasion.

Impeachment evidence Evidence that tends to undermine the credibility of the opponent's witnesses.

In camera In a judge's chambers, outside the presence of a jury and the public.

In camera review A judge's review of materials in the absence of the parties and the public

Incarceration Mandatory confinement in a facility that limits the ability to move around as the person wishes.

Inchoate crimes A crime that was planned but not completed.

Indeterminate sentencing A form of punishment in which the defendant is sentenced to a range of imprisonment with the actual release date determined by a parole board.

Indictment The formal criminal charge against a defendant returned by a grand jury. It is also referred to as "a bill of indictment."

Indictment jurisdictions Jurisdictions in which defendants accused of committing felonies have the right to be indicted by a grand jury.

Information The formal written charge presented by the prosecution without a grand jury indictment.

Information jurisdictions Jurisdictions in which prosecutors are authorized to initiate felony charges by either indictment or information.

Initial appearance The first time a person charged with a crime appears before a judge. This is also referred to as a "first appearance."

Insanity defense A defense that relieves people who are legally insane from criminal responsibility for their actions.

Interlocutory appeal An appeal from an order by a trial court that does not conclude the case.

Intimidation An act which involves putting someone in fear of something bad happening to them, their loved ones, or their property.

Involuntary intoxication The consumption of alcohol and/or drugs without knowledge or consent.

Irresistible impulse test A test that provides that the defendant is not guilty due to insanity if, at the time of the killing, the defendant could not control his or her actions.

Jail A facility controlled by a local governmental authority to hold criminal defendants awaiting trial and offenders convicted in state court of misdemeanors.

Joinder of defendants A process whereby individual defendants who are alleged to have committed the same offense(s) are tried together at the same time.

Joinder of offenses A process whereby a defendant is tried on multiple charges at the same time.

Judge A governmental official who presides at court proceedings. The judge decides all legal issues presented and determines the facts in non-jury cases.

Judicial notice An action taken by a judge to formally recognize something as being a fact without requiring the attorneys to prove it through the introduction of other evidence.

Judicial precedent An earlier judicial decision that is relied upon by judges in deciding a case.

Judicial review The legal doctrine that courts have the power to strike down statutes and void other government actions that are not consistent with the court's interpretation of the constitution.

Jurisdiction The geographic area within which a political entity has the right to exercise authority.

Jurisdiction also refers to a court's power to decide a case or issue an order.

Jury box The specific location in the courtroom where the jury sits during the trial.

Jury box system The method of jury selection in which prospective jurors fill the jury box and are replaced as they are stricken by other prospective jurors, until everyone left in the box is acceptable to both sides or all peremptory challenges are exhausted.

Jury instructions Written directions given by the judge to the jury pertaining to the controlling principles of law in the case.

Jury instructions conference The meeting of the parties with the judge following the close of the evidence for the purpose of determining the appropriate instructions to be given to the jury.

Jury nullification A term used to describe a situation in which a jury votes to acquit a defendant even though the facts clearly establish a violation of the letter of the law.

Juvenile A young person who has not yet attained the age at which persons are considered to be adults under the criminal law.

Juvenile courts Special courts established to deal with juveniles who commit acts that are violations of the criminal law or who are adjudged to be abused or neglected.

Juvenile delinquent A juvenile who has been adjudicated to have committed acts that are violations of the criminal law.

Knowingly Not intending to cause a specific harm, but being aware that such harm would be caused.

Larcecy A crime that involves the taking away of the goods or property of another without the consent and against the will of the owner or possessor and with a criminal intent to convert the property to the use of someone other than the owner.

Law A rule of conduct promulgated and enforced by the government.

Lay witness A witness who is called to testify about things personally observed through his or her senses.

Laying a foundation A process by which an attorney asks a witness a series of preliminary questions designed to identify potential evidence and explain how it relates to the issues involved in the trial.

Leading questions   Questions worded in such a way as to suggest what the answer should be.

Legal defense   A set of facts or legal arguments that, if accepted by the court, relieves a person of criminal liability for having committed an act that is defined as a crime.

Legal questions   Issues related to the interpretation of the meaning of the law, including procedures used in the trial and the admissibility of different kinds of evidence, as well at the type of behavior that is covered by the terms of the statutes being applied.

Lesser included offense   A crime that shares some, but not all, of the elements of a more serious criminal offense. Thus, the greater offense cannot be committed without committing the lesser crime.

Magistrate   A judicial officer vested with limited authority to administer and enforce the law.

Making false statements to federal investigators   The act of lying to or concealing information from a federal official.

Malice aforethought   The level of intent shown by the actor's premeditation, the cruelty or conscious disregard for the safety of others or demonstrated by the intent to commit another felony.

Mandatory sentence   A requirement, by the legislature, that the judge impose a minimum prison term for a specified crime.

Manslaughter   A homicide where the act was committed recklessly or under the influence of extreme mental or emotional disturbance.

Marshal   A court officer who serves summonses and other court documents, collects money as required by court judgments, provides security for the courthouse, and otherwise helps in carrying out the court's orders.

Material evidence   (For purposes of determining the prosecution's disclosure obligations under *Brady*), evidence is material if there is a reasonable probability that had the evidence been disclosed to the defense, the result of the proceeding would have been different.

Materiality   A requirement that the evidence be more probative than prejudicial.

Mens rea   A Latin term referring to what was going on in someone's mind at the time he or she committed an illegal act.

Misdemeanor   A minor crime that is punishable by a fine and/or less than a year in jail.

Mistrial   The early termination of a trial because of extraordinary circumstances such as a deadlocked jury, prejudicial trial error, or the illness or death of a trial participant.

M'Naghten test   A test that provides that the defendant is not guilty due to insanity if, at the time of the killing, the defendant suffered from a defect or disease of the mind and could not understand whether the act was right or wrong.

Model Penal Code   A model criminal code prepared by the American Law Institute (ALI) to promote improvements in and greater consistency among state criminal codes.

Model Rules of Professional Conduct   A set of recommended ethics standards for attorneys promulgated by the American Bar Association. Most of the states have adopted some or all of the model rules.

Motion   An application made to a court for the purpose of getting a ruling on an issue in favor of the moving party.

Motion for a change of venue   A formal request to the court to move the trial to a different location.

Motion for a competency hearing   A formal request to the court to hold a hearing to determine if the defendant is competent to stand trial.

Motion for bill of particulars   A defense motion that requests the court to order the prosecution to file a supplementary document that gives the specifics of a charge that were not set forth in the original charge.

Motion for continuance   A formal request to the court to postpone the date of an upcoming court proceeding.

Motion for entry of a protective order   A formal request to the court to protect either the opposing party or a third party from an unreasonable or invasive request for discovery.

Motion for judgment of acquittal   A formal request to have the judge acquit the defendant notwithstanding the jury's verdict to the contrary.

Motion for judgment of acquittal/motion for directed verdict   A request to have the judge enter a verdict of not guilty on the basis that the prosecution failed to present enough evidence to establish a prima facie case of guilt.

Motion for a new trial   A request to have the judge order a new trial on the basis of errors that were made in the pre-trial and trial stages.

Motion for substitution of judges   A formal request to the court to substitute a different judge for the one that is currently assigned to the case.

Motion in limine   A formal request to the court to prohibit mention of specified information because it is not sufficiently relevant to the issues being tried and would have a prejudicial effect on the jury.

Motion to compel   A formal request to the court to order either the opposing party or a third party to take some action. Typically, this motion is filed in connection with discovery disputes.

Motion to dismiss   A formal request to the court to drop a pending criminal charge against the defendant.

Motion to sever   A formal request to the court to require separate trials for individual defendants who are scheduled to be tried together, or for individual charges against a specific defendant.

Motion to suppress   A request that the court prohibit specified material from being admitted into evidence at a trial because it was gathered in an illegal manner.

Movant   The party filing a motion with the court.

Murder   A homicide that was committed purposefully, knowingly, or where the person acted recklessly with extreme indifference to the value of human life.

Necessity   A defense requiring proof that the defendant was forced to take an action to avoid a greater harm.

Negligence   A failure to act reasonably under the circumstances.

Negligent homicide   A homicide based on a negligent act.

Neutral witness   A witness who has no relationship with either the defense or the prosecution.

No bill   The grand jury's determination that there is no probable cause that an individual committed a crime.

No-knock warrant   A warrant that allows law enforcement officers to enter a property without knocking and without identifying themselves.

Nolo contendere   A "no contest" plea in which the defendant neither admits nor denies the charges but concedes that if the case went to trial, the prosecution would have sufficient evidence to prove its case beyond a reasonable doubt.

Non-pattern jury instructions   Jury instructions that were not created as part of the uniform pattern instructions for the jurisdiction.

Not guilty by reason of insanity   A verdict finding that the defendant carried out the actions constituting a crime but lacked the mental capacity to have intended to commit the crime.

Notice of appeal   A formal document filed with the clerk of the trial court stating that a party is appealing the decision of the trial court.

Notice of filing notice of appeal   A document filed with the clerk and served on the opposing party stating the date on which the appellant filed a notice of appeal.

Notice of hearing   A court document that states the time, date, and judge who will hear arguments on a particular motion.

Notice to appear   A notice informing a party that he or she must appear in court or risk losing the matter set for hearing.

Noticing the deposition   The process of sending a written notice to the other party informing the opposing party of the time, date, and place of a deposition of a named witness along with the method of recording testimony, such as stenography or audio recording.

Noticing a motion   The process of sending a written notice to the other party informing the party that the motion will be argued in front of the judge on a particular date at a specific time.

Nunc pro tunc   A Latin term meaning "now for then." In the courts, this refers to the modification of an order or record retroactively to show what actually happened at the time.

Objection   A request to the judge to not allow specific questions or comments by another attorney or types of answers/comments from witnesses.

Objection on the record   A challenge to the judge's ruling that is memorialized either by the electronic or stenographic capture of a verbal objection or a written notation of the objection by docket entry or otherwise.

Obstruction of justice An act that intentionally interferes with the work of police, prosecutors, and other government officials.

Offer of proof A procedure whereby excluded testimony is placed into the record for possible appellate review of the judge's decision to exclude it.

On the record Statements made in court that are recorded by either a court reporter or by the clerk of the court as a written entry in the case file.

Open plea A plea agreement under which the defendant pleads guilty and the judge determines the sentence without a joint recommendation from the parties.

Opening statement The speech each side presents to the jury before testimony is presented outlining what the attorney expects the evidence will show.

Order of protection A court order entered to forbid an individual from harassing, abusing, or otherwise interfering with the liberty of a particular person. Typically, the order protects a victim from a household or family member.

Ordinance A form of law that is created by local legislative bodies such as city councils.

Overbreadth A reason for invalidating a statute that criminalizes constitutionally protected activities along with those that it can legally prohibit.

Overbreadth doctrine A principle of constitutional law that any regulation of expression must be narrowly tailored to meet the government's legitimate object.

Overruled objection The judge's unfavorable ruling on an evidentiary objection.

Own recognizance (OR) *See* **Personal recognizance bond**

PACER The acronym for Public Access to Court Electronic Records, an online public-access service that permits users to retrieve case and docket information from the federal courts and the U.S. Party/Case Index.

Paralegal A person qualified by education, training, or work experience who is employed by a lawyer, law office, corporation, governmental agency, or other entity who performs specifically delegated substantive legal work for which a lawyer is responsible.

Parole A conditional release from incarceration after actually serving part of the sentence.

Partial defense A defense that reduces a crime to a lesser included offense.

Pattern discovery Model discovery requests that use generic, boilerplate language to request all of the information allowable under the applicable criminal discovery rules.

Pattern jury instructions Uniform basic jury instructions typically prepared by committees of judges, lawyers, and scholars for use by the trial courts in a specific jurisdiction.

Penalty enhancement statute A law providing for a stiffer penalty for the violation of a criminal statute due to the presence of an aggravating factor, such as the age or race of the victim, the heinous nature of the offense, etc.

Peremptory challenge A method an attorney can use to remove a prospective juror without being required to state a reason.

Periodic imprisonment A probation option that permits a defendant sentenced to imprisonment to leave custody for work or school.

Perjury The act of lying or knowingly making false statements while under oath in court or in affidavits or depositions.

Personal recognizance bond (PR) [also known as Own recognizance (OR)] A defendant's promise to appear in court without posting cash or other security.

Petit jury A court-appointed panel of citizens who consider the evidence presented by both sides at trial and determine the facts in dispute.

Petition to revoke (also called PTR) A motion filed by the prosecutor seeking to revoke probation and resentence the offender.

Petty offense A violation of the law that is considered less serious than a misdemeanor.

Physical evidence Material objects related to the case.

Plain error The exception to the waiver rule that permits an appellant to raise on appeal a mistake that was not preserved in the trial court because it was a highly prejudicial error affecting the fundamental rights of the defendant.

Plain view doctrine The legal theory that law enforcement officials have the right to seize contraband items or evidence of a crime when they see such items in public or from a location where there is no reasonable expectation of privacy.

Plaintiff The party who initiates a civil lawsuit.

Plea bargain An agreement whereby the defendant pleads guilty to a criminal charge in exchange for a reduction in the charges, the number of counts, or a lesser sentence.

Plea colloquy The in-court examination of a criminal defendant entering a guilty plea to determine whether the defendant is entering the plea intelligently, knowingly, and voluntarily.

Plea of convenience A guilty plea for a crime the defendant does not acknowledge committing that is made in order to conclude the case on terms the defendant feels are in his or her best interest.

Pocket brief A short memorandum of law used to advise the court on a discreet point of law.

Polling the jury After a jury's verdict has been announced, the procedure in which the judge asks each juror to confirm his or her vote.

Post-conviction relief A statutory collateral challenge to a judgment of conviction.

Post-verdict motion (also known as post-trial motion) A defense motion filed after a guilty verdict that seeks court action on various case-related matters.

Prayer for relief A short, unnumbered paragraph near the end of a motion in which the moving party presents the relief being sought from the court.

Preliminary hearing The initial hearing by a judge to determine whether there is probable cause for the charge against the defendant.

Presentence Investigation Report (PSR) The document which reports the results of the probation officer's post-trial investigation of a convicted defendant, including all factors the court should take into account when determining the sentence.

Prima facie case Evidence that, if not contradicted by other evidence, is sufficient to meet the burden of proof required for that type of case.

Principal A person who actually commits the crime.

Prison (also known as a penitentiary) A facility controlled by the state or federal government to house convicted state court felons and federal offenders.

Private counsel (Retained counsel) A private attorney chosen by the defendant to represent him or her.

Privilege against self-incrimination An individual's constitutional right to refuse to answer questions or to otherwise provide statements that could be used as evidence against the individual.

Probable cause The reasonable belief based on specific facts that a person committed a crime or that something will be found in a specific location.

Probation A criminal sentence discharging the defendant to the community subject to conditions, which may include reporting to a probation officer.

Pro bono The Latin term for "for the good," used to describe legal work that is performed for free as part of the attorney's professional responsibilities.

Procedural due process The series of procedures that federal and state government are constitutionally required to follow before they can deny anyone life, liberty, or property.

Proof of service A sworn statement by a member of the attorney's office attesting to the service of the document on the opposing side by mail, personal delivery, or other means.

Pro se party A party to litigation who is unrepresented by counsel.

Prosecutor The lawyer authorized to represent a particular unit of government in criminal court.

Prosecutor's rebuttal case The phase of the trial in which the prosecution calls witnesses to dispute the evidence presented by the defense in its case-in-chief. This is also referred to as "the rebuttal."

Protective order A court directive to protect a party or witness from unreasonable or invasive discovery requests.

Public defender An attorney paid by the government to represent indigent persons accused of committing crimes.

Public trial A trial open to the public.

Purposeful Intending to cause a specific harm.

Rape Traditionally defined as non-consensual sexual intercourse between a male and a female who was not his wife. (Exceptions for forced intercourse with a wife no longer apply in some states.)

Reasonable force The amount of force necessary to protect oneself or one's property.

Reasonable suspicion   A reasonable belief in the context of the specific facts of the situation. This standard is greater than a mere hunch but less than a probable cause.

Rebuttal evidence   Evidence presented to explain, repel, counteract, or disprove facts given in evidence after a party had rested its case.

Recklessness   Disregarding a substantial and unjustifiable risk that harm will result.

Record on appeal   ("the record") The common law record and the report of proceedings.

Re-cross   The portion of a witness's testimony during which the side that conducted the initial cross-examination has an opportunity to ask additional questions designed to clarify issues raised during the re-direct.

Recusal   The judge's voluntary removal of himself or herself from a case because of bias or the appearance of impropriety if he or she continues to preside over the case.

Redaction   The process of masking some part of the content of a document before making it available for inspection.

Re-direct   The portion of a witness's testimony during which the side that conducted the initial direct examination has an opportunity to ask additional questions designed to clarify issues raised during cross-examination.

Relevant evidence   Evidence that leads one to logically conclude that an asserted fact is either more or less probable.

Report of proceedings   The transcripts of testimony as well as any other oral statements made in the trial court.

Respondent   The party who receives the motion from the opposing side of a case.

Resting the case   A phrase used by attorneys to announce that they have presented all of the evidence they intend to present at the current stage of the trial.

Restitution   A component of a sentence entered against a defendant to be used to compensate the victims of the crime for their losses.

Retreat exception   The rule that in order to claim self-defense there must have been no possibility of retreat.

Return of search warrant   A court document that specifies when a search warrant was executed and lists the items of the property seized.

Return of service   The written verification establishing that a document has been served.

Reversible error   A mistake that is considered sufficiently prejudicial to warrant reversing the trial court's decision/action.

Robbery   A crime in which someone uses force or fear to take something of value from the possession of another against that person's wishes.

Rule of law   A collection of legal principles that all relate to the placement of limitations on the exercise of political power and the operation of government. These principles include: (1) government must follow its own rules; (2) government must apply the law impartially; and (3) government must provide due process for those accused of breaking the rules.

Search warrant   A written court order that authorizes an officer to search a specific place for specific objects. A neutral judge must determine that there is probable cause in order to issue a search warrant.

Self-defense   The justified use of force to protect oneself or others.

Sentence   A judgment formally pronouncing the punishment to be imposed on a person who has been convicted of a crime.

Sentence bargaining   A plea bargain in which the defendant enters a plea of guilty in exchange for a lighter sentence.

Sequestering a jury   A procedure for protecting jurors from outside influences by having them stay in hotel rooms where bailiffs can monitor their activities and block access to newspaper, television, radio, and Internet news related to the trial.

Sidebar conference   The discussion between the judge and the attorneys that takes place during the trial outside of the hearing of the jury. (Usually the attorneys stand in front of the bench.)

Solicitation   The crime of encouraging someone to commit a crime.

Speedy Trial Act   A law that sets forth a maximum time limit between the time that formal charges are filed and the start of a trial on those charges.

Stalking The act of following another person or placing them under surveillance when these actions place that person in reasonable apprehension of bodily harm, sexual assault, confinement, or restraint.

Statute of limitations A law that sets forth a maximum time limit between the occurrence or discovery of a crime and the date at which formal charges must be filed.

Statutes A form of written law that is enacted by federal and state legislative bodies.

Statutory law A form of law that is created by legislative bodies in the form of statutes and ordinances.

Statutory rape An act of sexual intercourse (even if it was consensual) with a person under a certain age.

Stipulation An agreement by both sides to accept something as being true so as to simplify and expedite the trial by dispensing with the need to present formal proof.

Street crime A crime that usually involves violence and is typically carried out by a person considered to be from a low socioeconomic class.

Struck jury method The jury selection process in which the judge randomly selects the number of jurors required for the case plus those numbering the total of peremptory challenges and a few extras. After the lawyers exercise all of their challenges, those remaining in the jury box are the jurors and alternates.

Subpoena An order issued by the authority of a court that commands an individual to appear to testify or produce documents at a judicial event such as a trial or grand jury proceeding.

Subpoena *duces tecum* A special form of the subpoena used to compel the witness to bring documents or other tangible items to court or to a grand jury proceeding.

Substantial capacity test (Part of the Model Penal Code) A test that provides that the defendant is not guilty due to insanity if, at the time of the killing, the defendant lacked either the ability to understand the act was wrong or the ability to control the behavior.

Substantive due process The constitutional limitation placed on the federal and state governments barring the deprivation of anyone's life, liberty, or property by means of a law found to be arbitrary and/or unreasonable.

Suicide The deliberate termination of one's own life.

Summary suspension The automatic cessation of driving privileges of an individual who has a specified blood alcohol (BAC) percentage in his or her bloodstream as shown by a blood test or a breathalyzer. A driver may also have his or her license suspended by refusing to submit to the breathalyzer test.

Summons An official notice issued under seal of the court informing a party that he or she must appear in court or risk losing the case.

Surrebuttal The phase of the trial in which the defense calls witnesses to dispute the rebuttal evidence offered by the prosecution.

Sustained objection The judge's favorable ruling on an evidentiary objection.

Taking case under advisement The judge's deferral of a decision on a case or issue raised in a case.

Temporary insanity The defense that the accused was momentarily insane when the crime was committed and therefore was incapable of understanding the nature of his or her actions.

***Terry* stop** A law enforcement officer's stop of a person for a brief period of time to ask a few questions when the officer has "reasonable suspicion" that the person has committed, is in the process of committing, or is about to commit a crime.

Testimonial evidence Verbal statements that are given under oath at a trial for the purpose of helping the jury and/or judge to understand the facts of the case.

Theft A crime involving taking property without the owner's consent.

Transactional immunity Prosecutorial immunity that protects a witness from prosecution for the offense revealed in his or her testimony.

Transferred intent doctrine The concept that when an actor who intends to injure one victim unintentionally harms another, the *mens rea* from the original offense is transferred to the crime involving the unintended victim.

Treason An attempt to overthrow the government of one's country or of assisting its enemies in war.

Trespass An unauthorized intrusion onto private land or into a building that belongs to someone else.

Trial notebook A three-ring notebook with appropriately tabbed sections containing materials required for a specific trial.

Trial subpoena A document prepared under the authority of the court that commands a witness to appear at a trial to give testimony.

True bill A grand jury's determination that the evidence before it constitutes probable cause that an individual committed a crime.

U.S. Attorney The chief federal law enforcement officer of the judicial district to which he or she is assigned. The U.S. Attorney is responsible for prosecuting persons accused of committing federal crimes.

U.S. Magistrate Judge A federal trial judge appointed by the life-tenured federal judges of a district court. Magistrates often try misdemeanor and petty offense cases and handle felony preliminary proceedings.

Use immunity Prosecutorial immunity that bars the government from using the testimony in the prosecution of the witness, except on charges of perjury. Use immunity is also known as "derivative use immunity."

Variance A federal sentence that is not within the guidelines or based on a departure from the guidelines.

Venire The group of potential jurors from which the jury for a specific case is selected.

Victim impact statement A written or oral statement made by the victim of the crime (or the family members of a deceased victim) that is presented at the sentencing hearing for the convicted offender.

Void for vagueness defense A claim that a criminal charge should be dismissed because the statute being applied fails to fairly inform ordinary people as to what is commanded or prohibited.

Voir dire An examination of prospective jurors to see if they are fit to serve on a jury in a specific case.

Voluntary intoxication The knowing and voluntary consumption of alcohol and/or drugs.

Waiver rule The rule of appellate procedure that an issue not presented in the trial court is waived and cannot be argued on appeal.

White-collar crime A non-violent crime characterized by deceit, concealment, or violation of trust that is committed by an individual in the course of his or her occupation or by a company in the course of its business.

Writ of habeas corpus A court document ordering public officials to produce the person named so that a neutral judge can determine if there is a lawful basis for detaining that person.

Index